HEALTH CARE
POLITICS
and
POLICY
in
AMERICA

HEALTH CARE POLITICS
and
POLICY
in
AMERICA

Kant Patel
Mark E. Rushefsky

Second Edition

M.E. Sharpe
Armonk, New York
London, England

Library of Congress Cataloging-in-Publication Data

Patel, Kant, 1946– .
Health care politics and policy in America / by Kant Patel and Mark E. Rushefsky.—2nd ed.
p. cm.
Includes bibliographical references and index.
ISBN 0-7656-0389-6 (c : alk. paper).   ISBN 0-7656-0390-X (pbk : alk. paper).
1. Medical policy—United States. 2. Medical care—Political aspects—United States.
I. Rushefsky, Mark E., 1945– . II. Title.
RA395.A3P285 1999
362.1′0973—dc21   98-56200
CIP

Printed in the United States of America

The paper used in this publication meets the minimum requirements of
American National Standard for Information Sciences
Permanence of Paper for Printed Library Materials,
ANSI Z 39.48-1984.

BM (c)   10   9   8   7   6   5   4   3   2
BM (p)   10   9   8   7   6   5   4   3

To Kahlua.
—K.P.

To my children, Rachel and Leah.
If you have your health, you have everything.
—M.E.R.

Politics is how society manages conflicts about values and interests. . . . And no issues trigger battles over values and interests more quickly and acutely than do the source and use of money in health reform proposals.

—Lawrence D. Brown

Contents

List of Tables, Figures, and Boxes

Figure

Box

Preface

We are gratified by the reception with which the first edition of *Health Care Politics and Policy in America* was received. It was well reviewed, it sold well, and it was adopted by many colleges and universities, running through five printings. The first edition was the first joint research project between Patel and Rushefsky. Since that time we have published another book on health care with M.E. Sharpe, *Politics, Power and Policymaking: The Case of Health Care Reform in the 1990s*, and our article on health policy elites was published in *Health: An Interdisciplinary Journal for the Social Study of Health, Illness and Medicine* in late 1998. Patel began working on the first edition of the book while on a sabbatical in the spring of 1991. Rushefsky joined the project in 1994. It continues to be an interesting experience for both of us. We do not have the same kind of work habits. One of us (we won't tell you which one) is very meticulous and organized; the other is considerably more scattered and sloppy. This has sometimes led to noisy discussions and scampering to find things. This is the kind of book Felix and Oscar, the Odd Couple, might have written! One adjustment we did make was that the neat, meticulous one kept all the papers and files because the other misplaced his. That we remain close friends who share common interests in professional basketball (and computer games) helped the relationship. Patel, who is from Houston, roots for the Houston Rockets. Rushefsky, from New York, is a lifelong, avid, irrational Knicks fan.

Both of us have had a long involvement in health care, dating back to the 1970s. Rushefsky first became interested in health care when his wife, Cynthia, began teaching childbirth classes in rural Rocky Mount, Virginia. She trained some of the nurses and the wife of the administrator of the local rural hospital (about ten miles along winding mountain roads from where they lived), and that hospital maintained its maternity ward rather than close it. That was fortunate for the Rushefskys when their second child, Leah, was born shortly after midnight on Halloween. They just made it that ten miles to the hospital. Had that hospital not maintained its birthing facilities, they would have had to go another twenty-five miles to Roanoke. Given the speed with which Leah was born (so fast that she beat the doctor to the delivery room!), Rushefsky half-jokingly says she would have been born in Boones Mill (about halfway between Rocky Mount and Roanoke), which had no hospital.

Patel's interest in health care was developed more conventionally, as an academic. He has a lifelong belief that access to good health care is a right! The two of us agree that the health care system has problems and that, before publication of the first edition of this book, there was no text that addressed those problems from a political perspective.

A second edition of a book should go easier and faster than a first edition. After all, with a first edition we are beginning with a blank slate. The second edition should build on the first and merely update it (as we describe below). That was not the case for this second edition. While both Patel and Rushefsky experienced delays, the major cause of delay can be laid at the feet of Rushefsky. His life became complicated!

In 1997, his wife Cynthia, the chief assistant prosecuting (and drug) attorney in Greene County, decided to run for a judgeship. The response Rushefsky should have made, given this book, her political race, and the normal teaching and other workload, was to ask for a sabbatical for the fall of 1998. But he did not do that. The campaign took much of his time during the spring, summer, and fall of 1998, much more than he realized. The campaign was an educational experience, as Cynthia unsuccessfully sought to become the first female judge in the county, running against a little-known but better-financed opponent.

Anyway, we have made some changes in this second edition. All the chapters have been brought up to date, and there are two new chapters. One chapter looks at the issue of medical liability. The other brings the story of health care policy up to the end of the millennium; it focuses on policy initiatives of the late 1990s and the managed care revolution and reaction. Ironically, that chapter is labeled "The Triumph of Incrementalism," noting that the incrementalism refers to government policy amid the vast changes in health care wrought by the private sector. We have also enhanced our discussion of equality; we focused a bit more on women's issues and included more of a philosophical discussion on equality and the notion of a right to health care.

Another important change, noticeable only to those who look at endnotes and bibliographies, is our significant new reliance on the Internet. There is a wealth of easily available material on the Net, and it has made our research easier.

Acknowledgments

As is typical of any book, this text is not the product of its authors only. We would like to thank Pauline Woods for her work on the bibliography, and our graduate research assistants, Julie Atwater and Kelly Layman, for their invaluable help in finding journal articles for us and for performing the really boring task of checking citations. Patel would like to thank the Faculty Leave Committee at Southwest Missouri State University for the spring 1991 sabbatical that made the initial research for this project possible. We would also like to thank Patricia Kolb, executive editor for social sciences at M.E. Sharpe, for her insightful judgment in continuing to support this project, as well as her assistant, Elizabeth Granda. Thanks are also due to Eileen Maass, production editor, and to her staff for the copyediting. Of course, any remaining errors are ours.

Kant Patel
Mark E. Rushefsky

List of Abbreviations

AAHP	American Association of Health Plans
AAPCC	Adjusted average per capita cost
AARP	American Association of Retired Persons
ADR	Alternate dispute resolution
AFDC	Aid to Families with Dependent Children
AFL-CIO	American Federation of Labor–Congress of Industrial Organizations
AHA	American Hospital Association
AHCA	American Health Care Association
AHCCS	Arizona Health Care Cost Containment System
AHCPR	Agency for Health Care Policy and Research
AHPs	Accountable Health Plans
ALTCS	Arizona Long-Term Care System
AMA	American Medical Association
AMPAC	American Medical Political Action Committee
APHA	American Public Health Association
BBA	Balanced Budget Act
BCBSM	Blue Cross and Blue Shield of Minnesota
CalPERS	California Public Employees' Retirement System
CBO	Congressional Budget Office
CCHP	Consumer Choice Health Plan
CDF	Children's Defense Fund
CHAMPUS	Civilian Health and Medical Program of the Uniformed Services
CHIP	Child Health Insurance Program
COBRA	Consolidated Omnibus Reconciliation Act
CON	Certificate of need
CPI	Consumer price index
CPS	Current Population Survey

DCE	Designated compensable event
DDT	Dichlorodiphenyl Trichloreothane
DNC	Democratic National Committee
DRGs	Diagnosis-related groups
EFM	Electronic fetal monitors
EKG	Electrocardiogram
EPSDT	Early and Periodic Screening, Diagnosis, and Treatment
ERISA	Employee Retirement Income Security Act
ESRD	End-stage renal disease
FDA	Food and Drug Administration
FEHBP	Federal Employees Health Benefit Program
FELA	Federal Employees Liability Act
FEMA	Federal Emergency Relief Administration
FFS	Fee-for-service
FSHCA	Federally Supported Health Centers Assistance Act
FTCA	Federal Tort Claims Act
FY	Fiscal year
GAO	General Accounting Office
GATT	General Agreement on Tariffs and Trade
GDP	Gross domestic product
HBC	Health Benefits Coalition
HCA	Hospital Corporation of America
HCFA	Health Care Financing Administration
HEDIS	Health Plan Employer Data and Information Set
HHA	Home Health Agency
HHS	Health and Human Services, Department of
HI	Hospital insurance
HIAA	Health Insurance Association of America
HIPAA	Health Insurance Portability and Accountability Act
HIOS	Health insuring organizations
HMOs	Health maintenance organizations
HSAs	Health systems agencies
HUGO	Human Genome Organization
IOGs	Illness outcome groups
IPAs	Independent practice associations

JCAH	Joint Commission on Accreditation of Hospitals
LTC	Long-term care
MAI	Medical adversity insurance
MCCA	Medicare Catastrophic Coverage Act
MCO	Managed care organization
Medi-Cal	California Medicaid program (Medi-Cal)
MEG	Magnetoencephalography
MMIA	Medical Malpractice Immunity Act
MRI	Magnetic resonance imaging
MSA	Medical savings account
NAFTA	North American Free Trade Agreement
NAIC	National Association of Insurance Commissioners
NCHSR	National Center for Health Services Research
NCI	National Cancer Institute
NCQA	National Committee for Quality Assurance
NFIB	National Federation of Independent Businesses
NHI	National health insurance
NIH	National Institutes of Health
NSF	National Science Foundation
OBRA	Omnibus Budget Reconciliation Act
OECD	Organization for Economic Cooperation and Development
OHTA	Office of Health Technology Assessment
OMB	Office of Management and Budget
OTA	Office of Technology Assessment
PAC	Political action committee
PCCM	Primary care case management
PET	Position emission tomography
PGPs	Prepaid group plans
PHPs	Prepaid health plans
POS	Point-of-service health plan
PPOs	Preferred provider organizations
PPRC	Physician Payment Review Commission
PPS	Prospective Payment System
PROs	Peer Review Organizations
PSOs	Provider Sponsored Organizations

PSROs	Professional Standard Review Organizations
QMB	Qualified Medicare beneficiaries
R&D	Research and development
RBRVS	Resource-based relative value scale
RVS	Relative value scale
RVU	Relative value units
S-CHIP	State Children's Insurance Program
S/HMOs	Social health maintenance organizations
SLMB	Specified low-income Medicare beneficiaries
SMI	Supplementary medical insurance
SSI	Supplemental Security Income
TANF	Temporary Assistance to Needy Families
TEFRA	Tax Equity and Fiscal Responsibility Act
UCR	Usual, customary, and reasonable (fees payment system)
USPHS	U.S. Public Health Service

Chronology of Significant Events and Legislation in U.S. Health Care

1798   President John Adams signs into law an act providing for relief of sick and disabled seamen, which approved the establishment of the first Marine Hospital.

1799   The first Marine Hospital is established.

1847   The American Medical Association (AMA) is founded.

1863   The National Academy of Sciences is established to assist in caring for the Union Army.

1870   First Reorganization Act federalizes the Marine Hospital Service.

1872   The American Public Health Association (APHA) is founded. This organization is concerned with the social and economic aspects of health problems.

1878   The National Quarantine Act is signed into law. This legislation is designed to prevent entry into the country of persons with communicable diseases.

1899   The National Hospital Superintendent's Association is created. It later becomes the American Hospital Association (AHA).

1904   The Council on Medical Education is established by the AMA.

1912   The U.S. Public Health Service (USPHS) is formed from the Marine Hospital Service.

1921   The Sheppard-Towner Act is signed into law. It establishes the first federal grant-in-aid program for local child health clinics.

1928   The Sheppard-Towner Act is terminated.

1929   Blue Cross is established.

1930   The National Institutes of Health (NIH) is established for the purpose of discovering the causes, prevention, and cure of disease.

1934   The Federal Emergency Relief Administration (FEMA) gives the first federal grants to local governments for public assistance to the poor, including financial support for health care.

1935   The Social Security Act of 1935 is signed into law. The act provides for unemployment compensation, old-age benefits, and other benefits.

1937   The National Cancer Act is passed by Congress, establishing the National Cancer Institute (NCI).

1939   The Murray-Wagner-Dingell bill is introduced, proposing national health insurance.

1946   The National Hospital Survey and Construction Act (Hill-Burton Act) mandates the provision of federal funding to subsidize the construction of hospitals.

The National Mental Health Act is signed into law, providing federal grants to states for research, prevention, diagnosis, and treatment of mental disorders.

1951   The Internal Revenue Service rules that employers' costs for health care insurance premiums are tax deductible.

1952   The nongovernmental Joint Commission on Accreditation of Hospitals (JCAH) is established.

The Health Insurance Association of America (HIAA) is formed.

1960   The Kerr-Mills Act (Medical Assistance Act) is signed into law, providing federal matching payments to states for vendor payments.

1965   The Medicare and Medicaid programs are passed as amendments to the Social Security Act of 1935.

1966   The Comprehensive Health Planning Act is signed into law. This legislation is an attempt to implement health care facilities planning through the states.

1971   Ralph Nader's Health Research Group is founded.

Senator Edward Kennedy introduces the Health Security Act, which calls for a comprehensive program of free medical care.

1972   President Nixon, in response to Kennedy's plan, introduces the National Health Insurance Partnership Act.

The Professional Standards Review Organizations (PSROs) are created through the Social Security Amendments of 1972. The PSRO creates a regulatory mechanism to encourage efficient and economical delivery of health care in the Medicare and Medicaid programs through peer review.

The Office of Technology Assessment (OTA) is established. This organization maintains, in part, a concern for medical technology assessment.

1973   The Health Maintenance Organization Act is signed into law. This legislation encouraged the development of health maintenance organizations (HMOs) in an attempt to induce competition in the health care market.

The U.S. Supreme Court legalizes abortion in *Roe v. Wade.*

1974   The Congressional Budget and Impoundment Control Act is signed into law.

The National Health Planning and Resource Development Act is signed into law. This legislation develops certificate-of-need (CON) requirements.

The Employee Retirement Income Security Act (ERISA) of 1974 is signed into law. This legislation is concerned with protection of private employee benefits.

1976   The Quinlan case (concerning the right to die) is decided by the New Jersey Supreme Court.

1981   The Omnibus Budget Reconciliation Act (OBRA) of 1981 is passed. This legislation affects growth rates in Medicaid, reduces the number of those eligible for welfare, and changes Medicaid policy.

The Health Care Financing Administration (HCFA) grants waivers to states to pay for home health care.

1982   The Tax Equity and Fiscal Responsibility Act (TEFRA) of 1982 is signed into law, giving states discretion to require Medicaid beneficiaries to pay nominal fees for medical services.

1983   The Prospective Payment System (PPS), a mandate of the Deficit Reduction Act of 1982, begins. This system classifies illnesses into categories for reimbursement.

1984   The Deficit Reduction Act of 1984 requires Medicaid beneficiaries to assign to the states any rights they had to other health benefit programs.

1985   Congress creates the Physician Payment Review Commission (PPRC), which is charged with making recommendations regarding payment systems.

1986   The Omnibus Budget Reconciliation Act (OBRA) of 1986 gives the states the option to extend Medicaid coverage to pregnant women and infants who are members of households with incomes as high as 100 percent of the federal poverty level.

1987   The Omnibus Budget Reconciliation Act of 1987 increases the income requirements of pregnant women and infants to 185 percent of the federal poverty level.

1988   The Medicare Catastrophic Coverage Act is passed.

The Pepper Commission Report is released, calling for coverage for long-term care and for universal coverage for those under the age of sixty-five.

1989   The Omnibus Budget Reconciliation Act of 1989 requires provision of all Medicaid- allowed treatment to correct problems identified during early and periodic screening, diagnosis, and treatment (EPSDT).

The Office of Health Technology Assessment (OHTA) is established. This office is responsible for advising the Health Care Financing Administration (HCFA) about technology as it is applied to Medicaid and Medicare programs.

The Agency for Health Care Policy and Research (AHCPR) develops guidelines on the appropriate treatment of common illnesses.

The U.S. Supreme Court, in *Webster v. Reproductive Health Services*, gives states the authority to regulate and thus restrict abortions in public clinics.

The Medicare Catastrophic Coverage Act is repealed.

1990   The U.S. Supreme Court rules on the Cruzan (right-to-die) case.

1993   President Bill Clinton unveils his Health Security Act.

1994   Congress fails to pass any health reform bill.

November elections result in Republican control of Congress.

1995   It is reported that the Medicare Hospital Insurance Trust Fund will go bankrupt by the year 2002.

Republicans adopt balanced budget target of 2002, calling for reductions in spending for Medicare and Medicaid.

President Clinton announces balanced budget target of 2005, with smaller reductions in Medicare and Medicaid.

President Clinton proposes federal regulation of private insurance.

Budget disputes between President Clinton and Congress result in two government shutdowns.

1996   Federal welfare program replaced as Congress passes Personal Responsibility and Work Opportunity Act.

Congress passes Health Insurance Portability and Accountability Act.

Congress passes legislation insurance plans to cover at least two-day hospital stay for women given birth and four days for caesarian births.

Congress also gives mental health the same status as physical health.

States begin passing patients' rights bills, regulating health maintenance organizations.

1997   Congress passes Balanced Budget Act, which calls for budget surplus by 2002 and reforms Medicare, creating Medicare+Choice program.

Texas passes patients' rights law allowing enterprise liability suits.

Columbia/HCA charged with massive fraud, revamps hospital operations. Oxford Health Plans shows significant financial losses.

Business and insurance companies lobby to thwart federal regulation of managed care plans.

1998   President Clinton proposes to extend Medicare to those aged 55–64 who are uninsured.

Federal government ends fiscal year with first surplus in almost three decades.

Congressional Budget Office predicts surplus of $1.6 trillion over next decade.

House passes patients' rights bill. Senate fails to act.

Federal investigators say portability law passed by Congress in 1996 is not working.

Number of uninsured in United States exceeds 40 million people, almost 16 percent of the population.

Some HMOs drop out of Medicare program, citing high costs and federal refusal to raise payments.

House of Representatives votes to conduct impeachment inquiry against President Clinton.

CHAPTER 1

Health Care Politics

Health care is the largest single industry in the country. Health policymaking in the United States involves a complex web of decisions made by various institutions and political actors across a broad spectrum of public and private sectors. These institutions and actors include federal, state, and local governments in the public sector. In the private sector they include health care providers such as hospitals and nursing homes; health care professionals; and health care purchasers such as insurance companies, industries, and consumers. In addition, a wide variety of interest groups influence and shape health care politics and policymaking.

These institutions and actors are involved throughout the policy cycle. The policy cycle includes getting problems to the government and agenda setting; policy formulation and legitimation; implementation of, evaluation of, and decisions about policy continuation; and modifications and/or termination.[1] These institutions and actors interact at every stage of the policy cycle. No one institution or actor dominates any one stage of policy development. Each contributes to the process by providing input that often is designed to promote the institution's or the actor's own interests.[2]

Some of the problems in health care policymaking are rooted in this diversity of institutions and actors. Any decision designed to affect the health care system generates immediate and heated responses. Any attempt to regulate the health care system also produces pressures from opponents of regulation who favor market-oriented approaches to delivery of health care. Government regulations have often been thwarted by those being regulated as well as by actors in the system who oppose a strong government role.[3]

The development of a comprehensive and consistent health care policy is made difficult, if not impossible, by the shotgun approach followed by many policymakers, such as the president and Congress. For example, Congress deals with most pressing problems one at a time and not in the framework of overall health care policy. Such an approach is often necessitated by the political realities of producing tangible results on a short-term basis for the purpose of reelection. Consequently, health care policy in the United States is

1

in a constant state of fluidity. It lacks consistency and often encompasses a mishmash of programs involving conflicting values. It is not too surprising that the American health care system is often described as scandalous and wasteful.[4]

Policymakers' discretion is often limited by a wide variety of restraints imposed by the policy environment. Just as a policy environment can help facilitate policymaking, it can also hinder policy development by the number and types of constraints it imposes on policymakers. The constraints imposed by the policy environment make it difficult for the government to resolve issues in a new or innovative manner.[5] The health policy environment can be thought of as a total matrix of factors that influence and shape the health policy cycle. These factors include constitutional or legal requirements, institutional settings, shared understandings about the rules of the game, cultural values of a society, political ideology, economic resources, and technological innovations and their impact on the cost and delivery of health care services.

This chapter has two goals: to provide a detailed and systematic analysis of the health policy environment that shapes health care policymaking, and to examine the role played by key actors in the health care field. Chapter 2 provides a historical perspective on the development of health care policy in the United States. The remaining chapters discuss contemporary issues in health care: Medicaid and Medicare; the problems of the uninsured; women, minorities, and children; cost containment; medical liability and malpractice; health care technology; health care reform; and incrementalism. These policy issues are examined from the perspective of the conflicting values of access, quality, cost, regulation, market approaches, and generational conflicts involved in the distribution of health care resources.

The Health Policy Environment

Constitutional Environment

Over 200 years ago, the Founding Fathers established a constitutional system of government that had two purposes. First, it established a government with powers to act. But second, it attempted to prevent a tyranny of the majority. Having experienced the repressive measures of concentrated power under British rule, the Founding Fathers opted for a decentralized structure of government. The major features of the American system of government, discussed next, reflect these two conflicting objectives.

Separation of Powers, and Checks and Balances

The Constitution created a system that disperses political power and decision-making authority among various branches of government. The powers of the national government are divided among the legislative, executive, and judicial branches of government. This is known as the separation of powers. The powers of the three branches are not totally separated, however, and thus it is more accurate to describe this arrangement as three coequal branches of government sharing powers. The underlying principle behind such a sharing of powers was that it would lead to checks and balances. It is based on the assumption that other branches would check an attempt by one branch of government to assume too much power or abuse its powers. James Madison, one of the most influential delegates at the Constitutional Convention, argued in *The Federalist Papers* (No. 51) that "ambition must be made to counteract ambition."[6]

Such a constitutional arrangement creates constant competition among these institutions for preeminence in various policy areas. It necessitates lengthy negotiations and compromises and bargaining in policymaking between the president and Congress. This makes it difficult to formulate a consistent and comprehensive set of policies. The result often is a government of deadlock and inaction. The problem becomes more pronounced during the periods of divided government, when different political parties control the White House and Congress. Between 1948 and 1992 we have experienced divided government 59 percent of the time (26 out of 44 years) and between 1969 and 1992, 83 percent of the time (20 of 24 years).[7] During the first six years of the Reagan administration (1981–86), the control of Congress itself was divided, with Republicans in the majority in the Senate and Democrats in the majority in the House. In the health policy area, this necessitated a number of compromises between the president and Congress. For example, the Reagan administration proposed the consolidation of some thirty-five health programs into block grants. Congress authorized four block grants covering twenty-four programs accompanied by a 25 percent reduction in federal funding. Similarly, President Ronald Reagan proposed putting a cap on federal Medicaid dollars, but Congress refused.[8] Even during periods of unified government, one of which occurred after the 1992 elections, institutional jealousies and prerogatives made policymaking a problematic adventure (see chapter 9). However, this period of unified government lasted for only two years. The 1994 congressional elections again produced a divided government with the White House controlled by a Democrat (President Bill Clinton) and both houses of Congress controlled by Republicans.

Federalism

The Constitution also created a federal system of government in which governmental authority is dispersed and divided between the national and state governments. The controversy over whether power and authority should be more centralized in the national government or more decentralized in state and local governments has been a perennial question in American politics. In addition, both the national and the state governments have often delegated important functions to thousands of units of local government. As a result, it is difficult to find many governmental activities that do not, to some extent, involve all three levels of government. Thus, despite the increased role of the federal government in the health care field during the 1960s, overall authority over health policy remains divided and shared among the national, the state, and the local governments. This is especially true with respect to implementation of many health policies and programs. In fact, the Reagan administration's desire to decentralize authority led to an increased role for state governments in the implementation of health programs.[9] In 1995, the Republican-controlled Congress proposed shifting more authority over social programs, including health care, to the states.

A federal system of government adds to the fragmentation of authority and thus increases complexity, jurisdictional competition, delays, duplication, finger pointing, and often the dodging of responsibilities by different levels of government in the health policy cycle. Attempts to reconcile many different geographical interests become problematic and tend to perpetuate a belief in organized chaos and flexible rules over central policymaking authority. The problem of regionalism and localism is accentuated by the need to satisfy the demands of a diverse and heterogeneous society. Thus, no single institution representing the nation as a whole defines the public interest and serves the public good. The result is a health care system made up of multiple "little governments" and "little empires" that pursue their own goals and interests. This in turn generates health policies that are vaguely defined and designed to serve "special publics."[10]

Institutional Environment

The institutional environment consists of the rules, structures, and settings within which major institutions involved in policymaking and implementation operate. These include the legislative, executive, and judicial branches of government. Congress is the primary policymaking institution, while the executive is primarily responsible for implementing policies. The judiciary's principal responsibility is to resolve constitutional and legal conflicts. In the twentieth century, however, these areas of responsibility have become increasingly blurred, with all three branches of government sharing powers in the areas of policymaking, implementation, and adjudication.

Congress

Policymaking in Congress takes place in an environment of decentralized and thus fragmented power structure where political power is dispersed among numerous committees and subcommittees in both chambers. This decentralization of power and authority in the committee structure has led some to describe Congress as a "kind of confederation of little legislatures."[11] One of the consequences of this in health policymaking is competition among committees within and between the Senate and the House. The second consequence for health policymaking is bargaining and compromises. Thus, health policy formulation in Congress occurs in numerous subsystems with little coordination.[12] In the 104th Congress (1995–96), the Republican majority attempted to coordinate committee action under tight leadership control.

Senators and representatives are elected to represent their respective states and smaller congressional districts, which leads to an emphasis on pork-barrel politics to capture federal goods and services for their constituencies. This creates a tendency to promote state and local interests and less sensitivity to national interests and needs in health care policymaking.

The Executive

The Constitution assigns the president and the executive branch agencies (i.e., the bureaucracy) the role of implementing policies approved by Congress. During the 1960s, concerns about issues of access, quality, equity, and efficiency in the health care area led Congress to create many new programs, such as Medicare and Medicaid, to increase access. In addition, concerns over spiraling costs have resulted in the creation of programs designed to contain rising health care costs through planning, peer review, regulation, and encouragement of the development of new health care delivery organizations such as health maintenance organizations (HMOs).

Congress routinely delegates the authority for making many decisions to bureaucratic agencies. For example, Congress created the Occupational Safety and Health Administration (OSHA) and gave it the authority to write regulations concerning workers' health and safety in the workplace. In addition, Congress often passes laws that are vague, very broad, or both, leaving bureaucratic agencies a significant amount of discretionary power to fill in the details of the law. Congress uses its legislative oversight and budgetary powers to exercise control over bureaucratic agencies. Nevertheless, the fact remains that congressional delegation of authority and discretionary power enjoyed by bureaucratic agencies gives them a significant role in health policymaking and implementation.

As with Congress, power and authority in the bureaucracy is highly dispersed and fragmented. Various health policies are under the jurisdictions of many different federal agencies, which leads to overlapping jurisdictions, authority, and responsibilities. In addition, as we discussed earlier, in a federal system of government, state bureaucracies implement many federal programs either partially or totally. Such dispersal and fragmentation of authority creates competition and conflicts along both vertical and horizontal planes throughout the health policy cycle. Turf fighting over program implementation, authority, and resources becomes the name of the game. The health policy cycle operates in a dynamic environment of constantly changing alignments of bureaucratic agencies, congressional committees, policymakers, and various interest groups shaping and reshaping health policy.

The Judiciary

Courts and judges influence health policymaking and implementation through their interpretation of the Constitution and congressional laws. They make sure that implementation of laws meets constitutional standards and that administrative agencies discharge their assigned responsibilities. Federal courts are also responsible for enforcement of the Administrative Procedures Act, which governs administrative procedures in all federal agencies. In addition, individuals and groups who feel that the executive and legislative branches have failed to redress their grievances often resort to seeking help from the courts.

The federal courts, and the U.S. Supreme Court in particular, have come to play a significant role in policymaking in certain aspects of the health care field. The Supreme Court's 1973 decision in *Roe v. Wade*, legalizing abortion, was a major policy decision and a victory for groups supporting a woman's right to have an abortion. But a 1989 decision by the Supreme Court (*Webster v. Reproductive Health Services*) whereby the Supreme Court granted states authority to regulate and thus restrict abortions in public clinics also suggests that the Court's position may change with changes in the composition of justices on the Court. Whether a more conservative Supreme Court in the future overturns *Roe v. Wade* remains to be seen.

The impact of health care technology on the treatment and delivery of health services and the ethical concerns raised by medical technology have drawn state and federal courts into such varied topics as organ transplants, fetal tissue research, health care surrogacy, quality of life, and the right to die with dignity, among others (see chapter 8).

Political Environment

The political environment includes a shared understanding among policymakers about how policy decisions should be made and the underlying values, political feasibility, electoral cycles, influence of organized interest groups, and political ideologies. The political environment itself is influenced

and shaped by the constitutional, legal, institutional, economic, and technological environment of a given policy area.

Consensus Building

We have already discussed how the constitutional and institutional environ-
ments create diffused and fragmented systems of authority and responsibility
in the health policy cycle. This in turn creates a political environment that is
conducive to constant bargaining and compromises among major institutions
and key actors in the health policy field. Since no single institution or actor is
in a position to dominate the process, coalition building becomes inevitable.
It also injects logrolling (trading votes to secure favors) and pork-barrel politics (obtaining government projects for one's legislative district) into the policy
adoption and implementation stages. One of the consequences of this is that
the policymaking process is invariably driven toward consensus building
among diverse and conflicting interests. This often results in contradictory
policies or policies that contain conflicting values.[13] Thus, the policymaking
process, instead of being a science of creating policy that solves a problem,
becomes an art of creating a consensus that holds conflicting and diverse interests together in order to create majority support for that policy. The political
logic of coalition building in order to create a consensus creates a situation in
which any measure that is successful, be it congressional or presidential, will
have been changed in ways its proponents did not foresee or desire.[14] Attempts at comprehensive change, as in the health care reform debate of the
1990s and other attempts at national health insurance, often fail. Thus, what
change does come about is piecemeal and incremental, epitomized by Medicaid and Medicare.

Incrementalism

Policymakers also share decision-making values that favor incremental
policymaking, that is, relatively small or incremental changes and modifications in existing policies. Thus, rather than consider all possible alternatives
in a comprehensive manner, policymakers concentrate only on marginal values or relatively few alternatives that bring about marginal changes in existing
policies.[15] Incrementalism is politically attractive to policymakers because
small policy adjustments reduce the impact of negative and politically risky
consequences. Nevertheless, incremental policymaking can also inhibit imagi-
nation, innovation, and fresh new approaches to the solution of problems.[16]
Policymakers end up creating policies aimed at "satisfying" diverse interests,
rather than problem solving.

Political Feasibility

Policymakers are also influenced and guided in their policy deliberations by political feasibility.[17] This involves judgment about whether it is possible to enact a policy given the political realities. One of the major political realities that policymakers face is the potential public reaction to a proposed policy. All the major institutions and actors involved in policymaking are influenced by considerations of political feasibility. This is especially true of elected public officials. Members of Congress are more apt to support and vote for a policy that is likely to be popular with their constituents than a policy that may produce a strong negative reaction from their constituents.

Electoral Cycle

Policymakers are influenced in their deliberations by the electoral cycle and the necessity of reelection. Thus, policy decisions are viewed from the perspective of potential electoral consequences. This is all the more true near election time. The policymaking process is driven by the need to produce short-term tangible benefits. The fact that the president, senators, and representatives not only have different constituencies to serve but different term lengths in office make electoral calculations a permanent fixture of the political environment. For example, during the 1980 primary campaign, Senator Edward Kennedy (D-Massachusetts), who was challenging the incumbent, President Jimmy Carter, for the Democratic party's nomination for the presidency, advocated a plan for universal national health insurance. When his proposal proved to be popular with the general public, the Carter administration was forced to propose a scaled-down version of a health insurance plan. President Carter went on to win the Democratic party's nomination but lost the general election to Ronald Reagan. The issue of national health insurance also receded from prominence on the national policy agenda because of the Reagan administration's commitment to deregulation and decentralization in health care, as well as the economic realities of the federal budget deficit. Health care reform came back on the health care agenda as a result of a special senatorial election in Pennsylvania in 1991 and the presidential campaign of 1992 (see chapter 9).

Public Philosophy and Political Ideology

Political ideology is the set of political beliefs and values by which policy actors in all policy arenas operate.[18] Within the health care system it is possible to identify the ideology of the medical profession, health care administrators, planners, and policymakers. The term "public philosophy," in contrast, is a broader concept and can be defined as an outlook on public affairs shared by a wide coalition in a nation.[19] A public philosophy often may not be explicit, but the ideological debate on issues takes place within its confines.

The underlying principle in American public philosophy, resulting from constitutional guarantees of freedom of speech, expression, and petition, is that organized interests should have an important role in influencing public policies. The public philosophy in the United States was influenced greatly by the writing of John Locke, a seventeenth-century English philosopher. A central feature of Locke's argument is the belief that ultimate authority resides in the individual's inalienable right to seek his or her own self-preservation. According to Locke, people form a government to protect their natural right of self-preservation. For Locke, the right to self-preservation is closely associated with the right to acquire property. This Lockean idea pervades American political thought and institutions.[20]

The clearest integration of this Lockean idea is found in James Madison's "Federalist 10." According to Madison, a faction constituted a number of citizens united by a common passion or interest adverse to the rights of other citizens or to the permanent and aggregate interests of the community. Madison argued that factions were evil and could lead to tyranny. Yet, elimination of the causes of factions was not a solution because it could also destroy liberty. Therefore, Madison advocated controlling the effects of factions. Since the American society is composed of a large number of geographic, ethnic, racial, economic, and religious groups, the way to control the negative effects of factions, according to Madison, was to create a representative form of government. In such a representative government, public views can be refined and enlarged by passing them through the medium of a chosen body of citizens (legislature) whose wisdom can help determine the true interest of the country. Madison also asserted that a large republic was less susceptible to tyranny than a small one because in a large republic many different interests will exist, making it difficult for any one interest regularly to dominate all other interests.[21]

This in turn helped create a philosophy of liberalism, which argues that all interests should be able to penetrate the political arena. Theodore Lowi describes this philosophy as interest group liberalism.[22] Such a political system is called a pluralistic system, which is characterized by many channels of access with various interest groups exercising countervailing veto power. This system is justified in terms of equality and openness that guarantees political freedom, which in turn can be used to achieve social and economic freedoms.[23]

The decentralized governmental structure based on separation of powers, checks and balances, and federalism is designed to give interest groups access throughout the policy cycle. Thus, ironically, a Madisonian system designed to prevent a tyranny of the majority and control the mischiefs of factions (interest groups) also gives these factions many opportunities for devilment. To formulate health policy under such a system requires public officials and institutions to reconcile the conflicting interests of many organized groups. In theory, the role of the government becomes one of neutral arbitrator resolving conflicts among organized groups. The broad and diffused distribution of political influence across numerous and diverse interest groups blurs the distinction between public and private power.

Private interests battle with one another and define themselves in terms of the public interest. But because all interest groups do not have equal resources, those with more economic resources have greater access to channels of influence and thus more opportunities for engaging in mischief. As McConnell has persuasively argued, small groups monopolize political power by successfully defining their own narrow interests as the general public interest.[24] For example, for many years, the American Medical Association (AMA) based its opposition to national health insurance on the ground that socialized medicine would be against the general public interest because it would deprive patients of their freedom of choice and would lead to poor-quality medical care. In a pluralistic system based on the public philosophy of interest-group liberalism, private economic, regional, and constituency interests are justified as public interests by appealing to values of individualism, constitution, democracy, freedom, and equality, which make up an important part of American culture and belief systems. Private interests as well as public officials do this. The consensus created from compromises and bargaining among competing interests gets defined as the public interest. The role of the government, according to the pluralistic formulation, becomes one of protecting these diverse and competing interests by creating a consensus through the give-and-take of politics.

Reforming the present health care system becomes difficult because every reform proposal gets trapped in pluralistic processes designed to safeguard all existing professional and organizational interests. Ideological conflicts between those who want to protect the professional monopoly and autonomy of the medical profession and those who want more health care planning and regulation are contained within a pluralistic institutional framework that prevents either side from generating enough power to bring about significant reforms designed to integrate and coordinate health care.[25] Market reformers blame bureaucratic interference and cumbersome regulations for the problems of the health care system. They call for less regulation and more incentive-based reforms to increase and diversify health care facilities and delivery of services. The libertarian ideology of distributive justice is most evident in arguments for competitive market reforms. According to this ideology, increased reliance on market competition for allocative decisions would result in a more efficient allocation of resources than we now have. Republicans in general, and conservatives in particular, support this position. Bureaucratic reformers blame market competition for the defects of the present system and call for more regulation and planning. This argument is based on the egalitarian ideology, which emphasizes the just distribution of health care resources based on need. The concern is to provide equal access to decent-quality health care for everyone at a reasonable cost. Democrats in general, and liberals in particular, support this position.[26]

Thus the health care system exhibits a continuous conflict and strain between the values of efficiency, access, equality, rights, and freedom. This is reflected in the contradictions between people's expectations for equal access to decent-quality health care, the failure of the private sector to provide equal access, and the inability of the public sector to compensate for the inadequacies of the private sector.

Which health policies are pursued at a given point in time depends on which ideology is dominant at that time. During the 1960s and early 1970s, the dominance of egalitarian ideology resulted in bureaucratic reformers' success in creating health policies designed to increase access to health care and at the same time provide quality care at a reasonable cost through such policies as Medicare, Medicaid, health care planning, and regulation. The ascendancy of libertarian ideology during the 1970s, and particularly the 1980s, led to the creation of health policies—supported by market reformers—aimed at cost containment and economic efficiency. This was attempted through deregulation, cuts in federal funds, encouragement of development of alternative health delivery organizations such as health maintenance organizations, and the establishment of a prospective reimbursement system of hospital payment for Medicare patients through diagnosis-related groups (DRGs). These policies were designed to induce diversity and competition in the health care system through market incentives.

Economic Environment

Decisions about health care policies are invariably intertwined with economics. Health care affects and is affected by the economic environment in a number of ways. The economic environment consists of a network of institutions, laws, and rules that deal with primary questions such as what goods and services to produce, how they should be produced, and for whom.[27] The economic point of view is also rooted in three fundamental assumptions: (1) resources are limited or scarce in relation to human wants, (2) resources have alternative uses, and (3) people have different wants and do not attach the same importance to them.[28] Because economic resources are limited and have alternative uses, decisions must be made with regard to how and for what purposes to use these resources. The concept of opportunity cost suggests that when deciding to use resources in a certain way, one loses the opportunity to obtain benefits of using resources in some other way.

The economic environment affects policy decisions in health care in a number of ways. At any given point in time, health policymakers are influenced in their decisions by the notion of economic feasibility. When an economy is growing at a healthy rate, making economic resources available, policymakers find it economically feasible to establish new programs. Such was the case during the 1960s and to an extent in the early 1970s, when a number of new programs designed to increase access to health care were created. But corresponding increases in health care costs, a slowed rate of economic growth, the massive federal budget deficits, and an executive branch dominated by a conservative political philosophy during the 1980s not only made it economically difficult to establish new health care programs but made it possible to cut expenditures on federal health programs.[29] If one accepts the assumptions of scarcity of resources and the existence of competing goals, then the question faced by health policymakers becomes how to bring about the optimum distribution of health care resources.[30] What is needed is not simply cost containment but a cost-effective health care system.[31] Former Secretary of Health, Education, and Welfare Joseph A. Califano, Jr., has argued that one of the major problems with the U.S. health care system is that it is less cost effective than health care systems in other industrialized countries.[32] In a constrained economic environment health policymakers are confronted with making choices and establishing priorities that are not easy to make. One of the major issues in health care is that of deciding how to value health. An environment of limited resources and constantly changing health care needs requires value judgments by policymakers about priorities.[33] How much of society's resources should be devoted to health care? What priorities should be assigned to different groups competing for the same health care resources? Should more priority be given to the health care needs of the elderly or to those of infants and children? Should everyone be entitled to an organ transplant, regardless of cost or the ability to pay? In recent years, a constrained economic environment has increased concerns about values of cost effectiveness and efficiency. It has prompted some states to attempt health care rationing. This has generated significant controversy and public debate over the conflicting values of efficiency, access, and equality.

Technological Environment

Dramatic advances in health care technology in the past thirty years have revolutionized the nature and delivery of health services in the United States. The rapid pace with which new biomedical technologies are developed and the swiftness with which they are adopted have transformed many hospitals into very complex and resource-intensive institutions, and have changed the very nature of medical practice.[34]

New health care technologies have been linked to the problems of cost and quality of health care in the United States.[35] Since every change in technology involves costs and benefits, the formulation of a good public policy depends on an accurate assessment of the relative magnitudes of costs and benefits. The nature of technological change can have profound effects on resource requirements.[36]

The technological revolution in biomedicine also raises questions about what medical technology should be developed and what is the proper and appropriate level of medical intervention to treat an illness. Since health care costs make up an increasing part of the government budget, the role of the government becomes crucial with respect to allocation of health care resources. Should health care technologies be available to all persons on an equal basis? If not, what criteria should be used to decide who gets scarce health resources and who does not? Should government be involved in technology assessment and play a role in encouraging or discouraging the development of particular technology through its funding? Should the government establish legal and ethical guidelines not only with respect to biomedical research but also regarding application of biomedical technology? We explore these questions in chapter 8.

Key Health Policy Actors

The key policy actors in the health care system include a variety of public and private institutions and groups: health care providers, health care practitioners, health care purchasers, health insurers, and a variety of other groups. The remainder of this chapter examines the role of the key health policy actors.

Health Care Purchasers

In 1996 federal, state, and local governments combined spent $483.2 billion to fund health care services. This represents 46.7 percent of the total national health care expenditures of $1,035.1 billion during the same year.[37] This alone makes the federal, state, and local governments key actors in the health care system. Since health expenditures continue to climb and require an increasingly larger share of the budget, the role of all three levels of government in health care has also increased.

The Federal Government

Today the federal government is one of the major purchasers of health care. In 1996 the federal government alone spent $350.9 billion on health care, representing 33.9 percent of total national health care expenditures.[38] The majority of federal health spending is for health services provided to low-income individuals and others eligible through Medicaid, people over sixty-five years of age through Medicare, military personnel and their dependents, veterans, federal civilian employees, and Native Americans.[39] Of these, the major bulk of the expenditures is taken up by Medicare and Medicaid programs. Medicare accounted for 60.3 percent of total federal funding for health care in 1996, with Medicaid accounting for another 27.3 percent.[40]

The three major branches of government play a crucial role in the health policy cycle. The primary policymaking responsibility lies with Congress. Most federal programs are implemented by numerous bureaucratic agencies in the executive branch of government. This makes the president and the bureaucracy important actors, especially during the implementation stage of the health policy cycle. In recent years the federal courts, especially the U.S. Supreme Court, have become major actors in the health policy cycle. The number, frequency, and complexity of legal, constitutional, and ethical issues is on the increase as a result of advances in medical technology. The federal courts are increasingly called on to resolve some of these conflicts.

The Department of Health and Human Services (HHS) is headed by a secretary who is appointed by the president with Senate confirmation. He or she is responsible for administering federal health care programs and activities. It advises the president and Congress on legislative measures and carries out congressional mandates in the health care (and social services) field. The Department of Health and Human Services has five operational divisions, three of them in the health care area.[41]

The Office of Human Development Service provides leadership and direction in the areas of human services programs for the elderly, children and youth, families, Native Americans, disabled persons, and people living in rural areas. It recommends to the secretary policies designed to improve coordination of human services programs within HHS, with other federal agencies, state and local governments, and private-sector organizations. It also supervises the use of research and impact evaluation funds.

The Public Health Service is responsible for conducting medical and bio-medical research; developing and administering programs to prevent and control diseases and alcohol and drug abuse; providing resources, expertise, and direction in the delivery of physical and mental health services; and enforcing laws in the areas of efficacy of drugs, protection against impure and unsafe foods, cosmetics, and medical devices. The Public Health Service performs these responsibilities through its various agencies, such as the Agency for Health Care Policy and Research; the Health Resources and Services Administration; the Centers for Disease Control; the Food and Drug Administration; the Indian Health Services; and the Alcohol, Drug Abuse, and Mental Health Administration. Many of these agencies are further subdivided into different components. For example, the Alcohol, Drug Abuse, and Mental Health Administration has various components that include agencies such as the National Institute on Alcohol and Alcoholism, the National Institute on Drug Abuse, and the National Institute of Mental Health.

The Health Care Financing Administration is responsible for the oversight of Medicare and Medicaid programs. It is also responsible for implementation of quality-assurance provisions of the Medicare and Medicaid programs and for professional review provisions.

State and Local Governments

Because of the federal system of government, state and local governments are important actors in the health care field. During 1996, state and local governments spent $132.2 billion on health care. This amounted to about 12.7 percent of the total national health care expenditures. In 1996, Medicaid accounted for about 44 percent of state and local expenditures for health.[42]

The public health programs of state health agencies and local health departments are primarily involved in four program areas. These include personal health, environmental health, health resources, and laboratory services. In addition, they perform general administrative and service functions. A sizable part of state health agencies' expenditures goes for maternal and child health, mental health, communicable disease, and handicapped children.[43] State governments have traditionally been involved in licensing and accreditation of health care providers, as well as insurance regulation. In recent years, state governments have also become involved in rate setting, negotiated or competitively bid fixed-price arrangements, and health care rationing to control health care costs. Some states have also been in the forefront of health care reform. We consider the role of the states more fully in chapters 6 and 9.

Industries

Large industries and firms are also major purchasers of health care. Many major industries and firms provide health insurance coverage to their employees as part of a benefit package. Today a majority of workers in the United States are employed by firms that offer health insurance.[44] Factors that seem to have a bearing on whether employers provide health insurance benefits or not are employer size, employee job tenure, wage level, full-time work status, industry, and union membership.[45] The health insurance coverage provided by employer group insurance plans also varies widely with respect to the scope of covered services, conditions of eligibility, and the share of employees' contribution to the plan.[46]

Major industries and firms have become key actors in the health care system because of the cost they incur in providing health insurance for their workers. A survey of 2,000 companies by Foster Higgins & Company, a New York consulting firm, set the average cost of medical benefits at $3,161 per employee in 1990. This represented a 22 percent increase over the 1989 average of $2,600. Similarly, from 1988 to 1989, the average cost of medical benefits jumped 46 percent, from $2,160 to $2,600.[47] Such dramatic increases in health care costs have made businesses more conscious of their costs and have led them to use a variety of cost-cutting measures such as managed care, increased cost sharing and cost shifting, and encouraging or requiring employees to enroll in prepaid group plans for health services.

Health Care Providers

The major health care providers include health care institutions such as hospitals, nursing homes, and pharmacies, as well as health care professionals such as physicians, nurses, and dentists. They are important actors in the health care system because they not only deliver health care services but also influence the way in which services are delivered and the type of services that are delivered. The major feature of the American health care system is its entrepreneurial nature. Pharmacies and manufacturers of pharmaceutical and medical equipment and suppliers are private, profit-making enterprises. Similarly, many nursing homes are for-profit institutions. Most physicians are private practitioners.

Hospitals

There are almost 4,856 short-term general hospitals with over 1 million beds, of which 592 hospitals were for-profit (i.e., investor owned).[48] Hospitals have become the primary setting for the delivery of health care services because most of the sophisticated medical technology and equipment are located there. Hospitals vary by purpose and ownership. Not-for-profit hospitals (those that are community run or church affiliated) provide short-term care. States run psychiatric hospitals. The federal government operates veterans' hospitals. There are also an increasing number of proprietary or profit-making hospitals.

Since the early 1980s, the number of health corporations that own profit-making hospitals, health care facilities, and health care suppliers has grown very rapidly. Corporate medicine has become such a major American growth industry that some refer to it as the medical-industrial complex.[49] Hospital Corporation of America (HCA) is the largest hospital management company. It owns about twenty-five psychiatric hospitals. Similarly, Humana is one of the largest acute-care chain hospital companies in the United States.[50]

Nursing Homes

Today there are over 20,000 nursing homes with about 2 million beds.[51] A majority of nursing homes are proprietary, that is, operated for profit. A small number of voluntary or not-for-profit nursing homes are operated by charitable organizations, mainly religious.[52] Nursing homes generally provide long-term care, and most of the people they serve are elderly. A sizable portion of their revenues comes from the government. In 1993, for example, 60 percent of nursing home revenues came from the government, with Medicaid constituting 51.7 percent and Medicare 8.8 percent of the payment.[53] Nursing homes are also heavily regulated by state and local governments.

Physicians

Physicians are key actors in the health care system, because they are the primary caregivers. They enjoy considerable professional autonomy. There are about 620,000 physicians in the United States.[54] A majority of them are specialists who conduct their practices in a hospital setting. Over the years, the number of generalists or family doctors has declined considerably.[55] Physicians play a pivotal role and occupy a unique position in the health care system. Since they not only diagnose an illness but also prescribe treatment, they control the supply of as well as the demand for health care services. In the process, they exert substantial influence over the pattern of health resources utilization in general and hospital resources in particular.

In addition to these key actors there are a number of other health care providers, such as 1.9 million registered nurses, 630,000 licensed practical nurses, 24,000 nurse practitioners, 25,000 physician assistants, and 160,000 dentists. They play if not a primary then a secondary role in influencing the health care system and health care policies. The U.S. health care system employs nearly 11 million people.[56]

Third-Party Payers

The U.S. health care system over the years has undergone dramatic changes. One of the fundamental changes that have occurred since the early 1930s is the method of payment for health care services. Before the rise of the modern health insurance system, the nature of financial transactions between patient and health care provider was largely a direct one-on-one transaction. Under this system the patient paid for health services directly to the health care provider out of his or her own pocket. The birth of the modern health insurance system came in 1929 with the establishment of the Blue Cross plans for hospital insurance. A third-party-payer system was created under which a consumer paid predetermined monthly premiums to an insurance company. In return, the insurance company agreed to pay the health care provider for a specified range of health services received by the consumer. The Blue Shield plans, initiated by physicians, followed, based on a similar concept. Over the years, the number of private health insurance companies increased. Between 1930 and 1950, health insurance companies not only continued to cover more and more people under such plans but also expanded the scope of coverage. In 1965 the federal government entered the picture by creating two major insurance programs—Medicare for the elderly and Medicaid for the poor.

In 1995, out of a total population of 264.3 million, more than 223 million Americans, or 84.6 percent of the population, were covered by private or public health insurance plans, or sometimes both, while 15.4 percent of the population, or 40.6 million people, were uninsured.[57] Of the 223 million insured Americans, 185.9 million (83 percent) were insured by private insurance companies.[58] The cost of providing health coverage has risen dramatically for private health insurance companies. In 1993 private health insurers spent an estimated $273.7 billion for medical care and disability claims, compared to $143.5 billion paid in 1986 and $73.4 billion in 1980.[59]

Such cost increases and pressure from employers have led insurance companies to look for ways to cut costs as well as increase the premiums they charge. Many insurance companies have begun to develop managed care systems. The concept of managed care involves arrangements with selected providers such as health maintenance organizations (HMOs) and preferred provider organizations (PPOs) to furnish a comprehensive set of health care services to its members, formal programs for ongoing quality assurance and utilization review, explicit standards for selection of health care providers, and financial incentives for members to use providers and procedures covered by the plan.[60] The role of health insurers is changing significantly.[61] This has led Robert M. Brandon, vice-president of Citizen Action, an advocacy group, to charge that health insurance companies are engaging in "cream-skimming and cherry-picking" that eliminate or penalize firms and employees that could put them at risk of high payments, rather than offering coverage to all at rates that pool the risk. The Health Insurance Association of America (HIAA), an industry group, denies such charges.[62]

Consumers

The public can exert influence on health care policies not only as purchasers of health care but also by the perceptions, attitudes, and values they bring to the health care system as consumers. In 1996 consumers spent $171.2 billion in out-of-pocket expenses for health services (18.9 percent) out of a total of $907.2 billion of personal health care expenditures.[63]

The public's perception of the American health care system is negative. A study examining the public's feeling about health care systems found that of the ten countries included in the study, the lowest degree of satisfaction with health care systems was in the United States and the highest was in Canada.[64] Surveys by the *Los Angeles Times* in March 1990, NBC in 1989, and Louis Harris & Associates in 1988 all showed that majorities of at least 61 percent of those polled supported establishing a Canadian-style comprehensive national health system. Despite escalating health care costs, the general public also shows a preference for more spending for health care, but they themselves do not want to pay the bill. They want the government to pay the cost of health care.[65] In 1987 a Harris poll asked a random sample of 1,250 Americans whether some limit should be set, say $5 million, on what we can afford to spend to save a life. Fifty-one percent of the respondents said that no limit should be set.[66] Surveys also show that Americans want more health care, not less. About half of all Americans believe that the United States spends too little on health care. Polls also suggest that the public does not believe the increased health care costs have been matched by similar increases in the quality of treatment.[67]

Those who are dissatisfied with the current system cite the high cost of care and lack of access—lack of availability of health care or health insurance—as primary reasons for their dissatisfaction. While a majority of Americans express a preference for a Canadian-style national health system, many also think that a government-run system would adversely affect their freedom of choice and lower quality of care, and they express doubt that such a system would lower costs.[68] Public dissatisfaction with the current health care system leads many people to support a change, but they are also ambivalent about the options that would change the system.

Such perceptions and attitudes in the general public present interesting dilemmas and value conflicts for health policymakers. The general public does not want to pay the bill but wants more spending on health care by the government. On their part, health policymakers concerned with the impact of escalating health care costs on the budget want to contain costs and at the same time provide access to quality care for all Americans.

Interest Groups

The role of interest groups in American politics has been debated intensely from the time of the founding of the Republic. The philosophy of interest-group liberalism has accorded interest groups a dominant role in American politics. Proponents have praised interest groups for advancing the cause of American democracy by providing access for citizen participation in the political process. Opponents have argued that special interests are stealing America[69] and destroying democracy.[70] Regardless of how one feels about interest groups, there is no denying the fact that they have become important political power brokers in American politics.[71] Since the 1970s, American society has also witnessed a rise in the number of public interest groups, that is, citizens' lobbies, to counter the influence of special interest groups in American politics.[72] Public interest groups presumably champion the cause of the public interest or the common good, while special or private interest groups work to advance narrow causes for the benefit of their members.[73]

Health care affects everyone in society. A wide variety of interests—health care providers, purchasers, third-party payers, suppliers, consumers—are affected by what happens within the field of health care. Thus it is not too surprising that the number and variety of interest groups involved in health care politics and policymaking is very large.[74] For example, over 1,000 health-related groups are listed in the *Encyclopedia of Associations 1991*.[75]

The universal nature of illness gives health care professionals such as physicians important psychological and political leverage. Given their unique position, they are able to influence developments in the health care field. The introduction of government-sponsored health insurance programs such as Medicare and Medicaid has also made hospitals and skilled nursing facilities important players. The technical nature of modern medicine gives drug and medical supply companies significant leverage in the health field. Similarly, insurance companies as third-party payers have also come to play an important role.[76]

One of the major ways in which these groups try to influence the political process is through their political action committees (PACs). According to an analysis by the Center for Responsive Politics, a Washington-based research group, health PACs accounted for 6 percent of all campaign contributions in the 1987–88 election cycle. Health PACs gave nearly $10 million to congressional candidates. The largest donor among health PACs was the political action committee of the AMA. Pharmaceutical and other health-product manufacturers were the next largest segment, followed by hospitals and nursing homes.[77] By the 1991–92 election cycle, the 199 health-related PACs had given almost $13 million in congressional elections.[78]

While it is impossible to discuss all the interest groups involved in the health care field, some of the major groups should be mentioned. Many of them are professional or trade associations of key actors in the health care field.

American Medical Association

The American Medical Association (AMA) is one of the largest and most influential health-related groups.[79] It is a professional association of physicians with a membership of about 283,000.[80] It is the voice of organized medicine and as such acts as an umbrella organization of American medicine. Its main functions include representing the interests of its members; providing scientific and socioeconomic information; keeping data on the profession; and developing and maintaining standards of professional education, training, and performance.[81]

The AMA has grassroots political power and is very active in lobbying Congress on health-related issues. It is very well financed. It has one of the largest political action committees. During the 1991–92 election cycle, the American Medical Political Action Committee (AMPAC) spent $2.3 million on contributions to congressional candidates, "with another $1 million in 'independent expenditures.'"[82] AMPAC ranked fourth among all PACs in overall spending and third in contributions to federal candidates.[83]

The AMA has acted as a voice of free enterprise and fee-for-service independent medical practice in the health care field. Much of its effort has been directed toward protecting the economic interests of its members and opposing policies that threaten those interests or threaten their professional autonomy. For example, for a long time the AMA has successfully argued against a national health insurance program because of the fear of losing its professional autonomy and a decline in physicians' income. But the organization has articulated its opposition to national health insurance not on the ground of protecting self-interest but by using the rhetoric of defending free enterprise and patients' freedom to choose their own doctors. It has argued that adoption of national health insurance would lead to lower quality of health care and services. The AMA has not been above using scare tactics to achieve its objectives.

The AMA is not the only physician group that has attempted to influence the political process. PACs representing such specialists as pathologists, plastic surgeons, anesthesiologists, chiropractors, and emergency physicians also contributed funds to political campaigns.[84]

American Hospital Association

The National Hospital Superintendents' Association was created in 1899. The membership in this organization was limited to chief executive officers of hospitals. A few years after the organization's founding, its name was changed to the American Hospital Association (AHA). In 1917 it changed from an individual membership organization to an organization of institutions.[85] Today, the AHA represents individuals and health care institutions including hospitals, health care systems, and pre- and postacute health care delivery organizations. It has a membership of about 45,000. In addition to conducting research and education projects, it acts as the voice of hospitals and represents their interests in national health care legislation.[86]

Hospital and other health care groups' political action committees are relatively small compared to AMPAC, but they are increasing their political power by raising more money for their political activities. The AHA's political action committee's spending has been relatively small compared to AMPAC's; however, in recent years there has been a significant growth of PACs among state hospital associations.[87]

Health Insurance Association of America

The Health Insurance Association of America (HIAA) was founded in 1956 and has a membership of 350 companies. It represents the voice of accident and health insurance companies. Through HIAA the health insurance industry attempts to present a united front. This has led some to criticize the health cost-containment record of the insurance companies and to suggest that insurers have colluded to prevent cost containment.[88] It has been argued that health insurers have advocated policies aimed at reducing the competitive pressures on themselves by investing resources in seeking legislation designed to suppress competition.[89]

Among the health insurers, two of the major commercial insurers are Blue Cross and Blue Shield. The Blue Cross plans were developed by the hospitals through the AHA, while the Blue Shield plans were developed by physicians through the AMA. In 1988, of the 182.3 million Americans insured by private insurance companies, an estimated 74 million were covered by Blue Cross and Blue Shield.[90]

American Health Care Association

The American Health Care Association (AHCA) is a federation of state associations of long-term health care facilities with a membership of 9,800. It provides continuing education to nursing home personnel and promotes standards for professionals in long-term-care delivery. The organization focuses on issues of availability, quality, affordability, and fair payment in health care. The American Health Care Association also maintains a liaison with government agencies, Congress, and other professional health care associations.[91]

Other Groups

A number of other groups represent hospital equipment suppliers and manufacturers of drugs and health care products and attempt to influence health care politics and policies. The increased cost of providing health care to employees has led many businesses and industries to form health coalitions to search for solutions to spiraling health care costs. Such coalitions are rapidly expanding in number.[92] The many major health coalitions include the Alliance of Business for Cost Containment; the Coalition on Health Care Costs, Quality, and Access; the National Leadership Coalition for Health Care Reforms, and the Washington Business Group on Health. A consortium of business groups representing small companies, called the Partnership on Health Care and Employment, was formed to oppose legislative proposals requiring all employers to offer health insurance to its employees. It includes the chamber of commerce, the American Farm Bureau Federation, the National Restaurant Association, and about 350 corporations.[93]

The number of health-related public interest groups has also increased. One of the most active groups is Ralph Nader's Health Research Group, founded in 1971. Its main objectives include protecting consumers and increasing public awareness on a variety of health issues.[94] Similarly, the National Insurance Consumer Organization was established in 1980 to help consumers buy insurance wisely and to serve as a consumer advocate on public policy matters.[95] Public interest groups typically rely on methods such as coalition forming, litigation, lobbying, testifying before congressional committees, and participation in regulatory proceedings to influence health care policies.

Conclusion

Health care politics and policies in the United States are shaped by a variety of factors. Health policy reflects a combination of initiatives taken by institutions and actors in the public and private sectors. The health policy cycle is influenced and shaped by the constitutional, institutional, political, economic, ideological, and technological environment within which it operates. The public philosophy of interest-group liberalism combined with constitutionally guaranteed freedom of speech, association, and petition allow a variety of interest groups to promote policies for private profit and to successfully defeat policies they perceive as harmful to their interests. Interest groups promote their narrow private interests using the rhetoric of the common good. The consensus created through compromise and bargaining between narrow private interests is often defined as the public interest. Such a policy process makes the establishment of a comprehensive national health policy highly improbable, if not impossible. The result is a series of health care programs and policies that often reflects conflicting values of access, equality, quality of care, and efficiency.

CHAPTER 2

Health Care Policy in the United States

There are substantial differences in the health care systems of various countries. They differ with respect to financing, delivery of health care, and the role of the government. Today there are three primary models of health care. In a mostly private health care system, workers and their dependents are covered through private insurance, even though the insurance is generally bought through employers. Government provides public insurance programs for those not covered by private insurance. Mostly private hospitals and doctors deliver health care. The United States is an example of such a system. Other countries have a health care system that is mostly public. Health care is paid out of general taxation or through payroll taxes. It is provided by publicly owned hospitals and salaried doctors. Examples of countries with such a system include Great Britain, Sweden, and Italy. The third model of health care system is a hybrid model. In such a system, health care is mostly publicly financed, generally through payroll taxes, but is delivered by private hospitals and doctors. Germany, Japan, Canada, France, and Holland exhibit variants of this model. However, it is important to keep in mind that none of the countries follows these models in their purest form. In reality, most countries incorporate public and private elements in their health care systems.[1]

As mentioned, the U.S. health care system follows the model of the mostly private health care system. A majority of Americans are covered through private insurance, usually bought through their employers. The government provides public insurance programs to cover the health care needs of groups such as the poor, the elderly, and veterans. Nevertheless, public insurance programs do not cover all uninsured Americans. Public programs do not cover a sizable number of individuals who cannot afford private health insurance for one reason or another.

The United States spends proportionately more money on health care than all other Western industrialized nations. Statistics compiled by the Organization for Economic Cooperation and Development (OECD) indicate that in 1989 health spending in the United States amounted to 11.8 percent of gross domestic product (GDP), compared to 8.7 percent for France and Canada, 8.2 percent for Germany, 6.7 percent for Japan, and 5.8 percent for Britain. Similarly, during the same year the United States spent $2,354 per person on health care, compared to $1,683 in Canada, $1,274 in France, $1,232 in Germany, $1,035 in Japan, and $836 in Britain. By 1993, the United States was spending almost 14 percent of GDP on health care, an average of $3,299 per person.[2]

Despite the fact that the United States spends proportionately more money on health care than most other Western countries, it does not rank very high on many health care indicators. For example, the United States has the highest infant mortality rate, 9.7 per 1,000 live births, of the countries mentioned above. It has the lowest life expectancy at birth, 71.5 years for males, among the same countries.[3] The U.S. health care system also has other problems. Health care costs continue to soar. The number of uninsured Americans continues to rise and is currently estimated to be around 40 million. By the early 1990s, many hospitals in large cities were reporting long waiting lines in emergency rooms, with many Medicaid patients leaving in frustration without receiving treatment.[4] The City Hospital Visiting Committee, in its annual report in 1991, described hospital care in New York City's municipal hospitals as the worst in recent memory.[5] Rising malpractice insurance costs also forced many of the nation's community health centers to cut or eliminate services for low-income patients.[6] Law enforcement officials in several states were investigating private psychiatric hospital chains on charges that they had systematically misdiagnosed, mistreated, and abused patients to increase their profits from insurance claims.[7]

As mentioned in chapter 1, a majority of Americans express very low satisfaction with the U.S. health care system and believe that increased health care expenditures have not been matched by similar increases in the quality of treatment. The American health care system has been referred to as "broken,"[8] "sick,"[9] "a disgrace,"[10] "wasteful,"[11] "built for waste,"[12] and "scandalous."[13] It is not too surprising, then, that by early 1990s, 60 percent of Americans expressed a view that fundamental changes were needed in the U.S. health care system, while another 29 percent believed that the entire system needed to be rebuilt.[14]

In this chapter we examine the historical development of health care policies in the United States. We discuss private- and public-sector policy initiatives and various factors that have shaped health care policy. The major emphasis is on the development of federal health care policies and how these policies have attempted to address the goals of equity, quality, and efficiency. The chapter also briefly explores the roles of state and local governments.

Health Care in the Nineteenth Century

The progress of medicine, or the "healing arts," was very slow in the 1700s and 1800s. Neither health care nor the biosciences received a great deal of popular support in the United States in the early 1800s. The biological sciences were not very popular with the general public. During the 1840s, a proposal for the establishment of a National Institute of Science, funded by the federal government, was rejected repeatedly by Congress. Finally, during the Civil War, the National Academy of Sciences was established in 1863 on the grounds of its usefulness to the Union armies.[15]

The American Medical Association was formed in 1847. During the latter part of the nineteenth century, physicians and pharmacists were the sole dispensers of professionally recognized health services. Most physicians were trained through apprenticeships with practicing physicians. Physicians also established "diploma mills" to train several students at a time. Later, private and public schools set up medical schools to train physicians. Physicians made their living treating patients for fees and received very little money from the government. The same was true of pharmacists, who later developed drugstores to supplement their income from prescriptions. Thus, private practice and fee for service became firmly established in the early American health care system.[16]

During the nineteenth century, public health activities were devoted to preventing the spread of communicable diseases and were confined primarily to major cities until the Civil War. In response to epidemics, a city board or commission was appointed to establish regulations for the maintenance of a sanitary environment. Only after the Civil War did state boards of health become popular. By the end of the nineteenth century, boards of health had been established within the governments of most large cities and at the state level. Their functions were limited to enforcement of sanitary regulations and control of certain communicable diseases. The scope of the health departments did not expand until the turn of the century.[17] Public health services were separated from the private practice of medicine, and public health officers were not allowed to practice medicine.

General hospitals, as we know them today, did not exist. Poorhouses and almshouses provided care for destitute persons. The origin of a hospital system in the United States is associated with the establishment of the first Marine Hospital in 1799.[18] Both the army and the navy had their own requirements for treating sickness, and they differed from those of the U.S. Marine Service. Between 1830 and 1860, marine hospitals proliferated. During the Civil War, the Marine Hospital System was very much neglected and the number of hospitals decreased. In 1869, Congress reviewed the Marine Hospital System and passed the first Reorganization Act in 1870. Under this law, the Marine Hospital Service was federalized and formally organized as a national agency with a central headquarters.[19]

The building of mental hospitals also preceded the development of personal health services. Mental hospitals were and continue to be largely publicly owned and operated.

The last quarter of the nineteenth century saw a steady advance in medical science. Antiseptic surgery was highly developed by 1875. The science of microbiology was introduced, and techniques of vaccination were developed. The advent of anesthesia and antisepsis made general hospitals a relatively safe place for surgery. Mostly voluntary community boards and churches established the early general hospitals. The growing economy made it possible for hospitals to obtain capital funds from philanthropists and operating funds from paying patients. Voluntary hospitals, because of their charitable and nonprofit charters, were obligated to provide care for the poor. Physicians began to admit patients to hospitals for surgeries. Patients paid for hospital charges and physicians' fees. In return, hospitals provided physicians with their facilities to provide free care for the poor. In 1875 there were very few general hospitals in the country. By 1900, there were about 4,000 general hospitals in the United States.[20]

The Transformation of American Medicine: 1900–1935

During the first decade of the twentieth century, the process of consolidation of medical education and the transformation of American medicine began to take shape. For a number of years, the American Medical Association had been trying to force inferior medical schools to close in order to reduce the numbers of institutions competing for philanthropic support.[21] Reform of medical schools was the top priority of the AMA. The Council on Medical Education, established by the AMA in 1904, elevated and standardized requirements for medical education for physicians. In addition, in order to identify and pressure weaker institutions, the council began to grade medical schools and later extended its evaluation to include curriculum, facilities, faculty, and requirements for admissions.[22]

Philanthropic foundations often had power and influence, but they lacked authority. Their financial power was limited by their fear that legislatures that chartered them would restrict their power or tax them out of existence. Nevertheless, placing medical education on a more scientific basis had also become their top priority. Several foundations began to finance studies that recommended reorganization of medical education and medical care. The AMA Council invited an outside group, the Carnegie Foundation for the Advancement of Teaching, to investigate medical schools. Abraham Flexner, as a representative of the Carnegie Foundation, visited each of the medical schools in the country during 1909 and 1910. He saw a great discrepancy between medical science and medical education. His report, known as the Flexner Report, was published in 1910 and recommended adoption of the German model of medicine with scientifically based training, the strengthening of first-class medical schools, and the elimination of a great majority of inferior schools.

Following the Flexner Report, the process of consolidation of medical education proceeded at a rapid pace. By 1915, the number of medical schools had decreased from 131 to 95. Similarly, the number of graduates from medical schools dropped from 5,440 to 3,536. Mergers between class A and class B schools became common. The AMA Council became a national accrediting agency for medical schools, and many states came to accept its judgments regarding medical schools. The new system increased the homogeneity and cohesiveness of the medical profession and made the AMA a powerful force in American medicine.[23]

Another significant development during this period was the rise of the third-party payment system in American medicine. Prior to the 1930s, medical insurance programs were nonexistent. During the Great Depression of the 1930s, the incomes of hospitals and physicians declined. Many people could not afford to pay hospitals or physicians for their medical services. Realizing that they could operate better with a steady income, hospitals began to sponsor prepayment plans, which came to be known as the Blue Cross plans. Similarly, prepayment plans for physicians' services in the hospital, especially surgery, also began to appear. Sponsored by state medical societies, they became known as Blue Shield plans. Both the Blue Cross and the Blue Shield plans were very successful. During the 1940s, the federal government encouraged the development of private, voluntary insurance plans. For example, Congress gave voluntary plans a financial boost by legislating that health insurance and pensions were fringe benefits and exempt from a wartime freeze on wages. Thus, employers could offer their workers health care fringe benefits by paying for part or all of the cost of their insurance premiums. A ruling by the Internal Revenue Service in 1951 that employers' costs for premiums were a tax-deductible expense made large-scale development of private health insurance viable.

The rise of third-party payment led to increases in visits to physicians and admissions to hospitals. The third-party payment system replaced the financing system based on one-on-one financial transactions between patient and physician. Third-party payers insulated health care consumers from the realities of health care costs, leading to overconsumption, a problem called "moral hazard" by economists. Physicians and hospitals prospered. Since insurance companies reimbursed hospitals for the charges and/ or costs of hospital services received by the patient, third-party payments made hospitals financially secure and independent because they could count on a steady income. Physicians prospered because they were paid by voluntary health insurance according to generous fee schedules negotiated by the Blue Shield plans.

The Role of the Federal Government

The Beginnings: 1800s

During much of the nineteenth century, the role of the federal government in health care was limited to providing public health services. In 1798 President John Adams signed into law an act that provided for the relief of sick and disabled seamen. This led to the development of marine hospitals during the nineteenth century. The American Public Health Association (APHA), composed mainly of social workers, was founded in 1872. Its main concern was the social and economic aspects of health problems. Following the Civil War, Congress in 1878 passed a National Quarantine Act for the purpose of preventing entry into the country of persons with communicable diseases. The period from 1870 to 1910 witnessed the maturation of the government's public health services. Health boards and health departments became widespread features of local and state governments; their functions were limited to the enforcement of sanitary regulations and control of communicable diseases. The AMA began to attack all proposals designed to extend the role of government in health care.

Limited Federal Role: 1900–1930

During the late nineteenth and the early part of the twentieth century, countries in Europe were establishing compulsory sickness insurance programs. Germany established the first national system of compulsory sickness insurance in 1883. Similar systems were established in Austria in 1888, Hungary in 1891, Norway in 1910, Britain in 1911, Russia in 1912, and the Netherlands in 1913. France and Italy required sickness insurance in only a few industries. Countries such as Sweden, Denmark, and Switzerland gave extensive state aid to voluntary funds and provided incentives for membership.[24]

The federal government in the United States, in contrast to happenings in Europe, took no action to subsidize voluntary funds or to make sickness insurance mandatory. This partly reflected existing political conditions and institutions in the United States, where, as a result of the influence of the public philosophy of classical liberalism, government was highly decentralized and played a very small role in regulation of the economy or in promoting social welfare.

Health insurance became a political issue in the United States on the eve of World War I. The progress of a workmen's compensation law between 1910 and 1913 encouraged reformers to believe that adoption of compulsory insurance against industrial accidents would lead to the adoption of compulsory sickness insurance. But the progressive reformers' hopes of strengthening government and adopting compulsory sickness insurance were soon dashed. Opposition from physicians and pharmaceutical and insurance companies defeated their reform proposals. In addition, both labor unions and business, fearing competition from government in social welfare programs, failed to support the reformers. By 1920, the movement for compulsory sickness insurance had faded from the political agenda.

Under pressure from the labor movement and children's advocates, Congress passed the Sheppard-Towner Act in 1921. It established the first federal grant-in-aid program for local child health clinics. But many local health departments refused to accept these grants because the AMA and local medical societies strongly opposed the program. Congress allowed the program to terminate in 1928.[25] Thus, the federal government's role in health care remained very limited during the nineteenth and early twentieth centuries.

Expansion of Health Facilities and Services: 1930–1960

A number of significant developments took place in the health care field during the 1930s. One major development, as mentioned earlier, was the start of a third-party payment system with the establishment of the Blue Cross and Blue Shield insurance plans. This revolutionized health care financing and led to employer-based health insurance programs. A second development concerned advances in medical technology and the discovery of antibiotics. Antibiotics changed the focus of medical care from prevention of disease through inoculation and hygiene to cure of illnesses.[26] For the first time, sulfa drugs and penicillin gave physicians their true power to cure.[27] The third development was the shift from local control of health and welfare issues to state and especially federal government control. Workmen's compensation, pensions, unemployment insurance, and certain medical services came to be perceived by the people as the responsibility of the federal government.[28] This was because of the Great Depression and the economic problems of state and local governments. The problems facing the country were too large for any but federal solutions.

The establishment of the National Institutes of Health (NIH) in 1930, with a broad mandate for ascertaining the cause, prevention, and cure of disease, reflected the increased role of the federal government in health care in general and in public health services in particular. It also paved the way for public funding of biomedical research through NIH and later through the National Science Foundation (NSF). In 1934, during the Great Depression, the Federal Emergency Relief Administration gave the first federal grants to local governments for public assistance to the poor, including financial support for medical care.

During the depression, there was also an increased demand for social insurance as differentiated from insurance against specific risks. Most Western countries had placed a higher priority on establishing health insurance programs as a natural outgrowth of insurance against industrial accidents. Old-age pensions and unemployment insurance programs received a lower priority in these countries. In the United States, with millions of people out of work as a result of the depression, unemployment insurance and old-age pensions received the higher priority. Thus the United States, rather than move in the direction of providing free medical care or reimbursement for its costs, as many Western European countries had done, attempted to supply more general social security benefits.

The Social Security Act of 1935 provided for unemployment compensation, old-age pensions, and other benefits. The early planning of the legislation had initially included health insurance as part of the package. However, the Roosevelt administration did not want to jeopardize the enactment of the entire law because of strong opposition to health insurance by the medical profession. Therefore, national health insurance was omitted from the final legislative proposal. The Social Security Act did extend the role of the federal government in health care by including provisions designed to strengthen public health services. These provisions called for federal matching grants-in-aid to states for maternal and infant care and diagnosis and treatment of crippled children. Federal grants were also made available for general public health purposes under the administration of the U.S. Public Health Service (USPHS), which had evolved in 1912 from the Marine Hospital Service.

In 1937 Congress passed the National Cancer Act. It established the National Cancer Institute (NCI) and set a national pattern for the federal support of biomedical research. The law authorized the NCI to conduct research in its own laboratories and to award grants to nongovernment scientists and institutions for training scientists and clinicians.

During 1935–36 the USPHS conducted a national health survey that revealed many untreated diseases in the population, especially in low-income groups. This led Senator Robert Wagner (D-N.Y.), sponsor of the Social Security Act, to introduce an amendment to the act that would have provided federal grants to the states for the organization of health insurance plans covering workers and their dependents. The onset of World War II postponed any serious consideration of such a plan.[29] Similar attempts to establish a health insurance program under the Truman administration were defeated during the 1940s. The medical profession had succeeded in defeating proposals for any national health insurance.

After the war, the Truman administration called for the expansion of hospitals, increased support for public health, maternal and child health services, and federal aid for medical research and education. The administration's aim was to expand the country's medical resources and facilities, reduce the financial burden for their use, and in the process expand access to medical care.[30] One major problem was that no new hospital construction took place during the depression or World War II, a period of some sixteen years.

In 1946 Congress passed the National Hospital Survey and Construction Act, also known as the Hill-Burton Act. This program provided federal funds to subsidize construction of hospitals in areas of bed shortages, mainly in rural counties. State public health agencies were made responsible for surveying the hospital bed supply in each state, and for developing a master plan for the construction of new hospitals. They were also assigned the task of inspecting and licensing all hospitals and related facilities.

Physicians welcomed Hill-Burton funds and actively sought them for construction of new hospitals for reasons of prestige, convenience, and service. Many physicians did not have privileges to treat their patients in the limited number of hospitals that were in existence. These physicians, faced with a limited supply of hospitals and beds and restricted access to them, supported the construction of new hospitals in the hope that they would enjoy the privilege of treating their patients in newly constructed hospitals. In addition, local pressure favoring nearby facilities, tax-favored bonds, and assured income from insurance companies and later from Medicare contributed to the proliferation of hospitals.[31]

As the number of hospitals increased, a nongovernmental Joint Commission on Accreditation of Hospitals was established in 1952. Between 1947 and 1966, the number of voluntary, not-for-profit hospitals increased from 2,584 to 3,426. During the same period, state and local government general hospitals increased from 785 to 1,453. The total number of hospitals (for-profit, state and local government, and voluntary not-for-profit) increased from 4,445 to 5,736. The rate of hospital admission per 1,000 population increased from 54 in 1935 to 129 in 1960.[32]

Congress, in 1946, also passed the National Mental Health Act. This law provided federal grants to states for research, prevention, diagnosis, and treatment of mental disorders. During the 1950s, there was also further expansion of public health services at the federal level. The NIH greatly expanded support of biomedical research. By the end of the 1950s, the role of the federal government in health care had increased significantly compared to its role in the early 1900s. There was a corresponding increase in the role of state and local governments in the field of public health services.

Increasing Access to Health Care: The 1960s

From the 1920s to the 1950s, efforts to establish a system of national health care or insurance for the entire population had failed because of charges from the medical profession and others that such plans would constitute "socialized medicine." The concept of socialized medicine went against the general public philosophy of classical liberalism, which advocates a limited role for government, and the specific philosophy of interest-group liberalism, wherein different interest groups exercise countervailing veto power over governmental policy decisions.

Faced with opposition to comprehensive change, advocates of a national system of health care or insurance changed their strategy and objectives. They began to advocate increasing access to health care for the needy. Rather than push for a universal coverage, under which the federal government would provide health insurance to all on a compulsory basis, they began to push for a limited system of health insurance for specific needy groups such as the elderly. The elderly were a perfect target group for providing help because of their greater medical need, inadequate financial resources, and the loss of employment-based group medical insurance upon retirement. Additionally, the elderly were deemed worthy and were not stigmatized as a failed group, as were welfare recipients. The health care problems of the elderly would be faced by most of us; almost everyone grows old, after all. This new approach also accommodated the federal structure of government by emphasizing that such programs would be administered by state governments with the federal government providing financial aid to states.

The result was the passage of the Kerr-Mills Act (also known as the Medical Assistance Act) by Congress in 1960. The law provided federal matching payments to states for vendor (provider) payments and allowed states to include the medically needy (i.e., elderly, blind, and disabled persons with low income who were not on public assistance). The act also suggested the scope of services to be covered, such as hospitals, nursing homes, physicians, and other health services. It also required each state to plan for institutional and noninstitutional care as a condition of federal cost sharing. State participation in the program was optional, and states were left free to determine eligibility and the extent of services provided. Most important, the act established the concept of "medical indigency."

The Kerr-Mills program proved to be neither effective nor adequate.[33] It failed to provide significant relief for a substantial portion of the elderly population. An investigation by the Senate Subcommittee on the Health of the Elderly in 1963 revealed that only 1 percent of the nation's elderly received help under the program. The report also highlighted several other problems such as stringent eligibility rules and high administrative costs of state governments.[34] Clearly, the issue of financing health care for the elderly had not been resolved and remained on the political agenda.

The Kennedy administration, on assuming office in 1961, was committed to increasing access to health care for millions of Americans. Having won a narrow victory in the 1960 presidential election, however, President Kennedy was not in a position to push for a universal insurance program. He faced a Congress that was not very amenable to his legislative proposals. He hoped that the 1962 congressional elections would produce a more receptive Congress. But he was able to keep the issue of health care needs of the elderly alive and on the political agenda.[35] On 21 February 1963, Kennedy delivered his "Special Message on Aiding Our Senior Citizens." The message contained thirty-nine legislative recommendations. The key proposal was Medicare to meet the medical needs of the elderly. It had two objectives. One was protection against the cost of serious illness. The other was to serve as a base of insurance protection on which supplementary private programs could be added.[36] The assassination of Kennedy in November 1963 left the task of carrying on the battle for Medicare to his successor, Lyndon Johnson.

Lyndon Johnson adopted most of John F. Kennedy's unfinished legislative proposals and incorporated them into the Great Society's War on Poverty program. After civil rights, Medicare was second in priority with the Johnson administration. Johnson saw Medicare as an essential part of his War on Poverty.[37] Johnson won a landslide victory in the 1964 presidential election, which allowed him to claim a public mandate for his programs. Equally important was the fact that Democrats also won major victories in congressional elections. The administration now had enough votes in the House and the Senate for the passage of its health care proposals.

Health insurance was at the top of the legislative agenda in 1965. The Johnson administration proposed hospital insurance for the elderly, financed through payroll taxes. Republicans offered a proposal for subsidized, voluntary insurance for the aged, including coverage for physicians' services financed through general revenues. The AMA opposed both plans and advocated expansion of the Kerr-Mills program of matching grants to the states for vendor payments for the needy. Both opponents and proponents used traditional concepts, symbols, and clichés in the debate. Opponents, especially the AMA and insurance companies, opposed the Johnson administration's proposal on the grounds that it was compulsory, it represented socialized medicine, it would reduce the quality of care, and it was "un-American." The proponents defended the plan as designed to help the needy by providing them with access to medical care and thus compatible with American ideals of equity and equality.[38]

Congress in 1965 passed the Medicare program for the elderly and the Medicaid program for the poor as amendments to the Social Security Act of 1935. This final product was a classic compromise between three competing proposals. It included a compulsory health insurance program for the elderly, financed through payroll taxes (Medicare Part A, the Johnson administration proposal), a voluntary insurance program for physicians' services subsidized through general revenues (Medicare Part B, the Republican proposal), and an expanded means-tested program administered by the states (Medicaid, the AMA proposal).

In addition to Medicare and Medicaid, a number of other health programs, such as Maternal and Infant Care (MIC), the Children Supplemental Feeding Program, and community health centers, were created during the 1960s as part of Johnson's War on Poverty.

The principal objective of the Medicare and Medicaid programs was to provide equal access to health care for the elderly and the poor. Both programs dramatically increased access to health care.[39] Medicare helped alleviate substantial financially related barriers to equal access to health care that existed before the program's enactment.[40] It greatly expanded financial access to acute care for the elderly and disabled.[41]

 In recent years, concern over rising health care costs and efforts at cost containment have led to tradeoffs between cost containment and access to health care. This has created new problems and gaps in access to health care. The next section provides a brief overview of the federal government's efforts at health care cost containment. Chapter 6 provides a more detailed examination and evaluation of major policy initiatives undertaken by federal and state governments, as well as the private sector, to contain health care costs.

Efforts at Health Care Cost Containment: 1970s–1980s

The 1970s represented a decade of transition in the American health care system. Prior to this time, federal health care policy was shaped by a number of assumptions. One of the major assumptions was that the health care system suffered from too few health care facilities and services. The health care system needed more hospitals, physicians, technology, and biomedical research. Biomedical research was encouraged through federal funds for the National Institutes of Health, while new hospital construction was encouraged with federal funds provided through the Hill-Burton program. The second assumption was that one of the serious problems with the health care system was limited financial access to health care among disadvantaged citizens. The establishment of Medicare and Medicaid by the federal government was an effort to increase access to health care for the needy. The third assumption was that competitive markets and regulatory strategies do not work in the health care field.[42]

By the 1970s, these assumptions had come under increased scrutiny. As we discussed earlier in the chapter, the Hill-Burton program led to a significant expansion in the number of voluntary, not-for-profit, and state and local government hospitals. Policymakers came to recognize that the health care system was too large. This was in sharp contrast to the assumption before the 1960s that the health care system was too small. By the 1970s there was an increasing concern with the nation's sizable surplus of hospital beds and physicians. There was a realization that one of the reasons for increased health care costs was unconstrained diffusion of biomedical technology and an excess supply of hospitals and physicians, which encouraged excessive tests and treatments. Similarly, while Medicare and Medicaid had increased financial access to health care for the elderly and the needy, increased access had also led to increases in health care costs. From the beginning, outlays for Medicare and Medicaid greatly exceeded initial projections. When Medicare was established, the federal government had deliberately chosen to reimburse physicians in a generous manner to win their political support.

By the 1970s health care costs had risen dramatically. Total national health care expenditure increased from $27.1 billion in 1960 to $74.3 billion in 1970. During this same period, federal health care expenditures increased from $2.9 billion to $17.8 billion, while state and local governments' health care expenditures increased from $3.7 billion to $9.9 billion. Similar increases were evident in hospital care and physician services.[43] From 1966 to 1970, Medicare expenditures increased from $1.6 billion to $7.1 billion, while Medicaid expenditures increased from $1.3 billion to $5.3 billion. Increases in medical care inflation outstripped overall inflation. (See Tables 2.1–2.3.)[44]

Policymakers' concerns began to shift from providing access and quality health care to containing rising health care costs. Ironically, there was an increased tolerance for government regulation of the health care system and at the same time encouragement of a competitive market strategy to contain health care costs. During the 1970s and 1980s, the federal government and the states

Table 2.1

Selected Health Care Expenditures, 1960–1996
(in billions of dollars)

	1960	1970	1980	1990	1991	1992	1993	1994	1995	1996
National health expenditures	26.9	73.2	247.3	699.5	766.8	836.6	895.1	945.7	991.4	1,035.1
Federal health expenditures	2.9	17.8	72.0	195.8	225.8	257.0	279.6	304.1	328.7	350.9
State and local health expenditures	3.7	9.9	32.8	88.5	95.9	101.6	109.3	119.8	126.5	132.2
Hospital health care	9.3	28.0	102.7	256.5	282.3	305.3	323.0	335.7	346.7	358.5
Physician services	5.3	13.6	45.2	146.3	162.2	175.9	183.6	190.4	196.4	202.1
Medicare expenditures	7.3	36.4	109.3	121.1	137.9	149.0	165.6	183.4	197.8	
Medicaid expenditures[a]	5.3	24.8	71.4	89.6	101.5	114.6	123.3	131.4	139.7	

Source: Katharine R. Levit et al., "National Health Expenditures, 1996," *Health Care Financing Review* 19, no. 1 (Fall 1997): 161–200.
[a]Medicaid figures combine federal, state, and local expenditures.

Table 2.2

Percentage Change in Health Care Expenditures, 1970–1996
(average annual percent change)

	1970	1980	1990	1991	1992	1993	1994	1995	1996
National health expenditures	10.6	12.9	11.0	9.6	9.1	7.0	5.6	4.8	4.4
Federal health expenditures	19.8	15.0	10.5	15.3	13.8	8.8	8.8	8.1	6.7
State and local health expenditures	10.2	12.7	10.4	8.3	5.9	7.6	9.5	5.6	4.5
Hospital health care	11.7	13.9	9.6	10.1	8.2	5.8	3.9	3.3	3.4
Physician services	9.9	12.8	12.5	10.8	8.5	4.4	3.7	3.1	2.9
Medicare expenditures[a]	10.8	13.9	8.1	11.1	10.8	7.6			
Medicaid expenditures[a,b]	25.5	13.3	12.9	7.8	6.6	6.3			

Source: Katherine R. Levit et al., "National Health Expenditures, 1996," *Health Care Financing Review* 19, no. 1 (Fall 1997): 161–200.
[a]Calculated from Table 2.1.
[b]Medicaid figures combine federal, state, and local expenditures.

undertook a number of regulatory and market-oriented policy initiatives in an effort to contain costs. These policy initiatives are examined in more detail in chapter 6, which discusses cost containment.

During its first two years in office, the Nixon administration proposed only moderate changes in the health care programs and proposed to hold the line on appropriations. In fact, President Nixon signed into law various acts designed to extend community mental health centers, migrant health centers, and programs designed to support training of health care personnel, among others.

Beginning in 1971, the Nixon administration sought to curtail health care programs. In his health message to Congress on 18 February 1971, Nixon argued that "costs have skyrocketed but values have not kept pace. We are investing more of our nation's resources in the health of our people but we are not getting full return on our investment."[45] Nixon sought curtailment in federal categorical grant programs and vetoed legislation designed to renew and expand these programs. He also relied on the strategy of impounding funds already appropriated. A struggle between the executive branch headed by a Republican president and a Congress controlled by Democrats ensued. The Democratic Congress was able to override some of Nixon's vetoes, and the battle over impoundment of funds ended up in the federal courts. It also ultimately led Congress in 1974 to enact the Congressional Budget and Impoundment Control Act, which Nixon signed into law a few days before he resigned from the presidency in the aftermath of the Watergate scandal. Despite Nixon's conflicts with Congress, a number of cost-containment initiatives were begun during this time.

Table 2.3
Consumer Price Index, 1960–1995

	All items	Medical care
1960	29.6	22.3
1965	31.5	25.2
1970	38.8	34.0
1975	53.8	47.5
1980	82.4	74.9
1985	107.6	113.5
1990	130.7	162.8
1995	152.4	220.5

Source: U.S. Bureau of the Census, *Statistical Abstract of the United States, 1996,* Government Printing Office, Washington, D.C., 1996.

PSROs and HMOs

One of the factors often cited as responsible for increased health care costs was the overutilization of health care resources. The rising costs of Medicare and Medicaid created concern in Congress about the cost and quality of care provided in these programs. Congress created the Professional Standards Review Organizations (PSROs) through the Social Security Amendments Act of 1972. It created a regulatory mechanism to encourage efficient and economical delivery of health care in the Medicare and Medicaid programs through peer review. More than 200 local PSROs were created and staffed by local physicians to review and monitor care provided to Medicare and Medicaid patients by hospitals, skilled nursing homes, and extended-care facilities. The PSROs were given the authority to deny approval of payment to physicians who provided services to Medicare and Medicaid patients.

In 1971, Senator Edward Kennedy (D-Massachusetts) introduced the Health Security Act in Congress, which was backed by organized labor. The bill called for a comprehensive program of free medical care and would have replaced all public and private health plans in a single federally operated health insurance system. The act would have set a national budget, allocated funds to regions, and obligated private physicians and hospitals to keep within budget constraints.

In his remarks introducing the plan, Kennedy blamed the insurance industry for failing to control costs, for providing partial benefits, and for ignoring the poor and the medically indigent. He also recognized the political difficulty of making his plan become reality when he stated that "throughout our society today, there is perhaps no institution more resistant to change than the organized medical profession."[46]

Opponents immediately described the plan as socialized medicine, a pejorative term used to help polarize debate. In reality, it was not socialized medicine, because the plan did not involve nationalization of health care facilities such as hospitals and did not require doctors to work on salary.

Nixon was interested in seeking reelection in 1972. The president felt compelled to respond to Kennedy's political challenge by proposing the National Health Insurance Partnership Act, which consisted of two parts. The first part, Family Health Insurance Plan, was a federally financed plan to provide health insurance for all low-income families. The second part, the National Health Insurance Standards Act, would be financed by private funds, would set standards for employer health insurance programs, and would require coverage of employees. But this plan could not win the necessary support for passage, since up to 40 million persons would still lack coverage.[47]

Nixon was not interested in starting a national health insurance program. The administration wanted some kind of plan to control health care costs that would look uniquely Republican. Nixon hoped to promote market-oriented reforms designed to encourage competition in the health care market as a way of controlling costs. He was interested in developing a health strategy that would create a more efficient health care system, balance the supply of health care resources and demands, and at the same time assure equal access to health care. The Nixon administration's key proposal was to provide federal funds for the development of health maintenance organizations (HMOs). In 1973, nearly three years after Nixon first sent his proposal to Congress, the Health Maintenance Organization Act was passed. It was a much more modest plan than originally conceived and reflected the necessity of bargaining and compromises between the president and Congress. For example, the first Senate bill had authorized $5.2 billion over three years for start-up costs. The version signed into law authorized $375 million over three years for projects more limited in scope.[48]

HMOs are a system in which enrollees pay a fixed fee (capitation) in advance, and in return they receive a comprehensive set of health services. The Nixon administration believed that HMOs would promote competition with traditional health care delivery systems by creating incentives for shifting health services utilization from more costly inpatient services such as hospitals and skilled nursing facilities to less costly outpatient services such as visits to doctors' offices. We consider HMOs and market reforms in later chapters.

Controlling Costs by Planning

The federal government during the late 1960s and the 1970s also emphasized health planning to contain rising health care costs. The rationale for planning was based on the argument that there was an abundance of health care facilities and services—too many hospitals, too many hospital beds, and too much medical equipment. Unnecessary expansion and duplication lead to overutilization of health care resources. The Comprehensive Health Planning Act of 1966 was an attempt at health care facilities planning through the states. Comprehensive health planning agencies were to be established in every state and in local areas. Their principal focus was hospital planning. The law also established the goal of providing the highest level of health care attainable to every person. Thus the law attempted to synthesize the goal of cost containment with the goal of providing access and quality care to everyone.

In 1972 the federal government, through the section 1122 amendments to the Social Security Act, limited Medicare/Medicaid reimbursements to approved expansions. Congress in 1974 passed the National Health Planning and Resource Development Act. This law replaced the Comprehensive Health Planning Act and such other health planning programs as the regional medical programs and the Hill-Burton programs. The law required all states to adopt certificate-of-need laws by 1980. Certificate-of-need laws require hospitals to document community need to obtain approval for major capital expenditures for expansion of facilities and services. The law also established a network of health systems agencies at state and local levels to administer the certificate-of-need laws.

Despite these efforts, overall health care costs continued to soar. The Medicare and Medicaid programs were also experiencing dramatic increases in expenditures. A recession combined with inflation during 1974–75 made efforts at expansion in medical programs politically impossible. The movement for national health insurance was stalled despite the election of a heavily Democratic Congress in 1974. Having assumed the office of the presidency following Nixon's resignation, President Gerald Ford proposed a national health insurance plan in his first message to Congress in 1974. In his 1976 State of the Union address, however, he withdrew the administration's plan on the ground that it would be inflationary.

Jimmy Carter, as a Democratic candidate for president in the 1976 election, also pledged his support for a comprehensive national health insurance program. His support during the Democratic primaries was a response to a political challenge by Senator Edward Kennedy, who was also seeking the party's nomination. Carter's continued support for a national health insurance program during the general election partly reflected his desire to win labor's support for his election.

Nevertheless, after assuming office in January 1977, Carter was hampered by budget constraints and was less anxious to push for a national health insurance program. From 1971 to 1974, under the Economic Stabilization Program, economywide wage and price controls were in effect. Hospital prices were subject to control under this program; however, this had a limited effect in controlling hospital costs. In 1977, the Carter administration proposed a series of all-payer revenue controls on hospitals, known as the hospital cost-containment proposal. The Carter administration argued that controlling hospital costs was necessary because traditional market forces would not keep those costs down. The proposal was strongly opposed by the medical industry in general and hospitals in particular. It also did not receive enthusiastic support in Congress. After three years of legislative battles, the proposal was defeated in favor of a promised voluntary effort by hospitals to contain costs. During the 1980 Democratic primary season, Senator Kennedy again challenged Carter. The president promised a national health care program, but one that would be implemented only when the economy, reeling from energy shocks and high interest and inflation rates, stabilized. Thus, the second half of the 1970s represented a political stalemate in the health policy area. Opposing and conflicting interests prevented adoption of any systematic and comprehensive set of health policies.[49]

The Reagan-Bush Years

After having campaigned on a platform of antiregulation and less government, Ronald Reagan became president in January 1981. Reagan sought to reduce expenditures for social programs, including health care. His "new federalism" proposal of 1982 attempted to decentralize authority and responsibility, giving state and local governments more discretion.

During the first two years of the Reagan administration, Congress enacted significant changes in federal health programs to restrain budget deficits, provide states with greater authority over health funding, and at the same time reduce federal funding for some health programs. Funding for health planning and health maintenance organizations was eventually eliminated. The PSRO program was renamed Peer Review Organizations (PROs) and its funding was reduced from $58 million in 1980 to $15 million in 1983. The Reagan administration also succeeded in replacing twenty-one categorical grant programs in the areas of prevention, mental health, maternal and child health care, and primary care into four block grants. Funding for Medicare and Medicaid was also reduced.[50]

The Reagan administration proposed a swap (the new federalism proposal) in which the federal government would assume full responsibility for funding Medicaid in return for state governments taking over responsibility for Aid to Families with Dependent Children (AFDC) and the food stamp program. Intense opposition from state governments caused the administration to drop this proposal from its legislative agenda.

The biggest innovation of the Reagan administration was the introduction in 1983 of the Prospective Payment System (PPS), mandated by the Deficit Reduction Act of 1982, for reimbursement to hospitals under the Medicare program in the hope of reducing Medicare costs and making hospitals more efficient. As discussed earlier, when Medicare was created, it provided for a generous reimbursement to hospitals based on a retrospective, reasonable cost basis for services provided to Medicare patients. Under the new system, illnesses are classified into one of 468 diagnosis-related groups (DRGs). Each category is assigned a treatment rate, and hospitals are reimbursed according to these rates. If hospitals spend more money on treatment, they have to absorb the additional costs. If they spend less money than the established rates, they can keep the overpayment as profit. The new system was phased in over a period of time and did not go into full effect until 1987.

By the mid-1980s it was also becoming clear that the Medicare program was unable to meet the health expenses of its beneficiaries. Their out-of-pocket expenses for services covered by Medicare were on the rise. In addition, the Medicare program did not provide coverage for certain basic services such as outpatient prescription drugs, custodial care, and most of the cost of nursing home care. The Reagan administration tried to address this problem of "medigap." In his 1986 State of the Union message, President Reagan unveiled his proposal for an expansion of Medicare. Congress passed his proposal in 1988 as the Medicare Catastrophic Coverage Act.

The law modified both program benefits and financing with changes to be phased in over a period of several years beginning in 1989. The act provided for coverage of outpatient prescription drugs such as home intravenously administered antibiotic and other FDA-approved drugs, as well as mammography screening for elderly and disabled beneficiaries. The act also expanded coverage of inpatient hospital days from ninety days to an unlimited number of days per year. Similarly, the act increased the number of days of coverage for skilled nursing facility, home health care, and hospice coverage. The act also reduced the amount of deductibles and coinsurance for certain coverage. The new benefits were to be financed entirely by the beneficiaries themselves through supplemental premiums. The act increased monthly premiums for Part B of Medicare and increased the tax liability of higher-income beneficiaries.

The Medicare Catastrophic Coverage Act was very unpopular, particularly among the affluent elderly. One reason for their opposition was the fact that they would shoulder most of the burden of financing the proposed changes through increases in their taxes. Many elderly did not like the idea of paying additional taxes to finance the new coverage. A second reason for the opposition was the fact that many of the elderly were satisfied with the supplemental private insurance coverage they had purchased to cover the gaps in the Medi-care program. Another major criticism of the act was that while it made modest changes in Medicare nursing home benefits, it did not extend Medicare cov-erage to long-term nursing home care.[51] Long-term care is the type of care most likely to devastate the elderly financially.[52]

Significant protests against the Medicare Catastrophic Coverage Act forced Congress to repeal the act in November 1989. This defeat of one of the most significant expansions in the Medicare program since its creation in 1965 is likely to make Congress, at least in the near future, less enthusiastic about reforms in Medicare or about undertaking any new initiatives with respect to long-term care.[53]

The Clinton Administration and Health Care Reforms

As health care costs continued to skyrocket (see Table 2.1), polls in the early 1990s indicated that a majority of Americans had a negative view of the Ameri-can health care system and were in favor of reforming the system. President George Bush, in February 1992, announced new health care initiatives. He proposed a series of reforms, including tax credits of up to $3,750 per year for families with income up to $70,000 and a voucher for the same amount for poor families. The estimated cost of the program, about $100 million, was to be paid for by placing limits on Medicare and Medicaid programs. Under the plan, the self-employed would receive a tax deduction equal to the size of the premiums. Small business would receive a tax inducement. There was also a proposal for mild insurance reform.[54] The Bush initiative was clearly in re-sponse to the coming presidential election and to the promise of Bill Clinton, Arkansas governor and Democratic candidate, that he would offer a plan for comprehensive reform of the U.S. health care system. By October 1992, both President Bush and Governor Clinton (as Democratic nominee for president) had endorsed managed care as the centerpieces of their health care plans. The comprehensive reform of the U.S. health care system became one of the major campaign issues in the 1992 presidential election. During the campaign, Bill Clinton promised that, if elected, he would deliver a comprehensive reform package for the U.S. health care system that would provide universal coverage to all Americans. Bill Clinton won the presidency. However, he had managed to garner only 43 percent of the popular vote in a three-candidate race.

President Clinton's plan was presented to the nation in a speech before the joint session of Congress in September of 1993, and a bill was sent to Congress in October. The proposal, entitled the Health Security Act, was very comprehensive; it proposed a fundamental restructuring of the American health care system. The bill provided universal coverage through an employer mandate. It also provided subsidies for poor persons and workers without insurance. The plan would provide a minimum benefits package covering a variety of services such as hospital, emergency, clinical preventive, mental health and substance abuse, family planning, pregnancy-related, hospice, home health care, extended care, outpatient laboratory, vision, hearing, and dental services among others.[55] "Health care plan that is always there" became the slogan for the Clinton plan.[56] The plan was based on the concept of managed competition. For more detailed analysis of the Clinton plan and competing plans, see chapter 9.

The initial reaction to the Clinton plan was positive. Deliberation over health care reform in Congress did not begin until 1994, an election year. Several competing plans emerged in Congress on both sides of the aisles. The competing plans ranged from a more radical proposal of a single-payer system to plans that proposed only minor changes to the system, designed to deal with specific concerns. As the debate over these competing plans intensified, none of the plans managed to attract majority support. The initial positive reaction to the Clinton plan turned more negative as the plan was criticized and attacked by a variety of interest groups and Republicans in Congress. Republican leaders had made a strategic decision not to support the Clinton plan and to make Clinton administration's failure to reform the health care system a campaign issue in the 1994 Congressional elections. It was classic election-year politics. As the debate continued, public support for the Clinton plan as well as support for fundamental reform of the U.S. health care system also declined. Opponents of comprehensive reforms argued that the U.S. health care system was not facing a crisis requiring major changes and that the problems of the health care system could be addressed through incremental reforms.

Ultimately, this was the view that prevailed, and by the late summer of 1994 President Clinton's Health Security Act was declared dead and buried. Several factors account for this failure. Some of the important reasons included the Clinton administration's miscalculation and mismanagement of the issue, attack from interest groups opposed to the plan, partisan politics, election-year politics, a decline in President Clinton's popularity, and declining public support for comprehensive reform.[57] Another window of opportunity for reform of the U.S. health care system had opened and closed without any comprehensive reforms.[58]

Republicans used a three-pronged approach in the 1994 election campaign: develop a positive governing agenda, derail Clinton's agenda, and amass a large campaign war chest.[59] The Republican party also came up with the Contract with America, a ten-point platform that included a balanced budget amendment, a line-item veto for the president, a crime bill, welfare reform, a family tax-cut plan, and parental rights in education. In addition, the Republican strategy of not cooperating with the president on the issue of comprehensive health care reform and then blaming President Clinton for its failure—on the basis that it was a bureaucratic, big-brother, big-government reform plan—paid handsome dividends in the 1994 congressional elections. The voters delivered the worst midterm repudiation that any president had received since Harry Truman in 1946. Republicans gained control of both the House and the Senate. The Republican victories extended to gubernatorial and state legislative races as well. A post-election survey conducted by President Clinton's pollster Stanley Greenberg identified the health care plan as the single item that directly linked Clinton with big government.[60] According to a survey of voters conducted on election day, President Clinton's failure to reform the health care system was a major reason Democrats suffered at the polls. Furthermore, polls also showed that the voters were strongly opposed to the comprehensive health care reform and instead favored incremental solution of the nation's health care problems.[61]

The Republicans came up with a budget plan and the Congress adopted a budget resolution for fiscal year (FY) 1996. It promised to balance the budget within seven years. It called for a $245 billion tax cut. It advocated reducing projected spending (growth rate) on Medicare by $270 billion and Medicaid spending by $182 billion over the next seven years. The Medicaid program was to be turned into a block grant and turned over to the states. The Democrats went on the offensive and portrayed themselves as the savior of the elderly and the poor (Medicare and the Medicaid) and argued that Republicans were willing to cut these programs to provide a tax cut for the wealthy. President Clinton refused to accept the Republican plan. He was determined not to cave into Republican demands. The stalemate between the president and the Republican Congress led to partial shutdown of government two times. This confrontation backfired on the Republicans, as they saw public support for the Contract with America decline sharply. No action was taken on the proposed reduction in spending for Medicare and Medicaid.

In 1996 legislation on the FY 1997 budget, the Republican leadership proposed block grants to replace the Medicaid and AFDC programs. They also wanted welfare reform. President Clinton had indicated that while he supported welfare reforms, he was strongly opposed to turning Medicaid into a block-grant program. Two times he vetoed legislation that tried to turn both Medicaid and the AFDC program into block grants. Finally, the Republicans dropped their proposal to turn Medicaid into a block grant. Once this was done, the welfare reform bill easily passed Congress, and President Clinton signed into law the bill known as the Personal Responsibility and Work Opportunity Act of 1996. The new law included changes in welfare, supplemental security income, child support enforcement, and food stamp and social services. The main feature of the law is the Temporary Assistance to Needy

Families (TANF) program, under which states are given a block grant to design their own welfare program. The Medicaid program was left virtually intact.

Despite the partisan acrimony that dominated the 104th Congress in 1995 and 1996 over the issue of a balanced budget amendment, Congress did succeed in passing some incremental reforms. One of the crowning achievements of the 104th Congress was the passage of the Health Insurance Portability and Accountability Act of 1996, which President Clinton signed into law in August. Two of the major provisions of the bill include placing limits on insurance companies' authority to deny coverage or to impose preexisting condition exclusions, and guaranteeing portability of insurance coverage when a person leave his or her job voluntarily or involuntarily.[62]

President Clinton won an impressive reelection in 1996. The Republicans managed to retain their majorities in the House and the Senate with narrower margins. President Clinton and the Republican-controlled Congress managed to address another issue that had become an area of concern, the increased number of children who lacked health insurance coverage. The Balanced Budget Act of 1997 provided funds to expand health insurance coverage for children by creating the State Children's Health Insurance Program as part of title XXI of the Social Security Act. Several states have taken advantage of this program and have expanded health insurance coverage to uninsured children in their states.[63]

The expansion of managed competition in the health care marketplace as a way to cut costs has led to dramatic increase in the enrollment of millions of Americans in health maintenance organizations (HMOs) and preferred provider organizations (PPOs). This in turn has raised concerns about managed care plans that deny or limit provision of health care services to their members, in order to cut costs. Some legislators and consumer advocates have suggested the passage of a patients' bill of rights to protect patients against unfair, arbitrary, and capricious decisions by managed care plans. President Clinton has proposed just such a bill, which would allow patients' to sue their managed care plans and/or managed care organizations such as HMOs and PPOs. The Republicans in Congress have proposed their own version of a patients' bill of rights, which does not allow patients to sue their health care plans or provider organizations. What, if anything ultimately, will come out of this struggle in the form of congressional legislation remains to be seen.

The Role of State and Local Governments in Health Care

The distribution of authority and responsibility between different levels of government within a federal system is a topic of continuous debate. Health care policy has not been exempt from this debate. Initially, the role of the federal government and of state and local governments was very limited. In the previous section we discussed how the federal government became increasingly involved in health care policy and how it plays a major role today with respect to access, quality, efficiency, and cost containment. This section briefly discusses the changing role of state and local governments in health care in our federal system.

During much of the nineteenth century, the role of state and local governments was confined to public health activities. The role of local governments in public health was stimulated by the great epidemics of the late eighteenth and early nineteenth centuries. Municipalities established health boards or health departments to deal with problems of sanitation, poor housing, and quarantine. For example, health departments were established in Baltimore in 1798, Charleston in 1815, Philadelphia in 1818, and Providence in 1832.[64]

Similarly, the states' role in public health was initially limited to special committees or commissions to control communicable diseases. The first state health department was established in Louisiana in 1855. State governments also played a significant role in personal health care through the establishment of state mental hospitals.[65]

By the beginning of the twentieth century, state and local governments were active in the delivery of personal health services. During the first decade of the 1900s, state governments also began the regulation and licensure of hospitals. But it was not until the end of World War II that detailed state regulations and licensure procedures for hospitals became more common.[66]

During the 1960s and 1970s, state governments took on many new functions; some of them fundamentally changed the traditional public health activities of subnational governments.[67] The federal health programs of the 1960s dramatically changed the functions of state and local governments in health care. There was increased federal support for the delivery of health care services by institutions that traditionally served the poor (i.e., public hospitals and local health departments). The establishment of the joint federal-state Medicaid program also increased revenues available to public hospitals and local health departments. Thus, by the 1980s, state and local governments were not only heavily involved in traditional public health activities such as health monitoring, sanitation, and disease control but were also key participants in the financing and delivery of personal health care services, particularly to the poor through Medicaid and other programs. The traditional public health focus on sanitation and communicable diseases also expanded to cover a broad range of protection against human-made environmental and occupational hazards to personal health.[68]

State governments are heavily involved in the regulation and licensure of health care facilities, such as hospitals and nursing homes, and in licensing health care professionals such as physicians and nurses. They also regulate hospital costs and prices through hospital rate setting. Furthermore, they have become important purchasers of health care services, especially for the poor. Thus, state and local governments play an important role, not only in public health activities, but in health care financing, delivery, and regulation of services as well. This increased role is reflected in the fact that between 1979 and 1981 alone state and local government health expenditures increased by 35 percent.[69]

The new federalism policies of the Nixon administration and especially the Reagan administration created new challenges for state and local governments. The Reagan administration placed heavy emphasis on decentralization, increased sharing of responsibilities and authority, and more discretion for state and local governments in the implementation of health programs. The diminishing federal responsibility for health care in the early 1980s resulted in increased cost shifting from the federal to state and local governments.

This has led some to argue that the Reagan administration's new federalism strategy was largely a means of cutting the federal budget rather than sharing responsibilities.[70] The increased discretion granted to state governments in the implementation of health policy raises the question of commitment, capacity, and progressivity of state governments. Conservatives have placed great emphasis on devolution of authority and financial responsibility back to the states, without much concern for adequate access to health care for all segments of the society.[71] This concern is heightened by some evidence that state and local governments may be even more susceptible to the influence of special interests than the federal government. Thus, compared to the federal government, some have argued that state governments are less likely to make decisions in the public interest.[72]

Federal budget reductions made in an effort to contain rising health care costs have left many states unable to meet the financial burden of meeting the health care needs of the poor under the Medicaid program. State governments have resorted to the practice of "bootstrapping." Thirty-seven states have passed "bootstrapping" laws that charge doctors, hospitals, and other Medicaid providers an extra tax. The idea is to force the federal government to pay more of the cost of the program because it reimburses states between 50 and 83 percent of the states' Medicaid costs. The more a state charges, the more it gets back.[73] The Bush administration announced new rules under which the federal government would no longer match spending by states for Medicaid if the state money came from donations or special taxes paid by hospitals and nursing homes rather than from a state's general revenues. According to state governors, these new rules would cut medical coverage for women and children.[74] The Clinton administration, headed by a former governor, has been somewhat more sympathetic to state concerns. More stringent Medicaid eligibility rules also have left a sizable number of poor people with no access to health care under the Medicaid program. Over the past ten years the number of Medicaid recipients has remained stable, while the poor population has grown substantially.[75] Thus, the Medicaid program is increasingly confronted with a tradeoff between cost containment and access to health care.[76]

This again raises a concern about the impact of new federalism initiatives on the issue of access to quality health care on the part of the elderly, the poor, and the uninsured. But the liberals' vision of a national health insurance program is likely to remain illusive, confronted with the reality of enormous federal budget deficits and the antitax mood prevalent in the country.

Despite this, it should be noted that states have become major actors in health policy reform, from regulation to rationing to innovative competitive strategies to cut health care costs. This has become all the more true with some of the changes and incremental reforms passed by Congress and signed into law by President Clinton during the 1990s in the area of welfare reform, health insurance reforms, and children's health insurance. This devolution of authority to state governments has given them more autonomy and more freedom to innovate, and state governments are likely to become even more important players in the future. State governments have already provided significant leadership in the area of expanding health insurance coverage to children and medical liability reforms. We consider these changes in later chapters.

Conclusion

The United States remains the only major Western industrialized nation without a national health insurance system. Health care policy in the United States results from a combination of decisions made and initiatives undertaken by various levels of government and the private sector. Though the role of federal, state, and local governments in health care policy has expanded significantly in the twentieth century, the U.S. health care system remains a mostly private system. Policymakers in the United States have mainly followed a middle road between a totally private health care system and a publicly financed national health care system.

The federal government's health policy initiatives have focused on concerns about values of access (equality), quality of care, and cost efficiency. The federal role in health care has gone through three distinct stages. The first stage was characterized by policies designed to increase access through expansion of health care facilities, services, and resources. The second stage was characterized by policies specifically designed to provide equal access and quality care to needy groups such as the elderly and the poor. The third stage was characterized by policies designed to contain rising health care costs.

Nevertheless, with respect to providing equal access to health care, federal policies have never displayed or practiced a broad commitment to ensuring that all Americans receive needed health care. Instead, the federal government has always followed an incremental approach by creating specific policies such as Medicare, Medicaid, and numerous categorical grant programs targeted at narrowly defined groups or problems.[77]

Medicare, Medicaid, and other federal grant-in-aid programs have increased access to health care by removing some of the financial obstacles faced by needy groups. Problems remain, however, and recent evidence suggests the emergence of new difficulties. The demise of the Medicare Catastrophic Coverage Act has left many poor elderly with significant gaps in their Medicare coverage because they cannot afford to buy supplemental private insurance. This problem is likely to grow as the number of elderly in the population increases. One of the biggest problems is Medicare's failure to provide coverage for long-term care. Similarly, a significant number of poor people are not covered under the Medicaid program. More and more people are falling through the cracks in the health care safety net, as reflected in the increased number of uninsured Americans. Moreover, hospitals in many major cities are facing a crisis situation.[78]

Because government intervention in American politics takes place within the context of the public philosophy of interest-group liberalism and cynicism about government regulation, governmental input has tended to occur at the margin rather than the core of the problem.[79] Powerful interest groups have been able to exercise veto power over proposed policies. For example, since the 1920s numerous attempts by the federal government to establish some form of national health insurance that would guarantee health care access to everyone have been defeated by powerful interests such as the AMA and insurance companies. Such groups have successfully defended and protected their narrow and selfish interests, even if they have done so in the name of protecting the public interest by appealing to the value of freedom to choose one's doctor and by raising the specter of "socialized medicine," which they argue would lower the quality of health care. In recent years the issue of national health insurance has been pushed back on the legislative agenda because of an economic environment characterized by huge federal budget deficits and a protracted recession.

Both liberals and conservatives have had difficulty in carrying out an ideologically faithful health care policy. Thus, for example, while the Nixon administration advocated a competitive market strategy and successfully pushed for federal support for the development of HMOs, it also had to accept increased federal government regulations in the form of peer review organizations. Similarly, the important innovation of the Prospective Payment System (PPS) for Medicare reimbursement under the Reagan administration relied on regulatory price-control mechanisms to encourage efficiency in the health care market. Both liberals and conservatives had to contend with powerful interest groups. For example, insurance companies, hospitals, and the medical profession have welcomed some regulatory relief, but they have not shown a great deal of enthusiasm for the conservative program of increased competition in the health care market.[80] Liberal efforts at major reforms to increase health care access have been successfully thwarted by these same interest groups.

The constitutional structure of separation of powers and checks and balances combined with the increased frequency of divided government have necessitated constant bargaining and compromises between the two houses of Congress and between the president and Congress. The federal structure of government has produced a continuous debate in health care policy over the proper distribution of authority and responsibility between the different levels of government. Different presidents have stressed different objectives in this regard. The Johnson administration in the 1960s placed more emphasis on increasing health care access by the federal government. In contrast, the Reagan administration in the 1980s emphasized deregulation and devolution of authority to state and local governments. The changing political climate and public mood and the desire to win election or reelection to office make short-term approaches to the solution of problems appealing. Under such circumstances, a comprehensive and consistent set of policies directed at long-term solutions to problems becomes difficult to attain.

We finish this chapter with a brief overview of the remainder of the book. Chapter 3 examines Medicaid. We explore Medicaid's structure and the coverage provided by the program, with an emphasis on its federal nature. We look at problems with Medicaid and latest developments in the program. We explore gaps in Medicaid coverage and attempts by states to control costs.

Chapter 4 looks at Medicare and the problem of long-term care. The chapter describes Medicare, the primary program of health care for the elderly and certain categories of the disabled. It looks at the cost and financing problems, recent changes, and gaps in the program. The major gap is long-term care, the subject of the second part of the chapter. We discuss the participants in the long-term-care industry and the financing of this difficult problem.

Chapter 5 has as its principal topics access and equity. In particular, we discuss two overlapping aspects. One is the uninsured. We look at the access aspect: the problem of those without adequate health insurance or with more. We seek answers to the question of why the numbers of uninsured have increased in recent years. We tie these answers to current pressures for health care reform. The second, related, part of the chapter looks at the equity aspect: disadvantaged groups in American society. Here we specifically concentrate on minority groups, women, and low-income persons. There is some overlap between the low-income group and the other two groups, as there is between these groups and the uninsured.

Chapter 6 spotlights perhaps the major driving force behind change in the health care field, the ever-increasing costs of health care. We explore explanations for cost increases and attempts at cost containment. This chapter highlights efforts at the state and federal levels as well as by the private sector.

Chapter 7 examines the issue of medical liability and malpractice. We explore the origins and development of the concepts of negligence and liability, the pros and cons of the current tort system, and proposed alternatives and attempts at reform by the federal and state governments. The chapter ends with a discussion of the changing concept of liability with the advent of managed care and new alternative health care delivery organizations such as HMOs and PPOs.

The subject of chapter 8 is technology and health care. Technology is one of the factors that have been implicated in health care cost increases. Some commentators point to advances in health care technology in the United States as indicating the virtues of the system, while others suggest it is responsible for overuse of care. Technology also presents numerous ethical concerns. In this chapter we discuss the factors that have contributed to the growth of medical technology, the cost of medical technology, the issue of technology assessment, and the ethical dilemmas raised by high-tech medicine.

Chapter 9 explores attempts at comprehensive health care reform in the 1990s. We examine the health care reform proposal of President Clinton, competing proposals, and the politics surrounding the various reform proposals. We also discuss market-reform concepts as an integral part of health care reform.

Chapter 10 explores incremental reforms that have taken place following the failed attempt at comprehensive and fundamental reform of the U.S. health care system during 1993 and 1994. The chapter begins with a discussion and an analysis of the Republican proposals in 1995 and 1996, focusing on Medicare and Medicaid. It then discusses the proposals that did pass, such as portability of insurance, moderate federal regulation of managed care plans, and welfare reforms. The chapter ends with an examination of the 1997 balanced budget agreement, which included changes in Medicare and expansion of health insurance for children.

Chapter 11 summarizes the major issues and problems of the U.S. health care system discussed in the previous chapters. We also present our prognosis and recommendations for change.

CHAPTER 3

Medicaid: Health Care for the Poor

The establishment of Medicare and Medicaid in 1965 was the result of a lengthy debate during the early part of the twentieth century over the role of the federal government in financing health care. The debate among policymakers focused on two competing models. One was a universal coverage model, under which the federal government would provide health insurance to all people on a compulsory basis financed by taxes on earnings. The second model envisioned a more limited role for the federal government. This model would limit the federal government's role to providing assistance to needy groups in society. In the past, most federal laws dealing with health care had followed the second model.[1] The political environment—structure and processes—made such an incremental approach feasible. Thus, during the 1950s and the 1960s policymakers followed the same approach.

The 1950 amendments to the Social Security Act authorized matching grants to the states for direct vendor (provider) payments for treatment of individuals on public assistance. During the late 1950s, the debate focused on the problem of hospital costs faced by the aged. The cost of hospital care doubled in the 1950s. Support increased for addressing the problem of hospital costs of the elderly. The aged could be presumed to be both needy and deserving.[2] In 1960 Congress passed the Kerr-Mills Act. This act expanded federal matching funds to the states for vendor payments, and more important, it allowed states to include the "medically needy"—that is, elderly, blind, and disabled persons with low incomes who were not on public assistance. However, many states moved very slowly or failed to move at all to take advantage of the Kerr-Mills Act.

The Democratic party's sweep of the 1964 elections guaranteed further action with respect to the role of the federal government in health care. Lyndon Johnson was elected to the presidency with an overwhelming popular vote. The Democrats gained a two-to-one majority in the House of Representatives. This made it possible for Congress in 1965 to create the Medicare and Medicaid programs. Both were in the forefront of Lyndon Johnson's Great Society programs designed to help the poor and the disadvantaged.[3] Medicare was established as a program for the elderly, while Medicaid was a program for the poor. The final shape of both programs represented compromises among competing models and approaches. The Democratic plan for a compulsory hospital insurance program, financed through payroll taxes under Social Security, became Part A of Medicare. The Republican-supported plan of a government subsidized, voluntary insurance program financed through general revenues to cover physicians' bills became Part B of Medicare. The AMA opposed both plans and pushed a plan of its own to expand the Kerr-Mills program to the needy. An expanded means-tested program for the poor administered by the states became the Medicaid program.

The generally accepted political explanation for the creation of Medicaid is that the program was created almost as an afterthought to Medicare.[4] Medicaid was intended to "pick up the pieces" left over by Medicare. It was designed to cover deductibles and coinsurance for indigent Medicare patients. The program was intended to pay for services not covered or covered only inadequately by Medicare (i.e., outpatient and nursing home care), and to pay the cost of medical care of indigent persons other than the elderly.[5]

Although Medicare and Medicaid were adopted at the same time, there are fundamental differences between the two. The Medicare program has enjoyed public popularity and legitimacy because it is tied to Social Security, a program that is contributory in nature (i.e., through Social Security taxes paid by workers). In contrast, from the beginning, Medicaid has been burdened by the stigma of being a public assistance (i.e., welfare) program. Medicare has uniform national standards for eligibility and benefits. In sharp contrast, Medicaid lets states decide on eligibility and benefit standards. Another major difference is that physician reimbursement under Medicaid is much lower than under Medicare or private insurance; consequently, very few physicians participate in the Medicaid program.[6] In addition, Medicare is financed and administered solely by the federal government, while Medicaid is financed by both the federal and the state governments on a matching basis and is administered by the state governments.

Program Objective and Structure

Medicaid was established to increase the access of the poor to health care by providing them with financial assistance to meet their medical needs. Although federal law created the program, the intent was to encourage state governments to set up a "unified system of health care" for certain low-income individuals.[7] The federal government encouraged state participation and compliance with the program in several ways. The federal government provided matching funds to encourage states to expand their existing medical assistance programs. Today, the federal Medicaid matching ratio varies from a minimum of 50 percent to a maximum of 83 percent. Second, state governments were given the responsibility for establishing program requirements. Finally, states were given the option of making the administration of the program a local as opposed to a state responsibility.

Thus the Medicaid program was created as a partnership between different levels of government to improve access and quality of health care for the poor. The national government establishes broad program guidelines, promotes and monitors program development, and provides financial assistance through matching grants. State governments are given significant control over important aspects of the scope and structure of the program. For example, state governments enjoy discretionary authority for establishing eligibility standards, the nature and scope of benefits provided, and mechanisms used to reimburse health care providers.

Medicaid is an excellent example of how the federal structure of government shapes the dynamics of policymaking and implementation. On the one hand, the federal structure, with its multiple governments, shared authority, political autonomy, and constitutional ambiguities, has allowed states to act as laboratories for innovation and experimentation in the Medicaid program. On the other hand, the same federal structure of government produces overlapping jurisdictions and wastefulness, and encourages the promotion of narrow and parochial interests that make it difficult to solve serious problems. It allows one level of government to pass the buck to another level by playing the federalism game.

Medicaid Coverage

The program's main target groups are children and mothers who receive Aid to Families with Dependent Children (AFDC), the elderly poor over the age of sixty-five, and disabled or blind persons who qualify for the Supplemental Security Income (SSI) program—a federal program for the aged, blind, and disabled. The federal government sets the income limits for the SSI program. Thus, state Medicaid programs are required to include all "categorically needy" persons—those receiving cash assistance under Old Age Assistance, Aid to the Blind, Aid to Families with Dependent Children, and Aid to the Permanently and Totally Disabled.[8]

States may elect to provide coverage to people who are not required to be covered by federal law. State governments can receive federal matching funds for providing coverage to these optional groups. Such optional groups include "medically needy" families with dependent children whose incomes are above state AFDC limits and elderly persons who do not qualify for cash assistance but have large medical or nursing home bills.[9]

Mandatory benefits covered under Medicaid include hospital and physician services, family planning consultation, care in skilled nursing facilities, diagnostic services, and screening and treatment of children for various sicknesses and impairment. Optional benefits include prescription drugs, dental care, and nursing home care in intermediate-care facilities.

States are permitted to restrict the amount of services per beneficiary. For example, a state may limit the number of days in hospitals or number of visits to physicians per year that it would cover. States also enjoy significant discretion with respect to the method of payment to health care providers. Originally, under the Medicaid program, states had to pay hospitals according to the same principle used by Medicare—the "reasonable cost" principle—that is, all costs associated with the care of a patient. Today, states can use any method for reimbursement as long as payments are "reasonable and adequate." Similarly, in the Medicare program, physicians are reimbursed for their charges, which are subject to screening for "reasonableness." However, physicians are permitted to charge the patient more than the amount considered reasonable by Medicare. Under Medicaid, states can pay physicians according to the Medicare principle or on the basis of a fee schedule. All providers must accept Medicaid's reimbursement as payment in full. Because of the very low physician rate paid by many states, a large number of physicians refuse to treat Medicaid patients.[10]

Originally, Medicaid was viewed as a limited entitlement program. Over time, the scope of the program has expanded considerably. Today, Medicaid also pays for health care services for low-income "first-time" pregnant women who do not qualify for programs such as AFDC. In addition, Medicaid finances long-term institutional care for the elderly, disabled, and mentally retarded.[11] From 1984 to 1990, Congress imposed various federal mandates requiring states to expand Medicaid coverage to women and children.

Major Trends in the Medicaid Program

Program Costs

As the data in Table 3.1 document, the Medicaid program has experienced dramatic increases in overall program cost from the beginning. Total Medicaid expenditures increased from $5.3 billion in 1970 to $24.8 billion in 1980. In the early years of the program, the primary reason for increases in program cost was the growth in the number of eligible recipients. As the data in Table 3.2 demonstrate, between 1981 and 1984, spending for Medicaid increased at a much slower rate than between 1978 and 1981. Factors contributing to this slowdown were the recession, the reduction in federal matching rates, and the programmatic changes introduced in the Omnibus Budget Reconciliation Act (OBRA) of 1981.[12] As a result of new federal mandates imposed by Congress between 1984 and 1990 that expanded Medicaid coverage, the annual growth rate increased again. By 1990, the total Medicaid cost had increased to $71.7 billion. From 1989 to 1990 Medicaid expenditures increased 21.3 percent. Even more dramatic was the increase that came during 1991 when the total program cost jumped to 89.6 billion. This represented an increase of 24.9 percent, the fastest annual growth in the history of the program. Factors that contributed to this dramatic increase were the expansions in Medicaid eligibility and a slowdown in the economy. Both factors caused additional individuals to qualify for coverage.[13]

Table 3.1
Medicaid Expenditures and Percent Change from Previous Year, 1970–1996
(in billions of dollars)

Year	Total	Percent change from previous year[b]	Federal	Percent change from previous year[c]	State/local	Percent change from previous year[d]
1970	5.3		2.9		2.4	
1975	13.6		7.6		6.0	
1980	24.8		13.7		11.1	
1985	39.7		21.9		17.8	
1990	71.7		40.7		31.1	
1991	89.6	24.9	54.3	33.4	35.3	13.5
1992	101.6[a]	13.4	65.4	20.4	36.2	2.5
1993	114.6[a]	12.8	73.5	12.4	41.1	13.5
1994	123.3[a]	7.6	77.7	5.7	45.6	11.0
1995	131.4[a]	6.6	82.0	5.5	49.4	8.3
1996	139.7[a]	6.3	87.4	6.6	52.3	5.9

Sources: For the years 1970 and 1975, Robert M. Gibson and Daniel R. Waldo, "National Health Expenditures, 1980," *Health Care Financing Review* 3, no. 1 (September 1981): 45–46. For the years 1980, 1985, and 1990, Suzanne W. Letsch et al., "National Health Expenditures, 1991," *Health Care Financing Review* 14, no. 2 (Winter 1992): 27–28. For the years 1991–96, Katharine R. Levit et al., "National Health Expenditures, 1996," *Health Care Financing Review* 19, no. 1 (Fall 1997): 197–199.

[a]Totals calculated from columns 4 and 6.
[b]Calculated from column 2.
[c]Calculated from column 4.
[d]Calculated from column 6.

Table 3.2

Total Medicaid Expenditures and Number of Recipients, 1966–1995

Year	Total expenditures (in billions of dollars)	Number of recipients (in millions)
1966	1.3	—
1967	3.0	—
1968	3.4	—
1969	4.0	—
1970	5.3	—
1971	6.4	—
1972	8.0	17.6
1973	9.1	19.6
1974	10.6	21.5
1975	13.6	22.0
1976	14.5	22.8
1977	16.6	22.8
1978	18.5	22.0
1979	21.2	21.5
1980	24.8	21.6
1981	28.9	21.9
1982	30.6	21.6
1983	33.6	21.5
1984	36.0	21.6
1985	39.7	21.8
1986	42.9	22.5
1987	48.2	23.1
1988	52.1	22.9
1989	59.2	23.5
1990	71.7	25.2
1991	89.6	27.9
1992	101.6	31.1
1993	114.6	33.4
1994	123.3	35.0
1995	131.4	36.2

Sources: Compiled from Katharine R. Levit et al., "National Health Expenditures, 1990," *Health Care Financing Review* 13, no. 1 (Fall 1991): 41; Katharine R. Levit, et al., "National Health Expenditures, 1996," *Health Care Financing Review* 16, no. 1 (1997): 197–199; *Health Care Financing Review*, Medicare and Medicaid Statistical Supplement (1997): 191.

The cost to the federal government alone increased from $2.4 billion in 1970 to $11.1 billion in 1980 and $73.5 billion in 1993. The federal spending by 1996 had increased it to $87.4 billion.

State governments have also experienced significant increases in their program costs. The combined cost of state and local governments for Medicaid increased from $2.9 billion in 1970 to $13.7 billion in 1980, $21.9 billion in 1985, and $40.6 billion in 1990. By 1996, state and local governments were spending $52.3 billion. Needless to say, program costs, eligibility standards, and benefit levels vary significantly among the states. The amount of optional services (those beyond the ones mandated by the federal government) and the mix of services provided by the state governments also vary a great deal. "The maze of eligibility rules is enough to make anyone sick."[4]

Overall, two factors have contributed to the steady growth in program expenditures. First, since Medicaid is an "entitlement" program, individuals who meet eligibility criteria are automatically covered. Thus, program costs increase any time the size of the population in need increases. Second, Medicaid, like other health insurance systems, pays health care providers and not the recipients who receive treatment. Thus, overall health care costs directly influence Medicaid expenditures. During the 1970s and 1980s, the cost of medical care increased annually by an average of 8.5 percent. Some of the increases in the Medicaid expenditures are attributable to general medical cost inflation.[15]

However, it is interesting to note that, since about 1994, there has been a considerable reduction in growth rate of the program costs. The total Medicaid expenditures increased in only single digits during 1994, 1995, and 1996, compared to the double-digit growth rates in the early 1990s. Similarly, during the same years growth rate in the federal and state-local costs of the Medicaid program also experienced considerable decline. There are a number of factors that might help explain the decline in the growth rate of the program costs. One possible explanation is that there was a decline in AFDC rolls due to improved economy and state efforts to reduced welfare rolls. Second, during this time, growth in the coverage for children and pregnant women also declined. Third, growth in the number of blind and disabled Medicaid recipients also declined. Fourth, the rapid growth in Medicaid managed care might also explain the decline in program growth rate. Another possible explanation is the drop in average annual medical price inflation during the mid-1990s.[16]

Despite the dramatic increases in spending for Medicaid, the program fails to insure millions of poor people who are ineligible to receive Medicaid because they do not fall into one of the eligible categories. It is not surprising that Medicaid is often called a monster.[17] Since its creation, the Medicaid program has occupied center stage in the debate over the proper role of the federal and state governments in meeting the health care needs of the poor.

The Number of Beneficiaries

Medicaid has also experienced a steady growth in the number of recipients. Those receiving Medicaid nationwide increased from 17.6 million in 1972 to 21.6 million in 1980. By 1990, the number had grown to 25.2 million people. By 1995, the total number of recipients had increased to 36.2 million. Still, it is important to note that the number of recipients has fluctuated over the same period. In the early years of the program's history, the number of recipients increased because eligibility for Medicaid increased. Paul Ginsburg cites four main reasons for this: states increased their need standards for AFDC, making more people eligible for Medicaid; the number of female-headed households (i.e., those categorically eligible for AFDC) increased as this demographic trend continued during the 1980s; organizations mounted public information campaigns to increase awareness and participation in the program; and additional states initiated Medicaid programs.[18]

The number of recipients declined slightly and remained steady during the early 1980s but began to rise again beginning in the mid-1980s and has continued to rise during the 1990s (see Table 3.2). The decline in the number of recipients can be attributed to the fact that from 1980 to 1984, eligibility for Medicaid was either directly or indirectly limited. Medicaid coverage for poor and near-poor people declined from 53 percent in 1980 to 46 percent in 1985. Factors contributing to this decline included failure to update state income standards, changes in Medicaid eligibility policy, and federal and state changes in AFDC eligibility policy. The 1981 Omnibus Budget Reconciliation Act (OBRA) established new limits on both income and resources for AFDC and Medicaid eligibility. It also limited cash assistance and Medicaid for certain groups of potential beneficiaries.[19] By 1985, however, this downward trend in the number of Medicaid recipients was reversed, and the number of recipients began to increase. This was largely caused by new federal mandates imposed by Congress between 1984 and 1990. Most of these mandates significantly expanded Medicaid eligibility for women and children. Between 1989 and 1991, the number of recipients increased by 4.8 million, with a significant portion of the increase attributable to federal mandates. For example, about one-half of the 3 million additional recipients qualifying for Medicaid between 1990 and 1991 were eligible because of mandated program expansions. The major beneficiaries of the mandated program expansions were children.[20] The changes introduced in the Medicaid program during the 1980s and 1990s are discussed in more detail later in the chapter.

Again, beginning with the mid-1990s, the growth rate of program recipients had slowed to single digits compared to double-digit growth rate of the early 1990s.

Changes in the Composition of Medicaid Beneficiaries

Over the years, the composition of the Medicaid clientele has changed. This in turn has affected patterns of Medicaid expenditures and enrollments. Between 1975 and 1995, the proportion of low-income aged, and other Medicaid beneficiaries declined while the proportion of disabled persons and children increased. In 1975, disabled persons accounted for 11.2 percent of the total Medicaid population; in 1995, they accounted for 16.1 percent. Similarly, the proportion of children in the Medicaid program increased from 43.6 percent of total beneficiaries in 1975 to 47.3 percent in 1995 (see Table 3.3).

In 1975, disabled persons accounted for 27.7 percent of Medicaid payments; in 1995, they accounted for 41 percent of the payments. Children accounted for 17.8 of total Medicaid payments in 1975 and 14.9 percent of payments in 1995.[21] Thus, even though the number of children recipients increased from 11 million in 1991 to 17 million in 1995, their proportionate cost declined. Today, children constitute the largest and fastest-growing component of the Medicaid population. Yet children are the least costly recipients covered by the program. The average payment per child is one-third the average payment for all recipients.[22]

The elderly and the disabled are the most costly recipients covered by the program. The elderly averaged about $8,868 per recipient, while the disabled averaged about $8,435 per recipient in 1995. In contrast, low-income children averaged only about $1,047 per recipient. The average for all recipients in 1995 was $3,311.[23]

There has also been a shift in the nature of the program. This shift has been away from an acute-care program for the disabled, poor adults, and children toward a long-term-care program for the elderly and chronically ill. In view of this shift toward long-term care, it is not surprising that elderly, blind, and disabled people are consuming a major share of Medicaid resources.[24] As the data in Table 3.4 reveal, Medicaid's share of total nursing home care expenditures has increased from $0.9 billion (out of total expenditures of $4.2 billion) in 1970 to $37.5 billion (out of total expenditures of $78.5 billion) in 1996. Medicaid accounted for 21.4 percent of total nursing home care expenditures in 1970. By 1996, Medicaid accounted for 47.8 percent of total nursing home care expenditures.[25]

Table 3.3

Number of Medicaid Persons Served by Eligibility Group, FY 1975–1995

	Total served	Low-income children (in millions)	Percentage	Low-income adults (in millions)	Percentage	Low-income aged (in millions)	Percentage	Low-income disabled (in millions)	Percentage	Other	percentage
1975	22.0	9.6	43.6	4.5	20.6	3.6	16.4	2.5	11.2	2.5	8.2
1976	22.8	9.9	43.5	4.8	20.9	3.6	15.8	2.7	11.7	2.7	8.1
1977	22.8	9.6	42.3	4.8	21.0	3.6	15.9	2.8	12.3	2.9	8.6
1978	22.0	9.3	42.7	4.6	21.1	3.4	15.4	2.7	12.4	2.7	8.4
1979	21.5	9.1	42.3	4.6	21.2	3.4	15.6	2.7	12.8	2.7	8.0
1980	21.6	9.3	43.2	4.9	22.6	3.4	15.9	2.9	13.5	2.9	4.8
1981	21.9	9.6	43.6	5.2	23.6	3.4	15.3	3.0	14.0	3.0	3.5
1982	21.6	9.6	44.3	5.4	24.8	3.2	15.0	2.9	13.4	2.9	2.6
1983	21.5	9.5	44.2	5.6	25.9	3.4	15.6	2.9	13.6	2.9	0.6
1984	21.6	9.6	44.8	5.6	25.9	3.2	15.0	2.9	13.5	2.9	0.8
1985	21.8	9.7	44.7	5.5	25.3	3.0	14.0	3.0	13.8	3.0	2.1
1986	22.5	10.0	44.5	5.6	25.1	3.1	13.9	3.2	14.1	3.2	2.3
1987	23.1	10.1	44.0	5.6	24.2	3.2	14.0	3.4	14.6	3.4	3.2
1988	22.9	10.0	43.8	5.5	24.0	3.2	13.8	3.5	15.2	3.5	3.1
1989	23.5	10.3	43.9	5.7	24.3	3.1	13.3	3.6	15.3	3.6	3.2
1990	25.2	11.2	44.4	6.0	23.8	3.2	12.7	3.7	14.7	3.7	4.4
1991	27.9	12.8	46.0	6.7	24.0	3.3	11.9	4.0	14.4	4.0	3.7
1992	31.1	15.2	48.8	7.0	22.6	3.7	12.0	4.5	14.4	4.5	2.2
1993	33.4	16.3	48.7	7.5	22.4	3.9	11.6	5.0	15.0	5.0	2.3
1994	35.0	17.1	49.1	7.6	21.6	4.0	11.5	5.4	15.6	5.4	2.2
1995	36.2	17.1	47.3	7.6	21.0	4.1	11.4	5.8	16.1	5.8	4.2

Source:Health Care Financing Review, Medicare and Medicaid Statistical Supplement (1997), 191.

Table 3.4

Medicaid's Share of Total Nursing Home Care Expenditures, 1970–1996

Year	Total nursing care expenditures (in billions of dollars)	Medicaid share (in billions of dollars)	Medicaid share (in percent)
1970	4.2	0.9	21.4
1980	17.6	8.8	50.0
1990	50.9	23.1	45.4
1991	57.2	27.5	48.0
1992	62.3	30.2	48.5
1993	66.3	32.4	48.9
1994	70.9	34.3	48.4
1995	75.2	35.5	47.2
1996	78.5	37.5	47.8

Source: Katharine R. Levit et al., "National Health Expenditures, 1996," *Health Care Financing Review* 19, no. 1 (Fall 1997): 195.

The Medicaid Program during the Reagan and Bush Years: 1980–1992

Two significant developments occurred in the Medicaid program during the 1980s. First, the Reagan administration introduced major changes in the early 1980s designed to decentralize Medicaid. State governments were given more autonomy and more flexibility, to enable them to attempt innovative approaches to providing health care for the poor while also containing rising Medicaid costs. Second, beginning in 1984–85, Democrats in Congress succeeded in imposing various mandates on the states designed to expand Medicaid coverage.

Reagan's New Federalism and the Decentralization of the Medicaid Program: 1981–1984

One of the major goals of the Reagan administration was to restructure the role of the federal, state, and local governments through the concept of "new federalism." New federalism was designed to decrease the role of the federal government and increase the role of the state governments in domestic policy areas. The Reagan administration tried to restrict the open-ended matching feature of the Medicaid program by proposing to limit the growth rate of the federal government's annual contribution to Medicaid to 5 percent. Congress did not support this proposal.

The most important spending and policy shift affecting health care for the poor was incorporated in the Omnibus Budget Reconciliation Act (OBRA) of 1981. This legislation contained three major changes affecting the Medicaid program. First, the federal contribution to Medicaid was directly reduced by 3 percent in 1982, 4 percent in 1983, and 4.5 percent in 1984. Second, changes in the federal welfare eligibility policy reduced welfare rolls and thereby the number of eligible Medicaid recipients. Third, the law contained many fundamental policy changes with far-reaching implications for Medicaid itself.[26] For example, although Medicaid had historically followed Medicare's reasonable-cost reimbursement principle, the act allowed states to pay health care providers (hospitals, nursing homes) on a basis other than reasonable cost.

OBRA also authorized formal retreat from the principle of free choice about provider eligibility. The act gave states wide discretion, on approval from the secretary of health and human services (HHS), to limit Medicaid recipients' freedom to choose their doctors or hospitals. Other provisions made it easier to use new kinds of health care providers, particularly health maintenance organizations (HMOs). The law also granted states wide discretion in deciding whom they would cover under Medicaid. It also authorized a provision allowing payment, through waiver from the secretary of HHS, for a wide range of home and community services that states could cover as an alternative to nursing home care. OBRA also allowed the states to buy laboratory services and medical devices via competitive bidding.

The Tax Equity and Fiscal Responsibility Act (TEFRA) of 1982 created new financing initiatives that allowed shifting costs to beneficiaries and third parties by granting the states discretion to require Medicaid beneficiaries to pay nominal fees for medical services.

In 1982 President Ronald Reagan, as part of his new federalism, proposed a swap of programs between the federal and the state governments. He proposed that the federal government take over full responsibility for Medicaid in return for state governments taking over food stamp and AFDC programs.[27] Reactions to the proposal were mixed. State governors liked the idea of the federal government's assuming full responsibility for the Medicaid program, but they wanted to defer action on the AFDC-food stamp portion of the swap.[28] The reaction on Capitol Hill ranged from tepid to frigid. The majority of Democrats were hostile to the plan.[29] New York City's Democratic mayor, Ed Koch, termed the Reagan plan "a con job, a snare and a delusion, a steal by the feds."[30] Because of the controversy surrounding the proposal, the plan was dropped and never submitted to Congress.

The Deficit Reduction Act of 1984 required Medicaid beneficiaries to assign to the states any rights they had to other health benefit programs. This allowed the states to collect from such programs any available payments for medical care for the covered beneficiaries.

President Reagan's new federalism initiatives posed a different challenge to the health policies established over the past fifty years.[31] The new federalism's emphasis on decentralization, with its focus on state- and local-level decision making, raised some fundamental questions. Could the state governments contain dramatically rising costs and provide access and quality care to the poor? How states respond to this challenge will shape the future course of Medicaid policy in particular and health care policy in general.

Congressional Expansion of the Medicaid Program: 1984–1990

By 1984, the 1981 Reagan initiative to prune the AFDC rosters was beginning to be challenged, and Congress began to ease eligibility standards. Since 1984, many incremental extensions of the Medicaid program have been aimed primarily at covering more low-income pregnant women, infants, and children. Thus, for example, under the Deficit Reduction Act of 1984 Congress required states to broaden their Medicaid coverage to include more low-income women during their first pregnancy, pregnant women in two-parent families in which the principal breadwinner was unemployed, and poor children up to the age of five in two-parent families.

The impetus for further expansion came from a 1985 Institute of Medicine report, which showed that every $1 spent on prenatal care saved $3.38 on care needed by low-birth-weight babies. The Omnibus Budget Reconciliation Act of 1986 gave states the option to extend Medicaid coverage to pregnant women and to infants up to the age of one year who are members of households with incomes of as much as 100 percent of the federal poverty level. The law also allowed coverage to be gradually implemented for children up to age eight in households with income less than the federal poverty level. By January 1989, twenty-nine states had adopted the option.[32]

The Omnibus Budget Reconciliation Act of 1987 allowed states to expand Medicaid eligibility to include pregnant women and infants up to age one year who live in households with incomes of as much as 185 percent of the federal poverty level. States were also given the option of immediately covering all children younger than age five living in households with incomes below the federal poverty level. The National Governors' Conference reported that as of January 1989, nine states were using the higher threshold established in the 1987 OBRA.[33]

In 1988 Congress passed a law to help avoid impoverishing the spouses of patients who receive Medicaid-financed nursing home care. The "spousal impoverishment" benefit—one of the few provisions to survive the Medicare Catastrophic Coverage Act repealed in 1989—substantially raised the amount of income that spouses could retain before handing the balance over to Medicaid to help defray the cost of a patient's nursing home care. The federal law allows states to let "at-home" spouses retain as much as $66,480 of the couple's combined assets and as much as $1,662 in monthly income.[34]

The Omnibus Budget Reconciliation Act of 1989 required provision of all Medicaid-allowed treatment to correct problems identified during early and periodic screening, diagnosis, and treatment (EPSDT), even if the treatment is otherwise not covered under the state Medicaid plan. The act also required periodic screening under EPSDT if medical problems were suspected. The Budget and Reconciliation Act of 1990 required Medicaid coverage of children under age eighteen if the family income is below 100 percent of the federal poverty line.

President Reagan's new federalism initiatives posed a new challenge to the health policies established over the past fifty years.[35] The Reagan administration was willing to grant states more discretion when such discretion promised cost reductions.[36]

Federal Government's Response to State Taxes on Hospitals and Health Care Providers

The incremental expansion in Medicaid coverage for pregnant women, infants, and children through the 1986 and 1987 OBRAs, and the "spousal impoverishment" benefit of 1988 has led to a significant increase in the number of Medicaid recipients. The total number of recipients increased from 21.6 million in 1985 to 28.3 million in 1991. This expansion in coverage and the increased number of recipients, combined with the 1990–91 recession, forced many states into a situation of fiscal crisis. According to a national survey conducted in 1991 by the National Association of Budget Officers and the National Governors' Association, the recession and Medicaid expansion mandates from the federal government forced more than half of all states to cut spending or increase revenues to avoid deficits in fiscal year 1991. Twenty-eight states faced total revenue shortfalls totaling $9.6 billion in 1991. Thirty-two states reported that their Medicaid spending would exceed their projections for the year.[37] According to a report by the General Accounting Office, expansion of Medicaid through federal mandates helped improved coverage, however, the fiscal problems faced by the states were likely to jeopardize further progress.[38]

In response to Medicaid program expansion under federal mandate and increase in program costs, state governments came to rely on a very controversial and growing practice known as "bootstrapping," also called "FTF" for "Fool the Feds." The practice involves states ordering doctors and other health care providers to hike up their fees so that the cost can be passed on to Washington.

Prior to 1985, the Health Care Financing Administration (HCFA) had allowed states to finance their share of Medicaid training expenditures through donation to the program by hospitals and other providers. However, states were not allowed to count such donations as part of the state-matching fund for the Medicaid program. In November of 1985, HCFA reversed this position and began to allow states to count private and public donations from hospitals and other providers as part of their matching funds.

State government wasted very little time in trying to take advantage of the new rule. Thirty-seven states passed laws that charge doctors, hospitals, and other Medicaid providers an extra tax. The money then can be returned to hospitals in the form of higher Medicaid reimbursements. Since the federal government reimburses anywhere from 50 to 83 percent of state Medicaid costs, the more a state charges, the more it gets back. If hospitals are unwilling to play along with the "voluntary donation" scheme, the states can pull the same trick by charging "provider taxes." The state levies a uniform tax on all hospitals, doctors, and other health care providers. The tax revenues are routed back to the providers of Medicaid services in the form of higher Medicaid reimbursements.[39] According to Richard Kusserow, inspector general of HHS, such provider taxes and donation programs "may change the very nature of the whole federal-state partnership."[40] By 1990 all but six states had a donation or provider tax program.

Concerned over this development, the Bush administration in September of 1991 proposed new rules intended to eliminate what it described as a "scam" used by the states to extract $3 billion to $5 billion a year from the federal government. Under the proposed rule, the federal government would not match spending by states for Medicaid if the state's money came from donations or special taxes paid by hospitals and nursing homes. The administration claimed that this practice of raising federal money by counting donations and taxes as part of a state's Medicaid share is a major reason for the explosion of the federal government's Medicaid costs. A statement issued on behalf of the National Governors' Association warned that if the proposed rules were adopted they could lead to the closing of hospitals, and women and children would lose eligibility for Medicaid.[41] After strong opposition from state officials, a deal was struck in which states could continue the program if every hospital is taxed by the method.

The new rules imposed several important restrictions. First, health care-related taxes eligible for federal matching funds must be broad based and uniformly imposed, and must include all members of a class, such as all inpatient hospitals, all physicians, or all HMOs and other prepaid entities. Second, these taxes cannot make up more than 25 percent of a state's share of Medicaid. Finally, the taxes cannot contain a "hold harmless" provision, which guarantees that health care providers will have the tax they paid returned to them.[42] Based on the above rules, Congress in 1991 passed a law, Medicaid Voluntary Contribution and Provider-Specific Tax Amendments of 1991 that closed the "provider taxes" loophole. With few exceptions, the law eliminated federal matching payments for provider donations. Second, it held out the possibility of a federal matching for provider-specific taxes only if these were uniform, were broad based, and did not exempt providers from the cost of the tax. The law also capped the revenue from such taxes for purposes of state matching at 25 percent of state Medicaid spending. Finally, the law prohibited states from guaranteeing that DHS payments would exceed the tax payment for each hospital.[43] But the story did not end with the 1991 law. According to the rules published by the Health Care Financing Administration in August 1993, the provider taxes must be broad based and uniform. In addition, states must drop "hold harmless" clauses. Nevertheless, almost half the states continued to make the assessments. The HCFA sent letters to nine states claiming that they were violating the law. In another letter to twenty-three states the HCFA argued that their programs were neither broad based nor uniform. The HCFA has disallowed millions of dollars worth of claims made by many states.[44]

Lawsuits over State Medicaid Reimbursements

The 1981 OBRA eliminated altogether the federal requirement for reasonable-cost reimbursement. As we discussed earlier, under this act, states are now required to pay only the "reasonable and adequate" rates needed to meet the costs of "efficiently and economically operated facilities." This is also known as the Boren Amendment, named after Senator David Boren (D-Oklahoma). States have to consider only the special needs of institutions serving a disproportionate number of poor persons and to assure "reasonable access" to services and "adequate quality."

State governments facing budget problems have begun to change their rate-setting formulas to reduce reimbursements to hospitals and nursing homes. This in turn has led hospitals and nursing homes to file lawsuits against states to force them to increase Medicaid payments to levels that more closely reflect what it costs to treat patients. Not only has the number of Medicaid lawsuits increased, but also so have the legal and political complexities involved in such lawsuits.[45] In February 1990 a federal judge ordered the state of Pennsylvania to increase its reimbursements to Temple University Hospital, the state's largest provider of health care to the poor. The judge declared that Pennsylvania's Medicaid rates were arbitrary and that the rate-setting formula used by the state was simply a mechanism to keep the total medical assistance cost within the welfare department budget.[46] In a decision handed down in June 1990, the U.S. Supreme Court upheld the right of hospitals and other providers to sue the states for higher Medicaid payments.[47]

According to a survey of hospitals by the American Hospital Association, hospitals, on average, receive 78 cents for every $1 it costs to care for Medicaid patients. Judges in several cases have reached similar conclusions. In many states, judges have ruled that Medicaid payments to health care providers do not meet the standards of "reasonable and adequate" compensation under the law. Judges in several states have also concluded that states often base their payments simply on budget considerations. The result is that federal and state spending has increased by several billion dollars a year as a result of court judgments, settlements, and rate increases granted by states in anticipation of lawsuits.[48]

Despite various strategies attempted by the federal and state governments to control the cost of Medicaid, total Medicaid expenditures increased from $24.8 billion in 1980 to $112.8 billion in 1993. During the same period, the federal government's Medicaid costs increased from $13.7 billion to $73.2 billion, while state costs increased from $11.1 billion to $39.6 billion. Thus, despite many innovative approaches utilized by state governments, the overall cost of the Medicaid program continued to grow.[49]

Further Devolution of the Medicaid Program during the Clinton Administration: 1992–1998

The failure of President Clinton's effort to reform the U.S. health care system through the Health Security Act of 1993, and the resulting Republican control of Congress in the 1994 elections, shifted the focus to incremental reforms. The 104th Congress, under the leadership of the Republican party, tried to bolster the role of the states in providing health care to the poor by transforming the Medicaid program into a block grant as part of the Balanced Budget Act of 1996. President Clinton vetoed the measure, and other similar attempts by Republicans to turn Medicaid into a block grant met with the same results.

President Clinton pursued his own vision of Medicaid devolution.[50] The Clinton administration allowed states more flexibility on Medicaid funds and supported states' efforts at innovation and experimentation. For example,

President Clinton ordered the federal government to make it easier for states to use Medicaid funds to introduce new health care programs for the poor. The administration also eased paperwork requirements related to states' requests for waivers in two ways. First, the Department of Health and Human Services was no longer allowed to make numerous requests for information and clarifications on a state's waiver application. Second, the Health Care Financing Administration was ordered to develop a list of state programs already approved for waiver. The purpose of this was to allow other states seeking to start similar programs to adopt them immediately, without having to go through the paperwork themselves.[51]

Upon assuming office in 1992, the Clinton administration had begun to provide states with waivers to experiment with their Medicaid programs. The HCFA, relying upon the demonstration authority embedded in Section 1115 of the Social Security Act, approved dramatic changes in the Medicaid programs of many states. Prior to this, in the absence of a special waiver from the federal government, states were restricted to running their Medicaid programs under a traditional fee-for-service delivery system. Three major restrictions were imposed on the states. First, under the freedom-of-choice requirement, states were required to allow Medicaid beneficiaries to seek services from the provider of their choice. Second, states were required to offer the same benefit package to all mandatory Medicaid eligibility groups under the comparability requirement. Finally, every managed care program must be established on a statewide basis. Two main options are available to states for gaining immunity from these requirements: They may either establish voluntary managed care programs or seek waivers from the federal government.[52] There are two basic types of waivers available. The 1915(b) waiver gives states the right to waive the freedom-of-choice, comparability, and statewide requirements. Under this waiver, states are not required to give Medicaid beneficiaries a choice of providers, even though they still must offer beneficiaries some choice of health plans. However, states cannot use the 1915(b) waiver to expand coverage to new populations, to change the Medicaid benefit package, to restrict access to family planning providers, or to restrict access to federally qualified health centers.[53]

States that want more flexibility than is allowed under a 1915(b) waiver can apply for a Section 1115 research-and-demonstration waiver. This waiver gives states freedom from many of the Medicaid program's federal requirements. Like a 1915(b) waiver, a 1115 waiver allows a state waiver from freedom-of-choice, comparability, and statewide requirements. Furthermore, states under a 1115 waiver can contract with managed care plans that do not meet all the federal criteria, and may be allowed to limit voluntary disenrollment to a single period each year. Under a 1115 waiver, a state must test an innovative approach in administering the Medicaid program and must allow the federal government to monitor and evaluate its activities. States are prohibited from altering the medical assistance given to pregnant women and children, from imposing copayments on Medicaid-eligible individuals, and from waiving spousal impoverishment protections for institutionalized persons, among other prohibitions. The Clinton administration has demonstrated even more flexibility by granting waivers to states whose proposals include the modest goal of advancing health care reform initiative. Thus, a 1115 waiver can be used to establish a statewide demonstration program or to run a small-scale reform project.[54]

The Personal Responsibility and Work Opportunity Reconciliation Act of 1996 repealed the Aid to Families with Dependent Children (AFDC) program and replaced it with Temporary Assistance for Needy Families (TANF). This is a block-grant program to the states. The Medicaid program itself remained essentially intact; however, its traditional ties to the welfare program were severed. Thus, as welfare rolls are reduced and as individuals and families lose their eligibility, they may continue to be eligible for the Medicaid program. The key issue faced by the states is how to reach the growing number of low-income parents and, even more important, children who will continue to be eligible for Medicaid but not for TANF. These parents and children used to be tracked through the welfare offices.[55] According to a 1994 study by the Center for Budget and Policy Priority, 2.7 million children under the age of eleven were not on welfare but were eligible for Medicaid.[56] With welfare reform, the number of uninsured children is certain to rise. According to the *Wall Street Journal*, welfare reform may increase the percentage of uninsured children from the current 20 percent to 30 percent by year 2002.[57] Advocates argue that uninsured children are a logical group for whom to expand coverage. They are relatively inexpensive to insure and they can benefit a great deal from coverage.

The Balanced Budget Act of 1997 provided about $40 billion in federal funds over the 1998–2007 period to expand health insurance coverage for children by creating the State Children's Insurance Program (S-CHIP) as part of title XXI of the Social Security Act. The formula for allocating federal S-CHIP funds among states depends on estimates of the number of uninsured and low-income children in each state. To qualify for S-CHIP funds, a state must submit a plan to the HCFA detailing how it intends to expand coverage for children. States have the freedom to use their S-CHIP funds to expand Medicaid to cover children by raising their Medicaid income-eligibility standards, to develop or expand other insurance programs for children, or to provide services directly.[58]

Medicaid Program and the State Governments: Innovations and Experimentation, 1980–1990s

The decentralization of the Medicaid program under the Reagan, Bush, and Clinton administrations, on the one hand, and significant expansion of the program through federal mandates between1984 and 1990, on the other, raises a fundamental question: Can the state governments contain the rising cost of the Medicaid program and still provide increased access and high-quality care to the poor? How states respond to this challenge will shape the future course of Medicaid policy. In the rest of this chapter we analyze how state governments have responded to the Medicaid program's decentralization and expansion during the 1980s and the 1990s.

By the early 1980s, health care cost containment had emerged as a major issue for state and local governments. Confronted with more discretionary authority and the need to reduce Medicaid expenditures, state governments responded to new federal initiatives of the 1980s and 1990s in many different ways.[59] The story of Medicaid reform varies from state to state.[60] The discussion that follows focuses on some of the major responses of state governments.

Cutbacks in Eligibility, Benefits, and Coverage

During the 1980s, in response to federal cuts in matching funds, many states turned to strategies such as placing limits on income eligibility standards, reducing coverage of optional groups, and reducing the amount of services covered in an attempt to reduce state expenditures under Medicaid.

States selected options that were easy to implement and promised the quickest savings. Some states attempted Medicaid cuts by reducing the number of people on the program, reducing benefits for those covered, or both.[61] These are attractive options for state governments because state agencies are the ones that make such decisions, and they have the machinery to calculate the amount of savings that can be generated. Nevertheless, these cost-saving methods are most likely to affect low-income patients adversely.[62]

In a nationwide survey, the Intergovernmental Health Policy Project at George Washington University found that in 1981 alone more than thirty states reduced Medicaid benefits or limited Medicaid eligibility. Since January 1982, twenty-four states had restricted use of medical services by placing limits on the number of visits to doctors, emergency rooms, and outpatient facilities. Eleven states had placed limits on the number of hospital days covered under Medicaid, while another eight states had eliminated certain optional services.[63] Many states had used a combination of stringent income criteria and limited optional service coverage to constrain enrollments and outlays.

By 1982, most of the states had made only small increases in AFDC ben-efit levels, or none at all, thereby allowing inflation to raise earnings of employed welfare recipients above the eligibility ceiling. People between the ages of eighteen and twenty-one were declared ineligible for AFDC in sev-eral states. Some states, such as California and Washington, reduced patients' medically needy coverage by increasing the amount that recipients must "spend down" before Medicaid eligibility begins. Thus, by 1982 most states had re-duced eligibility.[64] The number of total Medicaid recipients declined from 22 million in 1981 to 21.6 million in 1982. Reduction in Medicaid eligibility is an area where one of the goals of OBRA was realized by the early 1980s.[65]

Similarly, states have been active in reducing service coverage. States such as Illinois, Massachusetts, Michigan, Missouri, and Rhode Island placed limits or increased existing limits on hospital days, eliminating weekend ad-missions, reducing the coverage of preoperative days, and ending payment for inpatient surgery when the service could be provided on an outpatient basis. California, Connecticut, Illinois, New Jersey, and North Carolina di-rectly limited physician visits to "lock in" overutilizing patients or to "lock out" providers found to provide too many services or poor-quality care. Sev-eral states also added controls on the number of nursing home days (in either skilled nursing or intermediate-care facilities) they will pay for. Several states extended limits on drug coverage. Other states placed limits on optional ser-vices such as dentists, chiropractors, and optometrists, or eliminated coverage for such services completely.[66]

As we discussed earlier in the chapter, federal mandates imposed between 1984 and 1990 designed to expand coverage to women and children dramati-cally increased the number of recipients. The result is that despite state governments' attempts to reduce program cost and enrollments, both increased dramatically in the late 1980s and early 1990s. While federal mandates have helped increase access to the health care system, especially for poor women and children, they have also significantly increased program costs at both the federal and state levels of governments. Again, we were faced with the con-flicting values of access versus cost.

Increased Use of Copayments for Medicaid Services

During the 1980s, use of copayments became common in many states. Sev-eral states today require copayments for many Medicaid services.[67] The assumption here is that copayments force the beneficiary to ask whether the care is really worth paying for and thus make him or her more cost conscious. Some view copayments as an ideal mechanism for eliminating services not highly valued by Medicaid recipients. Others fear that even small copayments will result in drastic reductions in the use of health care services by the poor. Some early studies have suggested that copayments indeed reduce expenditures on medical services. More important, the effects of copayments, at least with income-related upper limits, did not vary significantly with the family income of those participating in these studies. Thus, supporters of use of the copayment approach argue that the fear of reduced use of health services by the poor because of copayments is unfounded.[68] However, it should be noted that states that have received 1915(b) and 1115 waivers are now significantly restricted in their use of copayments.

Competitive Bidding: Contractual and Prudent Buyer Arrangements

Another approach—a competitive strategy—used by the states is to attempt a fundamental reform in their approach to Medicaid. This involves replacing a fee-for-service system with negotiated or competitively bid fixed-price arrangements for Medicaid services. For example, California relies on negotiated fixed-price arrangements. Selective contracting of hospitals by the California Medicaid program (Medi-Cal) was established in 1983. During that year the state negotiated all-inclusive per diem rates on an individual basis with eligible hospitals. Once the rate was determined, hospitals had to absorb costs that exceeded the negotiated level. Medi-Cal patients are required to go to a contracting hospital, and contracting facilities must treat patients coming to them. Contracting applied to more than half of California's hospitals and more than 75 percent of its Medicaid hospitalizations.[69]

The Arizona Health Cost Containment System (AHCCS), implemented in 1982, relies on provider bidding for the delivery of health care to the indigent. The Arizona Medicaid program puts out various types of care for per capita bids, and counties as well as private-sector providers compete for prepaid contracts. In such a prepaid, capitated system of health care, financial risk bearing is shifted, partially from the consumer and totally from the third-party insurer, to the provider. According to proponents, such a system internalizes economic incentives.[70] Competitive bidding is also becoming increasingly popular for health care services such as clinical laboratory services, home health care, and mental health care.[71]

An analysis of the Arizona system in 1985 revealed that, overall, a lower proportion of the poor were enrolled in AHCCS in 1984 than in county programs in 1982. Access to care increased for AHCCS enrollees in 1984 compared to county patients in 1982. Nevertheless, the study also discovered significant undercoverage of the medically indigent and the medically needy. The study concluded that AHCCS may be a viable alternative to conventional

Medicaid programs, but poor persons who were financially ineligible for AHCCS were experiencing decreased opportunities for health services.[72] Thus it remains to be seen whether a competitive bidding approach helps contain costs without sacrificing access or quality of care.

The 1981 OBRA greatly expanded state authority by allowing states to purchase in bulk durable medical equipment, lab tests, and X-ray services. Some states are using bulk purchase arrangements for goods such as eyeglasses, hearing aids, and laboratory services. The objective is to buy from the lowest bidder, rather than to reimburse every retail seller at his or her price.

Rationing of Medicaid Services

The state of Oregon is in the process of implementing an innovative approach to address problems of cost and access in its Medicaid program. In 1987 the state decided to stop financing most organ transplants for Medicaid patients, and to use the money instead for prenatal care for pregnant women. In 1990 the state produced a more revolutionary Medicaid plan. As we discussed earlier, a large number of poor people do not have access to Medicaid because they do not meet eligibility criteria. The state proposed that under its plan, Medicaid would cover all poor people in the state but may not cover all medical services. In other words, the plan proposed a tradeoff—increased access in return for reduced benefits. The state ranked most medical services as more or less economically worthwhile to treat under the plan. If money ran out before all services were covered, the lowest-priority services would not be covered. In March 1993, the HCFA under the Clinton administration granted the state of Oregon a waiver from federal statutes to implement such a program. This is likely to encourage other states to adopt similar plans. Colorado is considering doing away with the Medicaid program and establishing its own health care program for the poor.[73] Critics charge that the plan targets the poor—mainly women and children, who make up most of the Medicaid population.[74] They also argue that such a meat-ax approach to health care will inevitably lead to gross misallocation of resources.[75]

Use of Medicaid Waivers for Home- and Community-Based Services

Section 2176 of the 1981 OBRA allowed states to seek waivers from the Department of Health and Human Services (HHS) for a variety of home- and community-based services provided to certain individuals—the elderly, the physically disabled, the developmentally disabled, and the mentally ill—who would otherwise require nursing home care. States that have approval from HHS can receive matching funds. The objective of section 2176 was to encourage a move away from the use of more expensive treatment in nursing homes and other long-term-care facilities and toward less expensive home- and community-based services when appropriate. The traditional purpose of the waiver process has been to allow HHS to conduct demonstrations on alternative delivery and financing schemes. The waiver provisions of the 1981 OBRA were based on early successes of demonstration projects in this area.

Such waiver programs have become popular with many states and have grown rapidly since their creation in 1981. By 1985, forty-two states were providing a broad range of health and social services under seventy-five waiver programs. The number of recipients had increased steadily under such waiver programs. For example, the number of aged and/or physically disabled recipients increased from 6,389 in 1981 to 45,934 in 1984. Similarly, the number of developmentally disabled and chronically mentally ill recipients increased from 10,000 to 21,823 during the same period.[76] Nevertheless, the popularity of waiver programs does not mean that all states find them cost effective. The waiver also provides states with a way to secure additional federal funding for services that otherwise would have to be funded entirely through state revenues.[77]

New Approaches to Reimbursing Providers

Payments to Physicians

States have generally enjoyed significant discretion over Medicaid payments to physicians. The Medicaid program has traditionally paid physicians much less than Medicare or private insurers. For example, under the Medicare program, states are mandated to pay physicians "usual, customary, and reasonable" fees (UCR payment system). The Medicaid statute, however, never imposed any specific method of payment on the states except that the fee be high enough to assure reasonable access to care for Medicaid beneficiaries.

Through waivers, states have also been able to pay physicians a set fee or capitation payment rather than a fee-for-service payment. States also can establish case management programs linking patients to solo or group practice physicians or with an HMO.[78] States may, under a waiver program, enroll Medicaid patients in an HMO and restrict their use of other providers.

Several state Medicaid programs have imposed significant limits or ceilings on physician payment. Some states have turned to the use of fee schedules. The average Medicaid payment for a visit to a physician is estimated to be only 65 percent of the average charge for visits of other patients. Medicare pays about 84 percent on the average. The result is that many physicians do not accept Medicaid patients; the willingness to accept them varies with the level of Medicaid payments.[79] This raises questions about access of Medicaid recipients to physicians. When Medicaid cuts have to be made, state programs often attempt to impose further restrictions on physicians' fees. Such efforts are often misguided. In general, physicians' fees constitute a very small percentage of total Medicaid spending. Thus, trying to save money by limiting payments to physicians may not be the best way to reduce program costs. In fact, reduced physician participation may drive many beneficiaries to substitute services at a greater cost to Medicaid.

Payments to Hospitals

In contrast to physician payment, Medicaid has generally been required to pay hospitals on the same basis as Medicare, that is, using a "reasonable cost" reimbursement method. With the 1972 amendments to the Social Security Act, however, there has been a gradual trend toward paying less than the actual cost. The amendments allowed states with approval from HHS to use alternate (to Medicare) payment methods for Medicaid.

The 1981 OBRA gave states more flexibility to develop and implement new Medicaid hospital payment methods as long as those payments were reasonable and adequate to meet the costs of "efficiently and economically operated facilities." The only requirements were that payment levels take into consideration the circumstances of hospitals serving a disproportionate number of low-income persons and that payments be sufficient to ensure Medicaid patients reasonable access to adequate-quality services.[80]

Faced with reduced revenues and increased health care costs, state governments have tried various strategies to contain costs. By 1982, seventeen states had legislation requiring the disclosure, review (such as HSAs and CON), or regulation of hospital rates or budgets. States such as California converted their hospital payment approach to selective contracting on the basis of price negotiated for services provided.

One major alternative payment method used by state governments is rate setting. Many states have adopted some form of hospital rate review or prospective reimbursement system. In some states, rate setting applies only to Medicaid, while in others the rate applies to all payers.[81] Rate-setting programs fall into three broad strategies to control Medicaid costs: multiple-payer rate setting, Medicaid-only prospective payment, and selective contracting.[82]

The state rate-setting strategy emerged, in the mid-1970s, in several eastern industrial states as a regulatory device in response to Medicaid's financial crisis. Limited prospective payment schemes for Medicaid reimbursement were adopted in Kentucky, Missouri, Alabama, Georgia, Mississippi, and North Carolina.[83]

State rate-setting programs have produced mixed results. Proponents have argued that some mandatory prospective rate-setting programs have been successful in reducing hospital expenditures per patient day, per admission, and per capita.[84] Other studies have also demonstrated that states have achieved modest success in containing Medicaid payments to hospitals under different rate-setting strategies—multiple-payer rate setting, Medicaid-only rate setting, and selective contracting—with some being more effective than others.[85] States that use all-payer rate setting are able to force down hospital prices for all payers. In states where the payment systems apply only to Medicaid, savings appear to be temporary and may not be sustained over a long period.[86]

Medicaid Managed Care in the 1990s

In response to problems of cost and access, state governments have increasingly turned to managed care systems in the Medicaid program. Many state governments have also moved in the direction of "privatization" of their Medicaid programs. States and the federal government continue to fund the program jointly, but the day-to-day control of health plans for the poor is being turned over to Health Maintenance Organizations (HMOs) or similar organizations and private insurers. Many states require Medicaid recipients to enroll in an HMO or other preferred provider organizations (PPOs). Case managers or primary-care physicians are assigned to watch Medicaid patients' health. They act as gatekeepers to control and coordinate the delivery of health services in a cost-conscious manner. The emphasis is on low-cost preventive care, outpatient services, and less reliance on emergency hospital care and costly specialists as a way of reducing costs.[87]

The 1981 OBRA gave states more flexibility to design managed care plans. In addition, HCFA allowed states to experiment with innovative approaches to Medicaid through research and demonstration projects. In most instances, states must obtain a waiver of federal statutory requirements from HCFA. Most states rapidly began to develop managed care programs. According to a study by the General Accounting Office, Medicaid-managed care enrollment more than doubled between 1987 and 1992 and included about 3.6 million beneficiaries nationwide, representing about 12 percent of the total Medicaid population as of June 1992. Thirty-six states were operating one or more mandatory managed care programs for Medicaid beneficiaries in February 1993.[88]

As discussed earlier in the chapter, the use of managed care for Medicaid program was given a significant boost during the Clinton administration by

HCFA's announcement of new rules pertaining to the Medicaid program that made it easier for the states to gain 1195(b) and 1115 waivers from the federal government.

As of June 1994, thirty-eight states had one or more 1915(b) waivers. States can have multiple 1915(b) waivers to cover different target groups or geographic areas. Thirty-six of the thirty-eight states used the 1915(b) waivers to enroll AFDC recipients and/or pregnant women and children in managed care. Half of the states with 1915(b) waivers enrolled aged, blind, physically or mentally disabled, mentally ill, or other special groups of Medicaid recipients in managed care. As of March 1996, under 1115 waiver, nine states had implemented statewide programs, five additional states had received permission to proceed with implementation, and another six had submitted waiver proposals. Eight states were relying on 1115 waivers for small-scope reform projects, such as a program for all intensive care for the elderly that seeks to integrate the delivery of primary, acute, and long-term care for elderly and disabled people.[89]

States participating in managed care share a common approach but employ a variety of models. There are four primary models utilized by states.[90] Some state plans utilize HMOs. HMOs can be public or private entities authorized by state law that are either federally qualified or meet a state plan's definition of HMO. While states have considerable flexibility to define HMOs as they wish, their definition must require HMOs to give Medicaid enrollees the same access to services as other plan participants and to protect Medicaid enrollees from losses if the HMO becomes insolvent. Most HMOs are risk-based programs that agree to provide beneficiaries with a substantial portion of the Medicaid benefit package they are entitled to in exchange for a capitated payment. If the payment falls short, the HMO suffers a loss. By the same token, if the plan can reduce the cost of services provided to less than the capitated payment, it makes a profit. HMOs can also contract with state Medicaid agencies on a partial-risk or nonrisk basis. In a partial-risk plan, HMOs can suffer losses if actual costs exceed capitated payment but they are responsible for providing a less than comprehensive set of services. Under a nonrisk plan, if the cost of providing services is larger than expected, the state can adjust the size of its capitated payment to the plan.

Some states utilize what are called health insuring organizations (HIOs). HIOs assume the risk of loss if the payment is inadequate to cover beneficiaries' health care expenses. However, unlike HMOs, HIOs generally do not deliver care. Congress since 1995 holds HIOs to the same regulatory standards as HMOs, if they offer a full-risk comprehensive set of services. However, if they do not offer a comprehensive set of services, they face fewer federal regulatory requirements.

Another delivery model utilized by states is called prepaid health plans (PHPs). These plans fall into two categories. One type of PHP provides services on a nonrisk basis or provides less than comprehensive range of services on a risk basis. The second type of PHP, often referred to as a "grandfathered" PHP, is statutorily defined, and is allowed to engage in comprehensive risk contracting without having to meet the same regulatory standards as an HMO or a regular PHP.

Finally, some states use primary care case management programs (PCCMs). These are not plans or separate organizations. They are programs under which Medicaid beneficiaries select a primary care provider. Generally, a primary care provider contracts directly with a state Medicaid agency and is paid on a fee-for-service basis to provide primary care services directly to the assigned beneficiaries. In some states, such as California, PCCM providers operate on a partial capitation basis, while in other states PCCM providers are at risk for outpatient services only.

There are several explanations of why states governments are using their increased discretion to encourage or require Medicaid beneficiaries to enroll in managed care. One primary reason is the belief that moving beneficiaries into managed care will significantly help reduce program costs. A second is the belief that managed care will provide beneficiaries better access to high-quality care. A third reason is that managed care fits into the general trend toward privatization and contracting out in the health care sector.[91]

The 1990s have witnessed an unprecedented increase in the number of Medicaid patients enrolled in managed care programs. Table 3.5 provides

Table 3.5

Medicaid Managed Care Enrollment—National Trends, 1991–1997

	Total Medicaid population (in thousands)	Fee-for-Service (FFS) population (in thousands)	Managed care population (in thousands)	Percentage managed care population	Percentage change from previous year
1991	28,280,000	25,583,603	2,696,397	9.53	
1992	30.926,390	27,291,874	3,634,516	11.75	34.8
1993	33,430,051	28,621,100	4,808,951	14.39	32.0
1994	33,634,000	25,839.750	7,794,250	23.17	62.1
1995	33,373,000*	23,573,000*	9,800,000*	29.37*	25.7
1996	33,241147	19,911,028	13,330,119	40.10	36.0
1997	32,092,380	16,746,878	15,345,502	47.82	15.1

Source: Health Care Financing Administration, Medicaid Managed Care Page. http://hcfa.gov/medicaid/trends97.htm.

*Approximate numbers.

Table 3.6
National Summary of Medicaid Managed Care Enrollment by Plan Type,
June 30, 1997

	Number of plans	Number (in thousands) of enrollees	Percentage of total enrollment
Health insuring organization	6	351,053	1.8
HMOs, federally qualified	118	2,752,264	14.1
HMOs, state plan defined	252	5,654,681	29.0
Primary care case management	60	4,337,486	22.3
Prepaid health plan	113	3,850,589	19.8
Other	19	2,510,808	13.0
Total	568	19,456,881	100.0

Source: Health Care Financing Administration. Medicaid Managed Care Page. http://www.hcfa.gov/medicaid/plansum7.htm.

nationwide data on Medicaid managed care enrollment. In 1991, only 9.53 percent of Medicaid beneficiaries were enrolled in managed care plans. The number of Medicaid managed care enrollees had reached 23.1 percent by 1994, and 47.8 percent by 1994. On average, Medicaid managed care enrollment has increased by over 30 percent annually.

With respect to different organizational models, the HMO (federally qualified or state plan defined) appears to be the most popular model utilized by the states (see Table 3.6). In June 1997, there were 370 such organizations enrolling about 43 percent of the Medicaid managed care population in the states. Another 22.3 percent of the Medicaid managed care population was enrolled in sixty PCCM programs, while 19.8 percent of the Medicaid managed care population was enrolled in 113 prepaid health plans. Over 85 percent of the Medicaid managed care population was enrolled in one of the four major organizational models we have described, while about 13 percent belonged to other organizational forms.

Table 3.7 provides data on Medicaid managed care enrollment on a state-by-state basis as of June 1997. A quick glance at the data suggests significant variations in Medicaid managed care enrollment among fifty states and U.S. territories. It ranges from zero percent of the Medicaid population enrolled in managed care plan in states such as Alaska and Wyoming to 100 percent of Medicaid patients enrolled in managed care plans in states such as Tennessee and Washington. In half of the states, 50 percent or more of the Medicaid beneficiaries were enrolled in managed care plans. Thus, there is no denying the fact that the Clinton administration's grant of 1915(b) and 1115 waivers to states and the decentralization of the Medicaid program encouraged states to move in the direction of managed care as one of the cost-saving measures.

The results of managed care experiments by state governments in containing Medicaid costs have been mixed. Some of the studies have found that managed care can save money. One study examined twenty-five managed care programs and found that per-member costs were 5 to 15 percent lower than in conventional Medicaid programs.[92] Many other studies of managed care plans have demonstrated that such plans have largely failed to improve recipients' access.[93] A General Accounting Office study concluded that "managed care plans have had mixed results in improving access to care, assuring the quality

Table 3.7

Medicaid Managed Care Enrollment by States, June 30, 1997
(in thousands)

State or area	Medicaid enrollment	Managed care enrollment	Percentage enrolled in managed care
Alabama	497,434	407,643	81.9
Alaska	87,475	0	00.0
Arizona	431,813	349,142	80.9
Arkansas	267,525	159,458	59.6
California	4,791,253	1,854,294	38.7
Colorado	228,558	184,000	80.5
Connecticut	360,246	231,966	64.4
Delaware	80,561	65,061	80.8
Florida	1,410,881	896,559	63.5
Georgia	881,632	560,771	63.6
Hawaii	166,725	135,200	81.1
Idaho	80,553	32,428	40.3
Illinois	1,370,354	187,048	13.7
Indiana	405,000	220,000	54.3
Iowa	217,668	88,282	40.6
Kansas	185,301	94,430	51.0
Kentucky	527,211	268,205	50.9
Louisiana	635,672	40,469	6.4
Maine	155,524	12,511	8.0
Maryland	465,136	347,640	74.7
Massachusetts	716,465	461,989	64.5
Michigan	1,115,903	865,434	77.5
Minnesota	402,787	169,239	42.0
Mississippi	543,560	81,255	15.0
Missouri	614,783	264,496	43.0
Montana	70,821	62,004	87.5
Nebraska	144,238	93,085	64.5
Nevada	88,500	26,376	29.8
New Hampshire	70,922	9,102	12.8
New Jersey	684,880	384,644	56.1

State or area	Medicaid enrollment	Managed care enrollment	Percentage enrolled in managed care
New Mexico	242,454	139,337	57.5
New York	2,296,479	660,725	28.8
North Carolina	825,464	351,043	42.5
North Dakota	45,303	24,295	53.6
Ohio	1,095,268	352,833	32.2
Oklahoma	437,161	222,818	50.9
Oregon	376,345	312,345	83.0
Pennsylvania	1,585,807	870,365	54.9
Rhode Island	114,162	70,944	62.1
South Carolina	393,475	14,311	3.6
South Dakota	60,412	41,542	68.7
Tennessee	1,188,570	1,188,570	100.0
Texas	2,079,297	275,951	13.3
Utah	118,343	93,785	79.2
Vermont	96,000	22,946	23.7
Virginia	522,080	306,804	58.8
Washington	730,052	730,052	100.0
West Virginia	310,710	125,521	40.4
Wisconsin	422,870	205,523	48.6
Wyoming	48,348	0	00.0
District of Columbia	125,000	80,721	64.6
Puerto Rico	1,261,769	702,250	55.7
Virgin Islands	16,654	0	00.0
Total	**32,092,380**	**15,345,502**	**47.8**

Source: Health Care Financing Administration. Medicaid Managed Care Page. http://www.hcfa.gov/medicaid/mcsten97.htm.

of services, and saving money."[94] More recent studies have also raised doubts about Medicaid managed care's ability to save significant amount of money for state and local governments. State governments' earlier estimates of savings they expected to gain due to managed care were about 15 percent relative to fee-for-service care. However, most states today anticipate savings to be in the range of 5 to 10 percent. One reason is that despite the dramatic growth in Medicaid managed care enrollment in this decade, very few states are enrolling elderly or the disabled, who are the most expensive Medicaid beneficiaries.[95]

Michael Sparer has provided five excellent explanations of why expected savings from the Medicaid managed care programs are likely to be more modest than earlier projections. First, many Medicaid initiatives by the states have focused on welfare mothers and their children, who are the least expensive part of the Medicaid population. Second, most states are paying high capitation rates to build up managed care capacity. Third, the technology of risk adjustment is not very advanced. Fourth, the start-up cost for new Medicaid initiatives by the states is often very high. Finally, the extent of managed care savings depends on the fee-for-service expenditure patterns in a particular state. States that already have an inexpensive fee-for-service program are not likely to realize a great deal of savings.[96]

Whether managed care plans have had substantial effect on Medicaid cost reduction or not may remain the subject of much discussion and debate. However, one thing is clear. Since 1994, the growth rate in Medicaid program cost has been slowed considerably and has averaged in single digits, as compared to double-digit growth in prior years. This is true for the overall cost of the Medicaid program as well as for the cost of the program to the federal government and to the state and local governments.

However, managed care programs are also plagued with other problems. In states that do not monitor HMO behavior, such plans may offer impressive marketing but poor care. Such HMOs are often referred to as "Medicaid mills." Some HMOs snap up the healthiest patients, leaving traditional Medicaid to deal with sicker people. In addition, paperwork is always a problem because many Medicaid recipients go on and off program rolls as their income and family status change.[97]

State Governments, Medicaid, and Children's Insurance Program

As we discussed earlier in the chapter, the failure of attempts at comprehensive reform of the U.S. health care system after the 1993–94 period led advocates of reforms to push for incremental changes. In the past, Medicare and Medicaid programs had targeted specific groups of Americans for protection. Following this model, the advocates of reforms argued that the next logical group that needed government protection was uninsured persons. The Health Insurance Portability and Accounting Act of 1996 provided some protection to uninsured adult Americans by placing limits on insurance companies' ability to deny coverage for preexisting conditions and by allowing portability of insurance from one job to the next. The next logical group to target was the large number of children who lacked any health insurance.[98] The result was the creation of the State Children's Health Insurance Program (S-CHIP) as part of title XXI of the Social Security Act under the 1997 Balanced Budget Act. Under the program, the federal government will provide matching funds to assist states in providing health insurance coverage for uninsured children.[99]

State governments have several options for the use of S-CHIP funds.[100] They can use the funds to expand the Medicaid program to cover more chil-

dren.[101] In such a case, states will be building on existing institutional structures and will need to make very few program modifications. Many advocates
favor this approach because Medicaid already provides a comprehensive benefit package for children. Opponents argue that some low-income families
may not apply for coverage because of the perceived stigma associated with
the Medicaid program. Medicaid expansion may also expose state government to financial risks.

Another alternative for states is to fund an alternative new insurance program with the S-CHIP funds. Such an approach may be more attractive to states
that already have such a program in place funded by state and local governments. For example, California, Colorado, Florida, Massachusetts, Minnesota,
New York, Pennsylvania, Tennessee, and Washington had already developed
their own children's health insurance programs. This also gives them the advantage of not having to satisfy all the federal requirements of the Medicaid
program, such as the mandatory benefits and limits on cost sharing. Since such
a program will not be an individual entitlement, program outlays can be capped.

Other options available to states are to provide the services directly through
expansions of local health department clinics or through more funding for
federally qualified health centers, and to make direct contracts with hospitals
that serve large number of low-income families. However, such an approach
is not likely to provide more coverage to children and would restrict the choice

Table 3.8

Medicaid Coverage of Children in the States, 1996

State or area	Number of children covered by Medicaid (in thousands)	Percentage of children covered by Medicaid
U.S. total	23,254,568	28.0
Alabama	357,152	27.1
Alaska	52,497	23.8
Arizona	454,952	32.8
Arkansas	199,713	25.0
California	3,682,510	34.8
Colorado	208,303	17.4
Connecticut	212,762	23.0
Delaware	56,946	26.9
Florida	1,245,241	30.5
Georgia	771,308	32.8
Hawaii	21,943	5.9
Idaho	82,762	19.5
Illinois	1,109,535	29.9
Indiana	360,442	20.3
Iowa	171,964	20.1

88

Table 3.8 *(continued)*

State or area	Number of children covered by Medicaid (in thousands)	Percentage of children covered by Medicaid
Kansas	161,121	19.8
Kentucky	348,045	29.3
Louisiana	466,503	31.0
Maine	96,652	27.3
Maryland	320,632	21.0
Massachusetts	419,973	25.3
Michigan	805,528	26.9
Minnesota	369,339	25.4
Mississippi	318,420	34.3
Missouri	468,126	28.5
Montana	58,925	20.7
Nebraska	111,327	21.2
Nevada	91,112	18.7
New Hampshire	60,418	17.7
New Jersey	465,523	20.1
New Mexico	224,007	37.1
New York	1,753,424	32.6
North Carolina	644,270	29.2
North Dakota	34,868	17.2
Ohio	877,582	26.0
Oklahoma	253,374	23.7
Oregon	170,906	17.6
Pennsylvania	936,185	27.5
Rhode Island	76,001	27.7
South Carolina	313,790	27.3
South Dakota	54,018	22.1
Tennessee	633,961	39.6
Texas	1,847,355	28.1
Utah	128,353	15.6
Vermont	61,559	35.6
Virginia	439,778	22.2
Washington	543,411	31.6
West Virginia	262,343	50.0
Wisconsin	334.921	21.2
Wyoming	35,153	21.5
District of Columbia	80,335	58.9

Source: Children's Defense Fund, "Medicaid Coverage of Children in States, 1996," March 15, 1998. http://www.childrensdefense.org/health_coverage.html.

Note: The number of children covered by Medicaid includes any persons under 21 years of age enrolled in Medicaid for any length of time in FY 1996. The percentage of children in each state covered by Medicaid represents the percentage Medicaid child enrollees composed of all children in the state, based on census estimate of the total population under age 21 as of July 1, 1996, adjusted for undercounting.

of providers. It is because of such concerns that the law limits the proportion of S-CHIP funds that could be used for direct services.

As can be expected, the number of children covered by Medicaid program varies from state to state based on a variety of factors such as poverty, eligibility standards, and the state's commitment (see Table 3.8). For example, Medicaid covered 5.9 percent of the children in Hawaii and 50.0 percent of the children in West Virginia.

Similarly, the number and the percent of children who are uninsured also vary from state to state. Furthermore, often the estimate of the number of uninsured children by states reported by different organizations also varies considerably depending upon what age category is used to define children. Some estimates use the age of eighteen while others use the age of nineteen to calculate the number of uninsured children. Table 3.9 reports the number of uninsured children by state. The numbers are based on three-year averages for 1994, 1995, and 1996.

As can be seen, the percentage of children at or below 200 percent of the federal poverty line without health insurance varies from a low of under 5 percent in states such as Hawaii, Massachusetts, South Dakota, Vermont, and Wisconsin to over 15 percent in states such as Texas, Oklahoma, New Mexico, and Arkansas.

Table 3.9
Low-Income Uninsured Children by State:
Three-Year Averages, 1994, 1995, and 1996

State or area	Total children under age 19, all income levels (in thousands)	Number of children at or below 200% of poverty (in thousands)	Percentage of children at or below 200% of poverty	Number of children at or below 200% of poverty without insurance (in thousands)	Percentage of children at or below 200% of poverty without insurance
Alabama	1,221	576	47.1	145	11.9
Alaska	215	63	29.4	12	5.3
Arizona	1,341	714	53.1	239	17.6
Arkansas	716	380	52.8	98	13.7
California	9,464	4,674	49.4	1,259	13.3
Colorado	1,064	341	32.0	92	8.6
Connecticut	883	303	34.2	55	6.2
Delaware	182	70	38.5	15	8.1
Florida	3,627	1,735	47.8	421	11.6
Georgia	2,070	927	44.8	215	10.4
Hawaii	297	120	39.8	14	4.5
Idaho	347	163	47.0	31	8.9
Illinois	3,365	1,317	39.2	196	5.8
Indiana	1,595	618	38,2	121	7.6
Iowa	849	312	36.7	71	8.4

Table 3.9 *(continued)*

State or area	Total children under age 19, all income levels (in thousands)	Number of children at or below 200% of poverty (in thousands)	Percentage of children at or below 200% of poverty	Number of children at or below 200% of poverty without insurance (in thousands)	Percentage of children at or below 200% of poverty without insurance
Kansas	748	323	43.2	52	6.9
Kentucky	1,056	511	48.4	116	11.0
Louisiana	1,273	708	55.6	180	14.2
Maine	296	107	36.1	27	9.0
Maryland	1,384	475	34.4	101	7.3
Massachusetts	1,555	495	31.8	75	4.8
Michigan	2,749	1,029	37.5	142	5.1
Minnesota	1,353	441	32.6	60	4.5
Mississippi	806	481	59.6	114	14.1
Missouri	1,346	525	39.1	104	7.7
Montana	247	120	48.1	19	7.9
Nebraska	497	183	36.9	28	5.5
Nevada	418	161	38.5	45	10.8
New Hampshire	298	82	27.8	18	6.0
New Jersey	2,063	577	28.0	159	7.7
New Mexico	598	358	59.6	109	16.4
New York	5,008	2,268	45.3	441	8.8
North Carolina	1,736	729	42.1	163	9.3
North Dakota	182	64	35.0	10	5.3
Ohio	3,192	1,238	38.7	210	6.6
Oklahoma	924	461	49.8	142	15.3
Oregon	865	375	43.4	82	9.5
Pennsylvania	3,139	1,182	37.7	192	6.1
Rhode Island	236	83	35.1	17	6.9
South Carolina	1,033	529	51.0	129	12.5
South Dakota	219	90	41.4	10	4.5
Tennessee	1,528	746	48.8	166	10.8
Texas	5,841	2,958	50.6	1,074	18.4
Utah	711	275	38.7	47	6.6
Vermont	166	65	39.1	6	3.8
Virginia	1,636	625	38.4	111	6.8
Washington	1,482	545	36.7	109	7.3
West Virginia	400	206	51.6	29	7.2
Wisconsin	1,498	501	33.4	62	4.1
Wyoming	145	58	40.1	15	10.1
District of Columbia	139	79	57.4	12	8.9

Source: U.S. Census Bureau, "Low Income Uninsured Children by State." http://www.census.gov/hhes/hlthins/lowinckid.html.

Note: Percentages listed are averages over the three years' percentages, not the percentage of the average number (calculated as "number" divided by "total children). Results may differ slightly, based on the method used.

As of August 1998, forty-seven states had already submitted their plans on how they propose to spend the federal funds under S-CHIP program to HCFA for approval. Of these, HCFA had approved twenty-six state plans. Of the forty-seven states that had submitted plans, twenty-seven states planned to use the federal funds to expand their current Medicaid programs to increase insurance coverage for uninsured children, fourteen states had proposed creating separate state child health insurance programs, and eight states had proposed a combination of the two methods. Thus, it appears that a majority of state governments are going to rely on using the current Medicaid program to expand insurance coverage for children.[102] How successful state governments are in significantly expanding health insurance coverage to children remains to be seen.

Medicaid: Middle-Class Entitlement?

During the late 1980s, Medicaid came under attack because the affluent elderly were misusing the program. Critics of the program charged that it was increasingly used to provide expensive benefits, that is, nursing home care for the middle-class and affluent elderly. The "spousal impoverishment" benefit expanded Medicaid's role for the middle class. Many families began to see Medicaid as middle-class entitlement, as a way to preserve the family's life savings and property in the event that one or both parents require high-cost nursing home care.[103] The middle-class and affluent elderly were increasingly utilizing ways not sanctioned by the government to retain family wealth and at the same time take advantage of Medicaid benefits. Numerous techniques for sheltering assets or transferring them to family members as a prelude to getting Medicaid to pay the bills for nursing home care were employed. These included maneuvers such as opening joint bank accounts, holding property in joint tenancy, investing in irrevocable and nontransferable annuities, and paying family members for services such as shopping and providing transportation. An army of lawyers and financial advisors were counseling affluent Americans on how to shuffle, shed, or shelter an elderly family member's assets to qualify for Medicaid nursing home benefits. Such maneuvers, often called "Medicaid estate planning," were legal but ran counter to the intent of the law. By 1996, Medicaid was paying about 47.8 percent of the nation's $78.5 billion nursing home bill. The Health Care Financing Administration has estimated that Medicaid's nursing home costs will grow two and a half times by the year 2000.[104]

The state of Virginia tried to close some of these loopholes and gaps in the Medicaid program. The state's General Assembly rejected a proposed tax on hospitals, nursing homes, and doctors. Nevertheless, one of the measures approved would allow state Medicaid officials to recover up to $92,000 in assets transferred within four years of a patient's becoming eligible for Medicaid by going after the heir or recipient. Federal law bars transfer within two and one-half years of eligibility and allows states to extend that period.[105]

A few states tried to find ways to allow more of the affluent elderly to benefit from the Medicaid program. Some states devised experiments that allowed these elderly to hang on to more of their assets and be entitled to Medicaid benefits provided that they bought long-term-care insurance. Under such experimental plans, elderly participants were required to contribute to the cost of their care in a more rational way, by pooling risks. Such a plan, supporters argued, would save states money. The more middle-class people who bought long-term-care insurance, the fewer would "spend down" their savings and end up on Medicaid at public expense.[106]

The federal government tried to address this problem in the Health Insurance Portability and Accountability Act of 1996 by making it a federal crime, under certain circumstances, to transfer assets to qualify for Medicaid coverage for nursing homes or other long-term care. The law stated that anyone who knowingly and willfully disposed of assets (including any transfer in trust) in order to become eligible for medical assistance was guilty of a federal crime. It also would lead to imposition of a period of ineligibility for such a person. This law squarely targeted middle-class elderly.[107] This became a very unpopular and controversial provision, and the Balanced Budget Act of 1997 amended it. Under the new provisions, as amended, criminal penalties are now imposed on anyone who knowingly and willfully counsels and assists an individual to dispose of assets in order to become eligible for medical assistance. Thus, the amended provision makes attorneys and others who advise middle-class elderly Medicaid estate planning the direct targets.[108] The law is already facing challenge in the courts. What impact such a law produces remains to be seen.

Conclusion

Medicaid policy has, in a sense, come full circle. The Reagan administration, in the early 1980s, used the conservative rhetoric of decentralization as a way of giving states more discretionary authority and reducing Medicaid enrollment. In the process, the administration also attempted to reduce the federal costs of the program and pass along some of its financial burden to the states. The Democrats in Congress during the mid-1980s used the liberal rhetoric of equal access and quality of care to expand the Medicaid program incrementally through the use of federal mandates. The 1990s have again witnessed significant decentralization of the Medicaid program under the Clinton administration.

The decentralization of the Medicaid program by the Reagan administration in the early 1980s gave state governments greater flexibility to experiment with new approaches in delivering health care to the poor. The subsequent program expansion through congressional mandates significantly increased the number of recipients, as well as program costs. Concerned with the dramatically rising cost of a program that is consuming an ever-larger portion of state budgets, state governments have used the Medicaid program in innovative ways to respond to the access and health care financing issues. Some have experimented with service delivery, payment reforms, and outreach programs. These approaches have included the rationing of Medicaid services, the increased use of Medicaid waivers for home or community-based services, fixed-price arrangements with health care providers, hospital rate setting, and the bulk-rate purchase of equipment and services. More emphasis has also been placed on case management and managed care. Many states have established new programs designed to provide preventive and primary care. Today, many states are trying innovative ways to expand coverage and at the same time control rising costs.[109]

The results of these experiments have been mixed. While a few have been successful in containing specific costs, the overall cost of the program continues to rise both at the federal and the state levels. Rationing in the Medicaid program leads to concerns about reduced access and limited choices. The same concerns arise in managed care programs. Reduction in payments to physicians has often made them more reluctant to accept Medicaid patients. Hospital rate-setting programs, especially those confined to the Medicaid program, in general have not been very successful.

Increased micromanagement of the Medicaid program by the federal government through congressional mandates in the late 1980s created additional problems for states. State governments' ability to fund the program was severely tested. Growing caseloads, declining revenues, and balanced-budget requirements compounded the problem. Hospitals and other health care providers began to sue states over reimbursement rates. In a majority of cases, states lost. The crisis of escalating Medicaid costs is not likely to be resolved until the problems of long-term care, reimbursement levels, and the uninsured are addressed in one form or another.

State governments alone are not likely to solve the problem of Medicaid and its cost because of fundamental impediments in the federal system. As Deborah Stone has argued, state governments lack sufficient autonomy from the federal government in the area of health care financing. Nor do they have sufficient power over private insurers, doctors, and hospitals. Federal law governing Medicaid limits the options available to state governments. The problem is too big and too complex for state-based solutions.[110]

Medicaid policy reflects the dictum that the more things change, the more they stay the same. The Medicaid policy process is driven to a significant extent by forces of federalism that often produce policies geared toward short-term, patchwork answers, rather than long-term solutions. All the new state experiments and innovations have failed to produce any consensus on how best to contain costs. These experiments have offered many different models of cost containment, but none that is satisfactory to all parties. It is clear that the program cannot continue on its current course, given stagnant or declining resources, on the one hand, and pressure to provide coverage to more people, on the other. Additional ad hoc, stopgap fixes are likely to produce more dissatisfaction with the program among groups such as policymakers, health care providers, program administrators, and advocacy groups.

CHAPTER 4

Medicare: Health Care for the Elderly and Disabled

Much of the current debate about Medicare's future mistakes what Medicare is and what it is designed to achieve. Medicare isn't just a trust fund. Medicare isn't just a certain kind of health care system, called fee for service. And Medicare is a lot more than just another number in the federal budget debate. Medicare is designed, at bottom, for two purposes. First, Medicare helps assure that older Americans and those with disabilities have access to the same standard of quality health care services as most Americans. Second, Medicare is an essential part of economic security. It is an insurance system that protects beneficiaries and their families from the high and unpredictable costs of health care services.[1]

Medicare is the largest public-sector health care program in the United States, in terms of both dollars and numbers of people covered. It began as an alternative to national health insurance and remains one of the most popular government programs. Despite its popularity, it has often been a target for those seeking to curtail government spending. Further, significant changes in the course of the thirty-plus-year history of the program provide lessons for the possible expansion of government provision of health care services. The 1990s, especially the late 1990s, saw a significant transformation in Medicare. Cost and coverage problems remain an issue, as does the lack of coverage for long-term care.

In this chapter, we closely examine Medicare. We begin by looking at its origin and structure. We then look at some of the changes and problems with the program and how those problems have been addressed. We close this portion of the chapter by examining proposed solutions. We next turn to the problem of long-term care and how that has been addressed in the United States. We look at some solutions to those problems and make some final conclusions about Medicare.

The Origins of Medicare

As mentioned in chapter 2, national health insurance (NHI) was first considered in the early twentieth century, during Woodrow Wilson's administration. But the onset of World War I, the linkage between NHI and Germany (which was the first to adopt NHI), and opposition to national health insurance on the part of the AMA killed the program. During the development of what eventually became the Social Security Act of 1935, policy formulators (the Committee for Economic Security) considered and rejected the idea of adding a national health insurance provision. They believed, based on responses to the mere mention of national health insurance, that including national health insurance would sink the entire Social Security bill.[2] Beginning in 1939, bills for national health insurance were introduced in Congress (e.g., the Murray-Wagner-Dingell bill). Marmor points out that, though the Democrats had a numerical majority, they did not have a "programmatic majority" to enact the legislation.[3] That is, there was insufficient unity within the majority Democratic Party, a problem that was repeated in 1994 (see chapter 9). The 1948 Democratic national platform called for national health insurance. Despite Truman's victory in that election, the Murray-Wagner-Dingell legislation died, never coming out of committee in Congress.

Advocates of national health insurance then tried an alternative strategy. The new strategy was incremental in nature, focusing on a group or groups that had reasonably high status but could not afford health insurance. The ideal group was the elderly.[4] Marmor describes the political strategy behind the new strategy:

> The concentration on the burdens of the aged was a ploy for sympathy. The disavowal of aims to change fundamentally the American medical system was a sop to AMA fears, and the exclusion of physician services benefits was a response to past AMA hysteria. The focus on the financial burdens of receiving hospital care took as given the existing structure of the private medical care world, and stressed the issue of spreading the costs of using available services within that world. The organization of health care, with its inefficiencies and resistance to cost-reduction, was a fundamental but politically sensitive problem which consensus-minded reformers wanted to avoid when they opted for 60 days of hospitalization insurance for the aged in 1951 as a promising "small" beginning.[5]

The above quote contains several important points. It shows the attempt to accommodate potential opposition, primarily the medical profession. It did this in several ways. This incremental strategy excluded coverage of physician services (though Medicare as enacted did include such coverage but treated it differently from hospital care). It limited the number of hospital days covered, the "small beginning," a feature that remains an integral part of Medicare. Finally, it left the structure of American medicine alone. That structure was the private practice of physicians and the fee-for-service system.[6] Some of these features would eventually be changed in the 1980s and 1990s. But they were at least partly responsible for some of the problems that Medicare has faced. A final note: the attempt at political accommodation was also a feature of the Clinton administration's Health Security Act. In any event, the finance committees in Congress held hearings on Medicare from 1958 to 1965.[7]

In 1960 Congress passed the Kerr-Mills bill, which provided federal assistance (50–80 percent) to states to help with hospital care for the aged poor. In other words, Kerr-Mills was a welfare program, with all the accompanying problems and stigma of means-tested (income-based) programs. By 1963, many states had not enacted programs to use Kerr-Mills.[8]

John F. Kennedy's campaign platform in 1960 included health insurance for the aged. Attempts were made to push a narrow program for the elderly from the beginning of the Kennedy administration. The conservative coalition (Republicans and southern Democrats) that had long opposed liberal legislation was able to delay enactment of the program, but the great electoral victory of Lyndon Johnson in 1964 accompanied by a large liberal Democratic majority in Congress allowed passage of a number of programs, part of the Johnson administration's Great Society. For our purposes, the important bill was Medicare, passed in 1965.

The law (title 18 [XVIII] amendments to the 1935 Social Security Act) was broader than envisioned under the incrementalist strategy following the Truman administration. It included physician services and covered a large section of the aged population, not just those who were poor but those covered by Social Security. Thus it embodied a social insurance concept, where subscribers made contributions, rather than assistance to the poor, which required means testing. Medicare would cover a large portion of the population, and virtually all would contribute and benefit.[9]

Program Objectives and Structure

Objectives

The original design or theory of the program has been aptly stated by Thompson: "If Washington paid mainstream rates to providers for delivering medical care to the elderly, they would receive increased amounts of needed care."[10]

The problem facing the elderly was that, for several reasons, they could not afford health insurance. First, health insurance was available to individuals and families largely through the workplace. As retirees, the elderly were (in most cases) no longer eligible to receive health insurance benefits. Second, because retirees were no longer part of a larger group through their jobs, they would not be able to gain the benefits of group insurance. Individual insurance rates are considerably higher than group rates. Finally, the elderly were (and are) more at risk of needing medical care (more likely to experience periods of illness, especially extended illness) and expensive care than those of working age. The combination of these three factors meant that few private health insurance companies would offer a policy to retirees, and those that were offered were prohibitively expensive. In 1963, only about 54 percent of the elderly (sixty-five years and older) had hospital insurance.[11]

Medicare resolved many of these problems. In 1995, 99.7 percent of those sixty-five or older were covered by insurance. By comparison, nearly 10 percent of those under eighteen had no health insurance.[12] Medicare had achieved its primary goal of providing health insurance for the elderly. Whether it was adequate is another story.

Structure

Medicare is open to those over sixty-five years of age, those disabled and receiving Social Security cash benefits, and those suffering from end-stage renal disease (ESRD, or kidney failure).[13] Table 4.1 presents data about Medicare enrollment and expenditures.

The program has two parts, hospital insurance and the supplementary medical program. The hospital insurance (HI, or Part A) program covers inpatient hospital expenses for specified periods. Recipients are covered for up to ninety days for a benefit period and have a lifetime reserve of sixty hospital

Table 4.1

Trends in Medicare Enrollment and Program Expenditures, 1970–1995

	Total enrollees (in thousands)	Aged enrollees (in thousands)	Disabled enrollees (in thousands)	Total program expenditures (in millions)
1970	20,491	20,491	——	$4,239
1975	24,959	22,790	2,168	$14,549
1980	28,478	25,515	2,963	$33,725
1985	31,083	28,176	2,907	$63,677
1990	34,213	30,961	3,252	$101,419
1995	37,566	33,157	4,409	$158,980

Source: Health Care Financing Administration, "Medicare and Medicaid Statistical Supplement, 1997," *Health Care Financing Review*, 23, 36–37.

Table 4.2

Medicare Part A, Covered Services, by Place of Service

Type of covered service	Inpatient hospital	Skilled nursing facility	Home health agency	Hospice
Accommodations, semiprivate, including special diets	X	X	—	X
Blood transfusions	X	X	—	X
Counseling	—	—	—	X
Dental services requiring hospitalization	X	—	—	X
Doctors' services	—	—	—	X
Drugs and biologicals	X	X	—	X
Durable medical equipment	X	X	X	X
Emergency services	X	—	—	—
Home health aides	—	—	X	—
Homemaker services	—	—	—	X
Intern and resident service and teaching physicians in hospitals	X	X	X	—
Medical social services	X	X	X	X
Medical supplies and appliances	X	X	X	X
Nursing and related services, excluding private duty	X	X	X	X
Nursing, intermittent skilled nursing care	—	—	X	—
Occupational therapy	X	X	X	X
Other diagnostic services	X	X	—	—
Outpatient services	—	X	X	—
Physical therapy	X	X	X	X
Respite care and procedures necessary for pain control	—	—	—	X
Speech pathology	X	X	X	X
White blood and packed red blood cells	X	X	—	—

Source: John T. Petrie, "Overview of the Medicare Program," *Health Care Financing Review*, 1991 Annual Supplement, 1–12.

days. Payment is made for room and board in semiprivate rooms and for such hospital services as nursing and pharmaceuticals. Part A also pays for hospice services and limited skilled nursing care. Table 4.2 lists the services covered under Part A.

The other major portion of Medicare is the supplementary medical insurance program (SMI or Part B). This is a voluntary program, though most Medicare recipients subscribe to it. SMI covers a wide range of physician and outpatient services, including diagnostic and surgical procedures and radiology. It also covers outpatient services, including ambulance services, medical

---

Table 4.3

Medicare Part B, Physician and Outpatient Covered Services

Physician services	Outpatient services
Chiropractic services (manual manipulation of the spine to correct subluxation)	Ambulatory surgical centers Ambulatory transportation Antigen and blood-clotting factors
Dental services that involve surgery on the jaw or the setting of fractures	Blood transfusions, blood, and other components
Diagnostic tests and procedures	Certified registered nurse anesthetist Clinic services
Medical and surgical services, including anesthesia	Comprehensive outpatient rehabilitation facility
Optometrists, excluding routine eye examinations	Dialysis services Drugs and biologicals Durable Medical equipment
Podiatrist services, excluding routine foot care	Emergency room services
Radiology and pathology services while hospital inpatient or outpatient	Independent clinical laboratory Laboratory tests billed by hospital
Second opinions	Medical supplies Mental health services
Services furnished in a doctor's office:	Nurse-midwife
Blood and blood components Drugs and biologicals	Occupational therapy

Medical supplies
  Occupational therapy
  Physical therapy
  Speech therapy
	Physical therapy
	Physician assistant
	Portable diagnostic X-ray
	Psychological services

X-rays	Speech pathology
	Vaccines, hepatitis, and pneumococcal
	X-rays and other radiology services billed by the hospital

Source: John T. Petrie, "Overview of the Medicare Program," *Health Care Financing Review*, 1992 Annual Supplement, 1–12.

---

supplies, clinical services, and blood transfusions. Table 4.3 lists the services covered under Part B.

As important as what is covered is what is not covered. In three major areas, Medicare coverage is extremely limited. First, Medicare does not pay for prescription drugs unless a patient is hospitalized. Thus, a Medicare patient, unless otherwise insured, must pay the full cost of medication, which can be expensive. We address this gap later in the chapter in connection with so-called medigap policies and the Medicare Catastrophic Coverage Act of 1988. A second, related limitation of Medicare is catastrophic coverage, that is, coverage of hospital stays that exceed the specified limits. Finally, Medicare has extremely limited long-term-care coverage. We also address this issue later in this chapter.

Financing Medicare

Medicare is financed through a combination of subscriber and tax payments. The Hospital Insurance and Supplementary Medical Insurance programs are financed differently. We begin with the hospital program.

The bulk of funds for the hospital insurance trust fund comes from the payroll tax (1.45 percent), a part of the Social Security tax that employees and employers pay (1.45 percent each).[14] In addition, there are copayments when Medicare recipients use hospital services. There is a one-time deductible (paid before Medicare starts paying) equal to the average cost of one day in the hospital. For 1998, that amount was $764 for each benefit period. Medicare then pays for the entire cost of hospitalization for the next fifty-nine days. If the hospitalization lasts longer than sixty days, there is a deductible equal to one-quarter of a hospital day ($191 as of 1998) for days sixty-one through ninety. Each Medicare recipient has a reserve equal to sixty hospital days, which can be used past day ninety. The deductible is then half of the inpatient hospital deductible ($382 as of 1998) per day. Under Part A, Medicare also pays for hospice and home health care with very limited deductibles. For example, those eligible for skilled nursing home services do not have to pay a deductible for the first twenty days. For the next eighty days, the deductible is $95.50 per day (as of 1998).[15]

The Supplementary Insurance Program, or Part B, is financed through a combination of general federal revenues and Medicare subscriber premiums. Federal government revenues accounted for more than 73 percent of the trust funds in 1991. Premiums and tax contributions were approximately equal in 1971; since that time, tax contributions have dwarfed premiums. That is why, even given the cost increases in Part B copayments, SMI remains a bargain. One can see this in the beneficiary cost-sharing liability percentages. Liability for Part A has remained relatively stable over the years, but the liability for Part B has decreased significantly, by about 37 percent (see Table 4.4).

Virtually all Medicare recipients (almost 98 percent) are enrolled in the Supplementary Insurance Program (Part B).[16] The 1998 premium (the amount paid each month) is $43.80 and is deducted from Social Security checks. There is also a $100 deductible.[17] Medicare pays 80 percent of physician charges as determined under the physician fee scale phased in beginning in 1992. The

Table 4.4

Medicare Beneficiary Cost-Sharing Liability, 1977, 1985, and 1995
(percent of costs)

	1977	1985	1995
Total	18.0%	7.0%	37.0%
Hospital insurance	17.6	8.3	17.6
Supplementary medical insurance	14.0	7.6	23.4

Source: Health Care Financing Administration, "Medicare and Medicaid Statistical Supplement, 1997," *Health Care Financing Review*, p. 53.

Medicare recipient is responsible for the other 20 percent. Physicians elect each year whether to accept full assignment, that is, whether to accept the Medicare fee schedule (participating). If the physician does accept the fee schedule, Medicare is billed by the physician and the recipient pays the balance (what is known as balance billing). Physicians do not have to accept full assignment. They can charge up to 115 percent of the Medicare fee schedule. The Balanced Budget Act of 1997 specifies a third payment relationship between patient and doctor, private contracts. This controversial provision will be discussed below and later in this chapter.

An example may help explain the fee schedule. Assume that you are a Medicare recipient who needs to visit a doctor for a Medicare-approved service. Your doctor would normally charge $200, given the services provided. According to the Medicare physician fee schedule, the visit is worth $142.[18] Medicare then will pay 80 percent of the $142, or $113.60. Now it gets complicated. Consider these two cases: In case 1, the physician accepts full assignment, or the $142. He or she then sends in the paperwork to Medicare and receives a reimbursement of $113.60. You, the Medicare patient, pay the balance, or $28.40, to the doctor. Now take case 2: The physician does not accept full assignment. He or she can charge up to 115 percent of the $142, or $163.30. The physician bills the patient for the entire amount. The patient pays the doctor and files for reimbursement from Medicare. The Medicare recipient receives $113.60 from Medicare and has to pay the physician $49.70. From the standpoint of the recipient, using a physician who does not accept full assignment would cost an additional $21.30, an increase in the copayment of 75 percent. It obviously pays the Medicare recipient to use physicians who accept assignment.

Now consider case 3. Under a private contract, the physician does not and cannot participate in Medicare because of the contract. The physician can then charge the full amount, $200, to the patient. The physician must notify you, the patient, prior to receiving the service that Medicare will not reimburse you for any of the costs. Thus your costs for the service are $200. That raises the interesting question of why Medicare recipients would want to see a physician under a private contract. Again, we will address this issue in connection with the Balanced Budget Act of 1997.

Over time, Medicare cost sharing has become a higher proportion of the elderly's income. In 1975, cost sharing was about 6.2 percent of the elderly's average median income. By 1996, that figure had risen to over 11 percent.[19] Another way of looking at this issue is to consider what percentage of income of the elderly, by far the largest group of Medicare recipients, is spent on health care. In 1987 the elderly spent about 15 percent of their income on health care. In 1994 that figure had increased to 21 percent.[20]

Medicaid Buy-In and Medigap

In 1991, almost 90 percent of the elderly population had some kind of health coverage in addition to Medicare. Of these, 35 percent were covered through a current or former employer, 37 percent owned individual coverage, 7 percent had both individual and employer coverage, and 12 percent were eligible for Medicaid.[21]

Medicaid Buy-In

As can be seen from the above discussion, Medicare does not cover everything. Nor does it pay for everything it covers. This has created a situation known as *medigap*. The gap can be covered in several ways. First, for Medicare beneficiaries who are also eligible for Medicaid (i.e., low-income individuals), there is state buy-in coverage. In 1995, some 4.8 million people (about 12.9 percent of Medicare recipients) were eligible for both programs.[22] States pay the premium under Part B and any cost sharing. What is covered under Medicare is paid for by Medicare and what is covered under Medicaid (such as prescription drugs or long-term care) is paid for by Medicaid. About a third of those eligible for the state buy-in either are disabled or suffer from kidney failure (end-stage renal disease), though they represent only about 10 percent of Medicare recipients.[23] "Medicare beneficiaries in the Medicaid group are more likely to be women, be nonwhite, reside in nursing homes, and have annual incomes below $10,000."[24]

There are three groups of Medicare beneficiaries who qualify for the Medicaid buy-in. One group are those who are either categorically (eligible for programs such as Supplemental Security Income) or medically needy. Additionally, there are two low-income groups that also qualify for the buy-in: those whose income is below the poverty line with limited assets (qualified Medicare beneficiaries, or QMBs) and those whose income are just over the poverty line (120 percent of the poverty) with limited assets (specified low-income Medicare beneficiaries, or SLMB). QMBs are limited to help with paying for Part B premiums and cost sharing while SLMBs are limited to help with Part B premiums.[25]

Medigap

Another solution is private supplemental medical insurance, so-called medigap policies. Such policies are provided by insurance companies or group organizations such as the American Association of Retired Persons (AARP). In 1991, some 13 million people purchased Medigap policies.[26] Medigap policies raise the average cost of health care because policyholders pay the full cost of that insurance, which includes administrative and advertising costs plus profits for insurance.[27] Such policies, as might be expected, are expensive. Those most likely to have supplementary policies are those who are better educated, younger, and in better health; who have higher incomes; and who are white.[28]

The 1980 amendments (the "Baucus Amendments") to the Social Security Act made it illegal knowingly to sell medigap policies that duplicate other policies. Of course the key word here is "knowingly." Nevertheless, analysis in 1987 suggested that while about 20 percent of Medicare recipients purchased more than one medigap policy, duplication was not a serious problem. There was duplication of policies that paid cash benefits or were specific to certain diseases. Between duplication and premium increases, some regulation was seen as necessary.[29]

In 1990 Congress passed legislation, as part of the Omnibus Budget Reconciliation Act (OBRA),[30] that regulated medigap policies. Earlier federal regulation over medigap policies was limited, requiring only minimal benefits. OBRA required insurers to obtain a written statement outlining the purchaser's insurance coverages.[31] Medigap policies could be offered in one of ten standardized forms developed by the National Association of Insurance Commissioners.[32] Perhaps more than the question of duplication of policies, Congress was concerned about the increase in medigap premiums. The increase in medigap premiums from 1989 to 1990 was 19.5 percent. Congress was also looking at medigap policies in the wake of the repeal of the Medicare Catastrophic Coverage Act in 1989 (see below).[33]

As a result of the mandated changes, Medicare recipients now choose from these ten standardized policies, labeled "A" (least comprehensive) to "J" (most comprehensive). The thirteen possible services that can be covered under the medigap policies are Part A hospital coinsurance for days 61–90; Part A hospital coinsurance for days 91–150; all charges for the Part A blood deductible; Part B coinsurance, skilled-nursing facility coinsurance for days

21–100; the Part A deductible; emergency care in foreign countries; the Part B deductible; excess charges under Part B; in-home health care following surgery, illness, or injury; prescription drugs; and preventive medical care.[34]

According to an analysis of medigap policies and insurance company practices by Consumers Union, agents try to sell Plan F, which is very profitable for them and perhaps unnecessary for consumers. The difference between Plan F and Plan C is one benefit, coverage of Part B excess charges. But since Congress has limited such charges, coverage for them is not, on the average, a wise investment.[35] Consumers Union also argued that insurance companies are selling what are known as "attained age" policies. Such policies have low premiums for the younger years, sixty-five to sixty-nine, but become increasingly expensive as the insured becomes older. The report compared Plan F policies from two different companies. In the first company, the premium depends on the age of the buyer at first purchase and then rises only with inflation. The second company has an attained-age policy. At age sixty-five, the second company's policy is $114 per year cheaper than the first company. But in the next fifteen years, the second company's policy would cost the insured $5,000 more than the first company's.[36] Despite Congress's attempt to tighten the medigap policy market, problems remain.

The new medigap policies have simplified some of the choices available to purchasers. More specifically, the most popular benefits are retained and in a hierarchical order so that a purchaser does not have to give up the basic benefits for other desired benefits, and the number of choices is limited to the ten standardized policies. Rice and Thomas, like McCormack et al., suggest that the new law and regulations promote the use of information about policies to make informed judgments. They also suggest that the legislation promotes market stability.[37] This experience with medigap regulations suggests how health care reform based on competition among competing plans might be structured.[38]

While the objectives of the 1990 legislation appear to have been met,[39] problems remain. Adverse selection (insurance carriers favoring those less likely to use the service) remains something of a problem, and there are some limitations on consumer choice. For example, McCormack et al.[40] point out that there is no "catastrophic-only coverage." That is, there is no policy that has a high deductible and pays expenses only above that high deductible. Such policies are cheaper than any of the other medigap policies and also retain cost-sharing, which tends to reduce utilization and thus reduce budgetary pressures on Medicare.

Another important problem McCormack et al.[41] mention is the advent of managed care alternatives, such as health maintenance organizations (HMOs). HMOs are yet a third way to obtain additional coverage. There are differences between medigap and HMOs in terms of regulation, whether the policy can vary premiums by age (medigap can, HMOs cannot) and open enrollment features. These differences compound the choices faced by Medicare recipients.

One reason that managed care became attractive to the elderly is that their out-of-pocket health costs, including medigap policies, were increasing. In 1961, four years before the enactment of Medicare and Medicaid, the elderly paid, on the average, about 11 percent of their after-tax income on health care; in 1994, that number had risen to 18 percent.[42] Much of this was due to increases in the premiums for Medigap policies, which in some cases increased by more than 40 percent in 1996.[43]

Medicare and Managed Care

In the 1980s, Medicare began enrolling recipients in managed care organizations such as health maintenance organizations as a means of restraining cost increases while maintaining quality of care for recipients. In addition, it was hoped that Medicare recipients would gain access to the same range of services as other patients while restraining costs.[44] In addition, the plans often offered important additional services that Medicare did not offer, such as prescription drugs. The plans also did not charge for their services and allowed Medicare beneficiaries to avoid the high costs of medigap policies.[45]

Among Medicare recipients, 3.1 percent were enrolled in risk-based HMOs in 1989.[46] This represented about 3.2 percent of HMO subscribers. By 1995, Medicare risk-based HMO enrollment exceeded 8.2 percent, constituting about 6.7 percent of HMO subscribers.[47] The Congressional Budget Office has projected that risk-based HMO Medicare enrollment could be as large as 34.2 percent of total enrollees by the year 2008.[48]

Under the Medicare risk program, HMOs provide Medicare recipients with all Medicare covered services for a set payment (known as capitation). The capitation payment, 95 percent of what Medicare would normally pay and known as adjusted average per capita cost (AAPCC), is calculated through a complicated formula. Medicare should therefore save 5 percent. The theory behind this provision was that

> HMOs, which act as insurers but have control over the set of providers from which members can choose and how much they are paid, have an incentive to provide care in the most cost-effective manner possible. This cost-effectiveness is achieved by reducing unnecessary services and providing health care in the least expensive but appropriate setting. The market power of HMOs can also help them negotiate favorable prices for provider services.[49]

A four-year evaluation found that these "risk" plans tended to enroll healthier-than-average Medicare recipients. Those enrolled in risk plans had

20 percent lower Medicare reimbursements than those not so enrolled. Further, they were less likely to be disabled or have chronic health problems than those enrolled in risk plans. Such a pattern of enrollment, called favorable selection, has often been charged to HMOs. The evaluation study estimates that given favorable selection, costs to Medicare were actually 5.7 percent higher than with the fee-for-service system.[50]

On the other hand, HMOs do tend to reduce the length of hospital stays over the fee-for-service system, though they do not reduce the number of admissions. For other services, HMOs tend to reduce the intensity of services (the number of services provided) from 10 to 20 percent.[51] The effects are greatest for those who are chronically ill.[52] Quality of care for HMO Medicare recipients was about equal to that of fee-for-service Medicare recipients.[53]

One question that could be asked is how satisfied Medicare recipients are with managed care plans. A study by Nelson[54] found that most Medicare HMO enrollees were satisfied with their access to care, such as being admitted to a hospital, seeing a specialist, making an appointment, or receiving desired home health care. Most were able to select their primary care physician and had received enough information to obtain care. Those more likely to report access problems were from "vulnerable subgroups,"[55] such as the nonelderly disabled, those whose heath was less than good, the oldest beneficiaries, and those with functional disabilities. African Americans seemed less satisfied with their HMOs than whites. Even so, most of these groups said they would recommend the plan to others with health problems. Adequacy of home health care services appears more likely under Medicare fee-for-service than under managed care.

A more recent study by Tudor, Riley, and Ingber[56] compared Medicare HMO enrollees with Medicare nonenrollees. The study found that HMO enrollees were more likely to receive preventive services (such as flu shots) than were nonenrollees. HMO enrollees were more satisfied with their cost of care and with receiving care at a single location than were nonenrollees. Otherwise, there seemed to be about the same level of satisfaction between the two groups. Nonenrollees were more likely to express satisfaction with the doctor-patient relationship than were HMO enrollees.

In general, Tudor et al. found that Medicare beneficiaries, regardless of whether they were enrolled in an HMO, seemed satisfied with their care. They even noted that enrollee satisfaction had increased, though they also noted that those who were highly dissatisfied with their HMO simply disenrolled and were not part of the analysis.

Riley, Ingber, and Tudor[57] also looked at those who had disenrolled from their HMOs. They noted that the disenrollment provisions provided a kind of a safety valve for those who were extremely dissatisfied with their plan. They also pointed out that disenrollment has declined. Those who disenrolled were older and less healthy than those who stayed, but many of those who disenrolled switched plans (sometimes because the beneficiaries moved). The authors also observed that those who enrolled with a preexisting chronic condition (such as cancer) were much more likely to disenroll than those who developed the condition after enrolling.

Disabled Medicare enrollees had about the same level of satisfaction with HMOs as elderly HMO enrollees, though the former group faced somewhat higher levels of access problems than did the latter group, particularly concerning specialists and home health care services.[58]

HMOs faced two problems that did not bode well for its Medicare patients. First, under the provisions of the Balanced Budget Act of 1997 (discussed below), payments to managed care organizations were cut to help balance the budget. Second, the cost of prescription drugs has increased significantly. As a result, some HMOs, for the first time, began to cut back benefits (such as free eye examinations and prescriptions) and to charge fees or even premiums. This is part of a trend in the managed care sector in general (see chapter 10). If the trend were to continue, the advantages of managed care, savings, especially for the elderly, would disappear, and the reliance on managed care to save Medicare money would be tenuous.

The Disaster of the Medicare Catastrophic Coverage Act

One of the more interesting episodes in the history of Medicare (and American health care policy in general) revolves around the Medicare Catastrophic Coverage Act (MCCA) of 1988. The notion of catastrophic coverage is that there may be medical expenses that can cause financial hardship or ruin to a family. Preventing financial ruin is one of the purposes of health insurance in the first place, certainly of the Medicare program. Such catastrophic expenses might include diseases such as cancer or AIDS that progress over a lengthy period of time and thus are very costly. Long-term care (to be considered in detail below) can also deplete the life savings of the average family in a couple of years.

As we have seen, Medicare does not cover everything. There is extremely limited long-term-care coverage, there is no coverage of prescription drugs outside of hospitals, and there are limits on hospital and physician services. Medigap policies were developed by the private sector to cover some of the holes in Medicare coverage. HMOs can also provide additional services. Nevertheless, there were (and are) Medicare recipients who cannot afford medigap policies (low-income and disabled recipients) and whose copayments would wreak hardship on families.

With this as background, the road toward the Medicare Catastrophic Coverage Act began in January 1986 with President Reagan's State of the Union address. The president discussed the problem of catastrophic expenses and suggested that coverage should be broadened for all sectors of the population, not just the elderly. Reagan also suggested that any solution should rely on the private sector.[59]

The president set up a commission headed by Otis Bowen, then secretary of the Department of Health and Human Services (HHS). The commission was supposed to look at both long-term and acute-care problems. Indeed, testimony before the Bowen Commission emphasized the problems of long-term care; however, the commission decided to focus on acute care for Medicare recipients as the easiest step that could be taken.[60]

The commission's original idea was to add a cap or limit of $2,000 on yearly expenses paid by Medicare beneficiaries. Once the limit had been reached, Medicare would pay Part A and B deductibles and coinsurance. The cost to the beneficiary would be $59 a month added to Part B premiums. The cost of this proposed expansion was $2 billion. Congress accepted the administration proposal as a framework for change. As is typical of congressional-presidential relations, this was seen as an opening bid by a Republican administration. The Democrats would try to expand benefits but keep the self-financing provisions.[61]

MCCA was passed in June 1988 with significant changes from the Bowen proposal. It eliminated limitations on hospital benefits including coinsurance, with the exception of a yearly deductible. It increased limits on stays in skilled nursing facilities. It increased provisions for home health care. It provided for a limit on Part B services (to $1,370 for 1990 and with adjustments to the cap in subsequent years). It provided for coverage of outpatient prescription drugs, with a deductible and coinsurance dropping to 20 percent by 1993.[62]

The act also included a self-financing provision. A surtax was assessed on Medicare beneficiaries in a progressive manner. That is, low-income recipients would pay $22.50 (if their tax liability was $150), with the highest surtax limited to $800 for an individual with income greater than $35,000 or $1,600 for a couple with incomes greater than $70,000 a year. The law also required that the surtax be paid beginning in 1989, though benefits would not begin until 1990.[63]

At first glance, there should have been considerable support for the new law. Groups representing the aging population, especially the AARP, were enthusiastic advocates of the legislation. But there was opposition. The drug industry opposed the legislation, fearing the imposition of cost controls (a stance it also took in regard to health care reform in 1993–94). The National Committee to Protect Social Security and Medicare was against the financing package because it would require beneficiaries to pay for all the new benefits, rather than rely on a combination of taxes and beneficiary contributions.[64]

It was also true that MCCA had redistributive implications. As we have seen, those least likely to have supplemental medical insurance (medigap policies) were at the low end of the income scale. They would have benefited more by the law than those at the high end. The progressive nature of the financing enhanced the redistributive effect.[65]

Additionally, Medicare beneficiaries did not understand the law, despite the considerable publicity that surrounded its enactment. A telephone survey of Medicare recipients documented this problem. For example, only 19 percent of the respondents knew that Medicare did not cover the costs of an extended nursing home stay. Few knew about the financing details or about the drug benefit. Once respondents were briefed about the new law, many were opposed. Indeed, those opposed held that opinion more strongly than those who favored it. The elderly were concerned about all costs, such as the deductibles for prescription medication. They also seemed satisfied with their medigap policies.[66]

From the standpoint of wealthier Medicare recipients, MCCA did not appear to be much of a bargain. They were more likely to have private insurance that already gave them what MCCA would do, plus they were asked to make a larger contribution to the program. Thus they did not see themselves as benefiting, but as having to pay for the expansion nevertheless.

Apart from the opposition of the two groups mentioned above that financed mail campaigns against the law, it appeared that the new premiums would build up faster than anticipated, yet the costs of some benefits (particularly the drug benefit) had been underestimated. Town meetings held by Congress in the summer of 1989 demonstrated the discontent. Given all this, Congress repealed the law in November 1989, about eighteen months after it had been passed.[67]

Controlling Costs

From the beginning, a chief concern about the Medicare program was cost. Several dimensions of costs play a role. One that has been discussed earlier was costs to the Medicare beneficiary. Here we can look at the copayments and deductible that recipients have to make under Parts A and B and premiums under Part B. We have also looked, to a certain extent, at the problem of cost through HMOs and medigap policies.

The other major dimension of cost control is costs to the federal government. As Medicare became more expensive for a variety of reasons, federal administrators and policymakers sought ways to curb those costs. Some of

Table 4.5

Personal Health Expenditures, 1970–1995
(in billions of dollars)

	Total health expenditures	Federal expenditures	Medicare expenditures
1970	$64.8	$14.7	$7.3
1980	217.0	63.4	36.4
1985	376.4	111.3	70.3
1990	614.7	178.1	109.6
1995	878.8	303.6	184.0

Source: Katharine R. Levit et al., "Data View: National Health Expenditures, 1995," *Health Care Financing Review* 19, no. 1 (Fall 1996), 205.

this could be done by raising premiums and deductibles for Medicare recipients. But by far the largest target of cost control was providers: physicians, hospitals, and so forth. From the beginning, the politics of Medicare revolved around the issue of provider payment, beginning with hospitals and then expanding to doctors.[68] In addition, the size of the Medicare program made it a tempting target for those seeking either to cut government spending and/or reduce the budget deficit. Medicare played a key role in the 1995–97 budget debates, a debate that ultimately led to significant changes in the program.

Consider, first, the increase in enrollments and expenditures in Medicare (see Tables 4.5 and 4.6). Medicare expenditures in 1970 were about $7.3 billion, about 49.7 percent of public personal health expenditures and 11.3 percent of total personal health expenditures. By 1995, Medicare expenditures were $184 billion, representing almost 61 percent of public personal health care expenditures and almost 21 percent of total personal health care expenditures.[69] One could argue that because Medicare began only in 1965, it would surely make large increases starting from such a small base. Nevertheless, doing similar calculations for 1980 to 1995 showed how much quicker Medicare was growing than the overall health sector. Overall personal health care expenditures increased by about 305 percent, public health expenditures increased by about 379 percent, but Medicare expenditures during the same period increased by about 406 percent. Considering the concern about overall increases in health care, such rapid increases in Medicare could not help but raise alarms.

One of the reasons for the increase in program expenditures was the increase in the number of Medicare beneficiaries. When the program began operation, in 1966, there were a little over 19 million enrollees. By 1970, that

Table 4.6

Medicare Enrollees, 1970–1995
(in thousands of enrollees)

	Total enrollees	Aged enrollees	Disabled enrollees
1970	20,491	20,491	
1980	28,478	25,515	2,963
1985	31,083	28,176	2,907
1990	34,213	30,961	3,252
1995	37,566	33,157	4,409

Source: Health Care Financing Administration, "Medicare and Medicaid Statistical Supplement, 1997," *Health Care Financing Review*, 23.

number had increased to over 20 million people. The 1972 amendments to the Social Security Act added the disabled and those suffering from end-stage renal disease (ESRD, or kidney failure). By 1995, there were approximately 37.5 million Medicare enrollees, 4.4 million of whom were disabled and about another 75,000 suffering from ESRD.[70] That represents an increase of about 83 percent in total recipients. Another reason is the growing generosity of Medicare in the sense that cost sharing on the part of Medicare recipients has become relatively smaller. In 1977, cost sharing amounted to about 18 percent of total expenditures. By 1983, the number had decreased to 17.6 percent. By 1995, that figure had decreased to about 14 percent.[71] Other reasons include increases caused by general inflation, health care inflation over and above general inflation, and changes in the technology of health care.

When policymakers began to seriously consider imposing cost-control measures on Medicare they focused first on hospitals. As is true for overall national health care expenditures, hospitals accounted for the largest single portion of Medicare expenditures. In 1995, hospital inpatient services were almost $79 billion, approximately 50 percent of total Medicare payments. By contrast, physician services accounted for over $41 billion, approximately 26 percent of total Medicare payments.[72]

When Medicare began, it contained the usual compromise provision "that the federal insurance program would not interfere in the practice of medicine or the structure of the medical care industry."[73] But it was inevitable that the federal government would have to take steps as the program became relatively more expensive. One way to understand that inevitability is to consider the theory of imbalanced political interests and its application to Medicare.[74]

At the beginning of the program, Medicare amounted to a relatively small percentage of federal expenditures. In fiscal year (FY) 1970, five years after

Medicare was established, Medicare expenditures amounted to about 4 percent of federal expenditures. Hospitals and physicians were faced with concentrated benefits and costs of payment and regulatory policies. The program was too small in the early years for the federal government to pay much concern. Ten years later, however, Medicare had increased to about 6.4 percent and by 1997 an estimated 11.9 percent of federal expenditures.[75] As Medicare spending continued to increase faster than overall spending, the federal government developed its own set of interests in cost containment that would counterbalance provider interests.[76] Additionally, there was, and is, the continual concern that the hospital trust fund will be insolvent by the end of the twentieth century. In the early 1980s, the federal government looked at hospital cost containment in Medicare. During the latter part of the decade it turned to physician payments. Eventually, other providers, such as nursing homes and home health care agencies, were covered by prospective payment.

Prospective Payment System and Cost Containment

The strain on the federal health budget (mentioned above) laid the political foundation for federal regulation of hospital costs.[77] Proponents of regulation claimed that it could reduce waste and inefficiency without sacrificing quality of care.[78]

The Omnibus Budget Reconciliation Act of 1981 made minor changes in the Medicare program. It tightened limits on Medicare reimbursement to generate cost savings. The Tax Equity and Fiscal Responsibility Act (TEFRA) of 1982 established a limit on the rate of increase over time in Medicare hospital payment rates, incorporated a case-mix index based on diagnosis related groupings (DRGs), and provided incentive payments to hospitals defined as efficient. The law also directed the Department of Health and Human Services (HHS) to design a prospective payment plan for the Medicare program. The TEFRA system was replaced in 1983 by the Prospective Payment System (PPS) for Medicare reimbursement to hospitals.

The PPS for Medicare reimbursement was modeled after a New Jersey program.[79] Faced with health care cost increases, inadequate care for the poor, pressure on the state Medicaid budget, and rising hospital charges, New Jersey adopted in 1978 a prospective reimbursement mechanism for all payers based on 467 DRGs. Implementation of PPS in New Jersey was phased in between 1980 and 1982. The Health Care Financing Administration (HCFA) in the Department of Health and Human Services had been supporting research, development, demonstration, and evaluation in cost control since the early 1970s, and the New Jersey DRG system was one of its demonstration projects. The adoption by the federal government in 1983 of a prospective payment mechanism based on DRGs for Medicare reimbursement to hospitals was a natural outgrowth of the New Jersey experiment.[80]

The rationale behind replacing the retrospective payment system was that under that system hospitals had no incentive to economize in their use of health care resources in treating Medicare patients. If anything, such a system encouraged overutilization of health resources because hospitals were assured that they would be reimbursed for all reasonable costs incurred. PPS was based on the assumption that given built-in incentives hospitals would be forced to consider cost factors in treatment and would be encouraged to be economically more efficient. Thus, inefficient hospitals would be forced to close. An economically more efficient hospital sector would help contain increases in hospital costs. PPS was viewed as a method of influencing hospital activities, creating cost-containment constraints, and introducing incentives into hospital payments.[81] The cost-control incentive was the primary purpose in establishing PPS.

Under PPS, hospitals are paid according to a schedule of preestablished rates linked to 468 DRGs. All major categories of diagnosis are classified into 492 categories. Each category is assigned a treatment rate, and hospitals are reimbursed according to these rates. There are economic incentives in the form of rewards and punishments built into the system. If a hospital spends more money than the preestablished rate for a particular diagnostic treatment, the hospital must absorb the additional cost. If the hospital spends less money than the preestablished rate, it is still paid the preestablished rate, and it can keep the overpayment as profit. The Health Care Financing Administration was assigned the responsibility for establishing the DRG payment schedule. To safeguard against reduction in quality of care as a result of PPS, Congress assigned to Peer Review Organizations (PROs) the responsibility for monitoring the quality and appropriateness of care for Medicare patients. If a PRO finds inappropriate or substandard care, the hospital may be denied Medicare payment. If a pattern of inappropriate or substandard care is discovered, the hospital Medicare provider agreement may be terminated.

The shift in the Medicare payment method to hospitals from a retrospective reimbursement system to a prospective payment system based on DRGs was the most far-reaching change in the Medicare program since its inception, equaled only by the move toward managed care and the Medicare+Choice program.[82] The changeover to PPS was the first major change in Medicare expected to revolutionize the economics of American health care.[83] DRGs change the incentive structure facing providers (hospitals in this case) using a regulatory approach. Managed care, on the other hand, changed the incentives structure using a market or private sector approach.

The implementation of PPS slowed the growth rate of hospital costs, largely through reduced hospital admissions. Concerns about cost shifting to third-party payers have not materialized, and there is no evidence to support the fear that Medicare patients were being denied beneficial care. Hospitals (and doctors) have accepted PPS, and it has become an accepted, if not liked, part of Medicare.

While PPS reduced the growth rate of hospital costs somewhat, national health care expenditures continued to rise, though they have slowed down in the mid- and late-1990s. This may partly reflect cost shifting to other sectors of the health care market, such as nursing home facilities or home health services.

Controlling Physician Costs

As we have seen, the Prospective Payment System focused on hospitals, but it also had an indirect effect on doctors. Hospitals are the structure or framework, but doctors decide medical or surgical treatment. The PPS, by creating a ceiling on hospital reimbursements, caused hospitals to pressure doctors so as to limit hospital expenditures. But physicians had independent effects on Medicare expenditures and government budgets.

General revenues make up a significant portion of Part B expenditures. After the 1972 Social Security amendments, increases in premiums were limited by increases in Social Security beneficiary payments. Thus, whereas in 1972 beneficiary premiums almost equaled general revenue contributions, by 1995 beneficiary premiums accounted for a little over 27.4 percent of Part B program payments.[84] With hospital expenses easing a bit, attention naturally turned to expenditures on the next biggest item, physicians. By 1995, such expenses accounted for 21.7 percent of total Medicare spending.[85]

In some ways, though Medicare based payments on usual and customary fees, the process was administratively complex and created inequities in physician income and dissatisfaction among physicians. In 1984, Congress froze Medicare physician reimbursements and then limited balance billing (the amount doctors could charge above Medicare). Further, there were significant increases in Medicare beneficiary cost sharing above increases in Social Security benefits. A final factor leading to change was the passage and implementation of the Prospective Payment System for hospitals. As Oliver points out, PPS "demonstrated that health cost containment was both technically feasible and politically feasible."[86]

Although the Reagan administration did not consider a physician payment schedule program, Congress acted.[87] It froze physician fees in Medicare and ordered the Office of Technology Assessment to evaluate different payment schemes. In 1985, Congress created the Physician Payment Review Commission (PPRC), through an omnibus budget reconciliation act, and ordered it to make recommendations regarding a payment system. It simultaneously ordered the Department of Health and Human Services to develop a fee schedule, based on a resource-based relative value scale (RBRVS). Such a scale was adopted in 1989, again through an omnibus budget reconciliation act. The Health Care Financing Administration began implementing the fee schedule in 1992 and it was fully implemented in 1996.[88]

A relative value scale (RVS) compares the complexity and time of services offered.[89] Thus a simple office visit would have a lower RVS than a coronary bypass operation. The fee schedule also contains adjustments for geography, and there is a conversion factor that translates the results into dollar amounts. Additionally, volume standards help in establishing growth rates in physician payments.[90]

The impact of the fee schedule varied, depending on the kind of service. Fees for office and hospital visits were generally increased; fees for surgery were significantly reduced. It is no wonder that physicians and their associations were unhappy with the fee schedules. Political pressure by interest groups, Congress, and the Bush administration led HCFA to liberalize the fee schedule.[91] In 1998, HCFA began using a single conversion factor for all physician services, effectively raising the conversion factor for primary care and nonsurgical care and lowering it for surgical services.[92] The 1997 balanced budget called for changes in the fee schedule components to be fully implemented by 2002.[93]

The Problem of Long-Term Care

Although the impetus behind the nation's quest for health care reform is public dissatisfaction over glaring deficiencies in America's acute-care health system—primarily excessive cost and the inability of millions of Americans to get health insurance—the way the nation provides for the financing and delivery of long-term care (LTC) may be even more badly in need of reform. Strong considerations, both public policy and moral, argue for addressing health care for the uninsured first, before long-term care. Yet no other part of the health care system generates as much passionate discontent as does long-term care.[94]

1. An estimated 13 million people currently need LTC, and the number is expected to increase dramatically in the future.

2. States are worried about providing a safety net for the growing number of older people, given that Medicaid B, which they finance jointly

with the federal government B, is the primary source of public financial assistance for LTC.

3. A large percentage of people who need LTC do not receive the necessary assistance.

4. The systems for financing LTC are irrational in that they are patched together with a combination of out-of-pocket and government funds.

5. Medicaid primarily funds institutional care, even though most consumers prefer to remain in their homes and communities for as long as possible.

6. The delivery structures are fragmented, duplicative, and difficult for consumers to negotiate.[95]

As we saw in the discussion of the Medicare Catastrophic Coverage Act, one of the important gaps in Medicare pertains to long-term care. We begin this section by looking at some of the data concerning long-term care.

A first point is the significant increase in expenditures on nursing homes. In 1970, about $4.2 billion was spent on nursing homes. By 1995, that figure had risen to $77.9 billion, an increase of 1,754 percent. By contrast, overall personal health care expenditures increased by 1,277 percent over the same period. For hospital services, the increase was 1,150 percent and for physician services, the increase was 1,382 percent. By the year 2018, we may be spending $168.2 billion (in 1993 inflation-adjusted dollars) for home health and nursing home care.[96]

Second, Medicare (and most private medical insurance) focuses on short-term or chronic care. It provides limited coverage for skilled nursing care, and then only after a hospital episode on physician orders. The bulk of spending on nursing homes is from Medicaid and out-of-pocket expenditures. Out of the $77.9 billion spent on nursing homes nationally, Medicare accounted for only about 9.4 percent.[97]

Consider 1995 data. Out of $184 billion spent by Medicare, nursing home care accounted for $7.3 billion.[98] Medicaid paid about $36.2 billion for long-term care, or 46.5 percent of nursing home care. Private health insurance paid for only 3.3 percent of nursing home care ($2.5 billion), while out-of-pocket payments were 36.7 percent of such costs ($28.6 billion).[99] Further, though the elderly constitute a small portion of Medicaid recipients, about 11.4 percent in 1995, over 30.4 percent of Medicaid spending is on this group.[100]

Having looked at expenditure data, we can look at the population likely to need long-term care.

Today [1994], approximately 11 million Americans of all ages are chronically disabled and depend on others for assistance in the basic tasks of daily living such as eating, bathing and other activities that most of us take for granted. In this highly diverse population are people with both physical and cognitive disabilities, including the frail elderly, quadriplegics and paraplegics, persons with developmental disabilities, persons with severe mental illness, and children with chronic conditions. Of the 11 million Americans with disabilities, about 3 million are considered to be severely disabled.[101]

Further, some 7.1 million of the elderly need some kind of long-term care, and about 1.5 million are in nursing homes.[102] The number of elderly (those sixty-five and over) is growing rapidly, and the segment of the elderly population growing the fastest is eighty-five and older. Thus there are projections that the need for long-term-care services, especially nursing homes, will double over the next twenty to thirty years. The projection is that the nursing home population will increase to 3.6 million people in 2018, while those needing home health care will increase to 7.4 million.[103]

Interestingly, it appears that disabilities among the elderly are declining while they are increasing in the under sixty-five group. One reason is that AIDS has become more of a chronic than an acute disease; thus survival times of those suffering from AIDS, especially given the advent of new medical therapies, have increased.[104] As the baby-boom generation ages, long-term-care needs will increase, though estimates of the dimensions of the problem vary.[105]

The nursing home industry was born of two actions by the federal government. One, in 1950, was an amendment to the Social Security Act prohibiting payments to residents living in institutional settings such as boardinghouses that did not provide health care. The other major development was the establishment of Medicaid. Though Medicaid does not pick up all the nursing home bill, it does pay for the medically indigent in nursing homes. These two developments created a situation in which long-term care became synonymous with nursing homes.

Long-term care can be delivered outside nursing homes, either home- or community-based. Much care for the elderly is given by relatives. This is free care and does not figure into the estimates of long-term care expenditures. Indeed, considerably more is spent on home and community-based care than on nursing homes.

Despite the relatively small number of the elderly in nursing homes, the threat of a nursing home stay is that it can wipe out lifetime savings. In 1988, nursing homes cost an average of $25,000 a year. By 1995, that figure rose to $41,000 a year.[106] Eligibility for Medicaid requires spending down one's savings. Many who start out in nursing homes as privately paying patients end up as Medicaid recipients. Further, the middle class has increasingly seen Medicaid has a middle-class entitlement, a way to protect life savings. Thus, families transfer funds from the elderly person to other members of the family so that the elderly person can become eligible for Medicaid. While Congress has tightened the rules (states and HCFA can look at transfers up to three years prior to placement in a nursing home), the problem remains.[107]

Long-term care thus presents several problems at different levels. At the level of the individual, the problem is financial: being able to afford long-term care, or in some cases being able to arrange it. From the standpoint of government, the problem is the ever-increasing costs of long-term care. From a societal standpoint, the problem is the increasing demand for long-term care in the twenty-first century.

Home and Informal Care

Much care for the elderly is given in the home by relatives, that is, unpaid informal assistance. Some 2 million elderly receive formal assistance at home or in the community. This includes meals, transportation, and home health care. About 1.5 million elderly are so severely disabled that they live in nursing homes. Thus, only a small minority of the elderly at any one time live in a nursing home. At the same time, relatives caring for the elderly need help and understanding as they deal with work and home conflicts.[108]

One way that these informal caregivers, the overwhelming majority of whom are women, can be assisted is by employers (both public and private) in the workplace. They can provide options for their employees that will help them assist their disabled relatives. Some 23 million Americans work in companies that have plans, such as leave policies (both paid and unpaid) or flexible work schedules, to help their employees in these situations. These and similar programs could reduce the chances of institutionalization of the disabled elderly by about a third.[109] Such policies are generally not available through small businesses, and there is considerable variation among employers. "Elder care" is also available to public-sector employees at all levels of government. While the options are available, however, they are not widely encouraged or promoted.[110] Although it appears that there will be some expansion of elder care in both the public and private sectors, the potential cost of such programs is a limiting factor.

An alternative to informal home care and nursing homes (institutionalization) is the use of home health care agencies. Under Part A, Medicare will pay for services if the enrollee is "under the care of a physician, confined to home, and need[s] skilled nursing services on an intermittent basis."[111] Since 1989, Medicare has, after a Supreme Court decision, relaxed eligibility requirements for home health care. The result has been a massive increase in use of services and increased costs. Table 4.7 presents the data on use and costs. As can be seen from the table, there was a massive increase in use and an even larger increase in costs. An additional statistic adds to the data about home health care. Since the 1989 liberalization of the home health care benefit (for example, only about one-third of home health care beneficiaries had a hospital stay during the year in which they were receiving services),[112] the number of home health agencies has grown, from 5,692 in 1989 to 7,864 in 1994. Over 80 percent of the growth was by proprietary agencies. This is significant because proprietary agencies tended to provide more visits (an average of 78 per recipient) than either nonprofit or government agencies (an average of 46).[113] At the same time the ability to control costs and utilization has suffered. The General Accounting Office (GAO) suggested that this combination opens the way for fraud and abuse. The GAO reached the following conclusions:

- Physicians tend to depend on home health agencies (HHAs) to design plans of care, especially for less complex cases, and agencies as a rule have incentives to furnish as many visits as possible. This combination can lead to overprovision of services.

- Medicare has reduced on-site audits and reviews so that HHAs have less incentive to follow Medicare rules. The percentage of claims that are reviewed has decreased from over 60 percent in 1987 to approximately 3 percent in 1994. We have testified on a number of occasions that program safeguard activities are cost effective, returning close to $14 in savings for each $1 invested in 1994, and cuts in payment safeguard areas translate into increased program losses from fraud, waste, and abuse. When claims volume increases and medical review of claims declines, intermediaries' ability to detect and prevent erroneous payments is substantially lessened. Further, even when claims are denied, they were often paid because the HHA qualified for a waiver of liability.

- It is nearly impossible for intermediaries to assess from paper review alone whether a beneficiary meets the eligibility criteria, whether the services received are appropriate given the beneficiary's current condition, and whether the beneficiary is actually receiving the services billed to Medicare. Coverage criteria, such as confined to home or intermittent, are not meaningful when the HHAs are in effect the only ones monitoring beneficiaries.[114]

A more recent GAO report found that HCFA's certification process was not very effective in removing problem home health care agencies from Medicare participation.[115]

Table 4.7

Medicare Home Health Care Enrollees and Costs, 1974–1995

	Number of persons served (in 000s)	Total Medicare payments (in $000s)	Medicare payments per person served	Medicare payments per enrollee	Percent of all Medicare program payments
1974	392.7	$141,464	$360	$ 6	1.3
1980	957.4	662,133	692	23	2.0
1985	1,600.2	1,773,048	1,116	57	2.8
1990	1,967.1	3,713,652	1,892	109	3.7
1995	3,469.4	15,391,094	4,441	452	9.7

Source: Health Care Financing Administration, "Medicare and Medicaid Statistical Supplement, 1997," *Health Care Financing Review*, 126.

A related issue concerns *hospices*. A hospice is a service that provides specialized care, usually for people who are near death. Hospices can provide counseling to both the patient and the family, as well as drugs, medical supplies, and a variety of services. Hospice services can be delivered in hospitals, or nursing homes, or at home. To be eligible for Medicare reimbursement, the patient must be diagnosed as within six months of dying. Hospice services are also one of the fastest-growing components of Medicare, costing about $2 billion in FY 1997. The problem is that there is apparently great potential for recipients who do not qualify for the service to bilk Medicare and/or patients.[116]

The home health care and hospice fraud issue is part of the larger problem of abuse in Medicare. Other institutions and services have been implicated as well, such as ambulances and some hospital services.[117] A 1997 study by the DHHS inspector general estimates Medicare overpayments at between 14 and 17 percent, with home health care being the worst offender.[118] To deal with the problem, the Clinton administration issued a temporary moratorium on new home health care agencies and said that HCFA would issue new standards requiring all home health agencies to reapply for Medicare certification every three years.[119] One part of the 1997 Balanced Budget Act provided for new funds to investigate fraud and new criminal penalties for those caught. There has also been a significant increase in investigators (both Federal Bureau of Investigation and DHHS) from 1995 to 1997. Fraud nevertheless remains difficult to ferret out.

Congress addressed some of the cost problems associated with home health care in the 1997 Balanced Budget Act. One change was to place a ceiling on reimbursements for individual home health care agencies. Another was to restrict agency reimbursement to only those services provided for under Medicare law. The intent of the changes was to restrict home health care to short-term therapy or skilled nursing services. There have been reports of home health agencies threatening to leave their patients because of the changes.[120] Despite the problems, home health care remains an important service for those confined to their homes.

Long-Term-Care Policy Alternatives

One policy alternative increasingly investigated is long-term-care (LTC) insurance. This would be similar to health insurance. Insurance could be sold to the elderly, say when they become sixty-five years old, or to younger people where they work so that a reserve fund could be established.

The long-term-care insurance market is relatively new and still small. The product was almost nonexistent before 1986; by June 1990, some 1.6 million policies had been sold. The policies are generally indemnity policies; that is, they pay a specified amount per day to the beneficiary. Janet Shikles, of the General Accounting Office, testified before Congress that the long-term-care insurance market looked like the "medigap" insurance market prior to congressional reforms. "Early Medigap policies varied greatly in value and coverage. State regulation was inconsistent, with sales and market abuses a recurring problem."[121]

The problem Shikles identified is that policies vary as to what is covered, whether prior hospitalization is necessary, inflation adjustments for coverage, amount of premiums, increases in premiums, and length of time the policy is in effect. A study by the Brookings Institution found that only wealthier people are likely to buy long-term-care insurance and that such insurance would reduce total nursing home care costs by 7 to 20 percent in the next century.[122]

Thus, while private long-term-care insurance has the potential for alleviating some of the cost problems, the long-term-care issue has not been fully dealt with. It is not yet a mature policy and requires considerable standardization.

Further, long-term-care insurance is expensive. The average premium for a policy at age sixty-five in 1991 was $2,525 a year. At age seventy-nine, the premium rises to $7,675 a year. There are two reasons for the high premiums. First, unlike regular health insurance, long-term-care insurance is sold to individuals rather than groups, and thus administrative costs are high. The population that buys it is limited generally to those sixty-five and older, the group most likely to need the insurance. Thus the insurance is sold to high-risk individuals.[123] One possible solution to this problem is to combine long-term-care insurance with Medicaid.[124] A small number of states (Connecticut, New York, Indiana, and California) have begun such a partnership program. The program works as follows:

As a public/private venture, the Partnership teams the state with private insurance companies to offer affordable long-term-care coverage. Consumers
who buy Partnership-approved policies are covered by private insurance until
the policy runs out, at which point Medicaid pays for their care without forcing them to spend down or transfer assets.[125]

The policies are more affordable than solely private LTC insurance policies. Medicaid saves as well because it does not have to pay for long-term
care until the private insurance runs out.[126]

The Forum for State Health Policy Leadership recommends, among other
things, that the long-term-care system try to accommodate the desire of consumers (patients) to have home-based health services and to be independent,
and should place greater reliance on private funding sources than on Medicaid.[127] Arizona has adopted (beginning in 1989) a capitated long-term-care
program for Medicaid. Its focus is to substitute home- and community-based
care for institutionalized care. It has appeared to save the state money while
at the same time expanding the alternative types of care.[128]

Long-Term Care and Health Care Reform

Given the problems of long-term care, to what extent was it considered in the
debate over health care? Two of the plans, the Clinton administration's Health
Security Act (based on managed competition and caps on insurance premiums) and the Wellstone-McDermott American Health Security Act (a single-
payer plan), had detailed provisions concerning long-term care.[129]

The Health Security Act maintained the traditional distinction between
long-term care and acute care. The program would have been state administered and available to all (not means tested). The Health Security Act provided
for both institutional care and home- and community-based care. It would
have built on the Medicare program and extended coverage to the medically
needy. It would have provided national standards for long-term insurance and
increased tax deductions. Finally, there would have been increased federal
funding for the new provisions.[130]

The American Health Security Act (single-payer bill) folded long-term-
care services (institutional, community-based, and home-based) into an overall
package of national health insurance. It would phase out Medicaid and provide for copayments for long-term-care services and subsidization for
low-income people.[131]

Because no health care reform bill passed in 1993–94, the long-term-care
issue remains unresolved. A Republican plan, under the Contract with America,
contained provisions that would help some of the elderly (largely upper-in-
come people). The plan would allow drawing from pension plans to pay for

long-term insurance. It would also provide tax credits for such insurance. The plan would also allow those needing long-term care to draw death benefits from life insurance to pay for the care.[132] This was never formally proposed.

Other proposals include expanding Medicaid, allowing recipients to keep more of their assets, and using the social insurance approach of Medicare that would cover everybody.[133] The latter has the advantage of providing a universal benefit and avoiding the stigma of the means-tested Medicaid program. The Medicaid option would be cheaper, however. In either case, the creation of a new entitlement program runs up against the fiscal constraint of the large budget deficits, though the budget surplus that appeared in 1998 changes the politics some. Further, the costs of such a new program are uncertain.[134]

There is one last perspective on long-term care. Except for the single-payer proposal mentioned earlier, most discussions of long-term care consider such care separately from the more familiar acute care. But it may be that integrating the two, say within Medicare, might prove in the long run to provide better care and control costs. One such model of how such integration might work is provided by the social health maintenance organizations (S/HMOs). Though there are only a few S/HMOs in existence, there is evidence that such an approach works. Further, such a policy would focus not just on nursing homes but also on home and community-based care.

In March 1998, Congress began considering a number of health insurance initiatives, based largely on tax credits. A bill developed by Bill Archer (R-Texas), the chair of the House Ways and Means Committee, would use money from tobacco taxes to finance the credits. One use of the credits would be to help cover long-term care, such as long-term-care insurance and nursing homes.[135]

Medicare, Balanced Budgets, and Change

Financial considerations have been an important part of the politics and policy deliberations surrounding Medicare since the program began. One such problem, already mentioned, is the sheer size of the program combined with its rapid growth and its impact on the federal budget. Another aspect is that the increase in the size of Medicare beneficiary population (especially when the massive baby boom generation begins to retire) places increased pressure on Medicare. This is most clearly seen in estimates as to the future solvency of the Hospital Insurance (Part A) Trust Fund. The trust fund and budget impacts of Medicare came together in the politics of balanced budgets in the 1990s.

Medicare was retained in President Clinton's 1993 Health Security Act proposal (see chapter 9), but spending on the program was to be cut by $124 billion to help finance the rest of the bill (Medicaid was to be cut by $114 billion).[136] More important, Medicare (and Medicaid) became a part of the battles over the budget between President Clinton and the Republican-controlled Congress after 1995.[137]

Congressional Republicans passed a budget resolution in June 1995 designed to balance the budget by fiscal year 2002. The resolution called for $983 billion in total deductions, with about $270 billion in reductions in spending over the 1996–2002 period. The plan included $245 billion in tax cuts. Medicare was such a large program that Republicans would be unable to meet its goal without the Medicare reductions. Republicans were aided by an April 1995 report of the Social Security and Medicare trustees that estimated that the Medicare trust fund (Part A) would go bankrupt by 2002. Republicans could then argue that they were not trying to cut or destroy Medicare, but to save it.[138]

Senate Republicans focused on reducing benefits and provider payments. House Republicans had a more elaborate plan that concentrated on beneficiaries: raising Part B premiums, requiring higher payments by wealthier beneficiaries, allowing more choice of plans for beneficiaries, and permitting medical savings accounts (taxfree savings accounts that could be used to pay for medical expenses).

Clinton and House Democrats adamantly opposed Republican plans for Medicare and budget cuts, though the president eventually embraced the balanced budget goal. In the 1996 elections, Democrats continually hammered away at the Republican proposals, continually pointing to cuts in Medicare, Medicaid, education, and environmental programs. The impasse led to two government shutdowns (in 1995–96). Clinton was reelected in 1996 and Republicans saw their majority in the House shrink, though the Republican majority in the more moderate Senate increased slightly.

In 1997, Republicans and Democrats made an effort to reach a bipartisan budget agreement. The Balanced Budget Act (BBA) of 1997 was signed by President Clinton on August 1, 1997. The Act provides for a balanced budget by FY 2002 (a goal met in FY 1998), with most of the program savings coming from Medicare.

The Balanced Budget Act is potentially the most important change in the Medicare program since the inception of provider fee schedules in the 1980s. First, it calls for $115 billion in estimated savings from Medicare over a five-year period, and for an estimated $393.4 billion in savings over a ten-year period (through FY 2007). This is the major source of savings in the legislation. The changes, to be described below, slow the yearly cost increases to an estimated 5 percent from the projected almost 7 percent.[139]

Much of the savings comes from reductions in payment to providers, especially in the fee-for-service sector ($78.1 billion through FY 2002 and $200.9 billion through FY 2007). Hospital payments reductions account for about 30 percent of the overall savings. The legislation also mandates the creation of a prospective payment system for skilled nursing, home health care, and outpatient services. Approximately 20 percent of the savings will be from reductions in payments to private plans, such as HMOs. The changes specified here would move the date for Part A trust fund insolvency to 2007.

The final source of savings is an increase in the Part B premiums. The BBA sets the Part B premium permanently at 25 percent of Part B costs. Additionally, a portion of the home health care benefit will be transferred from Part A to Part B. Services after the 100th visit in a year or services unconnected to hospital stay will be covered in Part B. The effect of both these changes is to make the monthly premium in 2007 about $45 higher than it would be prior to the BBA.

The law also includes new benefits, primarily in preventive services for specific cancers (such as breast and prostate cancer), osteoporosis, and management of diabetes. It also gradually reduces the copayment for hospital outpatient services.

These changes, though important, are fairly conventional. Raising beneficiary premiums, cutting provider payments, and instituting prospective payment plans have been done before, but the BBA creates a new set of options that promise (or threaten, depending on one's perspective) to change the nature of Medicare.

As discussed previously, a growing, though still relatively small, number of Medicare beneficiaries have switched from the standard Medicare fee-for-service system to managed care. The BBA extends the options. Beginning in 1999, Medicare recipients will effectively be able to choose from three sets of plans. One option is the traditional Medicare fee-for-service system. The second option is the Medicare+Choice program. This option contains a number of alternatives and is effectively Part C of the Medicare legislation. The options are described in Table 4.8.

Clearly, the new legislation seeks to move more Medicare recipients out of the traditional fee-for-service system and into managed care-type plans. The hope is that Medicare recipients will choose less costly plans and thus save money for both recipients and the program. The Medicare+Choice program also presents recipients with the responsibility for picking the plans, a responsibility that has been labeled a "dizzying array of choices" and a "Brave New World."[140] Managed care, both inside and outside Medicare, has been

Table 4.8

Medicare Choices

Plan	Description
Fee for service	The beneficiary can visit any doctor. Medicare pays a set fee for each service. Most beneficiaries, however, purchase private supplemental insurance to pay for uncovered costs.
Health Maintenance Organization (HMO)	The beneficiary can use only the doctors and health facilities on a limited list, but often receives extra benefits. A gatekeeper oversees the patient's total care and makes referrals to specialists. Medicare pays the HMO a set fee in advance to cover all patient services for a period of time.
Point of service	In this special kind of HMO, the beneficiary can visit doctors outside the network but must pay an additional cost.
Preferred provider organization (PPO)	The beneficiary can visit any doctor in the health care network without a referral, or see doctors outside the network at an additional cost. Medicare pays a set fee in advance to cover all patient services for a period of time.
Provider-Sponsored Organization (PSO)	PSOs are new health plans that will be created, owned, and operated by doctors and hospitals. They will resemble managed care plans, in which Medicare pays the health plan a monthly fee for each recipient.
Medical Savings Account (MSA)	Medicare provides catastrophic insurance coverage and advances a portion of the high deductible. At the end of the year, the beneficiary may keep any unused Medicare money.
Privately contracted fee-for-service	The beneficiary may visit any doctor or purchase any health plan but pays extra for noncovered or expensive services.

Source: Marilyn Werber Serafini. "Brave New World." *National Journal* 29, no. 33 (August 16, 1997): 1637 (1636–1639).

controversial, and we discuss this in chapters 9 and 10. The law allows beneficiaries who choose one of the options to return to the traditional Medicare program or to switch options. However, when a Medicare beneficiary chooses an option, such as an HMO, the recipient gives up any supplementary medical insurance (medigap) policy. If the recipient then decides to go back to the traditional Medicare program, he or she may be unable to purchase a medigap policy because of previous health problems.[141]

Perhaps the most controversial option is the private fee-for-service or private contracts plan. Recipients contract with doctors for a negotiated fee, but one not based on Medicare schedules. Medicare does not pay; rather, the patient is responsible for the full cost. Medicare continues to cover other services. An important feature of this option is that any physician who participates in this plan in any manner, even limited to one treatment, becomes ineligible for Medicare reimbursement for two years. Given the harsh nature of this feature, why would patients and doctors choose it?

Understanding this option requires us to return to the basic Medicare Part B program. Medicare has a fee schedule and doctors are limited in what they can charge their patients. Private contracting eliminates this feature. Some 85 percent of physicians accept (participate in) Medicare fee schedules. "Nonparticipating" physicians are limited to charging no more than 15 percent above what Medicare allows, as discussed above. About 5 percent of doctors refuse to limit themselves to the 115 percent and by law cannot treat Medicare patients for Medicare-covered services. The private contracting provision now allows Medicare patients to be seen by nonparticipating physicians.[142]

Some have argued that private contracting might lead to beneficiaries leaving Medicare for a strictly private system and that more doctors would refuse to participate in Medicare. The result might be the creation of a two-tiered health care system. The Clinton administration insisted on including the penalty (the two-year prohibition mentioned above) in the BBA.[143] The chief sponsor of the private contracting feature, Senator Jon Kyl (R-Arizona) wants to eliminate the two-year penalty. Supporters of Kyl's position, such as the United Seniors Association, have sent letters out decrying the limitation and arguing that Medicare recipients will not be able to receive some services even if they want to pay more.[144] This is an argument that can be seen in a commentary in the local paper published where the authors live.[145] Consider the following argument:

> Imagine you are a heart patient with severe symptoms who has already had bypass surgery and Medicare will not pay for it again. You are scared. Then an acquaintance tells you about a treatment he claims saved his life when he was in your situation. You investigate and decide it is worth a try even though it is not covered by Medicare and you must pay for it out of your own pocket. Until recently, no problem. However, as of August, a little noted amendment to the Medicare Act makes it illegal for a doctor to take payment for such treatment from Medicare-eligible patients. Doctors may, however, accept payment for this same treatment if you are not Medicare eligible (i.e., under age 65).[146]

There are two problems with this reasoning. First, the commentary says this is not a Medicare-covered service. At no time, including the BBA, are doctors limited in taking payments or charging whatever they want for non-Medicare-covered services. Second, under the private contracting feature of the BBA, even if the service were covered by Medicare, the doctor and patient could negotiate the private contract for a mutually agreeable fee, though the doctor would not be able to participate in Medicare for two years.[147]

Robert Pear pointed out the significance of these changes, especially the private contracting option:

> The options, which represent a radical departure from current Medicare policy, are likely to appeal to rugged individualists who resent Government interference with their medical care and can afford to pay more for it.
>
> The new alternatives would allow elderly people to drop out of the standard Medicare program, spend their own money and avoid the limits imposed by managed care and Medicare fee schedules.[148]

The Balanced Budget Act also sought to address the long-term issue of the solvency of Medicare by mandating a bipartisan commission, the National Bipartisan Commission on the Future of Medicare, to investigate ways to deal with the impact of the retirement of the baby boom generation. Commissions are a favored tool for putting off difficult decisions, though they can, under certain circumstances, work well (an example is the 1983 Greenspan commission on Social Security). The commission, under the BBA, must report to Congress by March 1999. Given the tight deadline, the commission got off to a slow start, wrangling over who would head the commission and deciding whether to consider President Clinton's proposals to expand Medicare to uninsured people age fifty-five and over (see below). Partisan conflict and disputes over whether additional taxes should be considered as part of the commission's recommendations made the outlook for a successful conclusion problematical.[149]

In late 1997 and early 1998, President Clinton proposed expanding Medicare coverage to uninsured people ages fifty-five to sixty-four. The president's proposal would allow people who are sixty-two to sixty-four to buy into Medicare for $300 a month. Those who are fifty-five to sixty-two could buy-in for $400. The proposal would cover those who did not have health insurance, those who lost health insurance because of loss of a job, and those who had an individual policy. The administration estimated that these premiums would fund the expansion without any additional strain on Medicare financial resources.[150] Such a plan, introduced by congressional Democrats in March 1998, would be another example of the incremental strategy of expanding public health insurance programs, a point reinforced by liberal commentator Robert Kuttner, who termed the plan politically brilliant.[151]

Republicans opposed the proposal, arguing that Medicare had serious financial problems and that bringing more people in would exacerbate those problems.[152] The health insurance industry also opposed the expansion, on similar grounds, noting that those who were less healthy (more likely to need health care services) would be most likely to buy in and that the actuarial projections were likely to be unsound (the expansion would cost more than the premiums would bring in).[153] Senator John Breaux (D-Louisiana), the head of the Medicare commission, asked Congress to delay consideration of the buy-in until the commission, had time to study the matter.[154] Breaux supported instead a plan to let the near elderly buy into the federal employees health insurance plan.[155]

Conclusion

> The challenges posed by rising costs today combined with the future burdens that will arise from an aging population will require that changes be made in Medicare. But we should not begin this process of reassessment under the mistaken claim that the program is a failure.[156]

> Seen from this angle, Medicare+Choice is the first step toward a two-tier system: strict managed-care plans where medical treatment can be rationed, and private fee-for-service for wealthier people who can afford the price.[157]

Medicare remains a popular program among the population at large.[158] But problems remain in both the long and the short term. First, the cost of Medicare and the increases in those costs affect both recipients and the federal government. Second, as the baby boom generation begins retiring in 2010–2011, additional pressures will be placed on the program. Additionally, Medicare has significant gaps in its coverage, particularly in long-term care, but also in areas such as prescription drugs. Finally, the issue of fraud and waste affects the short- and long-term viability of the program.

The 1980s and 1990s saw significant change in the structure of Medicare. The 1980s saw the imposition of fee schedules for hospitals and physicians, and the beginning of Medicare managed care. The Balanced Budget Act of 1997 brought more potentially fundamental restructuring of Medicare. It extended fee schedules to other providers (e.g., home health care agencies) and instituted the Medicare+Choice program, which increased the types of plans beneficiaries could choose, even giving some (the wealthier ones) an opportunity to effectively drop out of the program. The cuts in provider reimbursements called for in the BBA, combined with a surge in the economy, moved the projected insolvency of the hospital trust fund back to 2008.[159] Thus the short-term issue of insolvency appears to have been addressed.

Yet at the same time, the consensus that had existed from the beginning of the program about what Medicare would be began to dissolve. Oberlander argues that the politics of Medicare up to 1994 led to a consensus, first that Medicare would be a public program, one that was operated by the federal government. The other element of the consensus was that the politics of Medicare was bipartisan, supported by Republicans and Democrats. The politics of Medicare subsequent to the November 1994 elections saw the unraveling of the consensus. Medicare was depicted by some as a failure, a throwback to the 1960s Great Society programs, and a problem of intergenerational equity (younger people paying for older people). Medicare+Choice was the result, with its medical savings accounts and private fee-for-service provisions.[160]

Among other important elements affecting Medicare was the removal of federal budget deficits from politics. The BBA, combined with previous budget cuts (in 1990 under President Bush and in 1993 under President Clinton) and a vibrant expanding economy, projected the elimination of the federal deficit by FY 2002. However, by FY 1998, the deficit had disappeared, with projected budget surpluses running at least another ten years. This unexpected good news led President Clinton in 1997 and 1998 to propose expanding Medicare by allowing those aged fifty-five to sixty-four who had no health insurance to buy in to the program. While the proposal was attacked for expansion and for aggravating an already precarious financial status for Medicare, just President Clinton's making the proposal, another example of incremental reform, indicated a changed environment.

The longer-term problems (increasing costs and expansion of beneficiaries) do remain.[161] A variety of proposals have been suggested that would affect Medicare in the twenty-first century.

Some of the proposals, while significant, would not change Medicare's essential structure. One proposal would be to increase the hospital insurance trust fund tax from 2.9 percent (half paid by employee, half by employer) to perhaps 4.5 percent. Other possibilities include raising the eligibility age from sixty-five to sixty-seven (which would also save money, though it would run counter to proposals to expand Medicare to those below sixty-five) and means-testing Part B premiums (higher premiums for wealthier beneficiaries). Both proposals were rejected by Congress and the president during deliberations over the BBA. But those are still possibilities for the future and, like some of the other proposals such as private fee-for-service contracting and medical savings accounts, would change the nature of the program. For example, means-testing Medicare Part B premiums would make the program more like welfare and less like social insurance.[162]

Other proposals could change the nature of the program. The halting move toward managed care, now with increased incentives and choices as a result of the BBA, has always promised a limitation on use and therefore cost savings. But managed care has proved to be a mixed blessing. The BBA reduces payments to HMOs at the same time that HMOs are beginning to raise their fees to Medicare subscribers.

The private contracting and medical savings accounts elements could create, as the Quinn quote at the beginning of this section indicates, a two-tiered system. Wealthier recipients could effectively opt out of Medicare. Those who expect to need fewer services could also choose those options, knowing that at some point they could return to the more conventional Medicare program.

A more radical proposal is to rely on vouchers. Under a voucher program, recipients would be able to purchase any plan they chose. This would bring competition and consumer choice into Medicare, eliminating the program as we know it. Vouchers in health care are not new proposals[163] and are worth investigating. But they have proved controversial and are an unlikely near-term change.[164]

Another proposal, based on European experience, is to use price controls through limits on spending (program controls), using such policy instruments as "fee schedules, volume controls, and spending caps."[165] While the international experience does indicate the efficacy of program controls, in the political environment of turn-of-the-century America, a move toward regulatory controls seems unlikely. Further, the managed care revolution (discussed in chapters 9 and 10) points in the opposite direction.

Long-term care is an area that public policy has yet to come to grips with. The long-term-care insurance market has expanded, but not especially rapidly. Medicare can be expanded in a variety of ways to cover long-term-care needs.[166] To the extent that public programs cover long-term care, Medicaid, with all its faults, remains the primary program (see chapter 3).

The twenty-first-century Medicare program is being built around the ideas found in the Balanced Budget Act. We live in a brave and scary new world.

CHAPTER 5

Health Care and the Disadvantaged: Falling through the Cracks

By 1970, health care policy in the United States had reached its maturity. Medicare and Medicaid were passed in 1965; private insurance covered most of working America. But health care costs went up dramatically beginning in the mid-1960s, and portions of the population were left out of the system. Two of the major problems of the health care system are cost increases and access. We consider the problem of cost increases in the next chapter. This chapter focuses on the problem of access and the disadvantaged.

We concentrate on issues of access to the health care system, the problem of the uninsured and the underinsured, low-income groups, and minorities and women. To some extent, these problems overlap. While a good portion of the uninsured are low-income people, some are not. While minorities in general have lower incomes than whites, not all the problems of minorities and health care result from lower incomes. Rural areas have access problems to health care in the same way that inner cities do: lack of providers. We spell out these interrelationships as we go along.

Perhaps the underlying issue in looking at the disadvantaged and health care is equality and equity. We begin this chapter by considering this issue.

Equality and Equity

Equality and equity do not mean the same things. Equality means that we should treat people who are in the same situation the same way or treat people who are in different situations differently. That is, we should not discriminate against someone on account of race, religion, age, sex, ethnic group, and so forth. One reality of the health care system, to be discussed later in the chapter, is that there is discrimination based on income or at least based on health insurance. Those with private insurance plans, especially very generous ones, tend to get better service than those on public plans (such as Medicaid); those without health insurance tend to get the worst care.[1] Some have argued that the United States has a two-tiered health care system, one for most of us and another for the poor. In Krause's words,

> we have, combining the doctors and the office and hospital settings, a two-class medical care system. On the one hand, few practitioners and a few public settings for the poor in either the ghetto or rural areas; on the other hand, many practitioners and voluntary nonprofit hospitals for the middle class and the upper class in the suburbs.[2]

This leads us to the notion of equity, an extension of the concept of equality. Equity is related to another concept, social justice. Both ideas suggest that, given that some are disadvantaged in the health care system, there should be an extra effort made to help overcome those disadvantages. This is, in a sense, the idea behind Medicaid (and to a lesser extent, Medicare). Medicaid recipients do not have to pay for their health care. Instead, their health care is subsidized by the larger community (taxpayers) and to some extent by providers and their patients (in the sense that Medicaid reimbursements are lower than for privately insured patients and costs are shifted to privately insured patients). Compensatory education programs such as Head Start, where we devote more resources to children from impoverished backgrounds, are another example.

There are a number of philosophical concepts that support extending access to heath care services to those who do not have it. Daniels, Light, and Caplan argue that the appropriate philosophical ground is *fairness*.[3] To the authors, fairness is related to social justice and equal opportunity, or what they call fair equal opportunity. This concept, not especially well defined in our opinion, sees health care as instrumental in that it allows people to function normally. The lack of health care services, according to their reasoning, shortens peoples' lives or makes it more difficult for them to function normally and therefore to live on a level playing field with other people. They write:

> A commitment to fair equality of opportunity thus recognizes that we should not allow people's prospects in life to be governed by correctable, morally arbitrary, or irrelevant differences between them, including those that result from disease and disability. . . . By designing a health care system that keeps *all* people as close as possible to normal functioning, given reasonable resource constraints, we can in one important way fulfill our moral and legal obligations to protect equality of opportunity.[4]

Notice at the end of the quote the reference to resource constraints. Their view of fairness is balanced by a concern for liberty, social productivity, and efficiency.[5]

The bulk of their book develops ten benchmarks of fairness to evaluate health care policy and then applies those benchmarks to the current system, the Clinton proposals, and managed care. Their benchmarks include universal access, equitable financing, value for money, public accountability, comparability, and degree of consumer choice. The evaluation by Daniels et al. of the 1993–94 proposals (see chapter 9) gives the highest evaluation to the single-payer plan, lower marks to the Clinton proposal, and lowest marks to a market-oriented plan. Daniel et al. also conclude that the current trends (largely managed care and system integration; see chapter 10) would move the United States further away from fairness than any of the proposals considered in 1993–1994.

Baird[6] uses the concept of justice, in this case gender justice, to evaluate the U.S. health care system. The gender justice framework is summarized by Baird as follows:

> the framework of gender justice includes the principles of self-determination, which is composed of the criteria of self-development, recognition and democratic freedom; equality of gendered consequences; and diversity.[7]

Self-development refers to the ability of a policy to help people develop their capabilities. Recognition is accepting women's needs and experiences as legitimate, and respecting women. Democratic freedom refers to participating or determining actions that affect one's life. Equality of gendered consequences asks whether public policies, even those that are seemingly neutral, promote equality. Diversity recognizes differences between men and women, but also differences among women (minority versus white).

Others argue for the concept of a *right to health care*. Cust[8] contends that there is a moral right to health care, what he calls a *just minimum*. He writes that the moral right to health care is based on the fact that it can mean the difference between living and dying, and that it also affects a person's quality of life. The notion of rights, he continues, asserts an obligation to fulfill those rights. However, Cust, like Daniels et al., notes that the right is not unlimited because of resource constraints and the ever-increasing demand for heath care. Thus, he balances the moral right to health care with the notion of just minimum.

One aspect of this underlying issue is whether health care is a right, in the same way that there is a right to education (a state mandate). In most industrialized countries, health care is indeed considered a right. The United States and South Africa are the only industrialized countries without national health care systems.[9] And as we shall see, one of the problems to be discussed is the increasing number of people without health insurance.

Watson[10] argues that, at least for minorities, civil rights is at the base of health care inequities. He points to significant noneconomic barriers that lead to less access to health care and thus poorer health care for minorities. Thus, he advocates new civil rights legislation that would forbid discriminatory practices, including unintentional ones, "if they are not necessary to the provision of health care and if their goals cannot be substantially accomplished through less discriminatory alternatives."[11]

A human rights approach to health care, with similarities to the ideas discussed above, also provides justification for expanding access to health insurance and health care services. Chapman defines human rights as those rights people inherently have because they are human.[12] Human rights exist within the context of a community (see the discussion of community below) and are given high, though not absolute, priority. Chapman writes that these rights are "regarded as essential to the adequate functioning of the human being within the context of community and (society) accepts responsibility for its promotion and protection."[13] Thus there is the obligation on the part of society to fulfill those rights, though again there are limits to how much those rights, like some of the others we have discussed above, are fulfilled. Like Daniels et al., Chapman holds that health care as a human right would be limited to those services that would allow a person to function in society and to achieve his or her potential. Chapman goes further when she states that:

> The litmus test in this model of human rights is the extent to which the rights of the most vulnerable and disadvantaged individuals and groups are assured by these arrangements. A human rights standard assumes a special obligation or bias in favor of the needs and rights of the poor, the disadvantaged, the powerless, and those at the periphery of society.[14]

Aday argues that we should not base our health care system on a right to health care, which is within the individualistic, liberal tradition of American politics (see chapter 1). Instead, we should employ the notion of the common good, that it is in the best interest of the community, of society, not just the individual, that all its members have access to health care.[15] Kari, Boyte, and Jennings argue that health care should be seen as a civic question, where all participate in policy deliberations and emphasis should be placed on preventing disease and promoting health.[16]

Stone contends that in recent years, and for good financial reasons, the private insurance market has moved away from notions of community embodied in the civics and communitarian approach of Kari, Boyte, and Jennings. Insurance was originally intended as a means to spread the risk of individual misfortune among the larger community. Private insurers have increasingly sought to fragment the market, however, searching for those who are good health risks and placing more of the burden of financing care on those who are poor risks. This undermines the idea of community.[17]

The debates over national health insurance, Medicare, and health care reform are, in a sense, marked by notions of community. Do we help those who are vulnerable or disadvantaged, or is everyone on his or her own? The implications of the two choices are not trivial.

Jecker, likewise, suggests that the link between employment and health insurance itself creates injustices. She argues that there is discrimination in the distribution of jobs, focusing on gender-based discrimination, and that this creates discrepancies in the availability of health insurance. We consider the problems of women and the health care system in this chapter. As one example, consider that women are less likely to be employed in jobs that offer health insurance than men are.[18]

Thus, access to health care raises important ethical issues. What we must do now is document that the problems indeed do exist.

Uninsured and Underinsured

As noted, most people in the United States with health insurance have it through their jobs. In 1997, about 84.4 percent of the population were covered by health insurance (see Table 5.1). Of that 84.4 percent, about 23.2 percent were insured by public programs. Comparing the 1997 numbers with 1988, we see

Table 5.1

Sources of Health Insurance Coverage, 1988–1997

Year	Percent of population insured by all sources	Percent of total population insured through employer	Percent of total insured by employer	Percent of population insured by public insurance[a]	Percent of population with nongroup insurance
1988	87.3	61.5	70.4	20.8	5.0
1989	87.1	61.4	70.5	20.8	4.9
1990	87.0	61.3	70.5	20.6	5.1
1991	86.6	59.8	69.1	21.9	5.0
1992	86.4	58.8	68.1	22.8	4.8
1993	85.9	57.7	67.2	23.1	5.1
1994	85.3	57.0	66.8	22.9	5.4
1995	84.9	56.6	66.7	22.8	5.5
1996	84.5	55.7	65.9	23.1	5.7
1997	84.4	55.2	65.4	23.2	6.0

Source: Calculated from Health Insurance Association of America, *Sourcebook of Health Insurance Data, 1997–1998*, Health Insurance Association of America, Washington, D.C., 1998, 32.

[a]Includes Medicare, Medicaid, and the Civilian Health and Medical Program of the Uniformed Services (CHAMPUS).

that dependence on private insurance has gone down. Private insurance is generally linked to employment. Table 5.1 indicates that 55.2 percent of the population had employer-based insurance in 1997, compared to 61.5 percent in 1988. For those under sixty-five, employer-sponsored insurance in 1995 was 64.6 percent, a decline from 67.9 percent in 1990.[19]

Table 5.2 presents data about the number and percentage of uninsured persons. Note that the percentage of persons without insurance increased from 1988 to 1997 by about 22.8 percent. The number of uninsured persons increased by about 36 percent over the same period. The country's population increased by about 10.7 percent over the same time period; therefore, the increase in the uninsured population over and above general population increases was about 25 percent.[20] These numbers give an incomplete picture of the uninsurance problem. The data are, in a sense, a snapshot, a picture of those without insurance. A number of people experience spells of uninsurance during the year. One estimate is that about 27 percent of the population was without health insurance at some point during 1992–94, representing about 66.6 million people.[21] Another estimate was that some 51.3 million Americans were without health insurance for some time in 1993, most of them over four months.[22] Six percent of workers work in firms that offer health insurance but were not eligible for insurance. Fifty-four percent of these workers worked part time; 14 percent had not been in the job long enough (usually three to six months) to qualify for health insurance.[23]

Table 5.2

Number and Percentage of Uninsured Persons, 1988–1997

Year	Total uninsured (millions of people)	Total uninsured (percentage of population)
1988	30.6	12.7
1989	31.4	12.9
1990	32.0	13.0
1991	33.4	13.4
1992	34.2	13.6
1993	35.6	14.1
1994	38.2	14.7
1995	39.6	15.1
1996	41.0	15.5
1997	41.6	15.6

Source: Calculated from Health Insurance Association of America, *Sourcebook of Health Insurance Data, 1997–1998*, Health Insurance Association of America, Washington, D.C., 1998, 32.

The question to be raised is, why has health insurance coverage decreased? This is an important question, given two facts. One is that much health insurance coverage, as noted earlier, is linked to jobs. Second, such coverage has continued to decrease in the 1990s, even as job expansion has been impressive (9.3 percent increase from 1992 to 1997). The unemployment rate declined from 7.3 percent in 1992 to 4.3 percent by May 1998.[24]

One way of looking at this is to consider employment-based insurance for children. In 1996, about 64 percent of children, according to one estimate, were covered under private insurance, most of that through a parent's employer.[25] It should be noted that the number of children without any coverage has remained stable because of expansions in Medicaid, though a number of Medicaid-eligible children are not covered.[26] Seldin, Banthin, and Cohen estimate that about 4.7 million children who are eligible for Medicaid are not covered by the program.[27] The numbers show that the unique basis of medical insurance in the United States is declining.[28] Why?

The answer lies partly in the restructuring of the American economy. Insurance coverage is linked to size and type of firm. Larger firms are much more likely to offer health insurance than smaller firms. Almost 90 percent of firms with one thousand or more employees have health insurance, compared to about 86 percent in firms of twenty-five to ninety-nine employees. Among the smallest firms, under twenty-five employees, less than 72 percent have insurance.[29] Much of the growth in jobs has been in smaller businesses, exactly those that are less likely to offer health insurance.

Why is there so much more insurance coverage in larger as opposed to smaller firms? While there is probably more turnover in smaller firms, the size factor is most important. The idea behind insurance is to spread or pool the risk over a large population. Insurance companies view each individual firm or individual buyer as a self-contained unit, instead of pooling all those covered under the insurance company's policies. Therefore, smaller firms have more difficulty in negotiating favorable rates for their employees than do larger companies. Their costs per employee are higher than in larger firms. Further, when faced with rising health insurance costs, small firms are more likely to drop the benefit entirely rather than turn to managed care or self-insurance.[30]

Another reason there has been erosion in employer-based health insurance has to do with the sectors of the economy that are growing and shrinking. Manufacturing firms and unionized firms (with much overlapping) are more likely to offer insurance than service-based or agricultural firms. The service sector has experienced considerable growth, while the manufacturing sector and unionization has shrunk.[31]

Consider the following numbers. In 1970, some 20.7 million workers were in the manufacturing sector; by 1996, that number had declined to 20.5 million, a decrease of about 1.1 percent. By contrast, 20.4 million workers were in the service sector in 1970; by 1996, that number had increased to a little over 45 million workers, an increase of over 120 percent. Another way of looking at this is to compare the relative shares of manufacturing and service workers. In 1970, the share of workers in manufacturing was 26.4 percent; in 1996, that share had declined to 16.2 percent. The share of workers in the service sector in 1970 was 25.9 percent, a little less than the manufacturing share. But by 1996, the service-sector share of jobs had increased to 35.6 percent.[32] Thus, if there is less likelihood that the service sector will offer health insurance than the manufacturing sector, it is understandable why fewer workers have health insurance.[33]

One other element to this picture needs to be addressed. In the 1990s, the manufacturing sector began an impressive recovery, both from the recession of 1990–91 and from the impact of foreign competition. But the recovery did not translate into new jobs because corporations engaged in restructuring themselves, captured in terms such as "reengineering" and especially "downsizing."[34] Again, industrial recovery did not translate into more new jobs of the type that usually come with health insurance. As a result of all this, fewer firms are offering health insurance as a benefit. In 1990, 10.6 percent of workers in the manufacturing sector were uninsured; by 1995 that figured had risen to 13.5 percent.[35]

A related problem concerns younger retirees, those between fifty-five and sixty-five. Many such retirees once maintained their health care plans with their former companies. But the same trends can be seen: companies are increasingly withdrawing such coverage. Over half of the early retirees are in danger of losing their benefits.[36]

There are three other components to our understanding of the growth of the uninsured population. First is the growth in part-time or temporary workers. These are also unlikely to have health insurance, even if they work in firms that offer it to their full-time employees.[37] Second, a number of uninsured workers are covered as dependents under their spouses' health insurance. To the extent that this is the case, then the fact that not all firms offer health insurance is not quite as much of a problem. In 1991, some 89 million workers had health insurance and another 21 million workers had insurance as dependents of other workers.[38] Some of these 21 million are workers in jobs that offer health insurance, about 11 percent of workers in such jobs.[39] On the other hand, this amounts to a subsidy from firms that offer health insurance to firms that do not. Additionally, because of the changing job structure situation, sectors that provide dependent coverage are also shrinking, so it is not just those with insurance-covered jobs but the dependents in non-insurance-covered jobs that are losing coverage.[40]

Another part of the explanation for the uninsurance problem is that Medicaid, the health care program for the poor, covers only about 50 percent of those with incomes under the poverty line.[41] The federal poverty line is just an indicator, a measure (and a somewhat controversial one) of the number of people living in poverty.[42] Medicaid eligibility is set by states, and Medicaid is a costly program for them, even though the federal government picks up over half the costs. Medicaid increases combined with other budget pressures, including spending on crime and education, and resistance to tax increases led to efforts to constrain spending (see chapter 3 and chapter 10). Despite expansion of Medicaid coverage for children (chapter 3), many children still remain uninsured.[43]

But there is a more fundamental reason for people's being uninsured: Health insurance is expensive.[44] This is one of the reasons, discussed earlier, smaller firms are less likely to offer health insurance than larger firms. If it is difficult for small firms to afford insurance because of the small pool of workers, then it is even more difficult for individuals to afford it.[45] Such plans are not only costly in terms of premiums but are likely to have significant cost-sharing provisions.

One last aspect remains. The section heading refers to the uninsured and the underinsured. The underinsured are those who have health insurance but whose insurance is inadequate for their present or future needs. This refers especially to those who may have illnesses such as AIDS or multiple sclerosis, chronic diseases that are potentially expensive to cover. There have been cases in which an insured person was denied coverage after contracting HIV, the virus that leads to AIDS.[46]

Profiling the Uninsured

The obvious picture of the uninsured is that they should be poor. Insurance coverage is linked to income: those with lower incomes are less likely to be insured than those with higher incomes.[47] In terms of income, using 1995 data, over 36 percent of the uninsured had incomes below the poverty line and 66 percent had incomes below 200 percent of the poverty line.[48] The largest increase in uninsured persons from 1990–95 were in households with incomes between $50,000 and $60,000.[49]

A sizable number of uninsured people were in households where there were workers. Part-time workers had very high uninsurance or noncoverage rates, 22.4 percent as compared to 16.3 percent for full-time workers. Poor, full-time workers had a very high uninsurance rate, 52.2 percent.[50] Some 49 percent of the uninsured work in small firms or are self-employed.[51] "The profile of the uninsured is predominantly a picture of working people and their families. Most uninsured people—84 percent—are workers or the dependents of workers who do not receive health insurance through their jobs."[52] Younger adults were more likely to be uninsured than other age groups. Minorities and foreign-born people (especially noncitizens) had high uninsurance rates.[53]

Indeed, the increase in the number of uninsured working people accounts for most of the increase in the number of uninsured people. And welfare reform (see chapter 3 on Medicaid) exacerbates this situation. Though those leaving welfare can keep Medicaid for up to two years, they tend to move into precisely the kinds of jobs that do not provide health insurance.[54]

Consequences of Uninsurance or Underinsurance

There is a simple and easy, though not pleasant, answer to the question of the consequences of inadequate or no insurance. That answer is that such people are at higher risk of disease and death and are less likely to receive the services they need than are those who have insurance. This section documents that claim.

Uninsured people suffering from acute diseases are less likely, about a third less likely, to see a physician than those with acute illnesses who have health insurance.[55] For example, uninsured and Medicaid patients suffering from appendicitis are more likely to experience a ruptured appendix than privately insured patients.[56]

One common finding is that those lacking insurance also do not have a regular private physician. Therefore, they often use emergency rooms, particularly in public hospitals, as their primary source of care.[57] One result of delaying needed physician visits is that Medicaid patients and those without insurance are more likely to be hospitalized for conditions that could be avoided or treated outside hospitals than those with private insurance.[58] Uninsured hospital patients are more likely to enter hospitals sicker and have shorter stays and fewer procedures performed on them than privately insured patients. They also have a higher death rate than insured patients.[59]

Perhaps the most important impact is on children. Children whose families lack health insurance are less likely to see a physician than children in families with insurance.[60] Typical and treatable maladies of childhood, such as ear and throat infections, may go untreated and worsen.[61]

Further, barriers other than lack of insurance may hinder needed physician visits. These include cost-sharing provisions, lack of transportation, and lack of child care.[62] The General Accounting Office expressed the problem this way:

> But having health insurance is no guarantee that children will get appropriate, high-quality care. Some children live in families that do not understand the need for preventive care or do not know how to seek high-quality care. Some live in neighborhoods that have few health care providers, where they have to travel further and wait longer for care. Some live in families in which most of the members do not speak English or defer getting care because they have had difficulty getting care previously. Some children have health insurance that does not cover some of the services they need the most—such as dental care or physical therapy for the developmentally disabled. . . . Such barriers can reduce the likelihood that even insured children will get the care they need.[63]

Lack of insurance may affect the most helpless of people, newly born babies. Uninsured women are less likely to receive prenatal care than are privately insured women.[64] Uninsured (and Medicaid-insured) babies are likely to be discharged from hospitals sooner than privately insured babies. This is the case even though uninsured or Medicaid-insured babies experience more serious health problems than privately insured babies.[65]

The presence of health insurance also has an impact on the diagnosis of breast cancer. Women who have no health insurance or are covered by Medicaid are more likely to have breast cancer diagnosed later in the progression of the disease and are more likely to die as a result than women with breast cancer who have private health insurance.[66]

Quality of care for uninsured people is often lower than for those with insurance, particularly private insurance. Injuries resulting from negligence or substandard care appeared to be higher, according to a 1984 study in New York State, than for those with insurance.[67]

Those without health insurance also perceive themselves as less healthy than those with insurance.[68] Death rates may be higher for those who lack health insurance than for those with it. This may be because of both lack of access to medical care and lower quality of care when it is received.[69]

Uninsurance and underinsurance have impacts beyond those of the individual. Because uninsured people are more likely to use expensive emergency rooms than to use a regular physician, the cost of that care is shifted to others. Indeed, hospitals in particular engage in considerable cost shifting, given service to the uninsured and the low reimbursement rates for Medicaid patients. Those with private insurance are charged more (and pay higher premiums) because of such cost shifting. Because of the Medicare hospital Prospective Payment System (PPS), discussed in chapter 4, shifting costs to Medicare patients is virtually impossible. Given this cost shifting, portions of the community pay for uninsured care, but not on an explicit basis. Further, the use of underwriting creates a situation where those who most need the help are least likely to get it. That runs against the grain of the purpose of insurance.

Further, use of emergency rooms and trauma centers by uninsured patients places a heavy demand on those facilities.[70] Because of uncompensated care, hospitals and trauma centers face financial problems.[71] A further insight into the problem is that about a fifth of the uninsured people using emergency rooms are pregnancy- and childbirth-related cases and often do not get needed prenatal care.[72] The managed care revolution, discussed in chapter 10, may exacerbate some of these tendencies. Indeed, in the 1990s, while the number of uninsured people increased, the "relative amount of uncompensated care provided by hospitals" did not increase. Rather, fewer hospitals provided such care, and those that did provide it, especially public hospitals, faced significant financial pressures.[73]

There are responses to being uninsured or inadequately insured. One is financial difficulty and one way of handling such financial catastrophe is bankruptcy, much of it related to credit card debt. It appears that medical expenses are one cause of the increase in bankruptcy filings.[74]

What do underinsured people do to compensate for their potential financial risk? They face high premiums, coinsurance, and deductibles; stringent screening for preexisting conditions; exclusions of specific conditions; and limitations on maximum insurance benefits. Kinney and Steinmetz argue that they form essentially an "insurance underground." These authors studied people who suffered from multiple sclerosis in Indiana and found various coping strategies. These included staying in jobs so as not to lose insurance coverage ("job lock") and avoiding filing claims that would call attention to their condition. The result is even more inadequate insurance coverage and access to care, and aggravation of the chronic health problem.[75]

Another response to lack of adequate insurance, especially in this new age of managed care, is that more families are becoming caregivers, sometimes for their elderly parents (see chapter 4 on Medicare) but often for a child or spouse.[76]

Insurance and the Idea of Community

This brings us back to the issue of equity. Most health insurance provisions are put in place regardless of income. Consider a company that offers a health insurance plan covering dependents. The premiums are $200 a month and there are cost-sharing provisions. All employees are offered the same plan. The general manager of the company makes $100,000 a year and the janitor makes $15,000. Both have to pay the $200 monthly premium. The premium is only 2.4 percent of the general manager's income, but is 16 percent of the janitor's income. Now extend this example to those who try to buy health insurance as individuals rather than as part of a group. The premiums might be four times as high as in a group plan and the cost-sharing provisions less generous. The result is that "individuals and families with lower incomes who do seek medical care will spend a greater proportion of their income just to meet the cost-sharing requirements."[77]

There is another way in which ethical issues play a role in the uninsurance and underinsurance problem. This is the problem, briefly mentioned at the beginning of this chapter, of changes in insurance company policies. To simplify, health insurance policies can take two forms. On the one hand is community rating. This exists when everybody in the insurance pool pays the same premiums (though there may be differences based on age and other such factors, a practice known as risk adjustment). That way, the risk of using the insurance (needing health care) is spread over a larger population. Larger firms are more likely to have community rating than smaller firms. Because the pool of employees is larger, there is a larger group of workers over which to spread the risk. Smaller firms, with fewer workers, have a smaller group over which to spread the risk. Insurance companies could handle the problem by treating all those it insures as the community, so it would not matter whether the firm was large or small, or the policy was for an individual or a group. Note that pooling risk for individual policies by definition cannot be done.

There has been an increasing tendency for insurance companies to write policies based on experience rating. Under experience rating, the premiums are adjusted based on the likely risk of needing health care. A person with a chronic heart problem, for example, is more likely to need health care than one in good health with no chronic problems. Automobile insurance is written on this basis. Premiums are higher for those in the highest-risk groups. This includes those who have been in accidents and those in groups most likely to have accidents. For example, young single males have the highest auto insurance premiums of any group.

Such a practice makes sense from the standpoint of the insurance company, as well as policyholders in low-risk groups. Those more likely to need the service should pay more. Having community rating in auto insurance would mean higher rates for those in the low-risk groups and lower rates for those in the high-risk groups.

But health care and health insurance are not automobile insurance. People in good health can do more, can realize more of their potential, than those in poor health. Health care is instrumental in the sense that it enables one to do other things. If there is a systematic bias through community rating, then it carries over into other areas.

Stone brings the debate of community versus experience rating out into the open, looking at its philosophical underpinnings.

> Actuarial fairness—each person paying for his own risk—is more than an idea about distributive justice. It is a method of organizing mutual aid by fragmenting communities into ever-smaller, more homogeneous groups and a method that leads ultimately to the destruction of mutual aid. This fragmentation must be accomplished by fostering in people a sense of their differences, rather than their commonalities, and their responsibility for themselves only, rather than their interdependence. Moreover, insurance necessarily operates on the logic of actuarial fairness when it, in turn, is organized as a competitive market.[78]

Others have also noted the impact of the trend toward experience rating.[79]

The important idea here is that the insurance practice of experience rating breaks down the idea of community. This argument would support at a minimum insurance reform and at a maximum national health insurance. In-between policies might include tax subsidies and employer mandates.

There is another insurance practice, very much related to experience rating, that leads to some people being uninsured and others being underinsured. This is the practice of insurance underwriting. Underwriting occurs when an insurance company refuses to insure workers in an entire firm (a practice known as "redlining") or individuals with preexisting conditions. Examples of redlined firms include "those characterized by an older work force (over age fifty-five) or high employee turnover, those engaged in seasonal work or exposed to hazardous working conditions, those lacking an employer-employee relationship, and those 'known to present frequent claims submissions.'"[80] Those with preexisting conditions, such as cancer or AIDS, and those with conditions that are likely to result in costly claims in the future, may be denied insurance either permanently or during a specified time. In addition, limits may be placed on payments to such individuals. An alternative practice is to raise all the premiums for the groups significantly, sometimes to prohibitive levels.[81] It is not just insurance companies that engage in this practice. Employers that self-insure, and thus do not come under state regulation as do insurance companies, can also deny claims.

Apart from causing some people to be without insurance, others may be underinsured. Kinney and Steinmetz provide a definition and estimate of underinsurance, based on the 1990 Pepper Commission report: "those at risk of spending more than 10 percent of their annual income for health care in the event of serious illness."[82] Their estimate is that 20 million Americans are thus underinsured.

A Closer Look: Women and Minorities

In this section, we consider the health care problems of the disadvantaged, focusing on the poor, minorities, and women. To some extent, the material in this section overlaps with that in the previous section on the uninsured and the underinsured. But as we have noted, a sizable portion of the uninsured are not poor and do work. There are thus other problems that need to be addressed.

Minorities and Low-Income Groups

In general, minorities and low-income groups do not have the same access to health care, or do not compare on the same level on health statistics as those who are white and/or wealthier. In drawing this portrait of low-income and minority groups, we should point out that this is a statistical portrait. It applies in general to the groups discussed.

In looking at the health status of minority and low-income groups, we should note several important features. First, minority groups tend to have lower educational achievement, higher unemployment rates, higher crime rates, lower incomes and therefore higher poverty rates, higher proportions of female-headed families, and higher proportions of out-of-wedlock births. All of this seems to be correlated with health status. One of the confusing aspects of these data is that they are very much related to income. That is, many of these characteristics may be a result of poverty (socioeconomic class) rather than ethnicity (race).[83]

One issue related to low-income groups suggests that their poorer health status is largely attributable to "risky" behaviors that they engage in, such as smoking, drinking, being overweight, and not exercising. In a sense, this is an argument that can be labeled "blaming the victim."[84] That is, this hypothesis suggests that higher mortality rates are due to actions taken (or not taken) by each person. A study reported in the June 3, 1998, issue of *JAMA* found that even considering such behaviors, low-income groups had higher mortality rates than higher income groups. Changing the behaviors would certainly help some, but mortality differences would remain.[85]

McBride argues that health care policy toward blacks went through three stages. The first stage was engagement (mid-1960s to late 1970s), where health care services and financing were increased to the black community and discrimination was lessened. The second phase, submersion, from the late 1970s to the mid-1980s, saw a cutback in social programs. For example, as a result of the 1981 Omnibus Budget and Reconciliation Act, the working poor were taken off AFDC and Medicaid rolls. The third phase, crisis recognition, began in the mid-1980s. This is a recognition that there is a problem, particularly in the large urban cities. But McBride points out that this last phase has not yet resulted in changed policies. Thus the health care problems of minorities and low-income groups remain.[86] Indeed, a study of Chicago, Houston, and Los Angeles noted "the progressive deterioration in the delivery of health care to the poor and the indigent since the beginnings of the 1980s."[87]

Age-adjusted death rates are higher for minorities than for whites. Minorities tend to have less access to prenatal care and to give birth at earlier ages. This tends to result in higher rates of premature births and low-weight births. The low-birth-weight problem shows little change. There is, additionally, much variation within the Latino population. Puerto Rican women had the highest rate of low-weight births, while women from Mexico and Central and South America had low-weight birth rates close to the white rate.[88] Low-weight births in turn are associated with other problems (not just health) in later years. Infant mortality is higher among minorities. Indeed, the infant mortality rate among African Americans was comparable to the infant mortality rate in Costa Rica.[89]

Why do disadvantaged women not get full prenatal care? One reason is financial barriers. Minority and low-income women are less likely to have health insurance than the general population.[90] Clarke et al. find that minority women are somewhat less likely to receive prenatal care than white women, are more likely to begin such care in the third trimester of pregnancy, and are more likely to receive inadequate care. With a few exceptions, those living in rural areas are less likely to receive adequate services than those living in metropolitan areas.[91] African Americans compose about almost 13 percent of the population and account for over 17 percent of the uninsured. Latinos, less than 10 percent of the population, compose almost 20 percent of the uninsured.[92] Even though Medicaid has been expanded in recent years (since 1986) to cover more prenatal care, many states have not taken the appropriate action. Further, even if all the states covered the entire poverty population of expectant mothers (100 percent of those under the poverty line), those just over the poverty line would still be excluded. It should be noted again that even with expansions in the late 1980s and early 1990s, Medicaid covered less than half of those under the federal poverty line.[93]

Even if financial barriers did not exist, there are not enough doctors willing to work in low-income areas or with high-risk mothers. According to one report, fewer than one-third of the nation's doctors participate fully in Medicaid.[94] The Medicaid participation problem is most serious in the case of pediatricians and obstetricians.[95] Thus the services, even if affordable, might not be available.

Minorities also fare worse than the overall population in terms of chronic illnesses.

In general, Blacks are diagnosed and/or seek treatment later than Whites for many chronic diseases, and this may have significant implications for the efficacy of treatment and for survivorship for many chronic diseases. What is more, once under medical management or therapy, the treatment received by Blacks may be less aggressive than that received by Whites.[96]

For example, studies show that African-American women with breast cancer are less likely to receive surgery and more likely to receive no treatment than whites. A study of bladder cancer victims showed that African Americans were less likely to receive treatment than whites at similar stages of disease.[97]

Another health problem of minorities, though it may not appear that way, is homicide rates. Homicide rates of African-American males are 544 percent higher than those of white males. They are also higher for Latinos, though the difference is not as great.[98]

AIDS is another health problem that affects ethnicity differently. While a majority of AIDS victims are whites, the relative proportion of AIDS victims is twice as high among African Americans and Latinos as among whites.[99] The major transmission categories for AIDS are drug related (i.e., intravenous drug users). For minority women, having sex with someone who uses drugs is a major source of the disease.[100] Further, African Americans are less likely to have health insurance at the same time that they are at greater risk of getting AIDS.[101]

The use of health services for minorities increased beginning in the 1960s with the advent of Medicaid. Nevertheless, such utilization remains below that of whites. Further, minorities are less likely to have a private physician and more likely to seek primary care in hospital emergency rooms.[102] Cutbacks in Medicaid during the 1980s led to a decreased use of services among minorities.[103] Estimates are that just 41 percent of the population below the poverty line were covered by Medicaid and only about half of children in families below the poverty line.[104] Miller and Curtis note that even programs such as Medicare, where essentially all who are sixty-five or older have insurance coverage, have not reduced disparities between blacks and whites in the use of health services.[105]

Ginzberg argues that much of the problem of access to health care is not just the result of lack of insurance but has a supply dimension: the expansiveness of the state Medicaid program and the availability of institutions, largely public, that treat charity cases. New York City saw less deterioration in services for the poor because of the generous New York State Medicaid program, a large public hospital system, and voluntary hospitals that regularly treat uninsured patients. In contrast, Chicago saw the closing of eleven hospitals in the inner city, while Houston had both a restrictive Medicaid program (the Texas program was limited only to recipients of AFDC) combined with the lack of a tradition of charity cases being treated by voluntary hospitals.[106]

Ginzberg also notes that the number of physicians is much lower in impoverished neighborhoods than in wealthier areas. In the four cities studied, the physician-to-population ratio varied from one physician for every 10,000 residents to one per 15,000 residents. In the wealthier areas, the ratio was about one per 300 residents.[107] Thus, wealthier areas had thirty-three to fifty times more private physicians than poorer areas. Part of this reflects low Medicaid reimbursement rates. Further, "the majority of practitioners serving the poor consisted of foreign medical graduates, many with indifferent professional competence and language problems that impeded effective patient-physician communication."[108] One result is that useful medical and surgical procedures are often less available in minority, inner-city communities.[109]

The strongest perspective suggests that the American health care system shares characteristics with the South African health care system under apartheid. While the South African system was based on explicit racial segregation, the American system is based on socioeconomic differences. But again because of higher percentages of minorities in the lower socioeconomic classes, the effect is the same. Further, the fragmentation of the American health care system furthers the comparison. "Well babies may be seen at one location, but immunizations must be obtained at a different site, while ill children must travel to different clinics or county hospitals."[110] Most striking about the comparisons are health indicators. Both blacks in South Africa and in the United States have high infant mortality rates and high rates of preventable diseases.[111]

Americans of Latino descent appear to have the lowest level of health insurance coverage of any ethnic group, including blacks. Further, there are differences in health insurance coverage within the Latino population, with Puerto Ricans and Cubans having considerably higher levels of coverage than other Latinos.[112] Latinos also suffer from high rates of chronic diseases, such as cancer, diabetes, and AIDS.[113]

One important and careful study of the quality of care shows that neither race, gender, nor income status was associated with poor quality, defined as adverse events and negligence leading to adverse events. What was important was insurance status: those with no insurance suffered poorer-quality care. To the extent that minorities and low-income groups have high rates of uninsurance, then they are affected by quality of care.[114] An additional perspective suggests that cultural barriers for non-English-speaking patients appear to be minimal. The problem appears to be the structure of the health care system.[115]

It should be obvious by this time that the problem of the poor and the disadvantaged transcends the problem of lack of insurance. Privately insured expectant mothers begin prenatal care earlier than Medicaid-insured expectant mothers. "Thus, even when prenatal visits are provided free of charge, barriers such as transportation costs, lack of understanding of the importance of prenatal care, unfriendly or poorly organized clinics, poor scheduling, long waiting times, and inadequate social support inhibit access to care."[116]

One way to improve access to doctors, particularly for Medicaid patients, is to increase Medicaid reimbursements at least up to the level of Medicare reimbursements. Rowland and Salganicoff note that Medicaid reimbursements in general are 66 percent of Medicare reimbursements, and for pediatricians and obstetricians are about 55 percent of what private patients pay.[117] Such a change would increase participation in Medicaid. But increasing physician reimbursements (from $1.12 billion to $3.23 billion) makes such a policy difficult when states seek to reduce Medicaid expenditures. Because of the low percentages of physicians located in underserved areas, however, the problem of access will remain unless steps are taken to increase the number of doctors in those areas.[118] It is not clear that moving Medicaid recipients into managed care will successfully address this problem.

One last perspective, one that applies also to women: African Americans are relatively less likely to be included in medical research than are whites. Two reasons for this include distrust of the medical community on the part of the African-American community,[119] and lack of regular access to care, among other factors.[120]

Women

> [T]he issues of women's health cannot be understood only in biological terms, as simply the ills of the female of the species. Women and men are different, but we are also similar—and we both are divided by the social relations of class and race/ethnicity. To begin to understand how our social constitution affects our health, we must ask, repeatedly, what is different and what is similar across the social divides of gender, color, and class. We cannot assume that biology alone will provide the answers we need; instead, we must reframe the issues in the context of the social shaping of our human lives—as both biological creatures and historical actors. Otherwise, we will continue to mistake—as many before us have done—what is for what must be , and leave unchallenged the social forces that continue to create vast inequalities in health.[121]

To a degree, women's health issues overlap those of minorities (race/ethnicity) and low-income groups (class). To the extent that women's income, especially in families headed by women, is low, then all the health problems associated with low income show up here. For example, issues surrounding prenatal care, briefly discussed above, while obviously a concern for women, are generally associated with low income. If programs aimed at low-income people are cut, as was done in the early 1980s and may again be done in the late 1990s, then women will be affected.

On the other hand, there are certain issues that are unique to women, though of concern to men as well. Reproductive issues, such as abortion and family planning, are among the most controversial issues in health care or any policy field. In general, the availability of abortion, while not completely eliminated, has been reduced beginning in the late 1970s. Some of this has come about because of legislative changes, such as the Hyde amendment forbidding the use of federal Medicaid funds for abortion and similar action by some states. Some is a result of court decisions that have allowed restrictions, such as waiting periods. Another element has been the strong right-to-life movement, which has picketed abortion clinics. Medical schools are less frequently teaching abortion procedures.

Women are also less well protected by health insurance, both public and private. Fewer working women (37 percent) have employer-based health insurance than men (56 percent).[122] Baird notes that married men have higher rates of employer-provided insurance than married women. She also notes that divorce has a devastating effect on private health insurance for unemployed women. Women's employment careers tend to be intermittent (i.e., women may take time off for childbearing, or they may make job changes because their husbands move), and women are more often in lower-paying jobs that are less likely to offer health insurance.[123] Medicaid coverage is sporadic. Fewer than half those eligible are covered, and doctors do not have to accept Medicaid patients. Women are less likely than men to have supplemental Medicare health insurance and are less likely to have their illnesses covered under Medicare.[124] Further, because women, on the average, live longer than men, issues of long-term care and chronic illnesses are critical.[125]

The above paragraph probably understates the problem. First, the percentage of workers covered by employer-based health insurance has declined. Further, there is a growing trend toward using part-time or temporary workers, also unlikely to have health insurance benefits.

There have been changes in the workforce participation of women and in the family structure, where there are two-worker families or where the family is headed by a female. Adjustments to these changes have been slow (the Family Leave Act is one recent adjustment). Muller states:

> Independent coverage, benefit content and duplication, and cost sharing are issues that affect women differently in different family situations. Employ-

ers have expanded their use of peripheral or contingent workers who have few or no benefit entitlements, drawing on a largely female labor supply. It is not feasible to count on workplace arrangements as the social instrument for protecting individuals against health care costs.[126]

There is another important concern. There is some tendency for both private insurance and Medicare to reimburse at a lower rate for procedures unique to women. A study of gender-specific procedures by Barbara Goff et al. found that Medicare relative value units (RVUs; see chapter 4) were 50 percent higher for male-specific procedures than for a similar set of female-specific procedures. Furthermore, private insurance tends to use the RVU scale, and so whatever bias is found with the Medicare scale is replicated in the private sector.[127] One more example: The male-impotency drug Viagra was immediately covered by many insurance plans, but prescription contraceptives for women are covered by fewer than half of employer-based health insurance plans.[128]

The health care system treats women differently from men. Medicare tends to cover the kinds of diseases more predominant among men (i.e., heart attacks) better than the chronic diseases more prevalent among women. Men receive more preventive services than women. Women also tend to see a number of specialists, and so their care is often fragmented. Two observers label women's health care as a "patchwork quilt with gaps."[129]

Further, as Hafner-Eaton points out, women are likely to have unnecessary surgeries, such as caesarean births, radical mastectomies, and hysterectomies.[130] Despite this, much of the health research carried on in the United States uses the male as the model. Hafner-Eaton writes:

> Government notwithstanding, the National Institutes of Health, as recently as 1990, allocated a mere 13.5% of biomedical research funds to women's health. The remainder of funds went to research on men's health or research affecting both. . . . Women's different hormonal balance from men's means that pharmaceuticals used to treat jointly shared conditions might not work, or, worse yet, could be seriously injurious if used as tested safely on men. The use of the male body and its reactions as the norm has detrimental consequences for women and many times for their children as well.[131]

This bias in research has been somewhat alleviated. In 1991, the U.S. Public Health Service and other federal agencies began to devote more resources to research on women.[132] But the National Institutes of Health (NIH) research plan has been criticized for focusing too much on the trivial.[133] In some cases, women have engaged in interest group activity to lobby for more medical research on women's issue. Perhaps the most prominent of these efforts focused on breast cancer.[134]

A related area in women's health that needs further funding is lung cancer. Lung cancer affects more women than breast cancer and has been rising fairly consistently since the 1960s. The survival rate for lung cancer (14 percent) is much lower than that for breast cancer (67 percent). Federally allocated funds for breast cancer research are about six times higher than those for lung cancer research.[135]

There is also some evidence to suggest that women are not nearly as disadvantaged by the health care system and in research as suggested above.[136] Women seek care more frequently than men. The care received by women is at least as good as men's, and there is some tendency for women to receive more diagnostic tests than men. There is a gender difference in cardiac bypass procedures, largely because men who need the procedure tend to be younger (and thus to have fewer additional medical problems) and to have larger arteries (making the operation easier) than women.

Kadar points out that much innovative medical technology, such as ultrasound, was originally developed for women. He notes that women have a branch of medicine devoted strictly to them (gynecology) whereas men do not (urology probably being the closest).[137]

It was mentioned earlier that only a small fraction of NIH medical research was conducted on women. Kadar observes that much medical research uses both men and women as subjects; only about 6.5 percent of NIH research is devoted solely to men. As an example, the highest level of research funded by the National Cancer Institute is on breast cancer. By comparison, research on prostate cancer received only about a fourth as much funding as breast cancer research.[138]

Finally, Kadar mentions that at the beginning of the twentieth century, men had a slightly longer life expectancy than women. By the second half of the twentieth century, the life expectancy of women was about 10 percent higher then for men. One of the reasons for the change is that childbirth has become safer. A second reason is that many infectious diseases have been virtually eliminated, and those that remain affect men more than women.[139]

Granting Kadar's argument would mean that specific gender problems in health care are drastically overstated. To the extent that women are subject to the forces of ethnicity and class, however, the health of women remains an important concern.

Solutions to the Problem of Uninsurance and Underinsurance

One possible solution to the problem of those without health insurance or those who are underinsured is to expand Medicaid. This was mentioned by George Bush in 1988. There are some advantages to such a proposal, variations of which have been offered by the American Medical Association, the Health Insurance Association of America, the American Public Welfare Association, and the Health Policy Agenda for the American People.[140] Even with the expansions of Medicaid directed at children (see chapter 3), some 2.7 million children who were eligible for Medicaid coverage were not covered by either Medicaid or private insurance.[141] In the summer of 1997, as part of the Balanced Budget Act, Congress created the State Children's Health Insurance Program (S-CHIP), designed to cover children in medically indigent families. It is the states' responsibility to decide how to cover the children, whether through Medicaid or through some other mechanism. We consider the S-CHIP program in more detail in chapters 3 and 10.

Medicaid could be extended to medically indigent adults, but this seems unlikely at this point. While the administrative structure is already in place, and the adults could "buy in" to Medicaid, the costs to both the federal government and the states remain a stumbling block.[142]

Medicaid also offers a richer package of benefits (though lower provider-reimbursement rates) than private plans. This, combined with limitations on patient cost sharing, could encourage people to move from private insurance to Medicaid.[143] But there is another danger of expanding Medicaid. There is evidence, mentioned in this chapter and in chapter 3, that Medicaid patients do not have the same access to services as do either privately insured patients or Medicare recipients. This is because low Medicaid reimbursement rates lead to low physician participation in the program. Thus expansion of Medicaid might help the newly covered be insured but not necessarily provide more access.

A companion proposal would expand Medicare, essentially creating a "Part C" that would cover those not insured. It would have the same advantage as mentioned above concerning Medicaid: the structure is already in place. It would add two further advantages. First, Medicare is entirely a federal government program, so the fiscal impact on and program differences between states would not be a problem. Second, provider reimbursement is higher for Medicare than for Medicaid. Thus access to services would be greater. As we noted in chapter 4, President Bill Clinton proposed expanding Medicare to early retirees (55-64) who did not have health insurance and allowing them to "buy in" to the program. But the proposal stood little chance of passage. Given budgetary pressures, even with the new budget surpluses that appeared in the late 1990s, the long-term Medicare problems due to the aging of the baby boom generation have yet to be resolved.[144]

A proposal designed to address the "job lock" problem is the Health Insurance Portability and Accountability Act (the Kassebaum-Kennedy bill) passed in 1996. This bill guarantees the availability of health insurance to people changing jobs, though it does not guarantee affordable rates. This act is discussed in more detail in chapter 10.

Another proposal, typical of conservative and Republican proposals as opposed to the more liberal and Democratic Medicaid and Medicare proposals discussed above, would make use of tax credits and tax deductions. Tax credits would be available to the poor, and deductions to middle-income families (including the self-employed).[145] Such tax incentives would be provided to both individuals and employers.[146]

One problem that would have to be faced with the tax deduction approach is that health care and, concomitantly, insurance premiums would rise faster than the deduction, even if the deduction were indexed to cost-of-living changes.[147] Another problem with the proposal is that it does not guarantee coverage.

An example of such a tax credit-based bill is the 1991 plan offered by the conservative Heritage Foundation. Butler argues that the major problem of the health care system, at least as concerns the problem of the uninsured, is the tax code.[148] The tax code allows employers to treat health insurance as a business expense eligible for a tax deduction. This leads to three major problems, two of which are relevant to the uninsurance problem.

The first problem is that the system is inequitable. Assume that health insurance as a fringe benefit is part of the total employee compensation package. If this is so, then the cost of the health insurance if given as salary would be taxed at the highest marginal tax rate. Because high-wage workers are taxed at higher marginal rates than low-wage workers, the benefit would be highest for the high-wage workers. For those who must pay their own health insurance, the inequity is greater because they have only a limited tax deduction and thus must pay more from after-tax dollars.[149]

The second problem mentioned by Butler is "job lock," in which people keep their jobs for fear of losing health insurance coverage. By tying health insurance to employment, the tax code creates strong bonds between worker and job, a problem presumably dealt with by the Kassebaum-Kennedy bill. The final problem created by the tax code, though it is not directly related to the uninsurance problem, is that it creates inflationary pressures by severing the link between paying for the service and receiving it.[150]

The Heritage Foundation plan would eliminate the employer tax deduction for health care and replace it with a refundable tax credit for individuals. The tax credit would be available even to those who do not itemize their tax returns. If the health care tax credit were greater than the individual's tax obligation, the difference would be refunded to that individual. The credit would be geared toward the portion of family income spent on health care (insurance and out-of-pocket costs). If a family spent 10 percent of its income on health care, it would be eligible for a 20 percent tax credit.[151]

One interesting part of the proposal is the "health care social contract." Under the contract, all families would be required to join a health plan with a minimum package of benefits. Though Butler does not use the term, this plan is thus an individual mandate, rather than an employee mandate. The federal government would be part of the contract by guaranteeing the fiscal viability of the individual mandate, either through tax credits or through access to Medicaid and/or Medicare.[152]

The plan has important advantages. It severs the tie between work and health insurance. Employers would no longer have to worry about the increasing costs of health care and workers would not be tied to a job just because of the health insurance benefit. A second advantage is that it is equitable because it focuses on percentage of income regardless of size of income and would provide more help for those who need it more, such as low-income workers and those with chronic health problems. A third advantage is that the program would reduce the costs of welfare and Medicaid for both federal and state governments, thus reducing the strain on the federal budget or enabling the provision of somewhat more generous programs.[153]

Like all policy proposals, this one has its disadvantages as well. One is the equity consideration. The argument that Butler makes that the current tax deduction system is inequitable because those with higher incomes would pay at a higher tax rate than those with lower incomes is an assumption. The numbers, on the face of it, are correct. Consider the following:

Let us assume two families, one with a taxable income of $30,000 a year and the other with a taxable income of $90,000 a year. The families are the same size, and the primary workers for the two families work for the same company and get the same health insurance package from the employer. The employer contribution to both families' health insurance is the same, say $3,000 a year. If the tax deduction were removed and the employer kept the total compensation package the same, the workers would each receive an additional $3,000 in salary. This would increase their taxable incomes to $33,000 and $93,000, respectively. The tax for the lower-income family would increase by $450, an increase of about 10 percent (using 1994 tax rates) in tax obligations and a marginal tax rate of 15 percent ($450 ÷ $3,000 = 15%). The tax for the higher-income family would increase by $875, an increase of about 4.3 percent in tax obligations and a marginal tax rate of about 29 percent ($875 ÷ $3,000 = 29.2%). Thus the equity consideration, if it is a consideration at all, would apply only to those whose income was too low to pay federal income taxes. Otherwise, the current system, as Butler explains it, actually favors lower-income families as long as they pay taxes, if one looks at the actual increase in tax obligations versus marginal tax rates. So, in that sense, Butler is partially correct.

But he is incorrect in two other senses. First, workers get the health insurance but not the money. This is a "let-us-assume" proposition rather than the real world. Second, consider how the tax credit system would work. Let us take our families from the above example, the $30,000 income family and the $90,000 income family. Under the new system, both pay the same percentage of their income on health care. For the first family that amounts to $3,000; for the second family it amounts to $9,000. These are the same in percentage terms, but the impacts on the two families are much different, given the original sizes of their incomes. Both would be eligible for a 20 percent tax credit, but that would amount to $600 for the lower-income family (a cut of 13.3 percent in tax obligation). For the upper-income family, the 20 percent tax credit would amount to $1,800 (a tax cut of 8.9 percent in tax obligation). While the percentage decrease of tax obligation would be lower for the higher-income family, thus seeming to be equitable, the tax credit would be three times as large as for the low-income family. It would be proportional at best.

A final problem with the tax credit plan is that while it may guarantee insurance coverage, it does not deal with the other problems discussed: risk rating and so forth. It also does not guarantee access to health care in inner cities and rural areas, a topic to be discussed below. The proposal is worth considering as perhaps one component of health reform.

A related alternative, one enacted on a limited basis in 1996 and 1997, is *medical savings accounts* (MSA). As discussed in chapters 4 and 10, a medical savings account is money deposited into an account by the government, which can be used to pay for medical expenses. Then consumers could purchase relatively inexpensive health insurance policies ("catastrophic" health insurance) that would cover large expenses after cost-sharing provisions were met. The Health Insurance Portability and Accountability Act created a small MSA program as did the 1997 Balanced Budget Act for Medicare (see chapters 4 and 10).

A fourth alternative would be to expand the community health center program.[154] Community health centers (originally called neighborhood health centers) were created during the 1960s as part of President Lyndon Johnson's War on Poverty. These centers offer comprehensive health services to those in impoverished inner-city neighborhoods and rural areas at minimal or no cost to clients.[155] By 1991, there were some 550 such centers. Evaluations of community health centers have been very positive.[156] In 1991, the Advisory Council on Social Security recommended the addition of 250 more community health centers.[157]

There are two problems with such proposals. One is cost. A second, and probably more important issue, is ideological. Community health centers would put government in the business of more directly providing health services than Medicare or Medicaid.[158]

Another approach to expanding health insurance coverage would focus on employers. Such an approach would involve a combination of employer mandates, requiring employers to provide and help pay for health insurance for their employees, and subsidies to employers (especially smaller firms) either directly or through tax deductions, to enable them to afford such policies. A variation on this is the "play-or-pay" proposal, where the employer would either provide health insurance for employees (the "play" option) or contribute to a statewide or nationwide pool to help the uninsured (the "pay" option).

One advantage of focusing on the employer is that it builds on the present system. A second advantage is that it minimizes costs to government. Mandates do not require additional government expenditures of a sizable amount (the exception of course is subsidies, and these would be targeted and certainly less than the costs of a full national health care system).[159] A typical employer mandate proposal might require employers to pay for 80 percent of insurance premiums. Such a mandate would promote equity and be relatively easy to enforce through Social Security, though administration would be complex.[160] Of course, small businesses in particular have argued that they cannot afford the additional costs. Their opposition to the employer mandate portion of President Clinton's Health Security Act, discussed in chapter 9, was one of the reasons for its failure. A disadvantage of "play-or-pay" is that it might encourage employers to contribute to the uninsurance fund, effectively creating a national system. If that is the desire, a direct approach would be more useful.[161]

Another proposal would combine employer-based insurance with Medicare. This proposal would establish

> a common basic benefit package under both Medicare and employer plans, and [would also establish] common provider payment methods applicable to both Medicare and employer plans. It would be financed through a combination of employer and individual premium contributions, payroll taxes, personal income taxes, and other general tax revenues.[162]

A final approach is insurance reform. One such reform would be to place a cap or ceiling on insurance premiums. This was part of the Clinton health care plan. States would have the most important role here, as in other insurance reforms, because of their regulatory authority over the insurance industry. Two other insurance reforms might increase coverage of the uninsured. One would be to move back to community rating and away from experience rating. This would lower premiums, particularly for those in higher-risk groups (of course, it would raise premiums for those who are healthy). A related reform would restrict or eliminate underwriting, the practice of excluding or restricting those with preexisting conditions. Essentially this would guarantee that all who wanted insurance could get it at a reasonable price. Of course, insurance companies would raise overall premium rates to make up for the additional costs due to underwriting.

The experience of Rochester, New York, long a leader in health care reform, shows that requiring community rating, which the state of New York has done for several years, does increase access to insurance.[163] One drawback to the New York State requirement that insurers accept all applicants and use community rating is that it may encourage people to go without health insurance until they know it is needed and cannot be refused. Thus one paradoxical result of the New York plan is that the percentage of insured people in the state has decreased since the law was passed in 1992.

Conclusion

In this chapter we have considered one of the major problems of the U.S. health care system, that of the disadvantaged. The uniquely American mix of public and private insurance programs, a post–World War II development, covers about 85 percent of the population but leaves over 40 million people without any insurance at all. Especially in the case of private insurance, it also leaves a portion of the population underinsured and vulnerable to catastrophic medical expenses.

Incremental reforms, the kind that generally characterize public policy in the United States, have begun to address some of these problems. The S-CHIP program focuses on children. The Health Insurance Portability and Accountability Act addresses the "job lock" issue.

Medicaid, Medicare, or both, could be expanded to cover those without insurance, many of whom work. Using the tax system, through either subsidies to employers or tax credits for individuals or families, would also help. Insurance reforms, such as mandating community rating, would also be useful, though there are dangers in doing some of these things individually. A federal or state program of universal coverage, involving either employer or individual mandates, would likely be the simplest, though not necessarily the most politically feasible, way to deal with the problem.

Even were some or all of these policies undertaken, and they have been in some states, the problems of the disadvantaged would remain. Having insurance coverage is important. We know from a considerable body of evidence that those without health insurance have more health problems and receive less and poorer-quality service than those with health insurance. But if the providers are not in the geographical area, such as inner cities or rural areas, having insurance by itself is insufficient.

We also know that poverty, ethnicity, and gender play important and intermixing roles in health outcomes. We know that blacks and Latinos on the average have poorer health outcomes than whites. We know that minority women and their babies have poorer health outcomes: more troubling pregnancies, low birth weights, and so forth. Women are disadvantaged by a medical system that seems to take the white male as the model for research and insurance coverage.

These issues, which involve equality and equity, do not lend themselves to easy solutions. The managed care revolution, discussed in chapter 10, only minimally, if at all, addresses the problems discussed in this chapter. Perhaps the most viable solution is the community health center program, where providers are located in underserved areas. But the likelihood of the expansion of such programs is minimal. In the absence of a comprehensive transformation of the American health care system, it is likely that the problems of the disadvantaged will remain.

CHAPTER 6

Health Care Cost Containment

The 1960s saw a dramatic expansion in social programs. Civil rights, women's rights, educational opportunities, and improved housing and health care for citizens were the battle cries of a social revolution as the federal government attempted to expand individual opportunities. In the health field, health care came to be viewed as a right, rather than a privilege. Providing access to decent health care became the primary goal of the federal government.

The federal government in 1965, to provide increased access to health care for the elderly and the poor, established Medicare and Medicaid. These programs were successful in increasing access to health care for large numbers of people.[1] The creation and implementation of such programs was made possible by a healthy economy. Additionally, the Comprehensive Health Planning Act and Public Health Services Amendments of 1966 (PL 89-749) established the goal of providing the highest level of health care attainable to every person.

By the late 1960s and early 1970s, the focus began to shift from providing access to concern about rising health care costs. The cost of health care in the

Table 6.1

National Health Care Expenditures, 1960–1996

	1960	1970	1980	1990	1991	1992	1993	1994	1995	1996
National health care expenditures ($ billion)	26.9	73.2	247.3	699.5	766.8	836.6	895.1	945.7	991.4	1,035.1
As percentage of GDP	5.1	7.1	8.9	12.2	13.0	13.4	13.6	13.6	13.6	13.6
Average annual percent growth from previous year shown	10.6	12.9	11.0	9.6	9.1	7.0	5.6	4.8	4.4	

Source: Katharine R. Levit, "National Health Expenditures, 1993," *Health Care Financing Review* 19, no. 1 (Fall 1997): 187.

United States had been rising faster than the general growth rate of the economy. Health care expenditures accounted for an increased share of the national income.[2] As shown in Table 6.1, national health care expenditures increased from $26.9 billion in 1960 to $73.2 billion in 1970 and to $247.3 billion in 1980. In 1993, national health care expenditures had jumped to $895.1 billion and had reached $1,035.1 billion in 1996.[3] Spending for health care amounted to 12.2 percent of the gross domestic product (GDP) in 1990, more than double the figure of 5.1 percent in 1960. Another way of looking at the explosion in health care costs is to examine the third line in Table 6.1, which shows the percentage increase in health care expenditures from the previous period. Average annual percent growth remained in double digits from 1960 to 1990. It was only during the 1990s that the average annual growth dipped into single digit. In fact, from 1991 to 1996, average annual percent growth declined every year. It declined from 9.6 percent in 1991 to 4.4 percent in 1996.

Hospital and physician care accounted for more than half of all health care expenditures in 1996. Private sources (private insurance, out-of-pocket expenses plus other) accounted for about 53.3 percent of the total national health expenditures. Federal health spending of $350.9 billion in 1996 accounted for 34 percent of all national health care expenditures (see Table 6.2).[4]

Table 6.2

National Health Care Expenditures by Sources of Funds and Types of Expenditures, 1996 (in billions of dollars)

	Total	Out of pocket	Private insurance	Other	Federal	State and local
Total national health expenditures	1,035.1	171.2 (16.5%)	337.3 (32.6%)	43.5 (4.2%)	350.9 (34.0%)	132.2 (12.7%)
Hospital Care	358.5	9.2 (2.6%)	113.4 (31.6%)	15.3 (4.3%)	181.6 (50.6%)	39.1 (10.9%)
Physician services	202.1	29.6 (14.6%)	101.8 (50.4%)	4.2 (2.1%)	54.2 (26.8%)	12.3 (6.1%)
Dental services	47.6	22.1 (46.4%)	23.2 (48.7%)	0.2 (0.4%)	1.2 (2.5%)	0.9 (1.9%)
Home health care	30.2	5.9 (19.5%)	3.2 (10.6%)	3.3 (10.9%)	15.9 (52.5%)	2.0 (6.5%)
Drugs and other medical nondurables	91.4	50.3 (55.0%)	27.8 (30.4%)	0.0 (0.0%)	7.5 (8.2%)	5.8 (6.3%)
Nursing homes	78.5	24.7 (31.5%)	4.0 (5.1%)	1.5 (1.9%)	32.2 (41.0%)	16.1 (20.5%)

Source: Katharine R. Levit, "National Health Expenditures, 1997," *Health Care Financing Review* 19, no. 1 (Fall 1997): 191.

There are many causes for such dramatic increases in health care costs. To some, increased costs are the result of increased public expectations about the health care system, advances in health care technology and their success, and the prevailing sentiment that health care is a right.[5] Others see health care cost increases in fee for service, a medical arms race among hospitals, insurance companies and third-party payers, and the purchasers of health care, such as the federal government and industries that, for a long time, ignored the cost problem.[6] Still others argue that virtually all the medical care price inflation of recent years can be accounted for by general inflation, the labor intensity of health industries, the behavior of wage rates during inflation, and the pattern of labor-productivity changes.[7]

If there is any agreement among policymakers, health care practitioners, researchers, and health care consumers and purchasers, it is that health care costs too much. The federal government is one of the largest purchasers of health care. Federal health care expenditures constitute a significant portion of the federal budget, and the tax burden is large. Accordingly, federal policymakers and bureaucrats face great pressure to contain health care costs.[8] The question for policymakers has become one of how to contain costs and still maintain quality medical service.[9] The focus in the health care policy debate has shifted from "Should we contain costs?" to "How should we contain costs?"[10] This is not just a problem of public expenditures; the business sector also faces considerable health cost problems.

The debate over how to contain rising health care costs centers on two broad approaches or strategies.[11] One strategy relies on government regulation, while the other relies on increasing competition in the health care market.[12] During the decades of the 1970s, the 1980s, and the 1990s, the federal government tried both regulatory and competitive strategies to contain health costs. Similarly, state governments and the private sector have also undertaken many new initiatives in an attempt to contain rising health care costs.

This chapter has three purposes. First, it provides a brief theoretical rationale of regulatory and market strategies. Second, it examines the regulatory and market strategies used by the federal government to contain rising health care costs. Third, it analyzes state government and private-sector innovations and initiatives to contain health care costs.

Theoretical Framework: Government Regulation and Market Competition

The Regulatory Strategy

One of the most important assumptions of the regulatory strategy is that the health care market suffers from too many shortcomings. Government regulation can therefore help improve the performance of the market. Thus, one motivation for economic regulation of the system is the premise that the system suffers from serious market failures, including information disparities between providers and consumers of health services and an insurance system (third-party financing) that masks the costs of health services. This in turn produces excessive expenditures, inefficiency, and maldistribution of labor power and resources. A related market failure is that the health care system has a severe equity problem (differential access to services and financing). Thus the government must play a role, under this assumption, in providing greater access to the health care market for those who cannot afford it.[13] The second assumption of the regulatory strategy is that the health care market is different from other economic markets. In health care, physicians control both supply and demand because the physician is both the patient's consultant on what services are needed and the provider of these services. Physicians are not trained to think in terms of aggregate costs. Physicians not only influence cost decisions regarding individual patients but also influence the growth and expansion of health care institutions, thus affecting hospital costs. In addition, the third-party-payment system, based on private health insurance and government payment, tends to remove the patient from the effects of health care costs.[14]

Another important potential difference between medical care and other goods and services is the absence of consumer information about appropriate price and quality levels.[15] The role of information in facilitating choices about health care goods and services is crucial.[16] Some have argued that the medical market is on the verge of remedying the information deficit and that the determination of whether medical care is different from other goods and services is ultimately a political question.[17]

The third assumption of the regulatory strategy is that public regulation promotes important values of political accountability, public access to information, and public participation.[18] The regulatory process is characterized by a high degree of formal due process. The requirements of public notices, public meetings, adversary procedures, formal recordkeeping, and limits on appeals help inform consumers by providing access to information and extending to them an opportunity to participate in the policymaking process.

Thus, government regulation of the health care system is justified on many grounds: as a way of improving the workings of the health care market, providing equity, and promoting crucial public values with the hope that it will help contain health care costs. Some advocates of a regulatory strategy argue that a pure market in health care is unattainable and thus regulation is the second-best choice.[19] Others argue for a more tightly regulated health care system as the best policy.[20]

Critics of the regulatory strategy charge that examples of past regulatory failures suggest that government regulation does not work.[21] These critics argue that too many fundamental structural and incentive problems are stacked against good regulatory performance[22] and that comprehensive regulation will raise, not lower, the true cost of medical care,[23] thus contributing to health care cost inflation.[24] Regulation is not cost effective; it produces inefficiency and prevents technological innovations. Regulation often produces a cartel-like situation resulting in a monopoly on prices because regulatory agencies become captured by the regulated industry.[25] To the critics of a regulatory strategy the answer is competitive market strategy. "Competition" is the latest buzzword for many health policymakers and health care providers.

The Market Strategy

One of the major assumptions of the market strategy is that the principal source of rising health care costs is an attempt by the government to base the distribution of health care on the egalitarian principle of need, which does not allocate health care resources in an efficient manner.[26] The advocates of this strategy argue for creating incentives and mechanisms to increase competition and relying on the health care market for better and more efficient allocation of health care resources.[27] Some market reformers argue that health insurance creates a "moral hazard," masking the true costs of health care from both consumers and providers. From this it would follow that consumers must be presented with options that have genuine cost consequences.

New, alternative mechanisms of health care delivery must be found that will provide health care consumers with multiple choices having cost consequences. Creating conditions for fair market competition will produce competition in the market, which will help contain health care costs.[28] New incentives should be created. To make businesses more conscious of health care costs, tax laws should be altered to place a ceiling on the total amount of health insurance premiums that employers can deduct as a business expense. To make consumers more conscious of health care costs, insurance plans should rely on coinsurance and deductibles.[29] What is needed, some have argued, is to combine markets with a minimal but necessary amount of government regulation. This combination is known as managed competition.[30] Examples of programs or policies that rely on combining market-oriented competitive strategy with some government regulations include the Medicare Prospective Payment System (PPS), also known as diagnosis-related group (DRGs), and the use of organizations such as health maintenance organizations (HMOs) and preferred provider organizations (PPOs) to provide managed care on a precapitated basis to enrollees.

Some pro-competition advocates, such as Clark Havighurst, have argued that one of the most effective and least intrusive methods for assuring fair competition is enforcement of antitrust laws. Antitrust principles are based on the assumptions that competition promotes efficiency and innovation and encourages diversity through decentralization, and that competitive markets are more stable than noncompetitive markets because the former adjust continuously to market conditions. These assumptions, in turn, are based on social values of individual initiative, individual freedom of choice, and the dangers of big business and big government.[31] This does not mean that a competitive market would be unregulated; any competitive market requires monitoring and intervention from time to time to assure that competition is fair and open. According to antitrust enforcement advocates, given the potential for exercise of monopoly power by physicians, hospitals, and other health care providers, policing health care markets must be an integral part of reforms designed to enhance competition.[32]

In summary, advocates of the competitive strategy argue that improving structural mechanisms and changing incentives through introduction of competition in the health care market will result in better economic performance and reduced health care costs.

Critics of the competitive strategy are skeptical of the results of market competition. To some, the prospects of a competitive strategy are promising but uncertain technically and politically.[33] Others argue that markets in health care are usually pseudo-markets dominated by one side of the transaction,[34] and that the supporters of competition may be grossly overemphasizing the beneficial results.[35] It would take more than the stimulus from increased consumer cost sharing or reduced tax subsidies to produce competitive behavior on the part of health care providers.[36] Opponents of an antitrust enforcement strategy argue that professional autonomy and self-regulation produce significant social benefits. In addition, physicians are likely to oppose antitrust enforcement because a free market could be worse for physicians' economic well-being than government regulation. Physicians often reap substantial economic benefits from regulations they control and from the government programs that pay the bills.[37]

The Role of the Federal Government in Cost Containment

Over the years, the federal government has followed a middle road between the harsh realities of a private health care marketplace and a nationally planned and regulated health care system through a comprehensive national health insurance system. Thus, while the federal government has used both regulatory and competitive strategies in an effort to contain health care costs, the major efforts have been in the regulatory field. One of the regulatory strategies used by the federal government has been health care planning.

Health Care Planning and Cost Containment

During the late 1960s and early 1970s, the federal government responded to the concerns of rising health care costs by adopting various regulatory mechanisms. Health planning emerged as one of the major methods for controlling health care costs. While the federal government had always engaged in some planning, not until the late 1960s and early 1970s did health care planning became a dominant theme. Planning relies on a regulatory strategy and uses centralized decision making to guide the allocation of resources and ensure access to services.

The rationale for health care planning is based on the argument of excess capacity in the health care system in general, and in the hospital industry in particular, as a significant contributor to rising health care costs. The argument is that there are too many hospitals, beds, and medical equipment. This not only creates unnecessary expansion and duplication of expensive resources but also leads to overutilization of medical facilities.[38] Supply creates its own demand, following Roemer's argument that "a bed built is a bed filled is a bed billed."[39] This excess capacity, expansion, and duplication are encouraged by factors such as the third-party-payment system, the inability of the market to induce inefficient hospitals to reduce the number of beds or go out of business altogether, and competition among hospitals for prestige and physicians.[40]

While early approaches to planning were aimed at ensuring high-quality health care for everyone,[41] health planning in the 1960s and 1970s focused explicitly on the problem of rising costs. One of the significant regulatory developments in the area of health care planning was certificate-of-need (CON) law.[42] By 1973, twenty-three states had adopted such laws. The federal government got into the act with the passage of the 1972 amendments to the Social Security Act of 1935. This created the section 1,122 program, which called for review of hospital expansion proposals when Medicare funding might be involved.

Two years later, the federal government assumed control of the entire certificate-of-need process. The National Health Planning and Resource Development Act of 1974 (PL 93-641) provided an institutional framework for health care planning. It replaced three previous federal programs: Comprehensive Health Planning, the Regional Medical Program, and the Hill-Burton Hospital Construction Program.[43] The law required all states to adopt certificate-of-need laws by 1980. The law also established a network of state and local health planning agencies to shape local health systems based on national priorities. More than 200 local health systems agencies (HSAs) were established, each responsible for governing a specific area, to administer the certificate-of-need laws. State health planning development agencies roughly paralleled the roles and responsibilities of local HSAs. The law provided for the representation of consumer and provider interests in the HSAs.

Certificate-of-need laws require hospitals to document "community need" to obtain approval for major capital expenditures for expansion of physical plants, equipment, and services. The primary purpose of these laws was to prevent unnecessary investment in facilities and services. The laws were also designed to prevent the entry of new providers in the health care market unless a clear need was demonstrated.

Did the certificate-of-need laws and the HSAs help contain overall growth in hospital costs in particular and health care costs in general? The available empirical evidence overwhelmingly points to the failure of health care planning to control health care costs. Research findings show little evidence that CON constrained investment or had any significant effect on the total level of investment.[44] CON laws may have changed the composition of investment, but they may, in fact, have led to increased overall hospital costs.[45] There was some evidence that programs that focused on hospital beds alone may have had more success than those dealing with review of expansion of facilities, equipment, and services. Nevertheless, the effects of these narrowly focused programs were very weak. The investment in anticipation of regulation, rather than the effect of the CON laws, explain some initial decline in investment after adoption of the CON programs.

What accounts for the failure of CON laws and HSAs? There are many explanations. One possible explanation is the capture theory of regulation. This occurs when a regulated industry subverts or captures the regulatory agency through politically inspired appointments, lucrative employment prospects in the industry for cooperative regulators, regulated industry's ability to outspend the regulatory agency, and industry's influence with the elected officials who control a regulatory agency's appropriations. Thus, regulatory agencies adopt policies similar to the ones desired by the regulated industry, resulting in a cartel or monopoly situation. The fact that the American Hospital Association supported CON laws—and a fairly close correlation exists between the attitudes of the hospital industry and the regulators—may lend some legitimacy to this argument, even though it would be difficult to prove.[46]

A second explanation is that, despite consumer representation in the HSAs, provider interests have many more advantages in terms of information, expertise, and legal counsel.[47] In addition, consistent political participation by consumers in the form of attending public hearings was difficult to achieve because it required time, effort, and money.[48] Representatives of the health care providers dominated most public meetings.[49] It has also been argued that pluralist interest-group representation, as was the case with HSAs, leads to bargaining, log-rolling, and collusive competition among narrowly defined special interests in which the interest of the general public is not well served.[50]

A third explanation for the failure of the CON laws and HSAs lies in the lack of public support. A nationwide public opinion poll in 1978 revealed that the public had very little confidence in, and recognition of, HSAs and had little support for hospital cost-containment strategies and their consequences. There was also little support for the goals and consequences of cost-containment strategies among groups traditionally underrepresented in health planning activities.[51]

Within less than a decade, health planning, as established under the National Health Planning and Resource Development Act of 1974, was dismantled by the Reagan administration. Congress reduced health planning funding from $167 million in 1980 to $58 million in 1983.[52] Most of the states eliminated local HSAs. This is not to suggest that the concept of national health planning is dead. It is in a period of unsettlement and retrenchment. There is a danger that the total absence of hospital planning would lead to unnecessary duplication of facilities and equipment as strong hospitals attempt to increase their market share. Critics argue that a move toward free competition must embody an interim phase that eases regulation but does not do away with it entirely.[53]

Professional Standards Review and Cost Containment

One of the factors often cited as responsible for rising health care costs is overutilization of health care resources. The rise in health care costs since the enactment of Medicare and Medicaid programs in the mid-1960s created concern in Congress about the cost and quality of these programs. The Social Security Amendments of 1972 established the Professional Standards Review Organization (PSRO) program. The PSRO program was designed as a peer review mechanism to promote effective yet efficient and economical delivery of health care services for government-financed programs such as Medicare and Medicaid. Under the law, more than 200 local PSROs were created and staffed by local physicians to review and monitor care provided to Medicare and Medicaid patients by hospitals, extended-care facilities, and skilled nursing homes. The PSROs were responsible for determining whether the care provided was medically necessary, of professional quality, and delivered in an appropriate health care facility. They also had the authority to deny approval of payment for services to physicians who provide care to Medicaid

and Medicare patients. Two of the stated goals of the program were to eliminate unnecessary medical treatment and to eliminate unnecessary institutionalization. Thus, the PSRO program was created as a regulatory mechanism for
reducing the cost of federal health care programs.

Did the PSRO program succeed in achieving cost reductions? The majority of evidence suggests that it did not. A 1981 study by the Congressional
Budget Office concluded that the cost of the program exceeded its benefits.
Although the program slightly reduced Medicare utilization overall, it con-
sumed more resources than it saved. It had very little impact on the federal
budget.[54]

Many explanations are offered for this. One is that PSROs controlled by
local physicians have no incentives to reduce utilization because such reduction would lead to reduced federal payments to the locality. Second, the
program suffered from potential conflict between quality-enhancing and cost-
reducing goals, a persistent problem. Third, the PSRO program could be used
to advance the cartel objectives of health care providers.[55] Doctor-policing
laws such as PSRO or hospital peer review committees aimed at self-policing
are generally ineffective because of a reluctance to speak out against col-
leagues, concern over libel lawsuits, and problems of due process safeguards.[56]

The Reagan administration came to office in 1981 strongly supporting
the elimination of federal regulatory programs. The PSRO program was on
the administration's target list, but it failed to eliminate the program because
of opposition in Congress. Federal funding for the PSRO program was cut
from $58 million in 1980 to $15 million in 1983.[57] Congress, through the Tax
Equity and Fiscal Responsibility Act of 1982 (PL 97-248), renamed the program Peer Review Organizations (PROs). Today, PROs are responsible for
reviewing the appropriateness and quality of health care provided to Medicare beneficiaries. The Medicare program has relied on the PROs to safeguard
against inadequate medical treatment for individual patients. In 1987 the scope
of the program was expanded beyond hospital-based care to include review
of outpatient care. Hospitals, in general, view PROs as a nuisance causing
financial and administrative headaches or hassles. Hospitals in many states
report numerous problems with PROs, such as a lack of communication regarding review methods, lack of clear criteria on procedures to be reviewed,
and backlogs.[58] A telephone poll revealed that 70 percent of hospital chief
executive officers believe that the high cost of administering Medicare, including the utilization review requirements, is responsible for a significant
portion of the increases in health care costs.[59] Medicare PROs also suffer from
extreme variations in organizational structure and activities.[60]

While utilization review from a public standpoint remains weak, the private sector has moved in this direction. Indeed, one of the newer health care

reform concepts, to be discussed in chapters 9 and 10, is managed care. Though the term was not used originally, managed care is a fundamental part of the health maintenance strategy.

Health Maintenance Organizations, Managed Care, and Cost Containment

The CON, HSA, and PSRO programs were examples of behavioral regulations. These programs were designed to scrutinize decisions about utilization, expansion, and acquisition of health care resources by providers. They were based on the assumption that changing behavior and cutting waste could contain health care costs.[61] They were not very successful.

During the early 1970s, the federal government also tried a competitive market strategy to contain health care costs through prepaid group plans (PGPs), commonly known as health maintenance organizations (HMOs). The concept of PGPs was not new. Such plans had existed in the health care system without any federal assistance since the 1920s. During the early 1970s, the number of HMOs grew as a result of favorable market conditions and the rhetorical support provided by the Nixon administration. According to one estimate, the number of HMOs increased from 41 in 1970 to 133 in 1973.[62]

Dr. Paul M. Ellwood, Jr., a key health advisor to President Richard Nixon, is credited with bringing the competitive market strategy in the form of HMOs to the attention of national health policymakers.[63] In 1970 the Nixon administration asked Congress to create a new HMO option for Medicare recipients. In 1971 the administration began to use discretionary funds to plan the development of about a hundred HMOs around the country and asked Congress to create a special HMO development plan. The Department of Health, Education, and Welfare (now the Department of Health and Human Services) argued that there could be as many as 1,700 HMOs within a few years, with perhaps as many as 40 million people enrolled.[64] After long debate, Congress passed the Health Maintenance Organization Act (PL 93-222) of 1973.

The federal government assumed the role of venture capitalist.[65] It encouraged the development of HMOs in an attempt to induce competition in the health care market with the hope of containing health costs. This market strategy was designed to eliminate, or at least reduce, centralized health care bureaucracy and replace it with decentralized market building. This was to be accomplished through the use of federal funds to support efforts in developing new health care organizations and alternative means of health care delivery. It promised pluralism, choice, efficiency, and reorganization through competition, markets, and incentives.[66] The expectation was that HMOs would contain costs by (1) creating incentives for channeling health service utilization from costly inpatient settings (hospitals, skilled nursing homes, etc.) to less costly outpatient settings (visits to doctors' offices), (2) promoting competition with traditional health care delivery systems, and (3) exercising market power by obtaining preferential prices from various health care providers.[67]

An HMO is a prepaid medical practice delivering a comprehensive set of health care services to enrollees for a fixed fee (capitation) paid in advance. The Health Maintenance Organization Act of 1973 provided for an expenditure of $375 million over five years. Most of these funds were used to encourage development of HMOs by providing start-up costs. The law offered federally qualified HMOs three basic benefits: (1) money for development of HMOs; (2) overriding of certain restrictive state laws; and (3) a mandate to employers, covered by the Fair Labor Standards Act of 1938, that employ twenty-five or more employees to offer HMO coverage as an alternative to whatever other health plans they provide. This was designed to provide health care consumers with at least a dual choice in health plans. In return, to qualify for federal funds, HMOs were to deliver a comprehensive package of benefits to a broadly representative population on an equitable basis with consumer participation. This was to be done at the same price as or a lower price than traditional forms of health insurance.[68]

The original legislation so heavily burdened HMOs with special services (comprehensive benefits, open enrollment, dual choice, and limits on copayments) and pricing requirements (same premiums to be charged to all enrollees, that is, "community rate" as opposed to "experience rate")[69] that very few developers applied for federal support. By 1975, only five HMOs had qualified for federal support. Between 1974 and 1976, the growth in the number of federally supported HMOs was very slow.

To remedy this problem the HMO amendments of 1976 and 1978 deregulated service and pricing requirements, including a reduction in service requirements and the elimination of open enrollment with the exception of large and established programs. In 1981 the federal government stopped providing new grants to HMOs. Since then, the federal government has focused its attention on the promotion of competition in general, incentives designed to increase private-sector involvement in HMO development, and risk contracts to HMOs that agree to enroll Medicare beneficiaries. The federal government continues to designate HMOs that meet certain standards as federally qualified.[70]

Medicare Managed Care

During the late 1980s and particularly during the 1990s, the federal government particularly encouraged Medicare recipients to enroll in managed care

organizations such as HMOs. A study of the Medicare HMOs marketing activities in four major media markets suggests that, in general, the HMO
advertisements pitch lower costs and better benefits. Ads are also marketed to
healthy seniors and not to sick or to disabled persons under the age of sixty-
five. Finally, the study raises questions about the impact of marketing on
Medicare beneficiaries' insurance choices.[71]

Enrollment in Medicare managed care did increase about 50 percent between 1994 and 1997.[72] Enrollment in Medicare managed care has steadily
increased during the 1990s, and has particularly surged since 1994. Between
1994 and 1996, risk-contract enrollment increased at an average annual rate
of more than 40 percent, and such steady increase is projected to continue in
the next century.[73] However, it is important to point out that fewer than 11
percent of Medicare beneficiaries are enrolled in HMOs. Thus, the overall
impact of Medicare managed care on cost containment is likely to be very
small. A study of a stratified random sample of 3,080 Medicare beneficiaries
who were enrolled in a Medicare managed care risk plan found that a great
majority of Medicare managed care enrollees did not report any access problem, were relatively satisfied with the care they received, and would
recommend their plan to others. The study also found that Medicare HMOs
use resources more efficiently. It found only minor differences in access, quality, and beneficiary satisfaction compared with fee-for-service Medicare.
However, the study also found some problem areas. The study found that access to home health care services was particularly problematic and that
Medicare HMOs perform poorly for some vulnerable subgroups such as the
chronically ill.[74] One way to measure dissatisfaction among Medicare HMO
enrollees is to examine why persons who enroll in HMO leave their HMO
after a few years. A survey of disenrollees found that beneficiaries' reasons
for disenrolling often involve dissatisfaction with the physician or the plan,
problems with access to services, and misunderstandings on the part of enrollee about how HMOs operate. Other reasons include changes in enrollees'
residences, departure of plan physicians, and competition from other HMOs.[75]
The topic of Medicare managed care is discussed in more detail in chapter 4.

Prospective Payment System and Cost Containment

With the enactment of Medicaid and Medicare in the mid-1960s, the federal
government became a major purchaser of health services in the health care
market. Part of the increase in overall health care costs is attributed to dramatic increases in the cost of these programs. Federal spending for these
programs has almost doubled every five years. By 1980, spending had reached

about $61.2 billion, and it constituted about 27.8 percent of total national health spending—financing health care for about 50 million people.[76] At the same time, hospital costs were also rising dramatically. The cost of hospital care had increased from $28 billion in 1970 to $102.7 billion in 1980.[77] From 1977 to 1982, Medicare hospital expenditures grew at an average annual rate of 18 percent compared to a 14.6 percent increase in overall hospital spending.[78]

The burden on the federal health budget created the political environment for federal regulation of hospital costs.[79] Advocates of regulation argued that cost controls on hospitals would limit waste and inefficiency without sacrificing quality of care.[80]

President Carter, in response to rising hospital costs, proposed hospital cost containment legislation (HR 6575) designed to constrain the rate of increase in hospital costs and to limit the rate of increase in hospital revenues. The hospital industry strongly opposed such a measure and proposed a voluntary plan to control costs on its own. The controversy surrounding both plans led to their demise in 1979.

As mentioned earlier, President Ronald Reagan came to office in 1981 with the expressed intention of eliminating federal regulatory health care programs in favor of a market-oriented, competitive strategy to contain health care costs. Federal funding was cut for health planning programs, and the PSRO program was renamed PRO and given reduced funding. Budget cuts were made in Medicaid and Medicare, and new federal grants for HMO start-up were eliminated.

Minor changes were made in Medicare by the Omnibus Budget Reconciliation Act of 1981. This included tightening Medicare reimbursement payments. The 1982 Tax Equity and Fiscal Responsibility Act (TEFRA) limited the increase in Medicare hospital payment rates, created an early basis for prospective payment based on a case-mix index, and called for incentive payments to hospitals defined as efficient. TEFRA required that the Department of Health and Human Services (HHS) design a prospective payment plan for the Medicare program. That new system, implemented in 1983, was the Prospective Payment System (PPS) for Medicare reimbursement to hospitals. The PPS for Medicare reimbursement was based on the New Jersey program.[81] This is an example of the federal government embracing a program originally implemented at the state level.[82]

Under PPS, hospitals are paid according to a schedule of preestablished rates linked to 468 DRGs. All major diagnoses are classified into 468 categories, with each category assigned a treatment rate. Hospitals are reimbursed according to these rates. There are economic incentives in the form of rewards and punishments built into the system. If a hospital spends more money than the preestablished rate for a particular diagnostic treatment, the hospital must absorb the additional cost. If the hospital spends less money than the preestablished rate, it is still paid the preestablished rate and can keep the overpayment as profit. The Health Care Financing Administration within HHS was assigned the responsibility of establishing the DRG payment schedule. To safeguard against reduction in quality of care as a result of PPS, Congress assigned PROs the responsibility of monitoring the quality and appropriateness of care for Medicare patients. If a PRO finds inappropriate or substandard care, the hospital may be denied Medicare payment. If a pattern of inappropriate or substandard care is discovered, the hospital Medicare provider agreement may be terminated.

The shift in the Medicare payment method to hospitals from a retrospective reimbursement system to a PPS based on DRGs is the most far-reaching change in Medicare since its inception.[83] The changeover to PPS was expected to revolutionize the economics of American health care.[84]

There are three major kinds of hospital regulations: facilities and service regulation, utilization review, and rate and revenue regulations.[85] The first two were used by the federal government in programs such as CON, HSAs, and PSROs. The DRGs, under the PPS, involved rate and revenue regulations, commonly referred to as price regulation. Price regulation typically involves a regulatory agency that establishes a minimum, maximum, or range of prices an individual or an institution can charge for particular goods or services.[86] The rationale behind replacing the retrospective payment system was that under that system, hospitals had no incentive to economize in their use of health care resources in treating Medicare patients. If anything, such a system tended to encourage overutilization of health resources, since hospitals were assured that they would be reimbursed for all reasonable costs incurred. PPS was based on the assumption that given built-in incentives, hospitals would be forced to consider cost factors in treatment and would be encouraged to be economically more efficient. Thus, inefficient hospitals would be forced to close. An economically more efficient hospital sector would help contain increases in hospital costs. PPS was viewed as a method of influencing hospital activities, creating cost-containment constraints, and introducing incentives into hospital payments.[87] The cost-control incentive was the primary purpose in establishing the PPS.[88]

Evaluating the Prospective Payment System

How well has the prospective payment system constrained hospital cost increases? Early studies were encouraging, though not decisive. Any assessment of the impact of PPS must be viewed with caution for two reasons. First, PPS was not put into immediate implementation in 1983 but was phased in over a period of time. The complete transition to a PPS system occurred in November 1987. Thus, sufficient time needs to elapse to make any definitive conclusions about the impact of PPS.[89] Second, it is very difficult to assess changes in hospital behavior using aggregate data. It is even more difficult to disentangle the effects of Medicare PPS from other influences on hospital costs, let alone measure the magnitude of any effects.[90]

The initial years of PPS showed some reduction in the growth rate of hospital costs. Hospital expenditures increased more slowly in the first three years of PPS implementation as compared to the three previous years.[91] Cost reductions have largely resulted from reduced admissions. Occupancy rates fell, and length of hospital stay was reduced. There does not appear to have been any cost shifting, nor has the quality of care for Medicare patients declined.[92]

Between 1984 and 1991, PPS payment per caseload rose at an annual rate of 6.4 percent (2.5 percent faster than the CPI). Between 1991 and 1995, PPS payment per case had decelerated to 4.2 percent per year. PPS cost per case actually declined in 1994 and again in 1995.[93] The most recent data indicate that over the past several years the hospital industry has managed to improve the balance of revenue and expenses in the face of strong pressure from private payers. Although a little over 20 percent of all hospitals had negative total margins in 1995, this figure was lower than any year since PPS began in 1984.[94]

There have been criticisms of the new payment system. Some suggest that hospitals will seek ways to limit the impact of the new hospital regulations.[95] Because price regulation is a tax on hospital behavior, it not only affects price but also hospital output and quality and quantity of services. Hospitals respond by attempting to reduce the use of affected services or resources by modifying their practices and products.[96] Hospitals modify the cost of regulation by seeking an area unaffected by the regulation, that is, the "unregulated margin." Organizations respond to regulation through institutional, managerial, and technical changes.[97] Hospitals altered services, influenced practices, and changed the products offered to decrease the impact of regulation at the expense of Medicare patients. They also changed the mix of services offered in the inpatient Medicare market and expanded the surgical market because surgical DRGs are more profitable than medical DRGs. Often, services were cut.[98]

Despite the impact of PPS, national health care expenditures have continued to rise. Providers may have concentrated on other sectors of the health care system.[99] Thus, one response to PPS may be higher costs for outpatient and home care services.[100]

State Governments and Cost Containment

During the 1960s and 1970s, there was rapid growth in state and local governments' public health programs. They took on many new functions in the health care field by expanding their role beyond the traditional public health activities.[101] Their traditional role focused largely on problems of sanitation and communicable disease. During the 1960s and 1970s, state and local governments' role expanded to include a broad range of environmental concerns: air and water pollution, radiation control, hazardous waste, and occupational health and safety, as well as the delivery of medical services, particularly to the poor (as a result of the federal Medicaid program).

This expanded role also led to dramatic increases in health care expenditures of state governments. Their total health care expenditures increased from $9.9 billion in 1970 to $33.2 billion in 1980. Medicaid expenditures accounted for $11.4 billion in 1980.[102]

By the early 1980s, health care cost containment had emerged as a major issue for state and local governments. A number of factors contributed to this. One was the general taxpayer revolt in many states that followed the passage of Proposition 13 in California. The second factor was a national recession, which left state and local governments with reduced resources. Third, and perhaps most important, was the sharp cutback in federal aid that occurred during the first term of the Reagan administration. The consolidation of many categorical health grants into block grants substantially reduced available federal money. The federal Medicaid contribution was reduced 3 percent in 1982, 4 percent in 1983, and 4.5 percent in 1984. The administration showed considerable interest in granting states more discretion when such discretion seemed to promise cost reductions.[103]

Faced with reduced revenues and increased health care costs, state governments have attempted a number of different strategies to contain cost increases.[104] By 1982, seventeen states had legislation requiring the disclosure, review (such as HSAs and CON), or regulation of hospital rates or budgets.

The Rise and Demise of State Rate-Setting Programs

One major strategy used by the state governments during the 1970s and 1980s was rate setting. Rate-setting strategy was developed with the encouragement of the federal government through legislation and support from several administrations. This strategy emerged in the mid-1970s as the regulatory instrument of choice in several eastern industrial states as a response to Medicaid's financial crisis. By the 1980s hospital rate-setting programs were no longer confined to traditionally proregulatory states in the industrial Northeast. Limited prospective payment schemes for Medicaid reimbursement were adopted in Kentucky, Missouri, Alabama, Georgia, Mississippi, and North Carolina.[105] Some states introduced mandatory rate-setting programs, while others solicited voluntary compliance with the results of the review process or operated as disclosure programs. There was a considerable amount of diversity in these programs. Some related to revenues, others to costs. Most programs were revenue based and were concerned with the total financial needs of the hospital. The cost-based programs were used for establishing reasonable payment rates for hospitals.[106] During the 1980s more than thirty states had established some form of rate-setting program.

Proponents of regulation saw state rate setting as an approach most likely to win political support and argued that hospital expenditures exceed corresponding benefits. Therefore, American society in general, and government in particular, can no longer afford to finance the excess. In contrast, proponents of medical marketplace competition argued that the imposition of rate setting tends to remove flexibility and interest in innovation from the hospitals affected. State rate regulations involve a complex set of issues such as which providers to regulate, how the rate-setting body should be organized, and how it should set rates.[107]

State rate-setting programs have produced varying results. Proponents have argued that some mandatory prospective rate-setting programs have been successful in reducing hospital expenditures per patient day, per admission, and per capita.[108] Opponents argue that in many states, rate-setting programs have failed to produce the promised results, and the positive impact of state rate-setting programs has been overstated.[109] The failure of some state rate-setting programs is attributed to the fact that regulators often lack the necessary skills in the complex field of financial regulation and have fewer resources than the hospital industry. For example, the State Rate-Setting Commission in Massachusetts has only a few professionally trained people in a bureau that sets rates for 140 acute-care hospitals in the state. The staff of virtually every major hospital is larger than the state's.[110] In sum, state rate-setting programs have not provided a "quick fix" for the rapid rise in spending for hospital care.[111]

Beginning with Wisconsin in 1986, states that had been in the forefront of rate-setting strategy began to abandon it. By the mid-1990s, state rate-setting programs nearly disappeared because most states that had established rate-setting programs during the 1970s and 1980s had begun to deregulate and abandon them. John McDonough provides four reasons for the demise of the rate-setting program.[112] One reason was that during the early 1990s,

growth in HMOs directly collided with state rate-setting programs. All mandatory systems had to decide up-front whether to require HMOs to pay
state-regulated hospital charges or to permit negotiated rates of payment lower
than approved charges paid by Blue Cross, commercial carriers, and other
public payers. When public officials had to choose whether to bring HMOs
under the rate-setting scheme or to let all plans compete on the same basis,
deregulation won out. A second reason for the demise of rate-setting programs was that statutes and regulations dealing with rate setting were complex
and often incomprehensible. The confusion created suspicion that rate setting was subject to excessive gaming by powerful players (i.e., teaching and
urban hospitals). A third reason was the changing interest group landscape.
Again the steady growth of managed care was a key element in the changing
landscape. Furthermore, the American Hospital Association (AHA), which
had supported rate setting in the 1970s, dropped its support in the 1980s.
Finally, a fourth reason for the demise of the rate-setting programs was the
fact that states that deregulated their rate-setting programs had experienced
political change in the form of shifting from Democratic to Republican or
independent control.

Today, only two states still have rate-setting programs. The most successful state rate-setting program is in Maryland. It is unique because it operates
with the support of the Maryland Hospital Association. The four factors that
have allowed Maryland to keep its rate-setting program on track are: the ability to prevent HMOs from engaging in competitive discounting, flexibility
provided to regulators to adapt to changing environment, the maintenance of
a Medicare waiver that has placed regulatory opponents on the defensive, and
the maintenance of Democratic control in the executive and legislative
branches.[113] The result has been dramatic. Costs per hospital admission from
1980 to 1991 increased by the smallest percentage of any state in the country
and were well below the national average. Apart from the support of the Maryland Hospital Association, another reason for the program's success was that
it covers all sources of payment and thus prevents cost shifting. At the same
time, the program is flexible enough to account for inflation and to cover
losses for charitable or uncompensated care.[114]

Health Care Rationing

Some states have attempted Medicaid cuts by reducing the number of people
on the program, reducing benefits for those who are covered, or both.[115] A
new theme is being heard in the health care field. It implies that there are
limits to what we can expect and afford in the way of health care. It is based

on the notion that health care costs are rising disproportionately compared to the small or marginal gains in overall national health. Therefore, we must establish priorities in health services and become more rational in our health care spending.

Advocates of this new school of thought argue that health care costs are out of control and that regulatory controls on spending or competitive approaches based on economic incentives are doomed to fail. Regulatory approaches are, it is asserted, based on the faulty assumption that medical care produces health, and more care produces more health. The only realistic solution, therefore, is the rationing of health care resources. If the United States is serious about containing health care costs, society will have to forgo some medical benefits, and patients should not expect to receive all the care they want regardless of the costs.[116] Proponents argue that health care rationing already exists in the actions of insurance companies, legislatures, hospitals, physicians, and individual premium payers, and we need to get on with the public business of determining how health care rationing should be carried out ethically.[117] Observers call the existing de facto rationing "silent rationing," "under-the-table rationing," "rationing by finance," or "rationing by wallet."[118] Rationing can be explicit or implicit. *Implicit rationing* refers to discretionary decisions made by professionals, managers, and other health care personnel within the established budgetary guidelines. *Explicit rationing* refers to decisions made by an administrative authority regarding the amount of resources and types of resources to be made available, eligible populations, and specific rules for allocation. Explicit rationing is effected through constraining levels of available technology, locations of facilities and programs, expenditure levels, and the like.[119] The effort in the Medicaid program to establish treatment priorities represents the most explicit form of rationing in the United States.[120]

In Oregon, health care rationing has moved beyond the talking point to the way in which health care programs might be structured. The state provoked a national debate in 1987 when it decided to stop financing most organ transplants for Medicaid patients and use the money instead for prenatal care for pregnant women. In 1990 it produced a revolutionary Medicaid plan. Rather than offer a minority of the poor a comparatively full package of services, the state proposed to give all its poor access to health care but with a reduced level of services. The state ranked most medical conditions as least or most economically worthwhile to treat under the plan. If money ran out before all services were covered, the lowest-priority services would not be covered. Faced with intense criticisms of the listed priorities, in 1991 Oregon health officials overhauled the ranking and produced a new list. The Bush administration turned down Oregon's request for a Medicaid waiver, necessary to implement rationing, partly on the grounds that it might conflict with the Americans with Disabilities Act. The Clinton administration, however, did issue the waiver in 1993.[121]

Critics of rationing are skeptical of the process by which the state would determine what is high- or low-priority care. The state plans to blend public comments about what it values in health care with an elaborate system of medical cost-benefit analysis. Critics are cynical of health care by democracy. The most vehement reaction against the plan is that it targets the poor—mainly women and children, who make up most of the Medicaid population—and the disabled.[122] Another criticism of the plan is that the meat-ax approach of denying payment for treatment of a given condition makes very little sense. While the plan has good intentions, critics assert that it will inevitably lead to gross misallocation of resources and will provoke legitimate cries of outrage from patients, physicians, the media, and interest groups.[123]

David Mechanic provides five reasons to be skeptical about explicit rationing. One reason is that once bureaucratic decisions have been made and put in place (i.e., once explicit standards are established), they are resistant to change because constituencies develop to preserve the status quo. Developing explicit standards is difficult and often impossible. It is not a science. Second, medical care involves a process of discovery and negotiation between a patient and a health care provider, not simply application of technical means. Third, patients have different experiences, needs, tastes, preferences, and values. Two patients in comparable medical situations may require different treatments. Fourth, explicit rationing will result in inflexibility in responding to the contingencies of people's real lives. Fifth, explicit rationing will be susceptible to political manipulation. Once decisions are removed from a dialogue between patient and doctor to the public arena, they become subject to political, social, moral, and legal turf battles.[124]

Medicaid Managed Care

Another approach—a competitive strategy—used by the states is to attempt a fundamental reform in their approach to Medicaid. This involves replacing a fee-for-service system with negotiated or competitively bid fixed-price arrangements for Medicaid services. For example, California relies on negotiated fixed-price arrangements. The Arizona Health Cost Containment System (AHCCS) relies on provider bidding for the delivery of health care to the indigent. The AHCCS program began in October 1982 as an alternative to traditional Medicaid. In 1989 the Arizona Long-Term Care System (ALTCS) was incorporated into AHCCCS.[125] In such a prepaid, capitated system of health care, financial risk bearing is shifted, partially from the consumer and totally from the third-party insurer, to the provider. According to proponents, such a system internalizes economic incentives.[126] Competitive bidding is also becoming increasingly popular for such health care services as clinical laboratory services, home health care, and mental health care.[127]

As we discussed in chapter 3 on Medicaid, in response to problems of cost and access, state governments have increasingly turned to managed care in their Medicaid programs, with many states requiring Medicaid recipients to enroll in managed care plans. Consequently, Medicaid managed care enrollment has increased dramatically during the 1990s. In 1991, only 9.53 percent of Medicaid recipients were enrolled in managed care plans. The number of Medicaid managed care enrollees had reached 23.1 percent by 1994, and 47.8 percent of the Medicaid population was enrolled in some type of managed care plan by 1997. On average, Medicaid managed care enrollment has increased by over 30 percent annually.[128]

Has such a dramatic increase in enrollment of Medicaid beneficiaries into managed care plan resulted in cost savings or a reduced level of spending in the Medicaid program? The experience of the AHCCCS program has been positive. A comparison of Arizona with other comparable states indicated that for FY 1983 through FY 1993, the state of Arizona realized a savings of $197 million, an average saving per year of approximately 11 percent of medical service costs and 7 percent of total costs (medical service costs plus administrative costs). Similarly, ALTCS costs from 1989 through 1993, including medical and administrative costs, were on average 16 percent lower compared to the cost of a traditional program in Arizona.[129] Another study of Medicaid managed care plans in thirteen states concluded that contracting with mainstream HMOs rather than predominantly the Medicaid plan is becoming more common, and that mainstream plans tend to be more costly, which may limit Medicaid managed care's cost-saving potential. Realistically, expectations of savings from managed care should be in the range of 5–10 percent relative to fee-for-service.[130] The Health Care Financing Administration has estimated that about 80 percent of Medicaid managed care plans to date have saved money. However, many researchers urge the states to temper their expectations of cost savings to the 5–10 percent range rather than earlier expectations of 15 percent or more.[131]

Medicaid program growth has slowed considerably after 1992. Medicaid spending grew on average by only 9.5 percent per year between 1992 and 1995. Preliminary data also suggest that Medicaid expenditures grew by about 3.3 percent in 1996.[132] There are several possible explanations for the slowdown in the growth in Medicaid spending. One reason could be the decline in AFDC rolls in response to the improved economy. Another could be the fact that growth in coverage of children and pregnant women has declined after the initial increase caused by federal mandates. Similarly, the number of blind and disabled Medicaid recipients also began to slow down during this period.[133] Growth in spending per beneficiary fell from an average of 9.5 percent in 1988–92 to 4.9 percent per year in 1992–95.[134] This decline can be explained by two possible factors. One is the rapid growth in managed care, which seems to be achieving some short-term savings. The second explanation could be the fact that the average annual medical price inflation dropped from 8.2 percent in the 1988–92 period to 5.1 percent in 1992–95.[135] Both the Congressional Budget Office (CBO) and the Urban Institute project the Medicaid spending growth in future to remain slow. The Urban Institute and the CBO forecast growth rates of 7.5 percent and 7.7 percent, respectively, between 1997 and 2002.[136]

The Private Sector and Cost Containment

The dramatic rise in health care costs also has had significant consequences for the private sector. During the 1980s, many corporations spent 25 percent of their gross revenues to provide medical coverage for their employees. According to a national survey of 1,955 employers conducted by Foster Higgins & Company of New York, an average company spent 21.6 percent more in 1990 to provide doctor and hospital care to its employees than in 1989. During the 1989–90 period, the cost to employers of providing employee health care benefits rose 46.3 percent.[137] This has led the business community to search for solutions to contain health care costs. Many businesses participate in freestanding health policy groups or health coalitions. Business reformers have pushed the concept of managed care.[138] The term implies a stepped-up coordination and oversight of employee use of medical care for eliminating unnecessary care typically found in insurance plans. In managed care programs, companies limit the medical care of their employees to doctors and hospitals that agree to provide care for a set price.[139] As we saw earlier, health maintenance organizations embody the concept of managed care.

During the late 1970s, the business community was not very concerned about rising health care costs and was not very interested in acting to control them.[140] Since the early 1980s, however, faced with a dramatic rise in costs, the private sector has begun to look for solutions to the problem. As a major purchaser of health care services, business has become conscious of its capability and responsibility for controlling health care costs. The private sector has become concerned because soaring costs are having negative effects on profit margins.[141] The government has fostered the emergence of private-sector initiatives through legislative changes that alter incentives by providing technical assistance and/or financial support, and by demonstrating feasible options in its own cost-containment strategy as a major purchaser of health services.[142]

The cost-containment initiatives undertaken by the private sector fall into four major strategies: cost sharing, direct action, managed care, and wellness programs.[143]

Cost Sharing

One category consists of greater employee cost sharing for health services. The patient shares in the direct cost of health care services for his or her own coverage or that of dependents. Cost sharing can include deductibles, coinsurance, or copayments. A deductible is the fixed amount that must be paid by the patient before the insurance benefits begin. Coinsurance is the percentage contribution patients' pay once the deductible is exceeded. Copayments are generally a fixed contribution, rather than a percentage contribution, toward each unit of service. This strategy helps reduce the cost to the employers by shifting part of the cost to the patient. It is based on the belief that when patients are made to share a higher cost for treatment (negative incentive), they will reduce health service utilization. Some studies have demonstrated that cost sharing in the form of deductibles or coinsurance reduces the use of health care services.[144] Others have argued that increased cost shifting is not in the best interest of the workers, that some of the cost savings are illusory, and that other savings are likely to be one-time savings.[145] Whatever the case, more and more employers are seeking to reduce costs through cost sharing.

The cost-sharing requirements are increasing for all types of plans. Deductibles rose significantly between 1988 and 1993. During this period, the average deductible for conventional plans increased 9 to 10 percent a year. Increased cost sharing is also accomplished by increases in employee contribution for premiums; changes in covered benefits; and less coverage of active workers, dependents, and retirees. The share of premiums that employees pay has been rising slowly over the years. A major reason for this is the growing portion of workers who have to contribute to the cost of their own health insurance. For example, an analysis of the Current Population Survey (CPS) by the Lewin Group suggests that, of all full-time insured workers, 31 percent had health insurance premiums wholly paid by their employers in 1994, as compared to 40 percent in 1988. Another growing trend is for employers to "carve out" certain benefits such as mental health services, prescription drugs, and dental care.[146]

Perhaps the ultimate in cost sharing is a disturbing new trend. Companies have begun to eliminate certain coverage. This has taken two forms. In one, companies that self-insure, rather than use a third-party health insurer, have cut or drastically reduced benefits for employees with diseases that are very expensive. These diseases include cancer and AIDS.[147] In the other case, companies have reduced or eliminated medical coverage for their retired employees.[148] In both instances, the worker or former worker is left to use his or her own resources, or to rely on public-sector programs.

Direct Action

A second category of initiatives is designed to reduce health service utilization, especially the use of hospital services, through direct action. Here, initiatives include requiring a second opinion for surgery, doing a preadmission review (often prospective) of all nonemergency hospital admissions, making a more careful review of medical claims, providing coverage of certain services and procedures on an outpatient basis only, and providing incentives to shift care to an outpatient setting.

HMOs, PPOs, and Managed Care

The third set of initiatives consists of encouraging or requiring employees to use HMOs or PPOs for health care services. A PPO either restricts beneficiaries to a list of providers such as hospitals and physicians or provides financial incentives for beneficiaries to obtain their care from the list of preferred providers. Providers are generally selected on the basis of lower price or lower expected utilization. PPOs differ from traditional health insurance plans in two ways. In PPOs, the insurer takes an active role in negotiating payment rates or selecting providers, and the providers are on notice to comply with aggressive utilization review procedures.

PPOs also differ from HMOs. PPO providers are paid on a fee-for-service basis and thus are not at financial risk for services they provide, nor do they have incentives to reduce utilization. Under PPOs, beneficiaries can use providers outside the PPO plan, which is not the case with HMOs. Unlike HMOs, PPOs do not generally practice in a common location or in group practices.[149] PPOs are mainly sponsored by health care providers such as hospitals and physicians and by insurance companies.

Prepaid group practice plans such as HMOs and PPOs are based on the concept of managed care to contain costs. Allen Buchanan has outlined five cost-containment techniques that are commonly identified with the concept of managed care. One technique for cost containment is payment limits. An example of such a technique is the use of DRGs by the federal government to reimburse hospitals for Medicare patient fees. A second technique associated with managed care to save costs is requirement of preauthorization for medical services such as surgeries. A third technique is the use of primary care physicians as "gatekeepers" to control access to specialists. A fourth technique is "de-skilling" (i.e., using less trained providers to provide certain services). A fifth technique is to provide financial incentives to physicians to limit utilization of care. Managed care is a fancy name for rationing.[150]

In recent years the HMO market has gone through significant changes. A market previously dominated by traditional HMOs and traditional fee-for-service plans has been transformed into a variety of plans competing on the dimensions of premiums, provider choice, and coverage. The HMO programs have changed to such an extent that it is becoming harder to distinguish them from other health plans.[151] Current HMOs can be divided into four different models—staff, group, network, and independent practice associations (IPAs)—based on organization of physician services and the method of payment to physicians. All four HMO models may use one or a combination of three methods of payment. Under the capitation method, a physician is paid a fixed fee for each patient served. In the fee-for-service method, a physician is paid an agreed-upon fee for each service delivered. Under the salary method, a physician is paid a fixed salary regardless of the number of patients he or she serves.[152]

In the staff model, physicians are employed on a full-time basis. Neither the physicians nor the personnel employed by the staff model are at risk financially. A salary system with bonuses is utilized to pay physicians. In the group model, the HMO provides the facility, administrative support, and nonphysician staff. Physician services are obtained by contracts with one large, multispecialty medical group practice. The physician group is paid a fixed capitation fee for caring for each HMO member per month. Physicians are free to enter into various profit-sharing arrangements that generally are not available in the staff model. Many of the large group-model HMOs own and operate their own hospitals. The network model HMO contracts with more than one physician group. In this model, physician groups provide facilities and support personnel. Each physician receives a capitation payment. Most groups continue to see non-HMO patients in addition to HMO enrollees. In the IPA model, the HMO uses a percentage of practitioners' time to provide care for prepaid clients. They typically contract with a large number of solo practitioners as well as single or multispecialty group practices. Most IPA-model HMOs reimburse their physicians based on agreed-upon fee schedules or payment limits drawn from a collective account. The staff, group, and network model HMOs are commonly known as prepaid group plans (PGPs). The key point here is that prepayments, the premiums from subscribers, provide the vast bulk of revenues for the HMO. Thus the HMO, whatever the model, has an incentive not to overprovide services. HMOs do this by emphasizing primary care and reviewing the need for more specialized services as well as hospital services.

HMOs have grown considerably over the years. HMO enrollment in the United States has increased from 6 million in 1976 to more than 50 million in 1995. HMOs have expanded rapidly, particularly between 1985 and 1987. The years from 1987 to 1993 witnessed a period of consolidation. Since then the number of HMOs has increased again. A great deal of volatility in the number of HMOs is attributable to changes in the number of IPAs.[153] It is estimated that nearly three-quarters of U.S. workers with health insurance now receive their coverage through HMOs, PPOs, or other managed care plans. Today, managed care plans are commonplace in small companies as well as large companies. Managed care is now the dominant form of health insurance provided in the employment setting.[154] By 1995 there were about 571 HMOs in the country, of which 326 were IPAs and 245 were group model. There were 58 million people enrolled in HMOs in 1995. Of these 58 million, 23 million were enrolled in IPAs and 35 million were enrolled in group-model HMOs.[155] The number of PPOs in the country is estimated to be around 1,036, enrolling about 50 million Americans. Thus about 100 million Americans are enrolled in managed care plans.[156]

Jon Gabel has identified ten major changes that have occurred in HMOs during the 1990s. One of the trends is the rapid growth of for-profit HMOs. Another major change is the rapid growth of network and IPA models. Similarly, there has been a major growth of mixed models. For example, in 1990 only about one-third of staff models were mixed models. However, by 1994, that figure had increased to 57 percent. Employers increasingly have chosen to offer hybrid health plans: point-of-service (POS) plans and preferred provider organizations (PPOs). Other changes include mergers and acquisitions leading to consolidation, decline of community ratings, and increased patient cost sharing.[157]

The managed care revolution in turn has also produced some backlash from the consumers. A significant number of Americans report problems with managed care plans and indicate less satisfaction with managed care plans than with fee-for-service plans. Public backlash is also driven by rare but dramatic and threatening events experienced by very few consumers personally.[158] In response, forty-two states passed managed care regulations or benefit mandates in 1997. In states such as California and Oregon, opponents of managed care have succeeded in placing many initiatives on the ballot, asking citizens to vote yes or no on several anti-managed care proposals. The public backlash has also led to introduction of several bills in Congress designed to protect the consumers. President Bill Clinton has proposed the Patient's' Bill of Rights Act of 1998, which includes provisions dealing with consumers' choice of primary care providers, a procedure for referring enrollees to specialists, a grievance process, privacy and confidentiality, a nondiscrimination clause, and quality assurance. Republicans have introduced their own limited managed care consumer protection bill.

The Impact of HMOs and Managed Care on Costs

Has HMO development helped contain health care costs? The success of a competitive health strategy depends on the creation of health care delivery systems that are more efficient than the traditional system, and that are able to compete on price, benefits, access, style of medical care, and the existence of sufficient numbers of such systems throughout the country.[159] Available empirical evidence suggests that HMOs, especially PGPs, are more economical and more efficient than traditional health care plans. Studies indicate that total cost (premiums and out-of-pocket expenses) for HMO enrollees are 10 to 40 percent lower than those of comparable people with traditional health insurance.[160] Studies have also shown that HMO enrollees have a 20 to 40 percent lower hospitalization rate than traditional fee-for-service plans, because of incentives to reduce utilization (fixed payments), which in turn helps lower cost to HMO enrollees.[161] Nevertheless, critics have argued that reduction in hospital use cannot be easily attributed to HMO-induced competition but to factors such as biases in data, long-term trends predating HMOs, indirect effects of other policy changes, and other forms of competition.[162]

Some have argued that the lower cost and lower inpatient utilization rates reflect "creaming," or biased self-selection. Creaming is done when an HMO enrolls only younger or healthier persons, who use less medical care, and avoids enrolling elderly or high-risk groups and poor people.[163] Some HMOs use marketing strategies that encourage a favorable selection of patients by offering services such as sports medicine that are more likely to attract younger and healthier people, and by locating themselves in middle-class neighborhoods.[164] The practice of healthier people enrolling in HMOs is referred to as biased self-selection. HMO costs and utilization rates are lower because HMO enrollees are healthier and use fewer medical services.[165] Other studies have disputed such claims.[166]

While there is some evidence to suggest that HMOs reduce health care costs and utilization rates, does this translate into an overall reduction in hospital costs? The research in this area suggests that HMOs have not succeeded in reducing overall hospital costs or health care costs in general. A study of the impact of HMOs on total hospital costs and utilization rates in twenty-five cities from 1971 to 1981 concluded that the extent of HMO penetration in a community did not have any spillover effect on reducing overall hospital costs.[167] Studies of Minneapolis–St. Paul hospitals from 1979 to 1981 revealed that HMO-induced competition did not restrain hospital costs per admission. Hospitals with a large share of HMO patients did not have lower costs per admission compared to other hospitals. In addition, hospital profits demonstrated an upward trend.[168] Similarly, an analysis of hospital expenses in forty-three metropolitan areas revealed that while the nationwide HMO enrollment increased from 4 percent in 1980 to 7.1 percent in 1984, total hospital costs were reduced by only 0.9 percent.[169]

Though HMOs may offer lower costs, they have not been able substantially to alter the national pattern of medical care inflation and increasing resource use.[170] This may be because while the number of HMOs has grown over the years, the overall growth in HMOs and enrollment in them is not large enough to have a significant impact on national health care costs.

IPAs do not operate from a group setting and generally use a fee-for-service payment method. HMO enrollees may constitute a very small percentage of any IPA physician's practice. Thus, IPAs may be unable to reduce costs as effectively as other models of HMOs.[171] IPAs are growing three times faster than PGPs. As mentioned earlier, by 1995, of the 571 HMOs in the country, a majority of 326 were IPAs, while 245 were group-model HMOs. Purists in the PGP movement fear that the industry may be taken over by insurance interests using HMOs for their own ends. Other concerns are that, under IPAs, physicians may give their patients second-class care and save very little and that IPAs allow local medical societies to preempt real competition with real HMOs. There is some evidence that in recent years IPA physicians are given financial incentives to control costs.[172]

A recent study reports that hospital days per thousand HMO enrollees (private-sector and Medicaid) have declined steadily since 1985. However, analysis also suggests that IPAs use significantly more hospital days than other types of HMOs. In addition, group-model HMOs in highly competitive markets have premiums about 11 percent lower than those of the average HMO.[173] Health insurance premium increases have decelerated in recent years. For example, premiums for employer-sponsored family coverage rose by 2.3 percent in 1995 and premium increases were below the rate of general inflation.[174] Some attribute this development to intense price competition among HMOs.[175] However, others have argued that it is not clear whether there is a causal relationship between decline in premiums and the growth of managed care.[176]

Lawrence Brown has argued that a competitive strategy such as HMOs cannot have a significant impact on health care costs because it is based on an uncritical application of the concept of incentives. HMOs fail to influence all five of the crucial variables related to health care costs: consumers, medical technology, physicians, hospitals, and third-party payers.[177] The major sponsors of HMOs are laypersons, consumer groups, foundations, hospitals, and insurance companies. Since HMOs are an alternative to traditional insurance, one would not expect insurance companies to become involved in HMO development; however, insurance companies have entered the HMO market as a way of protecting their market share.[178] The HMO-insurer alliance has very little incentive to cut costs.[179] Hospital-sponsored HMOs are difficult to maintain because the two institutions are trying to pursue separate ends. Hospitals want to increase hospital utilization, while HMOs want to reduce hospital utilization.[180] Overall, HMO competition to date has failed to provide a powerful federal strategy of cost containment.[181]

Wellness Programs

The fourth set of initiatives consists of employee wellness programs. Larger employers are increasingly promoting programs designed to encourage healthier lifestyles and behavior. The emphasis is on preventive care to reduce the need for health care services. The assumption here is that prevention will lead to healthier workers and therefore reduced health care costs. Such employee wellness programs tend to penalize workers with unhealthy lifestyles by reducing their health care benefits. Some health care experts express concern over such meddling by employers because some of the health care problems of workers may be related to hereditary, environmental, or socioeconomic factors over which they have very little control. Some firms have also begun to consider lifestyles in hiring and firing decisions. This has led the American Civil Liberties Union to charge that some employers are overstepping their bounds. It argues that if employers are allowed to refuse to hire workers, or to fire them, because of something they do in their private lives, workers will not have any private lives left.[182]

Other Private-Sector Initiatives

In addition to the four major strategies discussed above, industries and firms are beginning to rely on other initiatives to contain rising health care costs. A number of organizations have moved toward self-insurance. Rather than contract out with private insurance companies, these companies try to reduce their health costs through administrative savings. One important feature of self-insurance is that such plans are not covered under the federal Employee Retirement Income Security Act (ERISA). This allows employer flexibility in maintaining or cutting coverage.[183] Some large businesses have begun to offer general medical services at in-house medical clinics, staffed by their own doctors or provided by contract medical firms as a cheaper alternative to constantly rising insurance rates. The Goodyear Tire and Rubber Co., for example, runs its own drugstore for workers and their families. The Gillette Co. provides its own X-ray services at the company's medical centers. Besides saving on drugs and tests, companies can save money by avoiding unnecessary hospitalization through careful monitoring of individual workers' health. A large company can also negotiate low fees with contracted medical firms. In addition to the cost savings, one of the most attractive features of such initiatives is the convenience it offers.[184]

Private-sector officials widely believe that these cost measures have been effective. Increased cost sharing by employees is perceived as the most effective. Others are more skeptical, arguing that cost shifting does not necessarily translate into cost containment. They express concern that cost shifting may have adverse effects on low-income patients or patients with serious health problems.[185] Because many of these initiatives have been in existence for only a short time, available empirical evidence is very limited. It is impossible to make any meaningful judgment about the impact of these initiatives on health care cost containment.

Private Insurers

Private insurers are also undertaking new initiatives. Some of them are moving away from spreading the cost of health insurance equally across all groups and are increasingly charging different rates for different people. Young and healthy employees are charged less at the expense of older and less healthy workers. Some experts on health care economics are troubled by such practices. Blue Cross and Blue Shield of Minnesota (BCBSM) has become the first national insurer to link health care reimbursement directly to patient outcomes. The plan, which went into effect in January 1991, uses a new system of risk classification called illness outcome groups (IOGs) to classify illnesses by their expected rate of adverse outcomes. In a major departure from past patient-assessment methodologies, this new system takes into consideration not only the severity of the patient's condition but also the anticipated risk from medical treatment. The plan is based on the assumption that severity itself is not the strong predictor of patient needs. Severity does not measure the risk of intervention. The new plan is designed to assess two risk dimensions. One is the illness the patient presents when he or she is admitted to the hospital, and the other is associated with the level of care provided by that hospital.

Under this system, four new outcome categories of IOGs will be used to group procedures by anticipated risks and outcomes. IOG-1 indicates a minimum risk, while IOG-4 indicates a high risk. The basic building block of each IOG will be the DRGs. Hospitals whose adverse outcomes exceed the outcome rates predicted by the BCBSM system will not get reimbursed for the extra cost associated with treating those excess adverse outcomes. The precise mechanisms of the programs are still being developed, but many see it as the wave of the future in American health care policy.

The Private Sector and Health Care Cost Containment

Sources of data on trends in health spending vary considerably in their completeness and consistency. Despite this, there are some positive and consistent results demonstrated by different sources. One is the fact that growth rate of private-sector health care spending during the 1990s has slowed significantly. Similarly, the rate of growth of employers' health care costs has also declined recently, which reflects slower growth in premium costs per enrollee.[186] The growth in employers' premiums or costs fell from double-digit rates early in the decade to 2 percent or less in 1995 and 1996.[187] The growth rate of private-sector spending for health insurance fell steadily between 1990 and 1994, reaching 2.5 percent in 1994 and staying at that level in 1995. In 1990, it was 14 percent.[188]

Conclusion

This chapter has examined various regulatory and competitive strategies by the federal and state governments and the private sector to contain health care costs. Federal strategies aimed at health planning and peer reviews have proved to be failures. There is some evidence that the competitive strategy of HMOs has lowered costs to enrollees and reduced their hospitalization rates. However, the impact of Medicare managed care on containment of overall health care costs has been very limited. The changeover from a retrospective payment to a prospective payment system for Medicare reimbursements to hospitals, through the DRGs, has reduced the average length of hospital stays and has slowed the growth rate in hospital costs for the initial years of PPS. Medicare costs have continued to climb upward, however, and PPS has had limited impact on overall health care costs. The growth rate in the Medicare program has not shown any decline or slowdown. Nonetheless, it is significant that the overall growth rate for all national health care expenditures has slowed considerably from a high of 12.1 percent in 1990 to 5.5 percent in 1995.

State efforts in cost containment have had a limited impact on overall health care costs. State rate-setting programs have shown mixed results. States' attempts to replace the fee-for-service system with a negotiated or competitively bid fixed-price arrangement for Medicaid services, as in California and Arizona, have shown some success in reducing costs. There is no denying the fact that state governments' push in the direction of Medicaid managed care has paid some dividends, as reflected in savings materialized and a slowed growth rate in spending for the Medicaid program.

Private-sector innovations have also resulted in some health care cost containment. However, cost shifting, utilization reviews, and increased reliance on HMOs and PPOs present a potential concern about access and equity. Wellness programs are increasing but are still not widespread among all industries.

Overall, a combination of regulatory and competitive strategies has produced some success in slowing the growth rate of health care spending. Overall health care spending has continued to rise, however, at a much slower rate than was common in the 1980s and early 1990s. How sustainable is the slowdown in national health care spending? Does the lower growth of spending represent a permanent reduction? Some analysts believe that the competitive transformation of the health care industry has resulted in a system in which market pressures will produce permanently lower rates of growth in health care spending. Other analysts are more skeptical. A number of factors are likely to influence the future direction of health care spending.

First, government efforts to formulate health policies directed toward cost containment must be made in a political environment. Just as in any other public policy area, the interplay between various interest groups and partisan conflicts leads to the formulation of policies built on compromises, bargaining, and consensus building, which fail to produce the desired results.

Second, the value of cost containment inevitably comes into conflict with the cherished values of access and high-quality care in American culture. Almost all government programs aimed at cost containment have also attempted to ensure access and quality of care. Public opposition is likely to be high in any program that attempts to reduce access or lower the quality of services or the number of services provided. Furthermore, many health care providers are likely to oppose rationing of health services.

Third, demographic changes are likely to create further pressures for more, not less, spending. When the baby boom generation begins to reach retirement age between the years 2010 and 2015, there is going to be a dramatic increase in the number of elderly people in our society. This is going to accelerate demand for health care resources.

Finally, technological advances in medicine are likely to continue at a rapid pace. Medical technology is very expensive, and it is one of the major contributors to increases in health care costs. We, as a society, have come to value medical technology regardless of the cost and regardless of the benefits it brings. Advances in medical technology have helped prolong life, and in some instances have eased pain and suffering, but they cannot cure many major illnesses. Nevertheless, the general public clings to the glimmer of hope offered by medical technology, and society's notions of health, life span, and life itself have changed. Until we as a society learn to resolve these value conflicts, future prospects for health care cost containment remain tenuous.

CHAPTER 7

Medical Malpractice and Medical Liability

The Origins

The problem of medical malpractice can be traced historically from the Code of Hammurabi established by the King of Babylon around 2200 B.C. to its acknowledgment, revision, and refinement by Egyptians, Greeks, and Romans and through its doctrinal development in fourteenth-century England.[1] The Hammurabi Code replaced the practice of personal violence against medical practitioners that was prevalent at the time through the establishment of a synonymous system of retribution. Thus, for example, if a doctor treated a patient with a knife and the patient died, the doctor's hand was cut off.[2] A similar notion of "an eye for an eye" was also advocated by the Mosaic Code of the Israelites. The limited size of their population and the need to preserve optimum manpower ultimately led to revision of the code by the eleventh century. The concept of an "eye for an eye" was replaced by the idea of monetary compensation for damages. The compensation was to be equal to the difference in value of the injured person before and after the incident if he were a slave being sold for six years of service.[3] In Greece, Hippocrates, the "father of medicine," around 460 B.C. promulgated an oath governing the conduct of physicians and surgeons. Part of the oath calls on the physician to follow a system of regimen for the benefit of the patients.[4] The Justinian Code, written between A.D. 529 and 564 A.D., made an attempt to control medical practitioners. It called for an examination to test the physicians' professional competency, a limitation on the number of physicians, as well as penalties for malpractice.[5]

As the legal and court systems evolved in England over the eleventh and twelfth centuries from "blood feuds" or "clan retribution" and lynching to a system involving a grand jury, a "petit jury," and trial by juries to resolve disputes, it also led to the accumulation of a large body of recorded decisions by the courts in both civil and criminal trials. This body of decisions and the custom of applying these previous decisions to new cases came to be known as the "common law." The actual practice of following the precedent also came to be known as "stare decisis." This was the same body of common law that was ultimately brought to the American colonies, and it became a basis for the American legal system.[6]

Development of the Common Law in England

Some of the early medical malpractice cases in England were brought against medical practitioners in the form of criminal proceedings. A case raising allegations of medical malpractice and the issue of professional liability involving a physician occurred around 1290. However, at that time there was no distinction made between those practicing legitimate medicine and those practicing quackery.[7] "Witch doctors," "medicine men," and so on, practiced their craft through potions, magic spells, and appeals to supernatural beings, along with legitimate medicine. Ultimately, codes were developed to protect the members of the community from inept and careless practitioners. However, it was not until the year 1511 that England provided for the licensure of physicians under which examinations were administered by the bishop of the diocese in which the physician wished to practice. Later on, the Royal College of Physicians was granted a charter for the self-regulation of the medical profession. The British Parliament confirmed the charter in 1522, paving the way for self-regulation by the medical profession.[8]

As the courts tried to find legal theories and remedies, the concept of "negligence" began to enter into court decisions. Soon after, the concepts of "duty" and "standard of care" came to be recognized as well. The term "tort" derives from the Latin word *tortus,* which means crooked or twisted. This term later came to be associated with a "body of law" that redressed wrongs other than breach of contract. Thus, tort actions are designed to protect individuals from being harmed. Those who considered themselves to be wronged and wanted to gain access to the court were required to file a writ. Two writs served as a basis for tort action. "Trespass" related to all forcible, direct, and immediate injuries, whether to person or to property, and "trespass on the case" was designed to afford a remedy for wrongful conduct resulting in injuries that were not forcible or direct. This paved the way for the theory of tort law. This notion of "trespass," or direct injury and "trespass on a case," or indirect injury, was ultimately replaced by notions of "intentional tort" and "unintentional tort," or negligence.[9]

Initially, the concept of negligence under the English common law was applied only in terms of "the nonfeasance," or the failure to perform within the contractual context. Negligence as carelessness in the performance of an affirmative act that caused harm was not considered. Physicians were basically regarded as members of public calling who had a duty to serve all comers, and their liability was defined accordingly.[10] The rise of commercialism led to a changed role of the physician, and the legal premise for liability focused on the contract itself. Under this new understanding, the physician's undertaking came to be regarded as the true foundation on which to base an action. It was an actionable wrong if a physician undertook to provide medical services for a fee and failed to do what was promised. It was an actionable wrong, not because the law obligated the physician to provide a service, but because the physician had agreed to assume the obligation toward the patient, that is, because of a breach of contract.[11]

Things changed dramatically in 1374 when a medical malpractice case helped set a major precedent. The case was heard in the court of the King's Bench in England with Chief Justice John Cavendish presiding. The case involved a London surgeon named John Swanlond who treated the crushed and mangled hand of Agnes of Stratton. The patient's hand was severely deformed, and she and her husband sued Dr. Swanlond for misfeasance (poor performance) under a breach of contract theory. According to the medical records, Dr. Swanlond guaranteed to competently cure the wound for reasonable payment. He later denied making such a statement. The suit charged that Dr. Swanlond had so negligently conducted his cure that the patient's hand was impaired and it was maimed by her injury.[12] The standards of the Hippocratic Oath were applied and the judge ruled that if the surgeon performed well, exercised the limits of his abilities, and acted with due diligence, he should not be held culpable. The court did not limit the scope of its consideration to whether the surgeon had performed his services under the contract. The court went a step further and scrutinized the quality of services rendered based upon a physician's assumed duty under the contract, as well as the legal duty imposed on him to exercise some degree of care in the treatment of his patients. This decision established the precedent for applying the negligence concept under a contract theory to cases of misfeasance (poor performance) by a medical practitioner.[13] While the physician in this case was held not liable, the court established a precedent that if a patient is harmed as a result of the physician's negligence, the physician would be held liable and the law will provide a remedy. This laid the foundation for the contemporary standards of the "ordinary reasonable/prudent physicians."[14] In 1553, an edict, the *Constitutio Criminalis*, by King Charles V, allowed judges to call expert witnesses to testify in medico-legal cases.[15]

The blurred lines of distinction between action in contract and tort following the 1374 ruling continued to create a dilemma for the court for many years to come. Finally, in 1615, Sir Edward Coke, known as the "father of the common law" decided a case that established the foundation in English common law for allowing an action against a physician for negligence to be brought under a theory other than contract. He ruled that the law gives the party sufficient remedy to recover for default of performance or for negligence in the performance. The negligence cases can stand alone, without a primary action in trespass and outside the contract.[16]

Medical Malpractice and Liability in the United States

Nineteenth Century

American laws in the area of medical liability were derived from the common law established in England.[17] Thus, the development of the concept of negligence as the major standard of civil liability in tort closely followed the British experience. The first recorded malpractice suit in the United States took place in Connecticut in 1794 in *Cross v. Guthrie*. A Connecticut physician, Dr. Cross, had performed a mastectomy on one of Mrs. Guthrie's breasts and she died three hours later. Her husband sued her surgeon, Dr. Cross, alleging negligence and claiming 1,000 pounds in damages for "his cost, expenses, and deprivation of the service and company of his wife." [18] It was argued that the physician had broken and violated his undertaking and promise to the plaintiff to perform the operation skillfully and safely. It further argued that the physician's "professional performance was unskilled, ignorant and cruel, contrary to all the well known rules and principles in practice in such cases." [19] The court agreed with the plaintiff and awarded him 40 pounds for the loss of his wife's companionship.

Between 1800 and 1835, medical malpractice was almost unknown in the United States, and between 1812 and 1835, *The New England Journal of Medicine and Survey* and its successor, *The Boston Medical and Surgical Journal*, reported only three malpractice cases. However, between 1835 and 1865, medical malpractice suits began to deluge the courts and the *Boston Medical and Surgical Journal* reported forty-five cases. By 1853, *the Western Journal of Medical and Physical Sciences* lamented the fact that malpractice suits occurred in every month of the year. This dramatic increase in the number of malpractice law suits has been labeled by some as America's first medical malpractice crisis.[20] Over a period of time prior to the Civil War, a variety of state courts rendered decisions that established the fundamental principles of medical malpractice in the United States. Analyzing the case law, C.R. Burns classified twenty-one pre-Civil War appellate court decisions between 1845 and 1861 into five groupings:[21]

1. with respect to physician's education and knowledge, the courts established the rule that a medical practitioner was legally responsible for what he said he was able to do;

2. the courts also established the idea that the level of skill expected of a medical practitioner was ordinary skill and not extraordinary skill;

3. the courts ascertained that physicians' contract required them to use reasonable and ordinary care in the application of their knowledge and skill;

4. whenever there was reasonable ground for diagnostic doubts and difference of opinion about treatment, if the physician exercised his best judgment, he was not liable for errors of judgment or mistakes;

5. legally, physicians were not required to guarantee or ensure a cure.

By the mid-1800s, various courts in the United States had delineated standards of professional conduct for tort action. Negligence as a separate and distinct basis of tort liability was recognized in the United States around 1825.[22]

One troubling problem dealt with regular versus irregular physicians. Regular or orthodox physicians received their training at medical schools that were often linked to a university. Irregular physicians included American Indian doctors, root doctors, and homeopaths who secured their medical education in a variety of ways. In the early 1800s, most of the state medical licensure laws were often weak or nonexistent. By 1830, medical societies had been established in many of the states, and they advocated examination and licensing of physicians. State legislatures responded by passing licensing laws that were statewide in coverage but varied widely from one state to the next.[23] The American Medical Association, founded in 1846, advocated reforms in medical education but made little progress. The early promise of the medical malpractice laws to protect the public was not fulfilled. In fact, between 1820 and 1870, licensing requirements deteriorated. From 1873, beginning in Texas, state boards of medical examiners were established, and by 1895 nearly all states had such entities. All states developed procedures for the examination and licensure of physicians.[24] Flexner, in 1910, called state boards "instruments through which the reconstruction of medical education will be largely effected."[25] Today, states through their medical practice laws not only decide who may practice in a state but also define the conditions under which a physician may practice.

Physicians' experience with malpractice between 1865 and 1900 followed a course set earlier in the century and became a prelude to the twentieth century. Physicians were encouraged when malpractice rates abated somewhat during the 1860s, and by the end of the decade the problem of medical malpractice was no longer perceived as urgent. However, by 1872 patients were suing doctors with renewed energy. Even though appellate court decisions are an ambiguous measure of trial court litigation rates, the fact remained that state appellate courts handled an increasing number of cases in each of the decades: twenty-five cases in 1860–70, forty-five in 1870–80, forty-seven in 1880–90, seventy-seven in 1890–1900, and one hundred sixteen in 1900–10.[26]

Between 1865 and 1900, damage awards also climbed slowly, and appellate courts refused to overturn or reduce the gradually increasing malpractice judgments. Doctors ceased to blame their fellow physicians for their medical malpractice woes and began to argue that the poor and laboring classes were their main tormentors and that greed, status, and class resentment led them to sue physicians for medical malpractice. It was further argued that physicians and corporations were often regarded as fair game by the penniless clients of desperate lawyers. Physicians felt that working-class juries were susceptible to lawyers who constantly drew contrasts between the poor laboring man, on the one hand, and the rich doctor on the other. Physicians also denounced the increased use of contingency fees by lawyers representing poor patients.[27] While it is true that class resentment existed against physicians, much of the antagonism against doctors was due more to their demand for social status and prestige for their learned profession than to their wealth. In early America, Jacksonians were repelled by the quasi-aristocratic views espoused by physicians. Physicians' average income still placed most of them only in the middle class.[28]

Physicians began to realize the problems of risking their reputation, legal fees, and court costs involved in fighting every case in court. This inspired the concept of group defense organizations. Legal defense associations sponsored by local medical societies very quickly became popular in many states. Organized physicians also became a potent political force, and many medical societies began to look for legislative remedies for malpractice lawsuits. However, most of their efforts were not very successful.[29]

Courts accepted a variety of substitutes for the term "ordinary" in the description of physicians' responsibilities. Appellate courts were in general agreement that terms such as "average skill," "fair knowledge and skill," "adequate care," and "reasonable skill" were valid synonyms for "ordinary." Furthermore, the courts also ruled that a physician could not be held liable for malpractice if a patient contributed in any way to his or her injury. However, some appellate judges fashioned an exception to the strict doctrine of contributory negligence: It was possible to hold a physician responsible for damages caused by his negligence even if the patient may have aggravated the injury. Courts also, over a period of time, ratified the locality principle. According to this principle, a physician's standard of skill should be judged by local circumstances.[30]

The Twentieth Century

By the beginning of the twentieth century, medical education had improved, medical societies were able to blunt the effects of intraprofessional competition, and licensure requirements were present in all states. However, medical malpractice suits continued partly due to the rapidly advancing medical technology. Medical discoveries in bacteriological science, nutritional advances, and pharmacological advances improved and routinized more treatments. It was during the 1930s and 1940s that scientists invented the miracle sulfonamide drugs and penicillin. Surgery had become common by the first half of the twentieth century. Discoveries in immunology, heredity, molecular biology, and chemistry, as well as the development of diagnostics and therapeutic technologies since the 1940s, dramatically improved modern medicine. Technology raised demands and expectations, which in turn led to higher dissatisfaction when treatments failed.[31]

Medical Malpractice Crisis of the 1970s and 1980s

During the 1950s, the medical malpractice insurance market was very stable. However, the malpractice insurance system in the United States underwent a "crisis" in the decades of the 1970s and 1980s.[32] Due to an unexpected surge in claims, many medical malpractice insurance companies either announced large hikes in premiums or withdrew from some state markets altogether. From 1974 to 1975, malpractice insurance premiums increased over 300 percent,[33] and physicians in some states could not find coverage at any price. By the mid-1970s, the malpractice insurance market was considered to be experiencing a crisis.[34] The frequency of malpractice claims (per 100 physicians) increased at about 10 percent a year during the 1970s and the 1980s, with sharp increases in the early 1970s and the early 1980s and slower growth in the second halves of both decades.[35] According to the General Accounting Office (GAO), malpractice premiums rose 45 percent from 1982 to 1984. Furthermore, malpractice premiums had risen to 9 percent of physicians' total costs,[36] whereas they represented only 1 percent of physicians' total costs in the 1950s.[37] According to the same GAO report, medical malpractice insurance costs increased, but also varied among physicians and hospitals. In 1988, internists experienced a 22 percent increase in their premiums. This was followed by general surgeons (20.5 percent) and pediatricians (20.2 percent). The percentage of orthopedic surgeons paying out $200,000 or more in premiums jumped from 30 to 45 percent and for internists it jumped from 3 to 8 percent.[38]

In Virginia, the largest insurer of medical malpractice in the United States, the St. Paul's Fire and Marine Insurance Company, raised the premiums of obstetricians from a national average of $12,481 in 1982 to $51,240 in 1987, an increase of 311 percent. By 1986, of the states' 600 obstetricians, 140 were without medical liability insurance coverage. Another major insurance carrier—Pennsylvania Hospital Insurance Company—left the Virginia market altogether in 1986. About 25 percent of the state's obstetricians could not get an insurance policy at any price.[39] When physicians in Florida went on strike to protest spiraling malpractice costs, some emergency rooms were forced to close down, while others had to manage with meager staffs. The situation was described as the "Beirut of American health care."[40]

There is also significant regional variations regarding where doctors get sued the most. Texas is one of the states where the incidence of malpractice suits against physicians is among the highest. One out of every seven physicians in Texas becomes a malpractice defendant every year. The percentage of doctors with claims filed against them rose from 10.8 percent in 1988 to about 15 percent in 1992, almost double the national average. The number of claims filed each year against the state's doctors jumped from 1,745 to 5,000 within a decade after 1983.[41]

Despite this predominant perception of crisis in medical malpractice insurance, some have argued that no such crisis existed during the 1970s and 1980s. For example, some researchers have expressed concern that medical malpractice insurance companies are obsessed with making a huge profit.[42] The argument goes that the high premiums charged to physicians generate the perception of crisis when, in fact, no crisis exists.[43] Some analysts have suggested that data from 1978 to 1986 show that medical malpractice insurance ranked only medium in underwriting profitability compared with other lines of insurance. In fact, during the 1985–86 period, it was the least profitable insurance business.[44] Others have argued that the perception of a crisis was based on the misleading notion that there were sudden and dramatic increases in malpractice liability of physicians from the 1960s to the 1980s. Historical data demonstrate that contrary to the common perception, recent increases in physician liability were neither sudden nor dramatic, and that the growth rates in physician liability between 1960 and 1980 are comparable to growth rates prior to the 1950s.[45]

The widely perceived crisis in the medical malpractice insurance market has raised a great deal of concern and criticism about the current system of tort, and has generated much debate and discussion about tort reform at the federal and state level. State governments, since the 1980s, have already initiated a significant number of reforms.

In the next section we briefly examine how the current tort system operates. This is followed by a discussion of the perceived weaknesses of the present tort system. Next, we examine a variety of reforms espoused by advocates of tort reform and then we examine reforms undertaken at the federal and state levels. Finally, we examine the new issues and concerns raised about medical liability by the rapid increase of managed care organizations such as HMOs.

The Current Tort System

Medical malpractice can be defined in a broad sense as "any unjustified act or failure to act on the part of a doctor or other health care professional that results in harm to the patient."[46] Within the legal framework of medical injury, negligence is a conduct that fails to achieve accepted standards of professional health care, and malpractice is negligent conduct that does harm to a patient. Negligence is treated as a civil wrong (tort), not a crime or breach of contract.[47] In order for a patient (plaintiff) to win a malpractice case in a court, it must be reasonably demonstrated that (1) the health care provider deviated from generally accepted medical practice, and (2) the medical injury/harm caused to the patient was the result of the health care provider's action or failure to act. It must be shown that the patient's injury resulted from negligence and not other causes such as the normal risk of medical treatment or the patient's prior health condition. If this is demonstrated with a preponderance of evidence, then the patient is entitled to recover compensatory damages for both economic and noneconomic losses (e.g., medical expenses, lost and projected earnings, and pain and suffering). Punitive damages can also be awarded in cases where the health care provider's conduct is viewed as willful and wanton.[48] In other words, the plaintiff must show three things: (1) the health care provider owed the plaintiff a duty of care, (2) the defendant failed to carry out this duty, and (3) the breach of duty caused damage to the plaintiff.[49]

In malpractice action, recovery against the physician is allowed only if one can demonstrate that there was an understanding between the physician and the patient (express or implied) that the physician would treat the patient with appropriate professional care, and that the patient would pay for such care, and that there was breach of professional duty to the patient. The breach of professional duty means that the doctor did something contrary to the recognized standard of medical practice in the community. There must be additional proof that the conduct of the doctor caused injury to the patient and the patient suffered damages. Finally, contributory negligence is another element in malpractice litigation. This involves breach of duty on the doctor's part to use ordinary care that a reasonable prudent person would use and which legally contributed to the injury of the patient.[50]

In the context of medical malpractice it is generally not difficult to establish the existence of a duty of care. To establish that the doctor has breached the duty of care is more difficult. Furthermore, to demonstrate causation sufficient to establish a link between the breach of duty and the injury or harm suffered by the patient is even more complex and difficult. With respect to determining reasonable medical care, the courts have generally looked to the customary practice of the medical profession as the benchmark of acceptable behavior.[51] The courts have further accepted the notion that the level of skill expected of physicians was ordinary skill and not extraordinary skills, and that physicians are expected to use reasonable and ordinary care in their application of knowledge and skill. Furthermore, the courts have also established that a physician's standard of skill should be judged by local circumstances.

Farber and White have outlined three stages of the litigation process in medical malpractice lawsuits.[52] The first stage of the litigation process generally involves the plaintiff filing a lawsuit against the physician. Often, the filing of lawsuits is preceded by communication in which the plaintiff attempts to extract a settlement offer without filing a suit. In medical malpractice cases the plaintiff's lawyers are paid on a contingency basis, that is, they receive a proportion (usually one-third) of the settlement amount if the case settles or of the damage award if the plaintiff wins at the trial. If the plaintiff drops the case or loses it, the lawyer receives nothing. This gives a potential lawyer incentive to screen cases carefully.

The second stage of the litigation involves pretrial discovery. This involves exchange of information, that is, evidence, between the plaintiff and the defendant. This includes many things. For example, the hospital provides the plaintiff with his or her medical records, while the hospital has a physician it names examine the patient (plaintiff) to verify damage claims. Each side in the case also deposes the other side's expert witnesses. The plaintiff's lawyer also deposes the medical personnel involved in the incident.

The third stage involves the actual trial itself. If the case goes to a local court, either side has the right to demand a trial by jury. Plaintiffs, in general, often demand a jury trial. Jury trials are not available in state courts. The judge or the jury decides whether the defendant is liable as well as the amount of damage to award if the defendant is found liable.

Very few cases actually go to trial. Most malpractice cases are either dropped by the plaintiff or settled out of court during the discovery period. Also, occasionally the judge may dismiss a case; this may be done for a variety of technical reasons at any stage of the litigation process.[53]

Today, medical practice and injuries are governed by some well-established principles of the common law tort system. They include the following: if a plaintiff is injured as a result of wrongful (i.e., negligent) behavior by a health care practitioner, the plaintiff is entitled to recover all losses, both financial and nonfinancial, caused by the fault of the medical practitioner. In the absence of negligent behavior, a medical practitioner is not legally responsible for injuries suffered by his or her patient; disputes over whether the medical practitioner was at fault and what injuries the patient suffered are resolved in a civil trial, often before a jury. Finally, if legal fault and liability are established through this process, compensation will be paid to the victim, generally by the liability insurer for the defendant or the institution that employed the doctor.[54]

The defenders of the present fault-based system argue that the system promotes two important values. One is the value of fairness, because the party at fault is punished and the victim is able to recover for damages. The second value that the current fault-based system promotes is deterrence, because the prospect of being sued and having to pay for losses deters physicians from providing substandard care. The financial and emotional incentives under this system are for the physician to provide careful treatment.[55]

Some have argued that a major problem is the fact that the current malpractice system operates on too many accepted presuppositions about medicine that need to be changed. For example, one is the notion that medicine can cure anything and everything, Medicine should be viewed as a cooperative venture with nature. Medicine may not be able to do much if the patient's body lacks the wherewithal to heal or recover. Second, the role of the patient in health care is as important as the role of the doctor. This includes the patient's cooperation, attitude, will, and ability to adopt to new circumstances, among other things. Third, modern medicine does not possess all the forms of expertise that are needed for contemporary health care to be successful. Finally, there is the need to distinguish between three sets of circumstances—medical intervention that leads to a bad outcome but no one's bad work is involved; medical intervention that leads to a bad outcome which results from a physician's bad work that is minor in nature and the recognition that all human beings are fallible; medical intervention that leads to a bad outcome resulting from physician's bad work that is gross and continual, that is, work that does great harm or happens repeatedly so as to suggest that there is a significant risk that the physician will produce a similar bad outcome in the future.[56] Many presuppositions about medicine are factually not very sound, and thus hinder our understanding of the concept of justice regarding medical care.[57]

Criticisms of the Current Tort System

One of the major criticisms of the current fault-based tort system is that it fails with respect to promoting values of fairness and corrective justice (by compensating victims for injuries suffered and by making the health care provider liable for injuries they cause) and deterrence (the potential threat of medical malpractice lawsuits that prevent doctors from providing substandard care). The system fails to produce fairness because only a very small percentage of negligent behavior actually generates claims, and of the claims that are filed, only 50 percent have any chance of success resulting in compensation for the victim.[58] The Harvard Medical Practice Study, based on randomly selected records of 30,000 patients from fifty-one hospitals in New York in 1990, estimated that eight times as many patients suffered an injury from negligence as filed a malpractice claim in the state of New York.[59] Patricia Danzon has estimated that only one out of ten victims of medical negligence ever files a claim.[60] Another study was based on a fifteen-year evaluation of medical negligence cases in the state of New Jersey. This study, after examining 8,231 cases involving 12,829 physicians, concluded that physicians usually win cases in which physician care was perceived as meeting community standards. Furthermore, severity of injury had very little bearing on whether a physician lost a case. Also, in only 6 percent of all cases reviewed did the settlement or jury award exceed $200,000.[61] Physicians often cite the fear of medical malpractice suits as the reason for the need to practice defensive medicine. To some, much of this is pure nonsense.[62] In Ohio, physicians prevail in 80 to 95 percent of all cases that go to verdict; that is, 80 percent of all cases are closed without any payment. However, to the defenders of the current system this does not suggest that plaintiffs are treated unfairly. Rather, it simply means that lawyers often file many frivolous lawsuits—that is, malpractice cases that have no merit.[63] Others have argued that the current system fails to compensate sensibly because no matter how passionately judges may want to compensate victims, they are constrained by the administrative structure of the tort law and the rules of damages. The current tort system leaves too many victims of medical malpractice uncompensated or undercompensated.[64] Sloan et al., in their study of a sample of 187 cases, found that when compensation is awarded, it tends to fall far short of the cost of injuries. Only about one-fifth of the claimants recovered more than economic loss. Punitive damages were not paid explicitly in any of the 187 cases included in the sample.[65] There is a fundamental mismatch between claims and injuries, and compensation tends to be inappropriate or unequal.[66]

In medical malpractice, punitive damages are seen as moderating abuses of power. Courts themselves have often indicated that punitive damages serve the important social function of punishment and deterrence. The policy underlying punitive damages is to teach both the potential and the actual wrongdoer that "tort does not pay." Punitive damages are also seen as a useful tool for augmenting the work of state licensing boards.[67] Critics also argue that the current tort system fails to act as a deterrent to physicians for a variety of reasons. One reason is the fact that, as we discussed earlier, very few victims of medical injury actually file a lawsuit, and of those that do, only about half have any chance of success. If malpractice litigation were effective in deterring physicians from providing substandard care, one would expect the incidence of substandard care to fall in response to increases in frequency or amount of claims. The empirical data do not support this. Despite increases in the frequency and amount of awards, there has not been any significant decline in incidents of medical malpractice.[68] Second, punitive damages are more likely to be effective in deterring an institution than a solo practitioner who may flee jurisdiction. The isolated nature of a solo practice also does not subject a deviant physician to peer review, common in institutional settings.[69] Third, the medical profession does a poor job of self-policing. Physicians often fail to report negligent behavior by fellow physicians, and state licensing boards are notorious for their inaction rather than action when negligent behavior does get reported. In 1985 only 2,108 of the 552,716 licensed physicians in the United States received any disciplinary action. Of the 2,108 who did receive disciplinary action, in only 641 cases were physicians' licenses to practice suspended or revoked.[70] A study of licensing boards in Florida found that even when licensing boards take disciplinary action, they are more likely to discipline older physicians and noncertified practitioners.[71] Finally, physicians often are ignorant of the common law of tort, and often seem to have an incomplete or incorrect understanding of the legal definition of negligence.[72]

Most of the medical malpractice lawsuits that end up in courts are tried before a jury. Juries make factual determinations and apply relevant laws to the facts to arrive at a verdict. The philosophy behind the jury system is that an impartial group of citizens can make decisions that reflect their common experiences and community values. For many years, jurors were seen as knowledgeable persons who had some specialized knowledge or expertise about the case that would help them resolve the dispute at hand. Today, however, jurors are seen as persons who have very little advanced knowledge about the case and thus, have no preconceived ideas or opinions regarding the dispute involved. The emphasis is on having laypersons as jurors.[73] The use of juries in medical malpractice cases has come under heavy criticism for a variety of reasons. Some have argued that jurors selected, at least in part, for their ignorance of the case are incompetent to decide issues involving complex scientific and medical evidence.[74] The heavy use of expert witnesses in medical malpractice cases poses a special problem for jurors when each side provides expert witnesses who testify in support of their respective position. It is argued that under this circumstance, jurors are left to determine which expert's testimony to believe since they themselves lack clear understanding of the testimony itself. They can also be easily misled by expert witnesses. Jurors are also susceptible to emotional ploys and irrelevant legal arguments.[75] A report by the American Medical Association's Specialty Society Medical Liability Project in 1988 argued that juries are not optimally suited to decide complicated issues of causation and duty of care, that jurors cannot independently evaluate testimony of experts, and that jurors cannot be very effective in deciding medical liability cases because their own experience and exposure to medical issues is very limited.[76] Critics also argue that juries are biased and unpredictable in their verdicts. Juries are also criticized for awarding extremely high awards to plaintiffs. Critics claim that this has become a "lottery" system rather than a rational system.[77]

The defenders of the jury system disagree with most of these criticisms. They argue that many of the criticisms of the jury system are based on anecdotal information rather than any hard scientific data. For example, after examining 24,625 civil jury verdicts from state trial courts of general jurisdiction in forty-six counties in eleven states, Stephen Daniels cautions about the danger of making sweeping generalizations about national trends or patterns. This research demonstrates the importance of local context, especially since local socioeconomic and environmental factors provide a primary explanation for variations in jury awards.[78] The findings raise doubts about the notion advanced by the critics of the jury system that the jury system has run amok. It has also been argued that some of the work criticizing the competence of juries is frequently based on misrepresentation of facts.[79]

Are jury decisions biased in favor of the plaintiffs? After examining many studies conducted over a decade in which data on rates at which plaintiffs won were collected, Neil Vidmar concluded that the win rates for the plaintiff ranged from a low of 13.5 percent to a high of 53 percent. However, the median win rate for all studies was 29.2 percent. In other words, plaintiffs won in only three out of every ten cases.[80] This questions the notion that juries tend to be biased in favor of the plaintiffs. He concludes that the data raise some doubts about extravagant claims of jury bias.[81]

Defenders of the present tort system also challenge the notion advanced by critics of the jury system that jurors are incompetent and incapable of understanding complex arguments. Some research demonstrates that jurors tend to correct each other during the deliberation process when an individual juror draws an inaccurate factual conclusion. Similarly, an individual juror's failure to recall some fact or instruction is overcome by the collective memory of all jurors.[82] Studies show that juries generally take their role very seriously and want to make the best judgment.[83] Defenders of the jury system argue that the notions that jurors are incompetent, and that juries have deep pockets and award outrageous damage awards, are simply myths and have no basis in reality.[84]

Another criticism that has been raised about the current tort system is the use of the expert witness in trials. Aside from the issue of whether jurors can understand the complex testimony of the expert witness, critics charge that the current system invites many forms of abuse. Many expert witnesses are motivated by money, power, or ego. As a result, they are willing to become partisan advocates of any opinion for the client that promises the most gratification.[85] Even well-meaning expert witnesses can end up being manipulated by skillful attorneys.[86] Defenders of the use of the medical expert argue that medical experts are given a bad rap, and unfairly portrayed as "hired guns" or marginally qualified whores willing to travel the country and say anything needed to win.[87]

The current tort system is also criticized for contributing to rising health care costs. Critics point to the costs of high premiums and the practice of defensive medicine as two major factors that contribute to rising health care costs. Average annual malpractice premiums for all physicians increased from $6,900 in 1983 to $14,500 in 1990. This figure is much higher for high-risk specialties. In 1988 an average annual premium was $38,200 for orthopedic surgeons, $35,000 for obstetricians and gynecologists, and $25,600 for anesthesiologists.[88] The amount of the premium continues to depend on the health care practitioner's specialty, location, and type of practice.[89]

Defensive medicine refers to physicians who, in order to protect themselves from potential malpractice lawsuits, overtreat a patient. Physicians often overprescribe diagnostic and treatment procedures as a defense against possible malpractice lawsuits. Research seems to confirm the presence of a defensive medicine, especially in the field of obstetrics. Exposure to malpractice suits seems to increase use of electronic fetal monitors (EFM), use of the label of fetal distress, and C-section rates.[90] According to a report published in 1994 by the U.S. Office of Technology Assessment, fewer than 8 percent of all diagnostic tests were performed by physicians, primarily because of fear of malpractice.[91] A survey conducted by the American Medical Association in 1986 found that 78 percent of physicians claimed that they practiced defensive medicine.[92] According to a study by the National Medical Liability Reform Coalition, malpractice insurance, unnecessary tests and procedures, and other measures to guard against malpractice suits cost 9.9 billion in 1991.[93] The American Medical Association's study concluded that the current malpractice system adds almost $21 billion a year to the cost of health care—$15.1 billion in defensive medicine and $5.6 billion in malpractice premiums.[94] According to Robert J. Rubin, president of Lewin-VHI Inc., a research firm, Americans could save $35 billion in medical bills over a five-year period by limiting malpractice awards and curbing defensive medicine.[95]

The defenders of the current system argue that claims about high premiums and the cost of defensive medicine contributing to spiraling health care costs are highly exaggerated. In 1985, the premium costs of 4.7 billion accounted for only 1 percent of the $425 billion national health costs. Furthermore, generally a small percentage of physicians account for most of the paid claims.[96] Medical malpractice insurance ranks only medium in underwriting profitability compared with other lines of insurance, discrediting the notion that the insurance companies are obsessed with making huge profits.[97] Defenders of the tort system also argue that many of the medical malpractice lawsuits that are filed are frivolous and lack merit. They suggest that the proliferation of lawyers results in lower income and increases their willingness to accept marginal medical malpractice claims.[98]

Critics further argue that the current tort system impairs doctor-patient relationships, and lowers job satisfaction among physicians.[99] According to the critics, the emotional and psychological costs of medical malpractice litigation is very high. For many physicians, being sued for medical malpractice is a major stress factor in their lives. It often leads to depression and anxiety and has led to retirement and suicide.[100] Research is scant with respect to the motivations that lead victims of medical injury to sue their physicians. Research does show that many of the noneconomic motives for suing stem from actual or perceived inadequate communication between the physician and the patient and his or her family.[101] Other hidden costs of the current system include a decrease in availability of medical malpractice insurance, reduced availability of services in certain specialties and geographic areas, and fear of new technologies and techniques.[102]

The criticisms of the current tort system have generated a great deal of debate about the reform of the current system and/or alternatives to the current system. In the next section, we briefly examine a variety of reforms and alternatives advocated by the critics of the current system.

Alternatives and Reforms

Legislative Reforms

Legislative (tort) reform is one of the most frequently proposed solutions to the problems of the medical malpractice crisis. One of the proposals is to place a reasonable cap on jury awards for noneconomic damages such as pain and suffering.[103] Proponents of caps on noneconomic damages argue that non-economic damages are difficult to measure and placing a cap will eliminate the lottery aspect of the current tort system and help reduce health care costs. Critics charge that caps are morally repugnant and unacceptable because they try to put a price on a patient's life, and because they fail to address issues of the patient's emotional vindication and deterrence.[104]

Another legislative proposal is to offset payment received by the plaintiff from collateral sources. Under the traditional collateral source rule, if a plaintiff receives compensation from a source independent of the tort, the payment cannot be deducted from the damages assessed against the defendant. Proponents argue that this is necessary to avoid double recovery from both a collateral source and the defendant. Opponents claim that such limits violate patients' right to due process and the equal protection clause of the Constitution.[105]

Shortening the statute of limitations for filing claims is another solution advocated by reformers. Proponents argue that a shortened time frame for filing claims will reduce the number of cases and discourage lawsuits filed as an afterthought after a long period of time. Opponents argue that often a medical injury may not manifest itself for a long period of time, and shortening the statute of limitations will be unfair to such a patient.[106]

Other legislative reforms proposed include limiting attorneys' contingency fees. Proponents argue that attorneys who get about one-third of the jury award as their fee have an incentive to seek larger and larger awards. Limiting attorneys' contingency fees would discourage lawyers from filing frivolous lawsuits. Finally, reformers have also advocated reform designed to allow large jury awards to be paid over a period of time rather than in one lump sum as a way of reducing the financial burden imposed by too large an award.

Alternate Dispute Resolution Methods

A variety of alternate dispute resolution (ADR) methods have been proposed as a way of addressing many of the perceived shortcomings of the present tort system. ADR methods and their variations are too numerous to discuss here. Some alternate dispute resolution proposals are moderate in nature and attempt to address problems of the current system, while others are more dramatic, designed to fundamentally change or replace the current system of tort.

In order to avoid and/or to address problems of the present tort system, one of the reforms advocated is the development of *medical practice guidelines*. Practice guidelines generally consist of systematically developed statements designed to help physicians in their health care decisions about patients and the appropriate health care for specific clinical circumstances. Practice guidelines may be developed by federal or state governments, professional medical societies, insurance companies, peer review organizations, and managed care organizations such as HMOs. Medical practice guidelines are viewed as providing a more direct link between quality of care issues and medical malpractice. Such well-established medical practice guidelines may help moderate exaggerated claims by expert witnesses and may provide some guidance to the courts.[107] Proponents of practice guidelines argue that predetermined prescriptive standards of care will provide clear legal standards for the practicing physician. Second, guidelines would help lower litigation costs because they would simplify trials, and some trial outcomes would become more predictable. Third, clear and precise practice guidelines may discourage and thus reduce frivolous lawsuits. Fourth, practice guidelines can help make malpractice legal proceedings shorter, simpler, and less costly. Potential problems with such practice guidelines include conflicts that can be created when more than one guideline has been developed for a specific medical condition or procedure. Moreover, if guidelines are very broad and unclear, difficulty could arise in applying such broad guidelines to resolve specific cases.[108]

Summary jury is another ADR method. In such a system, lawyers for both sides are given a limited number of hours (e.g., four to five) to call witnesses and make their arguments. Both parties may agree ahead of time to minimum and maximum damages if the jury decides the case in plaintiff's favor. This is designed to rule out jackpot awards.[109]

Another ADR method is to use a *neutral evaluator.* A disinterested third party looks at the evidence and provides an evaluation. The idea behind this concept is that if the assessment by a third-party evaluator shows that the plaintiff has a weak case he or she may decide not to pursue a costly court battle. By the same token, a physician who sees the evidence going against him or her, may decide to settle and award damages to the victim of medical injury.[110]

Mediation is often defined as a voluntary process in which a neutral third party helps participants reach their own agreement for resolving a dispute. However, the third party lacks the authority to impose a solution. The mediation process can take a variety of forms. In a pure mediation, parties communicate with one another in a joint attempt to reach a solution. Proponents of mediation claim that this has several advantages over the current tort system. Advantages claimed include: greater potential for improving the relationship between parties to a dispute through direct communication; enhancing the values of trust, caring, and respect; flexibility; low cost and speedy service; and the fact that the mediation process does not get bogged down by procedural and substantive rules.[111] However, some of the available empirical evidence suggests that mediation is not very effective in disposing of medical malpractice cases.[112]

Another ADR method is what is referred to as *pretrial screening panels*.[113] There are two types of review panels. One type is the medical quality review panel that is commonly found in a hospital. The second type of panel is created by agreement between bar associations and medical societies. The idea is to screen the cases for merit and promote early settlement, thereby reducing the number of cases that go to trial. Typical pretrial screening panels consist of physicians and lawyers, and the panels may occasionally also include laypersons. These panels review medical records and relevant evidence, consult with medical experts, and determine whether the patient's injury was caused by medical malpractice. If such is the case, it encourages settlement. If the panel finds that medical malpractice did not cause medical injury, it encourages dismissal of the claim by the victim. If the case does go to trial, the panel can provide experts who document its findings at the trial.[114]

Proponents view pretrial screening panels as potentially reducing tort cost by encouraging early settlement and by reducing the number of cases that end up in court. However, critics argue that a great deal of time and money is wasted if the case is not settled during the pretrial hearings. It has also been argued that review panels tend to favor the physicians since most panels have a physician on the panel. Finally, critics argue that pretrial screening panels are not very successful because their decisions are not binding and they do not have the power to discipline doctors.[115]

One of the most widely debated and discussed ADR methods is *arbitration*. In an arbitration, parties to a dispute voluntarily agree to refer a dispute to one or more impartial arbitrators for a final decision. The arbitrators are selected often by the parties to the dispute. The arbitrator's decision may or may not be binding. However, even when an arbitrator's decision is not binding, the arbitrator's opinion can exert a great deal of influence on the party against whom the judgment is rendered, to settle the case. Arbitration takes on several different forms and variations. It can be grouped into three broad categories.[116] In *traditional arbitration*, parties to a dispute, through agreement, create a private forum for the resolution of their disputes. Parties negotiate a set of rules for resolving their disputes and agree to be bound by the results. In a *facilitated arbitration*, the rules and procedures are specified by the state rather than being negotiated and agreed upon by the parties to the dispute. *Mandatory arbitration* is imposed by a state through the law. This form of arbitration often takes on the appearance of a screening panel for the court, since submission of the dispute to the arbitration is mandatory before parties can proceed to the court.[117]

Proponents of arbitration argue that it relieves overburdened courts of cases that might end up being litigated, saves time spent on resolving claims, and also reduces overall transaction costs and the average size of the awards.[118] Criticisms of arbitration include the fact that arbitration agreements themselves are of questionable validity—that is, questions can be raised as to when the agreement was signed, and whether the patient or his or her agent was fully informed of all the implications and was in a position to exercise free choice. Furthermore, physicians are often reluctant to ask patients to sign documents that discuss the consequences should something go wrong in treatment. Also, arbitration may not decrease the overall cost of malpractice claims. The final criticism of arbitration is that it does not give parties to the dispute an opportunity to reconcile their differences.[119]

In 1988, the American Medical Association proposed an alternative to the current tort system to reduce medical malpractice claims. The proposal has been referred to as the *fault-based administrative system*. The proposal calls for replacing the current court and jury system with an administrative claims tribunal. Under this system, medical malpractice claims would be adjudicated before an expert administrative agency. The proposal would create a state medical board as part of the state government. Its leadership would be appointed by the state governor. Claim adjustors would review claims submitted by patients. Claims with significant questions would be evaluated by a board medical specialist. This specialist would help the claimant evaluate settlement offers by the defendant. In a case that could not be settled, the board's general counsel would provide an attorney for the patient. An administrative judge or hearing examiner would supervise discovery and evaluate expert testimony. The judge could call his or her own witnesses. The judge would issue an opinion within ninety days. A medical board would also provide an appellate review. Appeals could be taken from the medical board's decision to an intermediate appellate court with a very high threshold designed to reduce the number of cases going to court. The state medical board would also handle credentialing and disciplinary functions and act as a clearinghouse for all information about individual providers and disciplinary actions. Overall, the AMA proposal retains the fault-based aspect of the current system.[120]

There are several advantages claimed for such a system. One is that it provides for an inexpensive screening mechanism. Second, it will provide a final resolution much quicker than is the case under the current system. Third, specialization of adjudicators will help streamline the process of presenting evidence, and expert adjudicators will perform the task of determining "standard of care," which is at the heart of most medical malpractice cases, much more efficiently than a jury of lay persons.[121] A potential major problem with such a system is financing. Would the system be adequately funded? It is almost impossible to estimate the cost of such a new system and it might end up costing more than the current system. Without sufficient resources and adequate manpower, the system might not be able to resolve claims quickly.[122] Finally, critics charge that such a system might be quick and efficient, but it ignores patients' interests and resolves disputes in a problematic fashion.[123]

Enterprise Liability

The concept of enterprise liability moves the focus from individual practitioner liability to institutional liability. This system will allow injured patients to sue either the hospital where they were treated or the health plan to which the provider subscribes. Such a system will immunize physicians from malpractice lawsuits. Instead of suing the physician, the injured patient will sue the enterprise in which a physician worked. The enterprise would defend the physician against a lawsuit. An argument in favor of enterprise liability is that it provides incentives to hospitals to improve their quality of care as well as to engage in risk management. It could also decrease administrative costs.[124]

Channeling

A variation of the enterprise liability reform is referred to as channeling. The idea is to remove the burden of malpractice liability from individual physicians to groups or institutions. Under one method of channeling, patients would be required to provide their own malpractice insurance. This would free physicians from malpractice liability. The problems with this approach are that poor persons may not be able to afford such insurance; that it provides very little incentive to physicians, medical institutions, or health plans to provide higher quality of care; and that it is likely to create greater distrust beween physician and patient. Under another method of channeling, hospitals and medical institutions would be required to provide insurance for both hospitals and physicians against any claim resulting from treatment received at the hospital.[125]

No-Fault Compensation System

One alternative advocated by the critics of the current fault-based system is what is often referred to as a no-fault system for compensation of medical injury.[126] In contrast to negligence or a fault-based tort system, a pure no-fault system would compensate patients for any injury arising out of medical care, regardless of whether it was caused by negligence of the physician or whether it was an unavoidable risk of normal care. The criterion used for compensation is not based on negligence but rather on medical causation. Thus, the issue of who is to be blamed or whose fault it is becomes irrelevant. Patients are compensated for medical injuries regardless of fault.

A wide range of options and alternatives are available in how one structures a no-fault compensation system. Professor Latz has provided one of the most comprehensive and excellent analysis of the various options available under the no-fault system. According to him, options fall under three main categories: (1) neo-no-fault early compensation system, (2) pure no-fault system, and (3) limited no-fault system.[127]

Under the *neo-no-fault early compensation system*, following any iatrogenic injury the provider has the option, within a limited time, to foreclose any actual or potential claim by offering the victim compensation for the full net economic loss (medical expenses and wage loss minus any payment from collateral sources) suffered and reasonable legal fees. The provider assesses his or her own liability and determines whether compensation is deserved. Once a provider extends a compensation offer, the injured patient has a limited time to accept or reject the offer but has no tort claim alternative. If the provider does not offer economic compensation, the victim has the full right to proceed in tort. The main reason behind this system is to preempt the tort system without abandoning the fault basis of liability.

Under a *pure no-fault system* the victim receives compensation for any injury resulting from medical care without assigning fault; that is, compensation is awarded regardless of whether the injury resulted due to negligence or a risk of normal care. Compensation comes from either the provider or the mandatory third-party insurer of the provider, or from the injured party's mandatory first party insurer. In a *limited no-fault system with specified events* the patients who have suffered negative outcomes that are specifically predetermined to be compensable are automatically compensated. What constitutes compensable outcomes is determined by law or by contract. The criteria used for deciding compensable outcomes are relative avoidability, or the likelihood of the outcome's having arisen as a result of medical error. For outcomes not included in the list of predetermined compensable events, the tort system would remain in place.

Two statutory variations under a limited no-fault system include the designated compensable events and the catastrophic no fault schemes. Under the designated compensable events scheme, health care providers would purchase from private insurers a policy of medical adversity insurance (MAI) to automatically indemnify a patient suffering from a designated compensable event (DCE). A statutory board of medical experts and consumer representatives would determine the list of compensable events. Providers would pay premiums rated for claims experience. Patients would be compensated for all medical and hospital expenses and for loss of wages up to a predetermined maximum.

A floor is also imposed on the wage loss compensation.[128] Under the second scheme, the law creates a compensation fund to cover participating physicians and hospitals for catastrophic injuries, such as severe brain and spinal cord injuries resulting from obstetrical care. The law excludes common law tort remedies for qualifying cases. The states of Virginia and Florida opted for such a scheme in 1987 and 1988, respectively. Other forms of limited no-fault designated compensable events schemes include elective no-fault and contractual neo-no-fault systems. The elective no-fault plan rests on elective contractual relations between patients and providers. It is meant for private implementation by health care providers as opposed to public-sector implementation. Health care providers would define all the negative outcomes for which fault-based claims would be foreclosed by automatic compensation. In a contractual neo-no-fault system, the provider obligates itself to offer economic compensation within ninety days of the occurrence of any adverse outcome specified in the patient-provider contract. The victim has the option of accepting the offer of compensation or pursuing the claim in court.

Advantages of a No-Fault System

Proponents claim that under a no-fault system removing the tort issue of whether a physician was at fault or not would remove a major source of litigation. Disputes would focus on technical questions of the exact source and extent of a patient's injury instead of on assigning blame. The system would also reduce expenditures on litigations. In addition, it would not place a doctor and a patient in an adversarial context, thus saving both sides the emotional and financial costs of such a context.[129] The money saved would free up funds to finance coverage for all victims of medical injury. It would also save time by avoiding a lengthy court battle, and victims would be compensated in a more timely fashion. Thus a no-fault system would be more efficient, both financially and administratively. Another advantage claimed for a no-fault system compared to a fault-based system is that it would be more fair, equitable, and rational. It would also remove the "lottery" aspect of the current tort system, in which only a few get large jury awards while others are undercompensated, and a large majority of victims are never compensated because they do not file a claim. In contrast, a no-fault system would compensate all victims of medical injury in a fair and equitable manner. Since a no-fault system guarantees coverage for all economic loss arising from covered or designated events, it would make compensation more predictable and rational by relating compensation to the loss incurred.[130]

Proponents also argue that if insurance premiums in a no-fault system are not experience-rated, it would remove one of the major factors responsible for defensive medicine, that is, fear of malpractice law suits.[131] This would eliminate a great deal of the costs of defensive medicine.

Disadvantages of a No-Fault System

Opponents of the no-fault system see many problems with it. They argue that a no-fault system would not deter negligent behavior on the part of health care providers, or at least it would deter such behavior less effectively than the tort system, for two reasons. First, because a no-fault system does not assign blame for specific negligent acts, there is no legal disincentive for the physician to correct his or her behavior. Second, a no-fault system would not provide any information to the medical community about which practices are considered unreasonable.[132]

Defenders of the no-fault system respond by arguing that of all cases involving medical injury, in a very small percentage of the cases medical injury is caused by negligent or incompetent behavior by the physician. Many medical injuries result from normal risks associated with medical procedures. Moreover, the current tort system does a very poor job of deterring negligent or incompetent behavior. For example, Danzon reported that even though 1,500 individuals were paid malpractice claims in California in 1976, only six disciplinary actions were taken against physicians for incompetence or gross negligence in that year.[133] A more recent study of Florida physicians concluded that none of the physicians with the most adverse claims experiences had their licenses suspended or revoked by the state medical board, and fewer than 10 percent of these physicians were disciplined in any manner.[134] However, this may not be a fair criticism, since existing disciplinary procedures in the medical profession are not designed to function as a shadow to the tort system.[135]

Another major criticism is that a no-fault system would encourage more claims to be filed by injured patients, thereby actually increasing the cost. The increased number of claims would more likely offset or exceed any savings a no-fault system might produce.[136] Furthermore, since the no-fault system makes causation rather than negligence the test for compensation, it might increase rather than reduce the administrative burden. Such a system would also abolish the notion of patient assumption of risk for possible adverse effects of adequate medical care. Any recovery that is less than perfect might become potentially compensable if there is any chance for alternative judgment, possible omission, or better treatment regardless of the cost.[137]

Another controversial aspect of the no-fault system is the fact that most no-fault plans would eliminate compensation for things such as pain, suffering, and the loss of enjoyment of life. In common law they are regarded as compensation for losses. They are also the traditional source of attorneys' fees. This would make it more difficult for patients to sue for medical injuries.[138] Another problem cited with the no-fault specified or designated event compensation plans is that the occurrence of compensable events is much easier to identify in cases of automobile and work-related accidents, but this is not true with the incidence of iatrogenic injury. Medical malpractice cases involve a variety of injuries, and it would be difficult to define a large number of comprehensible events with enough clarity. This could lead to extensive litigation over whether a particular case falls within a no-fault or a tort system.[139]

The general theme running through these criticisms is the notion that a no-fault system would be obtrusive and impersonal. It would focus only on the financial responsibility aspect of the health care provider, and would ignore assigning blame and holding individual health care providers accountable for their behavior and actions.[140]

Medical Liability: Federal Government Policy and Reforms

The federal role in the area of medical liability has been a limited one. Product liability provides a strong case for uniform treatment, and thus a case can be made for federal rules governing product liability. However, medical treatment decisions generally occur and have impact within a state. This is not to say that there are no spillover effects on service providers and consumers. Nonetheless, it is difficult to make a case for a strong federal role in the area of medical liability unless a strong need for national uniformity can be established or it can be demonstrated that there are overriding national interests involved.[141]

It is important to point out that the tradition of state tort law is a uniquely American tradition. In almost every other country, tort law is a national responsibility. In many other federal systems similar to the United States, such as India and Switzerland, tort law is all national law. In Canada and Australia, tort doctrines are developed by the judiciary in provinces or states, but disagreements are resolved by the national supreme court. In the United States, the tradition of state tort law in American society has held up quite well. In general, the Congress of the United States has respected tort law as a state prerogative.[142] This is not to suggest that the national government has never intervened in this area. In fact, in the twentieth century the national government has assumed an increasing number of responsibilities, and in the process has displaced state lawmaking authority. For example, at the turn of the century a large number of claims were brought by employees against their employers, especially railroad employees against the railroads. In 1908, Congress intervened and passed the Federal Employees Liability Act (FELA). This federal legislation preempted state tort law and governed the liability claims brought by employees against the railroads operating in interstate commerce.[143]

Under the doctrine of sovereign immunity, a government is not liable for the tortuous acts of its employees. However, the Federal Tort Claims Act (FTCA) provided a limited waiver of the federal government's sovereign immunity. It exposes the federal government to tort liability only to the extent that Congress has affirmatively waived sovereign immunity. Under FTCA, Congress gave plaintiffs the option of suing the government rather than the federal employee. However, plaintiffs were not barred from suing a federal employee. Over the years, Congress has given special protection to federal employees, especially medical personnel, who, because of the nature of their work, are at greater risk of being sued for tort committed within the scope of their job.[144]

In 1985, Congress passed the Medical Malpractice Immunity Act (MMIA). The purpose of the law was to protect medical personnel from any liability arising out of performance of their official medical duties. The MMIA removes plaintiff's option to sue the physician individually. The law is also intended to provide adequate compensation for legitimate malpractice claims. The law allows the attorney general to remove lawsuits from state to federal courts and to substitute the United States as defendant if he or she certifies that defendants were acting within the scope of their employment.[145]

Congress had also become concerned that state licensing boards were not adequately weeding out incompetent or unprofessional physicians and that it was too easy for a physician to move to another state (i.e., jurisdiction), and start their practice again. With this in mind, Congress in 1986 passed the Health Care Quality Improvement Act. This law restricted the ability of an incompetent physician to move from state to state without disclosure or discovery of his or her previous incompetent or damaging performance. To prevent such jurisdictional hopping, the law also created the National Practitioner Data Bank. The data bank stores information about physicians and other health care providers who have been defendants in malpractice cases and who, directly or through an insurance carrier, paid damages to claimant by settlement or by verdict after September 1990. The data bank is required to pass this information on to hospitals whenever a physician seeks appointment or reappointment to a medical staff. Information is also sometimes supplied to agencies such as HMOs. However, the information in the data bank is not available to the general public. Information is available upon request by physicians or state licensing boards. Attorneys may get the information only if a malpractice lawsuit has been filed against a physician and it is alleged that the hospital failed to inquire of the data bank about the physician being sued.[146]

Medical Liability Reforms: The Bush Administration

The perceived medical malpractice crisis of the 1970s and 1980s, combined with the criticisms of the current tort system, led to significant discussion and debate about medical liability reforms at the federal level. President George Bush argued that the skyrocketing costs of defensive medicine and malpractice litigation were threatening to make health care unaffordable to many Americans.

Congress made an attempt to develop practice guidelines when, in 1989, it amended the Public Health Service Act by enacting the Omnibus Budget Reconciliation Act. The law created the Agency for Health Care Policy and Research (AHCPR), with a primary mission of conducting or commissioning studies that focus on actual outcomes and effectiveness of various medical treatments. The law also established the Forum for Quality and Effectiveness in Health Care. The forum is a separate office of AHCPR and is responsible for appointing panels of physicians, experts, and consumer representatives to research and develop practice guidelines.[147]

In 1991, the Bush administration proposed a plan that would have given states three years to enact a set of very specific malpractice reforms. Under the plan, the federal government would have used financial incentives to compel states to adopt a series of reforms. Those states that failed to enact reforms would be fined 2 percent of their federal Medicaid administrative budgets and 1 percent of the annual increase in the operating cost portion of Medicare payments to hospitals. States that implemented these reforms would be paid bonuses from this money. The specific reform measures the Bush administration wanted states to adopt included the following: eliminating joint and several liability for noneconomic damages; placing a cap on noneconomic damage awards; requiring structured payments instead of a lump-sum payment for medical malpractice awards; promoting pretrial alternative dispute resolution methods; and eliminating the collateral source rule, among others.[148] It is important to emphasize that the Bush administration's basic approach was not to enact medical liability legislation at the federal level, but rather to encourage states to adopt reforms at the state level. However, the Bush plan did not get very far, and these initiatives came to an end with his defeat in the 1992 presidential elections.

Medical Liability Reform: The Clinton Administration

President Bill Clinton came into the office with a promise to overhaul the U.S. health care system. He had campaigned on the theme of establishing a national health care system that would make health care affordable and accessible to all Americans. After a very lengthy discussion and deliberation by the national task force on health care reform chaired by the First Lady, Hillary Clinton, the Clinton administration came up with a major reform proposal. The Clinton plan to overhaul the U.S. health care system was contained in the proposed Health Security Act of 1993, which was formally sent to Congress in November 1993. The detailed provisions of the Health Security Act and other major competing plans that emerged in the Congress are presented and discussed in chapter 9 on health care reform. Here, we highlight only those elements of the Health Security Act that dealt with the issue of medical liability for medical malpractice. President Clinton's proposed plan included several medical malpractice reforms. First, the plan advocated the creation of an alternative dispute resolution mechanism. Second, it required a certificate of merit as a prerequisite for filing a medical malpractice lawsuit. Third, it proposed placing a limit on attorneys' contingency fees. Fourth, it would have required malpractice awards to be paid in installments rather than one lump sum. Fifth, it would have provided the general public with increased access to information about repeat offenders. Finally, one of the cornerstones of the Clinton health care reform package was an attempt to relieve physicians of the burden of medical liability lawsuits by advocating enterprise liability instead of individual liability.[149] The Clinton administration believed that one of the most glaring problems with the current tort system is that it leaves individual doctors on the hook for malpractice. Under enterprise liability, malpractice risk would be transferred from individual physicians to institutions such as hospitals, insurance companies, and HMOs. Transfer of liability to managed care networks, also called Accountable Health Plans (AHPs), would help ensure that they would not skimp on needed services in a very competitive environment. Instead of paying malpractice premiums, physicians would pay a negotiated surcharge to their AHP. Proponents of enterprise liability argued that it had several benefits. One, it would remove doctors from the tug-of-war between payers. Second, physicians could end up spending a third less for malpractice coverage. Third, there would be a decrease in the practice of defensive medicine. Supporters also argued that enterprise liability would help improve health care quality. Needless to say, the insurance companies and HMOs that would have inherited malpractice risks strongly opposed this idea.[150]

Many other competing health care reform bills that emerged in Congress in response to President Clinton's Health Security Act also contained some provisions dealing with medical liability.[151] However, as discussed in chapter 9 on health care reform, for a variety of reasons no reform bill was able to garner majority support in Congress, and by the late summer of 1994, health care reform was declared dead. None of the bills even came up for a vote in Congress.

In 1995, Congress passed the Federally Supported Health Centers Assistance Act (FSHCA). The law extends coverage under the Federal Tort Claims Act (FTCA) to community health centers that receive federal funding under a federal program sponsored by the Department of Health and Human Services. It was implemented as a three-year experiment in 1992 and reauthorized permanently in 1995. The FTCA claims are first handled as administrative claims. If a claim is not settled within six months, the claimant can file a civil suit in federal court. FTCA cases are heard by a judge and not a jury. Attorney fees are limited to 20 percent of administrative claims and 25 percent on settlement of lawsuits.[152]

Congress, in April 1996, passed a broad tort reform bill titled the Common Sense Product Liability Legal Reform Act of 1996. The law would have restricted the amount of punitive damages that can be awarded in a civil action not to exceed three times the amount of damages awarded to the claimant for economic loss, or $250,000, whichever is greater. In the health care liability action, noneconomic damages in excess of $250,000 would be reduced to $250,000 before entry of judgment or by amendment of the judge after entry. On May 3, 1996, President Clinton vetoed the bill, complaining that it would intrude on state authority. Anthony Lewis, after reviewing congressional tort reform, concluded that tort law has been state law for 200 years and stated that "substantive tort law should be left to state courts and legislatures." Similarly, Joan Claybrook, president of Public Citizen, condemned the proposed law for infringing upon state sovereignty. Pamela Liapakis, then president-elect of the American Trial Lawyers Association, used similar language in disapproving federal action in the tort area. The spokesperson of the American Bar Association called federal action unwise and an unnecessary intrusion on the longstanding authority of the states to promulgate tort law.[153]

President Clinton, did however, on June 18, 1997, sign into law the Volunteer Protection Act of 1997. This law protects America's volunteers from meritless, costly, and time-consuming lawsuits. The law protects softball coaches, playground monitors, and emergency service providers, among others. The law establishes uniform rules and creates immunity from litigation for those volunteers who act within the boundaries of their responsibilities, who are properly licensed or certified when necessary, and who do not cause any harm intentionally.

Medical Liability Reforms at the State Level

Most of the action in the area of medical liability reform has been at the state level. In response to the medical malpractice "crisis" of the 1970s and the 1980s, many state governments passed a variety of reforms. The nature and type of reforms passed ranged from establishment of medical practice guidelines, no-fault system for certain specified types of injuries and mandating alternate dispute resolution, to a host of legislative reforms such as capping punitive damages, eliminating joint and several liability, requiring use of certificate of merit for filing a lawsuit, placing limits on noneconomic damages, shortening the statutes of limitation for filing claims, raising standards for expert witnesses, and imposing sanctions for frivolous lawsuits, among others. It is impossible to discuss each and every action taken by a variety of state governments with all types of subtle variations and differences. Thus, we will discuss only some of the major actions taken by a significant number of states and whether these actions have been effective or not.

Several states, including Maine, Florida, and Maryland, passed health care legislation that included provisions mandating the development of medical practice guidelines in certain specialty areas. Maine has incorporated into state law twenty practice guidelines in four specialties: anesthesiology, emergency medicine, obstetrics, and gynecology. Florida's legislation requires the state agency for health care administration to develop practice guidelines that are intended to reduce unnecessary variations in the delivery of medical treatment and to improve the quality of care. Maryland's legislation calls for a fifteen-member advisory committee to propose practice guidelines for medical specialties. The State Human Resources Planning Commission makes final determination on which guidelines to adopt.[154]

The states of Virginia and Florida in the late 1980s established a no-fault compensation system for birth-related injuries. The Virginia law, called the Birth-Related Neurological Compensation Act, went into effect on January 1, 1988. The Florida law, which went into effect on January 1, 1989, is also called the Birth-Related Neurological Compensation Act. Both laws provide compensation for severe birth-related neurological injuries caused by medical care regardless of fault or negligence of the health care provider. Both laws allow physicians to choose whether they want to participate in the no-fault plan. In Florida, hospitals are required to participate. Part of the funding for the program comes from levies on physicians and hospitals and assessment on insurers writing other lines of insurance in the state.[155] Doctors in Florida challenged the fees placed on them in the court in February 1992; however, the court ruled that the fees did not violate doctors' constitutional rights. In Virginia, the Virginia Medical Society was successful in getting the State Assembly to pass a bill that requires the state to suspend physician assessment any time the compensation fund is adequately funded for birth-related injuries.[156]

The two laws are similar in many respects. A claimant files a petition with a commission. A medical advisory board composed of physicians evaluates the merits of the claims and files a response within thirty days (in Virginia) or forty-five days (in Florida). The commission is required to hold a hearing within 120 days from the time of the filing of the petition. The commission determines whether the injury is a birth-related neurological injury. The infant is awarded compensation if the commission concludes that the injury suffered by the infant falls within the law. Any amount received from the collateral source is deducted from the compensation award. The commission's decision is final.

Most of the reforms adopted by state governments are legislative reforms designed to address specific problems or criticisms of the current tort system. For example, by December 1996, thirty-one states had placed a cap on punitive damage awards, thirty-four states had prohibited joint and several liability, while ten states had placed a cap on noneconomic damage awards.[157]

Twenty-nine states have enacted laws that either had mandatory or discretionary rules regarding collateral source damages. Fourteen states have placed limits on attorney's fees, while about twenty-nine states have adopted rules that address the issue of periodic payment of awards rather than one lump-sum payment. Finally, every state has some statute of limitation rule for filing a medical liability claim.[158] Needless to say, even among states that have adopted specific reforms, there is considerable variation regarding the mandatory or discretionary nature of the rules, the length of the statute of limitations, the ceiling at which awards are capped, and the nature of limits on attorney's fees. Thus it is easier to discuss state-level reforms at the aggregate level rather than at the individual state level. Clearly, the state governments have been very active in the 1980s and 1990s, enacting a variety of medical liability reforms.

How effective have these state medical liability reforms been? Perhaps not too surprisingly, the available evidence points to mixed results. With respect to practice guidelines, the jury is still out. Practice guidelines are generally developed to assist health care providers, especially physicians, in making clinical decisions regarding treatment choices, appropriate use of tests, and so on. How successful practice guidelines become ultimately depends on how courts use and interpret them. For medical practice guidelines to be admitted in a medical negligence case against a physician, the general standard of care required of a physician in a given clinical setting must be an issue. Furthermore, the proponents of the guidelines are required to establish that the guidelines are probative of a fact of consequence. This generally requires expert medical testimony. Once the guidelines have been admitted into evidence, they do not constitute a predetermined standard of care that a court is forced to apply. The court is free to consider other evidence regarding what the standard of care should be. Furthermore, studies also show that physicians often do not comply with the guidelines, and the compliance rate is estimated to be slightly over 50 percent. Medical practice guidelines have not been in existence for a long period of time and as a result there currently is not a great deal of information available on how courts use these guidelines. More experience with medical practice guidelines is needed before one can make any judgment about their effectiveness.[159]

Very few states have adopted a no-fault system of compensation for very specific types of medical injuries, as Florida and Virginia have. The usefulness of such a no-fault system of compensation based on available evidence in these two states is questionable. In Florida, the law did help alleviate the crisis of lack of availability of malpractice insurance. For example, 90 percent of all obstetricians in Florida were participating in the program in 1993, and the medical malpractice premium rates for obstetricians had also declined significantly.[160] In Virginia, the number of obstetricians participating in the no-fault compensation plan had jumped to 96 percent by September 1992. On the negative side, both states have experienced many difficulties with their plans. In Virginia, injury definition is so narrow that very few birth-related injuries fall within the definition, making very few victims eligible to file a claim under such a plan. For example, between 1988 and 1994, a total of only eight claims were filed. Of the eight claims, six were accepted for compensation. By February 1994, in Florida only eighty-nine claims were filed, of which twenty-seven were accepted and paid. Though it is important to remember that since the statute of limitation is seven years, final numbers may be different.[161]

With regard to the effectiveness of many of the legislative reforms, the results are again mixed. On the positive side, limits on noneconomic damages showed some promise in reducing the number of claims filed. For example, in the state of Ohio, payment of medical malpractice claims declined from 3.7 percent prior to the enactment of cap to 2.9 percent after the adoption of cap on noneconomic damages. Similarly, Patricia Danzon found that a cap on noneconomic damages reduced claim severity 23 percent on average over the decade in which she studied claims.[162] On the negative side, caps on noneconomic damages have been found unconstitutional under the state constitutions in Alabama, Florida, New Hampshire, Ohio, North Dakota, and Texas, and have been challenged in other state courts.[163]

Similarly, punitive damage caps have been found unconstitutional under the state constitution in Alabama and have been challenged in other courts. Periodic payment schedules have been found unconstitutional in Arizona, New Hampshire, and Ohio. Statutes of limitations have been found unconstitutional in Arizona and New Hampshire. The modification of the collateral source rule and the establishment of a contingency fee schedule for lawyers has been found unconstitutional under the state constitution in New Hampshire.[164] Most of the court challenges have been raised with respect to individual rights, right to a jury trial, and due process, among others. More court challenges are likely to follow.

Review of the empirical literature suggests that all reforms have encouraged plaintiffs to drop more of the claims filed. Yet, only limiting contingency fees and modifying the collateral source rule increases the likelihood of settlement. Thus, limiting contingency fees and modifying collateral source rules are two promising reforms to reduce litigation costs.[165] On the other hand, some studies have concluded that efforts to reform medical malpractice laws have not resulted in reduced medical costs or improved care. Even when cost savings are realized, they are not passed on to consumers.[166]

Medical Liability and Managed Care

There has been a dramatic increase in the number of persons enrolled in managed care organizations such as HMOs and PPOs in the last twenty years. Dramatic increases in health care cost to the government, consumers, and businesses have forced them to look for alternative methods for delivering health care as compared to the traditional method. The competitive environment of managed care has forced hospitals and managed care organizations to become economically more efficient. This shift from traditional fee-for-service plans to prepaid group health plans has raised some troubling questions and concerns about medical practice and medical liability.

Medical malpractice insurers are worried about the impact that managed care will have on physicians' practices. Insurers are worried that heavy demands placed on primary care physicians under managed care may lead some into areas of care they are not comfortable with. On the other hand, specialists may be forced to assume some primary care responsibilities they cannot readily handle in order to stay competitive. Thus, some fear increases in medical insurance premiums due to managed care.

Even more important issues have to do with how managed care is changing the nature of medical practice and what impact it has on the issue of medical liability. As a result of managed care, more and more physicians are to some extent losing their professional autonomy and finding themselves working for a hospital or a managed care entity such as an HMO or a PPO. Many doctors are now employees of managed care organizations or of group practices. Managed care organizations control patients' access to health care in which referral to a specialist is made only through a primary care physician who acts as the "gatekeeper." Increasingly, medical malpractice lawsuits are being filed against managed care organizations or hospitals rather than individual physicians.[167] The emergence of managed care and capitation has created additional grounds for shifting physician liability for medical malpractice to institutions such as hospitals and managed care organizations. Wrongful denial of care or access is an increasingly common tort allegation aimed at health care organizations. Claims can be made under the theories of vicarious liability for treatment exclusion or for denial of access or coverage. Improper utilization review can also create liability. Sacrifice of quality medical care for cost savings can also result in liability.[168]

In *Sloan v. Metropolitan Health Council of Indianapolis, Inc.* (Indiana Appeals Court, 1989) the court held the HMO liable for the negligence of its physician on the ground that since the HMO medical director controlled its staff physicians, an employer-employee relationship existed between the negligent physician and the HMO. The HMO was held vicariously liable. In *Scheleier v. Kaiser Foundation Health Plan* (D.C. Circuit Court, 1989), applying the doctrine of *respondeat superior*, the court held that the HMO could be vicariously liable for the actions of an independent consulting physician (an outside cardiologist requested by the Kaiser physician), because a "master-servant" relationship may have existed between him and the Kaiser physician. Under the theory of ostensible agency, a plaintiff can sue an HMO if he or she can prove that the patient looked to the HMO rather than the individual physician for care, and if the HMO "held out" the physician as its employee.[169]

Similarly, the established doctrine of corporate negligence holds that a hospital owes an independent duty to its patients to exercise reasonable care in ensuring that the physicians selected as members of the hospital staff are competent. This duty is not subject to delegation. Also, the hospital has a duty to maintain safe and adequate facilities, equipment, and so on. A hospital with actual knowledge that a physician lacks competence can be held liable for the physician's malpractice. Courts in at least twenty-one states have found hospitals liable on this basis.[170]

Thus it appears that courts are increasingly holding institutions that provide health care liable for the actions of individual health care providers. This has encouraged some state legislators to make health care organizations liable for medical negligence when patients incur injury or death. However, such a state-level effort is likely to run up against the fear that a HMO liability would drive up costs.[171] The concept of enterprise medical liability, to impose liability on health care organizations such as hospitals, HMOs, PPOs, and other health plans rather than on individual physicians, will continue to be an attractive alternative to advocates of medical liability reform.[172]

Conclusion

This chapter has examined the complex but very important issue of medical liability and malpractice in the American health care system. We have traced the origins of the concept of tort from early history to its development and refinement in Great Britain. British common law concepts and practices were adopted in America's legal system with very few modifications.

One point that should be emphasized is that whereas, in almost all federal systems in the world, tort is a federal responsibility and is covered under federal law, the United States remains one of the few exceptions. In the United States it is accepted that tort is a state responsibility. Even though occasionally the federal government has passed federal laws dealing with some aspect of medical liability, a 200-year history has established state sovereignty over the subject matter.

The crisis in the health insurance market of the 1970s and 1980s, accompanied by many criticisms of the current tort system, stimulated a nationwide debate and discussion of alternative and alternative dispute resolution mechanisms. Attempts at fundamental and comprehensive reform of the U.S. health care system, including medical liability reform, have met with failure at the federal level during the 1980s and so far during the 1990s. However, during the same period a considerable number of reform measures have been adopted at the state level. These legislative reforms have produced mixed results. Their record in controlling medical malpractice costs and malpractice insurance premium costs, in reducing the number of malpractice claims filed, and so on, is very weak, suggesting only minor successes. Furthermore, many of these reforms have been declared unconstitutional under the state constitutions in many states. We are unlikely to know the overall success or failure of these reforms until a considerable amount of time has passed and many of the constitutional conflicts surrounding these reforms have been settled. The dramatic increase in the number of persons enrolled in managed care health plans is significantly changing the nature of medical practice and raising questions about the future of medical liability. The concept of enterprise liability, holding health care organizations liable for the negligent behavior or incompetence of their physicians, rather than holding individual physicians liable, may look more attractive.

CHAPTER 8

Health Care Technology

Health care technology was mentioned in chapter 6 as one of several factors that have contributed to spiraling health care costs. This chapter focuses on the role of technology in the U.S. health care system. Technological developments in the past twenty years have dramatically changed the methods for diagnosing illnesses and the delivery of health care services in the United States. In the next ten to fifteen years the rate of technological change and the magnitude of the impact of technology on the health care delivery process are expected to be of quantum proportions compared to what they have been in the past.[1] These medical technologies have created high levels of expectations on the part of health care providers as well as consumers and have opened diagnostic and treatment avenues once unimaginable. These technological advancements encompass not just diagnoses and treatment abilities but also patient monitoring. For example, patient monitoring systems are making increased use of computer technology for data display and retrieval.

The past twenty-five years have seen significant developments in physics, electronics, computer science, and biotechnology, which are increasingly felt in the field of health care.[2] This in turn has raised questions about the factors that have contributed to the growth of medical technologies, the cost and effectiveness of such technologies, and the ethical dilemmas they raise. If technology is to be used effectively and efficiently, we must understand not only the technological tools used by modern medicine but also the ethical dilemmas involved, and must learn to make decisions that are individually and socially correct.[3] In this chapter we address these issues. First, we examine the growth of medical technology and the factors that have contributed to this growth. Second, we analyze the cost of the medical technology and its relation to overall health care costs. Third, we address the issue of the assessment of medical technology. Fourth, we examine the potential implications of managed care on medical technology. Finally, we examine the ethical concerns and dilemmas raised by medical technology by analyzing some specific cases.

The Growth and Diffusion of Medical Technology

Before we discuss the growth of medical technology and the factors that have contributed to its growth, it will be helpful to define medical technology. *Medical technology* can be defined simply as drugs, devices, and medical or surgical procedures used in medical care.[4] More recent medical technology has been defined by some to include medical techniques, equipment, and pharmaceuticals.[5] Examples of medical technology under these definitions include pharmaceutical drugs such as azidothymidine (AZT), medical devices such as computerized tomography (CT) scanners, and organ transplants.[6] "High-tech medicine" is the term often used to refer to developments in the field of medical technology in the past twenty or so years. *High-tech medicine* has been defined as the "sum of all the advances in medical knowledge and techniques that have been translated into improved diagnostic, therapeutic, and rehabilitative procedures during the last several decades."[7]

The transformation of medicine is associated with the Renaissance, when different applications of scientific methods were introduced. Disciplined observation of the empirical symptoms of illness was brought about by the influence of Francis Bacon (1561–1626) and Thomas Sydenham (1624–1689). During the seventeenth century, there was a significant increase not only in the ability to understand illnesses but also to classify them. By the nineteenth and twentieth centuries, medicine had progressed to the point where it was capable of healing illnesses and preventing illnesses from starting.[8]

The practice of medical technology emerged in the late 1800s as an outgrowth of scientific advances that created a need for clinical pathology laboratories. Before the 1890s, physicians were expected to perform and interpret almost all laboratory tests themselves. By the early 1900s, interns in larger hospitals had begun to perform laboratory tests as part of their responsibilities. The years 1890 to 1928 marked the emergence of clinical laboratory practice as an occupation separate from medicine and nursing. Pathology became established as a recognized specialty after World War I. Laboratory testing and interpretation of results became the responsibility of the pathologist.[9]

The professionalization of medical technology occurred between the 1920s and 1930s. In 1928 the American Society of Clinical Pathologists set up the national Board of Registry for clinical laboratory technicians. For the first time, educational and training standards for students were established. The Board of Registry also assumed responsibility for accreditation of schools of medical technology and for certification of clinical laboratory technicians. The professionalization of medical technology was also reflected in the establishment and publication of professional journals: the *Bulletin of the*

American Society of Clinical Laboratory Technicians in 1933 and the *American Journal of Medical Technology* in 1935. The latter journal was renamed the *Journal of Medical Technology* in 1984, and in 1988 it came to be called *Clinical Laboratory Science.*[10]

Some of the major advances in medical technology during the first fifty years of the twentieth century included X-rays for diagnoses (1901); insulin (1921); the first sulfa drug (1937); penicillin (1943); dichlorodiphenyl; trichloroethane (DDT) (1944); renal dialysis (1945); streptomycin, the first anti-tuberculosis drug (1948); and tetracycline, the first broad-spectrum antibiotic (1949).[11] These early developments, particularly antisepsis techniques and anesthesiology, made a critical contribution to the advancement of medicine and the health of human beings.

In the fifty years since the end of World War II, dramatic developments in medical technology have revolutionized the American health care system. Almost all of today's disease diagnosis and treatment devices and techniques were unknown forty to fifty years ago. The role of the physician was mainly that of diagnostician, limited to identification of illness, prediction of likely outcome, and the provision of guidance to the patient and his or her family while the illness ran its course. All this has changed dramatically. Today the scope of medical intervention includes kidney dialysis, organ transplants, laser surgery, arthroscopic surgical techniques, computed tomography scanners, nuclear magnetic resonators, and much more. New miracle drugs are being marketed each year. Of the prescription drugs, about 10 percent of the 200 top-selling drugs are new each year, while only 25 percent of the 200 top-selling drugs in 1972 remained in the group fifteen years later.[12]

Not too long ago, except for X-rays, the only way a doctor could see inside a patient's body was through exploratory surgery. Today a variety of medical technologies are available that are nonintrusive to the patient. One such technique is the CT scan, or computerized tomography. A CT scan provides a detailed X-ray of the entire body and converts a two-dimensional picture into three-dimensional images. Magnetic resonance imaging (MRI) uses a combination of radio waves, a computer, and a magnetic coil that allows a doctor to see tissues hidden or surrounded by bone. This is not possible to do with a simple X-ray. MRI scans are used by doctors to diagnose tumors, arthritis, and problems associated with tissues and organs. Magnetic resonance spectroscopy uses a similar technology to gather information about body chemistry, while magnetoencephalography (MEG) allows the doctor to measure brain activity. Another imaging technique—PET scan, or position emission tomography— uses a low-level radioactive chemical that travels through the body. PET scans are used to diagnose strokes, epilepsy, schizophrenia, and Parkinson's disease.[13]

As diagnostic abilities have improved, so have the treatment options available to doctors. For example, surgeons have been using lasers instead of scalpels since the 1970s to cut skin, remove growths, and unclog blood vessels. The new free-electron laser has made possible photodynamic therapy that makes it possible to kill viruses in the blood.[14] Surgical techniques have also undergone dramatic changes in the past thirty to forty years. Organ transplants have become increasingly common, especially with respect to heart, liver, and kidney. Replacement of human body parts with artificial parts is also becoming a reality. Today it is possible to replace a human arm or hand with a realistic artificial arm or hand that can perform almost the same functions. Soon it may be possible to replace eyes, ears, bones, and other vital organs.

Most of the developments in the field of medical technology can be classified as of two types.[15] One is replacement technology, which replaces an old procedure with a new one. Replacement technology enables doctors to do more efficiently and effectively what they have already been doing. One example includes diagnostic tests such as the CT scanner, which replaces intrusive exploratory surgery. A second development is what might be called "new technologies." These allow doctors to do things that were not being done or that were not possible to do before. Some examples include organ transplants, reproductive technologies, and life-extending and life-sustaining technologies. Both types of technology are developing rapidly.

Lewis Thomas provides another useful way of classifying three levels of technology in medicine.[16] "Nontechnology" tides patients over diseases that are not well understood. This mainly involves reassuring patients and providing nursing and hospital care, but offers little hope for recovery. Nontechnology is applied in cases including intractable cancer, multiple sclerosis, and stroke. The second level of technology is called "halfway technology." This represents the "kinds of things that must be done after the fact, as efforts to compensate for the incapacitating effects of certain diseases whose course one is unable to do very much about. It is a technology designed to make up for disease, or to postpone death."[17] Examples include organ transplants and the use of artificial organs, among others. Halfway technology for chronic kidney failure means dialysis or kidney transplant. For heart disease, the halfway technology can mean open heart surgery, a pacemaker, a transplant, or an artificial heart. Such halfway technologies are generally very expensive.[18] John Cooper, president of the American Association of Medical Colleges, in 1973 congressional testimony, described halfway technology as not "really evidence of success in dealing with disease," but rather "confessions of failure, of a lack of understanding to prevent disease before clinical signs and symptoms appear. They are the consequence of partial understanding."[19] The final level of technology, "high technology" is exemplified by immunization, antibiotics for bacterial infections, and prevention of nutritional disorders. High technology "comes as a result of genuine understanding of disease mechanisms, and when it becomes available it is relatively inexpensive to deliver."[20]

In recent years, most of the growth in medical technology has been in the area of halfway technologies, which is the most expensive.[21] What accounts for the growth of medical technology in general and halfway technologies in particular?

Factors Responsible for the Growth of Medical Technologies

Many factors have influenced the dramatic growth in medical technologies in the United States. In this section we discuss some of the major influences on the growth of medical technologies. These factors are not discussed in any particular order. Thus we do not suggest the relative contribution of each factor to the overall growth in medical technologies.

The Public and Private Sectors

Vannevar Bush, science adviser to President Franklin Roosevelt, in his 1945 report, *Science: The Endless Frontier*, recommended a significantly enlarged federal government role in support of science. The federal government not only dramatically increased its funding for biomedical research but made large amounts of federal funds available to outlying communities for construction of hospitals. During the 1960s, the federal government played a role in expanding physician supply (heavily weighted toward specialists) through funding of medical schools and medical students. It also created Medicare and Medicaid, enlarging federal funding. One of the results of the massive flow of federal dollars into the health care system was the rapid development of academic health centers. Given the availability of a large amount of federal dollars, leading medical schools changed their focal interest from the training of medical students to biomedical research. This, combined with the increasing supply of medical specialists, set the stage for rapid growth in medical technologies.[22] Modern hospitals became repositories of high-tech medical equipment. Similarly, private-sector spending in research and development (R&D) has exploded. At present, the industry invests 7 to 13 percent of its annual gross profit in R&D.

All parties in health care—hospitals, clinics, physicians, consumers, and manufacturers of medical devices—have a stake in the development and diffusion of medical technology.[23] From World War II to the early 1970s, health care financing in most countries was very generous, based on retrospective pricing. The result was the emergence of very expensive halfway technologies such as organ transplants, MRI, and high-priced drugs with marginal value. Such financing also contributed to the development of such "high-technology" items as new antibiotics and vaccines that were cost effective.[24]

The Health Insurance/Finance System

The usual method for limiting demand in the marketplace is to raise prices. The third-party payment system has made such a mechanism largely irrelevant in the health care market. The third-party payment system insulates the consumer from the high cost of the treatment. Consumers have little incentive to question expensive care since the third party (the insurance company) is going to pay most or all of the entire bill.[25] The reimbursement system used by the insurance companies—retrospective payment, which pays a provider on the basis of costs incurred—has stimulated demand for medical technology by encouraging any innovation that promises some benefit, regardless of the cost. Victor Fuchs has claimed that hospitals operate under a technological imperative that drives them to adopt the latest technology, regardless of the cost. The incentive system helps explain the rapid and indiscriminate adoption of medical innovations.[26] The retrospective payment mechanism also sends a clear message to research and development. The message is to develop new technologies that enhance the quality of care, regardless of the cost. Examples of high-cost medical innovations made possible by a retrospective payment system might include natural organ transplants and artificial organs.[27]

The new prospective payment finance mechanism, which pays health care providers sums that are independent of the costs incurred, sends a different signal to the R&D sector. The message here is to develop new technologies that reduce costs as long as quality does not suffer too much. The shift to this new system under Medicare, while not resulting in decreased use of intensive-care units, does seem to have helped decrease the use of diagnostic procedures such as chest X-rays.[28] But the long-term effect of the Prospective Payment System (PPS) on Medicare is far from conclusive.

In most industries, before a new cost-increasing technology is adopted it must satisfy two criteria: it must represent advancement beyond what we currently have, and there must be a market for it. Unfortunately, in the health care market, whether a technological change occurs or not is largely determined by the first criterion. The presence of a third-party-payer system makes the second criterion irrelevant. Insurance leads to technological change, and more costly technological change increases demand for insurance, since most patients cannot pay for costly technology out of their own pockets.[29] Some of the evidence gathered thus far suggests that insurance coverage largely determines whether or not a new technology is developed, manufactured, and used.[30]

The Hospitals

Aside from the influence of a retrospective insurance payment system, hospitals have other reasons for the acquisition of the latest medical technology.[31] By stocking hospitals with the latest medical technologies, hospitals hope to recruit physicians and attract patients. From the physician's perspective, a hospital with the latest technology and empty beds promises little delay in admitting and treating his or her patients. Hospitals also hope to attract patients by portraying themselves as state-of-the-art facilities. The result is a medical arms race between hospitals as each hospital tries to maximize its own status, prestige, and profits. The result often is a tremendous duplication of very expensive medical technologies among many hospitals within the same community. This is helped by the fact that there is a lack of incentives for hospitals to cooperate and coordinate efficient use of medical technology.[32] The acquisition of diagnostic imaging technologies (CT scan, MRI, etc.) by hospitals requires a significant initial capital investment and a high level of operating costs. To avoid the financial risks involved and generate profit requires a high volume of use of such technologies. Thus, once a hospital buys an expensive new technology, there is pressure to use it more frequently to produce sufficient demand to cover the operating costs and increase profit margins.[33] This has often led to excesses and overuse of medical technology in the United States.

Physicians

According to Eric Cassell, five human characteristics help explain physicians' enchantment with medical technology. One is wonderment about something new that can do fantastic or inexplicable things. This causes physicians to use and overuse medical technology. It also helps solve the problem of boredom and loss of motivation. A second reason for physicians' attraction to technology is that technology tells them directly what it means in immediate terms. For example, computer-generated Electrocardiogram (EKG) interpretations provide immediate information and answers. The third reason for technology's hold on physicians is that virtually all technology is characterized by unambiguous values. Lack of ambiguity is generally considered essential for good science of medicine. Thus, technological values and medical values reinforce each other because both are intolerant of ambiguities. A fourth and related factor has to do with the fact that one of the main problems physicians confront is uncertainty. This is caused by shortcomings in the individual physician's knowledge and/or the inadequacies of the profession's knowledge. Technology helps physicians reduce some of the uncertainty. A medical problem is often redefined in terms of a technological answer. The final reason technology lures physicians is the power it confers on them. Every therapeutic and diagnostic test is a demonstration of a physician's efficacy and thus of his or her power.[34]

According to David Freed, physicians have capitulated to the growth of medical technology at both the structural and the applied level. At the structural level, medical education has emphasized the scientific basis of medicine and downplayed its role as a healing "art." Physicians and the science community's compulsion about avoiding uncertainty have stimulated excessive dependence on clinical tests and treatments of marginal value in pursuit of certainty. Another structural factor is a strong tradition of professional autonomy in the medical profession. Physicians are the key decision makers with respect to the use of medical technology, and as long as physicians believe that a new technology might benefit a patient, they are likely to use it. At an applied level, physicians are trained to be advocates for their patients. They are also comfortable doing what they learned to do in their training. There are no general decision-making models that all physicians can apply with respect to the use of technology, and thus decisions are made at an individual level, resulting in a wide variance in physician practice. Finally, the fear of malpractice lawsuits and medical liability risks has also encouraged tremendous growth of expensive diagnostic imaging technologies.[35] How physicians will respond to the new era of economic constraints and the changing health policy environment and market forces—managed care, managed competition, HMOs—remains to be seen.[36]

The Health Policymaking Environment

The diffusion of medical technology has taken place in the United States in an environment of both regulation and free enterprise. Attempts at regulating the diffusion of CT scanners through certificate-of-need (CON) programs were not very successful. By the 1980s, the use of CT scanners had become widespread, and CON agencies were either abandoned in some states or had become liberal in their requirements. Supporters of the marketplace model (i.e., the free enterprise system) argue that the health care delivery system should operate according to the principle of supply and demand. Thus the diffusion of medical technology in the United States has taken place between the two competing models—the regulation model and the free-enterprise, marketplace model. Health care providers have manipulated each, to some extent. Overall, the market model has continued to operate in the medical technology area, despite some attempts at regulation.[37]

Societal Culture and Values

American society places a great deal of emphasis on individual autonomy, self-determination, personal privacy, and shared belief in justice and equality. This is reflected in the health care field by a belief held by many that health care is a right to which everyone is entitled. Access to the latest medical technology is also viewed as a right, and demand for it has increased because of greater public awareness of the latest technological innovation. Compared to many other countries, the American public is more aware of the latest technological advances in medicine because of considerable coverage in the mass media. The public demands the newest and the best in medical technology, even though it continues to express dissatisfaction with high cost and low efficacy.[38]

In addition to significant emphasis on individual autonomy, rights, and self-determination, American culture is heavily predisposed toward progress through technological means and faith in scientific progress. Our culture equates reduction of uncertainty and gaining control over ambiguities with progress. This has often led to an unrealistic dependence on technology to fix problems of the health care system and exclusion of nontechnological solutions. We have come to equate sophisticated medical procedures with better health care.[39]

We are a culture that believes that "we can have it all." We want the latest, the most sophisticated medical technology, and we want to use it indiscriminately for the very young, the very old, and the hopelessly ill. We want the physician to do everything possible for the patient even when there is little or no hope for survival. We want the best, yet we want to pay the least. We admire countries that place limits and global budgets on health care and want to adopt their health care systems, but we do not want to accept any limits.[40]

In view of the above discussion, it is not too surprising that we have witnessed a rampant growth in medical technology in the United States, and such a growth is likely to continue in the future. The biotechnology industry is expected to grow from an $8 billion (revenue) industry in 1992 to a $50 billion industry by the year 2000.[41] The availability of large-scale technology has been much greater in the United States than in Western European countries. The concentration of medical equipment in the United States is far greater than in other countries that have good-quality health care systems.[42] For example, the United States has 11.2 MRI units per million population compared to 1.1 units per million in Canada and 3.7 units per million in Germany. Similarly, in 1992, the United States had 3.7 installed open-heart surgery units per million population compared to 1.3 units per million in Canada and 0.8 units per million in Germany.[43]

The rapid proliferation of health care technologies has raised concerns in many quarters about the costs of such technologies and the strain they put on the nation's resources. It also raises issues about the cost-effectiveness of such technologies.

Health Care Technology and Costs

A great deal of modern technology—medical equipment, medical techniques, and pharmaceuticals—is very expensive. New medical technology and the overuse of such technologies helps drive health care costs upward.[44] One of the most significant advances in medical technology, and one of the most costly, is the spread and increased use of such diagnostic tools as MRI and CT scans. Since such new diagnostic therapies are simpler and safer than exploratory surgery, they are used at a much higher rate, adding to health care costs. MRI equipment costs between $2 million and $3 million, and the cost of one MRI scan ranges from $600 to $800. In fact, MRI equipment has proved to be so popular that today it is available not only in hospitals and doctors' offices but in roadside facilities and shopping centers.[45]

A free-electron laser device is likely to cost about $2 million, and portable laser equipment costs about $70,000.[46] Many other technological advances, such as coronary bypass surgery and hip-replacement operations are also very expensive and contribute to overall health care costs. Liver transplants cost about $200,000 per transplant, on the average. The discovery in the early 1980s of the drug cyclosporine, which prevents the body's immune system from rejecting organ transplants, has been instrumental in increasing the number of yearly liver transplants from 15 in 1980 to 3,056 in 1992.[47]

The field of neonatology is another example of how technology has allowed us to save lives at increased cost. Due to numerous medical breakthroughs—incubators, intravenous feeding, advances in cesarean section, controls for infection—that were made during the 1950s and 1960s, doctors have succeeded in saving the lives of babies with increasingly lower birth weights. However, the cost has been very high. In 1984 constant dollars, the cost per survival of an infant born weighing between 750 and 1,000 grams is estimated to be about $125,000, while the cost for an infant born weighing less than 750 grams is about $175,000.[48] Many economists argue that we would be better off providing intensive care for babies over 1,000 grams than spending resources on children with birth weights of less than 800 grams. They justify such arguments on the ground that we could actually reduce suffering by targeting only those newborns who are most likely to benefit from medical intervention.[49] This example demonstrates the complexity as well as the difficult nature of the problems created by medical technology.

Many economists argue that new health care technology is the largest factor driving up health care costs in the United States. They believe that technology accounts for as much as 50 percent of the growth in health care cost beyond overall inflation.[50] Furthermore, the diffusion of these technologies has outpaced our ability to evaluate their need and their cost effectiveness. Despite regulatory and competitive strategies to control diffusion of technology, excessive supply exists.[51] Most analysts believe that advances in medical technology have been largely responsible for a 4 to 5 percent annual rate of growth in the industrialized nations' health care costs.[52] According to Henry Aaron, medical technologies that did not exist twenty to thirty years ago account for most of the rise in health care spending in the United States.[53] He argues that developments in medical technology affect outlays in two ways: new technology adds new treatments, and because of its less intrusive nature, many more patients benefit from it, resulting in increased use and costs.[54]

The hospital is the major center of high-tech medicine, and hospital care constitutes the single largest component of our health care spending, about 40 percent. The most important factor stimulating hospital cost increases is the rapid adoption of new medical technology, according to a report by the General Accounting Office (GAO). Competition among hospitals combined with a third-party reimbursement system provides incentives for rapid advancement of medical technologies in hospitals. Since hospitals do not compete for patients on the basis of price, hospitals try to gain market advantage by offering the most up-to-date services, and the cost of these technologies is passed on to the third-party payers—insurance companies.[55]

Attempts to control costs associated with medical technology immediately produce confrontation between two powerful interests in the health care system, insurance companies and manufacturers of medical devices. Medical device manufacturers argue that they are unfairly singled out and that many new inventions provide less costly alternatives for diagnosis and treatment. Today, many surgeries require shorter hospital stays and significantly reduced recovery time.[56] Any technology that allows us to produce existing goods or services at a lower cost, while maintaining or increasing quality, is to be welcomed. Nevertheless, rapid cost escalation related to wasteful technologies deserves scrutiny.

Insurance companies generally try to limit coverage to care that is "reasonably necessary" or "medically necessary." These terms are generally interpreted broadly to cover any nonexperimental technology accepted by the medical community that is not considered unsafe or ineffective. Courts have often expanded the scope of insurance coverage by relying on the notion that all ambiguities should be interpreted against the insurer and in favor of the beneficiary. Courts have often forced insurance companies to cover technologies and treatments still considered to be in an experimental stage. Extra insurance rights established through the courts are often called "judge-made insurance."[57]

The relationship between health care technology and health care costs is a complex one because technology affects costs in many different ways. Not all technology is good or bad. On the positive side, technology can play a significant role in supporting the provision of adequate care in the areas of prevention and rehabilitation. Mobile health care units can help overcome the challenge of geographic maldistribution by helping extend service areas and helping make medical service distribution more equitable.[58] On the negative side, technology can be unsafe, ineffective, and inefficient.

Some technologies can increase costs considerably through introduction of new diagnostic or treatment therapy and improved health. In other words, some technologies are both high cost and high benefit. Some technologies may decrease costs by allowing care to be given in a lower-cost setting, replacing expensive procedures, keeping people healthier, reducing hospital stay and recovery time, and returning people to work sooner. Such technologies may be both low cost and high benefit. In contrast, some technologies may be very costly but produce only marginal benefits. It is these technologies—the high-cost and low-benefit technologies—that raise serious concerns among critics of the U.S. health care system. Some technologies are unsafe, while others are ineffective. Some technologies are medically effective, but they are not cost effective. Technologies that are unsafe, ineffective, or not cost effective are called "wasteful technologies."[59]

Examples of wasteful technologies abound. An estimated 50 percent of all U.S. births are electronically monitored. Eight controlled studies have found that electronic monitoring has no advantage over a stethoscope placed on the mother's stomach, even in high-risk pregnancies. Yet electronic monitoring is growing at a cost of $1 billion a year.[60] U.S. doctors perform about 600,000 hysterectomies a year at a cost of $5 billion. Almost a third of women undergo the operation by the time they are sixty. Yet it is not clear how many of these women gain anything from it.[61] In recent years, late-stage breast cancer victims have turned to a treatment known as autologous bone marrow transplant. The procedure is considered risky and costly, costing about $100,000 a patient; however, there is no solid evidence at the present time that it works better than less expensive treatments.[62] Every year, about 400,000 patients undergo heart bypass surgery at a cost of about $12 billion. Studies show that it is no better than drug treatment for less dire conditions. About 300,000 Americans receive angioplasties a year at a cost of $10,000 a procedure. Drug treatment generally yields similar benefits at a fraction of the cost. The procedure has not been shown to prevent heart attacks.[63]

Neither procompetitive policies nor regulation has dealt effectively with oversupply of technology services. Regulatory loopholes have allowed hospitals to escape CON reviews before expanding capacity. Market-based incentives to rationally distribute health care services also seem to have failed, because hospitals have competed to attract and retain physicians and patients by acquiring new technologies. Furthermore, cost-based reimbursement and cost shifting by providers often mitigate potential financial losses associated with oversupply of technology.[64] Currently in the United States, most drugs and medical devices are assessed for safety and efficacy only and not for cost effectiveness. Most medical and surgical procedures are not formally evaluated at all. It is clear that what is needed is a systematic assessment of medical technologies that would allow us to weed out wasteful technologies.

Technology Assessment

The rate of diffusion of high-cost technology varies between countries. In mainly public, government-funded, and planned nonmarket health care delivery systems, such as those in Great Britain and Scandinavia, there are generally more built-in constraints that limit the introduction of new technologies. In the United States, market forces are the most influential with respect to diffusion of high-cost technologies, often resulting in a medical arms race.[65]

The late 1990s may witness even more dramatic developments in health care technology.[66] Currently, biotechnology is the most radical research area. At present, more than 100 biologically derived drugs are in clinical trials. Some of the products now in the developmental stage are likely to cost as much as $5,000 per therapeutic regimen; portable EKG units are already on the market.[67] According to M. Roy Schwartz, senior vice president of medical education and science with the American Medical Association (AMA), most of America's economic growth comes from technology, specifically biotechnology, and technological development pays off in the long run.[68]

Nevertheless, the country is facing some tough decisions about access, funding, distribution of health care resources, and cost containment. Today, evaluating health technology is one of the most important challenges facing policymakers and researchers alike. Improving the process of technology diffusion requires continuous monitoring of technological development, identifying technologies for assessment, and conducting early assessment before technology is marketed.[69] With more availability of outcome data, employers, insurers, and researchers are beginning to question the value of certain high-cost technology.[70]

The history of technology assessment in the United States is a very brief one. The dramatic growth in medical technologies in the 1970s raised some concerns about technology. In 1972, the Office of Technology Assessment (OTA), a congressional staff agency that maintains a concern for medical technology assessment, was established. The Republican majority in Congress eliminated OTA as a cost-saving measure. Another congressional agency, the General Accounting Office, often analyzes the role of technology in its health reports. In 1978, the National Center for Health Care Technology was established by law; it was responsible for examining the cost effectiveness of new technologies. Although the agency was reauthorized in 1981 at the urging of the medical device industry, the Reagan administration did not seek any funding for the agency in its 1982 budget. No funds were appropriated, and the agency went out of existence in 1982. At the urging of the Reagan administration, Congress also cut off funds for state health planning agencies that required hospitals to seek approval of large capital investment in technology.

Skyrocketing health care costs and evidence of inappropriate use of technological devices and procedures led both Congress and President George Bush to revisit the issue of health care technology assessment in the late 1980s. The result was the establishment in 1989 of the Office of Health Technology Assessment (OHTA) in the National Center for Health Services Research (NCHSR). OHTA is responsible for advising the Health Care Financing Administration (HCFA) about technology as it is applied to Medicaid and Medicare, but the influence of OHTA is indirect and limited.[71] In 1989, the Agency for Health Care Policy and Research (AHCPR) was also created within the NCHSR, to develop guidelines on the appropriate treatment of common illnesses. The agency also evaluates the effectiveness and cost of specific technologies related to federal health programs.

Another agency, the Food and Drug Administration (FDA), is responsible for regulating the safety and efficacy of drugs and medical devices, but not their cost effectiveness. The FDA's role in the regulation of drugs has been shaped by the 1906 Food and Drug Act; the 1938 Federal Food, Drug and Cosmetic Act; and 1962 amendments. The drug companies are required to get advance permission from the FDA for every important step in testing, production, and marketing new drugs. The 1938 Federal Food, Drug and Cosmetic Act gave the FDA jurisdiction over medical devices for the first time. The 1976 Medical Device amendments to the act strengthened the FDA's hand in regulating medical devices. The 1990 Safe Medical Devices Act also strengthened the FDA by controlling the entry of new products and monitoring the use of marketed products.[72] Nevertheless, it is important to emphasize again that the FDA is mainly concerned with the safety and efficacy of drugs and medical devices, and it is not heavily involved in assessing cost effectiveness. Furthermore, as mentioned earlier, most medical and surgical procedures are not evaluated at all in the United States.

The private sector's record in technology assessment has been uneven. The Council on Health Care Technology of the Institute of Medicine, created in 1986, operated for four years and became defunct in 1990. Other organizations in the private sector that continue to engage in some technology assessment are Blue Cross and Blue Shield, the American Medical Association, and the American Hospital Association.[73]

What is clear is that the efforts at technology assessment in the United States have been sporadic, uncoordinated, and limited. According to the Office of Technology Assessment, less than 20 percent of all existing medical technology has been subjected to systematic study via controlled clinical trials.[74] Spiraling health care costs in the 1980s have again revived interest in technology assessment. Technology assessment raises a number of questions: What is technology assessment? How is it conducted? Who should conduct technology assessment?

Traditionally, technology assessment concerned itself with evaluating the safety and efficacy of drugs and medical devices. In recent years, there has been a broadening of perspective in defining technology assessment. Proponents of technology assessment argue that technology assessment should go beyond the traditional concerns of safety and efficacy to include evaluation of the cost effectiveness of various technologies, including therapeutic and surgical procedures. Some go even further.[75]

David Banta and Stephen Thacker have argued that "technology assessment is a comprehensive form of policy research that examines short and long-term social (e.g., clinical, societal, economic, ethical, and legal) consequences of the applications of technology."[76] As the perspective on technology assessment has changed, so has the nature of researchers who engage in that assessment and the methods of assessment. In the past, scientists and physicians mainly carried out technology assessments. Today, with its emphasis on cost and quality-of-life concerns, among others, the approach to technology assessment has become more interdisciplinary, requiring more collaborative effort on the part of researchers trained in economics, epidemiology, operations research, ethics, and other social sciences.[77] Americans, on the one hand, demand more and more technology. On the other hand, they are reluctant to pay for it and believe they are not getting good return (benefits) for their money. Given this, one of the tasks of technology assessment is to connect the costs of medical service to the value attached to it.[78]

In traditional technology assessment, where safety and efficacy were the two main concerns, the most important methodological tool was clinical testing or randomized clinical trials. The new perspective on technology assessment, with its emphasis on cost effectiveness and medical, social, and ethical results, requires the use of many different methodological tools. Today, technology assessment relies on epidemiologic tools, biological and medical models, laboratory tests, clinical trials, the use of samples, control groups, replications, and cost-benefit analysis. A highly developed set of rules and conventions governs sampling, random selection, reliability, and validity. Statistical analysis has contributed to technology assessment with techniques of sample designs, proper testing methods, and the use of confidence intervals. In short, methodologies for technology assessment have become more varied and more sophisticated.[79] However, it is important to remember that despite better and more sophisticated methodologies, technology assessment is still not a perfect science and subjective factors may influence the assessment itself or the interpretation of results.[80]

Another relevant question about technology assessment is who should do the assessment. Medical device manufacturers and professionals who perform high-tech procedures have fought government efforts to assess health care technology on the ground that it would lead to a small number of people deciding whether Americans have access to new technologies. They also argue that government involvement would lead to cost controls and national spending limits, which would have a detrimental effect on technological innovations. Critics of the medical device industry argue that the industry opposes the government's role in technology assessment for purely selfish reasons—out of the fear that technology assessment by the government will lead to useless products and procedures being weeded out of the marketplace, cutting into industry's profit. Given the huge economic self-interest involved on the part of the medical device industry, we cannot leave the task of technology assessment to the manufacturers and marketers of new medical products and procedures.[81]

Insurers and different health plans argue that they are not in a position to assess new technologies because of the scarcity of information about new products and lack of resources to develop the information base. When individual health or insurance plans do engage in assessment, the results are kept in-house for competitive reasons. Even if individual insurers or health plans conduct their own assessment, they may reach different conclusions about the value of various technologies because of differences in methodologies used or differences in interpretations.[82]

Governments play a more prominent role in health care technology assessment in many Western European countries than in the United States. Given the fragmented nature of technology assessment in the private sector and the economic and profit motives at work, it seems to us that the federal government needs to play a more active role in technology assessment. The federal government can influence the diffusion of technology in two ways. First, the government could issue regulations or directives. These could include premarket controls, pricing decisions, reimbursement methods, licensing of advanced medical facilities, and generating and distributing information about the cost effectiveness of medical devices and procedures. Second, the government could use economic incentives. These could include changing the financing or fee system, requiring cost sharing, or inducing competition in the marketplace. At the present time, this second approach seems to be gaining momentum.[83]

Technology assessment can add a great deal of information that can help policymakers make decisions about the allocation of scarce resources. It can inject rationality and scientific knowledge into the policymaking process. Nevertheless, it is important to remember that technology assessment is not a miracle cure that will solve all problems. There is a limit to how much policymaking can be guided strictly by scientific knowledge and rational processes. Policymaking is a very complex process that attempts to integrate a variety of economic, social, political, and ideological values and belief systems.[84] Policymaking often involves the "science of muddling through."[85] Even good cost-effectiveness analysis may have only a limited impact on policymaking.[86] Technology assessment may tell us something about cost effectiveness; however, it cannot tell us how much we should be willing to pay for a given health effect. This involves making explicit value judgments, something that both the old and the new technology assessment abhors.[87]

Despite these weaknesses, health care technology assessment can play an important role in societal decision making about the allocation of scarce resources and the acceptance or rejection of new technologies. Technology assessment raises two issues. One has to do with the value of economic efficiency, that is, whether the new technology is cost effective. This involves making societal judgments about whether to accept or reject new technology. The other issue has to do with the value of equity. This involves making societal judgments about relationships between needs and demands, distribution of health care spending, and access to high-cost technology for different groups in society. These issues have ethical implications. Ethical issues become more prominent when values of efficiency and equity come in conflict.[88] The ethical implications of and concerns raised by biomedical technology have created a new field of bioethics.[89] At present, there is an ambivalent relationship between medical technology assessment and ethics. The current method of technology assessment treats ethics itself as just another problem-solving technology. Ethics needs to play a more critical role in technology assessment by better understanding the complex relationship between society, medicine, and technology and by recasting how problems are defined.[90]

Before we turn to the discussion of health care technology and ethics, let us briefly examine how the health care marketplace has changed because of the managed care revolution and whether managed care can contain the growth of medical technology and, thus, health care costs.

Managed Care and Health Care Technology

Earlier we cited two contributions to growth in medical technology and, thus, to health care costs: first, the third-party payment system, which insulates the consumer from the cost of health care, and second, the cost-based reimbursement system, which allows hospitals to acquire and stock medical technology without fear of financial losses. The managed care revolution with its capitation system has changed many economic incentives as the country has moved from traditional fee-for-service health care system to capitated payment under managed care system. Under capitation, providers have contracts from insurance companies that call for them to provide care for a fixed par capita annual payment regardless of what the provision of certain services costs. Under such a system payments to providers are drastically reduced. This gives health service providers economic incentives to reduce their costs by adopting cost-cutting strategies.[91]

Today, health maintenance organizations (HMOs), insurance companies, and the employers that ultimately pay the bills have resorted to the capitation method of payment. In all managed care programs, the primary care physician plays the role of a technology gatekeeper who controls patients' access to hospitals and specialists.[92]

Considerable evidence supports the idea that managed care health plans, specifically HMOs, reduce expenditures on health care services, as compared to traditional fee-for-service health plans. However, the evidence is mixed with regard to HMOs' ability to moderate growth in health care costs.[93] Furthermore, despite the fact that considerable evidence suggests that the development, adoption, and diffusion of new medical technology increases health care expenditures, very little is known about how HMOs control the diffusion of new medical technology. A significant challenge for an HMO is to control the use of medical technology for which there is a strong patient demand but the value of which is questionable.[94]

Today, hospitals find themselves saddled with large and expensive excess capacity of hospital beds and sophisticated medical equipment. In a new era of managed care such excess capacity has become unaffordable. Yet, surprisingly, relatively little of the excess inpatient capacity has been closed. Consequently, insurance companies and other purchasers of health care such as HMOs have begun to join together to demand deep discounts, as large as 40 percent. The rate paid for heart bypass surgery has dropped from as much as $45,000 under indemnity insurance to $15,000 under a managed care plan.[95]

Despite such examples, it is unclear whether managed care plans will succeed in restraining the growth of medical technology. A recent study analyzed how cholecystectomy (surgical removal of gallbladder) rates in different types of health delivery systems (health plans) changed following the introduction of an important new surgical technique, laparoscopic cholecystectomy. The study found no systematic difference between HMOs and the general population in the rate of growth in utilization following the introduction of this new technology.[96] However, it is important to point out that, as of today, very few studies have systematically examined how managed care plans have dealt with adoption and diffusion of new medical technology. Until this is done, it is premature to come to any conclusion regarding the implications of managed care and capitation systems with regard to development, adoption, and diffusion of new medical technology. As the system for health care delivery continues to undergo further changes in the coming years, it becomes all the more important that the federal government improve the measurement of the costs and benefits of health care research so that it can make informed decisions about federal funding for health care research and recognize the tradeoffs among alternative policies for promoting innovation in health care.[97]

The capitated method of payment under the new managed care system will require cost assessment and rationing with respect to new medical technology. Physicians and other health care providers under the financial pressures imposed by capitation will face increased ethical dilemmas as they try to act as health care rationers. Physicians' single-minded devotion to patient's medical interests without concern for cost will come into direct conflict with financial pressures to contain costs.[98]

Health Care Costs, Technology, and Ethics

Technology assessment has been highly fragmented and sporadic in the United States. As a society, we have failed to make systematic decisions about research and development of medical technologies, such as: who should determine whether a particular technology should be developed and funded? On what basis should individuals be provided access once a technology is available in the marketplace? What level of technological intervention is appropriate for a specific medical problem, and what is the total impact of the rapid spread of high-cost medical technologies on society in general and on the U.S. health care system in particular?[99]

The rapid proliferation of halfway technologies and spiraling health care costs raise many ethical concerns and dilemmas that we as a society must confront and address through public policies related to health care. The term "dilemma" in a popular sense is understood to mean a difficult choice between two or more alternatives. An ethical dilemma refers to a situation in which all the alternatives are morally problematic, that is, each alternative seems to involve a wrong act or action.[100]

In the following pages, we discuss some of the ethical dilemmas raised by medical technology at two levels. First, at a broad level, we discuss the issue of health care rationing and the ethical concerns it raises. Second, we discuss the ethical dilemmas raised by specific medical technologies such as life-sustaining technologies, organ transplants, and reproductive technologies.

Health Care Rationing

The state of Oregon adopted a rationing plan for Medicaid to contain rising health care costs. The Oregon plan has been praised by some and criticized by others.[101] We discussed the plan in chapter 3 on Medicaid and in chapter 6 on cost containment. Here, our discussion focuses on health care rationing in general.

As past efforts at cost containment have failed, and as health care costs have continued to escalate, the debate over health care rationing has intensified. How much can we afford, and for how many people? Should everyone or every group have equal access to high-cost technology? If not, what criteria do we use to allow access to some and deny access to others? Do patients have a right to receive the best technology available, regardless of their ability to pay? Should patients be denied medical treatments when social costs outweigh individual benefits? Should patients' medical needs or economic status (i.e., ability to pay) determine the treatment they receive? Given limited resources, what is the best and the most efficient way of allocating scarce resources? How do we limit access and allocate resources in a way that is acceptable to society?[102]

The term "rationing" can be used in two different ways. One way in which rationing occurs is when market economies deny goods or services to those who cannot afford them. Like many other goods, health care is certainly rationed in this manner, especially for the poor and the uninsured, who cannot afford a variety of expensive health care services (see chapter 5). This type of rationing affects only about 15 percent of the population.

The current debate about health care rationing focuses on the second type of rationing. The question is: should certain health care goods and services (e.g., halfway technologies) be denied or their availability limited even to those who can afford to pay? This type of rationing raises intense debate, since it would cover about 85 percent of the population—those who have access to health insurance.[103] Such rationing is not common in the United States, but it has been practiced in other countries, such as Great Britain, for a long time. For example, virtually every patient suffering from chronic kidney failure is treated in the United States; in Britain, most are not treated. The British society is much more willing to deny treatment for chronic kidney failure to older patients. Similarly, in Britain, patients over the age of sixty are generally not considered suitable for kidney transplants. Limited resources and age are two factors that act as a basis for a great deal of rationing in Britain. Consequently, the rate and the cost of treatment for certain health services are much lower in Britain than in the United States.[104]

In the United States, Medicare provides major funding for acute health care of persons over sixty-five and for the permanently disabled between the ages of fifty-five and sixty-five. But there is no comparable source of funding for the young, except through Medicaid, which provides limited support. Some people feel that it is unethical for a society to devote so much of its resources to the care of the elderly and to spend so little on the young. They argue that this imbalance is more the result of the political clout of the elderly, who are organized and vote in large numbers, than of a rational allocation of resources.[105] Some find the use of age as a criterion in allocating resources unjustifiable.[106] Still others express concern over keeping extremely low-weight babies alive even when there is a high probability that they will be confined to a life of severe and permanent disability, and when many of them will require continuing institutional or specialized care for the remainder of their lives.

Some observers have argued that if the U.S. government is serious about containing health care costs, it needs to seriously consider rationing. One of the prominent proponents of health care rationing is Daniel Callahan, a philosopher who is the director of the Hastings Center.[107] Callahan argues that in the United States, from the beginning, bioethics has gravitated toward an emphasis on individual autonomy and integrity, because it fits very well with the dominant ideology and values of American society. According to Callahan, this has led to ignoring the value of the common good or public interest. What is needed, he argues, is a communitarian ethic—a blending of cultural judgment and personal judgment.[108] In his book *Setting Limits: Medical Goals in an Aging Society*, Callahan addresses the question of how much health care the aged should have.[109] In a more recent book, he addresses the question of how much health care Americans are entitled to have. Callahan argues that individual demand for health care is limitless, and he blames the "liberal society" for not curbing individual desires and needs.[110] John Kilner challenges the popular myth that Americans have enough resources to treat every terminal disease and argues for rationing.[111] Others have also argued for rationing health care in the United States.[112] Critics of health care rationing argue that any attempt to justify rationing using principles such as social worth, ability to pay, or age leaves enormous potential for mischief. Furthermore, arriving at any societal consensus about these principles would be very complex and problematic at best.

Life-Sustaining Technologies and the Right to Die

Today's life-support technologies are capable of keeping patients alive for a long time, even when they have no chance of regaining consciousness. Mechanical ventilators can keep patients breathing and artificial nutrition and hydration can sustain severely debilitated and dying individuals for many years. This raises the specter of individuals being kept alive in a vegetative, helpless state, sustained by a host of tubes and machines.[113] The question of who shall live and who shall die, and the question of who shall decide—raise difficult ethical and legal issues.[114] Some well-publicized court cases help illustrate the complexities involved in such situations.

One of the early cases to highlight the ethical and legal dilemma involved a New Jersey woman named Karen Quinlan who, at the age of twenty-one, slipped into a deep coma. She was hooked up to a respirator in a hospital. Her doctor informed her parents that their daughter was never going to come out of her coma because her brain was severely damaged. She might not necessarily die and, kept on a life-support system, might live for many years. Quinlan's parents asked the doctor to turn off the respirator. The doctor refused, and they went to court. The judge in the lower court disagreed with the parents. They then appealed the decision to the N.J. Supreme Court, and on March 31, 1976, the parents won the right to have the respirator turned off. The state supreme court ruled that Karen had a constitutional right of privacy, which her guardian could assert on her behalf.[115] Ironically, Karen Quinlan was able to breathe on her own. She was moved from a hospital to a nursing home, where she died in June 1985.

A different dilemma was presented in the case of twenty-six-year-old Elizabeth Bouvia, who in September 1983 admitted herself to the psychiatric unit of California's Riverside General Hospital. She had had a very difficult life and was almost totally paralyzed from cerebral palsy. Once admitted, she asked for assistance in starving herself to death. What was unique about this case is that Ms. Bouvia was not terminally ill, but wanted the hospital staff to provide her with pain-killing drugs and hygienic care while she waited to die. The hospital refused. Elizabeth Bouvia went to court and lost; the court ordered that she be force fed. On April 7, 1984, she left the hospital. The hospital bill for 217 days, excluding physicians' fees, was more than $56,000; it was paid by the hospital and the state of California. After repeated court appeals, the California Court of Appeals found in her favor. The court said that she could refuse life-sustaining medical treatment. The court ruled that the right of a competent adult patient to refuse treatment is a constitutionally guaranteed right. After her victory, Ms. Bouvia changed her mind and did not kill herself.[116]

A more recent case involved thirty-two-year-old Nancy Cruzan of Missouri. She had been in a persistent vegetative state for seven years since a car accident. Her prognosis was hopeless. Her cerebral cortex had atrophied, but she was not dead, and she could have lived in such a vegetative state for many more years. The cost of her medical treatment was about $130,000 a year, paid by the state. In 1987 her parents requested that Nancy's feeding tube be removed so she could die. A lower court granted the request in July 1988, but the state supreme court in November 1988 reversed the decision, agreeing with the state's argument that the state of Missouri had an "unqualified" interest in preserving life. According to the court, the state's interest was not in the "quality" of life; the state's interest was in "life."[117] Nancy's parents appealed the decision to the U.S. Supreme Court. In June 1990, the court, in a five-to-four decision, agreed with the decision of the Missouri Supreme Court. The court found that a competent person has a constitutionally protected right to refuse life-saving hydration and nutrition. If the person is incompetent, the court ruled, the state is entitled to require rigorous proof that this person, when competent, would have requested removal of a feeding tube in the event of his or her future incompetence. According to the court, the state of Missouri was entitled to require clear and convincing proof that a surrogate decision maker was choosing what Ms. Cruzan herself, when competent, desired.[118] It is interesting to note that the court based its ruling, not on the ground of a fundamental privacy right, as was the case with Quinlan, but on the ground of the liberty interest. The court argued that the state's interests must be balanced against the interests of the patient.[119] On December 14, 1990, the Circuit Court of Jasper County, Missouri, declared that there was clear and convincing evidence that if Nancy Cruzan was mentally able, she would want to terminate her nutrition and hydration, and she would not want to continue her present existence. Her parents were authorized to remove the nutrition and hydration tube. After the removal of the feeding tube, Nancy Cruzan died on December 26, 1990.

On the other side of the ledger was a case in Minnesota in which a public hospital sought permission to remove a respirator from an eighty-seven-year-old woman who was in a persistent vegetative state. The hospital argued that continuing treatment was not in the woman's best medical or personal interest; however, the family of the woman opposed the request. The family won, and the woman died a year later.[120]

These cases illustrate the legal and ethical complexities created by today's life-sustaining technologies. Who should live and who should die? Who decides? When is life worth preserving? Who determines what is quality of life? How does one measure a person's quality of life? Should the courts be involved in making such decisions? Can euthanasia ethically be justified? What should be the ethical role of the physician and other caregivers? Does a patient have a right to demand unending medical treatment in a hopeless case?

Today, approximately 10,000 patients live in a vegetative state in the United States. The complexities created by the life-sustaining technologies have given rise to the "right-to-die" movement across the country. Proponents of the right to die argue that individuals have a right to die with dignity and to determine when to end their lives. Proponents argue that passive as well as active euthanasia is justified. Passive euthanasia refers to a situation in which death results from omitting or terminating treatment. Active euthanasia—that is, actively assisted suicide—refers to a situation in which the health care provider gives the patient a means to kill himself or herself, or assists in the administration of the means. The publicity surrounding pathologist Jack Kevorkian of Michigan, who has assisted numerous terminally ill patients in killing themselves, has heightened the debate over the issue of the right to die. In fact, it has led the state legislature to pass a law making it a crime to assist someone in euthanasia.

Opposition to the right-to-die movement has come from many sources, including the right-to-life movement. These opponents argue that suicide is wrong on religious and theological grounds, as well as being harmful to the community and the common good, and that it produces harmful consequences for other individuals in society.[121] Others have argued that no human being has a right to decide, for himself or herself or for others, when life is no longer worth living. Opponents of this view argue that there is a danger that such decisions may be based on wrong or ulterior motives. An example would be an agreement to end the life of a patient whose continual stay in the hospital was a financial burden to his or her family, or of a patient whose family members stood to benefit financially by inheritance. It can be argued that, once a society agrees that at some stage a life is not worth sustaining, the society is on a "slippery slope." Once passive euthanasia becomes acceptable, the next step will be active euthanasia, which in turn can easily lead to forced or involuntary euthanasia. Another worry is that if active euthanasia became a common practice, it could undermine the role of doctors as healers and caregivers.[122]

Public sentiment seems to favor the right-to-die movement. A poll conducted in 1990 for Time/CNN by Yankelovich Clancy Shulman revealed that 80 percent of those surveyed said that decisions about ending the lives of terminally ill patients should be made by their families and doctors and not by lawmakers. Eighty-one percent believed that if a patient is terminally ill and unconscious but has left instructions in a living will, the doctor should be allowed to withdraw life-sustaining treatment—passive euthanasia. Fifty-seven percent went even further and said that in such cases it is all right for a doctor to administer a lethal injection or provide a lethal pill—active euthanasia.[123]

Washington state's "death-with-dignity" initiative, also known as Initiative 119 on the state ballot in a 1991 election, failed to garner a majority vote and lost by a margin of 54 percent to 46 percent. The initiative was supported by a large majority of voters for much of the campaign, but it lost support in the last few weeks before the election. A similar initiative in California in 1992 was defeated by the same margin as in Washington state.[124]

On November 8, 1994, Oregon voters approved the Death with Dignity Act by a margin of 52 percent to 48 percent. Known as Ballot Measure 16, the act allows physicians in the state to write lethal drug prescriptions for terminally ill patients who are expected to die within six months.[125] Opponents of the law took the issue to the federal courts and lost. The Ninth U.S. Circuit Court of Appeals rejected the argument that depressed terminally ill adults would be prevented under the law from making informed decisions. The court stated that the specter of involuntary suicides was merely speculative. The U.S. Supreme Court, in October 1997, refused to hear the challenge and without comment issued an order letting the ruling of the Ninth U.S. Circuit Court of Appeals decision stand.[126] On June 9, 1997, the Oregon legislature, declining to either amend or repeal the act, placed it on the ballot for a second vote. In the November 4, 1997, election 60 percent of voters voted against repeal of the law, while 40 percent voted in favor of repeal.[127] Since the enforcement of the law in late 1997, preliminary indications are that, contrary to opponents' fears, only a handful of terminally ill patients have requested and received assistance in ending their lives.

Individual health care providers and society have tried to address some of the problems arising out of life-sustaining technologies in a variety of ways. Many hospitals have established ethics committees to help with ethical and related issues arising out of treatment of terminally ill patients. They often perform the functions of educating the hospital staff, developing policies in problem areas, and acting as advisory consultants to health care providers and occasionally to family members. Some have expressed concerns that the committee's decisions, instead of being advisory, may turn into de facto binding decisions, diminishing the role and rights of patient, family members, and health care providers.[128]

There has also been a significant interest in "living wills" and "durable power of attorney." A living will is signed by a competent person in good health and gives permission to his or her doctor to turn off life-support systems in the case of terminal illness or a permanent coma. Thus the living will gives the person some control over his or her last few days or weeks of life. Because both the National Conference of Commissioners of Uniform State Laws and the American Bar Association have given their stamp of approval to the Uniform Rights of the Terminally Ill Act, the number of persons signing living wills is expected to increase. To prevent abuse, state laws in the area of living wills often stipulate specific conditions that must be met. For example, some states require that at least two physicians certify that the patient's illness is terminal. Some states require that the living will be witnessed by people who are not health care providers or beneficiaries of the person's last will.

An option to a living will is for an individual to assign a permanent power of attorney to another person. In this scheme, another person (for example a spouse, a family member, or a friend) is designated as a surrogate health care decision maker in case a person is unable or incompetent to make decisions for herself or himself due to serious illness.

Genetic Research and Ethics

Another controversial area involves genetic research. Genetic research is producing a great deal of genetic knowledge that raises troublesome ethical questions. One of the most controversial issues is the cloning of animals and humans. Some of the other significant moral issues involving genetic research relate to genetic knowledge. Do individuals have a moral right to pursue their own goals without contributing to society's knowledge of population genetics? Is there a presumed right to genetic ignorance?[129] Right to know or not to

know is linked to issues of privacy and confidentiality. While gene enhance-
ment for a particular trait, such as intelligence, or a talent for music or sports,
at present remains technically unfeasible, in the future it may become possible. The real danger is one of commercialization, and the fear is that
politicians may be influenced by biotechnology company lobbyists.[130]

On the one hand, genetic research offers some positives. Testing for pre-
dictive diagnosis and carrier identification can help treatment. However, since
gene "diagnosis" will generally highlight susceptibility to later disease (e.g.,
cardiovascular disorders), would an individual's failure to adjust his or her
lifestyle (for instance, by exercising, by eating well) make that individual less
deserving of health interventions? How would resources be allocated, since
all people are somewhat guilty (e.g., they have hazardous lifestyles, they work
in occupations that present health hazards, they engage in risky behaviors,
etc.)? Who would make the rules? Once genetic research establishes clear
links with specific disease, what about the potential for discrimination in employment and health insurance?[131]

The issue of who has access to and control of DNA samples and genetic
information—collection, storage, and retrieval—is an important one from the
perspective of patient privacy and confidentiality. The Ethical, Legal, and
Social Issue Committee of the Human Genome Organization (HUGO) has
recently drafted some guidelines on the use of genetic material and information. HUGO is an international organization of scientists and others involved
in the Human Genome Project. One of the goals of this organization is to
foster international collaboration within the project. The organization also
organizes workshops designed to encourage consideration of social, ethical,
legal, and intellectual property issues arising from this project.[132] We as a
society have barely begun to scratch the surface and have a long way to go in
addressing a host of issues raised by genetic research.

Conclusion: Medical Technology, Ethics, and Public Policy

The discussion of life-sustaining technology exemplifies the complexities of
legal and ethical issues raised by modern medical technology. Similar complex issues are raised by health care technology in areas such as organ
transplants[133] and reproductive technologies,[134] to name two. Organ transplants
raise many ethical issues for donors, recipients, health care providers, and
society as a whole. When is it ethical to donate organs? What criteria should
be used in deciding who gets an organ transplant and who does not? Is it
ethical to sell organs? Since it is reasonable to assume that there will always
be more demand for than supply of available organs, would allowing the
selling of organs produce an economic market for organs, in which organs

would be bought and sold as other goods and services are? What are the ethical issues related to the living donor versus the living but terminal donor? Is it ethical to end the life of a terminal patient in order to make an organ available?

Health care technology has also produced a revolution in reproductive processes that raises many difficult ethical problems. Ethical objections to artificial insemination are often raised on religious or theological grounds. Objections are also raised on the ground that artificial insemination produces harmful consequences for society when the woman is not married, when the donor is not screened, or when the identity of the donor is concealed. Similar ethical concerns are raised with in vitro fertilization (i.e., test-tube fertilization), surrogate parenthood, embryo transfers, and the use of frozen embryos and sperm banks.

Health care technology is developing at a rapid pace, while our capacity and our ability to comprehend and deal with the legal and ethical issues raised by medical technology are lagging behind. As we enter the twenty-first century, policymakers will be increasingly confronted with the challenge of formulating public policies that require an understanding of legal and ethical implications of rapidly emerging new technologies. Despite this, at present no formal mechanism or forum is available at the national level in the United States that can allow for systematic examination of and debate about the legal and ethical issues dealing with health care technology. This is in sharp contrast to many other countries, where government-sponsored or government-encouraged bioethics forums have flourished. For example, governments of at least twenty-seven countries have established a national commission of some kind or have legislation pending to do so.[135]

Australia was one of the first countries to adopt legislation in 1984 regulating in vitro fertilization. In general, efforts to enact regulations in Australia have met with success at both the state and the federal levels. At both levels of government, formal bodies exist that reflect on bioethical issues and have the authority to recommend regulatory responses.[136] Canada also has developed a national ethics forum with specific mandates to address ethical issues. This includes groups such as the Advisory Committee on Medical, Ethical, Legal and Social Issues; the Royal Commission on New Reproductive Technologies; and the National Council on Bioethics in Human Research.[137]

Developments in the United States can be best characterized as a patchwork approach to bioethics. Most initiatives have tended to be private rather than government-sponsored. This has the advantage of producing multiple or pluralistic approaches that foster diversity. Private bodies also are under less political pressure.[138] But such approaches often lack the necessary authority to produce meaningful and timely responses. Kathi E. Hanna, Robert M. Cook-Deegan, and Robyn Y. Nishimi have advocated that the United States adopt a new approach to addressing issues of bioethics. They have called for the establishment of a centralized national forum, along the lines of a presidential commission, which would conduct research, hold hearings, and address issues of broad public interest dealing with, for example, assisted suicide and life-sustaining and reproductive technologies. They have also recommended creation of an entity within the Department of Health and Human Services to establish protocols for federally funded biomedical experiments and research.[139] Such proposals have come under criticism from some quarters. For example, Ira H. Carmen argues that "good" biomedicine or "ethical" biomedicine cannot be defined in the abstract. According to Carmen, our constitutional and political order requires a delicate weighing and balancing of competing interests by policymakers. The Madisonian model that underlies our political system requires that the people's representatives, not some presidential commission, work through the political branches to formulate national policies.[140] Whether the Congress of the United States is up to the task remains to be seen.

CHAPTER 9

Reforming the System

Politics is how society manages conflicts about values and interests. The United States, a large, heterogeneous society with complex cross-cutting divisions by race, ethnicity, class, region, and more, naturally presents many such conflicts to manage. Health care, an arena of high popular expectations, settled professional prerogative, and expenses that now total nearly $1 trillion per year, piles on further problems of its own. The conflict management that is politics, therefore, is not some nonrational and inefficient sideshow that threatens the reformist visions of the best and the brightest but rather a challenge central to making health reform come out for the better—indeed, come out at all. And no issues trigger battles over values and interests more quickly and acutely than do the source and use of money in health reform proposals.

—Lawrence D. Brown

As Brown states, reforming the health care system presents a huge challenge.[1] Previous chapters have concentrated on specific aspects of health care. Chapter 3 looked at Medicaid and chapter 4 examined Medicare. Chapter 5 examined the problems of the disadvantaged. Chapter 6 focused on cost control, chapter 7 on medical liability issues, and chapter 8 on technology. Chapters 1 and 2 presented some background material for understanding the context of health care policymaking in the United States. Chapter 1 discussed the politics of health care and chapter 2 presented a history of health policy in the United States. But none of these chapters provided a systematic examination of the health care system as a whole. That is the purpose of this chapter.

We begin by looking at some of the problems of the health care system, in a sense bringing together much of the material of the previous chapters. We then look at economic critiques of the health care system, which suggest major reform. Following that, we present some policy history of attempts to inject competitive reforms into the health care system. In particular, we examine the development of ideas that eventually became known as "managed care" and "managed competition." Using this as a focus, we look at the attempt to reform health care in the early and mid-1990s and why that attempt failed. We also examine the role of the states and the private sector in the transformation of the American health care system.

Systemic Problems

Various problems of the health care system have been dealt with at length in this book. The underlying problem is one of finance. From an individual perspective, medical care is expensive. For those with adequate and secure sources of health insurance, medical costs are ameliorated. Even then, premiums for health insurance continue to rise. For those with no health insurance, public or private, cost is a key barrier (though not the only one) to obtaining care. Medicaid covers fewer than half the people whose incomes are below the poverty line. A growing number of people find that their health insurance is either inadequate or insecure.

Cost is also a problem for the business sector. Smaller firms are less likely to provide health insurance for their employees than are larger firms, again primarily because of cost. Larger firms do provide health insurance, but the cost of providing that insurance has risen markedly. Firms have sought to manage those costs by cutting back, shifting more costs to employees, and moving their employees toward managed care plans.

For governments, health care costs are barely controllable. On the state level, Medicaid is one of the fastest-growing budgetary items. At the federal level, Medicare costs have grown faster than either the growth of the overall economy or government budgets. Governments have sought to control costs through reimbursement policies in both Medicaid and Medicare (diagnosis-related groups, or DRGs, and physician fee schedules), with some success. But the result has been either some cost shifting or fewer physicians participating in the programs (especially Medicaid).

Other problems exist. For residents of inner cities and rural areas, there is an insufficient supply of providers. Medicaid eligibility does not guarantee service if few doctors are willing to accept Medicaid patients. Certain sectors of society, the poor and minorities, have less access to care and thus higher rates of health problems than the population at large. And some 14 percent of the population is not covered by health insurance.

From the systemic perspective, the United States spends more on health care (absolutely and relatively) than any other country. Health care is the largest sector of the American economy. Yet, by many health indicators (such as infant mortality rates), the population is not necessarily healthier. Medical technology is most developed in this country, yet that same technology presents problems. It is one of the reasons for the cost problem, and it creates ethical problems surrounding the issue of quality of life. Much of the technology is "halfway" technology, which does not cure "but requires months or years of extremely expensive life-prolonging therapies."[2]

Furthermore, and paradoxically, the United States has both the most complex regulatory control over health care and the least control over the system. Because of numerous decisions that have been largely left medical care in the hands of providers, insurers, and pharmaceutical and medical technology companies, government response has been at best reactive and piecemeal. Medicare and Medicaid (as well as other programs of the 1960s) reinforced the predominant "values and interests," to use Lawrence Brown's term in the book's epigraph, of health providers and insurers. The federal tax code aided in the development of private insurance but never challenged the medical establishment.[3]

In various chapters we have looked at attempts to overhaul the system through national health insurance. Some six tries have failed, most recently in 1994. But alongside those attempts at nationalizing health care were critiques of the system and of government's role based on an economic analysis of health care, which led to calls for reform. These critiques would eventually become married to some form of national health insurance, relying on competition strategies and peaking in the 1990s.

The Economic Critique

The economic critique begins with a consideration of some classic works in economics. The "bible" of economics is Adam Smith's *The Wealth of Nations*, published in 1776.[4] Smith argued that unfettered markets, free from government or monopoly interference, would produce the greatest benefits for humankind. Such markets were the most efficient, producing precisely the amounts of a good or service that producers want to sell and that consumers want to buy through the price mechanism. Anything that impeded the price mechanism would lower efficiency.

Smith's work formed the basis for classical (and neoclassical) economics and remains an important part of American ideology. The American bias has always been toward free markets and away from government control, though, as we see below, in health care (as in other areas) the viability of free, competitive markets is questionable.

Frederick Hayek, writing just at the end of World War II, warned the country of moving toward more government control.[5] Most influential was Milton Friedman's *Capitalism and Freedom*. Friedman argued that economic freedom, a capitalist society, supported political freedom. He discussed a number of policy issues showing how free markets would work better than government intervention or control.[6]

So what is the economic critique of the health care system that dates back to Adam Smith? The critique is that the incentive structure of health care moves the system toward inefficiencies. It does this in several ways. Consider the traditional *fee-for-service, third-party payment system*.[7]

There are four parts to the transaction: the patient with health insurance seeks a service; the patient sees a doctor, who provides that service; the doctor's charges depend on the amount of services provided; the more services, the higher the charge (that is why it is called fee-for-service). The doctor knows that the patient is covered by health insurance provided by the employer through an insurance company. The patient pays the bill and then files a claim with the insurance company for reimbursement. In some instances, the health insurance policy is so generous that the patient does not have to pay anything. In other cases, the doctor's office files the claim and bills the patient for the balance after the claim is paid. Depending on the policy, the patient may have met the deductible for the year and may have limited copayments. The insurance company processes the claim and either pays the doctor or reimburses the patient. The employer pays the premiums on the employee's health insurance and may also (if the policy is especially generous) pay premiums for dependents. If not, then the employee pays the premiums, but at a group rate.

Who is concerned about the cost of care and the quality and efficiency of care (whether a particular test or treatment is really necessary) under such a system? If the doctor and the patient both know that third-party insurance will cover the cost, they have little concern. As long as the premiums cover the reimbursements (plus a profit), the insurer does not care. As long as premium costs are reasonable, and the federal government allows a business tax deduction for premiums (an incentive to cover or continue coverage), the employer does not care. The same situation is true for hospital care.

That is exactly the point that economic reformers seek to make. Under this kind of situation, typical up through most of the 1980s, the cost and the price of service are irrelevant. Economists argue that in the absence of paying the true cost of care, consumers will demand more health care than they really need, a problem labeled *moral hazard*.[8]

Health care suffers from another problem that impedes the operation of free, competitive markets: *imperfect information*. Providers have considerable information and expertise (though not complete information) and are in a power position compared to other actors, especially consumers, or patients. Thus additional treatments are not the result of consumer demand for them, but of provider requests. In that sense health care is provider driven, rather than consumer driven. Furthermore, consumers do not shop around comparing service and price at critical times (e.g., during a heart attack). Imperfect information, power asymmetries, and lack of a clear price mechanism work together to create market failures in health care. The question is how to solve these problems.

Market Reforms

The simplest way to reform health care markets is to focus on the consumer and insurance. The more generous the insurance policy, the less likely it is that costs are a consideration. The obvious solution would be to make health insurance less generous. Insurance may have what is known as *first-dollar coverage*, beginning coverage with the smallest illnesses. Rather than cover everything, a *catastrophic health insurance policy* might be substituted. Such a policy would go into effect after a rather high deductible was met, perhaps as a percentage of family income.

A typical health insurance policy might have a $300 deductible (some have no deductibles). After the first $300 of medical expenses, 80 percent or more of further medical expenses might be covered by insurance. But what if the policy were changed so that the deductible were $2,000, or 10 percent of a family's income? Then the consumer, or patient, would have to bear the expenses of further care and might not go to the doctor for every cold or sniffle. Only truly needed care would be undertaken. Further, the family would be protected from very high medical expenses (such as a cancer operation and treatment) after the deductible was met. Moreover, as we know with automobile insurance, the higher the deductible, the lower the premium to the worker and/or the employer.

There is an element of simplicity to such plans, which were proposed in the late 1970s and early 1980s. Such analysis largely underlies the relatively new policy proposal of *medical savings accounts* (MSAs). Such policies were first included in Medicare in 1996 on an experimental basis and then in the larger population, also on an experimental basis in 1997. Chapter 10 discusses MSAs in more detail. But consumers preferred first-dollar coverage, and the plans never went anywhere.

Such catastrophic plans concentrated on what could be called the *demand side* of health care, the consumer, but most reform plans focused on the *supply side* of health care, the provider.[9] This would mean changing the incentives built into the traditional system and trying to create more competitive markets.

The first attempt at a supply-side, market-reform solution came in the 1960s and 1970s. This was the *health maintenance strategy* mentioned in chapters 2 and 6. The strategy, the brainchild of Dr. Paul Ellwood, was an elegant idea.[10] Based on already-existing *prepaid group plans* (PGPs), the idea was to limit the money available to providers through a *capitation* system. The health maintenance organization (HMO) enrolls subscribers, who pay a monthly premium. The premiums constitute the total budget for the HMO. Providing more services does not produce more revenues. So the incentive was not to overtreat, as market reformers argue is done in the fee-for-service system, but to treat only as necessary. The HMO became the prototype of a *managed care organization* (in 1990s language), one that would review services and try to eliminate unnecessary care.

There was a further hope behind the HMO strategy: HMOs would create competitive pressures on the fee-for-service system so that all providers and insurers would begin to look at costs. As HMOs penetrated a market, competitive pressures would increase. This idea was embodied in the 1973 *Health Maintenance Organization Act* to promote, with federal assistance, the development of HMOs. Into the 1980s, at least, the competitive impact of the strategy was questionable.

The second stage came in the late 1970s and early 1980s. Alain Enthoven took the competitive strategy a step further by suggesting a complete reorganization of the health care system, in essence national health insurance. Originally writing in the 1970s in the *New England Journal of Medicine* (and other journals) and then in his 1980 book *Health Plan*, Enthoven wanted to eliminate the employment-insurance connection.[11]

The *Consumer-Choice Health Plan* (CCHP) was a form of national health insurance that would work as follows:[12] Providers and insurers would organize into competitive health care plans. Each plan would then determine what its premiums would be. The federal government would estimate the average cost of care in various geographical areas and pay a percentage of that average cost through tax credits or 100 percent of the average cost for the poor via vouchers. CCHP featured an open-enrollment period, community rating (see chapter 5), and a limit on out-of-pocket costs. Consumers would then choose among the competing plans, which could include a traditional fee-for-service plan, an HMO, a plan with a very high deductible, and so forth. Each plan would charge a different premium, but the federal government would pay the same amount regardless of the plan chosen. Thus, consumers would face the decision of what plan to choose depending on the financial consequences for them. The newly regained place of price signals plus open enrollments would create the competition among the plans and (it was hoped) restrain the costs. Thus health care would be consumer driven rather than cost driven.

A somewhat less ambitious version of CCHP built on the employment-based insurance system already in place. For those with work-based insurance, the employer would pay the same premium for each employee regardless of which plan was chosen. Employees would have a choice of plans, with similar features, as mentioned above. For the poor or those without employment-based insurance, vouchers from the federal government could be used.

Competition plans created a great deal of interest in the late 1970s and early 1980s.[13] Congressmen Richard Schweiker (R-Pennsylvania) and David Stockman (R-Michigan) offered bills based on the CCHP. In 1981 Schweiker became the secretary of the Department of Health and Human Services (HHS) and Stockman became director of the Office of Management and Budget (OMB) in the Reagan administration. A task force within HHS was created to investigate competitive ideas; however, nothing further came of the effort, perhaps because CCHP or a variant was essentially a form of national health insurance at a time when the Reagan administration was seeking to reduce the federal government's role.

In addition, several practical developments began to move toward competitive plans. One was a focus on deregulating the health care industry but engaging in vigorous anticompetitive regulation.[14] For example, the American Medical Association (AMA) had for a long time opposed the group practice of medicine, arguing that it trespassed on the traditional autonomy of the individual practitioner. Over time, this opposition lessened, though the AMA still has some problems with managed care organizations.

Two developments among public employers provided some experience with choosing among competitive plans. The Federal Employees Health Benefits Program (FEHBP) allows federal employees to choose among competing plans, while the federal government provides level premium contributions. A similar program established in California, the California Public Employees' Retirement System (CalPERS), enrolls nearly a million public employees at all levels of government. CalPERS is a purchasing cooperative that negotiates with a number of different plans, such as HMOs, *preferred provider organizations* (PPOs), and traditional fee-for-service plans.[15]

In the late 1980s and early 1990s, Ellwood, who had moved from Minnesota to Jackson Hole, Wyoming, formed a working group to develop a strategy for change based on the idea of managed competition. The work group and guests "included academics, public officials and leaders of the insurance and health industries."[16]

Enthoven, perhaps the chief theorist of the Jackson Hole group, began advocating *managed competition* in the late 1980s and continued into the

1990s.[17] Managed competition is an attempt to marry several different ideas—national health insurance, insurance reform, managed care, organization of providers and purchasers, and choice for consumers—while building on the present system.

Managed Competition

The managed competition proposal was designed, according to Enthoven and Kronick, to meet two major goals: "to provide financial protection from health care expenses for all . . . and to promote the development of economical financing and delivery arrangements."[18] This would be done by enabling those not already in Medicare or Medicaid to purchase health insurance either through their employer or through a public sponsor organized by the states. The purpose of aggregating purchasers of insurance, either through employment or through sponsors (*health care alliances*), would be to allow them to bargain and contract with provider organizations, such as HMOs, PPOs, or the traditional fee-for-service system (or some other of the many possibilities).

Employers would pay a specific amount for full-time employees and dependents, and would pay a payroll tax for those not covered.[19] An employer's contribution would be 80 percent of an average of the price of plans offered (a *defined contribution* regardless of the plan chosen); subscribers would pay the difference. The tax laws would be changed to limit contributions by employers beyond the specified amount. Those not covered by an employer plan, such as the self-employed, would pay into the public sponsor plans, up to an income ceiling. The program would also include subsidies to pay for the premiums of the poor (not covered by Medicaid) and for small businesses.

Employers and sponsors would then negotiate with qualified health plans, made up of some combination of providers and insurers, who would offer a variety of plans. Subscribers would elect a plan each year. The federal government would collect the funds and make determinations about average costs of plans. The program could be run entirely by the federal government or by both the states and the federal government. Medicaid and Medicare would be left alone, at least at first, though recipients would be encouraged to join HMOs.

Like the earlier CCHP, the intent is to promote efficient organization of health providers and provide competition among those organizations. The major difference between the earlier and later plans is that purchasers would also be aggregated and would be in a position to bargain with providers, not at the time of the occurrence of an illness but at the point of purchasing coverage.[20] While the plan does not attempt radical surgery on the health care system, the hope is that forces put into place will in fact create significant changes, cover virtually the entire population, and cost less than the present system.

Moving toward Reform

The push for managed competition was one of the forces that led to a renewed focus on health care in the 1990s. The problems of the health care system were also creating a momentum toward change. The increasing costs of heath care to business and government and the associated rise in the cost of premiums were major problems (see chapter 6). There were other difficulties as well, many created by cost problems. Fewer workers found themselves covered by employer-based health insurance. The number of uninsured kept rising, with about 14 percent of the population lacking health insurance (see chapter 5). The problem of the uninsured was compounded by growing economic insecurity. Even those with health insurance were fearful that if they or their dependents became sick, their health insurance would be inadequate. Changing jobs might result in losing coverage for a preexisting problem. Medicaid seemed to cover smaller and smaller proportions of families with incomes below the poverty rate. All of this was exacerbated by the recession of 1990–91 and the reengineering of corporations to become more efficient and more competitive (i.e., more productive with the same or fewer workers).

One response to the growing problems was the report of the *Pepper Commission*, originally known as the U.S. Bipartisan Commission on Comprehensive Health Care. Created in 1988, the report called for coverage for long-term care and for universal coverage for those under the age of sixty-five. Medicare would be retained, but Medicaid would be phased out. The report proposed the elimination of experience rating among insurance companies.[21] While there was more consensus on long-term coverage than on universal coverage, there was no agreement on financing. Nevertheless, the Pepper Commission report was another factor in moving toward consideration of change.

Perhaps the most important factor was political.[22] The political aspect was set off by an unusual off-year senatorial election in Pennsylvania. Republican Senator John Heinz died in a plane crash in 1991, and Democratic Governor Bob Casey appointed Harris Wofford to the seat. Wofford would have to run in a special November 1991 election to see who would fill the remainder of Heinz's term (which was up in 1994). Wofford's Republican opponent was one of the most popular politicians in Pennsylvania, Richard Thornburgh. Thornburgh, at the time attorney general of the United States in the Bush administration, had previously been governor of the state. He resigned his position and was widely expected to win against the little-known Wofford.

To the surprise of everyone, Wofford won. In his campaign, Wofford played up the economic insecurity issue, focusing on heath care. His memorable campaign sound bite was that if we had the right to a lawyer, we should have the right to health insurance. Wofford's call for national health insurance resonated well among the voters and was widely considered to be one of the major factors in his victory.

The Pennsylvania off-year election demonstrated that health care could be a powerful campaign tool. In December 1991 Democrats began holding "town meetings" to discuss health care. Potential Democratic presidential candidates met on television to discuss health care. A group of touring Democratic senators held hearings and news conferences around the country. A majority of House Democrats held a simultaneous town meeting in January 1992.[23]

In February 1992 President Bush announced a health care initiative that would cost an additional $100 billion over a five-year period, to be paid for by limits on Medicare and Medicaid. The plan was based on tax credits and vouchers. Tax credits of up to $3,750 per year would go to families with incomes ranging up to $70,000 (and phased out as incomes rose). For poor families, a voucher equal to that amount would be issued. For the self-employed, there would be a tax deduction equal to the size of the premiums. Small business would be given tax inducements to band together and spread risk. There would also be some mild insurance reform.[24] The plan was a limited one and vague in detail, especially concerning cost control. Further, the plan did not address long-term care and was administratively complex. Finally, the value of the tax credits, deductions, and vouchers would erode over time. This was true because their value would be indexed to the consumer price index (CPI), but the cost of insurance premiums generally climbs faster than the CPI. Thus the amount of insurance the voucher or tax incentives could buy would decrease over time. Nevertheless, the Bush plan was an important piece in moving health care reform forward.[25]

Even at this early stage of the health care reform debate, the outlook for change was troubling. This reflected the presence of interest groups representing the major financial stakes in health care. They included the American Medical Association and its specialty groups; the American Hospital Association; specialty hospital groups such as those representing the for-profit or proprietary sector; insurance groups such as the Health Insurance Association of America; a group representing the five largest insurers such as Aetna; and business groups of all sizes. While larger employers supported employer mandates, small businesses did not. The American College of Physicians came out in favor of a cap on spending and a managed competition plan.[26]

The lobbyists and lawyers for these groups continued their efforts into 1994, and their impact was largely one of impeding change or, to put it another way, of protecting their interests. According to one observer of the health policy scene:

On the whole, health-care lobbyists have had the effect of retarding change and blocking it. That's because most of the effort has come from smart, well-financed groups that have a vested interest in the status quo. They do a good job of pointing out the potential risks and costs of change, but there is little information about the broader public interest in the benefits of change.[27]

Meyer's comment is an example of a pervasive problem of American politics and government. As government, especially at the federal level, has sought to do more, additional groups with stakes in the outcome of government deliberations have risen. Each program that government undertakes, whether a subsidy, a tax credit, or services, has interest groups to protect it. In 1979 there were about 117 national health care interest groups; by 1992 that number had increased to 741, an increase of over 500 percent.[28]

The more general problem is one that has been labeled *demosclerosis*. As Rauch describes it, demosclerosis is analogous to hardening of the arteries, or arteriosclerosis.[29] As the number of interest groups increase, and as the numbers of their lawyers, lobbyists, and consultants increase, government is less likely to cut unneeded programs or to make needed changes that might adversely affect an interest.[30] This early stage of the health care reform debate started ominously.

The motivation for the Bush plan was clearly the coming presidential elections (as well as the 1991 Pennsylvania senatorial elections). Arkansas Governor Bill Clinton promised that he would offer a health care plan. To support Clinton, Democratic leaders in the House of Representatives offered a health plan in June 1992 similar to one that Clinton was discussing. The plan would extend coverage to most, but not all, of the uninsured, and it contained provisions to control costs (price controls). The politics of the situation was clear: the Democrats offered a plan knowing that President George Bush would veto it, thus giving them a campaign issue.[31] In a preview of the split among congressional Democrats in 1993–94, conservative Democrats in the House offered a plan, sponsored by Jim Cooper (D-Tennessee), based on managed competition but with spending limitations.[32]

By October 1992, both President Bush and Governor Clinton had endorsed managed competition as the centerpiece of their health care plans.[33] The difference between the two proposals was that the Bush plan relied on tax incentives, while the Clinton proposal also had mandates and spending limitations. Both proposals would, at least in the short run, increase health care expenditures.[34] With Clinton's election in November 1992, health care reform was placed solidly on the governmental agenda.

Health Care Reform on the Front Burner

It appeared that after all the previously failed attempts in this century, health care reform and national health insurance had finally arrived. Most thought that change would take place, and many sought to benefit from it. The insurance industry, long an opponent of federal regulation, began to advocate universal health insurance. The major interest group, the Health Insurance Association of America (HIAA), advocated tax incentives, an individual mandate to purchase insurance (and possibly an employer mandate), and insurance reform. Part of the reasoning behind the insurance industry move was to become a player in reform. The industry also felt that it would benefit substantially from reform because more people would be buying insurance.[35]

Further, early public opinion polls supported President Clinton's efforts. A strong majority of the public, which included supporters of President Bush, felt that the president would be successful in extending health insurance coverage.[36] A poll several months later found that support for change remained, but that it was in some cases shaky. There was backing for change and even for paying additional taxes, under some circumstances. Typically, most Americans expressed dissatisfaction with the health care system as a whole, but satisfaction with their own coverage and their own doctors. But the results of the poll also showed what would eventually become a problem for the Clinton plan: "the political conundrum that some analysts see at the heart of the health-care debate: The public wants the current quality of care, at a lower cost and with the assurance that they will never lose it."[37] Other poll results showed that physicians favored universal health coverage and supported managed competition. This was true even though managed competition would likely reduce physician income.[38]

To develop a health care reform plan, Clinton set up a series of task forces, composed of some 500 people, headed by First Lady Hillary Rodham Clinton and Ira Magaziner. The task force, composed of people in government and the private sector, met in secret over a period of months. Details of the plan leaked out, with the major roadblock being how to finance the plan. The alleged secretness of the task force meetings became a point of controversy. According to one account, Clinton and his aides had decided on the overall health care reform plan prior to the inauguration in January 1993.[39] The outlines of what became the Clinton plan were mentioned during the campaign with the slogan "Competition within a budget," and a proposal and rationale for such a plan were published in book form in 1992.[40] Some charged that the meetings violated the Federal Advisory Committee Act because private-sector people were involved. Others, especially industry representatives, complained that they were left out of the deliberations, though members of the task force met with outside groups as well as members of Congress and their staffs.[41]

The president's plan was presented to the nation in September 1993 and a bill was sent to Congress the next month. The proposal, entitled the Health Security Act, had several fundamental value premises. One, captured by the title of the bill, was security. The bill provided for universal coverage through an employer mandate and through subsidies for poor people and workers without health insurance. The Clinton motto was "Health care that's always there."[42] There would be a minimum benefits package covering the following services: hospital, emergency, physician, clinical preventive, mental health and substance abuse, family planning, pregnancy-related matters, hospice care, home health care, extended care, ambulance, outpatient laboratory and diagnostic service, outpatient prescription and biologicals, outpatient rehabilitation, durable medical equipment, vision and hearing, preventive dental services for children, and health education classes.[43] There were, of course, limitations on the services. For example, the extended-care services were limited to 100 days a year.

The plan was based on the concept of managed competition.[44] All would belong to a health alliance, a purchasing cooperative, that would be set up by the states. Large corporations (those with 5,000 or more workers) could set up their own health alliances. Similarly, insurers and providers would establish plans. The alliances and plans would negotiate and subscribers would be offered a minimum of three plans. One would be a health maintenance organization providing all services to subscribers. A second would be the traditional fee-for-service system, the most expensive plan in terms of premiums and copayments. The third alternative was a hybrid or combination plan. This might be a preferred provider organization, where subscribers would get discounts for providers on the approved list.

The plan also specified how people would pay for health care. For example, self-employed workers would pay their own health premiums up to a point ($1,800 for individuals and $4,200 for families), and all premiums would be fully tax deductible. In the case of employees, employers would pay 80 percent of the premiums and workers the remainder. Small employers (those with fewer than fifty workers) would receive government subsidies. The unemployed would receive government subsidies for premiums. Medicaid would be eliminated, but the federal and state governments would pay the premiums for the poor (though only for the low-cost plans). Medicare would remain and the federal government would pay the bills. For retired people under the age of sixty-five, the federal government would pay the premiums.

The plan continually mentioned that employers would pay 80 percent of the premiums. The reference was to 80 percent of the average cost of premiums for the alliances (a defined contribution). Subscribers would pay the additional amount. This, as mentioned earlier, was an essential component of consumer choice: give the consumer a financial stake in the decision of which plan to choose. The alliances would also work toward insurance reform, so that experience rating would not be allowed, but some premium adjustments based on risk could be granted.[45]

The Clinton proposal also discussed financing. Part of the financing would come from employers and subscribers. While mid-size and large businesses paid for health insurance under the current system, small employers were less likely to (see chapter 5). Through the employer mandate, they would now be brought into the system. Even those who were uninsured would be contributing. Thus about 75 percent of the financing for health care under the Health Security Act would come from the private sector.[46] A second source of funds was savings from Medicaid and Medicare. Medicaid would be eliminated entirely, and there would be savings in Medicare. The plan was less specific about new sources of financing. After considering a number of options, a tax on tobacco was the most politically feasible one.

The Health Security Act also focused on cost control. Both managed competition and managed care would help restrain cost increases. Analysts believed that a sizable portion of the population would choose a HMO or another managed care option. This would, as explained above and in chapters 2 and 6, change the incentive structure of medical care toward more efficient care and away from cost-increasing, dubious services. The competition-inducing effect, based on experience with the federal employees program, the system in use in California, and other programs, would also lower costs and change the system toward more integrated care. Finally, supporters of the plan argued that the Health Security Act would reduce administrative complexity. All these things, it was hoped, would eventually result in lowered costs.[47] The Clinton administration recognized that costs would rise in the near future because more of the population would have health insurance.

But what if managed competition and managed care did not restrain cost increases? The Clinton plan contained a set of backup regulatory provisions. This "second line of defense" was a cap or ceiling on growth of insurance premiums.[48] Paul Starr describes how the premium caps would work:

> Under the Clinton plan, the caps apply not to the premiums of individual health plans but to an alliance's weight-average premium (the average of all premiums weighted according to the share of enrollment in the various plans). Federal legislation would set a growth rate for premiums for covered benefits for the country as a whole, and the National Health Board would adjust that rate for specific alliances depending on demographic changes and other

factors. Alliances could meet their targets without any enforcement of caps as competition held down premium increases of individual plans or as consumers switched out of high-cost plans, thereby dragging down the average. If, however, health plans' bids threatened to push an alliance's average over the allowable growth, the federal government would deny full rate increases to the plans seeking the biggest jumps and require the plans to pass on these rate reductions to their providers.[49]

As can be seen from this brief description, the Clinton proposal was complex. It was also over 1,300 pages in length. It was a combination of ideas. It contained an employer mandate (and to some extent an individual mandate for the unemployed) combined with subsidies for both businesses and individuals. It promised universal coverage. It allowed for the possibility of a single-payer system, by permitting states to establish such a system if they wished. Most important, it sought to reform the health care system through a set of health care purchasing cooperative alliances and incentives for providers to integrate into more efficient units. It sought to marry competition with regulation.

The Clinton plan was therefore not a pure plan. While it provided for universal coverage, insurance, and administrative reforms, it did not adopt a single-payer system. Such a system is simpler than either the present system or the one envisioned under the Clinton plan. A single-payer system was not viewed as politically feasible, however, and the Clinton plan sought to build on the present employer-based insurance system. It was also designed to meet the needs of various constituencies.[50]

Insurance companies in general would benefit in two ways. First, a larger proportion of the population would be covered. Second, insurers could be major forces behind the provider plans. This would be more true for large insurance companies such as Aetna and Prudential.

Business would also benefit from the plan in several ways. It was true that there would be an employer mandate. This was good from the standpoint of large businesses, because with everyone covered and more paying, cost shifting would effectively be ended. For small businesses, there were subsidies and limitations on their contributions. Further, the Health Security Act would cover early retirees (those under sixty-five and therefore not yet eligible for Medicare), a growing cost burden for larger employers.

Thus there appeared to be something for everyone. States had an important role, managed competition would be tried, everyone would be covered. The plan, as originally estimated, would reduce the budget deficit in the long run, as health care costs were restrained.

The early reaction to the Clinton plan was positive. Initially, public opinion seemed to support the proposal, though there was some concern about the complexity of the plan and the additional layers of bureaucracy and government regulation that the plan proposed. In this early stages, both interest groups and Republicans supported the plan to remain part of the action.[51]

It should be further noted that, despite the complexity of the plan and the effort that went into the formulation stage, the Clinton administration never saw the plan as written in stone. They knew the plan would be modified in Congress; this was the opening move.[52] Indeed, some of the provisions, such as a generous benefits package, high employer cost sharing, and strict limitations on the growth of insurance premiums, were designed to allow some negotiating room.[53]

It was also clear that despite the administration's attempt to meet the needs of various constituencies, there would still be those who won and lost by the Clinton plan. Younger people would be asked to pay more, as would those in rural areas. Working couples would also be losers under the Clinton plan because both would have to pay for health insurance, rather than rely on one job for insurance. Couples with self-employed spouses, who currently paid nothing, would also be dramatic losers.[54] Similar estimates could be made among providers and insurers. Primary-care physicians would be winners, and specialists would be losers. This is true because under managed care arrangements, especially HMOs, primary-care physicians would act as "gatekeepers," deciding when additional services would be necessary. Specialists, therefore, would be more limited in their ability to offer services. Doctors who joined health care plans would be both winners and losers. They would be winners in that they would be guaranteed access to patients and losers in that they would lose some autonomy and perhaps some income. Doctors who did not join plans would likely be losers because they would not be able to hold onto their patients. Large insurers would be able to organize health care plans, whereas small and medium-size insurers would not.[55]

The Legislative Stage

Deliberations over the health care reform plan did not begin until 1994, an election year. One of the key aspects of the legislative process is that a complex plan such as the Health Security Act is generally shared among a number of congressional committees. The bill was divided among six committees in the House and five in the Senate.[56] To pass health care legislation would take strong leadership on the part of the majority Democrats. Only one committee in Congress, the Senate Labor and Education Committee, under the guidance of its chairman, the long-time national health insurance advocate Edward M. Kennedy (D-Massachusetts), approved even a modified version of the president's proposal.

One problem was financing. A study by Lewin-VHI, a health care consulting firm, found the cost estimates optimistic. The original estimate of the additional costs of the program was $286 billion over a five-year period. The Lewin study estimated that the program would cost about $78 billion more than the administration estimated over the same period. So, rather than reduce the budget deficit by $103 billion, it would decrease it by about $25 billion.[57] During the deliberations of the task force in 1993, economists in the Treasury Department argued that the cost figures were not reliable.[58] The Congressional Budget Office (CBO), which scored legislation (estimated how much bills would cost if enacted), came up with the estimate of the near-term negative impact of the Health Security Act on the budget deficit. It also made several rulings that decreased support for the plan, for example, that mandated premiums should be considered as part of the federal budgets and that the health alliances should be considered as federal agencies.[59]

Doubts were also expressed about various aspects of the health plan. For example, an early 1994 report by the Congressional Budget Office said that the regional alliances were being asked to do numerous complex tasks in a very short period of time. The tasks included "the functions of purchasing agents, contract negotiators, welfare agencies, financial intermediaries, collectors of premiums, developers and managers of information systems, and coordinators of the flow of information about themselves and other alliances."[60]

Even those whose support should have easily been forthcoming criticized the Clinton plan. The Jackson Hole group opposed the plan on a number of grounds. Enthoven wrote that the plan promised too much (covering everyone, restraining costs) and would likely not result in cuts in Medicare. He opposed the employer mandate. The group also did not like the price controls that were an important part of the plan. More important, Enthoven stated that the Clinton plan had taken the idea of health care cooperatives of a limited size and changed them into monstrous alliances.[61] Enthoven favored a bill by Congressman Jim Cooper (see below). In response, Paul Starr, a member of the Clinton health care reform task force and one of its leading advocates, argued that in some respects the Clinton plan was quite close to what Enthoven had previously written. For example, Starr pointed out that Enthoven had favored an employer mandate but no longer did so. Further, Starr noted that Enthoven took a strong antigovernment position about the Clinton plan, yet the Jackson Hole proposals would require significant government involvement to help restructure markets.[62]

The Clinton plan was not the only one put before Congress. Some six alternative plans were proposed, some by Democrats, others by Republicans.[63] The Clinton plan had 100 co-sponsors in the House and thirty-one in the Senate.[64] The Democratic proposals were divided among two widely disparate proposals. On the left, the bill by Senator Paul Wellstone (D-Minnesota) and Congressman Jim McDermott (D-Washington) called for a single-payer approach to be administered by the states. That bill had ninety-two cosponsors in the House and five in the Senate. On the right, Congressman Jim Cooper (D-Tennessee) and Senator John Breaux (D-Louisiana) sponsored a bill that was sometimes referred to as "Clinton-lite." Their bill would expand access to insurance through voluntary cooperatives, subsidies for low-income people, and insurance reform. The Cooper bill had fifty-seven cosponsors in the House and four in the Senate.

Republicans offered three different plans. One bill, offered by House Minority Leader Robert Michel (R-Illinois) and Senator Trent Lott (R-Mississippi), expanded access to insurance but contained no mandate. It was a voluntary program that expanded Medicaid and provided for insurance reforms. Employers had to offer their employees health insurance, though they did not have to pay for it. The bill had 139 co-sponsors in the House and ten in the Senate. A second Republican bill was offered by Congressman Cliff Stearns (R-Florida) and Senator Don Nickles (R-Oklahoma). The bill was a voluntary program but had penalties for individuals not purchasing catastrophic insurance. There would be tax changes regarding the deductibility of health costs and expansion of Medicaid. The bill had eighteen co-sponsors in the House and twenty-five in the Senate. The final bill was the one offered by Congressman William Thomas (R-California) and Senator John Chafee (R-Rhode Island). The bill was basically an individual mandate to purchase insurance and enroll in a plan (either government, employer, or purchasing cooperative). Employers had to offer coverage but did not have to pay for it. Those not purchasing insurance would be penalized. The bill also called for an individual mandate to purchase long-term care insurance. The Thomas-Chafee bill had four co-sponsors in the House and twenty in the Senate.

The abundance of plans did not necessarily translate into support for health care reform. There seemed to be a consensus that some change would take place, given the Democratic majority in Congress and the priority placed on reform by the Clinton administration. But the motives of those proposing and supporting the other plans varied. Some wanted to show that they were involved and wanted to have a say in the final outcome. Others had particular features they wanted included in a health care reform bill. Some wanted to demonstrate their concern about the issue.[65]

As the debate over health care reform moved closer to congressional deliberation, however, support for the plan began to diminish. Interest groups began to attack individual portions of the plan. Perhaps the strongest opposition came from the National Federation of Independent Businesses (NFIB), the association of small businesses. NFIB opposed the employer mandate and lobbied against the Clinton plan from the beginning.

Another major opponent was the Health Insurance Association of America (HIAA). A trade association composed of most of the nation's insurance companies, its members felt that they were left out of the plan. Unlike the largest insurance companies, they would not be able to sponsor or work with alliances and so would be forced out of business. They, therefore, opposed alliances; they also argued that the Clinton plan reduced patients' choice of doctors. The insurance industry was not of one mind, however. The five largest insurance companies (Aetna, Cigna, Metlife, Prudential, and Travelers) formed the Alliance for Managed Competition and sponsored ads promoting managed competition and managed care. This did not, nevertheless, translate into support for the Clinton plan.[66]

This is not to say that no interest groups supported the Clinton plan. The Democratic National Committee was given a major role in sending out mail to contributors and potential contributors for their campaign in support of health care reform. The liberal group Families USA also engaged in direct-mail campaigns. Conservative groups likewise utilized direct mail.[67] Interest groups (about 650 of them) and lobbyists on both sides showered key congressmen and senators with campaign contributions. For example, from January 1, 1993, to May 31, 1994, the AMA political action committee gave almost $1 million in contributions.[68]

Interest groups on both sides also turned toward the grass roots, trying to mobilize supporters for their positions in the districts. Some of the grassroots support was genuine, especially on the part of employees of tobacco firms, who argued against additional taxes on tobacco products, and small business owners, who argued against employer mandates.[69] Other support was manufactured (sometimes known as "AstroTurf" lobbying):

> Pharmaceutical companies, for instance, are writing to their shareholders warning them that profits could suffer if price controls impede new drug research. Planned Parenthood is encouraging its members to deluge Congress with a post-card campaign demanding that abortion services, prenatal care and estrogen replacement therapy are covered under a proposed insurance blanket.[70]

A portion of the health care reform debate was fought through advertising, both print and electronic. The most famous of the television ad campaigns were the "Harry and Louise" and "Libby and Louise" ads by the Health Insurance Association of America. HIAA's major problems with the Clinton health care plan were threefold: HIAA opposed the ceiling or cap on insurance premiums, it opposed the requirement that people join the regional cooperatives (because smaller and midsize insurance companies would not be large enough to participate and would be forced out of the business), and it opposed community rating. As an example of the kind of pitch made in the HIAA ads, consider the following:

Harry: I'm glad the President's doing something about health care reform.
Louise: He's right, We need it.
Harry: Some of these details—
Louise: Like a limit on health care?
Harry: Really.
Louise: The Government caps how much the country can spend on health care and says, "That's it!"
Harry: So, what if our health plan runs out of money?
Louise: There's got to be a better way.[71]

A related HIAA ad saw Louise and her business partner, Libby, discussing the Clinton plan:

Libby: I want Congress to pass health care reform . . .
Louise: Make sure everyone is covered.
Libby: . . . but not force us to buy our insurance from these mandatory government "health alliances."
Louise: So we couldn't choose a plan that's not on their list even if we think it's better for our employees and their families.
Libby: Not according to this. (Holds up president's health plan.)
Louise: But Congress can fix that—cover everyone and let us pick the plan we want.
Libby: And they will, if we send them that message.
Announcer: For the facts you need to send a message, call today.[72]

Opponents of the Clinton plan used ads to attack various aspects of the proposal. Some, such as the Project for the Republican Future, argued that the greatest jeopardy to health care security was in fact the Clinton plan. Others, such as HIAA, attacked the plan as being bureaucratic and as restricting choice. Still others argued that the plan would cost more for people who currently had coverage.[73]

The ads were often incorrect or misleading. Some suggested that the Clinton plan would reduce choice of doctors. The reality is that the Clinton plan might in fact have increased choice for certain segments of the population.[74] Other ads attacked health care alliances long after that idea had been dropped by Congress.[75]

Supporters of the program were also active. The Democratic National Committee (DNC) ran a series of ads that counterattacked and parodied the "Harry and Louise" ads. In the DNC version, the couple get injured and lose their health insurance, and Harry loses his job. Louise turns to Harry and says: "You said universal coverage was too complicated. You said you'd never lose your job, so we'd always be covered. You said, what would we do when the government runs out of money? Well who's out of money now, Harry?" The ad closed with the tag line, "There is a better way. Tell Congress you want what they already have: the security of affordable, universal health care."[76] A coalition of consumer, labor, civic, professional, and other groups ran a newspaper and radio campaign touting the benefits of health care reform.[77] Pro-choice and pro-life groups ran ads on whether health reform should include or exclude abortion provisions.[78] Another parody of the "Harry and Louise" ads came from those sponsoring a single-payer system, with the tag line delivered by comedienne Anne Meara, "Harry and Louise, there is a better way." Of course the money raised by those supporting the single-payer plan was dwarfed by other interests.[79]

The ads may have made a bigger impact on the Clinton administration and on the media than on the public. The Clinton administration attacked the ads and, as noted, the Democratic National Committee ran ads parodying them. News media focused on the ads and the attacks on them and attributed to them more power than perhaps they had. A study testing the effectiveness of the "Harry and Louise" ads found little retention of the content of the ads and showed little effect of the ads on attitudes.[80]

Another way that opponents of health care reform had of attacking the plan was to suggest that while the country's health care problems were serious, they were not critical, requiring radical surgery. For example, Senate Minority Leader Robert Dole (R-Kansas) stated in January 1994 that there was no crisis in health care; Senate Finance Committee Chairman Daniel Patrick Moynihan (D-New York) made a similar point.[81] Public opinion polls gave ambiguous signs about whether the public saw a crisis. When asked to name the country's most important problems, only 7 percent listed health care (considerably behind the economy and crime). On the other hand, when asked whether the country faced a health care crisis, a problem, or no crisis, 57 percent said it had a crisis and 42 percent said a problem. Further, most people were satisfied with the quality of health care they received and with their health insurance. At the same time, a sizable majority favored universal health insurance.[82] To some extent, the idea of a crisis in health care in the early 1990s that could fuel an upset victory by Harris Wofford was caused by the economic conditions of that time. The recession of 1990–91, the continued increase in health care costs, and the diminishment of health insurance coverage among workers also contributed to the feeling of a crisis. But as the economy recovered from the recession and began to expand, and as health care cost increases moderated, the atmosphere of crisis diminished. Between the lessened crisis atmosphere, heavy lobbying, and advertising on the part of opponents, public support for the Clinton plan dwindled.[83]

Public Opinion and the Health Care Reform Debate

Early public opinion polls showed some support for the Clinton plan, though on a partisan basis. In a *New York Times/CBS News* poll, 61 percent said they would be willing to pay higher taxes so that universal coverage could be achieved. Forty-five percent felt that the president would be able to bring about reform, 41 percent said that the plan would being about needed changes, 40 percent said that it would be fair, and 46 percent said that it would make health care better. Republicans and independents expressed greater skepticism and much lower levels of support for change. The poll, like most others, showed the public's dissatisfaction with the system as a whole, though satisfaction with their care. A majority would support a limitation on choice of doctors and increased waiting for noncritical appointments if it meant that more could be covered. Only 36 percent, however, supported rationing (limiting coverage for expensive treatments with limited effectiveness). The poll showed majority support for employer mandates and for several ways to finance universal coverage: increased taxes on alcohol and tobacco and limitations on charges by doctors and hospitals through the Medicare program.[84]

A study of public opinion polls commissioned by the House of Representatives Ways and Means Committee found limited and declining support for increased taxes, though an increase in the number of people who felt that the country was spending too much on health care. The report concluded that "most Americans would rather see the scope of the Clinton reform plan scaled back than pay new taxes. In addition, the public is strongly opposed to increasing the deficit in order to pay for health reform."[85]

By March 1994, public support for the Clinton plan was declining precipitously. While there was support for the goals of the plan, more people disapproved of the proposal than approved of it. Part of the problem was that the complex plan was difficult to understand. Another part was the criticisms leveled at the proposal through ad campaigns. There was fear that the quality of care would decline, that rationing would occur, and that the middle class would be hurt by the proposal. A slim majority hoped that either nothing changed or that Congress would make changes in the plan. Nevertheless, the public still supported employer mandates and controls on premiums. Further, the public gave Clinton credit for trying to change the system.[86]

Two findings about public opinion were especially interesting. One was that while the public thought that the government could guarantee security of insurance coverage, there was doubt that the government could control costs. This was one reason the administration deemphasized cost control and emphasized security.[87] A second finding came from a March 1994 focus group presented with the Clinton plan without stating that it was the Clinton plan. The group preferred that plan to other alternatives. When the group was told that it was the Clinton plan, support dropped dramatically.[88]

It should be pointed out that part of the problem with public opinion polling is that slight differences in question wording can affect the results. When asked whether the Clinton plan was better or worse than the present system, a majority (52 percent) said better. When the phrase "or don't you know enough about the plan to say" was added, only 21 percent said it was better. The percentage of those who felt that the Clinton plan was worse declined to 27 percent from 34 percent. Thus a substantial portion of those polled (52 percent) admitted ignorance of the plan.[89]

As the struggle over health care reform continued in Congress, public support for change decreased. By September 1994, only about 40 percent approved of the way President Clinton was handling the health care issue. But the opinion of other players in the health care reform debate also diminished. Robert Dole's unfavorability ratings had increased by 10 points over the previous year. Strong support remained for universal coverage and the idea that the health care system was in crisis. The major targets for blame included the opposition to the Clinton plan and the high level of government regulation in the plan.[90]

Health Care Reform Defeated

While several committees in the House of Representatives passed a version of the Clinton health care reform bill, there was never a vote on the floor of the House. House Democrats, despite the crafting of a bill by House Majority Leader Richard Gephardt (D-Missouri) calling for universal coverage by 1999, never united behind a single plan.[91] By early August, House leaders decided that between Republican opposition and the hesitancy of a number of Democrats, they would let the Senate take the lead.[92]

One of the interesting things that happened during deliberations over health care reform was how little of the original plan remained. President Clinton said his major concern was universal coverage. Then the question raised was: What did universal mean? Was it 100 percent or would some lesser figure, such as 95 or 90 percent, be acceptable? The president agreed to a lesser figure. Lost in the debate was another major concern: controlling the cost of care.[93] But Senate Democrats were also not united. Senate Finance Committee Chairman Moynihan stated that he saw no crisis in health care that warranted emergency surgery. Several Republicans and Democrats on the Finance Committee proposed a plan that had an individual rather than an employer mandate.[94] The feeling of some of those on the committee was that even though the individual mandate was not desirable, it would help get a bill reported to the floor of the Senate. But a group of civic, consumer, and labor groups, known as the Health Care Reform Project, opposed the proposal. They wanted an employer mandate; they felt that the individual mandate would not achieve universal coverage and that middle-income families without insurance would still have financial problems.[95] At the same time, Senate Minority Leader Bob Dole moved away from his previous advocacy of universal coverage toward a much less ambitious goal of assisting the poor in purchasing insurance and prohibiting insurance companies from denying coverage to those with previous medical conditions.[96]

It also became clear that Republicans in both the House and the Senate were opposing reform with an eye on the forthcoming November 1994 elections, a strategy that would ultimately be successful. House Minority Whip Newt Gingrich (R-Georgia) told Republicans on the Ways and Means Committee not to support any amendments that would improve the chances of a committee bill passing. Further, Gingrich told Republicans that, if they supported a tax increase, one portion of the bill the Ways and Means Committee was considering, such support could be used against them by Democrats in the elections. To a small extent, the Republican strategy backfired. Democrats on the committee who had previously been divided on a bill came together to support one in a show of party unity.[97] Overall, the Republicans were emboldened in their opposition, as support for the Clinton plan eroded and House Democrats showed little unity.[98]

In early August, Senate Majority Leader George Mitchell (D-Maine) made one last try at a bill.[99] The Mitchell bill relied on individual mandates, with the goal of 95 percent coverage by the end of the century. The president supported the Mitchell bill.[100] A few days later, Mitchell agreed to compromise with a bill being prepared by Senator Chafee.[101] After debate began on the Mitchell bill, Senate Republicans began a filibuster to prevent a vote on the floor of the Senate. Mitchell was unable to get enough votes to end debate and at one point threatened to keep the Senate in an around-the-clock session to break the filibuster.[102] Mitchell's efforts would eventually fail, and health care reform was doomed. Moderate Republicans and Democrats, in what became known as the Mainstream Group, attempted to fashion a compromise bill but got little support beyond their group.[103]

By the end of August, it became clear that health care reform could not be passed in any version. Republicans were not only opposing any reform in both the Senate and the House but were threatening to drop support for the trade agreement, the General Agreement on Tariffs and Trade (GATT), which would be debated later in the year.[104]

The November elections brought a historic Republican victory. Health care was not an important issue in the campaigns, and the Republicans gained control of both houses of Congress for the first time in forty years.[105] Perhaps most symbolic were losses by two Democrats. Jim Cooper, the author of a major alternative to the Clinton health plan in the House, lost his bid for senator from Tennessee. Harris Wofford, whose unexpected victory in the special senatorial election in Pennsylvania in 1991 sparked political movement toward health care reform, lost his effort to serve a complete term.

The Failure of Health Care Reform

> After hundreds of town hall meetings, months of congressional hearings and markups by five committees, days of Senate consideration and an unprecedented lobbying campaign by special interest groups, neither the House nor the Senate ever did vote on a health care bill. As the 103d Congress adjourned, its unwillingness to act on what President Clinton described as his most important domestic priority stood as the most conspicuous symbol of Clinton's failure to implement the ambitious reform agenda.[106]

Why did health care reform fail to win approval in 1994?[107] A number of reasons have been put forth to explain the failure. One was the inability of the president to maintain public support, either for himself or for his reform proposal. While the initial returns from the president's September 1993 speech were quite positive, opinion polls always showed that support was tenuous. The public wanted change but was also satisfied with its care. It wanted security but feared government bureaucracy.[108]

This last point is an important one. The Clinton plan, rightly or wrongly, was characterized by opponents, such as the Health Insurance Association of America and congressional Republicans, as big government. This ran into the traditional American distrust of government, particularly at a time (1994) when government was under attack.[109]

The president's own approval ratings also were a problem. Bill Clinton won the 1992 election but captured only 43 percent of the popular vote. During his first two years in office, his approval ratings hovered in that area, only periodically exceeding 50 percent. Questions about his character and finances (Whitewater) also affected Clinton's approval ratings. Further, during the 1992 elections, he had run behind virtually all the congressmen and senators who ran that year. He clearly had no coattails that one could cling to in 1994.[110]

The process by which the Health Security Act was formulated also may have contributed to its defeat. The 500-person task force headed by First Lady Hillary Rodham Clinton and Ira Magaziner focused on technical issues and not political feasibility.[111] It was conducted in secret and created antagonism from the beginning. The bill produced was very complex, and its complexity and length (more than 1,300 pages) did not help win it public support.[112] The administration was urged by moderates within the White House to come up with a general set of principles and goals and to let Congress work out the details. Instead, the detailed, highly complex plan became a target for those opposed either to reform or to portions of it.

The administration did not respond well to attacks by interest groups, particularly via television advertisements. Nor was the administration able to portray its flexibility and willingness to negotiate.[113]

Time was also a problem.[114] The proceedings of the task force were lengthy, and a bill promised in April 1993 was not unveiled until September 1993. Even then, the bill was not delivered to Congress until the next month. The anticipation and buildup that accompanied the early stages of policy formulation dissipated with delay.

Other administration priorities blocked the way.[115] In 1993, this included the big deficit-cutting budget bill and the North American Free Trade Agreement (NAFTA). In 1994, the administration's crime bill got in the way. To a certain extent, Republicans' opposition to the crime bill in the House was designed to impede passage of health care reform.

Another thing that hurt the Clinton plan was the economy. While the 1990–91 recession was over by the time of the 1992 elections, the effects of the recession were still being felt because the recovery was slow. By 1994, things had changed. The economy was growing at a good clip and inflation was low. Further, medical inflation was relatively low in 1994. Thus, Senator Dole could with some reason claim that there was no health care crisis. The slowdown in health care inflation has been attributed to the reduction in overall inflation and to changes in the health care system as it moved toward managed care. The more cynical could argue that providers and insurers kept cost increases low as a means of deflating the drive for reform.[116]

Of course, a major portion of the failure is attributable to opposition on the part of interest groups, most prominently the National Federation of Independent Businesses (NFIB) and the Health Insurance Association of America. The financial resources devoted to the campaign for advertising, lobbying, and grassroots activity towered over those of supporters. One estimate is that interest groups spent about $300 million to oppose the Clinton plan.[117]

These groups, especially NFIB, were able to mobilize their members to contact their congressmen. NFIB was also able to convince groups that originally supported reform to come out in opposition to the Clinton plan. The AMA and the Chamber of Commerce are cases in point. Small businesses began to quit the chamber because of its support for the Health Security Act. The chamber reversed its position. Other groups that originally supported the plan, such as the Business Roundtable, eventually came out against it.[118]

Partisanship was also a problem. Democrats in both the House and Senate were divided. This was in contrast to the considerable unity among Republicans in opposition to the Clinton plan. As the Republicans saw that public support was low and that the outlook for a successful election in 1994 grew, they became less inclined to negotiate and see the passage of a bill.[119]

There was also division among policy experts as to what course of action to take. One study conducted shortly after the demise of comprehensive reform in 1994 found that while policy elites were pretty much agreed on the nature of the problems with the health care system (though disagreeing with the general public about what those problems were), there was no consensus about what to do.[120]

There was one last factor, an institutional one. The institutional perspective takes note of the structure of the American political system (discussed in chapter 1), such as checks and balances, separation of powers, and federalism, and sees how that structure affects policy debate. The system devised by the delegates to the Constitutional Convention of 1787 was designed for two purposes. The first was to create a government that could act. The second was to create barriers to precipitous action by what the Founding Fathers called "factions" (what we would call interest groups and political parties). The Founding Fathers were distrustful of democracy and sought ways to limit the power of factions and of government that could be controlled by them.

The history of attempts at health care reform and national health insurance in the twentieth century bears witness to the power of the Founding Fathers' vision of limited government. And so while other Western industrialized countries moved toward some form of national health insurance and universal coverage, the United States did not. The barriers created, especially in Congress, provided the access points for interest groups opposed to reform and made the development of broad majorities at several different points of the legislative process very difficult.

After reviewing the institutionalist argument and the history of health care reform attempts in the United States, two political scientists, Sven Steinmo and Jon Watts, predicted eight months before the Health Security Act was presented to Congress that comprehensive health care reform would fail:

> America cannot pass major comprehensive health care reform that will control costs and offer complete coverage to all Americans because her political

institutions are designed to prevent this kind of reform. To truly pass meaningful reform would require imposing costs on certain groups (factions).
Clearly the majority (faction) both want and would benefit from such a reform. But the fragmentation of authority designed into the U.S. Constitution
makes it virtually impossible for the majority's will to supersede the minority—at least when that minority is well financed and well organized. To
overcome the opposition of the minority faction, the majority must buy off
their opposition. The effect (in the case of health care reform at least) is to
throw fat onto the inflationary fire.[121]

The States and Comprehensive Health Care Reform

> Change is likely to be driven less by what Washington does than by the sky-
> rocketing costs to states of caring for the poor under the Medicaid program
> and the tactics used by health maintenance organizations and insurance com-
> panies to cut health care spending. Together, the pressures on state budgets
> and business bottom lines are changing medical care on a level hardly envi-
> sioned when Clinton unveiled his proposals last year.[122]

Although the federal government considered health care reform in 1992–94,
little was actually accomplished. In contrast, a number of states passed legislation that sought either to cover more of the population or to reform the
entire system.

There are several rationales for state action. One is flexibility. States differ along many dimensions—size, economic base, urbanization, and so forth.
From this perspective, a single plan from the federal government would not
be appropriate for all states.[123] A second rationale is that states already have
important roles in health care: insurance and hospital regulation, rate regulation, licensing, delivery of public services, and education and training.[124]

A third rationale for looking at states (and local governments) is that
even under a national plan, the states would have an important administrative
role. This is typical of other domestic policy areas, such as welfare. Medicaid,
building on the welfare system, is a joint federal-state program. Under the
Clinton plan, states would have had an important role in designing and over-
seeing regional health alliances.[125] Even with the demise of comprehensive
reform at the national level, states undertook new programs, encouraged by
the Clinton administration's waivers from Medicaid regulations.[126]

A fourth rationale was the pressure that health care costs, especially Medicaid, was placing on state budgets. It was hoped that some changes, such as
Medicaid reform, would alleviate that pressure.[127]

The earliest state health reform effort was in Hawaii in 1974. Hawaii has
an employer mandate, even covering part-time workers. For low-income

people, there is an insurance premium subsidy. The Hawaii program, including Medicaid, covers about 93 percent of the state's population.[128] More recently, Hawaii has experienced some budget difficulties and has moved more toward market reforms and cost control.[129]

Some thirteen states engaged in attempts at comprehensive health care reform (in some cases predating the federal effort), designed to cover more of the population as well as restraining Medicare costs. Some of the most far-reaching reforms were in Florida, Massachusetts, Minnesota, Oregon, Vermont, and Washington.[130]

One of the more interesting attempts at reform came when Oregon, beginning in 1989, sought to impose an explicit rationing program within Medicaid.[131] It did this by ranking some 709 medical procedures and then setting a line of what would be and would not be funded by the state. For example, medical therapy for AIDS patients was allowed, unless they were in the last six months of life. Liver transplants would be allowed for those suffering from cirrhosis of the liver unless it was related to alcohol consumption.[132] Oregon argued that this rationing scheme could cover up to 400,000 more people with the same amount of money.

The Oregon plan required a Medicaid waiver from the federal government, but the Bush administration rejected it. There were several reasons for the rejection. One was that the plan was too inflexible given the variety of medical conditions physicians are presented with. A second reason was that explicit rationing affected only Medicaid recipients. Thus the least politically powerful would bear the brunt of rationing. Third, if health care costs rose more than expected after rationing went into effect, the cutoff point would have to be drawn higher.[133]

Perhaps the most important reason was that advocacy groups and others felt that the rationing plan would discriminate against disabled persons and therefore violate the 1990 Americans with Disabilities Act. Those making this claim included pro-life groups, the liberal Children's Defense Fund, the Catholic church, and the Democratic vice-presidential candidate, Al Gore.[134]

Oregon's governor, Barbara Roberts, argued that the plan was well thought out, that it had the participation of a wide variety of interests, and that disability groups in Oregon supported it. Further, she asserted that neither the General Accounting Office nor the Office of Technology Assessment (both staff arms of Congress) had raised the disabilities issue. Finally, Governor Roberts said that the Justice Department had not said how the Oregon plan might violate the act.[135] After changing the plan to meet some of the objections, the Clinton administration approved the Medicaid waiver in March 1993.[136] A second waiver and an exception from the Employee Retirement Income Security Act

(ERISA) were not granted and the employer mandate was rescinded.[137]

The Florida reforms began with some insurance revisions and agency consolidation in 1992. In 1993, Florida passed legislation designed to bring managed competition to the state (mimicking some of the elements of the Clinton Health Security Act). Attempts to increase the use of managed care for Medicaid recipients and extend coverage to more working families failed. The state did modestly expand coverage for children and enrolled a small number of people in the health alliances program.[138]

By early 1994, eight states had enacted health care reform plans, some successfully, some not so successfully. Some states focused on insurance reform. One important failure was the insurance reforms enacted in New York. The combination of community rating and limitations on preexisting conditions restrictions induced healthier and younger residents to drop insurance coverage. A second failure was in Massachusetts. The state passed a comprehensive universal health care law in 1988, based on the "play-or-pay" formula, under Democratic Governor Michael Dukakis. But economic problems, some opposition, and the political destruction of Dukakis after his unsuccessful campaign as the Democratic nominee for president against George Bush in 1988 led to delay in implementation of the plan until 1995. The Republican governor, William Weld, supported repeal of the law, despite popular support for it.[139] Implementation of the law was delayed by the state legislature three times, and the employer mandate was finally repealed in 1996. Massachusetts then turned to extending Medicaid to more children and to long-term unemployed families and adults with incomes just above the federal poverty line.[140]

More encompassing health care reform programs have been adopted in Florida, Minnesota, and Washington. These programs generally seek to employ both managed competition and regulation, a goal of the Clinton Health Security Act. The Florida law provides for a basic benefits package and creates eleven regional alliances similar to those in the Clinton plan.[141] The Washington law has both an individual and an employer mandate. It also has controls over insurance premiums, organized provider delivery systems, and purchasing cooperatives.[142]

The first state to implement purchasing cooperatives was California. Beginning in July 1993, small businesses began enrolling their employees in the program. There are limitations on benefits and restrictions on what providers can be chosen. A few businesses have opted out, but their costs have been higher than the costs of those participating in the alliance. As of the middle of 1994, another thirteen states were moving in this direction.[143]

One of the motives for state reform is to limit the effect of Medicaid expenditures on state budgets. One way that states have done this is to try to enroll Medicaid recipients in HMOs.[144] Such plans require Medicaid waivers from the federal government, a policy that the Clinton administration supports. The most drastic plan was Tennessee's proposal to withdraw entirely from Medicaid and, still in partnership with the federal government, to enroll poor patients in managed care organizations.[145]

Cities and communities have also moved toward change. Rochester, New York, and Minneapolis–St. Paul have been leaders, especially in managed care and competition. Lancaster, Pennsylvania, and Mount Carmel, Illinois, are two smaller communities that developed their own plans. In Lancaster, managed care has been implemented and HMOs are growing. The two major hospitals support the change, forming integrated units of providers.[146] In Mount Carmel, a clinic has been set up to provide care for those without insurance.[147]

States and communities have thus begun to move toward reforming the health care system. Any further reform will either include other levels of government or perhaps be concentrated on states and communities. But with the elections of November 1994, when Republicans gained more control over state legislatures and captured more governors' offices, change may be impeded at the state level. There may be opposition to employer mandates and changes in ERISA.[148]

Conclusion

Comprehensive health care reform (i.e., national health insurance) found its way onto the policy agenda in the early and mid-1990s, fueled by economic distress and corporate restructuring, by political events such as the 1991 Pennsylvania special senatorial election and the 1992 presidential election, and by budget and fiscal issues. This was not, as we have seen in chapter 2, the first effort to enact national health insurance. This effort was different from the previous attempts in some ways but similar in one important way.

One difference was that a bill actually went further in Congress than any previous legislation. The most important difference was the incorporation of market-like mechanisms as part of the proposal, managed care, and managed competition.

The important similarity was that this effort, like all previous ones, also failed. A number of reasons have been offered to explain failure at the federal level: the structure of Congress, the opposition of interest groups, lack of public support, a weak president, disagreement among policy elites, political calculations by political opponents, and so forth.

If the federal government could not act, might the states? Here the message was mixed. A number of states enacted insurance reforms; some sought comprehensive coverage; others looked toward market reform. Many laws were, in fact, enacted. The Clinton administration aided this effort through the generous granting of Medicaid waivers. Yet this effort by the laboratories of democracy[149] was ultimately unsatisfactory. Ambitious attempts were followed by retrenchment.

That comprehensive efforts to change the health care delivery system in the United States and to ensure coverage for all citizens failed is not surprising. The political fallout from that failure, the Republican congressional victories in 1994, seemed to spell doom to the possibility for anything but cutbacks. But as the doomed attempt at national health insurance in 1948 eventually led to the establishment of Medicare and Medicaid, so too did the 1993–94 effort eventually lead to change at both the state and the federal level. Medicare and Medicaid became the focus of activity in the 1995–96 period. What emerged from that debate were new programs directed at managed care, insurance coverage, and extension of insurance coverage to children. This incremental movement, typical of public policy making in the United States, is the subject of chapter 10.

CHAPTER 10

The Triumph of Incrementalism: Revolution, Rationing, and Reaction

The demise of comprehensive health care reform, as represented by the Clinton administration's Health Security Act, did not end policy debates or action on health care. It is pretty much a given within political science and the policy studies field that the dominant style of decision making in the United States is *incrementalism*, defined as making small changes over a period of time.[1] *Comprehensive reform* is an attempt to change the whole system at one time.

This is not to say that comprehensive reform is impossible. The passage of welfare reform legislation in the summer of 1996 is an excellent example of such change. But health care affects far more people (everybody!), than welfare and the structure of the political system, the political system's values, and interest group activity make radical reform highly unlikely.

Just because policymaking is gradual, that does not mean that it is uncontroversial or unproductive. The mid- to late 1990s saw health care policy become, in some ways, even more important than the Clinton attempt. It helped lead to two shutdowns of government and was an important issue in the 1996 and 1998 elections. Health care policy, as the United States approached the twenty-first century, saw dizzying change, revolution, and reaction. Incremental or not, the pace of change was astonishing.

We begin this chapter by considering the fallout from the 1993–94 debates: the Republican congressional victories in 1994, the Republican agenda as set forth in the Contract with America, the big budget battles, and the role of Medicare and Medicaid in those battles. We look at health care policies that emerged from that struggle. We then turn to the "armistice" in that battle, the 1997 budget agreement and the changes it wrought. Our attention next focuses on the managed care revolution, concentrating on the private sector (though considering Medicare and Medicaid as well) and tracing the tremendous increase in managed care. This is followed by a look at the reaction to managed care in the guise of "consumer protection." We end the chapter with a look at the strengths and weaknesses of managed care.

Retrenchment

Prologue: The Republican Congressional Triumph

> The Republicans enjoyed a double triumph, killing reform and then watching jurors find the president guilty. It was the political equivalent of the perfect crime.[2]

Congressional Republicans, especially in the House of Representatives, saw health care as a wonderful opportunity to reclaim control of Congress. President Bill Clinton and congressional Democrats could be blamed both for their failure to fulfill the Democratic campaign promise to reform the health care system and for proposing a system that would mean, as Republicans depicted it, more bureaucracy, more taxes, and more government intrusion.

To separate themselves from the Democrats, who seemingly did not have a coherent program, House Republicans under the leadership of minority whip Newt Gingrich (R-Georgia) produced the Contract with America. The contract, in its various versions, promised change. The Republicans would pass (or at least vote on) term limits for office, a balanced budget constitutional amendment, welfare reform, a rollback of government regulations and so forth. Health care was not mentioned in any version of the contract. Most House Republican candidates signed on to the contract in a September 1994 ceremony in front of the Capitol building.

The Republican triumphs in the 1994 elections were of historic proportions. They picked up nine seats in the Senate, recapturing that body for the first time since 1986. More impressive were the gains in the House. Republicans picked up forty-two seats, ending the virtual Democratic lock on the House and gaining control of both bodies for the first time since 1954.

The Republican Agenda

The Republican agenda was originally focused on reducing government. Though all the proposals that the contract promised to consider in the first one hundred days of the 104th Congress were in fact voted upon in the House, a major defeat was the balanced budget amendment, which failed to get the required two-thirds vote in the Senate by one vote, with Republican Mark Hatfield (Oregon) voting against the measure.[3] With the failure of the balanced budget measure, Congress turned to the regular budget process to balance the budget. The goal was a balanced budget by fiscal year (FY) 2002.

President Clinton's FY 1996 budget proposal did not call for a balanced budget. The president's reasoning was that if the Republicans wanted to balance the budget, they should set out the plan to do so. In June 1995, Congress passed a budget resolution calling for $983 billion in total spending through

2002, including $270 billion in Medicare cuts and $180 billion in Medicaid cuts. The proposal also called for $245 billion in tax cuts.[4] Republicans, especially in the House, also proposed a series of rollbacks in consumer and environmental regulation. Clinton, while he eventually agreed to the 2002 balanced budget goal, opposed virtually the entire Republican set of proposals.

Medicare (and, to a lesser extent, Medicaid) proposals gave Democrats an opening to counterattack the Republicans. Democrats charged that Republicans were trying to cut a program that was immensely popular. Republicans replied that they were trying to save or strengthen the program, bolstered by the Social Security and Medicare trustees report that Medicare Part A would go bankrupt by 2001, though only about a third of the proposed cuts would have addressed the bankruptcy issue (see chapter 4). Democrats used the Republican proposals to mount a series of campaign attacks and continually employed the mantra of protecting Medicare, Medicaid, education, and the environment from Republican hands.

The budget battles led to a congressional-presidential standoff or, perhaps more appropriately, a train wreck. Clinton vetoed appropriations bills, and Congress refused to pass a new debt ceiling bill that would permit the federal government to borrow money and meet its obligations. The result was two government shutdowns, one in November 1995 and another in December 1995–January 1996.

Clinton's popularity rose as the confrontation tightened, and Republicans' approval ratings, especially those of the architect of the Republican revolution, Speaker of the House Newt Gingrich, fell. By spring 1996, congressional Republicans and the president had agreed on a budget, though provisions concerning Medicare and Medicaid were not dealt with.

The FY 1997 proposals by both Clinton and the Congress for the two huge public programs were considerably smaller than those under discussion (and rejected by Clinton). The most revolutionary proposal concerned Medicaid. Republicans, with the backing of the governors, wanted to transform Medicaid into a block grant, essentially eliminating the program as an entitlement. This was the same proposal that recommended welfare reform, and the two programs were thus linked together. Opposition to the Medicaid block proposal led to its being dropped. Welfare reform passed (in the Personal Responsibility and Work Opportunity Act of 1996) with some linkage to Medicaid eligibility (see chapter 3). Medicare reform would have to wait one year.

Health Care Legislation in the 104th Congress

While Medicare and Medicaid were an integral target of the budget battles during this period, other health legislation, with some difficulty, was enacted.

The new legislation moved the federal government into somewhat new ground, insurance reform.

One of the findings of public opinion surveys taken as early as 1991 was that a sizable number of Americans were concerned about what became known as "job lock."[5] People were concerned about losing insurance when they changed or lost jobs (say through downsizing). This was especially true for those with preexisting medical conditions.

A bill to address these issues was introduced in the Senate in 1995. Commonly known as the Kassebaum-Kennedy bill after its co-sponsors Nancy Landon Kassebaum (R-Kansas) and Edward M. Kennedy (D-Massachusetts), it became the focus of attention in 1996.

Senate Majority Leader Robert Dole (R-Kansas) delayed the bill, partly to ensure that medical savings accounts (MSAs) would be included (others such as House Speaker Newt Gingrich also wanted MSAs included), and partly because he saw delay as helping his presidential aspirations.[6] While the Senate passed a "clean" version of the bill, one that included only the portability issues, the House passed legislation including the MSA program as well as health insurance tax deductions. The conference committee to reconcile the differences between the two branches of Congress was delayed by Dole to get senators favorable to MSAs on the committee. Passage of the bill was facilitated when Dole resigned his Senate seat to concentrate on what became his ill-fated presidential quest. The conference committee agreed on a number of compromises, including the MSAs, and Congress overwhelming passed the legislation in the summer of 1996. President Clinton signed the bill in August.

The *Health Insurance Portability and Accountability Act* (HIPAA) built on previous federal-state relations regarding health insurance. In general, the states have the primary responsibility for regulating health insurance. Actions by the U.S. Supreme Court and Congress dating back to the mid-1940s carved out the relationship.[7] A 1944 Supreme Court decision, *United States v. South-Eastern Underwriters Association*, 322 U.S. 533, held that insurance companies were engaged in interstate commerce and therefore covered by federal antitrust law. In 1945, Congress passed the *McCarran-Ferguson Act*, which excused insurance companies from such regulations if the states were regulating. The 1973 Health Maintenance Organizations Act attempted to foster the growth of health maintenance organizations (HMOs) through subsidies, overriding prohibitions to group practices and requiring employers to offer HMO plans to their employees under certain conditions.

A critical law in this brief history is the *Employment Retirement Income Security Act* (ERISA) of 1974. The law was originally designed to protect employee pension funds, but it has been interpreted to also prohibit states from regulating health insurance plans financed and administered by employers (self-insured firms). This turned out to be a critical exemption, because almost half of those covered by job-related insurance are in self-insurance firms.[8] The final federal foray into insurance reform prior to HIPAA was the 1990 legislation regulating and standardizing private medigap policies (see chapter 4).

The major purpose of HIPAA is to eliminate health status from health insurance consideration. That is, for the small employer and individual insurance markets, the focus of reform, preexisting conditions cannot be considered by insurance companies when a person changes jobs. This is especially true for those who are "eligible individuals": those who

> have had eighteen months of continuous prior coverage (no coverage gap lasting longer than sixty-two days), most recently group coverage; have exhausted any Consolidated Omnibus Reconciliation Act (COBRA) benefits to which they are entitled and have no current access to group insurance or a public program; and are eligible for some type of guaranteed issue coverage in the individual market.[9]

In the spring of 1997, the three federal departments with responsibility for implementing HIPAA (the Treasury, Labor, and Health and Human Services departments) issued implementing regulations. The regulations required employers to certify that someone leaving a job had health insurance (and eventually whether dependents were covered). The Clinton administration estimated that 12 million of the 20 million people changed jobs every year (along with 7 million dependents). It predicted that administrative and higher premiums would cost businesses about $500 million a year in new costs.[10]

There are two interrelated ways of looking at the implementation of HIPAA: what states are doing and what private insurers are doing. The purpose of HIPAA, again, is to affect risk pooling, that is, that ability of insurers to segment or separate high-risk from low-risk (sick from healthy) clients. HIPAA constrains insurers with the preexisting restrictions and by guaranteeing renewal for eligible individuals and small groups. It does not, however, guarantee price. States have three implementation choices: leave implementation up to the federal government, pass a similar or stronger law, or provide some alternative mechanism for covering eligible people.

In a study of thirteen states, Nichols and Blumberg (1998) found that most of the states had passed laws covering small groups but few had the eligible person guarantee prior to HIPAA.[11] After passage, high-risk pools was the most frequently used tool to cover eligible individuals.

Private insurers, in some cases, took action that worked against the intent of HIPAA. A General Accounting Office (GAO) study issued in early 1998 said that implementation of the law by private insurers created problems. In some cases, extremely high insurance premiums were charged, 140–600 percent of standard premiums. In other cases, insurers refused to pay commissions to agents who sold such policies. Insurers also delayed telling potential clients about the availability of such policies, so that the sixty-two-day period was exceeded. Sometimes insurers simply did not tell clients about such policies.[12]

To get around these private insurers' efforts, President Clinton, in July 1998, issued an executive order that would exclude those insurers from participating in the Federal Employees Health Benefits Program (FEHBP). The president ordered the Office of Personnel Management to enforce the directive. Insurers have to certify that they are complying with the law to remain eligible for FEHBP participation. State insurance commissioners agreed to work with the federal government to find violators.[13]

Two other actions were taken by Congress in 1996. The first was to include mental health coverage on an equal basis with physical health. The second was to mandate minimum hospital stays of two days for regular births and four days for caesarian births. The latter involves consumer protection and managed care, which we will consider below.

Covering Children

If, in the 1960s, the incremental strategy for health insurance focused on the elderly as the deserving group that should be covered, in the late 1990s, it was children. We have noted, in previous chapters, gaps in insurance coverage. Coverage by employers, in terms of percentage of population, was decreasing. Even with the changes in Medicaid discussed in chapter 3, many children were still uncovered. According to the General Accounting Office, about one-third of Medicaid-eligible children were not covered by Medicaid, due to either ignorance of the program or application difficulties. Most of the uninsured children were in working families who had too much income even for the expanded Medicaid eligibility and who worked for firms that did not provide such coverage. The Medicaid expansion was useful and did begin to cover some children from working families who were not eligible for Medicaid, but there still was a large gap, about 3 million children in 1996.[14] All told, some 10 million children lacked insurance in 1996.[15]

As discussed in chapter 5, insurance coverage is important because it can lead, other things being equal, to better access to health services. A General Accounting Office review of the literature found that children with health insurance had better access to a wide variety of health care services than children without such coverage.[16]

The children's health insurance at the federal level became intertwined in two unrelated policy issues. The first was the federal budget. The 1995–96 policy debates revolved around the issue of federal budget deficits. Indeed, the fiscal constraint of the budget deficits have affected politics and policy at the federal level since the start of the Reagan administration. The conflict between President Clinton and the Republican-controlled Congress over the deficit and related issues (Medicare and Medicaid, as well as other issues) led to two partial government shutdowns and a shrinking of the Republican House majority. The budget politics of 1997 would play to a different beat.

Thanks to the 1990 and 1993 budget agreements and a good economy, 1997 (really FY 1998) looked more promising. Where once there were budget deficits as far as the eye could see, suddenly the word "surplus" appeared. By mid-1998, the Congressional Budget Office was predicting budget surpluses of over a trillion dollars for the next ten years. One question that was raised with this apparent turnover of budget politics is what to do with the surplus. It could be used to pay off the multi-trillion-dollar federal deficit; to ensure the financial viability of Social Security; to reduce taxes; or to expand programs, such as health insurance for children.

The other element in this mixture was tobacco. In 1997, the tobacco industry and most of the state attorneys general reached an unprecedented agreement to deal with the issue of the health effects of tobacco. The agreement had to be ratified by the federal government. The Clinton administration and congressional Democrats proposed a large tax increase on the price of a package of cigarettes, over $1 a pack, the revenues from which could be used for a children's health insurance program. It was also felt that the large price increase would reduce demand for cigarettes on the part of young people. Republicans balked at the proposal and it was dropped. Indeed, the whole tobacco agreement went up in smoke as the industry and its supporters successfully portrayed the issue not as a health one, but as a large tax increase, particularly on the lower and working classes.

Children's health insurance did become part of the Balanced Budget Act of 1997, which we discussed in connection with Medicaid in chapter 3. The State Children's Health Insurance Program (S-CHIP), a grant program to the states, became Title XXI of the Social Security Act.

In the move to extend coverage to uninsured children, states led federal action. By May 1997, more than fourteen states had passed legislation to extend coverage to uninsured children.[17] Three such states are Massachusetts, Florida, and New York.

In some ways, the Massachusetts plan served as a model for those seeking federal action. The plan, known as the Children's Medical Security Plan, followed on the failure to implement and eventually abandon a more global health insurance plan for Massachusetts citizens. It is financed by a twenty-five cent increase in the price of a package of cigarettes and is designed to cover children under eighteen years of age who are in families that do not qualify for Medicaid but are too poor for private health insurance. The law was passed over the veto of Republican Governor William Weld, who opposed any new taxes. The Massachusetts plan also expands Medicaid coverage to all families with incomes within 133 percent of the poverty line (approximately $16,400 for a family of four in 1998). Benefits under the plan are more limited than under Medicaid. In addition, there is a graduated series of premiums and copayments. It is estimated that the Medicaid expansion will cover about 40 percent of the state's approximately 150,000 uninsured children. The Children's Medical Security Plan is expected to enroll another 40,000–60,000 children.[18]

What is interesting about the plan is that its advocates suggested that the federal government follow form. Two Massachusetts Democratic senators— Edward M. Kennedy, a long-time proponent of national health insurance, and John Kerry—wanted to extend the idea to the national level. Marion Wright Edelman, head of a children's advocacy group, the Children's Defense Fund, urged both state and federal action.[19]

New York took a somewhat different approach to covering uninsured children. Child Health Plus is an insurance subsidy program on a sliding scale. Households with incomes of 120 percent or less of the poverty line make no contribution. Households with incomes of over 220 percent of the poverty line pay full premiums, though the premiums are less than for regular private insurance. Benefits are very generous, including "any type of outpatient care, including well-child checkups, ambulatory surgery, dialysis, immunizations, emergency care, lab tests, chemotherapy and medicines."[20] There are also some very small copayments.

One problem the program faces is marketing, getting families to sign up. Of New York's estimated 620,000 uninsured children, about 280,000 are eligible for Medicaid and another almost 200,000 are eligible for Child Health Plus but are not enrolled.[21] The New York plan is financed by a surcharge on insurance companies and is trying to double its enrollment by 1999.[22]

The third state that is a model for enhanced coverage of children is Florida. In 1988, Steve Freedman of the University of Florida wrote an article that was published in the *New England Journal of Medicine*, calling for a unique way of covering uninsured children. We mentioned in chapter 5 (about the disadvantaged) that small groups and individuals who want to purchase health insurance face very high premiums because of industry practices (and efficiencies associated with large groups). Freedman's idea was to "group children by schools districts and then to negotiate affordable rates."[23] The state legislature began testing the idea, called Health Kids, in one county in 1992 and expanded it by 1997 to sixteen counties. Financing of the program is considerably different from either the New York or the Massachusetts plan.

> About half the program's cost is paid by the state, 35 percent by family contributions and 16 percent by a mix of local sources, including school districts, hospitals, children's services councils and other groups.[24]

Further, the state has contracted with health maintenance organizations to provide health care to enrollees, for less than what Medicaid would cost.[25]

Of the three states, Florida's plan has the smallest reach, insuring 36,000 of the state's estimated 700,000 uninsured children. In 1998, an estimated 60,000 children will participate in Health Kids.[26] In Volusia County, where the program began, Hispanic and African-American children were somewhat less likely to make use of the program than were similarly eligible white children. This suggests that communication and transportation present barriers.[27]

Thus the federal government was faced with several questions, based on the states' experience, if it wanted, as it apparently did, to cover uninsured children. One question was whether to offer coverage through Medicaid or through a program created by the states. Another question was financing: Should tobacco taxes cover some, all, or none of the costs? A third question was whether the federal government should give the states a block grant (a set amount of money) and let states take full responsibility for designing and running the program (a position favored by the governors and echoing policy debates over welfare reform in 1996), or whether a categorical program should be used, leaving more control with the federal government.[28]

The final proposal included in the 1997 Balanced Budget Act (BBA) was co-sponsored by Senator Kennedy and Senator Orrin Hatch (R-Utah). They provided the rationale for the legislation:

> If the act succeeds, working families that do not earn enough to purchase health insurance on their own will no longer have to make heartbreaking decisions among spending scarce resources on groceries, rent or medical bills for their children.
>
> Investing in children's health yields high returns. Preventive health care early in life is extremely cost-effective in avoiding large long-run costs of disease and disability. The hospital emergency room should not be a child's family doctor.
>
> Health care pays dividends in education, too. Basic vision care and hearing care can make all the difference for many children in school. Children who have difficulty seeing the blackboard or hearing the teaching also have difficulty learning. No young mind should be lost for want of an eye test or hearing exam.

The Balanced Budget Act removes any excuse for the world's strongest
industrial nation to deny health insurance to any child.[29]

Not everyone was pleased with the program. David Frum, writing in the
New York Times, argued that the 1986 and 1990 expansions of Medicaid failed
to reach all the targeted children and that the cost of the program has skyrocketed.[30] He points out that Medicaid spent about $27 billion in 1986 and $105
billion in 1997. He notes that when the 2002 mandate to cover all children in
poverty-stricken families is reached, Medicaid will spend about $133 billion.
He also says that, despite this huge increase in spending, some 10 million
children (more than in the late 1980s) remain without insurance.

Frum's analysis is subject to several criticisms. First, Medicaid has indeed been covering more children. In FY 1990, 11.2 million children were
covered under the program; by FY 1996, about 16.7 million children were
covered. This is an increase of 49.2 percent. So one can see that Medicaid was
beginning to reach its goal (see Table 10.1).

A second problem with Frum's reasoning concerns expenditures. By citing total Medicaid expenditures, Frum suggests that all that additional money
has been spent on children. It is true that Medicaid is spending more on children, rising from $9.1 billion in FY1990 to $17.5 billion in FY1996. This
turns out, however, to be a small portion of total Medicaid expenditures. Certainly, we are spending more on children, $811 per child in FY 1990 versus
$1,480 in FY1996. But as a percentage of total spending, this amounts to a
slight increase. The real increase in spending is for the elderly and the disabled. Consider, again, Table 10.1. While the number of children on Medicaid
is larger than the number of elderly and disabled Medicaid recipients combined in the two years, expenditures on the elderly dwarf expenditures on
children, as do expenditures on the disabled. It is misleading to look at overall program statistics and imply that everything goes for children.[31]

Frum asserts that the real health insurance problem is the middle-aged
workers who have been downsized. He points out that the program might
provide an incentive for employers to stop providing health insurance. He
also notes that the amount of money allocated for the program ($5 billion a
year for four years) would probably not be sufficient to cover many children.
He proposes instead that government get out of the way (by providing less
regulation and fewer subsidies) and allow the sale of basic, affordable health
insurance to low- and middle-income families.[32] Douglas Besharov also suggests that the crowding-out phenomenon will hurt the program and private
health insurance.[33] He notes that S-CHIP calls for extremely generous benefits packages and could cover families with incomes up to $38,000 a year.[34]

The Children's Health Insurance Program is a block grant of $20 billion
over a five-year period beginning FY 1998 (October 1, 1997). The purposes

Table 10.1

Medicaid Recipients and Expenditures, FY1990 and FY1996

	FY 1990		
	Recipients	Expenditures	Expenditures per recipient
Total	25,255,067	$64,858,936,389	$2,568
Elderly (65+)	3,202,129	$21,508,078,280	6,717
Elderly as percent of total	12.7%	33.2%	
Under 21	11,219,969	$9,100,095,928	811
Under 21 as percent of total	44.4	14.0	
Disabled	3,634,678	$23,969,413,463	6,595
Disabled as percent of total	14.4%	37.0%	

	FY 1996		
	Recipients	Expenditures	Expenditures per recipient
Total	36,117,956	$121,684,650,21	3,369
Elderly (65+)	4,285,354	$36,947,324,235	8,622
Elderly as percent of total	11.9%	30.4%	
Under 21	16,738,800	$17,543,512,927	1,048
Under 21 as percent of total	46.3	14.4	
Disabled	6,126,397	$51,196,304,564	8,357
Disabled as percent of total	17.0%	42.1%	

	Percentage change		
	Recipients	Expenditures	Expenditures per recipient
Total	43.0	87.6	31.2
Elderly (65+)	33.8	71.8	28.4
Under 21	49.2	92.8	29.2
Disabled	68.6	113.6	26.7

Source: Medicaid Statistics, HCFA 2082 Report. http://www.hcfa.gov/medicaid/mstats.htm.

of the new law are to provide health insurance for uninsured children and to coordinate with other children's health programs.

S-CHIP gives states two implementation options, combining the two approaches mentioned above. States can either extend Medicaid to eligible uninsured children, or they can create or extend their own programs (such as

Florida's Health Kids). In either case, the state must pay some of the costs of the program, a matching requirement (which they would have to do under Medicaid anyway). Eligibility for a separate state program must be no lower than state children Medicaid eligibility levels as of June 1, 1997.[35]

If a state chooses the Medicaid route, benefits are the standard Medicaid benefits. For state-initiated programs, the benefits package is more complicated. Such a state can choose among four options:

1. *Federal Employees Health Benefit Plan Equivalent Coverage*—A state may offer health benefits coverage equivalent to the benefits offered under the standard Blue Cross/Blue Shield preferred provider option service plan offered to federal employees.

2. *State Employee Coverage*—A state may offer health benefits coverage equivalent to the benefits provided under a health plan that is offered and generally available to a state's public employees.

3. *HMO Coverage*—A state may offer health benefits coverage equivalent to the benefits offered by the HMO within the state that has the highest commercial enrollment (excluding Medicaid enrollment).

4. *Benchmark Equivalent Coverage*—A state can choose one of the three plans listed above to serve as a "benchmark" for an alternative package of benefits. The alternative must meet three criteria: (1) it must have an "aggregate actuarial value" equivalent to the benchmark plan selected by the state; (2) it must offer hospital, physician, lab and x-ray, and well-baby and well-child care (although the state can determine the scope of the coverage offered in each of these categories); and (3) *if* the state's benchmark offers coverage for prescription drugs, mental health, vision, or hearing benefits, the children's benefit package must offer some coverage in each of these areas. (Specifically, the coverage must have an actuarial value that is equal to at least 75 percent of the actuarial value of the coverage under the benchmark plan.)[36]

Each state submits a plan describing its child health program to the Secretary of Health and Human Services for approval.

An evaluation of state implementation of S-CHIP by the Children's Defense Fund (CDF) found some areas of concern, though most states were positively implementing the new program.[37] On the positive side, the CDF found that most states proposed income eligibility standards covering children in families up to 185–200 percent of the poverty line. About two-thirds of states that had made a decision about benefits were using the Medicaid benefits package.[38] Nine states chose to create or expand their own programs without using Medicaid.

On the other hand, the CDF report notes that implementation of the program has been slow, with most states not beginning the program until July 1998. Some states, such as Wyoming and Washington State, have decided not to participate in the program, whereas others—Alabama, Mississippi, and Texas—stop income eligibility at 100 percent of poverty level. The latter three states are simply speeding up coverage that is required under present law.

Nine states are charging what the CDF report considers unaffordable premiums ($200 or more per year) to low-income working families. Some states appear concerned that the S-CHIP program will simply replace private insurance (a phenomenon known as "crowding out"); that is, people or employers will drop insurance and let the states pick up the children, a problem that Besharov and the Congressional Budget Office pointed to. The CDF report cites three studies suggesting that crowding out is not a significant problem, affecting perhaps 2–3 percent of targeted children.[39] As a result, fifteen states have imposed waiting periods for coverage of children after parents have lost employment-based health insurance. Five states may deny coverage on the grounds that coverage should come through employment-based insurance.

To aid in the implementation of S-CHIP, President Clinton ordered the heads of federal agencies to send letters to their employees asking them to help enroll eligible children and to disseminate information.[40] A later federal effort will send Medicaid-eligible workers to "hospitals, clinics, day care centers, schools and factories" to get more eligible children enrolled. In addition, the administration wants the application process simplified.[41]

Managed Care

By managed care, we mean forms of coverage that integrate financing and delivery, as well as the organizations that provide this coverage—health maintenance organizations (HMOs), preferred provider organizations (PPOs), and point-of-service (POS) plans.[42]

> The bottom line is that the American public doesn't want to give too much power to *any bureaucrats*. It doesn't matter whether they work for the federal government or for the insurance industry.[43]

Definitions

One important and confusing aspect of policy debates and experiences with managed care is definitional. In this section, we offer some definitions so that we will all know what we are talking about.

We define *managed care* broadly as any health insurance plan that seeks to restrain the use of health care services. Such a plan can be as simple as requiring preauthorization for a nonemergency hospital stay.[44] It can also encompass more organized forms of provider delivery.

The classic type of managed care organization is the *health maintenance organization (HMO)*. An HMO is an organization whose providers, generally primary care physicians, are prepaid through monthly subscriber premiums (known as *capitation*) to deliver a comprehensive set of services. The HMO assumes the financial risk of providing those services. The original label for such an organization was prepaid group plan (PGP). PPGs were developed to provide health care services to employees in areas where medical services were thin. Kaiser-Permanente is typical of such plans.

To complicate the situation, HMOs come in various forms. A *staff-model HMO* is one in which the physicians are on a salary and members obtain services primarily from the HMO. In a *group-model HMO*, a multispecialty group of doctors works primarily for the HMO's members. There are hybrid versions of these HMOs.

A looser type of HMO is an *independent practice association (IPA)*. In this case, physicians contract to work for the HMO. A physician in an IPA can work on a fee-for-service basis or a capitation basis (so much money per patient). HMOs of any type can be nonprofit or profit.

Another type of managed care organization is the *preferred provider organization (PPO)*. Here the employer or insurer contracts with physicians for discount rates on services. Consumers can use providers outside the PPO but must pay higher copayments.

As physicians have been losing power and autonomy to managed care plans, they have sometimes sought to sponsor their own plans, known as *provider-sponsored organizations (PSOs)*. One last type of managed care plan, which is incorporated in the Balanced Budget Act of 1997 with Medicare is the *point-of-service (POS)* plan. Here the consumer chooses the provider at the time the service is needed.

The Development of Managed Care

While managed care has been increasingly a part of the public health care programs, Medicare and Medicaid, the push in the 1980s and 1990s came from the private sector, particularly large employers. The impetus was partly the drastically increasing cost of health insurance and partly due to decreases in corporate profits and a weak economy.[45] For example, the cost of employee health care for General Motors in the mid-1980s was twice the cost of steel.[46]

The first significant move by a large employer into managed care came in 1988 when Allied-Signal canceled its health care plans and transferred its employees into Cigna's HMO.[47] Other large companies soon followed. The trend toward managed care can be easily shown. Table 10.2 presents some data concerning growth of health maintenance organizations, one form of managed care. First, there has been a sizable increase in enrollment, from just over nine million people in 1980, to 33 million in 1990, to almost 67 million people by 1997. Second, most of this growth has come from the private sector. HMO growth in Medicare and Medicaid is much lower as a percentage of the appropriate population.

Third, the dominant type of HMO has become the independent practice association, followed by the mixed type. The classic HMO, the group model, has become less important. For this classic HMO, both the number of plans and enrollment has significantly declined.

One of the most recent and careful studies of managed care trends, though not with quite this much historical perspective, is that by Jensen et al.[48] This study, focusing on the private sector, found that nearly 70 percent of workers were covered by some type of managed care insurance plan. Jensen et al. examined four types of plans: conventional, health maintenance organization, preferred provider organization, and point-of-service plan. In 1993 nearly 50 percent (48.9 percent) of private-sector workers were covered by conventional plans. Two years later, that number was down to 27.4 percent, a decrease of almost 49 percent. While the three types of managed care plans all increased substantially in this two-year period, the greatest increase was in the POS plans, which grew from 9.1 percent of private-sector workers to 20.1 percent (an increase of 121 percent). The number of workers in HMOs grew from 22.4 percent in 1993 to 27.5 percent in 1995, an increase of 22.8 percent. The respective numbers for PPOs were 19.6 percent and 25 percent, an increase of 27.6 percent.[49]

The number of firms offering at least two choices of health plans (necessary for the managed competition aspect to work) increased slightly from 56 to 62 percent. While small firms moved vigorously from conventional to managed care, choice of plans was directly related to size of firm. That is, the larger the firm, the more likely there was some choice for workers.

The survey found that most employers self-insured, except for those with HMOs. The authors also found that insurance premium increases were inversely related to firm size; that is, the larger the firm, the smaller the increases. The survey also found that, between 1994 and 1995, conventional plans had the largest premium increases and HMOs the smallest. About one-third of employees who had a choice of plan had a level-dollar contribution from the employer (that is, the employer made the same contribution, known as a defined contribution, for each plan). The survey found that coverage of preexisting conditions increased, much of this due to new state laws. POS deductibles declined while HMO copayments increased.

Table 10.2

HMO Growth, Plans and Enrollment, and Percentage of the Population, 1980–1997

	1980	1985	1990	1991	1992	1993	1994	1995	1996	1997
Plans (number of plans)										
All plans	235	478	572	553	555	551	543	562	630	651
Model type										
Individual practice association	97	244	360	346	340	332	321	332	367	284
Group	138	234	212	168	166	150	118	108	122	98
Mixed	—	—	—	39	49	69	104	122	141	258
Enrollment (in millions of people)										
Total	9.1	21.0	33.0	34.0	36.1	38.4	45.1	50.9	59.1	66.8
Model type										
Individual practice association	1.7	6.4	13.7	13.6	14.7	15.3	17.8	20.1	26.0	26.7
Group	7.4	14.6	19.3	17.1	16.5	15.4	13.9	13.3	14.1	11.0
Mixed	—	—	—	3.3	4.9	7.7	13.4	17.6	19.0	29.0
Federal program										
Medicaid	0.3	0.6	1.2	1.4	1.7	1.7	2.6	3.5	4.7	5.5
Medicare	0.4	1.1	1.8	2.0	2.2	2.2	2.5	2.9	3.7	4.8
Percent of population enrolled in HMOs	2.8	4.0	8.9	13.6	14.3	15.1	17.3[1]	9.4	22.3	25.2

Source: National Center for Health Statistics, Health US, 1998, table 135, Washington, D.C.: Government Printing Office, 1998.

In many cases, employees are given no choice among plans; they use the chosen HMO (or other type of plan). Bodenheimer and Sullivan report that about 47 percent of employees in large companies have no choice of plans, while about 91 percent of employees in small firms have no choice.[50] The significance of this, apart from the lack of choice of provider that will be discussed below, is that competition among health plans, which managed competition sees as an important mechanism for ensuring both high quality of care and cost control, is missing.

Still, that means that a large number of employees do have a choice of plans. In that case, the driving concept is "'pay more for higher-cost health plan.'"[51] With this method, the employer pays the same amount of premiums for each employee, regardless of the cost of the plan. When the yearly open enrollment period comes around, employees can change plans, but there are financial considerations attached to those changes. This is an idea that Alain Enthoven has championed, going back to the 1970s.[52] Additionally, large employers use their clout (large numbers of potential subscribers) to directly contract with a health plan and negotiate rates.[53]

An important trend in managed care is for such organizations to offer more than one type of plan or product. The products referred to are traditional HMO, open-ended HMO, PPO with and without a primary gatekeeper, exclusive provider organization, and point-of-service plans. Seventy-one percent of the plans in one survey offered more than one product, with the group or staff model the least likely to offer more than one product. The reason for offering multiple products is twofold: "to expand choice in response to customer interest or to ease transition to more traditional managed care arrangements."[54]

Another important, critical managed care trend is the growth of national managed care companies and the related trend of the growth and dominance of for-profit companies. By 1994, a majority of managed care enrollees were in national plans, and most of these plans were for-profit.[55] Corrigan et al. describe the significance of this trend:

> Although it is often said that "health care, like politics, is local," it is likely the emergence of national managed care companies and national provider organizations will have some impact on how care is delivered in local communities. To the extent that national companies benefit from greater access to capital markets and economies of scale, there is the potential for these companies to improve quality and efficiency through investment in technology (e.g., clinical information systems), enhanced management systems (e.g., financial accounting systems, marketing), and access to specialized clinical and managerial expertise.
>
> But concerns have been voiced that national companies, almost all of which are for-profit, may seek returns on investment at the expense of ac-

cess and quality. There are worries that these firms may be less responsive to community needs, such as care of the uninsured and provision of public health services, the benefits of which accrue to society at large. There is also the concern that over time, national companies may engage in predatory pricing to drive out competition, leaving consumers with few choices.[56]

One can see the growth of for-profit health plans in the following figures. In 1981, for-profit HMOs accounted for 12 percent of HMO enrollees and 18 percent of HMO plans. By 1997, for-profits accounted for 18 percent of enrollees and 75 percent of plans.[57] For-profit hospitals have gained over the same time period but at a much smaller rate, accounting for only 15 percent of community hospitals and 13 percent of beds. Gabel also notes that, between 1988 and 1994, for-profit membership growth was nearly four times higher than that of nonprofits.

Gabel asks why for-profits grew so much. One explanation is that for-profits were more aggressive in seeking growth. A second explanation is their better access to capital (Wall Street) and this is why many HMOs converted their status. A third explanation is that nonprofits tended to prefer the group model that required expensive infrastructure, whereas for-profits favored IPAs or networks. It is these latter forms of managed care organizations that have grown the fastest.[58]

One way of understanding what is going on is by examining measures of stock market activity, especially with HMOs. Equity (a source of financing, as opposed to bonds or borrowing) rose from 20 percent of external capital in 1988–90 to 69 percent in the 1991–97 period. Market capitalization of HMO stocks was $3 billion in 1987 and rose to $39 billion in 1997, much faster than the stock market itself rose. HMO stocks have outperformed the market as a whole.[59]

One theme running through some of the literature is the consolidation of managed health care into managed care empires. Table 10.3 shows the top ten HMOs and their subscribers in 1995. Comparing total enrollment in 1995 (see Table 10.2), a rough calculation suggests that these ten companies accounted for nearly 86 percent of total HMO enrollment.

There are several reasons why such mergers are taking place. First, they allow companies to be big enough to resist doctors' and hospitals' efforts to squeeze their payments. Second, they strengthen companies' hands in negotiating low prices for medical suppliers so that they can keep their prices low to purchasers. Third, future competition may come from providers who may try to negotiate directly with employers (provider-sponsored organizations) and skip managed care organizations. One estimate is that in five years or so there may be only three to five major national companies.[60]

Table 10.3

Top Ten HMO Companies, 1995

Company	Number of Enrollees (in millions)
Blue Cross	8.5
United Healthcare	6.7
Kaiser Permanente	6.7
Aetna/U.S. Healthcare	5.7
Prudential	4.7
Cigna Healthplan	3.9
Humana	2.1
FHP	1.8
Health Systems	1.8
Pacificare	1.8
Total number of enrollees	43.7

Source: Milt Freudenheim, "Managed Care Empires in the Making," *New York Times*, April 2, 1996.

Another change caused by the managed care revolution concerns the types of organizational situations in which doctors practice. In 1983, 41 percent of physicians were in solo practice, 35 percent were in group practice, and 24 percent were employees of larger companies. The respective numbers for 1997 are 26 percent, 31 percent, and 43 percent. In 1988, 61 percent of physicians were in a practice with at least one managed care contract; physicians in that year received 23 percent of their income from managed care. In 1997, in contrast, 92 percent of physicians were in a practice with at least one managed care contract, and managed care accounted for 44 percent of physicians' revenues.[61]

The Successes of Managed Care

As the data indicate, there has been a dramatic move of consumers, or patients, from conventional fee-for-service indemnity plans into various kinds of managed care arrangements. The sustained movement suggests that managed care has had some successes, and that is in fact the case. As Easterbrook puts it, their successes have been in "restraining costs, avoiding unneeded surgeries, promoting prevention."[62]

The major accomplishment of management has to do with costs. After all, the major reason the public and private sectors have turned to managed care is save money. If managed care did not save money, given all the problems discussed below, there would be no point to it.

Table 10.4

Annual Percentage Increase in Employee Health Insurance Premiums or Costs, 1990–1996

Source	1990	1991	1992	1993	1994	1995	1996
Private sector[a]	15	12	10.5	7.75	2.75	1.26	-0.23
Federal Employees Health Benefits Program	9	6	7	10	2	-4	0.05
CalPERS	17	11	6	1	-1	-4	-1
Minnesota State Employees Insurance Plan	14	10	6	6	3	-5.00	n.a.

Source: Congressional Budget Office, *Trends in Spending by the Private Sector*, U.S. Congressional Budget Office, Washington, D.C., April 1997. Numbers are from tables 1 and 2.

[a]Calculated from Table 1 of source.

The data are clear. In 1990, depending on the source of the data, the cost of employment-based health insurance increased by an average of 15 percent. For three large public employee groups, the 1990 increase was between 9 and 17 percent (see Table 10.4). Table 10.4 shows that there has been a dramatic decline in the increases, and, in the latter years (1994–96), there have even been some declines.

One reason is the increasing shift of employees from conventional fee-for-service plans to managed care and the competition among insurance plans for business. Table 10.5 shows the change in health insurance premiums by type of insurance plan for large employers.

Another reason for the decline in cost increases is the dramatic decline in overall inflation. In 1990, inflation was around 5.4 percent; by 1996 it had declined to around 2 percent, where it has pretty much remained through 1998.[63]

Managed care has been able to control spending so quickly through a number of mechanisms. Managed care organizations have changed the incentives facing physicians and the way doctors practice medicine. The move toward capitation and away from fee-for-service just on its own changes the incentives. This is probably the most important change. Under fee-for-service, physicians (and other providers) get more money for each service provided. Under capitation, providers get no more money for more services. Indeed, the pressure may be to underserve rather than to overserve.

In a sense, managed care turns all the incentives around. Defenders of managed care, such as Susan Love, argue that the fee-for-service system was flawed. Because of third-party payments, neither the patient nor the doctor

Table 10.5

Annual Percentage Growth of Health Insurance Premiums for Large Firms (200 or More Employees), 1991–1996

Type of Plan	1991	1992	1993	1994	1995	1996
Conventional fee-for-service	12.0	11.0	8.8	5.1	2.7	1.2
HMO	12.1	9.8	8.3	5.3	0.4	-0.4
PPO	10.1	10.6	8.2	3.2	3.5	0.6
POS	n.a.	12.4	4.9	5.9	2.4	1.2
All plans	11.5	10.9	8.0	4.8	2.1	0.5

Source: Congressional Budget Office, *Trends in Spending by the Private Sector*, U.S. Congressional Budget Office, Washington, D.C., April 1997, table 8.

was concerned about the costs of care, and overtreatment occurred (it may also have been spurred on by the medical malpractice issue, discussed in chapter 7). Additionally, under fee-for-service or indemnity insurance, preventive treatments and services such as mammograms, physicals, well-baby checkups, and immunizations were not necessarily covered.[64] A good managed care organization will provide these services, usually at no extra cost, because they save money in the long run.

Managed care can also save money by limiting medication to a list of approved drugs, known as a formulary. Related to this is that managed care organizations negotiate fees with suppliers (medical supply companies, pharmaceutical companies, clinical laboratories) as well as providers (doctors, hospitals, nursing homes, home treatment companies).

The use of standardized procedures for disease treatment, along with monitoring the treatment practices of doctors, also saves money. Utilization review panels and preauthorizations also help, as does the use of primary care physicians as gatekeepers. Additionally, managed care saves money by paying only for actual services (as opposed to charges) and by enrolling healthier and younger people.[65]

The effectiveness of these techniques is clear. A study by the Lewin Group found that over the 1990–96 period, managed care saved between $116 and $180 billion. In 1996, employers saved about 11 percent of what they would have spent under the fee-for-service system.[66]

The successes of managed care are not just cost-related. Managed care organizations appeared to detect some kinds of cancers earlier than under the fee-for-service arrangement, largely, again, because of preventive screening. There is also some evidence that dying patients were less likely to be given futile but painful treatments and thus suffered less. Open-heart surgery managed care patients in California were directed to high-volume, high-quality facilities.[67]

Quality

In some ways, the underlying issue surrounding managed care is quality of care. All the anecdotal stories that depict the horrors of managed care concern denial of service or refusal to pay for services.

Quality is an important concern of managed care, though whether it outweighs cost concerns is questionable. There is an industry committee, the National Committee for Quality Assurance (NCQA), with its own set of standards. The American Association of Health Plans (AAHP) has its Patients' First program. There is an industrywide effort at data gathering, known as HEDIS—Health Plan Employer Data and Information Set. Employers have started using accreditation from the National Committee for Quality Assurance and collecting data on performance through HEDIS, which "measures preventive services such as immunizations, access to medical providers and services, and the medical outcomes of specific illnesses."[68] The HEDIS data set includes clinical measures (such as childhood immunizations, first trimester prenatal care, breast and cervical cancer screening and ceasarean section rates) as well as measures of patient satisfaction (including referrals to specialists, choice of physicians, and waiting times).[69] There is debate about how well these kinds of measures actually capture the quality of care in a managed care organization.[70]

Three studies, however, suggest that information about quality is not critical in evaluating HMOs. One study, a survey of large employers, found that employers (purchasers) did not make much use of the available clinical outcomes data. The authors of the study describe a decision process characterized by multiple factors and multiple goals. Given this complex decision-making situation, decision makers look to simplify the decision and avoid the overload of information.[71]

Two studies funded by the Commonwealth Fund support this finding. One study of firms with over 200 employees found that 99 percent of employers did not provide data on health quality to their employees, 91 percent did not require NCQA mandatory accreditation for plans, and 94 percent did not use HEDIS data to select plans. The second study of employers found the overwhelming majority of them (65 percent) were not even familiar with HEDIS or NCQA accreditation.[72]

A third study came up with a similar result. This time it looked at HMOs in the south Florida market and found that they did not channel their coronary artery bypass graft surgery to either low-mortality or high-quality hospitals. Low-quality hospitals offered lower prices. The implications the authors draw is that cost considerations may outweigh quality considerations.[73]

While the successes are undeniable, especially concerning costs, the same techniques that control costs have led to a managed care backlash. It is to this that we now turn.

Managed Care Backlash

We begin this section by first pointing out that the arguments against managed care come generally under the name of consumer protection or patients' rights.[74] Another point we want to make is that to a great extent, the issue is one of power, trust, and accountability.

It is an issue of *power* because managed care organizations have gained control over patients or consumers, and providers. Providers, physicians especially, have lost the professional dominance that had characterized the medical profession for decades.[75] For many years, the medical profession opposed both the group practice of medicine and corporate control of medicine. Both group practice and corporate control now characterize the practice of medicine. More and more, doctors see themselves as employees; the cottage industry of medicine has given way to corporate rationalization and industrialization. Thus some of the backlash comes from doctors.[76] Managed care has impinged upon doctors' incomes and their sovereignty. The review panels and practice guidelines combined with the financial incentives limit what managed care doctors can do. Some physicians have reasoned that if they are no longer professionals with complete autonomy over their medical decisions, they should act like employees. In response to managed care, they have begun considering unions as a countervailing power.[77]

Power is also important to the patients, consumers, or subscribers. Patients are generally assigned a primary care physician and restricted from using some services without the authorization of the physician and the plan. For example, consumers may be prohibited from seeing a specialist without a referral from the primary care physician (gatekeeper). The use of certain hospitals or treatment centers may be restricted because managed care organizations contract with specific facilities and negotiate fees.

The second important concept is *trust*. Patients place their health and lives, and those of their loved ones, in the hands of a provider. There is certainly an asymmetry of power, because patients generally lack information and providers possess it. The assumption is that doctors and other providers will furnish all the necessary services; this is a fiduciary or trust-based relationship.[78] Under the fee-for-service plans, some unneeded services were provided. Under man-

aged care, many have argued, all the incentives, for the provider and the organization, are to underserve. Subscribers who are satisfied with managed care,
in general, are those who are healthy and do not need much. The conflicts
arise when care, emergency or chronic, is needed. Can patients trust that providers have only their interests at heart, or are they influenced by other factors?
Related to trust is the issue of quality of care versus cost of care.[79]

In addition, managed care, according to Annas, has sought to change the
patient into a consumer. This makes the relationship with the organization
and its providers a business transaction, with the assumption that consumers
can make choices based on "cost, coverage, and quality."[80]

The third major concept at issue in the managed care backlash is *accountability*. Because managed care organizations make decisions about the
provision of care, and their decisions are sometimes different from what a
doctor might want, they should also be responsible, many have argued, for
the outcomes of that care. Holding a managed care organization accountable
for medical decisions is known as *enterprise liability* and is one of the most
controversial issues in this area.[81]

Public Opinion

One way of looking at the backlash is to ask whether in fact there is one. That
is, what is the public position on managed care? Newspapers, magazines, and
journals are filled with anecdotal information. Survey research can tell us
how the public as a whole feels. Public support, or lack of support, was critical in the eventual outcome of the Clinton Health Security Act.[82] There is
evidence to suggest that public support for action has motivated both Republicans and Democrats. [83]

A Kaiser Family Foundation/Harvard University study found that most
people are satisfied with their health insurance plans.[84] But the survey also found
considerable support for consumer protection regulation, even if costs were
increased (a point often made by those opposed to patients' rights bills). A
sizable portion of those surveyed believe that managed care is hurting the quality of health care being received and will do so in the future. Blendon et al. note
that those in managed care plans show less satisfaction about quality of care
than those in fee-for-service plans and also show more concern about obtaining
care; but they also note that public perceptions of managed care programs, which
affect only a relatively small number of people, are based on both personal
experience and reporting of problems with managed care. They conclude:

> Public concerns about the need for increased regulation of managed care are
> likely to be with us for the long term. Experience in other industries sug-
> gests that Americans have limits on how far they will allow marketplace

decisions to put them at individual risk. As with airline safety and banking, public support for regulation is being driven in part by the anxiety the public feels relating to the occurrence of visible events questioning the behavior of managed care plans, as well as the problems people experience in their own lives. As a result, debate about regulation of the managed care industry is likely to be a permanent fixture on the health care agenda for years to come.[85]

An August 1997 Louis Harris survey found growing dissatisfaction with managed care: 54 percent of those polled saw managed care as detrimental to their health care, compared to 43 percent the year before.[86]

Ladd argues, however, in an article entitled "Health Care Hysteria, Part II," that most people are satisfied with their health insurance, even those who had episodes of serious illnesses.[87] While most people would like regulation of managed care plans, only about one-quarter of those polled preferred government regulation over other choices. When the possible additional cost of such regulation is inquired about, support for government regulation drops substantially.

The Case against Managed Care

There appear to be three basic concerns that have fueled the managed care backlash.[88] The first, and most important, is *access to care. Quality of care* is another phrase that expresses this concern. Managed care organizations grew because of their promise of control of costs. The question is whether control of costs has come at the expense of access and quality of care. There has been, some have asserted, this very tradeoff.

The incentives that physicians face, the capitation fees, is one part of this concern. Easterbrook describes the impact of capitation on physicians and therefore on patient care:

> Consider what happens when an HMO member walks into a doctor's office. Many plans pay physicians a fixed fee per registered member, regardless of how much treatment each patient needs [capitation]. Primary-care doctors for HMOs that pay this way currently receive a median of about $150 per patient annually. If a patient is healthy or needs only incidental care, the physician keeps the $150 and comes out ahead. But if the patient becomes ill, that $150 can be wiped out fast—and if the patient needs extensive attention, the doctor may end up paying from his or her own pocket.[89]

A different type of financial incentive, bonuses to physicians based on how much they have limited care, essentially a quota system, also plays a role.

An interesting managed care practice is the use of formularies, medications that are on an approved list. Physicians in managed care organizations are usually limited to the listed drugs. Problems arise when plan doctors order a particular prescription drug and the plan's pharmacy on its own substitutes a less costly generic equivalent. Sometimes the generic equivalent can cause severe side-effects that the original prescription would have avoided. Apart from this, the use of formularies is seen by physicians and pharmacists as an interference in patient care. The formularies may be based on deals between plans and pharmaceutical firms.[90]

As the cost of drugs has continued to rise, one response on the part of HMOs has been to put doctors on a monthly drug budget. That is, they are not supposed to prescribe more than the budgeted amount, a specific amount per patient per month. This is another way that doctors are losing autonomy and weakening their roles as patient advocates. Patients may not know about the drug budget.[91]

Other managed care practices play a role. Limiting access to specialists, who are more expensive than primary care physicians, is another way that managed care organizations can save money. Limitations placed on emergency care visits—for example, requirements for prior authorization or contracting with some emergency clinics rather than others—have been among the most contentious issues. Out-of-area coverage has raised similar concerns. In the case of emergency care, hospitals are required to treat all those who need care, regardless of their ability to pay. When managed care organizations such as HMOs refuse to pay for such care, it creates conflict over reimbursement.[92]

Managed care organizations also make use of standardized protocols on how to treat patients and utilization committees to see if providers are within those standards. For example, surgical procedures such as bone marrow transplants for women with advanced breast cancer have been disapproved as experimental.[93] This helps explain public opinion surveys that show that most people, even in managed care organizations, are satisfied with their health coverage. Most people are healthy and thus do not need a great deal of care.

However, those who are severely or chronically ill, the kinds of cases that are most expensive, are the ones who have the most concern about managed care. These people represent losses, not profits, to managed care organizations.

This can be seen in rural Ohio, where Anthem Blue Cross and Blue Shield established a Medicare HMO, promising very attractive benefits over traditional Medicare:

> Prescriptions would cost just $5 to $15; doctor visits $5; there would be no deductibles, no premiums and no charges at all for hospitalization, and there would be free screenings and free preventive care.[94]

Further, Anthem engaged in door-to-door sales, promising all kinds of benefits. It was very successful in enrolling Medicare recipients. But the more people it enrolled, the more it lost money.

Some of the largest HMOs, such as Kaiser Permanente and Aetna U.S. Healthcare, have ended Medicaid HMO operations in twelve states. This has spread to Medicare, particularly in rural areas. Apart from the Anthem HMO mentioned above, HMOs announced reduced services and higher costs.[95]

Another concern raised about access to care and HMOs is whether the list of providers in the plan is accurate or stays up to date. People may join an HMO because of a particular practitioner who may later leave. One California HMO advertised some doctors who were dead. Even if a provider's name is on the list it does not mean he or she is still a participant in the plan. Some employer plans contract with only a portion of the plan's providers, a limited-provider network. So even if a physician is part of an HMO, he or she may not be covered by a particular employee's plan.[96]

Yet another issue, to illustrate the concerns about access to care, was the so-called drive-through deliveries. In this case, HMOs would require that women who gave birth, included those delivering by C-section, be released early. Federal law passed in 1996 required insurers to pay for at least a forty-eight-hour stay for a normal birth and a ninety-six-hour hospital stay for C-section delivery.

A second large managed care issue revolves around information: whether consumers have sufficient information about the plan, physicians, and practices so that they will have faith in what their health plans do.

Another issue that has raised questions about access to care refers to limitations managed care organizations have placed on what physicians can tell patients, say about such financial arrangement as mentioned above. While most of these so-called gag clauses are no longer around, largely because of state legislation that has restricted them as well as actions taken by HMOs and other types of managed care organizations (MCOs) in response to concern, the use of gag clauses does relate to the trust issue discussed above. The *New York Times* provided excerpts from some physician and HMO contracts to illustrate the gag clauses:

> Do not discuss proposed treatment with Kaiser Permanente members prior to receiving authorizations.
> Do not discuss the H.R.M. [Health Risk Management, the company that issued the set of practice guidelines used by Kaiser Permanente] process with members.
> Do not give out H.R.M. phone numbers to members.

> This agreement and the terms and conditions herein shall be treated by the parties as strictly confidential. Accordingly, the parties agree not to directly or indirectly disclose this agreement or the terms and conditions therein, including but not limited to all schedules and financial terms, to any third party.

> The provider expressly waives provider's rights to contact plan members in any way about the termination of this agreement, and expressly agrees not to communicate in any form or manner with such members concerning the termination; the options such members may have to join other health care service plans (including H.M.O.'s) or to switch to other providers as a result of the termination; or the fact that the provider will no longer be the member's health care provider.[97]

This relates to the trust issue discussed above.

The third concern is that managed care organizations may engage in what is known as *risk selection*, or marketing to healthy people. That is, some have argued that managed care plans reduce costs not just by limiting services (rationing) but by seeking to enroll healthier subscribers.

Risk selection (also known as "creaming" or "cherry picking") makes a certain amount of economic sense. Because managed care plans work on a largely capitated basis, such plans and their providers make money by limiting the provision of services. If their subscribers are generally healthy, they will use fewer services and covering them will be more profitable for the plans.

There are a couple of factors that lessen the fear of risk selection. First, Medicare-eligible managed care plans are not allowed to reject Medicare recipients. Second, employers, especially large ones, do not allow plans to risk-select.

Nevertheless, there are ways for HMOs and other managed care plans to engage in risk selection. One of the most prominent ways to engage in risk selection is through advertising campaigns designed to get more subscribers. Neuman et al.[98] have found that HMOs do market in such a way that healthier Medicare recipients are attracted to them. HMOs advertise their lower costs (as compared to traditional Medicare plus medigap policies) and additional benefits over traditional medigap.

The analysis of HMO television and newspaper marketing ads by Newman et al. indicates that most ads show healthy seniors engaging in hobbies and physically demanding activities. None show HMO beneficiaries in a hospital or a wheelchair, or using a walker, and almost none mention that Medicare recipients seeking to enroll in an HMO cannot be refused because of their health status. Neuman et al. also note that many of the seminars at which HMOs make presentations to potential subscribers are not accessible to people confined to wheelchairs. Nor do HMOs seem to market to the under-sixty-five group, or to the disabled. Television and newspaper ads either did not note limitations, such as those on pharmaceuticals, or did so only in fine print.

The economics of Medicare reimbursement shows why managed care organizations undertake such activities. Three pieces of information and some calculations show the problem. First, the average yearly cost of treating most

Medicare patients (about 90 percent of them) is $1,200. Second, a small per-
centage, the 10 percent who are the most seriously ill, average health care
costs of $37,000 per year. The final piece of information is the amount man-
aged care organizations receive on average for each Medicare enrollee,
$5,688.[99] Obviously, the seriously ill patients cause a loss of profit. Let's do
the calculations.

In our first example, the managed care organization has one hundred
Medicare enrollees, who match the above numbers, 10 percent seriously ill
and the other 90 percent generally in good health. That will produce revenue
of $568,800 ($5,688 × 100). The total cost of treating these one hundred enrollees will be $478,000 (90 × $1,200 = $108,000 + 10 × $37,000 = $370,000).
The net profit is $568,000 - $478,000, or $90,000.

Now let's change our example to ninety-five healthy patients and only
five ill patients, a fairly small shift in enrollment. The amount of revenue
generated remains the same, $568,000. Healthy patients now cost $114,000
(95 × $1,200) and seriously ill patients now cost $185,000 (5 × $37,000), for
a total cost of $299,000. The net profit is now $568,000 - $299,000, or
$269,000, an increase in net profit of almost 300 percent. The financial in-
centive to recruit healthy people (whatever their ages) and not to recruit ill
people is immense.

Another set of charges made about managed care is related to its profit
status. As we saw in an earlier section of this chapter, much of the growth in
managed care plans and managed care enrollment has come from for-profit
plans. For-profits can take advantage of equity financing and have proved to
be profitable on the stock market.

But the profits, some have feared, have come from cutting costs. Kuttner,
for example, distinguishes between socially oriented and market-oriented
HMOs.[100] Socially oriented HMOs attempt to be efficient in three ways: prevention and patient education, a lack of monetary incentive to undertreat, and
educating providers about the best practices, based on monitoring.

Market-oriented HMOs may require physicians to assume some of the
financial risks of providing care, to use primary care physicians as gatekeepers,
to select healthier patients, to underserve, and to use outside contractors for
utilization review and preapprovals.[101]

The basic question that Kuttner raises is whether the bad HMOs (market-
oriented) are driving out the good ones (socially oriented), or at least forcing
the good ones to change. He notes that nonprofit HMOs "tend to score better
on many objective indicators and in surveys of consumers."[102] For example,
he notes that an analysis of National Committee for Quality Assurance data
found that nonprofits composed 89 percent of the top thirty-seven HMOs. A

recent ranking of HMOs by *Newsweek* did not include some of the largest for-profit organizations because they refused to participate in the survey.[103]

Easterbrook argues that the entry of for-profit managed care organizations may be very disruptive:

> For-profit health care firms can engage in private extravagance unknown to the old system. J.T. Sebastianelli, for example, president of Aetna U.S. Healthcare, took home $4.9 million last year. And the firms may claim a fiduciary obligation to shift funds from patient care to stockholder dividends.[104]

Marketing expenses and compensation for chief executive officers (though not limited to for-profits) have also become part of national health care expenditures.[105]

Another concern raised by managed care, and especially the for-profits version, is that to reduce costs managed care has also reduced some important cross-subsidies. A portion of fees charged by physicians and hospitals has gone to charitable care, that is, care for those who are uninsured and cannot afford to pay their bills. This is especially true for emergency visits to hospitals. In negotiating low rates with doctors and hospitals, managed care organizations effectively squeeze out such charitable care. This is extremely short-sighted, because emergency care is costly and needed care is delayed.[106] Declining reimbursements by Medicare and Medicaid have a similar effect. Managed care is also putting pressure on research and teaching hospitals which also have benefited in the past from cross-subsidies.

The Role of the Media

One could argue that the case against managed care is heavily overstated and is largely a function of the mass media's search for stories that will catch the public's eye. Certainly cases about mismanaged care would meet that criterion. As Figure 10.1 shows, the media have paid increasing attention to managed care. As another indicator, for instance, the movie *As Good As It Gets* contains a scene in which the character played by Helen Hunt denounces HMOs for not providing sufficient care and coverage for her child.

A careful study of newspaper and television coverage of managed care found that, over the 1990–97 time period, media coverage became more critical or negative in tone. Most of the stories on managed care were neutral, but of those stories that had a tone, negative stories dominated positive stories by about seven to one. Such stories made heavy use of anecdotes, drama, and villains, and increasingly, managed care organizations were the villains.[107]

Brodie, Brady, and Altman write that "the vast majority of media coverage is neutral, but the most visible media sources—broadcast and special

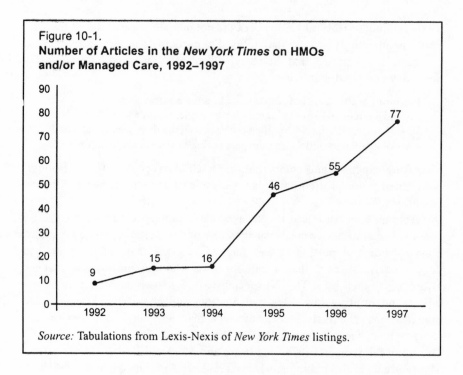

Figure 10-1.
Number of Articles in the *New York Times* on HMOs and/or Managed Care, 1992–1997

Source: Tabulations from Lexis-Nexis of *New York Times* listings.

series—are more negative and focus on more graphic examples of problems people have had."[108] This is important because, as the authors point out, people tend to generalize from the anecdotal stories that typify news reporting. On the other hand, the authors also cite survey data that indicate most people think that media coverage of managed care is fair and their opinions are largely based on personal experience or the experience of others that they know.[109]

Karen Ignagni, chief executive officer of the American Association of Health Plans, writes that managed care is a breaking revolution, a work in progress, and that the media are unduly negative in their coverage.[110] Ignagni provides three examples of poor media coverage that undermines public confidence: physician "gag" rules, "drive-through" deliveries, and outpatient mastectomies. As a result of inaccurate reporting, using the gag rule as an example, some thirty-two states have outlawed a problem she says is nonexistent. What managed care plans have to do is communicate better, demonstrate improvement, and provide comparisons, especially with fee-for-service plans. Additionally, managed care plans have to make the case that the development of managed care is ongoing. Ignagni gives the example of providing consumers with more choice of physicians.

Kuttner, however, points out that the GAO report referred to by Ignagni was issued in the summer of 1997. There were gag rules in effect in 1995 and 1996. They had been removed by 1997, according to Kuttner, because of the media pressure and legislation that Ignagni decried.[111]

What to Do about Managed Care

Assuming the problems with managed care are real, the question then is: What do we do about it? Moran suggests three sets of policy tools for dealing with the problems of managed care.[112] The first he calls "information utilities." These could include a requirement that plans disclose important information, such as financial incentives facing physicians. There could also be regulation of the form of disclosure so that the information is understandable. Etheridge suggests that a regulatory body similar to those that regulate securities in the United States might be appropriate.[113]

A second type of tool is what Moran calls "private enforcement." This would use the judicial system to take legal action against plans because of their medical decisions. Moran calls this "enterprise liability,"[114] and it is at the heart of the debate over federal patient protection legislation (see below).

The third type of tool is economic regulation of various aspects of managed care plans. This has been the providence of states, which have been concerned about the financial viability of plans and their structure at licensure time as well as enforcing a variety of consumer protection plans. Enthoven and Singer make some proposals for collective (though not necessarily public) action to work with private markets.[115] One proposal is to have risk pools to help cover the uninsured, though some type of voucher, government mandate, or tax credit may be necessary to achieve universal coverage. A second suggestion is to use managed competition, and a third is to protect consumers through a variety of mechanisms, such as contracts, liability, property rights, and antitrust regulation.

"Putting Patients First"

The response of the managed care industry, largely through the American Association of Health Plans, has been to adopt an industrywide set of standards known as Putting Patients First. AAHP has responded to issues that are usually publicly driven. Jones says that this is not cynical if it is responsive to public concern.[116] He provides a number of examples.

Jones argues that the drive-through maternity and breast cancer (requiring outpatient mastectomies) controversies were misinformed. For example, the drive-through maternity issue was really that physicians needed to get authorization for longer stays. As for the breast cancer issue, he says that there was confusion between lumpectomies and mastectomies. Lumpectomies are normally done on an outpatient basis, and most of the cases were in fact fee-for-service. Nevertheless, AAHP issued a policy statement saying that outpatient mastectomies are not required and that physicians and patients together should determine whether a mastectomy should be outpatient or inpatient.

A second area is information for patients. One controversy is whether plans consider certain medical procedures as experimental and therefore not covered by the plan. AAHP adopted a policy that

> health plans should (1) routinely inform members about their plan's struc-
> ture and provider network; the benefits covered and excluded, including
> out-of-area and emergency coverage; and cost-sharing requirements; and (2)
> provide information about precertification and other utilization review pro-
> cedures; the basis for a specific utilization review decision with which a
> member disagrees; whether a specific prescription drug is included in a for-
> mulary; a summary description of how patients are paid, including financial
> incentives and the procedures and criteria used to determine whether experi-
> mental treatments and technologies are covered services.[117]

Another area of controversy concerns whether physicians have to get au-
thorization for discussing services that the plan might not cover. This has been labeled a "gag clause" (as discussed above), though it occurred, according to Jones, in only a few plans. The AAHP went beyond supporting complete physician-patient communication to adopt a policy that health plans not prohibit doctors from communicating about medical treatment with patients, regardless of whether the treatment was covered by the plan.

A fourth area of concern was appeals and grievance procedures. The AAHP policy is that health plans must completely explain their appeals procedures, including a time frame for appealing and the patient's rights, and must expe-
dite appeals based on the condition of the patient.

A fifth area is emergency care. The AAHP policy, as described by Jones, is:

> (1) health plans should cover emergency screening and stabilization as needed
> for conditions that reasonably appeared to constitute an emergency, based
> on the patient's presenting symptoms; (2) emergency conditions are those
> that arise suddenly and require immediate treatment to avoid jeopardy to a
> patient's life or health; and (3) to promote continuity of care and optimal
> care by the treating physician, the emergency department should contact the
> patient's primary care physician as soon as possible."[118]

A sixth part of Putting Patients First has to do with quality improvements. The policy guidelines state that things such as practice guidelines and utilization management should be physician-directed and based on available scientific evidence.

Peter Lee, a consumer advocate, criticizes AAHP's Putting Patients First on two grounds: it assumes that there are no problems with managed care, just bad publicity or "anti-managed care misinformation." Further, Lee argues that just letting plans be accountable is not enough.[119] He suggests that an important problem with managed care is the incentives it offers physicians to refrain from giving care. Also, as managed care plans become increasingly for-profit, there is the tension, which Jones does not mention, of profits versus patients.

Lee points to two studies, which are not just consumer satisfaction studies, that survey managed care participants and ask whether they have had any problems. In one survey, almost one-fourth of respondents indicated problems. In another survey, which included CalPERS, about 17 percent of respondents indicated problems.[120]

Lee then turns to the weaknesses of self-regulation. First, he finds in a national survey that 59 percent of respondents said they could not trust their health plans. He also notes that AAHP does not review health plans for compliance with standards and that there are few if any penalties for violating the standards.[121] He also notes that some parts of the standards have already been enacted into state laws.

Lee lists the following set of problem areas:

(1) the need for fair and consistent grievance procedures; (2) the scarcity of valid information for purchasers and consumers on health plan performance; (3) the need for independent assistance for consumers who are confused or have problems; (4) assurance that physicians are providing their patients with the full range of information about treatment options: and (5) protections to ensure that qualified providers are making and are accountable for their own medical decisions.[122]

Clark Havighurst, a long-time advocate of legal changes that affect the health care industry such as antitrust action, argues that the AAHP Putting Patients First as described by Jones is essentially a "benign cartel theme."[123] Jones's article, according to Havighurst, contains themes of "collective action and collective responsibility."[124] Havighurst describes his concerns about Putting Patients First as follows:

My skepticism [is] that Putting Patients First may be just what he claims it is: a program for further centralizing decision making on important health care issues. As a politically inspired program to ward off public regulatory intrusions, the AAHP agenda could easily lead us by another route—industry self-regulation—deeper into the very centralization trap from which the managed care industry should be helping us to escape.[125]

The Public-Sector Response to Managed Care

State Action

Much of the public-sector action on managed care has been at the state level. According to a report by Families USA, the 104th Congress (1995–96, the Congress especially known for its battles with President Clinton) passed three pieces of health legislation. One was welfare reform (the Personal Responsibility and Job Opportunity Act), which had features that dealt with Medicaid eligibility. The second was the Health Insurance Portability and Accountability Act. The third piece of health legislation dealt with consumer protections: maternity stays and mental health parity. In 1996, state legislatures passed laws on health insurance in more than eight categories, from purchasing to maternity stays, gag clauses, access to providers, and so forth.[126] More than 1,000 pieces of legislation were proposed in state legislatures and thirty-three states took action.[127]

States have moved away from reforming the health care system to alleviating problems caused by managed care.[128] The major concern has been the impact of the financial incentives on care and providers have joined with consumers to effect change.[129] Much managed care legislation passed by the states beginning in 1995 and through 1998 was aimed at specific issues rather than at addressing the entire range of issues surrounding managed care (see Table 10.6). As Table 10.6 indicates, the states varied dramatically in their consumer protection bills. Vermont passed the most protections, eleven of the thirteen, while South Dakota was the only state that passed no protections. Further, ERISA denies some protections to consumers in managed care plans, such as remedies for delay or denial of services. That is why the Families USA report is entitled *Hit and Miss.*[130] At the same time, states have to make sure that they do not overregulate managed care organizations, which might increase costs and hurt creativity in creating integrated delivery systems.[131]

The Federal Government

The federal government began addressing managed care issues raised in 1996. Legislation was passed, as mentioned, to require minimum stays for deliveries. In 1997 and 1998 Congress and President Clinton debated managed care bills. One reason for considering federal action even in the light of state initiatives is the impact of the Employment Retirement Income Security Act (ERISA). That act, passed in 1974 to protect employee pension funds, has been interpreted as prohibiting state regulation of employer self-insured health plans. HMOs have claimed immunity from enterprise liability in employer-sponsored health plans under ERISA.[132] Because so many people (about ninety

Table 10.6

State Managed Care Consumer Protection Laws

States	E.R. services Services (prudent layperson standard)	Access to providers Referral to out-of-network providers	Specialists as primary care providers	Standing referrals to specialists	OB-GYN direct access	Continuity of care when physicians leave plan
Alabama				X	X	
Alaska						
Arizona						
Arkansas	X				X	X
California	X			X	X	X
Colorado	X	X			X	X
Connecticut	X				X	
Delaware					X	
District of Columbia	X					
Florida		X		X	X	X
Georgia	X					
Hawaii	X					
Idaho	X				X	
Illinois					X	
Indiana	X	X	X		X	X
Iowa	X					
Kansas				X		X
Kentucky	X	X				
Louisiana	X				X	
Maine	X	X			X	
Maryland	X				X	
Massachusetts						
Michigan	X					
Minnesota	X			X	X	X
Mississippi					X	
Missouri	X	X	X	X		X
Montana		X			X	X
Nebraska	X				X	
Nevada	X					
New Hampshire						
New Jersey			X		X	
New Mexico	X	X	X	X	X	X
New York	X	X	X	X	X	
North Carolina	X	X			X	X
North Dakota						
Ohio	X	X	X	X		
Oklahoma						
Oregon		X			X	
Pennsylvania	X		X	X	X	X
Rhode Island						
South Carolina	X				X	
South Dakota						

Table 10.6 (continued)

States	E.R. services Services (prudent layperson standard)	Access to providers Referral to out-of-network providers	Specialists as primary care providers	Standing referrals to specialists	OB-GYN direct access	Continuity of care when physicians leave plan
Tennessee		X	X	X	X	
Texas	X	X	X		X	X
Utah		X				X
Vermont	X	X	X		X	
Virginia	X			X	X	
Washington	X			X	X	
West Virginia	X			X		
Wisconsin			X			
Wyoming						

States	Prescription drug access (access to nonformulary prescriptions)	Appeals procedures (independent external reviews)	Consumer assistance (independent ombuds programs)	Patient–Provider Realtionship Disclosure of treatment options	Prohibition of physician financial incentives	Clinical trials	Liability (right to sue health plans for damages)
Alabama							
Alaska				X	X		
Arizona		X		X			
Arkansas	X	X		X		X	X
California	X			X	X	X	X
Colorado	X			X			
Connecticut		X		X			
Delaware				X			
District of Columbia				X			
Florida	X	X	X	X			
Georgia	X			X	X	X	
Hawaii		X		X			
Idaho				X	X		
Illinois							
Indiana	X			X			
Iowa				X			
Kansas				X	X		
Kentucky				X			
Louisiana				X	X		
Maine				X			
Maryland		X		X	X	X	
Massachusetts				X			
Michigan		X		X			
Minnesota		X		X			
Mississippi							
Missouri	X	X		X			X
Montana				X	X		
Nebraska				X	X		

States	Prescription drug access (access to nonformulary prescriptions)	Appeals procedures (independent external reviews)	Consumer assistance (independent ombuds programs)	Patient–Provider Realtionship		Clinical trials	Liability (right to sue health plans for damages)
				Disclosure of treatment options	Prohibition of physician financial incentives		
Nevada				X	X		
New Hampshire				X			
New Jersey		X		X	X		
New Mexico		X		X	X		
New York				X			
North Carolina				X			
North Dakota				X			
Ohio	X			X	X		
Oklahoma				X			
Oregon	X			X			
Pennsylvania		X		X	X		
Rhode Island		X		X	X	X	
South Carolina							
South Dakota							
Tennessee		X		X			
Texas		X		X	X		X
Utah				X	X		
Vermont	X	X	X	X	X		
Virginia				X			
Washington				X			
West Virginia				X	X		
Wisconsin				X			
Wyoming				X			

Source: Families USA, *Hit and Miss: State Managed Care Laws*, Families USA, Washington, D.C., 1998, 20–21. The report may be found at the following Web site: http://www.familiesusa.org.

million[133]) are in plans that have ERISA protection, states are limited in what they can do. Some examples will illustrate the problem:[134]

1. A federal appeal court in New Orleans ruled that an insurance company could not be sued for damages by a mother-to-be when her fetus died after her company refused hospitalization for her high-risk pregnancy.

2. A Denver appellate court judge said that a husband could not sue his HMO after his wife died when the HMO refused to approve a bone marrow transplant.

3. In St. Louis, an HMO was protected by ERISA after it refused to approve a heart surgery recommended by a patient's doctor. The patient died.

4. In Cincinnati, a utilization review company was protected after it refused approval of psychiatric treatment for a man who eventually committed suicide.

One action that President Clinton took in 1997 was to create by executive order the Advisory Commission on Consumer Protection and Quality in the Health Care Industry. Its charge was to make recommendations about changes in the health care system, with a special focus on consumer protections and quality. It consisted of thirty-four members from a broad spectrum of health care participants. Its interim report was issued in November 1997 and its final report in March 1998.

The commission drafted a Consumer Bill of Rights and Responsibilities, covering eight areas: information disclosure, choice of providers and plans, access to emergency services, participation in treatment decisions, respect and nondiscrimination, confidentiality of health information, complaints and appeals, and consumer responsibilities.[135]

In his 1998 State of the Union message, President Clinton called for the passage of consumer protection language and placed the debate in the context of what the federal government had accomplished over the previous two years:

> We have to make it possible for all hard-working families to meet their most important responsibilities. Two years ago, we helped guarantee that Americans can keep their health insurance when they change jobs. Last year, we extended health care to up to 5 million children. This year, I challenge Congress to take the next historic steps.
>
> One hundred sixty million of our fellow citizens are in managed care plans. These plans save money and they can improve care. But medical decisions ought to be made by medical doctors, not insurance company accountants. I urge this Congress to reach across the aisle and write into law a Consumer Bill of Rights that says this: You have the right to know all your medical options, not just the cheapest. You have the right to choose the doctor you want for the care you need. You have the right to emergency room care, wherever and whenever you need it. You have the right to keep your medical records confidential. Traditional care or managed care, every American deserves quality care.[136]

The Democratic congressional bill was the Dingell-Daschle bill, which included enterprise liability.

While Republican leaders were reluctant to push consumer protection or patients' rights bills, some Republicans were strong advocates of such legislation. Perhaps the chief Republican proponents were Representative Charles Norwood of Georgia, a dentist, and Greg Ganske of Iowa. House Republicans introduced their bill, the result of four months of deliberation by a fifteen-member task force.[137] Senate Republicans also proposed a bill. A bipartisan bill, sponsored by Senator John Chafee (R-Rhode Island) and Senator Bob Graham (D-Florida) was similar to the Dingell-Daschle bill.

The details of those bills showed interesting differences between the Democratic and Republican versions, apart from the fact that the Republican bill did not allow patients to sue plans over medical liability and would cover fewer people (because it excluded plans protected by ERISA).

One contrast concerns access to emergency medical services. The problem here is that some managed care plans will not pay for such services unless previously authorized. The Democratic bill in the House would require the plan, such as an HMO, to cover the emergency medical service without prior authorization using the "prudent layperson" standard. Essentially, this standard says that if the average person thinks that the absence of the emergency medical service would result in immediate and serious harm, the plan would have to pay.

The Republican House bill was more complicated. In stage one, the plan uses the prudent layperson standard for initial screening in an emergency ward. For further treatment in the emergency room, a "prudent emergency medical professional" standard is used to judge whether treatment is necessary and then "the need for such services must be certified in writing by 'an appropriate physician.'"[138] One doctor said that this new standard was "'invented out of thin air.'"[139]

Further, while the Democratic bill requires that the health plan charge no more for out-of-service emergency services than for in-area services, the Republican bill does not. According to the Congressional Budget Office, the Democratic bill would force plans to cover about half of the emergency services they currently deny.[140]

Another aspect of the patients' rights bills concerns privacy of records. Whereas the Democratic bill protects patients' privacy, the Republican House bill contains provisions that weakens those protections that already exist. *New York Times* reporter Robert Pear described this portion of the bill as follows:

> When privacy advocates read the fine print of the Republican bill, they were surprised to find a provision that explicitly authorizes the disclosure of information from a person's medical records for the purpose of "health care operations." In the bill, that phrase is broadly defined to include risk assessment, quality assessment, disease management, underwriting, auditing and "coordinating health care."[141]

A further important difference concerns enterprise liability. As can be seen in Table 10.6, only a few states provide for it. The Republican bill would preempt state law and eliminate the provision. Opponents of enterprise liability argue that it would significantly raise the cost of care. According to David

Sibley, a Texas state senator, a conservative, pro-business Republican and an oral surgeon, the only costs of the Texas law are for review by an independent panel of denials of service on the part of HMOs. He estimates that the average cost of this process is "less than 6 cents per enrollee per year."[142] A report in the *New York Times* estimated that the actual increase in monthly premiums per member due to enterprise liability was 0.1 percent; as of early September 1998, no one had filed a suit against an HMO.[143] The Congressional Budget Office estimates that establishing a grievance procedure, such as called for in the Daschle-Dingell bill, would add about 0.4 percent to premiums for employer-sponsored health insurance.[144]

Interest groups have become active in the debate over patients' rights. The controversy has altered somewhat the alliance of interest groups from what it was during the 1993–94 period. Then, consumer groups supported the plan, while business groups such as the Chamber of Commerce and the National Federation of Independent Businesses opposed it. Provider groups, especially the American Medical Association, were undecided. As an example, both the American Trial Lawyers Association and the American Medical Association support patients' rights, though for different reasons. Doctors want to protect themselves against the restrictions that managed care organizations place on them, while trial lawyers want to be able to sue managed care organizations for bad decisions. The coalition supporting patients' rights, the National Partnership for Women and Families, also includes labor unions, consumer groups, midwives, and chiropractors. Business groups, such as the Health Benefits Coalition, contain both huge and small employers and they agree on some issues, disagree on others. Some HMOs are more supportive,[145] and some of the larger insurers have quit the Health Insurance Association of America to better represent their own interests.[146]

As an example of this point, five organizations agreed on "legally enforceable standards" for managed care plans. Three of the organizations are large nonprofit health maintenance organizations, Kaiser Permanente, HIP Health Insurance Plans, and Group Health Cooperative of Puget Sound. Two of the organizations are consumer groups: the American Association of Retired Persons (AARP) and Families USA. The standards agreed to would amount to a consumer bill of rights.[147]

Box 10.1 contains the statement of principles agreed to by the organizations. It should be noted that other managed care organizations and AAHP did not approve of the principles.

Annas states that patients' bill of rights laws must have the following core provisions: the right to treatment information, the right to privacy and dignity, the right to refuse treatment, the right to emergency care, and the right to an advocate.[148]

Box 10.1
Summary of Preliminary Statement of Principles for Consumer Protection

The health plans and consumer organizations that drafted this agreement have identified 18 consumer protection principles to promote quality health care and restore trust in the health care system. It is intended that these principles will be incorporated into legally enforceable national standards. The principles are called "preliminary" because the health plans and consumer organizations are continuing discussions about a number of issues that are not included in this enumeration, including appropriate mechanisms for member grievances and appeals and the appropriate locus for oversight of health plan standards. The health plans and consumer organizations are committed to continuing joint work on these complex issues and intend to include them when we reach agreement on them. Below is a brief summary of those 18 principles:

1. Accessibility of Services. To ensure access to quality care, health plans should:
   - have enough physicians, specialists, and other providers to provide timely, appropriate care 24 hours a day, seven days a week; provide women members with direct access to obstetricians and gynecologists; provide access to specialists and specialty care centers affiliated with the plan pursuant to treatment plans, including standing referrals to specialists; provide out-of-network referrals at no cost to the member when the health plan does not have a network physician with the appropriate training or experience or when the health plan does not have an affiliation with a recognized specialty care center to meet a member's covered medical needs; and provide health care materials and services in a culturally and linguistically sensitive manner.

2. Choice of Health Plans. Individuals should be given a choice of health plans.

3. Confidentiality of Health Plan Information. There should be strong protections against improper disclosure by health plans of medical information. Health plans should ensure that the confidentiality of member or patient information is protected. Individual level information should not be disclosed except:
   - if necessary for quality assurance, for purchasers or providers (e.g., to determine eligibility for coverage or to administer payments), or to conduct research (but these data should not contain patient identifiers which could lead to violation of individual privacy and harm to patients);
   - if the individual provides consent; or if required by law or court order.

4. Continuity of Care. Members should be allowed to choose their own primary care physician and change their primary care physician at any time. Health plans should promote preventive care and ensure that medical

records are complete and available to members and their providers. Members who are being treated for a serious illness or who are in the second trimester of pregnancy should be allowed to continue to receive treatment from their physician specialists for up to 60 days or through postpartum when their doctors' contracts are terminated by a plan (for reasons other than quality of care) or when, under their group coverage, their former health plan is replaced and they no longer have the option of continuing to receive care from their previous physician specialists.

5. Disclosure of Information to Consumers. Health plans should provide consumers with information, such as: a description of the coverage provided and excluded, how to obtain service, select providers and obtain medically necessary referrals; members' cost-sharing requirements; the names and credentials of the plan's physicians; a description of the methodologies used to compensate physicians; procedures for utilization management; a description of restrictive prescription drug formularies; procedures for receiving emergency care and out-of-network services; procedures for determining coverage for investigational or experimental treatments; use of arbitration; disenrollment data; and how to appeal decisions, file grievances, and contact consumer organizations, such as ombudsman programs, or government agencies regulating the health plan.

6. Coverage of Emergency Care. Health plans should cover emergency services, including services provided when a prudent layperson reasonably believes he or she is suffering from a medical emergency. In order to assure continuity of care after the patient is stabilized, emergency departments should inform the health plan within thirty minutes after stabilization to obtain authorization for any medically necessary post-stabilization services. The health plan should respond to the request within thirty minutes of the initial call, and, upon request, provide access to a participating physician if it intends to deny the request for authorization. Health plans should educate their members about the availability, location, and appropriate use of emergency and other medical services, any cost-sharing provisions for emergency services, and the availability of medical care outside an emergency department.

7. Determinations of When Coverage Is Excluded Because Care Is Experimental. Health plans should have an objective process for reviewing new drugs, devices, procedures, and therapies. Plans should also have an external, independent review process to examine the cases of seriously ill patients who are denied coverage for experimental treatments.

8. Development of Drug Formularies. Health plans that cover prescription drugs and use restrictive formularies should allow physicians to participate in the development of the formularies and provide for an exception process when non-formulary alternatives are medically necessary.

9. Disclosure of Loss Ratios. In order to allow consumers to learn what percentage of their premiums are paid out in medical benefits, health plans should uniformly calculate and disclose how much of premium dollars

are going for health care delivery costs rather than for plan administration, profits, or other uses.

10. Prohibitions against Discrimination. Health plans should not discriminate in the provision of health care services on the basis of age, gender, race, national origin, language, religion, socio-economic status, sexual orientation, disability, genetic make-up, health status, or source of payment. Health plans should develop culturally competent provider networks. Health insurance reform should address discriminatory practices that discourage enrollment of high-risk, high-cost or vulnerable populations in health plans.

11. Ombudsman Programs. Consumers should have access to, and health plans should cooperate with, an independent, external non-profit ombudsman program that [will] help consumers understand plan marketing materials and coverage provisions, educate members about their rights within health plans, investigate members' complaints, help members file grievances and appeals, and provide consumer education and information.

12. Out-of-Area Coverage. Health plans should cover unforeseen emergency and urgent medical care for members traveling outside a plan's service area.

13. Performance Measurement and Data Reporting. Health plans should meet national standards for measuring and reporting performance in areas such as quality of care, access to care, patient satisfaction, and financial stability. There should be a collaborative effort to develop a national core data set of outcome-oriented, scientifically based measures, building on existing efforts. Standards should ensure appropriate confidentiality and protection of individual privacy. Health plans should disclose the results of performance assessments and be subject to independent audit to ensure accuracy.

14. Provider Communication with Patients. Health plans should not limit the exchange of information between health care providers and patients regarding the patient's condition and treatment options. Health plans should not penalize providers who in good faith advocate for their patients, assist patients with claims appeals, or report quality concerns to government authorities or health plan managers.

15. Provider Credentialing. Health plans and provider groups should develop written standards similar to those used by the National Committee for Quality Assurance for hiring and contracting with physicians, other providers and health care facilities. Health plans should not discriminate against providers who treat a disproportionate number of patients with expensive or chronic medical conditions.

16. Provider Reimbursement Incentives. Neither health plans nor provider groups should use payment methodologies that directly encourage providers to overtreat patients or to limit medically necessary care. Full-risk capitation should not be used for an individual provider. Where capitation is used for an individual provider, it should only apply to services directly

provided by that provider. Appropriate safeguards, such as reinsurance or stop-loss coverage, should be used when individual providers or small groups of providers are capitated or when providers are placed at substantial financial risk. General information about the types of reimbursement methodologies used for providers should be disclosed.

17. Quality Assurance. All health plans should be subject to comparable comprehensive quality assurance requirements. National standards for quality assurance should be non-duplicative and should provide latitude in the specific methods and activities employed to meet the standards to reflect differences in health plan organization. Standards should provide for external review of the quality of care, conducted by qualified health professionals who are independent of the plan and accountable to the appropriate regulatory agency.

18. Utilization Management. Utilization management activities of health plans should be subject to appropriate regulation, including requirements to use appropriately licensed providers to evaluate the clinical appropriateness of adverse decisions. Health plans should make timely and, if necessary, expedited decisions, and give the principal reasons for adverse determinations and instructions for initiating an appeal. Health plans should be prohibited from having compensation arrangements for utilization management services that contain incentives to make adverse review decisions.

Source: Families USA (1997), "Leading Health Plans and National Consumer Groups Announce Unprecedented Agreement for Consumer Protection Standards in Managed Care." http://www.familiesusa.orghmoagre.htm.

A number of groups are lobbying and advertising against patients' rights bills (both Republican and Democratic). One very active group is the American Association of Health Plans (AAHP), the association of managed care organizations. It began running television ads in June 1998 denouncing the bills, arguing that they would raise the cost of health care and that politicians were using the issue for political purposes. The ad read in part:

> Hear about the politicians' new game . . . bashing HMOs and other health plans to trick you into voting for them. The politicians' new laws and regulations could cause nearly two million hard-working Americans to lose their coverage.[149]

In mid-1997, AAHP prepared a list of talking points to use to lobby against a congressional proposal mandating payment for emergency services. The bill, sponsored by Bob Graham (D-Florida) and John Chafee (R-Rhode Island) would make severe pain a condition that required HMOs to pay. The talking points were that pain was subjective, that waiting times in emergency rooms were so long that people left without being seen, that coverage for pain drove up costs, and that wrong medications were often given. Another was that the bill was so vague that any kind of pain (e.g., stubbing one's toe) might be covered.[150]

AAHP has over 1,000 members, including the largest of the managed care companies. The Health Benefits Coalition (HBC), which is also advertising against patients' rights legislation, consists of over thirty organizations, including the Health Insurance Association of America, the Chamber of Commerce, the Business Roundtable, and the National Federation of Independent Businesses. The HBC ad referred to a "Congressman Frankenstein" while another accused Republican supporters of patients' rights bills of joining with liberals like Edward Kennedy.[151] Liberal groups like the American Federation of Labor–Congress of Industrial Organization (AFL-CIO) announced a nationwide media campaign to back the Senate Democratic bill.[152]

The House passed a patients' rights bill in July 1998 that was crafted by an ad hoc committee. As of September 1998, no federal legislation has passed and in the wake of the independent prosecutor's report on President Clinton released in that month, such legislation is unlikely. Senate Minority Leader Tom Daschle (D-South Dakota) proposed to bring up the House bill and then heavily amend it more to the Democrats' liking. However, Senate Republicans proposed instead to allow their bill and the Senate Democratic bill to come to the floor with limited amendments. The disagreement meant that no action would be taken.[153]

The Clinton administration was able to take some action unilaterally. In February 1998, Clinton issued an order that gave many patients' rights protections to federal employees and Medicare and Medicaid recipients. In August 1998, the president issued another executive order requiring a quick appeals process for managed care patients in plans covered by ERISA.[154]

State Action versus Federal Action

Why have the states been able to act while the federal government could do so little? One explanation is that legislative efforts at the state level have been bipartisan, whereas the federal government has seen a "bitter conflict" in Congress.[155] This has been exacerbated by scandals and investigations that have plagued the Clinton administration and have led to consideration of impeachment of the president in the fall of 1998. A second reason is that state legislators, whatever their political persuasion, perceive the issue of patients' rights and managed care as an opportunity to serve their constituents who have had problems rather than engage in conflict.[156] A third reason is that interest groups in the states, unlike those at the federal level, have cooperated on the legislation. At the least, insurance companies have accepted the legislation if not embraced it.[157]

Conclusion

The 1990s have seen almost a breathless amount of activity in both the public and the private sector. The federal government considered and then rejected comprehensive health care. It then turned to an incremental strategy, focusing on a specific range of problems: portability of health insurance, hospital maternity stays, and expanding coverage for uninsured children. In addition to the S-CHIP program, Congress also passed legislation that could potentially change the nature of Medicare (Medicare+Choice; see chapter 4). Congress and the president also considered legislation that would effectively establish a patient's bill of rights. But work on the patient's rights bill was stalled because of many of the same factors that led to the failure of the Health Security Act.

Many of the changes that took place in health care took place in the private sector. Led by big business's desire to curb employee health expenditures, a revolution in health care organization and financing took place, the managed care revolution. By 1998, the vast majority of people with employer-based health insurance were in some type of managed care organization. States were moving Medicaid recipients into managed care, and increasing, though small, numbers of Medicare recipients were making the same choices.

Along with this change came distress. Physicians found that they had lost a great deal of their power and autonomy. Provider reimbursement was squeezed. Members of managed care organizations (i.e., consumers) found that they faced limits on the choice of provider and plan, and that their faith that physicians had patients' best interests in mind, rather than various kinds of incentives to limit care, was lowered.

This is not to say that managed care has had only deleterious effects. Managed care has dramatically reduced cost increases. While the debate over the quality of care is inconclusive, there are certainly some areas where managed care excels. For those who are not disabled, or seriously or chronically ill, managed care has provided high-quality care. The focus on well-baby care, immunizations, and screening for breast and prostate cancer has been helpful. Both for those who need more than ordinary care, managed care has been shown to be, in too many cases, a maze worthy of Franz Kafka.

One of the major complaints about the Clinton Health Security Act was that it was too bureaucratic and would involve too much government intervention in medical care. Schneider argues that the managed care backlash in

1996–1998 is really a striking out at bureaucratic rationing. While most people are happy with their managed care plan, it is the basic concept "that a bureaucrat can control you health care" that creates the anxiety and the backlash.[158]

It is this backlash that the states have addressed to greater or lesser degrees. The patients' right movement, which unites consumers, physicians, and lawyers, seeks to provide a stopgap remedy to the problem. But state and (to a lesser extent) federal action has been, in the phrase of the consumer advocacy group Families USA, a "hit-and-miss" proposition. And the managed care revolution is incomplete; it does not (and perhaps cannot) solve all the problems of the health care system. We consider these points in our concluding chapter.

CHAPTER 11

Conclusion: Health Care Policy at the End of the Twentieth Century

In these final pages, we would like to summarize the discussion of the text, focusing on the features that help explain the course of health care policy in the United States. Based on this review, we end by making some reasonably educated guesses about the future of health care policy.

We began this text by examining various factors that affect the policymaking process, whether in health care or some other policy area. Policymaking and the policies that result from that process are profoundly affected by the constitutional structure of government. In the United States, that constitutional structure creates a bias against major changes. The system of separation of powers and checks and balances creates separate institutions that share power. Chief among them is the separation between executive and legislative powers. In a parliamentary system, such as in England, the party with a majority in the legislature would be able to enact its program (party discipline is important here too). In the United States, even under conditions of party control of both Congress and the presidency (i.e., 1993–94), the passage of programs is hardly assured. Separation of powers creates institutional jealousies that are difficult to overcome. When there is divided control (i.e., 1995–98), the institutional jealousies may be reinforced.[1] This is not to say that major changes cannot take place, only that they occur under constitutionally difficult circumstances.[2] And all three branches of government—executive, legislative, and judicial—are brought into policymaking.

A further constitutional feature is federalism, the division of powers between different levels of government. States (and local governments) are independent actors, and policy made at the federal level must consider its impact on states. The result of federalism and separation of powers (as in a system of checks and balances) is the deliberate fragmentation of power, vertically and horizontally. It would be little exaggeration to say that no other country faces as difficult a set of constitutional barriers as the United States.

Additionally, some states have shown great initiative in trying to control the costs of Medicaid, in attempting to extend insurance coverage through comprehensive reform, and in protecting patients' rights.

A second key set of factors is the political environment, which is shaped by constitutional structure and the institutional environment. Fragmentation of power requires that policies be adopted as a result of consensus building, especially in legislatures. It also means that rather than adopt major reforms or new ways of doing things, we in the United States tend to adopt smaller changes, tinkering as we go along. This incremental style of decision making characterizes policymaking in health care. Numerous attempts at comprehensive change in the twentieth century have failed, most recently in 1994 (see chapter 9).

Our political philosophy or ideology has a strong promarket, antigovernment bias. Those who seek positive government action have the burden of justifying new programs and then maintaining political support for them. This antigovernment bias, among other factors, helps explain why the public sector's role in health care is limited in the United States, as compared to other countries.[3] Even in other countries, some have argued that markets have become predominant.[4] As chapter 10 shows, the private sector has taken the lead in effecting change in the health care system.

The same political philosophy, along with the same constitutional and institutional factors, allows for another important feature of our political environment: the presence of interest groups. The right to assemble, the rights of free speech and press, the right of association, and the right to petition government create a constitutional basis for interest groups. Fragmentation in government, where there are multiple sources of power at different levels of government, invites interest groups to try to influence those sources of power. Recall the definition of politics offered by Lawrence Brown in the opening epigraph to chapter 9: politics involves the resolution of conflicts of values and interests. For every program, a set of interests is affected by it. Interest groups seek either to defend programs that benefit them or to get rid of programs that adversely affect them. They are also prepared to defend themselves against policy proposals that would hurt them. We certainly saw the mobilization of interests in chapters 9 and 10, but this occurs in other ways as well. Medicaid, Medicare, and the planning programs of the 1960s all contained provisions in their original legislation that effectively said that the program could not interfere with the practice of medicine. The danger of interest-group activity is that once programs are enacted and entrenched, their interest-group defenders man the barricades against change. The result is what Rauch calls demosclerosis.[5]

All these factors help explain the peculiar nature of the health care system in the United States. It is a combination of mostly private-sector coverage with substantial public programs and public regulation. If we were to develop a health care system from scratch, we would likely never produce the system we currently have.

This system has problems. Costs remain a problem, which affects governments, businesses, insurers, individuals, and providers. At the same time that the health care sector is the largest sector of the nation (about one-seventh of the economy), a sizable and increasing number of people (over 16 percent of the population) have inadequate access to quality care, largely but not entirely because of lack of health insurance. This is compounded by developments in biomedical technology that present ethical questions (such as: What is life? Is there a right to die?) we have not yet resolved and may never resolve.

Given these political features, problems, and policy failures (as in 1994), what is the future of health care policy in the United States? It is always hazardous to go out on a limb and make projections, but certain trends seem obvious, based on our analysis in the previous ten chapters.

First, whatever change is likely to take place will be incremental. Public health care programs, Medicaid and Medicare, have been tinkered with as a means of controlling costs and expanding access. Of the two, Medicare is perhaps the better example of incremental policymaking that can, over a period of time, result in significant change.

Consider the Balanced Budget Act (BBA) of 1997. Without altering some of the basic fundamentals of the program, potentially significant change has been enacted. Prospective payment, imposed first on hospitals and then on doctors, has been extended to other providers, such as home health care and nursing homes. Perhaps more important, the options available to Medicare recipients have been significantly increased through the Medicare+Choice program. Some commentators have argued that the policy consensus underlying Medicare has eroded.[6] On the other hand, there are questions about whether the Health Care Financing Administration (HCFA) can effectively implement the new program as scheduled, and about whether health plans will offer the options.[7]

A further change that was part of the BBA was expansion of health insurance to children in families lacking health insurance. This is the State Child Insurance Health Program (S-CHIP), in which, with federal grants and state matching funds, states can either extend Medicaid to children or create new programs.

Another incremental, but critical, policy initiative includes laws regulating managed care and patients' rights bills. The federal government passed some legislation in 1996 (affecting maternity care and portability of insurance) and discussed patients' rights bills in 1998. Meanwhile, over thirty states have enacted some version of managed care regulation.

How effective these bills will be is questionable. While the managed care industry and its supporters argue that the new regulations will be very costly,[8] Cohn has argued that at best such laws will be "cosmetic surgery." What advocates of managed care regulation really want, he argues, is national health insurance.[9]

Others, including some opponents of a greater public-sector role, have argued that, in fact, policy is moving us in the direction of national health insurance, one step at a time.[10] First children are covered, then the uninsured between ages fifty-five and sixty-four as President Clinton proposed. As managed care extends its reach, the federal government and states regulate the behavior of health plans. Pretty soon, so the argument goes, we effectively have a system of national health insurance. Whether this scenario works out is problematical, because the opposition to increased regulation, if not to increased coverage, remains strong.

Problems remain in specific policy areas. In the case of Medicaid, there has been considerable change, though the basic elements remain the same. Decentralization of authority to the states during the Reagan and Clinton administrations was accompanied by liberalization of eligibility so that more people, primarily children, could be covered. At the same time, states have taken steps to control costs, such as moving Medicaid recipients into managed care, limiting services, and restricting provider reimbursements. As we concluded in chapter 3, the states by themselves are unable to solve the problems with the program. The federal government still has a significant role to play. And certainly the demographic impact of an aging population will continue to place strains on the federal-state program.

The same demographic problem affects Medicare (chapter 4). Medicare remains a popular program and has, in a sense, weathered the storms of attacks upon it in 1995–96. The cost problems remain, especially as the population ages. The issue of the long-term financial viability of Medicare Part A (the hospital trust) has been postponed. It is not clear that 1997 changes, with their dizzying array of new choices, from medical savings accounts to private fee-for-service, can address this issue; it is not even clear whether they were intended to address the cost problem or whether, as some have charged, they were designed to change the basic nature of the program. There are certainly questions that can be raised as to whether the nation's senior citizens can make effective choices of plans, especially as they get even older. The move to managed care within Medicare has been much slower than either within Medicaid or in the private sector. Indeed, news reports in late 1998 suggested that some managed care companies were moving out of Medicare because of their inability to gain higher premiums.[11] The cost of Medigap policies has risen at double-digit figures.[12]

Related to Medicare and Medicaid is the issue of long-term care. It is one of the fastest-growing areas of health care spending, again a result, largely, of the aging of the population. Nursing home care is extremely expensive, and the long-term care insurance market is small and growing at a slow rate. Further, both nursing homes and home health agencies have been cited for fraudulent billing. No easy solution appears for an area where the private sector, including individuals and families, remains the largest provider and payer of services.

Equally discouraging, in some respects, is the issue of the disadvantaged, those who do not have the financial resources to afford health insurance and adequate health care. If there is one demonstrable finding in the health care literature, it is that lack of access to health care leads to poor health outcomes. There are ways to cover more people, as we mentioned in chapter 5. Medicare and Medicaid could be expanded; tax credits for purchase of health insurance would help. Medical savings accounts could provide insurance coverage to the uninsured who are working, especially the self-employed, though few people to date have opted for the program. National health insurance would, of course, largely end the lack of insurance problem, but as we have seen, it is the least likely policy to be enacted. Managed care has the potential to increase coverage, because cost savings can be used to extend care to others (Oregon is a prime example here); but the reality has been much different, as we will discuss below.

Even these programs could prove inadequate if providers are not available. Inner cities and rural areas suffer from an insufficient number of doctors. The literature also shows that minorities are more likely to lack access to services and insurance than whites.

Interestingly enough, some policies in other areas can impact on the distribution of providers. The attack on affirmative action, successful so far (as of fall 1998) in Texas, California, and Washington State and perhaps spreading to other states, may reduce the number of minorities in our nation's medical schools, especially the top medical schools.[13] Affirmative action, it turns out, is a health care program.

While access to services has been a perennial issue, the issue that drives change in the health care system remains cost containment (chapter 6). The initial efforts at cost containment were regulatory in nature. At the state level, this involved hospital price (which met with some success) and certificate-of-need (CON) regulation (which met with much less success). At the federal level, planning was tried (again with limited success) and then rate setting in Medicare (prospective payment first for hospitals, then for doctors, and eventually for other providers, such as home health care services). The prospective payment system (PPS) met with some success and has become an integral part of Medicare. Managed care has produced cost savings, at least in the short run.

Medical technology, the subject of chapter 8, raises a whole range of questions, apart from its impact on costs. Technology has enhanced what medicine can do and in the process has raised troubling ethical questions. These include issues such as how organs ought to be made available to those who need transplants and the ethics of ending life for terminally ill patients (either to end suffering or to make organs available). Developments in reproductive technology make it possible for people to have children under circumstances that had not even been thought of two decades before. Right-to-die movements, a reaction to life-sustaining technologies, confront those who object on religious grounds. How well the American political system is equipped to deal with these complex, difficult issues is an important question. Some, such as right to die, have been the object of voter initiatives (e.g., Oregon). Are initiatives, with all the trappings of political campaigns, the best forum for deciding these kinds of issues? Will genetic testing lead to some people being unable to obtain health insurance?

Regulation as a means of cost control has largely been eliminated (a few states like Maryland retain their programs). The private sector's attempt to control employees' health care costs has led to significant change. The increasing costs of premiums has led some employers to reduce or eliminate coverage, or to shift more costs to employees. And the move to managed care has become the dominant means of controlling costs (chapter 10).

Managed care has been successful, at least in the short run. Double-digit inflation in premiums in the late 1980s and early 1990s has been changed to low-single-digit inflation and, in some cases, to decreases in premium costs in the middle and late 1990s.

But there are signs that the managed care's effect on costs may not hold for the longer term. First, there is the conflict of cost control with access and quality, which we discussed in chapter 10. Second, the increase in population and particularly the aging of the baby boom population will place more pressure on costs. Technological advances also place pressure on costs.

Concluding Thoughts

While we noted above and in several other chapters that cost increases have plunged in the middle and late 1990s, the continuation of that trend is doubtful. A 1998 study released by the Health Care Financing Administration suggested that health spending would increase through the year 2007 and that the increases "will be driven almost entirely by rising expenditures in the private rather than the public sector."[14]

The managed care revolution has led to a reaction, as providers (largely physicians) and consumers (patients) have complained about the bureaucratic restrictions placed on them,[15] as well as about loss of autonomy and restrictions on income (reimbursement) for providers. The quality of care provided by managed care organizations, especially the for-profit versions, has been called into question.[16]

Employers have typically been more concerned about the cost of health care than about the quality of care received by their employees. This has fueled state regulatory efforts and discussion at the federal level (patients' rights bills). Employers have also begun to look at less restrictive plans, such as preferred provider organizations (PPOs) and growth in PPOs has exceeded growth in HMOs.[17] Managed care has clearly lost some of its luster, even among larger employees.[18]

Additionally, managed care organizations, apart from facing resistance, may have captured the easy savings (negotiating discounts, restrictions on care, risk selection); further savings may be more difficult.

An important area where managed care has had an impact is on access to care. Because managed care (that is, employer-based insurance) is largely a private-sector phenomenon, the concern for those who do not have health care is absent. Indeed, one could argue that managed care exacerbates the health insurance problem. Historically, hospitals, for example, have used charges to privately insured (and, to some extent, to Medicare) patients to cross-subsidize people who cannot afford care, especially those who use emergency clinics as their major source of care. Managed care organizations, however, in their attempts to restrain costs, create pressure to eliminate cross-subsidies. This has dramatically affected hospitals (especially teaching hospitals) and squeezed their revenue.

This may be one reason the proportion of those without health insurance increased in 1997 to 16 percent of the population.[19] According to the U.S. Census Bureau, it was those "ages eighteen to sixty-four who accounted for the increase in the uninsured."[20] The issue of the uninsured has been largely lacking from current policy debates.[21]

Yet another problem associated with managed care is that unless the federal government takes action, state patients' bills of rights will not affect those whose employers choose self-insurance. The Employee Retirement Income Security Act (ERISA) limits state regulation over some plans. Thus the backlash against managed care will be confined unless Washington acts.

A trend related to managed care is the consolidation of the health care industry. As we noted in chapter 10, a small number of managed health organizations enroll the bulk of beneficiaries. Hospital consolidation is a related trend. What we have, effectively, is the creation of health care empires, some surrounding hospitals, others surrounding insurers. Many of these are for-profit firms that have placed cost control over quality.[22]

Further, while managed care has been a good deal for larger companies, premium increases for smaller employers and the self-employed have been substantial. Even larger employers are facing demands for higher premiums.[23]

There are proposals that could make managed care more palatable. For example, independent reviews of appeals would help. Some have argued that allowing enterprise liability will have an impact. An important finding is that lack of choice of plans leads to dissatisfaction with the plan.[24] The term for proposals that offer a choice of plans is "managed competition."

A model for a managed competition (which was part of the debates in the early and mid-1990s) is the Federal Employees Health Benefits Program (FEHBP). Such a plan has been favorably looked upon by both liberals and conservatives. It has been described as follows:

> With nearly 10 million enrollees nationwide, FEHBP constitutes the largest medical plan in the United States. All federal employees—as well as members of Congress, the Supreme Court, and the Cabinet—are eligible for coverage. While employees elsewhere hope for "cafeteria plans," FEHBP enrollees are treated to a virtual Valhalla of smorgasbords: A total of 380 health plans nationwide participate in FEHBP, offering the average beneficiary at least a dozen options for coverage in her locality, ranging from managed care to traditional fee-for-service. It allows enrollees to choose their own physicians. Even before Kennedy-Kassebaum, it basically insured everyone in its population, regardless of pre-existing conditions. There is no cancellation for catastrophic illness. And if the plan you choose isn't working out for you, the annual "open season" allows you easily to switch insurers within a year. Consumer satisfaction is strikingly high: 87 percent for those in fee-for-service plans and 85 percent for those in HMOs.[25]

FEHBP has also kept prices and price increases relatively low through competition. At the federal level, however, there are no proposals that would allow people to buy into the program, so as to extend the program to nonfederal people.

One last set of predictions: Change in the heath care sector in the twenty-first century will be driven by the private sector. The public sector is likely to have mostly a reactive role. The title of one book on health care captures this notion: *The Private Regulation of American Health Care.*[26] Whether the managed care revolution, which may be faltering, can control costs in the long term is yet unknown. The failure of the Clinton health reform effort has doomed, at least for a while, any large-scale public-sector efforts at reform. The problems of cost, access, and quality have not been solved.

Some commentators have argued that, as long as the basic issue is one of trying to deal with the tradeoffs among these three values, the problems may never be solved:

> If you want an end to the health-care debate—don't hold your breath. It won't happen now. It won't happen 50 years from now. This is not because our politicians are incompetent, although they often are. Nor is it because doctors, hospitals, drug companies and insurers try to manipulate the system, although they do. The real reason is that we Americans want contradictory things from the health-care system: We want unlimited medical care without unlimited spending. Because this is impossible—and because our politicians reinforce our unrealistic demands—we are doomed to complain forever about the health system's defects.[27]

Notes

Chapter 1. Health Care Politics

1. Charles O. Jones, *An Introduction to the Study of Public Policy*; James E. Anderson, *Public Policy Making*.

2. Lawrence D. Brown, "The Formulation of Federal Health Care Policy," 48.

3. J.H.A. Brown, *The Politics of Health Care*, 15–16.

4. Susan Dentzer, "America's Scandalous Health Care," *U.S. News and World Report*, March 12, 1990, 25–30; Humphrey Taylor, "U.S. Health Care: Built for Waste," *New York Times*, April 17, 1990.

5. Walter A. Rosenbaum, *Environmental Politics and Policy*, 31.

6. James Madison, "Federalist 51," in *The Federalist Papers*, ed. Alexander Hamilton, James Madison, and John Jay, 320–25.

7. Calculated from Harold W. Stanley and Richard G. Niemi, *Vital Statistics on American Politics*.

8. Lawrence D. Brown, *Health Policy in the Reagan Administration*, 32–33.

9. See Frank J. Thompson, "New Federalism and Health Care Policy."

10. Christa Altenstetter, *Health Policy-Making and Administration in West Germany and the United States*, 26–27.

11. Ralph Huitt, "Political Feasibility," 410.

12. Brown, "Formulation of Federal Health Care Policy," 53.

13. Graham Allison, *The Essence of Decision*, 163.

14. Brown, "Formulation of Federal Health Care Policy," 53.

15. Charles A. Lindblom, "The Science of Muddling Through," 86.

16. Rosenbaum, *Environmental Politics and Policy*, 36.

17. Huitt, "Political Feasibility," 410.

18. Rudolf Klein, "The Political Ideology vs. the Reality of Politics," 83.

19. S.H. Beer, *Modern British Politics*, 5.

20. Jane H. Bayes, *Ideologies and Interest-Group Politics*, 42.

21. James Madison, "Federalist 10," in *The Federalist Papers*, ed. Alexander Hamilton, James Madison, and John Jay, 77–84.

22. Theodore Lowi, "The Public Philosophy."

23. David Wilsford, *Doctors and the State*, 69.

24. Grant McConnell, *Private Power and American Democracy*.

25. Robert A. Alford, *Health Care Politics*, 15.

26. S.E. Berki, "Health Care Policy."

27. Paul Samuelson, *Economics*.

28. Victor R. Fuchs, *Who Shall Live?*

29. Alan L. Sorkin, *Health Care and the Changing Economic Environment*, xiii, 1.

30. Victor R. Fuchs, *The Health Economy*, 13.

31. Ibid., 6.

32. Joseph A. Califano, Jr., "The Health-Care Chaos," *New York Times Magazine*, March 20, 1988.

33. Gavin Mooney, *Economics, Medicine and Health Care*, 21.

34. Alan B. Cohen and Donald R. Cohodes, "Certificate of Need and Low Capital-Cost Medical Technology," 307.

35. H.V. Fineberg and H.H. Hiatt, "Evaluation of Medical Practices."

36. Fuchs, *Health Economy*, 30.

37. Katharine R. Levit et al., "National Health Expenditures, 1996," 187.

38. Ibid.

39. Hospital Insurance Association of America, *Source Book of Health Insurance Data*, 35.

40. Levit et al., "National Health Expenditures, 1996," 200.

41. The description that follows is derived from Office of the Federal Register, National Archives and Records Administration, *The United States Government Manual 1990/91*, 287–315.

42. Levit et al., "National Health Expenditures, 1996," 187, 200.

43. Hospital Insurance Association of America, *Source Book of Health Insurance Data*, 38–39.

44. Ibid., 13.

45. Wesley S. Mellow, "Determinants of Health Insurance and Pension Coverage," 30–32.

46. Deborah J. Chollet, *Employer-Provided Health Benefits*, 31.

47. Reported in "Employees Finding 'Free' Health Insurance Costly, Survey Shows," *Springfield News-Leader*, July 10, 1991.

48. George A. Silver, "Health-Care Systems," *Grolier Multimedia Encyclopedia*, 1998.

49. Stanley Whol, M.D., *The Medical Industrial Complex*, 5.

50. Ibid., 111–17. For a detailed discussion of about thirty-five major medical corporations, see 101–76.

51. Silver, "Health-Care Systems."

52. Bruce C. Vladeck, *Unloving Care*, 8–9.

53. Calculated from Levit et al., "National Health Expenditures, 1993," 292.

54. Silver, "Health-Care Systems," 1998.

55. Elisabeth Rosenthal, "Medicine Suffers As Fewer Doctors Join Front Lines," *New York Times*, May 24, 1993.

56. Ibid.

57. U.S. Bureau of the Census, "Health Insurance Coverage: 1995." http://www.census.gov/hhes/hlthins/cover95/c95taba.html.

58. Ibid.

59. Helen C. Lazenby and Suzanne W. Letsch, "National Health Expenditures, 1989," 16–17; Sally T. Burner, Daniel R. Waldo, and David R. McKusick, "National Health Expenditure Projections Through 2030," 20.

60. Ibid., 19.

61. Milt Freudenheim, "Business and Health: Health Insurers Changing Role," *New York Times*, January 16, 1990; Peter Kerr, "The Changing Definition of Health Insurers," *New York Times*, May 10, 1993.

62. Spencer Rich, "Are Insurers Playing Favorites?" *Washington Post National Weekly Edition*, June 24–30, 1991, 37.

63. Levit et al., "National Health Expenditures, 1996," 188.

64. Robert J. Blendon et al., "Satisfaction with Health Systems in Ten Nations," 188. The countries included in the study are the United States, Canada, Great Britain, West Germany, Australia, France, Sweden, Japan, Italy, and the Netherlands.

65. Milt Freudenheim, "Business and Health: Most Want U.S. to Pay the Bill,"

New York Times, July 3, 1990.

66. Richard Morin, "Americans Want Health Care to Save Lives Whatever the Cost," *Washington Post National Weekly Edition*, February 5–11, 1990, 38.

67. Ibid.

68. Cindy Jajich-Toth and Burns W. Roper, "Americans' Views on Health Care," 151, 153.

69. Peter Navarro, *The Policy Game*.

70. James T. Bennett and Thomas J. DiLorenzo, *Destroying America*.

71. Judith G. Smith, ed., *Political Brokers*.

72. Stephen Miller, *Special Interest Groups in American Politics*, esp. 113–35.

73. H.R. Mahood, *Interest Group Politics in America*, 162.

74. For good discussions of public and private interest groups involved in the health care field and the techniques they use to influence health care politics and policies, see Paul D. Ward, "Health Lobbies," 28–47; Paul J. Feldstein, "Health Associations and the Legislative Process," 223–42.

75. *Encyclopedia of Associations 1991*, 25th ed., Gale Research, New York, 1990.

76. Jane H. Bayes, *Ideologies and Interest-Group Politics*, 222.

77. Reported in Lynn Wagner, "Health PACs Modest Donors—Study," 4.

78. Charles R. Babcock, "Health Care Fears Open Up the Pocketbooks," *Washington Post National Weekly Edition*, June 7–13, 1993, 14.

79. Dwight L. Wilbur, "The AMA in Washington," in Douglas Carter and Philip R. Lee, eds., *Politics of Health*, 48–60.

80. Foundation for Public Affairs, *Public Interest Profiles 1988–1989*, 302.

81. Frank D. Campion, *The AMA and U.S. Health Policy Since 1940*, 45–47.

82. Babcock, "Health Care Fears Open Up the Pocketbooks."

83. Stanley and Niemi, *Vital Statistics on American Politics*, 165.

84. Babcock, "Health Care Fears Open Up the Pocketbooks."

85. Lewis E. Weeks and Howard J. Berman, *Shapers of American Health Care Policy*, 195.

86. *Encyclopedia of Associations 1991*, 1414.

87. Cynthia Wallace, "Hospital PACs Ring Up More Clout," 52.

88. Clark C. Havighurst, "The Questionable Cost-Containment Record of Commercial Health Insurers," 243–45.

89. Ibid., 255.

90. Health Insurance Association of America, *Source Book of Health Insurance Data*, Health Insurance Institute, New York, 1991, 23.

91. Ibid., 1469.

92. Allen S. Meyerhoff and David A. Crozier, "Health Care Coalitions," 120.

93. Julie Kosterlitz, "Softening Resistance," 66.

94. Foundation for Public Affairs, *Public Interest Profiles 1988–1989*, 333–35.

95. Ibid., 343–45.

Chapter 2. Health Care Policy in the United States

1. "A Survey of Health Care," 4–5.

2. Ibid. Also see Craig R. Whitney, "British Health Service, Much Beloved but Inadequate, Is Facing Changes," *New York Times*, June 9, 1991; Philip J. Hilts, "Demands to Fix U.S. Health Care Reach a Crescendo," *New York Times*, May 19, 1991.

3. "A Survey of Health Care," 2–3.

4. Philip J. Hilts, "Many Leave Emergency Room Needing Care," *New York Times*, August 27, 1991; David W. Baker, Carl D. Stevens, and Robert H. Brook, "Patients

Who Leave a Public Hospital Emergency Department without Being Seen by a Physician," 1085–1090; Andrew Bindman et al., "Consequences of Queuing for Care at a Public Hospital Emergency Department," 1091–1096.

5. Lisa Belkin, "Hospitals Sacked, a Report Asserts," *New York Times*, October 22, 1991.

6. Robert Pear, "Health Clinics Cut Services As Cost of Insurance Soars," *New York Times*, August 21, 1991.

7. Peter Kerr, "Chain of Mental Hospitals Faces Inquiry in Four States," *New York Times*, October 22, 1991.

8. "The Health Care System Is Broken and Here Is How to Fix It," *New York Times*, July 22, 1991.

9. Anthony Lewis, "A Sick System," *New York Times*, June 3, 1991.

10. Barbara Ehrenreich, "Our Health-Care Disgrace," *Time*, December 10, 1990, 112.

11. Milton Terris, "A Wasteful System That Doesn't Work," 14–16.

12. Humphrey Taylor, "U.S. Health Care: Built for Waste," *New York Times*, April 17, 1990.

13. Susan Dentzer, "America's Scandalous Health Care," *U.S. News and World Report*, March 12, 1990, 25–30.

14. Erik Eckholm, "Rescuing Health Care," *New York Times*, May 2, 1991.

15. Lister Hill, "Health in America," 4–5.

16. Odin W. Anderson, *Health Services in the United States*, 13–15.

17. Milton I. Roemer, *An Introduction to the U.S. Health Care System*, 2d ed., 50–51.

18. Marshall W. Raffel, *The U.S. Health System*, 534.

19. U.S. Health Resource Administration, *Health in America: 1776–1976*, U.S. Department of Health, Education, and Welfare, Rockville, MD, 1976), 69–79.

20. Anderson, *Health Services in the United States*, 14.

21. Daniel M. Fox, *Health Policies, Health Politics*, 39.

22. Paul Starr, *The Social Transformation of American Medicine*, 117–18.

23. Ibid., 120–23.

24. Ibid., 237.

25. Milton I. Roemer, "The Politics of Public Health in the United States," 264.

26. Merton C. Bernstein and Joan Broadshaug Bernstein, *Social Security*, 253–54.

27. Gregg Easterbrook, "The Revolution in Medicine," *Newsweek*, January 26, 1987, 43.

28. Robert B. Greifinger and Victor William Sidel, "Three Centuries of Medical Care," 22–23.

29. Roemer, *Introduction to the U.S. Health Care System*, 57.

30. Starr, *Social Transformation of American Medicine*, 281.

31. Bernstein and Bernstein, *Social Security*, 256.

32. Rosemary Stevens, *In Sickness and in Wealth*, 229.

33. Bernstein and Bernstein, *Social Security*, 259.

34. U.S. Department of Health, Education, and Welfare, *Health in America: 1776 –1976*, 124–25.

35. Rashi Fein, *Medical Care, Medical Costs*, 60–61.

36. Sheri I. David, *With Dignity*, 90.

37. Ibid., 105.

38. For an excellent examination of the rhetorical debate over the issue of Medicare, see Max J. Skidmore, *Medicare and the American Rhetoric of Reconciliation*.

39. Helen Darling, "The Role of the Federal Government in Assuring Access to Health Care," 286.

40. Stephen H. Long and Russell F. Settle, "Medicare and the Disadvantaged Elderly," 644.

41. Henry J. Aaron, *Serious and Unstable Condition*, 61.

42. Lawrence D. Brown, "Introduction to a Decade of Transition," 572.

43. Katharine R. Levit et al., "National Health Expenditures, 1993," 285.

44. Ibid.

45. Richard M. Nixon, "Message to Congress."

46. Senator Edward M. Kennedy, remarks on introducing the Health Security Act (Senate Bill No. 3), 92d Cong., 1st sess., *Congressional Record*, January 25, 1971, 284.

47. Jonas Norris, *Searching for a Cure*, 61.

48. Ibid., 71–72. See also Joseph L. Falkson, *HMOs and the Politics of Health Service Reform*.

49. Starr, *Social Transformation of American Medicine*, 411.

50. For a more detailed and systematic analysis of the first two years of the Reagan administration's initiatives in the health area, see Lynn Etheredge, "Reagan, Congress, and Health Spending," 14–24.

51. Thomas Rice, Katherine Desmond, and Jon Gable, "The Medicare Catastrophic Coverage Act," 76.

52. Thomas Rice and Jon Gable, "Protecting the Elderly against High Health Care Costs," 5.

53. Thomas Rice, Katherine Desmond, and Jon Gable, "The Medicare Catastrophic Coverage Act," 76.

54. Michael Wines, "Bush Announces Health Plan, Filling Gap in Re-Election Bid," *New York Times*, February 7, 1992.

55. White House Domestic Policy Council, *The President's Health Security Act*, 21–22.

56. Adam Clymer, "Clinton Asks Backing for Sweeping Change in the Health System," *New York Times*, September 23, 1993.

57. James Fallows, "A Triumph of Misinformation"; Paul Starr, "What Happened to Health Care Reform?" 20–31; Richard Morin, "A Health Care Reform Post-Mortem," *Washington Post National Weekly Edition*, September 12–18, 1994, 37.

58. For more academic analysis of the failure of health care reform, see: David W. Brady and Kara M. Buckley, "Health Care Reform in the 103d Congress"; Mollyann Brodie and Robert J. Blendon, "The Public's Contribution to Congressional Gridlock on Health Care Reform"; John P. Canaham-Clyne, "The Health Care Debacle"; Lawrence R. Jacobs and Robert Y. Shapiro, "Don't Blame the Public for Failed Health Care Reform"; Vicente Navarro, "Why Congress Did Not Enact Health Care Reform"; Kant Patel and Mark Rushefsky, "Health Policy Community and Health Care Reform"; Sven Steinmo and Jon Watts, "It's the Institutions, Stupid!"; John W. Thomas, "The Clinton Health Care Reform Plan."

59. Dan Balz and Ronald J. Brownstein, *Storming the Gates*.

60. Ibid.

61. John K. Iglehart, "Health Policy Report," 972–75.

62. "Kassebaum-Kennedy Health Insurance Bill Clears Congress," 1996.

63. Congressional Budget Office, "Expanding Health Insurance Coverage for Children under Title XXI of the Social Security Act."

64. John T. Hanlon and George E. Picker, *Public Health*, 23.

65. Philip R. Lee and Carroll L. Estes, "New Federalism and Health Policy," 93.

66. David L. Rosenbloom, "New Ways to Keep Old Promises in Health Care," 50.

67. Bayless Manning and Bruce Vladeck, "The Role of State and Local Government in Health," 134.

68. Drew E. Altman and Douglas H. Morgan, "The Role of the State and Local Government in Health," 13–14.

69. Rosenbloom, "New Ways to Keep Old Promises in Health Care," 45.

70. Richard P. Nathan et al., "Initial Effects of the Fiscal Year 1982 Reductions in Federal Domestic Spending," 315–49.

71. Frank J. Thompson, "New Federalism and Health Care Policy," 665–66.

72. Lee and Estes, "New Federalism and Health Policy," 90.

73. Joseph P. Shapiro, "How States Cook the Books," *U.S. News and World Report*, July 29, 1991, 24–25.

74. Robert Pear, "U.S. Moves to Curb Medicaid Payments for Many States," *New York Times*, September 11, 1991.

75. Rick Curtis, "The Role of the State Government in Assuring Access to Care," 277–78.

76. See John F. Holahan and Joel W. Cohen, *Medicaid*.

77. Darling, "The Role of the Federal Government," 289.

78. Michael Specter, "Putting Michigan Hospitals on the Critical Care List," *Washington Post Weekly Edition*, June 4–10, 1990, 33; Patricia King, "The City as a Patient," *Newsweek*, February 19, 1990, 58–59; Melinda Beck, Daniel Glick, Nadine Joseph, and Peter Katel, "State of Emergency," *Newsweek*, October 14, 1991, 52–53.

79. David Mechanic, "Some Dilemmas in Health Care Policy," 8.

80. Starr, *Social Transformation of American Medicine*, 419.

Chapter 3. Medicaid: Health Care for the Poor

1. Paul B. Ginsburg, "Public Insurance Programs," 181.

2. Paul Starr, *The Social Transformation of American Medicine*, 368.

3. Karen Davis and Roger Reynolds, *The Impact of Medicare and Medicaid on Access to Medical Care*, 391.

4. Thomas W. Grannemann and Mark V. Pauly, *Controlling Medicaid Costs*, 5.

5. E. Richard Brown, "Medicare and Medicaid: Band-Aids for the Old and Poor," 60–61.

6. Starr, *Social Transformation of American Medicine*, 370.

7. Saundra K. Schneider, "Intergovernmental Influences on Medicaid Program Expenditures," 756.

8. Brown, "Medicare and Medicaid," 61.

9. Grannemann and Pauly, *Controlling Medicaid Costs*, 6.

10. Paul B. Ginsburg, "Public Insurance Programs," 183–86.

11. Saundra K. Schneider, "Intergovernmental Influences on Medicaid Program Expenditures," 757.

12. John F. Holahan and Joel W. Cohen, *Medicaid*, 9–10.

13. Suzanne W. Letsch et al., "National Health Expenditures, 1991," 13.

14. Michael Specter, "Medicaid's Crazy Quilt of Care," *Washington Post National Weekly Edition*, August 26–September 1, 1991, 33.

15. Schneider, "Intergovernmental Influences on Medicaid Program Expenditures," 757.

16. John Holahan and David Liska, "The Slowdown in Medicaid Spending Growth," 157–63.

17. Robert J. Samuelson, "Medicaid Monster," *Washington Post National Weekly Edition*, May 12–26, 1991, 29.

18. Ginsburg, "Public Insurance Programs," 190.

19. Karen Davis et al., *Health Care Cost Containment*, 75–78.

20. Letsch et al., "National Health Expenditures, 1991," 13.

21. Health Care Financing Review, *Medicare and Medicaid Statistical Supplement*, 1997, 205.

22. Ibid.

23. Ibid.

24. Holahan and Cohen, *Medicaid*, 10.

25. Katharine R. Levit et al., "National Health Expenditures, 1993," 288.

26. Drew E. Altman, "Health Care for the Poor," 112–13.

27. George Gross, "Reagan's 'Bold' Aid Reform," 1.

28. Fred Jordan, "Governors OK Alternative Plan on Federalism," 1.

29. David L. Barnett, "Reagan's Bold New Blueprint," *U.S. News and World Report*, February 8, 1982, 20.

30. Ed Magnuson, "New Federalism or Feudalism?" *Time*, February 8, 1982, 19.

31. Philip R. Lee and Carroll L. Estes, "New Federalism and Health Policy," 100.

32. Lynn Wagner, "Access for All People," 28.

33. Ibid.

34. Julie Kosterlitz, "Middle-Class Medicaid," 2728–2731.

35. Lee and Estes, "New Federalism and Health Policy," 100.

36. For a detailed analysis of the evolution of health care policy and its implications for federalism, see Frank J. Thompson, "New Federalism and Health Care Policy," 647–69; also see Lee and Estes, "New Federalism and Health Policy," 88–102.

37. Lynn Wagner, "28 States Face Potential Deficits," 2.

38. General Accounting Office, *Medicaid Expansions*.

39. Joseph P. Shapiro, "How States Cook the Books," *U.S. News and World Report*, July 29, 1991, 24–25. William Tucker, "A Leak in Medicaid," 46–48.

40. Ibid., 48.

41. Robert Pear, "U.S. Moves to Curb Medicaid Payments for Many States," *New York Times*, September 11, 1991.

42. Terese Hudson, "States Scramble for Solutions under New Medicaid Law," 52–56.

43. Frank J. Thompson, "The Faces of Devolution," 39.

44. "HCFA, States Spar—Again—over Medicaid Provider Taxes," *State Health Notes* 16, no. 200 (March 20, 1995): 1–3; Dan Morgan, "Medicaid Bills Come Home to Roost," *Washington Post National Weekly Edition*, February 6–12, 1995, 32.

45. David Durda, "Number of Medicaid Lawsuits Belies Complexities Involved in Such Filings," 31–32.

46. Robert Pear, "Ruling May Lead to Big Rise in States' Medicaid Costs," *New York Times*, July 5, 1990.

47. Ibid.

48. Robert Pear, "Suits Force U.S. and States to Pay More for Medicaid," *New York Times*, October 29, 1991.

49. Levit et al., "National Health Expenditures, 1993," 290–91.

50. Thompson, "The Faces of Devolution," 14–55.

51. Thomas L. Friedman, "Clinton Allowing States Flexibility on Medicaid Funds," *New York Times*, February 2, 1993.

52. Joycelyn Guyer, "States' Options for Implementing Medicaid Managed Care."

53. Ibid.

54. Ibid.

55. Sylvia Fubini, "Medicaid under Welfare Reform," 1.

56. J. Koppelman, "Impact of the New Welfare Law on Medicaid."

57. E. Graham, "Generation Y: When Terrible Twos Become Terrible Teens," *Wall Street Journal*.

58. Congressional Budget Office, "Expanding Health Insurance Coverage for Children under Title XXI of the Social Security Act."

59. Kant Patel, "Medicaid: Perspectives from the States."

60. Mark R. Daniels, ed., *Medicaid Reform and the American States.*

61. Drew E. Altman and Douglas H. Morgan, "The Role of State and Local Government in Health," 26.

62. Drew E. Altman, "Health Care for the Poor," 115.

63. Ibid.

64. Randall R. Bovbjerg and John Holahan, *Medicaid in the Reagan Era,* 30–31.

65. Holahan and Cohen, *Medicaid,* 99.

66. For a detailed look at how different states are tightening eligibility standards and cutting benefits, see Kathryn Johnson, "Major Surgery for Ailing Medicaid Program," *U.S. News and World Report,* October 17, 1983, 91–93.

67. Ibid.

68. Joseph Newhouse et al., "Some Interim Results from a Controlled Trial of Cost Sharing in Health Insurance," 1501–1507.

69. John Holahan, "The Impact of Alternative Hospital Payment Systems on Medicaid Costs," 519–20.

70. Ronald J. Vogel, "An Analysis of Structural Incentives in the Arizona Health Care Cost-Containment System," 14.

71. Jeffrey S. McCombs and Jon B. Christianson, "Applying Competitive Bidding to Health Care," 703–21.

72. Howard E. Freeman and Bradford L. Kirkman-Liff, "Health Care under AHCCCS," 245–66.

73. Mary Wagner, "Colorado Considers Establishing Its Own Health Plan for Needy," 5.

74. Julie Kosterlitz, "Rationing Health Care," 1590–1595.

75. William B. Schwartz and Henry J. Aaron, "The Achilles Heel of Health Care Rationing," 15; William B. Schwartz and Henry J. Aaron, *Health Care Costs.*

76. Susan S. Laudicina and Brian Burwell, "Profile of Medicaid Home and Community-Based Care Waivers," 528–29.

77. Ibid., 544.

78. Rosemary G. Kern and Susan R. Windham, with Paula Griswold, *Medicaid and Other Experiments in State Health Policy,* 54.

79. Frank Sloan, Janet Mitchell, and Jerry Cromwell, "Physician Participation in State Medicaid Programs," 211–45.

80. Bovbjerg and Holahan, *Medicaid in the Reagan Era,* 41.

81. Thomas W. Grannemann and Mark V. Pauly, *Controlling Medicaid Costs,* 71.

82. John Holahan, "Impact of Alternative Hospital Payment Systems on Medicaid Costs," 517.

83. David A. Crozier, "State Rate Setting," 66–83.

84. Craig Coelen and Daniel Sullivan, "An Analysis of the Effects of Prospective Reimbursement Programs on Hospital Expenditures," 1.

85. Holahan, "Impact of Alternative Hospital Payment Systems on Medicaid Costs," 531–32.

86. Karen Davis et al., *Health Care Cost Containment,* 85.

87. George Anders, "Many States Embrace Managed Care System for Medicaid Patients," *Wall Street Journal,* June 11, 1993.

88. General Accounting Office, *Medicaid,* 4.

89. Joycelyn Guyer, "States' Options for Implementing Medicaid Managed Care."

90. Ibid.

91. Michael S. Sparer, "Devolution of Power," 9.

92. Reported in Anders, "Many States Embrace Managed Care System for Medicaid Patients."

93. Ronda Kotelchuck, "Medicaid Managed Care: A Mixed Review," 4–11; Deborah A. Freund et al., "Evaluation of the Medicaid Competition Demonstrations," 81; Maren D. Anderson and Peter D. Fox, "Lessons Learned from Medicaid Managed Care Approaches," 80.

94. General Accounting Office, *Medicaid*, 4.

95. John Holahan et al., "Medicaid Managed Care in Thirteen States," 43.

96. Sparer, "Devolution of Power," 10.

97. Anders, "Many States Embrace Managed Care System for Medicaid Patients."

98. Samuel S. Flint, "Insuring Children," 79–81.

99. For detailed analysis of program features, see Sara Rosenbaum et al., "The Children's Hour."

100. Children's Defense Fund, "States Should Consider Building on Medicaid"; Congressional Budget Office, "Expanding Health Insurance Coverage for Children under Title XXI of the Social Security Act."

101. Alan Weil, "The New Children's Health Insurance Program."

102. Health Care Financing Administration, "Child Health Insurance Program: State Plans."

103. Donald P. Baker, "Squeezing through the Loophole in the Medicaid Law," *Washington Post National Weekly Edition*, March 2–8, 1992, 34.

104. Kosterlitz, "Middle-Class Medicaid," 2728–2731.

105. Baker, "Squeezing through the Loophole in the Medicaid Law," 34.

106. Kosterlitz, "Middle-Class Medicaid," 2728–2731.

107. "Congress Says Some Medicaid Planning Is a Federal Crime."

108. Institute of Continuing Legal Education, "Balanced Budget Act Targets Medicaid Planning Advice."

109. Teresa A. Coughlin, *Medicaid Since 1980*; Intergovernmental Health Policy Project, *Expanding Access to Health Care*.

110. Deborah Stone, "Why States Can't Solve the Health Care Crisis," 51–60.

Chapter 4. Medicare: Health Care for the Elderly and Disabled

1. John C. Rother, "A Medicare in the 21st Century," 1.

2. Paul Starr, *The Social Transformation of American Medicine*, 266–70; Theodore Marmor, *The Politics of Medicare*, 8–9.

3. Marmor, *The Politics of Medicare*, 10–11.

4. Ibid., 15–20.

5. Ibid., 20.

6. For a thorough discussion of how health policy promised not to interfere with the practice of medicine, see Elliot A. Krause, *Power and Illness*.

7. Marmor, *Politics of Medicare*, 23.

8. Starr, *Social Transformation of American Medicine*, 369.

9. This social insurance strategy, as described in Medicare, was a continuation of that initially incorporated into Social Security. The idea was that the program would be so popular, and everyone would have such an interest in it, that it would survive attack. That politically astute strategy seems to have worked well for both programs, though, as we discuss later in conjunction with the Balanced Budget Act of 1997, the consensus surrounding Medicare has unraveled.

10. Frank J. Thompson, *Health Policy and the Bureaucracy*, 155.

358   NOTES TO CHAPTER 4

11. Number calculated from U.S. Bureau of the Census, *Statistical Abstract of the United States 1966*, 72.

12. U.S. Bureau of the Census, *Statistical Abstract of the United States, 1997*.

13. John T. Petrie, "Overview of the Medicare Program," 1–14.

14. The Medicare Hospital Insurance tax is listed separately from the FICA tax on pay stubs.

15. Health Care Financing Administration, "Medicare, Deductible, Coinsurance and Premium Amounts (1998)." *Federal Register* 62, no. 212 (November 3, 1997), 59365–59366. This information comes from the HCFA Internet site: http://www.hcfa.gov/stats/mdedco98.htm.

16. Calculated from "Medicare and Medicaid: Statistical Supplement, 1997," *Health Care Financing Review*, 24, no. 16, 422–23, table 6.

17. Health Care Financing Administration, "Medicare, Deductible, Coinsurance and Premium Amounts (1998)."

18. The percentages are not pulled out of a hat. Medicare pays about 71 percent of private sector charges. Marilyn Moon, *Medicare Now and in the Future*, 77.

19. Ibid., 40.

20. Ibid., 10.

21. McCormack et al., "Medigap Reform Legislation of 1990," 158.

22. Health Care Financing Administration, "Medicare and Medicaid Statistical Supplement, 1997," 31. The percentage is calculated. Note that in 1991, the percentage was 11.8 percent of Medicare recipients, which indicates some increasing distress or poverty among the elderly. Katie Merrell, David C. Colby, and Christopher Hogan, "Medicare Beneficiaries Covered by Medicaid Buy-In Agreements."

23. Ibid., 177.

24. Ibid.

25. Ibid.

26. U.S. Bureau of the Census, *Statistical Abstract of the United States, 1992*, 105. See also McCormack et al., "Medigap Reform Legislation of 1990," 158.

27. Moon, *Medicare Now and in the Future*, 10–12.

28. Pamela Farley Short and Jessica Primoff Vistnes, "Multiple Sources of Medicare Supplementary Insurance," 42.

29. Ibid., 42–43.

30. OBRA was part of the deal between Congress and President Bush to reduce the budget deficit by about $500 billion over a five-year period.

31. Short and Vistnes, "Multiple Sources of Medicare Supplementary Insurance," 34.

32. Thomas Rice and Kathleen Thomas, "Evaluating the New Medigap Standardization Regulations," 194–207.

33. Ibid.

34. "Filling the Gaps in Medicare," *Consumer Reports*, August 1994, 524.

35. Ibid., 524–25.

36. Ibid., 526.

37. Rice and Thomas, "Evaluating the New Medigap Standardization Regulations." See also Peter D. Fox, Thomas Rice, and Lisa Alecxih, "Medigap Regulations," 31–48; and McCormack et al., "Medigap Reform Legislation of 1990."

38. Short and Vistnes, "Multiple Sources of Medicare Supplementary Insurance," 33.

39. McCormack et al., "Medigap Reform Legislation of 1990," 172.

40. Ibid., 173.

41. Ibid.

42. Geraldine Dallek, *The Crushing Costs of Medicare Supplemental Policies*.

43. Ibid.

44. Randall S. Brown et al., "Do Health Maintenance Organizations Work for Medicare?" 7–23.

45. Milt Freudenheim, "Medicare H.M.O.'s to Trim Benefits for the Elderly," *New York Times*, December 2, 1997.

46. There are three types of HMOs that Medicare recipients could enroll in prior to the implementation of the Medicare provisions of the 1997 Balanced Budget Act. By far the most numerous were the risk-based plans. These HMOs provided the Medicare services based on 95 percent of average Medicare recipient costs. In a second type, a cost-based plan, the HMO is reimbursed by Medicare for actual services given. The third type, also a cost-based plan, covered only Part B services on a prepayment basis. Outside the Medicare population, HMOs are entirely risk based. Congressional Budget Office, *Predicting How Changes in Medicare's Payment Rates Would Affect Risk Sector Enrollment and Costs*, 1.

47. Numbers based on the following sources: Health Care Financing Administration, "Medicare and Medicaid Statistical Supplement, 1997," 23; U.S. Bureau of the Census, *Statistical Abstract of the United States*, 1997, 121; Jo Ann Lamphere et al., "Surge in Medicare Managed Care," 128.

48. Lamphere et al., "Surge in Medicare Managed Care."

49. Brown et al., "Do Health Maintenance Organizations Work for Medicare?"

50. Ibid., 10. See also Congressional Budget Office, *Predicting How Changes in Medicare's Payment Rates Would Affect Risk Sector Enrollment and Costs*, 9–12; and Jonathan B. Oberlander, "Managed Care and Medicare Reform." For a discussion of alternative managed care payment methods, see Joseph P. Newhouse, Melinda Beeuwkes Buntin, and John D. Chapman (1997), "A Risk Adjustment and Medicare."

51. Congressional Budget Office, *Predicting How Changes in Medicare's Payment Rates Would Affect Risk Sector Enrollment and Costs*, 14.

52. Oberlander, "Managed Care and Medicare Reform."

53. Brown et al., "Do Health Maintenance Organizations Work for Medicare?" 14–15.

54. Lyle Nelson, "Access to Care in Medicare HMOs, 1996."

55. Ibid., 151–52.

56. Cynthia G. Tudor, Gerald F. Riley, and Melvin J. Ingber, "Satisfaction with Care."

57. Gerald F. Riley, Melvin J. Ingber, and Cynthia G. Tudor. "Disenrollment of Medicare Beneficiaries from HMOs."

58. Marsha Gold et al., "Disabled Medicare Beneficiaries in HMOs."

59. Claudia L. Schur, Marc L. Berk, and Penny Mohr, "Understanding the Cost of a Catastrophic Drug Benefit," 90.

60. Marilyn Moon, *Medicare Now and in the Future*, 110–11.

61. Ibid.

62. Description of the benefits comes from ibid., 116–17.

63. Ibid., 118–19. The reason for the delay in benefits was to build up a reserve to begin paying for them. The precedent for this is the original Social Security Act of 1935. Payments into the trust fund began in 1936, but the first Social Security checks did not begin until 1940.

64. Ibid., 121.

65. Ibid., 121–23.

66. Thomas Rice, Katherine Desmond, and Jon Gabel, "The Medicare Catastrophic Coverage Act," 75–87.

67. Moon, *Medicare Now and in the Future*, 124–27.

68. See Judith M. Feder, *Medicare*; and Frank J. Thompson, *Health Policy and the Bureaucracy*.

69. Katharine R. Levit et al., "DataView."

70. John T. Petrie and Herbert A. Silverman, "Medicare Enrollment," *Health Care Financing Review*, 1992 Annual Supplement, 14.

71. Calculated from Health Care Financing Administration, "Medicare and Medicaid Statistical Supplement, 1995," 54.

72. Calculated from Health Care Financing Administration, "Medicare and Medicaid Statistical Supplement, 1997," 44–45.

73. Feder, *Medicare*, 1.

74. Theodore R. Marmor, Donald A. Wittman, and Thomas C. Heagy, "The Politics of Medical Inflation," 61–75.

75. Calculated from U.S. Bureau of the Census, *Statistical Abstract of the United States, 1997*, 332, 334.

76. Marmor's theory would work best under a system of national health insurance. This is undoubtedly one reason providers have long opposed such programs in the United States.

77. Bruce Steunwald and Frank A. Sloan, "Regulatory Approaches to Hospital Cost Containment," 276.

78. Paul L. Joskow, "Alternative Regulatory Mechanism for Controlling Hospital Costs," 219–57.

79. For a detailed discussion and analysis of the all-payer DRG system in New Jersey, see *Bulletin of the New York Academy of Medicine* 62, no. 6 (July/August 1986). The entire issue is devoted to the discussion of New Jersey's DRG system.

80. For an excellent analysis of the political process through which the DRG system was initiated first in New Jersey and then at the federal level, see James A. Morone and Andrew B. Dunham, "Slouching toward National Health Insurance," 646–62.

81. Franklin A. Shaffer, "DRGs," 389.

82. Bruce C. Vladeck, "Comment on Hospital Reimbursement under Medicare," 269.

83. D.A. Dolnec and C.J. Dougherty, "DRGs," 19–29.

84. Calculated from Moon, *Medicare Now and in the Future*, 38; and "A Medicare and Medicaid Statistical Supplement, 1997," 28, 37.

85. Levit et al., "Data View," calculated from 205, 207.

86. Thomas R. Oliver, "Analysis, Advice, and Congressional Leadership," 120.

87. Gornick notes that the Medicare fee schedule was part of a stream of reforms that began in 1975 with the creation of an economic index to limit changes in physician charges. See Marian Gornick, "Physician Payment Reform under Medicare," 79–80.

88. Moon, *Medicare Now and in the Future*, 69–72.

89. Ibid., 73.

90. Ibid., 74–75.

91. Oliver, "Analysis, Advice, and Congressional Leadership," 165–68.

92. "Victory: Family Physicians Make Gains in Medicare Fee Schedule," *AAFD Directors' Newsletter*, November 13, 1997. http://www.aafp.org/dn;/971113dl/2.html.

93. See Physician Payment Review Commission, "A New Law Changes Practice Expense."

94. Joshua M. Weiner and Laurel Hixon Illston, "How to Share the Burden," 17.

95. Wendy Fox-Grage, *The Task Force Report*.

96. The 1970–1995 figures are calculated from Levit et al., "Data View," 201.

97. Ibid., 208.

98. Feder and Lambrew argue that Medicare is still important to people who need long-term care services. See Judith Feder and Jeanne Lambrew, "Why Medicare Matters to People Who Need Long-Term Care."

99. Ibid.

100. Ibid., 192, 203.

101. Jane L. Ross, "Long-Term Care," 1.

102. Ibid.

103. Wiener and Illston, "How to Share the Burden," 17.

104. Bruce C. Vladeck, Nancy A. Miller, and Steven B. Clauser, "The Changing Face of Long-Term Care," 8, 10.

105. See the discussion in the statement of William J. Scanlon of the General Accounting Office before the U.S. Senate Special Committee on Aging in *Long-Term Care: Baby Boom Generation Presents Financing Challenges*, U.S. General Accounting Office, Washington, D.C., March 9, 1998.

106. Joshua M. Weiner and David G. Stevenson, *Long-Term Care of the Elderly and State Health Policy*.

107. Esther B. Fein, "Elderly Transfer Assets to Qualify for Medicaid," *New York Times*, September 25, 1994.

108. Penelope Lemov, "Nursing Homes and Common Sense," 45–46.

109. General Accounting Office, *Long-Term Care: Private Sector Elder Care Could Yield Multiple Benefits*.

110. Ibid., 5–10.

111. Moon, *Medicare Now and in the Future*, 79.

112. General Accounting Office, *Medicare*.

113. Ibid., 2.

114. Ibid., 25–26.

115. General Accounting Office, *Medicare Home Health Agencies*. Both Congress and Medicare have begun to address the problem. See statement of Laura A. Dummit before the House Subcommittee on Oversight and Investigations, Committee on Commerce, March 19, 1998, "Medicare Home Health Benefit: Congressional and HCFA Actions Begin to Address Chronic Oversight Weaknesses."

116. See Douglas Frantz, "Hospice Boom Is Giving Rise to New Fraud," *New York Times*, May 10, 1998.

117. See Robert Pear, "Ambulances Overbill U.S., Report Shows," *New York Times*, November 9, 1997; and Kurt Eichenwald, "U.S. Contends Billing Fraud at Columbia Was 'Systematic,'" *New York Times*, October 7, 1997.

118. Marilyn Werber Serafini, "Medicare Crooks," *National Journal*, July 19, 1997, 1458–1460.

119. Robert Pear, "Citing Fraud in Home Care, Clinton Halts New Permits," *New York Times*, September 16, 1997.

120. Don McLeod, "Home-Care Patients Feel Unfairly Targeted," *AARP Bulletin* 39, no. 4 (April 1998): 1, 8–9.

121. Testimony of Janet L. Shikles, Director, Health Financing and Policy Issues, Human Resources Division, in General Accounting Office, "Long-Term Care Insurance: Risks to Consumers Should Be Reduced," 2–3.

122. Cited in Thomas Rice, Kathleen Thomas, and William Weissert, *The Impact of Owning Private Long-Term Care Insurance Policies on Out-of-Pocket Costs*, 7; and Joshua M. Wiener and David G. Stevenson, *Long-Term Care for the Elderly and State Health Policy*.

123. Wiener and Illston, "How to Share the Burden," 18.

124. For an analysis of state variations in long-term care spending, see Robert L. Kane et al. (1998), "Variation in State Spending for Long-Term Care."

125. Joshua Perin, "Long-Term Care Insurance," 4.

126. Ibid.

127. See Fox-Grage, *Task Force Report*, 25–43; and Joshua M. Wiener and David G. Stevenson, "State Policy on Long-Term Care for the Elderly."

128. William G. Wissert et al., "Cost Savings from Home and Community-Based Services."

129. Sharon M. Keigher, "Health Care Reform and Long-Term Care," 224–25.

130. Ibid., 224. See also: Kaiser Commission on the Future of Medicaid, *Health Reform Legislation*, Joseph F. Delfico, testimony before the Subcommittee on Aging, Committee on Labor and Human Resources, U.S. Senate, *Long-Term Reform: Program Eligibility, States' Service Capacity, and Federal Role in Reform Need More Consideration* (General Accounting Office, April 14, 1994); and Mark V. Nadel, testimony before the Subcommittees on Health and the Environment and on Commerce, Consumer Protection, and Competitiveness, Committee on Energy and Commerce, U.S. House of Representatives, *Health Care Reform: Supplemental and Long-Term Care Insurance* (General Accounting Office, September 9, 1993).

131. Keigher, "Health Care Reform and Long-Term Care," 224; Kaiser Commission on the Future of Medicaid, *Health Reform Legislation*.

132. Spencer Rich, "For the Elderly, A Promise of More Social Security and Less Taxation," *Washington Post National Weekly Edition*, December 26, 1994–January 1, 1995, 10.

133. In 1994, Vermont considered financing long-term care through a social insurance model. See Linda E. Demkovich, "Vermont Takes on LTC Financing," 1–2, 8.

134. Joshua M. Weiner and Laurel Hixson Illston, "How to Share the Burden," 19–21. See also Marilyn Moon and Janemarie Mulvey, *Entitlements and the Elderly*.

135. Robert Pear, "Health Insurance is G.O.P. Initiative for Election Year," *New York Times*, March 30, 1998.

136. Nicholas Laham, *A Lost Cause*; and Jeff Shear, "The Big Fix."

137. For a thorough discussion of the 1995–1996 budget battle between Congress and President Clinton, see Mark E. Rushefsky and Kant Patel, *Politics, Power and Policy Making*, esp. chap. 4.

138. For a critique of the notion that Medicare needed "saving," see Joseph White, "'Saving' Medicare—From What?"

139. Marilyn Moon, Barbara Gage, and Alison Evans, *An Examination of Key Medicare Provisions in the Balanced Budget Act of 1997*. http://www.urban.org/entitlements/moonfinal.htm. This is the source of all the numbers in the two paragraphs below.

140. Amy Goldstein, "Medicare Recipients to Face a Dizzying Array of Choices," *Washington Post*, August 18, 1997; and Marilyn Werber Serafini, "Brave New World."

141. Milt Freudenheim, "Medicare H.M.O.'s to Trim Benefits for the Elderly," *New York Times*, December 22, 1997.

142. "Medicare Privatization B The Issue in Brief," *Senior News Network*, January 1998. http://www.seniornews.com/senior-beacon/article639.html.

143. "Medicare Privatization"; Marilyn Werber Serafini, "A Return to Medi-Scare Tactics?"

144. Serafini, "A Return to Medi-Scare Tactics?"

145. Lori McGuire, "Do Not Let Government Steal Your Health Care Rights," *Springfield News-Leader*, October 19, 1997. See also Kent Masterson Brown, "Want to Pay for Something Medicare Doesn't Cover? Forget it?" *Wall Street Journal*, October 1, 1997.

146. McGuire, "Do Not Let Government Steal Your Health Care Rights."

147. See National Senior Citizens Law Center, "The Truth about the New Medicare Private Contract Provisions." http://www.nsclc.org.kyl.factsheet.html. See also

Mary Beth Franklin, "Uproar over Medicare Payments," *Washington Post*, January 13, 1998.

148. Robert Pear, "New Flexibility, but at a Price," *New York Times*, August 5, 1997.

149. See Robert Pear, "Wrangling Stalls Selection of Medicare Panel," *New York Times*, December 3, 1997; Alexis Simendinger, "Another Problem, Another Commission," *National Journal* 29, no. 50 (December 13, 1997): 2514–2515; David Rosenbaum, "Medicare in a Quandary," *New York Times*, December 6, 1997; Marilyn Werber Serafini, "The Deal Maker," *National Journal* 30, no. 7 (February 14, 1998): 332–37; and Robert Pear, "Study Panel on Medicare Begins Work, in Conflict," *New York Times*, March 7, 1998.

150. Robert Pear, "Clinton Pushes Medicare Plan for Millions Ages 55 to 64," *New York Times*, March 18, 1998.

151. Robert Kuttner, "Medicare Extension a Step in the Right Direction."

152. Allison Mitchell, "Clinton Plan on Medicare Is Opposed," *New York Times*, March 19, 1998.

153. Health Insurance Association of America, "Response to Democrats' Medicare Buy-In Bill." See also Robert Pear, "Clinton Plan to Widen Medicare Can't Pay for Itself," *New York Times*, January 20, 1998.

154. Robert Pear, "Clinton Is Urged to Defer a Plan to Increase Medicare Eligibility," *New York Times*, March 3, 1998.

155. Marilyn Werber Serafini, "Insuring Early Retirees," *New York Times*, March 14, 1998.

156. Marilyn Moon, "Ensuring a Future for Medicare."

157. Jane Bryant Quinn, "Medicare for Boomers." See also Jane Bryant Quinn, "Reinventing Medicare."

158. Madelyn Hochstein, "American Attitudes and Values Regarding Medicare."

159. Richard W Stevenson, "Surging Economy Lifting Social Security, U.S. Finds," *New York Times*, April 29, 1998.

160. See Jon Oberlander, "Medicare: The End of Consensus."

161. Robert Pear, "Greenspan, Issuing Warning, Urges Changes in Medicare." See also Moon, *Medicare Now and in the Future*.

162. Chapter 5 discusses the concept of social insurance. For a discussion of raising the eligibility age and means testing, see Ben Wildavsky, "Who's Entitled?"; Marilyn Moon, *Medicare Now and in the Future*, esp. chap. 7; and Robert D. Reischauer, "Two Years That Make a Big Difference," *New York Times*, July 13, 1997.

163. See Mark E. Rushefsky, "A Critique of Market Reform in Health Care."

164. See Moon, *Medicare Now and in the Future*, 176–79; Theodore Marmor and Jonathan Oberlander, "Rethinking Medicare Reform"; Henry J. Aaron and Robert D. Reischauer (1998), "'Rethinking Medicare Reform' Needs Rethinking"; Stuart M. Butler, "Medicare Price Controls."

165. Marmor and Oberlander, "Rethinking Medicare Reform," 62. For a detailed discussion of health care systems in other countries, see Joseph White, *Competing Solutions*.

166. See Moon, *Medicare Now and in the Future*, 205–15.

Chapter 5. Health Care and the Disadvantaged: Falling through the Cracks

1. Marc L. Berk and Claudia L. Schur, "Access to Care."

2. Elliot A. Krause, *Power and Illness*, 146.

3. Norman Daniels, Donald W. Light, and Ronald L. Caplan, *Benchmarks of Fairness for Health Care Reform.*
4. Ibid., 22. Emphasis in original.
5. Ibid., 24–25.
6. Karen L. Baird, *Gender Justice and the Health Care System.*
7. Ibid., 114.
8. Kenneth F.T. Cust, *A Just Minimum of Health Care.*
9. For a discussion of health care in the United States and other countries, see Joseph White, *Competing Solutions.*
10. Sidney Dean Watson, "Minority Access and Health Reform."
11. Ibid., 132.
12. Audrey R. Chapman, ed., *Health Care Reform,* "Introduction," 1–32.
13. Ibid., 5.
14. Ibid., 7.
15. Lu Ann Aday, "Equity, Accessibility, and Ethical Issues." Aday briefly discusses the liberal, individual rights tradition and the communitarian tradition that underlies the notion of the common good. See also Lu Ann Aday, *At Risk in America.*
16. Nancy Kari, Harry C. Boyte, and Bruce Jennings et al., "Health as a Civic Question."
17. Deborah A. Stone, "The Struggle for the Soul of Health Insurance."
18. Nancy S. Jecker, "Can an Employer-Based Health Insurance System Be Just?" For critiques of Jecker's argument, see Joan E. Ruttenberg, "Commentary—Revisiting the Employment-Insurance Link," 675–81; and David A. Rochefort, "Commentary—The Pragmatic Appeal of Employment-Based Health Care Reform," 683–93.
19. Kenneth E. Thorpe, *The Rising Number of Uninsured Workers,* 3. http://www.americashealth.org/emerge.uninsured.html. See also Linda J. Blumberg and David W. Liska, *The Uninsured in the United States: A Status Report,* Urban Institute, Washington, D.C., April 1996. http://www.urban.org/pubs/hinsure/uninsure.htm.
20. Calculated from Heath Insurance Association of America, *Sourcebook of Health Insurance Data,* 32.
21. Robert L. Bennefield, "Who Loses Coverage and for How Long?"
22. Diana Rowland, Barbara Lyons, Alina Salganicoff, and Peter Long, "A Profile of the Uninsured in America," 283.
23. Stephen H. Long and M. Susan Marquis, "Gaps in Employer Coverage," 284.
24. Statistics from U.S. Bureau of Labor Statistics.
25. Robin M. Weinick, Margaret E. Weigers, and Joel W. Cohen, "Children's Health Insurance, Access to Care, and Health Status."
26. See General Accounting Office, *Health Insurance for Children.*
27. Thomas M. Selden, Jessica S. Banthin, and Joel W. Cohen, "Medicaid's Problem Children." See also Weinick, Weigers, and Cohen, "Children's Health Insurance, Access to Care, and Health Status."
28. "Eroding Employer-Based Insurance," 4.
29. Thorpe, *Rising Number of Uninsured Workers,* 10.
30. General Accounting Office, *Employment-Based Health Insurance.*
31. Thorpe, *Rising Number of Uninsured Workers.*
32. Calculated from U.S. Bureau of the Census, *Statistical Abstract of the United States, 1997,* 415.
33. For an analysis of downsizing, see Steven Pearlstein, "The Downsizing Trap," *Washington Post National Weekly Edition,* January 10–16, 1994, 8–9; Steven Pearlstein, "Recessions Fade, but Downsizings Are Forever," *Washington Post National Weekly*

Edition, October 3–9, 1994, 21; and Deborah Chollet, "Employer-Based Health Insurance in a Changing Work Force." See also Thorpe, *Rising Number of Uninsured Workers*.

34. See *New York Times, The Downsizing of America*.

35. Thorpe, *Rising Number of Uninsured Workers*, 9.

36. See General Accounting Office, *Retiree Health Insurance*.

37. Thorpe, *Rising Number of Uninsured Workers*.

38. Chollet, "Employer-Based Health Insurance in a Changing Work Force," 314.

39. Stephen H. Long and M. Susan Marquis, "Gaps in Employer Coverage," 284.

40. Chollet, "Employer-Based Health Insurance in a Changing Work Force," 321. See also Alan C. Monheit and Jessica Primoff Vistnes, "Implicit Pooling of Workers from Large and Small Firms."

41. Blumberg and Liska, *Uninsured in the United States*.

42. The controversy arises because the poverty line looks only at money income, leaving out food stamps, Medicaid, housing allowance, and so forth. Adding those items in would bring more people over the poverty line, but the trends in poverty would remain more or less the same.

43. See General Accounting Office, *Health Insurance for Children*.

44. Phillip F. Cooper and Barbara Steinberg Schone, "More Offers, Fewer Takers for Employment-Based Health Insurance: 1987–1996."

45. See General Accounting Office, *Private Health Insurance*; and Kenneth E. Thorpe, *Changes in the Growth in Health Care Spending*. http://www.americas health.org/implications/implications.html.

46. See, for example, Robert Pear, "Insurance-Liability Curb Poses Problem for Bush," *New York Times*, May 19, 1992.

47. See Robert L. Bennefield, "Health Insurance Coverage: 1996"; Blumberg and Liska, *Uninsured in the United States*; and Thorpe, *Rising Number of Insured Workers*.

48. Calculated from table 11 of Thorpe, *Rising Number of Uninsured Workers*.

49. Thorpe, *Rising Number of Uninsured Workers*.

50. Bennefield, "Health Insurance Coverage: 1996."

51. Health Insurance Association of America, *Sourcebook of Health Insurance Data*.

52. Diana Rowland et al., "Profile of the Uninsured in America."

53. Bennefield, "Health Insurance Coverage: 1996."

54. Peter T. Kilborn, "Illness Is Turning into Financial Catastrophe for More of the Uninsured," *New York Times*, August 1, 1997.

55. Chris Hafner-Eaton, "Physician Utilization Disparities between the Uninsured and Insured, 787–82.

56. Paula Braverman et al., "Insurance-Related Differences in the Risk of Ruptured Appendix."

57. See David W. Baker, Carl D. Stevens, and Robert H. Brook, "Regular Source of Ambulatory Care and Medical Care Utilization by Patients Presenting to a Public Hospital Emergency Department," 1909–1912; and Kimberly J. Rask et al., "Obstacles Predicting Lack of a Regular Provider and Delays in Seeking Care for Patients at an Urban Public Hospital."

58. Joel S. Weisman, Constantine Gatsonis, and Arnold M. Epstein, "Rates of Avoidable Hospitalization by Insurance Status in Massachusetts and Maryland," 2388–2394.

59. Ibid.

60. Children's Defense Fund, *The State of America's Children*; P.W. Newacheck, J.J. Stoddard, D.C. Hughes, and M. Pearl, "Health Insurance and Access to Primary Care for Children"; and G. Simpson et al., "Access to Health Care. Part 1: Children."

61. J.M. Quintana, D. Goldmann, and C. Homer, "Social Disparities in the Use of Diagnostic Tests for Children with Gastroenteritis."

62. Jeffrey J. Stoddard, Robert F. St. Peter, and Paul W. Newacheck, "Health Insurance Status and Ambulatory Care for Children."

63. General Accounting Office, *Health Insurance: Coverage Leads to Increased Health Care Access for Children.*

64. Charles Oberg et al., "Prenatal Care Comparisons among Privately Insured, Uninsured, and Medicaid-Enrolled Women."

65. Paula A. Braveman et al., "Differences in Hospital Resource Allocation among Sick Newborns According to Insurance Coverage."

66. John Z. Ayanian et al., "The Relation between Health Insurance Coverage and Clinical Outcomes among Women with Breast Cancer." See also N. Breen, L.G. Kessler, and M.L. Brown, "Breast Cancer Control among the Underserved"; and J.F. Kerner, "Breast Cancer Prevention and Control among the Medically Underserved."

67. Helen R. Burstin, Stuart R. Lipsitz, and Troyen A. Brennan, "Socioeconomic Status and Risk for Substandard Medical Care."

68. Peter Franks et al., "Health Insurance and Subjective Health Status."

69. Cathy Schoen et al., "Insurance Matters for Low-Income Adults: Results from a Five-State Survey."

70. See Robert S. Stern, Joel E. Weissman, and Arnold M. Epstein, "The Emergency Department as a Pathway for Admission for Poor and High-Cost Patients"; and Luba Vikhanski, "Emergency Departments Face a Growing Crisis in Care."

71. See Bruce Goldfarb, "Uncompensated Care Pushes Trauma Centers Out of Business," 32; and Ellen S. Campbell, "Unpaid Hospital Bills: Evidence from Florida."

72. Terrel W. Zollinger, Robert M. Saywell, Jr., and David K.W. Chu, "Uncompensated Hospital Care for Pregnancy and Childbirth Cases."

73. Peter J. Cunningham and Ha T. Tu, "A Changing Picture of Uncompensated Care." See also Graham Atkinson, W. David Helms, and Jack Needleman, "State Trends in Hospital Uncompensated Care"; and Joyce M. Mann et al., "A Profile of Uncompensated Care, 1983–1995."

74. Kilborn, "Illness is Turning into Financial Catastrophe for More of the Uninsured."

75. Eleanor D. Kinney and Suzanne K. Steinmetz, "Notes from the Insurance Underground," 641.

76. Ian Fisher, "Families Providing Complex Medical Care, Tubes and All," *New York Times*, June 7, 1998.

77. Thomas Rice and Kenneth E. Thorpe, "Income-Related Cost Sharing in Health Insurance," 22. See also the analysis in Jon Gable, Kelly Hunt, and Jean Kim, "The Financial Burden of Self-Paid Insurance for the Poor and Near-Poor."

78. Deborah A. Stone, "The Struggle for the Soul of Health Insurance," 290.

79. See General Accounting Office, *Health Insurance: Cost Increases Lead to Coverage Limitations and Cost Shifting*; Alan C. Monheit and Jessical Primoff Vistnes, "Implicit Pooling of Workers from Large and Small Firms"; Gina Kolata, "New Insurance Practice: Dividing Sick from Well," *New York Times*, March 4, 1992; and Gina Kolata, "The Philosophical Fight over What Insurance Should Be," *New York Times*, March 8, 1992.

80. Wendy K. Zellers, Catherine G. McLaughlin, and Kevin D. Frick, "Small-Business Health Insurance," 174–75.

81. Ibid., 175.

82. Kinney and Steinmentz, "Notes from the Insurance Underground," 637.

83. For a discussion of the class versus race issue, see two works by William Julius Wilson, *The Declining Significance of Race* and *The Truly Disadvantaged.*

84. William F. Ryan, *Blaming the Victim.*

85. Paul M. Lantz et al., "Socioeconomic Factors, Health Behaviors, and Mortality."

86. David McBride, "Black America."

87. Eli Ginzberg, "Improving Health Care for the Poor," 464.

88. Michael Millman, ed., *Access to Health Care in America.*

89. U.S. Department of Health and Human Services, *Health Status of Minorities and Low-Income Groups,* 89.

90. M.O. Garner et al., "Ethnicity and Sources of Prenatal Care."

91. Leslie L. Clarke et al., "Prenatal Care Use in Nonmetropolitan and Metropolitan America."

92. Millman, *Access to Health Care in America.* For a general discussion of Latinos and health care, see Carlos W. Molina and Marilyn Aguirre-Molina, eds., *Latino Health in the US.*

93. U.S. Department of Health and Human Services, *Health Status of Minorities and Low-Income Groups.*

94. Diane Rowland and Alina Salganicoff, "Commentary: Lessons from Medicaid," 550–51.

95. Ibid., 551.

96. U.S. Department of Health and Human Services, *Health Status of Minorities and Low-Income Groups,* 131.

97. Ibid., 137.

98. Ibid., 167.

99. Ibid., 195; see also "Fighting on Two Fronts (Minorities and AIDS)," *Time,* January 25, 1993, 23; and Lu Ann Aday, *At Risk in America,* 52.

100. U.S. Department of Health and Human Services, *Health Status of Minorities and Low-Income Groups,* 196.

101. Ibid., 199.

102. Ibid., 325.

103. Ibid., 345.

104. Ibid.

105. Velvet G. Miller and Janis L. Curties, "Health Care Reform and Race-Specific Policies," 748.

106. Eli Ginzberg, "Improving Health Care for the Poor," 464–65.

107. Ibid., 465.

108. Ibid.

109. See, for example, David M. Carlisle et al., "The Effect of Race and Ethnicity on the Use of Selected Health Care Procedures."

110. Durado D. Brooks, David R. Smith, and Ron J. Anderson, "Medical Apartheid," 2746. This kind of travel to health facilities has also been seen in managed care. See George Anders, *Health Against Wealth.*

111. Brooks et al., "Medical Apartheid," 2747.

112. R. Burciaga Valdez et al., "Insuring Latinos against the Costs of Illness."

113. See Fernando M. Trevino et al., "Health Insurance Coverage and Utilization of Health Services by Mexican Americans"; and Fernando M. Trevino et al., "Hispanic Health in the United States."

114. Helen R. Burstin, Stuart R. Lipsitz, and Troyen A. Brennan, "Socioeconomic Status and Risk for Substandard Medical Care."

115. Millman, *Access to Health Care in America.*

116. Kevin G. Volpp and J. Sanford Schwartz, "Myths and Realities Surrounding Health Reform," 1372; see also Charles N. Oberg et al., "Prenatal Comparisons among Privately Insured, Uninsured, and Medicaid-Enrolled Women."

117. Rowland and Salganicoff, "Commentary: Lessons from Medicaid," 551.

118. Ibid., 552.

119. The infamous Tuskegee syphilis "experiments" and the view held among some that AIDS was designed to decimate the black community fit into this.

120. V.L. Shavers-Hornaday et al., "Why Are African Americans Under-Repre-sented in Medical Research Studies?"

121. Nancy Krieger and Elizabeth Fee, "Man-Made Medicine and Women's Health," 27.

122. U.S. Department of Health and Human Services, *Health Status of Minorities and Low-Income Groups,* 647. See also Chris Hafner-Eaton, "Will the Phoenix Rise, and Where Should She Go?"

123. Baird, *Gender Justice and the Health Care System.* Some of this may change with the implementation of the Family and Medical Leave Act of 1993. The act pro-vides employees with up to twelve weeks of unpaid leave because of the birth or adoption of a child, the illness of a family member, or a death in the family.

124. U.S. Department of Health and Human Services, *Health Status of Minorities and Low-Income Groups,* 648.

125. Charlotte F. Muller, *Health Care and Gender,* 104–14.

126. Ibid., 73.

127. See Barbara A. Goff, H.G. Muntz, and J.M. Cain, "Is Adam Worth More than Eve?"; Barbara A. Goff, H.G. Muntz, and J.M. Cain, "Comparison of 1997 Medicare Relative Value Units for Gender-Specific Procedures"; and Peter Cherouny and Col-leen Nadolski, "Underreimbursement of Obstetric and Gynecologic Invasive Services by the Resource-Based Relative Value Scale."

128. "Gender Bias at Work with Viagra, Physicians Say," *Springfield News-Leader,* May 13, 1998.

129. Carolyn M. Clancy and Charlea T. Massion, "American Women's Health Care."

130. Hafner-Eaton, "Will the Phoenix Rise, and Where Should She Go?" 851.

131. Ibid., 843.

132. Charles Mawrick, "Women's Health Action Plan Sees First Anniversary."

133. Barbara J. Culliton, "Critics Condemn NIH Women's Study," 11.

134. See Kay Kicersin and Lauren Schnaper, "Reinventing Medical Research." On the women's health movement in general, see Judy Norsigian, "The Women's Health Movement in the United States."

135. Jane Brody, "A Fatal Shift in Cancer's Gender Gap," *New York Times,* May 12, 1998.

136. The following is based on Andrew G. Kadar, "The Sex-Bias Myth in Medicine."

137. Ibid., 69.

138. Ibid.

139. Ibid., 70.

140. See Jeffrey A. Buck and Mark S. Kamlet, "Problems with Expanding Medic-aid for the Uninsured"; and Julie Kosterlitz, "Buying into Trouble."

141. See Chris Collins, "Qualified Children Living Without Medicaid," *Springfield News-Leader,* February 23, 1997; and Laura Summer, Sharon Parrott, and Cindy Mann, "Millions of Uninsured and Underinsured Children Are Eligible for Medicaid."

142. Buck and Kamlet, "Problems with Expanding Medicaid for the Uninsured," 3–4.

143. Ibid., 13–20.

144. On long-term Medicare problems, see Congressional Budget Office, *Long-Term Budgetary Pressures and Policy Options*.

145. Robert Pear, "National Health Care Policy: How Bush and Clinton Differ," *New York Times*, August 12, 1992.

146. Clifford Krauss, "Under Political Steam, Health-Care Issue Gains Wider Support in Congress," *New York Times*, January 12, 1992.

147. Robert Pear, "President Leaves Many Areas Gray," *New York Times*, February 7, 1992.

148. Stuart M. Butler, "A Tax Reform Strategy to Deal with the Uninsured," 2541.

149. Ibid.

150. Ibid., 2541–2542.

151. Ibid., 2542.

152. Ibid.

153. Ibid., 2542–2543. The article also examines how the refundable tax credit program would reduce inflationary pressures by making consumers more cost conscious.

154. Alice Sardell, *The U.S. Experiment in Social Medicine*.

155. See Paul Starr, *The Social Transformation of American Medicine*, 370–72; and Karen Davis and Cathy Schoen, *Health and the War on Poverty*, 161–202.

156. Davis and Schoen, *Health and the War on Poverty*, 177–85.

157. Robert Pear, "Panel Offers Health Plan to Bush on Uninsured," *New York Times*, December 20, 1991.

158. The most direct provision of health services by the federal government is done by the Department of Veterans Affairs Hospital System and the Public Health Service Hospitals.

159. Karen Davis and Cathy Schoen, "Universal Coverage," 11–12.

160. Ibid., 12–14.

161. Sheila R. Zedlewdki, Gregory P. Acs, and Colin W. Winterbottom, "Play-or-Pay Employer Mandates," 69.

162. Karen Davis, "Expanding Medicare and Employer Plans to Achieve Universal Health Insurance," 2525.

163. Howard Berman, "Rochester: Community Rating = Insurance Access," 56.

Chapter 6. Health Care Cost Containment

1. Karen Davis and Cathy Schoen, *Health and the War on Poverty*.

2. Robert G. Evans, "Finding the Levers, Finding the Courage."

3. Katharine R. Levit et al., "National Health Expenditures, 1996," 188.

4. Ibid., 191.

5. Maurice McGregor, "Hospital Costs," 92–93.

6. W. Bryan Latham, *Health Care Costs*, 11–26; for a discussion of business attitudes toward health care costs, see Harvey M. Sapolsky et al., "Corporate Attitude toward Health Care Costs," 561–85.

7. John R. Virts and George W. Wilson, "Inflation and Health Care Prices."

8. David Mechanic, "Some Dilemmas in Health Care Policy," 2–3.

9. James R. Jones, "Cost Pressures and Health Policy Reforms," 41.

10. Kevin Grumbach and Thomas Bodenheimer, "Reins or Fences: A Physician's View of Cost Containment," 120.

11. This is an old debate. See, for example, Charles E. Lindblom, *Politics and Markets*; Robert A. Dahl and Charles E. Lindblom, *Politics, Economics and Planning*.

12. Donald W. Moran, "Federal Regulation of Managed Care"; Lynn Etheredge, "Promarket Regulation"; Alain C. Enthoven and Sara J. Singer, "Markets and Collec-

tive Action in Regulating Managed Care," 26–32; Steve Zatkin, "A Health Plan's View of Government Regulation," 33–35; Thomas Rice, "Can Markets Give Us the Health Care System We Want?"; Robert G. Evans, "Going for the Gold."

13. Walter McClure, "Structural and Incentive Problems in Economic Regulation of Medical Care," 109–10.

14. Robert M. Ball, "Background of Regulation in Health Care," 8–9.

15. Mark V. Pauly, "Is Medical Care Different?" 22.

16. Theresa Varner and Jack Christy, "Consumer Information Needs in a Competitive Health Care Environment."

17. Pauly, "Is Medical Care Different?" 236.

18. Stephen M. Weiner, "On Public Values and Private Regulation," 278.

19. Stuart Altman and Sanford L. Weiner, "Regulation as a Second Best Choice."

20. Bruce C. Vladeck, "The Market vs. Regulation"; Bruce C. Vladeck, "Variation Data and the Regulatory Rationale."

21. S. Breyer, "Analyzing Regulatory Failure."

22. McClure, "Structural and Incentive Problems in Economic Regulation of Medical Care." The author outlines a series of structural and incentive problems such as diffused consumer interests versus concentrated producer interests, political setting problems, and technical content problems. For a theoretical argument against government regulation analogous to the concept of market failure, see Charles Wolf, Jr., "A Theory of Non-Market Failures."

23. John C. Goodman, *The Regulation of Medical Care*, 133.

24. David F. Durenberger, "The Politics of Health," 4.

25. Roger G. Noll, "The Consequences of Public Utility Regulation of Hospitals," 23–48.

26. S.E. Berki, "Health Care Policy," 235.

27. Paul M. Ellwood, Jr., "Alternative to Regulation."

28. Alain C. Enthoven, "Competition in the Marketplace," 18–19. For a more extended discussion, see Alain C. Enthoven, *Health Plan*.

29. Alain C. Enthoven, "Consumer Choice Health Plans" (first of two parts) and (second of two parts).

30. Alain C. Enthoven, "Managed Competition of Alternate Delivery System"; H.E. Frech III and Paul B. Ginsburg, "Competition among Health Insurers, Revisited."

31. Michael R. Pollard, "The Essential Role of Antitrust in a Competitive Market for Health Services," 263.

32. Ibid., 262.

33. Walter McClure, "The Competitive Strategy for Medical Care," 46.

34. Robert G. Evans, "Incomplete Vertical Integration in the Health Care Industry."

35. Eli Ginzberg, "Procompetition in Health Care."

36. Jon R. Gabel and Alan C. Monheit, "Will Competition Plans Change Insurer-Provider Relationships?" 635.

37. Paul Starr, "Changing the Balance of Power in American Medicine," 170.

38. Goodman, *The Regulation of Medical Care*, 117–18.

39. M.S. Roemer, "Hospitals Utilization and the Supply of Physicians."

40. Clark C. Havighurst, "Regulation of Health Facilities and Services by 'Certificate of Need.'"

41. The major example of the early planning effort was the Hospital Survey and Construction Act of 1946, better known as the Hill-Burton Act.

42. For an extensive analysis of federal and state laws and procedures in this area, see Medicine in Public Interest, *Certificate of Need: An Expanding Regulatory Concept: A Compilation and Analysis of Federal and State Laws and Procedures*, Medicine

in Public Interest, Washington, D.C., 1978; for an excellent annotated bibliography of certificate-of-need project reviews, see U.S. Department of Health, Education, and Welfare, *Certificate of Need/1122 Project Reviews*.

43. Louanne Kennedy and Bernard M. Baruch, "Health Planning in an Age of Austerity," 233.

44. Judith Gelman, *Competition and Health Planning*, 11. Also see David S. Salkever and Thomas W. Bice, "The Impact of Certificate of Need Controls on Hospital Investment."

45. David S. Salkever and Thomas W. Bice, *Hospital Certificate-of-Need Controls*, 75.

46. Clark C. Havighurst, "Regulation of Health Facilities and Services by 'Certificate of Need'"; and John C. Goodman, *The Regulation of Medical Care*, 121.

47. Salkever and Bice, *Hospital Certificate-of-Need Controls*, 16; and William J. Bicknell and Diana C. Walsh, "Critical Experiences in Organizing and Administering a State Certificate-of-Need Program."

48. Theodore Marmor and James Morone, "HSAs and the Representation of Consumer Interests."

49. Lewin and Associates, Inc., *Evaluation of the Efficiency and Effectiveness of the Section 1122 Review Process*, 1–17.

50. Bruce Vladeck, "Interest Group Representation and the HSAs."

51. Stephen S. Mick and John D. Thompson, "Public Attitude toward Health Planning Under the Health Systems Agencies."

52. Lynn Etheredge, "Reagan, Congress and Health Spending," 16.

53. Richard L. Johnson, "Should Hospital Planning Continue to Be Regulated?" 90.

54. Congressional Budget Office, *The Impact of PSROs on Health-Care Costs*. The other studies by the CBO using data for earlier years had come to similar conclusions.

55. Goodman, *The Regulation of Medical Care*, 126–27.

56. Charlotte L. Rosenberg, "Why Doctor-Policing Laws Don't Work"; John Varlova, "A $2.2 Million Lesson in the Perils of Peer Review"; Robert Cassidy, "Can You Really Speak Your Mind in Peer Review?"

57. Etheredge, "Reagan, Congress and Health Spending," 16.

58. "PROs: Peering Harder in the '90s," *Hospitals* 63, no. 3, February 5, 1989, 42–46.

59. Ibid.

60. General Accounting Office, *Medicare PROs*.

61. Lawrence D. Brown, "Introduction to a Decade of Transition."

62. Richard McNeil, Jr., and Robert E. Schlenker, "HMOs, Competition and Government."

63. See Joseph L. Falkson, *HMOs and the Politics of Health Service Reform*.

64. U.S. Department of Health, Education, and Welfare, *Toward a Comprehensive Health Policy for the 1970s*.

65. John K. Iglehart, "The Federal Government as Venture Capitalist: How Does It Fare?"

66. Paul M. Ellwood, "Health Maintenance Strategy"; Clark C. Havighurst, "Health Maintenance Organizations and the Market for Health Services."

67. Joseph L. Falkson, "Market Reform, Health Systems, and HMOs," 218.

68. Arnold J. Rosoff, "Phase Two of the Federal HMO Development Program."

69. Ibid.

70. Karen Davis et al., *Health Care Cost Containment*, 135.

71. Patricia Neuman et al., "Marketing HMOs to Medicare Beneficiaries."

72. Lyle Nelson et al., "Access to Care in Medicare HMOs, 1996," 148.

73. Jo Ann Lamphere et al., "The Surge in Medicare Managed Care: An Update," 127.

74. Nelson et al., "Access to Care in Medicare HMOs, 1996," 148–56.
75. Gerald F. Riley, Melvin J. Ingberg, and Cynthia G. Tudor, "Disenrollment of Medicare Beneficiaries from HMOs."
76. Katharine R. Levit et al., "National Health Expenditures, 1993," 285.
77. Ibid., 26.
78. Robert M. Gibson et al., "National Health Expenditures, 1983," 22.
79. Bruce Steunwald and Frank A. Sloan, "Regulatory Approaches to Hospital Cost Containment," 276.
80. Paul L. Joskow, "Alternative Regulatory Mechanism for Controlling Hospital Costs."
81. For a detailed discussion and analysis of the all-payer DRG system in New Jersey, see Bulletin of the New York Academy of Medicine 62, no. 6. The entire issue is devoted to the discussion of New Jersey's DRG system.
82. For an excellent analysis of the political process through which the DRG system was initiated first in New Jersey and than at the federal level, see James A. Morone and Andrew B. Dunham, "Slouching toward National Health Insurance."
83. Bruce C. Vladeck, "Comment on Hospital Reimbursement Under Medicare," 269.
84. D.A. Dolnec and C.J. Dougherty, "DRGs."
85. Frank A. Sloan, "Government and the Regulation of Hospital Care."
86. Kenneth J. Meir, Regulation, 1.
87. Franklin A. Shaffer, "DRGs," 389.
88. E.S. Quade, Analysis for Public Decisions, 294.
89. Davis et al., Health Care Cost Containment, 50–51.
90. Urban Institute, "Hospital Prospective Payment."
91. Davis et al., Health Care Cost Containment, 170–71.
92. Frank A. Sloan, Michael A. Morrisey, and Joseph Valvona, "Effects of the Medicare Prospective Payment System on Hospital Costs Containment."
93. Stuart Guterman, "The Balanced Budget Act of 1997," 161.
94. Ibid., 165.
95. Judith R. Lave, "Hospital Reimbursement under Medicare"; Donald W. Simborg, "DRG Creep"; William C. Hsiao and Daniel L. Dunn, "The Impact of DRG Payment on New Jersey Hospitals."
96. Karen Cook et al., "A Theory of Organizational Response to Regulation."
97. T.E. Parsons, "Suggestions for a Sociological Approach to a Theory of Organizations."
98. E. Green Gay et al., "An Appraisal of Organizational Response to Fiscally Constraining Regulation."
99. John Holahan and John L. Palmer, "Medicare's Fiscal Problems."
100. Stuart H. Altman and Marc A. Rodwin, "Halfway Competitive Markets and Ineffective Regulation," 335.
101. Sun Valley Forum on National Health, Harrison Conference Center, "The Role of State and Local Government in Health," 134.
102. Helen C. Lazenby and Suzanne W. Letsch, "National Health Expenditures, 1989," 14, 23.
103. For a detailed analysis of the evolution of health care policy and its implications for federalism, see Frank J. Thompson, "New Federalism and Health Care Policy."
104. Helen Leeds, Health Care Cost Containment in the States.
105. David A. Crozier, "State Rate Setting."

106. Alfonso Esposito et al., "Abstracts of State Legislated Hospital Cost-Containment Programs," 129.

107. Harold Cohen, "State Rate Regulation."

108. Craig Coelen and Daniel Sullivan, "An Analysis of the Effects of Prospective Reimbursement Programs on Hospital Expenditures," 1.

109. Samuel A. Mitchell, "Issues, Evidence, and the Policymaker's Dilemma."

110. David Rosenbloom, "New Ways to Keep Old Promises in Health Care," 53.

111. Frank A. Sloan, "Reviews: An Economist," 115.

112. John E. McDonough, "Tracking the Demise of State Hospital Rate Setting," 144–45.

113. Ibid., 146.

114. See Spencer Rich, "How One State Holds Down Costs in Its Hospitals," *Washington Post National Weekly Edition*, December 21–27, 1992, 33–34.

115. Drew E. Altman and Douglas H. Morgan, "The Role of State and Local Government in Health," 26.

116. Henry J. Aaron and William B. Schwartz, *The Painful Prescription*.

117. Paul T. Menzel, *Strong Medicine*.

118. Victor Cohn, "Rationing Medical Care," *Washington Post National Weekly Edition*, August 13–19, 1990, 11.

119. David Mechanic, "Muddling Through Elegantly," 83–84.

120. Ibid., 84.

121. John Kitzhaber, "A Healthier Approach to Health Care"; Timothy Egan, "Oregon Shakes Up Pioneering Health Plan for the Poor," *New York Times*, February 22, 1991; Patrick O'Neill, "Oregon's Health Care Rationing Plan Causing Fight"; Melinda Beck and Nadine Joseph, "Not Enough for All: Oregon Experiments with Rationing Health Care," *Newsweek*, May 14, 1990, 53–54; and B. Drummond Ayres, Jr., "States Hustle to Adopt Health-Care Overhauls," *New York Times*, April 25, 1993.

122. Julie Kosterlitz, "Rationing Health Care."

123. William B. Schwartz and Henry J. Aaron, "The Achilles Heel of Health Care Rationing"; William B. Schwartz and Henry J. Aaron, *Health Care Costs*.

124. Mechanic, "Muddling Through Elegantly," 85–86.

125. Nelda McCall, "Lessons from Arizona's Medicaid Managed Care Program," 194.

126. Ronald J. Vogel, "An Analysis of Structural Incentives in the Arizona Health Care Cost-Containment System," 14.

127. Jeffrey S. McCombs and Jon B. Christianson, "Applying Competitive Bidding to Health Care."

128. Health Care Financing Administration, *Medicaid Managed Care Page*, http://hcfa.gov/medicaid/trends97.htm.

129. McCall, "Lessons from Arizona's Medicaid Managed Care Program," 195.

130. John Holahan et al., "Medicaid Managed Care in Thirteen States," 59–60.

131. "Medicaid Managed Care: Promise and Pitfalls," http://www.rwjf.org/library/sum95cov.htm.

132. John Holahan and David Liska, "The Slowdown in Medicaid Spending Growth," 160.

133. Ibid., 160.

134. Ibid., 161.

135. Ibid.

136. Ibid., 162.

137. Cited in Frank Swoboda, "The Mercury Rises for Health Care Costs," *Washington Post National Weekly Edition*, February 4–10, 1991, 21.

138. Julie Kosterlitz, "Softening Resistance."

139. Frank Swoboda, "A Surgical Strike against Corporate Health Care Costs: Firms Try Managed Plans to Remedy Soaring Expenses," *Washington Post National Weekly Edition*, February 19–25, 1990, 20.

140. Harvey M. Sapolsky et al., "Corporate Attitude toward Health Care Costs."

141. John K. Iglehart, "Health Care and American Business."

142. Eileen J. Tell, Marilyn Falik, and Peter D. Fox, "Private-Sector Health Care Initiatives," 372.

143. Much of the discussion that follows is derived from Sean Sullivan, *Managing Health Care Costs*; Karen Davis et al., *Health Care Cost Containment*; and Tell, Falik, and Fox, "Private-Sector Health Care Initiatives."

144. Joseph P. Newhouse et al., "Some Interim Results from a Controlled Trial of Cost Sharing in Health Insurance," 1501–1507.

145. Davis et al., *Health Care Cost Containment*, 125–26.

146. Congressional Budget Office, *Trends in Health Care Spending by the Private Sector*, 19–29.

147. Milt Freudenheim, "Employers Winning Wide Leeway to Cut Medical Insurance Benefits," *New York Times*, March 29, 1992.

148. Milt Freudenheim, "Medical Insurance Is Being Cut Back for Many Retirees," *New York Times*, June 28, 1992.

149. Davis et al., *Health Care Cost Containment*, 115–16.

150. Allen Buchanan, "Managed Care," 619.

151. Roger Feldman, John Kralewski, and Bryan Dowd, "Health Maintenance Organizations."

152. Alan L. Hillman, "Financial Incentives for Physicians in HMOs."

153. Douglas R. Wholey et al., "HMO Market Structure and Performance: 1985–1996," 76.

154. Gail A. Jensen et al., "The New Dominance of Managed Care," 125.

155. Wholey et al., "HMO Market Structure and Performance: 1985–1995," 77.

156. "Facts about Managed Care," http://www.wnet.org/archive/mhc/overview/sidebar4.html.

157. Jon Gable, "Ten Ways HMOs Have Changed during the 1990s."

158. Robert J. Blendon et al., "Understanding the Managed Care Backlash," 90–91.

159. Donald W. Moran, "HMOs, Competition, and the Politics of Minimum Benefits."

160. Alan L. Sorkin, *Health Care and the Changing Economic Environment*, 124; Harold S. Luft, *Health Maintenance Organizations*; Harold S. Luft, "How Do Health Maintenance Organizations Achieve Their Savings?"

161. Sorkin, *Health Care and the Changing Economic Environment*, 119, 124; Harold S. Luft, "Trends in Medical Costs"; William G. Manninh et al., "A Controlled Trial of the Effects of a Prepaid Group Practice on Use of Services"; J.E. Ware et al., "Comparison of Health Outcomes at a Health Maintenance Organization with Those of Fee-for-Service Care"; Group Health Association of America, *HMO Industry Profile: Utilization Pattern*, Group Health Association of America, Washington, D.C., 1988.

162. Harold S. Luft, Susan C. Maerki, and Joan B. Trauner, "The Competitive Effects of Health Maintenance Organizations."

163. Sorkin, *Health Care and the Changing Economic Environment*, 128; Marie L.F. Ashcraft and S.E. Berki, "Health Maintenance Organizations as Medicaid Providers." The authors argue that HMOs have no incentives to enroll Medicaid beneficiaries and that Medicaid beneficiaries have no incentives to enroll in HMOs.

164. Gail Wilensky and L. Rossiter, "Patient Self-Selection in HMOs."

165. Stanley B. Jones, "Multiple Choice Health Insurance"; Ira Strumwasser et al., "The Triple Option Choice"; Harold S. Luft and R.H. Miller, "Patient Selection in a Competitive Health Care System."

166. F.J. Hellinger, "Selection Bias in Health Maintenance Organizations"; Mark S. Blumberg, "Health Status and Health Care Use by Type of Private Health Coverage," 633–55.

167. Jeffrey Merrill and Catherine McLaughlin, "Competition versus Regulation: Some Empirical Evidence."

168. Roger Feldman et al., "The Competitive Impact of Health Maintenance Organizations on Hospital Finances"; Allan N. Johnson and David Aquilina, "The Competitive Impact of Health Maintenance Organizations and Competition on Hospitals in Minneapolis/St. Paul."

169. Jack Hadley and Katherine Swartz, "The Impact of Hospital Costs between 1980 and 1984 on Hospital Rate Regulation, Competition, and Change in Health Insurance Coverage."

170. Harold S. Luft, "Trends in Medical Care Costs."

171. Davis et al., *Health Care Cost Containment*, 132–34.

172. W.P. Welch, "The New Structure of Individual Practice Associations."

173. Douglas R. Wholey et al., "HMO Market Structure and Performance: 1985–1995," 79–83.

174. Jensen et al., "The New Dominance of Managed Care," 134.

175. Gabel, "Ten Ways HMOs Have Changed during the 1990s," 143.

176. Jensen et al., "The New Dominance of Managed Care," 134.

177. Lawrence D. Brown, "Competition and Health Cost Containment," 157–58.

178. Peter Kerr, "The Changing Definition of Health Insurers," *New York Times,* May 10, 1993.

179. J.H.A. Brown, *The Politics of Health Care*, 27.

180. Odin Anderson et al., *HMO Development*, 146.

181. Lawrence D. Brown, "Competition and Health Care Policy," 51.

182. Annetta Miller and Elizabeth Bradburn, "Shape Up—Or Else," *Newsweek*, July 1, 1991, 42–43.

183. Robert Pear, "U.S. Is to Argue Employers Can Cut Health Insurance," *New York Times*, October 16, 1993.

184. Spencer Rich, "The Doctor Will See You Now at the Corporate, In-House Clinic," *Washington Post National Weekly Edition*, June 10–16, 1991, 22.

185. E.R. Brooks et al., "Does Free Care Improve Adult Health?"; Jack Hadley, *More Medical Care*; N. Lurie, "Termination from Medical Care: Does It Affect Health?"

186. Congressional Budget Office, *Trends in Health Care Spending by the Private Sector*, viii.

187. Ibid., 6.

188. Ibid., 13.

Chapter 7. Medical Malpractice and Medical Liability

1. Winsor C. Schmidt, D. Alex Keckert, and Alice A. Mercer, "Factors Associated with Medical Malpractice," 2.

2. Cyril J. Gadd, *Hammurabi and the End of His Dynasty*.

3. *Legal Medicine*, 35; N.S. Blackman and C.P. Bailey, *Liability in Medical Malpractice*, 7–11, 39.

4. V.M. Gordon, "The Origin, Basis and Nature of Medical Malpractice Liability."

5. C.H. Wetch, "Legal Medicine: An Historical Review and Future Perspectives."

6. Cece L. Wood, "Historical Perspectives on Law, Medical Practice and the Concept of Negligence," 821–23.

7. *Britton: Homicide*, 34.

8. S. Shindell, "A Survey of the Law of Medical Practice."

9. Wood, "Historical Perspectives," 823–24.

10. Ibid., 824.

11. Ibid.

12. Allen D. Spiegel and Florence Kavaler, "America's First Medical Malpractice Crisis: 1835–1865," 285.

13. Wood, "Historical Perspectives," 824–25.

14. Spiegel and Kavaler, "America's First Medical Malpractice Crisis: 1835–1865," 285–86.

15. Ibid., 286.

16. Wood, "Historical Perspectives," 825.

17. Kenneth Allen De Ville, *Medical Malpractice in Nineteenth Century America: Origins and Legacy*, 1990, 157–61.

18. Spiegel and Kavaler, "America's First Medical Malpractice Crisis: 1835–1865," 288–89.

19. V.M. Gordon, "The Origin, Basis and Nature of Medical Malpractice Liability."

20. Spiegel and Kavaler, "America's First Medical Malpractice Crisis: 1835–1865," 284–85.

21. Chester R. Burns, "Malpractice Suits in American Medicine Before the Civil War."

22. Wood, "Historical Perspectives on Law, Medical Malpractice and the Concept of Negligence," 826.

23. Robert C. Derbyshire, *Medical Licensure and Discipline in the United States*, 5–6.

24. Ibid., 6–7.

25. Abraham Flexner, *Medical Education in the United States and Canada.*

26. Hubert W. Smith, "Legal Responsibility for Medical Malpractice"; Charles J. Weigel II, "Medical Malpractice in America's Middle Years."

27. De Ville, *Medical Malpractice in Nineteenth Century America*, 191–95.

28. Ibid., 192.

29. Ibid., 206.

30. Ibid., 210–13.

31. Ibid., 227.

32. Frank A. Sloan, Randall R. Bovbjerg, and Penny B. Githens, *Insuring Medical Malpractice*, 4–6.

33. Patricia M. Danzon, "The 'Crisis' in Medical Malpractice," 48–58.

34. Patricia M. Danzon, *Medical Malpractice*; Sloan, Bovbjerg, and Githens, *Insuring Medical Malpractice*; Glen Robinson, "Rethinking the Allocation of Medical Malpractice Risks between Patients and Providers."

35. Patricia M. Danzon, "Liability for Medical Malpractice," 57.

36. General Accounting Office, *Medical Malpractice Insurance Costs Increased but Varied Among Physicians and Hospitals.*

37. Sloan, Bovbjerg, and Githens, *Insuring Medical Malpractice.*

38. Harry T. Paxton, "Which Practice Expenses Are Out of Control?" 91.

39. Cynthia L. Gallup, "Can No-Fault Compensation of Impaired Infants Alleviate the Malpractice Crisis in Obstetrics?"

40. A. Korcok, "I Will See You in Court: US Still Looking for Malpractice Cure."

41. Berkeley Rice, "Where Doctors Get Sued the Most," 99.

42. M.R. Schwartz, "Liability Crisis: The Physician's Viewpoint."

43. Mahmud Hassan, "How Profitable Is Medical Malpractice Insurance?" 74–80.

44. Ibid., 74.

45. Reed N. Olsen, "The Reform of Medical Malpractice Law," 2575–2576.

46. Marc S. Stauch, "Causation Issues in Medical Malpractice," 247.

47. Jeffery Mullis, "Medical Malpractice, Social Structure, and Social Control," 135–36.

48. Stephen L. Fielding, "Changing Medical Practice and Medical Malpractice Claims," 39.

49. Stauch, "Causation Issues in Medical Malpractice," 248.

50. Irving J. Sloan, *Professional Malpractice*, 31–37.

51. John A. Siliciano and James A. Henderson, Jr., "Universal Health Care and the Continued Reliance on Custom in Determining Medical Malpractice,"1384.

52. Henry S. Farber and Michelle J. White, "Medical Malpractice," 200–1.

53. For a detailed analysis of the litigation process, see Margaret C. Jasper, *The Law of Medical Malpractice*.

54. Paul C. Weiler et al., *A Measure of Malpractice: Medical Injury, Malpractice Litigation, and Patient Compensation*, 14.

55. Ibid.

56. David T. Ozar, "Malpractice and the Presupposition of Medical Practice," 146–48.

57. Ibid., 152.

58. Paul Weiler, *Medical Malpractice on Trial*.

59. "Incidence of Adverse Events and Negligence in Hospitalized Patients," 370–84.

60. Patricia Danzon, *Medical Malpractice Theory, Evidence and Public Policy*.

61. M.I. Taragin et al., "The Influence of Standard of Care and Severity of Injury on the Resolution of Medical Malpractice Claims," 780–84.

62. J. Michael Monteleone, "Trial Lawyers and the Health Care Crisis," 32.

63. William C. Ludwig, "The Medical Profession and the Health Care Crisis," 25–35.

64. Stephen D. Sugarman, "Doing Away With Tort Law," 592.

65. Frank A. Sloan et al., "Compensation," 206.

66. Patricia Danzon, "Tort Reform: The Case of Medical Malpractice," 87–88.

67. Michael Rustad and Thomas Koenig, "Reconceptualizing Punitive Damages in Medical Malpractice," 1044–1045.

68. David S. Starr, "Does Malpractice Litigation Deter Substandard Care?" 366.

69. Rustad and Koenig, "Reconceptualizing Punitive Damages in Medical Malpractice," 1045.

70. Buddy Rake and Bobby Thrasher, "Medical Malpractice Myths, Truths and Solutions," 23.

71. Gary M. Fournier and Melayne M. Mcinnes, "Medical Board Regulation of Physician Licensure," 125.

72. Bryan A. Liang, "Medical Malpractice," 68.

73. Jody W. Menon, "Adversarial Medical and Scientific Testimony and Lay Jurors," 283.

74. Stephen D. Sugarman, "The Need to Reform Personal Injury Law Leaving Scientific Disputes to Scientists," 823; Peter W. Huber, *Liability, The Legal Revolution and Its Consequences*; Peter W. Huber, *Galileo's Revenge: Junk Science in the Courtroom*.

75. Randall R. Bovbjerg et al., "Juries and Justice."

76. Neil Vidmar, "Are Juries Competent to Decide Liability in Tort Cases Involving Scientific/Medical Issues?" 889–90.

77. Jeffrey O'Connell and C. Brian Kelly, *The Blame Game*; Otis Bowen, "Congressional Testimony on Senate Bill S.1804," 816.

78. Stephen Daniels, "Tracing the Shadow of the Law," 4–39; Stephen Daniels, "Verdicts in Medical Malpractice Cases," 23–30.

79. Kenneth I. Chesebro, "Galileo's Retort: Peter Huber's Junk Scholarship."

80. Vidmar, "Are Juries Competent to Decide Liability in Tort Cases Involving Scientific/Medical Issues?" 892–93.

81. Ibid. 911.

82. Joe S. Cecil et al., "Citizen Comprehension of Difficult Issues: Lessons from Civil Jury Trials," 727, 749.

83. Bovbjerg et al., "Juries and Justice."

84. Neil Vidmar, *Medical Malpractice and the American Jury.*

85. Meron J. Levitats, "How to Get Rid of the Hired Guns," 21.

86. Ibid., 21.

87. Robert A. Harway, "'Hired Guns' Isn't a Synonym for 'Medical Whore,'" 41.

88. Harry T. Paxton, "Which Practice Expenses Are Out of Control?"; Richard K. Thomas, Loius Pol and William F. Sehnert, Jr., *Health Care Book of Lists.*

89. Harry T. Paxton, "Just How Heavy Is the Burden of Malpractice Premiums?" 168.

90. A. Dale Tussing and Martha A. Wojtowycz, "Malpractice, Defensive Medicine, and Obstetric Behavior," 172–91.

91. Office of Technology Assessment, *Defensive Medicine and Medical Malpractice.*

92. Elliot M. Abramson, "The Medical Malpractice Imbroglio," 293–310.

93. Brian McCormick, "Study: Defensive Medicine Costs Nearly $10 Billion," 4–5.

94. Carol Stevens, "Is George Bush the White Knight of Malpractice Reform?" 87–91.

95. Steve Brostoff, "Eliminate Defensive Medicine, Save $36B: Study," 5.

96. Winsor C. Schmidt, D. Alex Heckert, and Alice A. Mercer, "Factors Associated with Medical Malpractice," 160–61.

97. Hassan, "How Profitable Is Medical Malpractice Insurance?" 74–80.

98. Lawrence Southwick and Gary J. Young, "Layers and Medical Torts," 989–98.

99. J.S. McQuade. "The Medical Malpractice Crisis B Reflections on the Alleged Causes and Proposed Cures," 408–11.

100. Allen K. Hutkins, "Resolving the Medical Malpractice Crisis," 24.

101. Ellen W. Clayton et al., "Doctor-Patient Relationships," 50–71.

102. Hutkins, "Resolving the Medical Malpractice Crisis," 24.

103. Mitchell S. Berger, "Following the Doctor's Orders—Caps on Non-Economic Damages in Medical Malpractice Cases."

104. Risa B. Greene, "Federal Legislative Proposals for Medical Malpractice Reform," 569–70.

105. Ibid., 374–75.

106. Scott R. McMillen, "The Medical Malpractice Statute of Limitations."

107. Andrew L. Hyams, David W. Shapiro, and Troyen A. Brennan, "Medical Practice Guidelines in Malpractice Litigation," 289–90.

108. Lore Rinella, "The Use of Medical Practice Guidelines in Medical Malpractice Litigation—Should Practice Guidelines Define the Standard of Care?" 352–53.

109. "Can Malpractice Be Kept Out of the Court?" 111.

110. Ibid.

111. Andrew McMullen, "Comment: Mediation and Medical Malpractice Disputes," 373–74.

112. Walter O. Simmons, "An Economic Analysis of Mandatory Mediation and the Disposition of Medical Malpractice Claims," 69.

113. Jean A. Macchiaroli, "Medical Malpractice Screening Panels."

114. Hutkin, "Resolving the Medical Malpractice Crisis," 38.

115. Ibid., 39.

116. Mitchell and McDiarmid, "Medical Malpractice," 234–35.

117. Ibid.

118. Greene, "Federal Legislative Proposals for Medical Malpractice Forum," 577.

119. Hutkin, "Resolving the Medical Malpractice Crisis," 37–38.

120. Kirk B. Johnson et al., "The American Medical Association/Specialty Society Tort Reform Proposal"; Randall R. Bovbjerg, Esq., "Reforming a Proposed Tort Reform"; Herbert A. Ferrari, "Suing for Restitution"; Troyen A. Brennan, "Medical Malpractice Reform."

121. Mary Ann Baily, "The Administrative Approach to Medical Malpractice Disputes," 29–30.

122. Ibid., 31.

123. Hutkin, "Resolving the Medical Malpractice Crisis," 43.

124. Troyen A. Brennan, "Medical Malpractice Reform," 214–15; Greene, "Federal Legislative Proposals for Medical Malpractice Reform," 580.

125. Hutkin, "Resolving the Medical Malpractice Crisis," 35–36.

126. Paul C. Weiler, *Medical Malpractice on Trial*; Clark C. Havighurst and Laurence R. Tancredi, "Medical Adversity Insurance"; John Havard, "No-Fault Compensation for Medical Accidents"; Jeffrey O'Connell, "No-Fault Insurance for Injuries Arising from Medical Treatment"; Josephine Y. King, "No-Fault Compensation for Medical Injuries."

127. Ronald S. Latz, "No-Fault Liability and Medical Malpractice."

128. Clark C. Havighurst, "Medical Adversity Insurance"; Clark C. Havighurst and Laurence R. Tancredi, "Medical Adversity Insurance," 69; Patricia M. Danzon. *Medical Malpractice*, 217–18.

129. Paul C. Weiler et al., *A Measure of Malpractice.*

130. Latz, "No-Fault Liability and Medical Malpractice," 498.

131. Danzon, *Medical Malpractice*, 214.

132. Carter G. Phillips and Paul E. Kalb, "Replacing the Tort System for Medical Malpractice."

133. Patricia M. Danzon, "The Frequency and Severity of Medical Malpractice Claims," 115.

134. Frank A. Sloan et al., "Medical Malpractice Experience of Physicians," 3297.

135. Michael J. Trebilcock, Donald N. Dewees, and David G. Duff, "The Medical Malpractice Explosion," 563.

136. Hutkins, "Resolving the Medical Malpractice Crisis," 35; Marshall B. Kapp, "Solving the Medical Malpractice Problem."

137. Danzon, *Medical Malpractice*, 215.

138. Latz, "No-Fault Liability and Medical Malpractice," 501.

139. Patrica M. Danzon, *Medical Malpractice*, 216–18.

140. Weiler et al., *A Measure of Malpractice.*

141. James F. Blumstein, "A Perspective on Federalism and Medical Malpractice," 411–28.

142. Gary T. Schwartz, "Considering the Proper Federal Role in American Tort Law," 920–21.

143. Ibid., 920.

144. Bruce G. Hart, Jr., "Medical Malpractice Protection Under the Federal Tort Claims Act," 1107–1108.

145. Ibid., 1111–1112.

146. Nolan R. Atkinson, Jr., "How the National Practitioner Data Bank Affects Medical Malpractice Clients," 35–44.

147. Rinella, "The Use of Medical Practice Guidelines in Medical Malpractice Litigation," 345.

148. Jerry Geisel, "Bush Budget Proposes Malpractice Reform," 1, 26; Editorial, "Bush Plans a Good First Step on Tort Reform," 19; Adrienne C. Locke, "Bush Unveils Malpractice Reform Proposal," 3–4; Carol Stevens, "Is George Bush the White Knight of Malpractice Reform?" 87–91.

149. Robert N. Berg, "Malpractice Reform Under President Clinton," 364.

150. Carol Stevens, "Will the Clinton Plan End Your Malpractice Woes?" 29–30; William M. Sage, Kathleen E. Hastings, and Robert A. Berenson, "Enterprise Liability for Medical Malpractice and Health Care Quality Improvement," 1–28.

151. Marshall B. Kapp, "Medical Malpractice Reform as Part of Health Care Reform."

152. Don McNay and Thomas L. Gentry, "Structured Settlements and the Federally Supported Health Centers Assistance Act of 1995."

153. Gary T. Schwartz, "Considering the Proper Federal Role in American Tort Law," 918.

154. Rinella, "The Use of Practice Guidelines in Medical Malpractice Litigation," 342–43.

155. Patricia M. Danzon, "Liability for Medical Malpractice," 65.

156. Harris A. Meyer, "Doctors Fight Fees for No-Fault Patient Compensation Upheld"; Harris A. Meyer, "Doctor Fee for No-Fault Patient Compensation Upheld"; Howard Larkin, "Firm to Offer Insurance with No-Fault Features."

157. American Tort Reform Association, "Issue-by-Issue Look at the Number of States Enacting Tort Reform Legislation."

158. Health Care Liability Alliance, "State Enactment of Selected Health Care Liability Reforms."

159. Rinella, "The Use of Medical Practice Guidelines in Medical Malpractice Litigation," 354; Andrew Hyams, David D. Shapiro, and Troyen A. Brennan, 310–11.

160. A. Bilodeau, "Jury Still Out on Plan That Pays for Infants Injured at Birth"; L.B. Dickenson, "Medical Malpractice Guidelines in Malpractice Litigation," *Update on the Florida Birth-Related Neurological Injury Compensation Association*.

161. Kant Patel, "No-Fault Medical Liability in Virginia and Florida."

162. Danzon, "Liability for Medical Malpractice," 57.

163. Health Care Liability Alliance, *HCLA Fact Sheet: Non-Economic Damage Cap*; Health Care Liability Alliance, *HCLA Fact Sheet: State Constitutional Limitations*; James E. Magleby, "The Constitutionality of Utah's Medical Malpractice Damages Cap under the Utah Constitution"; Randall B. Keiser, "Does This Hurt?": Constitutional Challenges of Damage Caps and the Review Panel Process in Medical Malpractice Actions in Louisiana," 1233–1252.

164. Health Care Liability Alliance, *HCLA Fact Sheet: State Constitutional Impediments*; Thomas O. Depperschmidt, "The Legality of State Limitations on Medical Malpractice Tort Damage Awards," 417–26; Brett M. Wall, "Sympathy for the Devil"; Jacqueline Ross, "Will States Protect Us, Equally, from Damage Caps in Medical Malpractice Legislation?"

165. James W. Hughes and Edward A. Snyder, "Evaluating Medical Malpractice Reforms."

166. Annette Wencl and Margaret Brizzolara, "Survey of States."

167. Julie Brienza, "Changes Ahead for Lawyers Who Handle Medical Malpractice, Insurers Study Says."

168. John R. Penhallegon, "Emerging Physician and Organization Liability under Managed Health Care"; William T. Robinson. "New Deep Pocket."

169. Domenick C. DiCicco, Jr., "Liability of the HMO for the Medical Negligence of Its Providers."

170. David M. Kopstein and Karen R. Ristuben, "Privilege Denied—Hospital Liability for Credentialing."

171. Stephanie Anderson, "Revenge of the HMO Patients."

172. Kenneth S. Abraham and Paul C. Weiler, "Enterprise Liability and the Evolution of the American Health Care System," 381–436.

Chapter 8. Health Care Technology

1. John K. Kerr and Richard Jelinek, "Impact of Technology in Health Care and Health Administration."

2. D.W. Hill, "25 Years of Medical Technology."

3. Joseph D. Bronzino, Vincent H. Smith, and Maurice L. Wade, *Medical Technology and Society*, 34.

4. Kalb, "Controlling Health Care Costs by Controlling Technology," 1112.

5. Julie Kosterlitz, "Paying for Miracles," 1967.

6. Paul E. Kalb, "Controlling Health Care Costs by Controlling Technology," 1112.

7. Eli Ginzberg, "High-Tech Medicine and Rising Health Care Costs," 1820.

8. Kevin W. Wildes, "Health Reform and the Seduction of Technology."

9. Virginia Lotlarz, "History of Medical Techology in the United States."

10. Ibid.

11. Howard S. Berlinger, *Strategic Factors in U.S. Healthcare*, 112.

12. Burton A. Weisbrod, "The Nature of Technological Change."

13. Mary-Lan Kambert, "High-Tech Health Care."

14. Ibid.

15. Wildes, "Health Reform and the Seduction of Technology."

16. Lewis Thomas, *The Lives of a Cell*.

17. Ibid., 37.

18. Jonas Morris, *Searching for a Cure*, 197.

19. Quoted in ibid., 198.

20. Thomas, *Lives of a Cell*, 40.

21. "Health Care Dollars," *Consumer Reports*, July 1992, 435–48.

22. Ginzberg, "High-Tech Medicine and Rising Health Care Costs," 1821.

23. Frans F.H. Rutten and Gouke J. Bonsel, "High Cost Technology in Health Care," 567.

24. Ibid., 570.

25. David H. Freed, "Toward Redefining Expectations about Medical Technology," 22.

26. Victor R. Fuchs, *The Health Economy*; Annetine Gelijns and Nathan Rosenberg, "The Dynamics of Technological Change in Medicine."

27. Weisbrod, "The Nature of Technological Change."

28. Ibid., 27.

29. John Nyman, "Costs, Technology, and Insurance in the Health Care Sector," 108–9.

30. N. Kane and P. Manoukian, "The Effect of the Medicare Prospective Payment System on the Adoption of New Technology."

31. Paul F. Griner, "New Technology Adoption in the Hospital"; Gerald F. Anderson and Earl Steinberg, "Role of the Hospital in the Acquisition of Technology."

32. Freed, "Toward Redefining Expectations about Medical Technology," 23.

33. Jason H. Sussman, "Financial Considerations in Technology Assessment," 33.

34. Eric J. Cassell, "The Sorcerer's Broom."

35. Freed, "Toward Redefining Expectations about Medical Technology"; Charles E. Phelps and Stephen T. Parente, "Priority Setting in Medical Technology and Medical Practice Assessment."

36. Bruce J. Hillman, "Physicians' Acquisition and Use of New Technology in an Era of Economic Constraints"; Mark A. Fendrick and J. Sanford Schwartz, "Physicians' Decisions Regarding the Acquisition of Technology."

37. A. Everette James et al., "The Diffusion of Medical Technology."

38. Freed, "Toward Redefining Expectations about Medical Technology."

39. Robert H. Blank, *Rationing Medicine*, 4–5.

40. John W. Melski, "Price of Technology," 1517.

41. William R. Davis, "Medical Technology Investing in the '90s."

42. G. Lawrence Atkins and John L. Bauer, "Taming Health Care Costs Now," 56.

43. Dale A. Rublee, "Medical Technology in Canada, Germany, and the United States," 114–15.

44. Joel L. Nitzkin, "Technology and Health Care—Driving Costs Up, Not Down"; Mark McClellan, "Are the Returns to Technological Change in Health Care Declining?"

45. Kosterlitz, "Paying for Miracles."

46. Kambert, "High-Tech Health Care," 8.

47. Sara Collins, "Saving Lives Isn't Cheap," *U.S. News and World Report*, June 7, 1993, 57.

48. Robert P. Rhodes, *Health Care: Politics, Policy and Distributive Justice*, 76.

49. Ibid.

50. Kosterlitz, "Paying for Miracles," 1969.

51. Cindy L. Bryce and Kathryn Ellen Cline, "The Supply and Use of Selected Medical Technologies," 213.

52. Collins, "Saving Lives Isn't Cheap," 56.

53. Henry J. Aaron, *Serious and Unstable Condition*, 26.

54. Ibid., 48.

55. General Accounting Office, *Hospital Costs*, 2.

56. Kosterlitz, "Paying for Miracles."

57. Kalb, "Controlling Health Care Costs by Controlling Technology," 1114–1118.

58. G.G. Jaros and D.A. Boonzaier, "Cost Escalation in Health-Care Technology—Possible Solutions," 422.

59. Kalb, "Controlling Health Care Costs by Controlling Technology," 1112.

60. Geoffrey Cowley, "What High Tech Can't Accomplish," *Newsweek*, October 4, 1993, 60.

61. Ibid.

62. Kosterlitz, "Paying for Miracles," 1967.

63. Cowley, "What High Tech Can't Accomplish," 62.

64. Bryce and Cline, "Supply and Use of Selected Medical Technologies," 220–21.

65. Rutten and Bonsel, "High Cost Technology in Health Care," 570.

66. William B. Schwartz, "In the Pipeline."

67. "High Tech Medicine for the 90s"; Mary Wagner, "Weighing the Cost of New Technology"; Henry C. Alder, "Technology Assessment"; Suzanna Hoppszallern, Christine Hughes, and Robert A. Zimmerman, "MRI Acquisition."

68. "Cost/Benefits of High-Tech Medicine," 16.

69. David H. Banta and Hindrik Vondeling, "Strategies for Successful Evaluation and Policy-Making toward Health Care Technology on the Move."

70. Kathryn S. Taylor, "Technology's Next Test."

71. Patricia Huston, "Is Health Technology Assessment Medicine's Rising Star?" 1839.

72. Richard A. Merrill, "Regulation of Drugs and Devices."

73. Richard A. Rettig, "Medical Innovation Duels Cost Containment," 16.

74. Anne O. Kilpatrick, Krishna S. Dhir, and John M. Sanders, "Health Care Technology Assessment," 61.

75. Robin J. Strongin, "The Truth about Technology and Health Care Costs," 10–15.

76. David Banta and Stephen B. Thacker, "The Case for Reassessment of Health Care Technology," 235.

77. Victor R. Fuchs, "The New Technology Assessment," 673.

78. David M. Eddy, "Connecting Value and Costs."

79. Charlotte Muller, "Objective Health Care Technology Evaluation—It Isn't Easy," 121–24.

80. Ibid., 124–30.

81. Kosterlitz, "Paying for Miracles."

82. Ibid.

83. Rutten and Bonsel, "High Cost Technology in Health Care," 574–75.

84. Renaldo N. Battista, "Health Care Technology Assessment."

85. Charles E. Lindblom, "The Science of Muddling Through."

86. Wouter Van Rossum, "Decision-Making and Medical Technology Assessment."

87. Fuchs, "New Technology Assessment," 676.

88. Rutten and Bonsell, "High Cost Technology in Health Care," 571–73.

89. Alexander Morgan Capron, "Biomedical Technology and Health Care"; Joseph C. d'Oronzio, "Bioethics and the Body Politic"; Margot C.J. Mabie, *Bioethics and the New Medical Technology*; John Harris, *Wonderwoman and Superman*.

90. Henk A.M.J. ten Have, "Medical Technology Assessment and Ethics: Ambivalent Relations," 13–20.

91. Victor Tabbush and Gerald Swanson, "Changing Paradigms in Medical Payment."

92. Peter L. Spencer, "Technology Gatekeepers."

93. Michael Chernew, A. Amrk Fendrick, and Richard A. Hirth, "Managed Care and Medical Technology," 196.

94. Ibid., 197.

95. Tabbush and Swanson, "Changing Paradigms in Medical Payment," 357–61.

96. Chernew, Fendrick, and Hirth, "Managed Care and Medical Technology," 202–5.

97. Alan M. Garber and Paul M. Romer, "Evaluating the Federal Role in Financing Health-Related Research," 12717–12725.

98. Michael J. Malinowski, "Capitation, Advances in Medical Technology, and the Advent of a New Era in Medical Ethics," 331–60.

99. Robert H. Blank, "Introduction," vii–xiv.

100. Donald VanDeVeer, "Introduction," 20.

101. Martin A. Strosberg et al., eds., *Rationing America's Medical Care*; Norman Daniels, "Rationing Fairly."

102. Julie Johnsson, "High-Tech Health Care"; Robert Wright, "The Technology Time Bomb"; Lowell C. Kruse, "Some Thoughts about Resource Allocation in Health Care."

103. Henry J. Aaron and William B. Schwartz, "Rationing Health Care," 418.

104. Henry J. Aaron and William B. Schwartz, *The Painful Prescription*, esp. 29–56.

105. Eli Ginzberg, "Balancing Dollars and Quality," 4.

106. John F. Kilner, "Age as a Basis for Allocating Lifesaving Medical Resources."

107. Daniel Callahan, "Why We Must Set Limits."

108. David Callahan, "Bioethics: Private Choice and Common Good," 28.

109. Daniel Callahan, *Setting Limits*.

110. Daniel Callahan, *What Kind of Life*.

111. John F. Kilner, *Who Lives? Who Dies?;* John F. Kilner, *Life on the Line.*
112. Paul T. Menzel, *Strong Medicine*; Robert H. Blank, *Rationing Medicine.*
113. Norman L. Cantor, *Advance Directives and the Pursuit of Death with Dignity.*
114. Jerry Buckley, "How Doctors Decide Who Shall Live, Who Shall Die," *U.S. News and World Report*, January 11, 1990, 50–58.
115. Philip G. Peters, Jr., "The Constitution and the Right to Die," 13.
116. Gregory E. Pence, *Classic Cases in Medical Ethics*, 41–47; Maggie Shreve and June Isaacson Kailes, "The Right to Die or the Right to Community Support."
117. Marcia Angell, "Prisoners of Technology," 1227.
118. Gilbert Meilaender, "The Cruzan Decision."
119. Richard A. McCormick, "Clear and Convincing Evidence"; Peters, "The Constitution and the Right to Die."
120. Yale Kamisar, "Who Should Live—or Die? Who Should Decide?"
121. Thomas M. Garrett, Harold W. Baillie, and Rosellen M. Garrett, *Health Care Ethics*, 115–17.
122. Nancy Gibbs and Andrea Sachs, "Love and Let Die: In an Era of Medical Technology, How Are Patients and Families to Decide Whether to Halt Treatment—or Even to Help Death Along?" *Time*, March 19, 1990, 66.
123. Ibid., 64.
124. "Oregon's Assisted Suicide Law Stokes the Fires of Controversy," 1.
125. For a detailed discussion of various provisions of the law, see International Anti-Euthanasia Task Force, "The Facts about the Oregon 'Death with Dignity Act' Initiative."
126. Joan Biskupic, "Oregon's Assisted-Suicide Law Lives On"; "Challenge to Oregon's Assisted-Suicide Law Dies in Appeals Court."
127. "Oregon Upholds Suicide Law"; "Oregon's Right to Die Movement."
128. Garrett, Baillie, and Garrett, *Health Care Ethics*, 132–33.
129. Rosamond Rhodes, "Genetic Links, Family Ties, and Social Bonds, 10–31."
130. David McNamee, "Living with HUGO."
131. Ibid.
132. Joan Stephenson, "Ethics Group Drafts Guidelines for Control of Genetic Material and Information."
133. Linda R. Shaw et al., "Ethics of Lung Transplantation with Live Donors"; General Accounting Office, *Heart Transplants*; Keith J. Mueller, "Organ Transplant Legislation"; Garrett, Baillie, and Garrett, *Health Care Ethics*, esp. chap. 9, "Ethics of Organ Transplants," 177–97.
134. Mark Nichols, "Tinkering with Mother Nature"; Mary S. Henifin, "New Reproductive Technologies"; Melinda Beck and Geoffrey Cowley, "Mother Nature?" *Newsweek*, January 17, 1994, 54–57; Gina Kolata, "Reproductive Revolution Is Jolting Old Views," *New York Times*, January 11, 1994; Garrett, Baillie, and Garrett, *Health Care Ethics*, esp. chap. 8, "New Methods of Reproduction," 160–76; Janice G. Raymond, *Women as Wombs*; John A. Robertson, *Children of Choice*; Marilyn Strathern, *Reproducing the Future*; Elain H. Baruch, Amadeo F. D'Adamo, Jr., and Joni Seager, eds., *Embryos, Ethics, and Women's Rights*; Paul Lauritzen, *Pursuing Parenthood.*
135. Robyn Y. Nishimi, "From the Congressional Office of Technology Assessment."
136. Lynn Gillam, "Bioethics and Public Policy in Australia," 87.
137. Judith Miller, "What to Do Until the Philosopher Kings Come."
138. Cynthia B. Cohen and Elizabeth L. McCloskey, "Private Bioethics Forums."
139. Kathi E. Hanna, Robert M. Cook-Deegan, and Robyn Y. Nishimi, "Finding a Forum for Bioethics in U.S. Public Policy."
140. Ira H. Carmen, "Bioethics, Public Policy and Political Science," 80.

Chapter 9. Reforming the System

1. Lawrence D. Brown, "Politics, Money, and Health Care Reform."
2. Deborah A. Stone, "When Patients Go to Market: The Workings of Managed Competition," 111.
3. See Elliott A. Krause, *Power and Illness*; Betty Leyerle, *The Private Regulation of American Health Care*; and Paul Starr, *The Social Transformation of American Medicine*.
4. It is an extraordinary coincidence that Adam Smith's *The Wealth of Nations*, which extolled the virtues of free markets, appeared in the same year as the Declaration of Independence, which declared humanity's freedom.
5. Frederick Hayek, *The Road to Serfdom*.
6. Milton Friedman, *Capitalism and Freedom*.
7. This traditional structure is becoming less prominent, largely because of the press of cost increases and the development of managed care.
8. See Mark V. Pauly, *Medical Care at Public Expense*, 42–45.
9. Given the earlier statement, it might be more correct to argue that providers were both the demand and the supply side.
10. See Patricia Bauman, "The Formulation and Evolution of the Health Maintenance Organization Policy, 1970–1973"; and Joseph L. Falkson, *HMOs and the Politics of Health System Reform*.
11. Alain C. Enthoven, "Consumer-Choice Health Plans" (first of two parts), and "Consumer-Choice Health Plans" (second of two parts); Alain C. Enthoven, *Health Plan*.
12. This is based on Mark E. Rushefsky, "A Critique of Market Reform in Health Care," 724–25.
13. See, for example, Elizabeth Wehr, "Competition in Health Care"; and Linda E. Demkovich, "Adding Competition to the Health Industry."
14. Clark C. Havighurst, *Deregulating the Health Care Industry*.
15. For an evaluation of the California program, see General Accounting Office, *Health Insurance: California Public Employees' Alliance Has Reduced Recent Premium Growth*.
16. Robert Reinhold, "A Health-Care Theory Hatched in Fireside Chats," *New York Times*, February 10, 1993. See also Alain C. Enthoven, "The History and Principles of Managed Competition."
17. See Alain Enthoven and Richard Kronick, "A Consumer-Choice Health Plan for the 1990s" (first of two parts) and (second of two parts); Alain C. Enthoven, "Universal Health Insurance through Incentives Reform"; and Alain E. Enthoven and Richard Kronick, "Will Managed Competition Work? Better Care at Lower Cost," *New York Times*, January 25, 1992.
18. Enthoven and Kronick, "A Consumer-Choice Health Plan for the 1990s" (first of two parts), 31.
19. This is a variation of the play-or-pay rule and contains an employer mandate.
20. The managed competition plan has some resemblance to the German system, whereby Sickness Funds negotiate with organizations of providers.
21. John D. Rockefeller IV, "The Pepper Commission Report on Comprehensive Health Care."
22. John Kingdon argues that political and problem factors are the most important in placing an item on the governmental agenda. See John W. Kingdon, *Agendas, Alternatives, and Public Policies*. See also Mark E. Rushefsky and Kant Patel, *Politics, Power and Policy Making*; and Theda Skocpol, *Boomerang*.

23. Adam Clymer, "Democrats Call Town Meetings on Health Care," *New York Times*, December 22, 1991.

24. Michael Wines, "Bush Announces Health Plan, Filling Gap in Re-Election Bid," *New York Times*, February 7, 1992.

25. Robert Pear, "President Leaves Many Areas Gray," *New York Times*, February 7, 1992.

26. Robert Pear, "Doctors' Group Offers Plan to Curb Health-Care Costs," *New York Times*, September 15, 1992.

27. Quoted in Robert Pear, "Conflicting Aims in Health Lobby Stall Legislation," *New York Times*, March 18, 1992.

28. Ibid.

29. Jonathan Rauch, *Demosclerosis*. See also Mancur Olson, *The Logic of Collective Action*; and Mancur Olson, *The Rise and Decline of Nations*.

30. For a discussion of interest groups in the health policy debates of the 1990s, see Rushefsky and Patel, *Politics, Power and Policy Making*, 140–72, chap. 5.

31. Clifford Krauss, "Democrats Offer a Health-Care Plan," *New York Times*, June 26, 1992.

32. "Conservative Democrats Offer Health-Care Plan," *Springfield News-Leader*, September 17, 1992.

33. For a discussion of the acceptance of managed competition by many policy elites and decision makers during this time, see Jacob S. Hacker, *The Road to Nowhere*.

34. See "Editorial: The Bush-Clinton Health Reform," *New York Times*, October 10, 1992; and Robert Pear, "Bush and Clinton Aren't Saying It, but Health-Care Taxes Are Likely," *New York Times*, October 18, 1992.

35. See Robert Pear, "In Shift, Insurers Ask U.S. to Require Coverage for All," *New York Times*, December 3, 1993; and Peter Kerr, "Insurers Stand to Profit Big from a Health Care Overhaul," *New York Times*, December 4, 1992.

36. Adam Clymer, "Americans Have High Hopes for Clinton, Poll Finds," *New York Times*, January 19, 1993.

37. Robin Toner, "Support Is Found for Broad Change in Health Policy," *New York Times*, April 6, 1993. For a discussion of public opinion polls and health care reform, see Rushefsky and Patel, *Power, Politics, and Policy making*, 211–42, chap. 7. See also Robert J. Blendon, Mollyann Brodie, and John Benson, "What Happened to Americans' Support for the Clinton Plan?"; and Lawrence R. Jacobs and Robert Y. Shapiro, "Don't Blame the Public for Failed Health Care Reform."

38. Richard Morin, "Even Doctors Are on the Health Reform Bandwagon," *Washington Post National Weekly Edition*, April 19–25, 1993, 37.

39. David Wessel and Gerald F. Seib, "Clinton Had Devised His Health Package before the Inaugural," *Wall Street Journal*, September 22, 1993.

40. James Fallows, "A Triumph of Misinformation," 28. The book was the first edition of Paul Starr, *The Logic of Health Care Reform*.

41. This was mostly a political complaint. Whatever plan the president proposed would have to be approved by Congress, where the deliberations were open. This is opposed to situations during the Reagan and Bush administrations, when secret meetings with industry were held that affected regulations and would not be subject to open meetings or congressional oversight at a later time. On this point, see Richard Nathan, *The Administrative Presidency*; and Charles Tiefer, *The Semi-Sovereign Presidency*. On the openness of the task force to outside views, see Fallows, "Triumph of Misinformation," 28–30. See also Hacker, *The Road to Nowhere*; and Skocpol, *Boomerang*.

42. Adam Clymer, "Clinton Asks Backing for Sweeping Change in the Health System," *New York Times*, September 23, 1993.

43. White House House Domestic Policy Council, *The President's Health Security Act*, 21–22.

44. The following description is based on Patrick Rogers, "Healthtown, U.S.A.," *Newsweek*, October 4, 1993, 44–45. See also Hacker, *Road to Nowhere*.

45. As we shall see in chapter 10, some of these provisions become part of the incremental approach to health care, though not all get enacted.

46. Alice M. Rivlin, David M. Cutler, and Len M. Nichols, "Financing, Estimation, and Estimation Effects," 31.

47. See Walter A. Zelman, "The Rationale behind the Clinton Health Reform Plan," 20–21. See, in general, Starr, *Logic of Health Care Reform*.

48. Starr, *Logic of Health Care Reform*, 101.

49. Ibid., 102.

50. See Steven Pearlstein and Dana Priest, "Some Spoonfuls of Sugar Help the Medicine Go Down with Special Interests," *Washington Post National Weekly Edition*, September 27–October 3, 1993, 7.

51. William Schneider, "Health Care Reform." Some argued that the public did not support the proposal so much as they supported recognition of the problems with the health care system and a desire to do something about them. See, for example, Karlyn H. Bowman, *The 1993–1994 Debate on Health Care Reform*.

52. Richard E. Cohen, "Ready, Aim, Reform," 2582.

53. James Fallows, "A Triumph of Misinformation," 30.

54. Julie Kosterlitz, "Winners and Losers."

55. Milt Freudenheim, "Changing the Fortunes of the Medical Business," *New York Times*, September 19, 1993. See also David S. Broder, "Of Gored Oxen and Health Care," *Washington Post National Weekly Edition*, January 17–23, 1994, 4.

56. Cohen, "Ready, Aim, Reform," 2584.

57. See Robert Pear, "Analysis Says Cost of Health Effort Is Underestimated," *New York Times*, December 9, 1993. See also John F. Sheils and Lawrence S. Lewin, "Perspective: Alternative Estimate."

58. Robert Pear, "Early Doubts on Health, Papers Show," *New York Times*, September 8, 1993. See also Steven Greenhouse, "Many Experts Say Health Plan Would Fall Far Short on Savings," *New York Times*, September 21, 1993.

59. See Alissa J. Rubin, "CBO Turns Budget Spotlight on Health-Care Overhaul," *Congressional Quarterly Weekly Report* 52, no. 6 (February 12, 1994), 290–91.

60. Quoted in Jodie T. Allen, "New Blue Smoke and Mirrors," *Washington Post National Weekly Edition*, February 21–27, 1994, 23.

61. Alain C. Enthoven, "Why Not the Clinton Health Plan?"

62. Paul Starr, "Why the Clinton Plan Is Not the Enthoven Plan."

63. The following two paragraphs are based on the Kaiser Commission on the Future of Medicaid, *Health Reform Legislation*.

64. Co-sponsorship is an indicator of support for a proposal.

65. Adam Clymer, "Many Health Plans, One Political Goal," *New York Times*, October 17, 1993.

66. For a discussion of interest groups and health care reform proposals, see Rushefsky and Patel, *Politics, Power, and Policy Making*, chap. 5; and Haynes Johnson and David S. Broder, *The System*.

67. Julie Kosterlitz, "Health Lobby Cranks Up Its Postage Meter."

68. Katharine Q. Seelye, "Lobbyists Are the Loudest in the Health Care Debate," *New York Times*, August 16, 1994. See also Neil A. Lewis, "Medical Industry Showers Congress with Lobby Money," *New York Times*, December 13, 1993.

69. Clifford Krauss, "Lobbyists of Every Stripe on Health Care Proposals," *New York Times*, September 24, 1993.

70. Ibid.

71. Elizabeth Kolbert, "Health Plan Foes Try Campaign-Style Ads," *New York Times*, October 21, 1993.

72. Robin Toner, "Highlighting Fears about the Clinton Health Plan," *New York Times*, February 1, 1994.

73. Robin Toner, "Ads Are Potent Weapon in Health Care Struggle," *New York Times*, February 1, 1994. For a critique of the HIAA ad campaign, see Julie Kosterlitz, "Harry, Louise and Doublespeak."

74. One could argue that changes occurring in the health care system will in fact reduce choice more than the Clinton plan would have, had it gone into effect.

75. Steven Waldman and Bob Cohn, "Health Care Reform: The Lost Chance," *Newsweek*, September 19, 1994, 32.

76. "Spin Doctors Wreck Harry and Louise," *New York Times*, July 8, 1994.

77. Toner, "Ads Are Potent Weapons in Health Care Struggle."

78. "Muddling Through the Message," *Newsweek*, October 11, 1993, 44.

79. Robin Toner, "Ad Drive Opens for Canadian-Style Health Care," *New York Times*, May 3, 1994.

80. Kathleen Hall Jamieson, "When Harry Met Louise," *Washington Post National Weekly Edition* 11, no. 43, August 22–28, 1994, 29.

81. Adam Clymer, "Debate on Health Care May Depend on 'Crisis,'" *New York Times*, January 17, 1994.

82. Richard Morin, "Is There a Health Care Crisis? Yes and No," *Washington Post National Weekly Edition*, February 21–27, 1994, 37.

83. William Schneider, "Health Care: So Where's the Crisis?"

84. Robin Toner, "Poll on Changes in Health Care Finds Support amid Skepticism," *New York Times*, September 22, 1993. See also Toner, "Support Is Found for Broad Change in Health Policy."

85. Robert J. Blendon, quoted in Richard Morin, "Health Care Reform, Yes, but Not at Any Price," *Washington Post National Weekly Edition*, January 10–16, 1994, 37.

86. David S. Broder and Richard Morin, "Clinton's Health Plan: A Turn for the Worse," *Washington Post National Weekly Edition*, March 7–13, 1994, 15. See also Adam Clymer, "Poll Finds Public Still Doubtful over Costs of Clinton Health Plan," *New York Times*, March 15, 1994.

87. James Fallows, "Triumph of Misinformation," 30.

88. Ibid., 37.

89. See Richard Morin, "Don't Know Much about Health Care Reform," *Washington Post National Weekly Edition*, March 14–20, 1994, 37. See also Richard Morin, "A Bitter Pill to the Public," *Washington Post National Weekly Edition*, March 28–April 3, 1994, 37. This lack of information about policy issues is a fairly common finding. On the importance of looking at question wording to get a real sense of changes in public mood, see James A. Stimson, *Public Opinion in America*.

90. Robin Toner, "Health Impasse Sours Voters, New Poll Finds," *New York Times*, September 13, 1994.

91. Robin Toner, "House Democrats Unveil Proposal for Health Bill," *New York Times*, July 30, 1994; and Katharine Q. Seelye, "Some House Democrats Like Plan but Not Political Risks," *New York Times*, July 30, 1994.

92. Adam Clymer, "House Is Letting Senate Go First on Health Care," *New York Times*, August 5, 1994.

93. Robert Pear, "Cost Is Obscured in Health Debate," *New York Times*, August 7, 1994.

94. Adam Clymer, "Centrists on Senate Panel Near Compromise on Health Care Bill," *New York Times*, June 23, 1994.

95. See Adam Clymer, "Blind Eye Now, Eyeing Victory Later," *New York Times*, June 24, 1994; and Robin Toner, "Health Coalition Strongly Opposes Compromise Plan," *New York Times*, June 24, 1994.

96. Adam Clymer, "Dole Gathering Broad Backing for a G.O.P. Health Care Plan," *New York Times*, June 30, 1994.

97. Adam Clymer, "G.O.P. in the House Trying to Block Health Care Bill," *New York Times*, June 17, 1994.

98. Julie Kosterlitz, "Brinkmanship."

99. Adam Clymer, "Senate Leader Unveils His Plan for Health Care," *New York Times*, August 3, 1994.

100. Michael Wines, "Clinton Puts Onus for Health Care on Republicans," *New York Times*, August 4, 1994.

101. Adam Clymer, "Mitchell Sees Room for Dealing on Rival Health Care Proposals," *New York Times*, August 13, 1994.

102. Adam Clymer, "Mitchell Announces Plan to End G.O.P. 'Filibuster' on Health Bill," *New York Times*, August 16, 1994.

103. Robert Pear, "Diverse Elements Criticize 'Mainstream' Senate Plan," *New York Times*, August 21, 1994.

104. See Todd S. Purdum, "Clinton's Allies on Health Concede That Broad Plan Is All but Dead This Year," *New York Times*, August 27, 1994; and Adam Clymer, "Clinton Is Urged to Abandon Fight over Health Bill," *New York Times*, September 21, 1994.

105. Adam Clymer, "Defying Omens, Health Care Drops from Campaign Stage," *New York Times*, October 22, 1994.

106. Dana Priest and Michael Weisskopf, "Death from a Thousand Cuts," *Washington Post National Weekly Edition*, October 17–23, 1993, 9.

107. For a discussion of the failure of health care reform on the part of sympathetic observers, see Fallows, "A Triumph of Misinformation"; and Paul Starr, "What Happened to Health Care Reform?" See also Skocpol, *Boomerang: Clinton's Health Security Effort and Turn against Government in U.S. Politics*; Johnson and Broder, *The System*; and Rushefsky and Patel, *Politics, Power and Policy Making*.

108. Richard Morin, "A Health Care Reform Post-Mortem," *Washington Post National Weekly Edition*, September 12–18, 1994, 37.

109. For a discussion of trust in government, see Stephen C. Craig, *The Malevolent Leaders*; and Joseph S. Nye, Jr., Philip D. Zelikow, and David C. King, eds., *Why People Don't Trust Government*.

110. Helen Dewar, "Health Care's Real Issue: November," *Washington Post National Weekly Edition*, July 11–17, 1994, 12–13. For a discussion of President Clinton's approval ratings, see Rushefsky and Patel, *Politics, Power and Policy Making*, chaps. 3 and 7.

111. Dana Priest and Michael Weisskopf, "Health Care Reform." Also see Fallows, "Triumph of Misinformation."

112. See Stuart M. Butler, "Rube Goldberg, Call Your Office," *New York Times*, September 28, 1993; and Steven Waldman, "How Clinton Blew It," *Newsweek*, June 27, 1994, 28. One could argue that the health care system envisioned by the plan was no more and perhaps even less complex than the current system. That assertion was never made by the Clinton forces or its allies.

113. Adam Clymer, "Hillary Clinton Says Administration Was Misunderstood on Health Care," *New York Times*, October 3, 1994. See also E.J. Dionne, Jr., "Clinton's Health Care Crisis," *Washington Post National Weekly Edition*, March 14–20, 1994, 29.

114. Adam Clymer, Robert Pear, and Robin Toner, "For Health Care, Time Was a Killer," *New York Times*, August 29, 1994.

115. Fallows, "Triumph of Misinformation," 30–32.

116. David S. Hilzenrath, "Health Care Costs' Double-Edged Sword," *Washington Post National Weekly Edition*, December 27, 1993–January 2, 1994, 22. There is some precedent for this. In the late 1970s, President Jimmy Carter proposed legislation that would result in some federal controls over hospitals. The health care sector promised to restrain inflation through what became known as the Voluntary Effort. While Carter was president, medical inflation was restrained. With Carter's defeat in 1980, the Voluntary Effort was dropped.

117. Steven Waldman and Bob Cohn, "Health Care Reform: The Lost Chance," *Newsweek*, September 19, 1994, 28.

118. Ibid., 32.

119. Fallows, "Triumph of Misinformation," 36–37.

120. Kant Patel and Mark Rushefsky, "The Health Policy Community and Health Care Reform in the United States," *Health: An Interdisciplinary Journal for the Social Study of Health, Illness and Medicine.*

121. Sven Steinmo and Jon Watts, "It's the Institutions, Stupid." This is also essentially the argument made by journalists Haynes Johnson and David Broder, who wrote that "the system" itself was broken; see Johnson and Broder, *The System.*

122. Dan Morgan, "While Washington Fiddles, the States March On," *Washington Post National Weekly Edition*, October 10–16, 1994, 47.

123. Harry Nelson, *Federalism in Health Reform*, 1.

124. National Commission on the State and Local Public Service, *Frustrated Federalism.*

125. John J. DiIulio, Jr., and Richard Nathan, eds. "Introduction," 3.

126. See John Holahan, and Len Nichols, "State Health Policy in the 1990s."

127. For a discussion of the fiscal impact of health care spending on the states, see Steven D. Gold, "Health Care and the Fiscal Crisis of the States."

128. Harry Nelson, *Federalism in Health Reform*, 9. See also Deane Neubauer, "Hawaii: A Pioneer in Health System Reform," 31–39.

129. See Deane Neubauer, "Hawaii: The Health State Revisited."

130. See Thomas R. Oliver and Pamela Paul-Shaheen, "Translating Ideas into Actions: Entrepreneurial Leadership in State Health Care Reforms," *Journal of Health Politics, Policy and Law* 22, no. 3 (June 1997): 721–88; Daniel M. Fox and John K. Iglehart, eds., *Five States That Could Not Wait*; Holahan and Nichols, "State Health Policy in the 1990s"; and Pamela A. Paul-Shaheen, "The States and Health Care Reform."

131. For a thorough discussion of the Oregon plan and subsequent developments, see Howard M. Leichter, "Rationing of Health Care in Oregon."

132. Robert Pear, "Plan to Ration Health Care Is Rejected by Government," *New York Times*, August 4, 1992.

133. Robert Pear, "Too-Bitter Medicine," *New York Times*, August 5, 1992.

134. Ibid.

135. Barbara Roberts, "Bush Blows It on Health Care," *New York Times*, August 11, 1992.

136. John K. Iglehart, "Health Care Reform," 78.

137. Oliver and Paul-Shaheen, "Translating Ideas into Actions."

138. Ibid.

139. Iglehart, "Health Care Reform," 76.

140. Oliver and Paul-Shaheen, "Translating Ideas into Actions."

141. Iglehart, "Health Care Reform," 78; and Nelson, *Federalism in Health Reform*, 8.

142. Robert Crittenden, "Managed Competition and Premium Caps in Washington State."

143. Michelle Quinn, "California's Health Pool: Limits, but Lower Rates," *New York Times*, June 11, 1994.

144. General Accounting Office, *Medicaid: States Turn to Managed Care to Improve Access and Control Costs.*

145. See Penelope Lemov, "States and Medicaid: Ahead of the Feds"; Penelope Lemov, "An Acute Case of Health Care Reform"; and Stuart Schear, "A Medicaid Miracle?"

146. Dale Russakoff, "When Health Care Reform Hits Home," *Washington Post National Weekly Edition*, October 25–31, 1993, 31–32.

147. Melinda Henneberger, "Self-Help Overhaul of Health Care," *New York Times*, May 6, 1994.

148. Dan Morgan, "State Health Care Goes on the Critical List," *Washington Post National Weekly Edition*, December 5–11, 1994, 31; see also "Elections: What Impact on Health Care Reform?"

149. The phrase is from Supreme Court Justice Louis B. Brandeis. See the discussion by Oliver and Paul-Shaheen in "Translating Ideas into Actions."

Chapter 10. The Triumph of Incrementalism: Revolution, Rationing, and Reaction

1. The political scientist who has most strongly argued that incrementalism is the dominant style of policymaking is Charles Lindblom. See Charles E. Lindblom, "The Science of Muddling Through"; and Charles E. Lindblom and Edward J. Woodhouse, *The Policy-Making Process*. See also Michael T. Hayes, *Incrementalism and Public Policy*; and Charles O. Jones, *An Introduction to the Study of Public Policy.*

2. Paul Starr, "What Happened to Health Care Reform?" 20–21.

3. Term limitations was voted on in the House but failed.

4. George Hager and Alissa J. Rubin, "Last-Minute Maneuvers Forge a Conference Agreement," *Congressional Quarterly Weekly Report* 53, no. 25 (June 24, 1995): 1814–1819.

5. See Erik Eckholm, "Health Benefits Found to Deter Job Switching," *New York Times*, September 26, 1991.

6. See Mark E. Rushefsky and Kant Patel, *Politics, Power and Policy Making*, pp. 131–35; and Brian K. Atchinson and Daniel M. Fox, "The Politics of the Health Insurance Portability and Accountability Act," 148.

7. Len M. Nichols and Linda J. Blumberg, "A Different Kind of 'New Federalism'?" (the history is based on pages 26–30); and Kala Ladenheim, "Health Insurance in Transition."

8. Ladenheim, "Health Insurance in Transition."

9. Nichols and Blumberg, "A Different Kind of 'New Federalism'?" 33.

10. Robert Pear, "New Health Insurance Rules Spell Out Rights of Workers," *New York Times*, April 2 1997.

11. Nichols and Blumberg, "A Different Kind of 'New Federalism'?" 34.

12. See General Accounting Office, *Health Insurance Standards*; Robert Pear, "Health Insurers Skirting New Law, Officials Report," *New York Times*, October 5, 1997; and Robert Pear, "High Rates Hobble Law to Guarantee Health Insurance," *New York Times*, March 17, 1998.

13. Robert Pear, "Clinton to Punish Insurers Who Deny Health Coverage," *New York Times*, July 7, 1998.

14. General Accounting Office, *Health Insurance for Children*; and Laura Summer, Sharon Parrott, and Cindy Mann, *Millions of Uninsured and Underinsured Children Are Eligible for Medicaid.*

15. Sara H. Rosenbaum, Kay Johnson, Colleen Sonosky, Anne Markus, and Chris DeGraw, "The Children's Hour."

16. General Accounting Office, *Health Insurance: Coverage Leads to Increased Health Care Access for Children.* See also Robin R. Weinick, Margaret E. Weigers, and Joel W. Cohen, "Children's Health Insurance, Access to Care, and Health Status."

17. Mireya Navarro, "Group Plan Gives Florida Children Access to Affordable Health Care," *New York Times*, May 23, 1997.

18. Adam Clymer, "Cigarette Tax Rise Pays for Child Health Plan," *New York Times*, February 28, 1997.

19. Ibid.

20. Esther B. Fein, "New York Health Plan for Children Draws Attention," *New York Times*, April 27, 1997.

21. Ibid.

22. Navarro, "Group Plan Gives Florida Children Access to Affordable Health Care."

23. Ibid.

24. Ibid.

25. Marilyn Werber Serafini, "Children's Crusade."

26. Ibid.

27. Navarro, "Group Plan Gives Florida Children Access to Affordable Health Care."

28. See Robert Pear, "Capitol in Discord Over Plan to Aid Uninsured Youths," *New York Times*, June 17, 1997.

29. Edward M. Kennedy and Orrin Hatch, "Health Insurance for Every Child."

30. David Frum, "What's Wrong with This Plan?"

31. A similar argument (and mistake) has been made about spending for elementary and secondary public education. Those who denigrate public education point to the massive increase in spending for public education. Much of the increase in public education spending has gone to other programs apart from regular education, for example, special education. For a discussion of this point, see Richard Rothstein and Karen Hawley Mills, *Where the Money's Gone.*

32. Frum, "What's Wrong with This Plan?"

33. David Besharov cites Congressional Budget Office studies on this point. See Robert Pear, "Health Care Bills Don't Meet Goals, Budget Aides Say," *New York Times*, July 2, 1997.

34. Douglas J. Besharov, "Beware the Real Agenda," *New York Times*, August 5, 1997.

35. Cindy Mann, and Jocelyn Guyer, "Overview of the New Child Health Block Grant."

36. Ibid., 7.

37. Children's Defense Fund, *CHIP Checkup.*

38. The CDF report argues that the Medicaid has uniquely child-friendly benefits compared to private insurance packages.

39. Children's Defense Fund, *CHIP Checkup*, 7, footnote 7.

40. James Dao, "Clinton Details Efforts to Insure More Children," *New York Times*, June 23, 1998.

41. Robert Pear, "Clinton Ordering Effort to Sign Up Medicaid Children," *New York Times*, December 29, 1997.

42. Marsha Gold and Robert Hurley, "The Role of Managed Care 'Products' in Managed Care Plans," 29.

43. William Schneider, "Fear of Bureaucrats Strikes Again."

44. Jonathan P. Weinder and Gregory de Lissovoy, "Razing a Tower of Babel."

45. See Thomas Bodenheimer and Kip Sullivan, "How Large Employers Are Shaping the Health Care Marketplace," (first of two parts);" and Betty Leyerle, *The Private Regulation of American Heath Care*.

46. Susan Brink and Nancy Shute, "Are HMOs the Right Prescription?"

47. Bodenheimer and Sullivan, "How Large Employers Are Shaping the Health Care Marketplace" (first of two parts). See also George Anders, *Health against Wealth*.

48. Gail A. Jensen et al. "The New Dominance of Managed Care."

49. Ibid., taken from and calculated from exhibit 2. Marmor argues that the definition of managed care given by Jensen et al. is too broad. See Theodore R. Marmor, "Forecasting American Health Care."

50. Bodenheimer and Sullivan, "How Large Employers Are Shaping the Health Care Marketplace" (first of two parts).

51. Ibid., 1004.

52. Alain C. Enthoven, "Consumer Choice Health Plans" (first of two parts) and (second of two parts).

53. Bodenheimer and Sullivan, "How Large Employers Are Shaping the Health Care Marketplace" (first of two parts) and (second of two parts).

54. Gold and Hurley, "The Role of Managed Care 'Products' in Managed Care Plans," 31. See also Jon R. Gabel, "Ten Ways HMOs Have Changed during the 1990s."

55. Corrigan et al., "Trends toward a National Health Care Marketplace."

56. Janet M. Corrigan et al., "Trends toward a National Health Care Marketplace" (quote is from p. 12).

57. Srija Srinivasan, Larry Levitt, and Janet Lundy, "Wall Street's Love Affair with Health Care."

58. Gabel, "Ten Ways HMOs Have Changed during the 1990s."

59. Srinivasan, Levitt, and Lundy, "Wall Street's Love Affair with Health Care."

60. Milt Freudenheim, "Managed Care Empires in the Making," *New York Times*, April 2, 1996.

61. Sheryl Gay Stolberg, "As Doctors Trade Shingle for Marquee, Cries of Woe," *New York Times*, August 3, 1998.

62. Easterbrook, "Healing the Great Divide," 66.

63. Congressional Budget Office, *Trends in Spending by the Private Sector*.

64. Susan Love, "H.M.O.'s Could Save Your Life," *New York Times*, June 7, 1998.

65. Susan Brink, "HMOs Were the Right Rx."

66. Ibid.

67. Ibid.

68. Marilyn Werber Serafini, "Quality Time," *National Journal* 29, no. 21 (May 24, 1997): 1035–1037 quote is from pp. 1035–1036.

69. Joseph W. Thompson et al., "The NCQA's Quality Compass."

70. See, for example, Kathleen N. Lohr, "How Do We Measure Quality?" See also Gail R. Wilensky, "Promoting Quality?" The May/June 1998 and July/August 1998 issues of *Health Affairs* include a number of articles that address quality issues.

71. Judith H. Hibbard et al., "Choosing a Health Plan."

72. See Commonwealth Fund news release, "Majority of Employers Do Not Consider Reports on HMO Quality When Choosing Employee Health Plans," September 15, 1998. http://www.cmsf.org./media/gabel293-0915.html.

73. Jose J. Escarce, Judy A. Shea, and Wei Chen, "Segmentation of Hospital Markets."

74. For a brief history of the patients' rights movement and its linkage with consumer rights, see George J. Annas, "A National Bill of Patients' Rights."

75. On the issue of professional dominance, see Paul Starr, *The Social Transformation of American Medicine.*

76. It is the authors' observation that doctors as a whole do not like managed care.

77. See, for example, Steven Greenhouse, "Podiatrists to Form Nationwide Union; A Reply to H.M.O.'s," *New York Times*, October 25, 1996; and Peter T. Kilborn, "Devalued by Growth of H.M.O.'s, Some Doctors Seek Union Banner," *New York Times*, May 30, 1996.

78. George J. Annas, "A National Bill of Patients' Rights."

79. For discussions of trust and managed care, see Bradford H. Gray, "Trust and Trustworthy Care in the Managed Care Era"; and Lee N. Newcomer, "Measures of Trust in Health Care." Besides these, see especially two pieces by David Mechanic: "The Functions and Limitations of Trust in the Provision of Medical Care" and "Changing Medical Organization and the Erosion of Trust."

80. Annas, "A National Bill of Patients' Rights."

81. For a discussion of accountability in health care and, in particular, the role of standards in setting accountability, see Linda L. Emanuel, "Professional Standards in Health Care: Calling All Parties to Account." See also Norman Daniels and James Sabin, "The Ethics of Accountability in Managed Care Reform"; and Alice G. Gosfield, "Who is Holding Whom Accountable for Quality?"

82. See Rushefsky and Patel, *Politics, Power and Policy Making*, chap. 7.

83. Lizette Alvarez, "After Polling, G.O.P. Offers a Patients' Bill," *New York Times*, July 16, 1998.

84. Robert J. Blendon et al., "Understanding the Managed Care Backlash."

85. Ibid., 91–92.

86. Peter T. Kilborn, "Dissatisfaction Is Growing with Managed Care Plans," *New York Times*, September 28, 1997.

87. Everett C. Ladd, "Health Care Hysteria, Part II," *New York Times*, July 23, 1998.

88. Donald W. Moran, "Federal Regulation of Managed Care."

89. Easterbrook, "Healing the Great Divide," 64.

90. Milt Freudenheim, "Not Quite What the Doctor Ordered," *New York Times*, October 8, 1996. See also Bob Herbert, "Prescription Switches," *New York Times*, December 27, 1996.

91. Laura Johannes, "Some HMOs Now Put Doctors on a Budget for Prescription Drugs," *Wall Street Journal*, May 22, 1997.

92. Robert Pear, "H.M.O.'s Refusing Emergency Claims, Hospitals Assert," *New York Times*, July 9, 1995.

93. See Anders, *Health against Wealth*, chap. 7.

94. Peter T. Kilborn, "End of H.M.O. for the Elderly Brings Dismay in Rural Ohio," *New York Times*, July 31, 1998.

95. Peter T. Kilborn, "Largest H.M.O.'s Cutting the Poor and the Elderly," *New York Times*, July 6, 1998.

96. Carol Marie Cropper, "The H.M.O. Says the Doctor Is In. Is He Really?" *New York Times*, November 10, 1996.

97. Robert Pear, "The Tricky Business of Keeping Doctors Quiet," *New York Times*, September 22, 1996.

98. Patricia Neuman et al., "Marketing HMOs to Medicare Beneficiaries."

99. The three figures are taken from David J. Morrow, "Medicare Panacea Turns Patient," *New York Times*, September 9, 1998.

100. Robert Kuttner, "Must Good HMOs Go Bad?" (first of two parts).

101. Ibid., 1558–1559.

102. Ibid., 1562.

103. "Ranking the Health Plans," *Newsweek* 132, no. 13 (September 28, 1998): 67–70.

104. Easterbrook, "Healing the Great Divide," p. 67. See also Families USA, *Premium Pay II.*

105. Susan Brink and Nancy Shute, "Are HMOs the Right Prescription?"; and Easterbrook, "Healing the Great Divide."

106. Peter T. Kilborn, "The Uninsured Find Fewer Doctors in the House," *New York Times*, August 30, 1998.

107. Mollyann Brodie, Lee Ann Brady, and Drew E. Altman, "Media Coverage of Managed Care."

108. Ibid., 22.

109. Ibid., 23–24.

110. Karen Ignagni, "Covering a Breaking Revolution."

111. Robert Kuttner, "Must Good HMOs Go Bad? (second of two parts).

112. Donald W. Moran, "Federal Regulation of Managed Care."

113. A Securities and Exchange Commission model is proposed by Etheredge, See Lynn Etheredge, "Promarket Regulation."

114. Moran, "Federal Regulation of Managed Care."

115. Alain C. Enthoven and Sara J. Singer, "Markets and Collective Action in Regulating Managed Care."

116. David A. Jones, "'Putting Patients First.'"

117. Ibid., 118.

118. Ibid., 119.

119. Peter V. Lee, "The True Test of Whether Health Plans Put Patients First."

120. Ibid., 130–31.

121. Ibid. 131.

122. Ibid., 132.

123. Clark C. Havighurst, "'Putting Patients First,'" 123.

124. Ibid.

125. Ibid.

126. Families USA, "Health Legislation Enacted by the 104th Congress"; National Conference of State Legislatures, *Health Care Legislation 1996.*

127. Families USA, *HMO Consumers at Risk.*

128. Patricia A. Miller, "Health Care Reform: Not Dead Yet," *Politics Now*, July 19, 1996.

129. Families USA, *HMO Consumers at Risk.*

130. Families USA, *Hit and Miss.*

131. See Trish Riley, "The Role of States in Accountability for Quality"; and Len M. Nichols; *Health Care Quality.*

132. Robert Pear, "H.M.O.'s Asserting Immunity in Suits over Malpractice," *New York Times*, November 17, 1996.

133. Lizette Alvarez, "After Polling, G.O.P. Offers a Patients' Bill," *New York Times*, July 16, 1998.

134. Robert Pear, "Hands Tied, Judges Rue Law That Limits H.M.O. Liability," *New York Times*, July 11, 1998.

135. Advisory Commission on Consumer Protection and Quality in the Health Care Industry.

136. Bill Clinton, "State of the Union," January 27, 1998. The State of the Union address can be found at the White House Web site: http:// www.pub.whitehouse.gov.

137. Robert Pear, "G.O.P. Unveils a Bill to Define Patients' Rights," *New York Times*, June 25, 1998.

138. Robert Pear, "Common Ground on Patient Rights Hides a Chasm," *New York Times*, August 4, 1998. See also Robert Pear, "2 Patients' Rights Bill Take Divergent Roads," *New York Times*, July 4, 1998.

139. Pear, "Common Ground on Patient Rights Hides a Chasm."

140. Ibid.

141. Ibid.

142. David Sibley, "What the Texas Experiment Shows about H.M.O. Liability," *New York Times*, August 7, 1998.

143. Carol Marie Cropper, "In Texas, a Laboratory Test on the Effects of Suing H.M.O.'s," *New York Times*, September 13, 1998.

144. Congressional Budget Office, "H.R. 3605/S. 1890 Patients' Bill of Rights Act of 1998," July 16, 1998. This report can be found at the CBO Web site: http://www.cbo.gov. See also Cropper, "In Texas, a Laboratory Test on the Effects of Suing H.M.O.'s."

145. Robert Pear, "H.M.O. Group Backs Controls G.O.P. Rejects," *New York Times*, July 14, 1998.

146. Peter T. Kilborn, "Patients' Rights Debate Engenders Unlikeliest of Alliances," *New York Times*, July 21, 1998.

147. Robert Pear, "3 Big Health Plans Urge National Standards," *New York Times*, September 24, 1997; and Families USA, *Leading Health Plans and National Consumer Groups Announce Unprecedented Agreement for Consumer Protection Standards in Managed Care*. For a brief critique of the principles, see Annas, "National Bill of Patients' Rights."

148. Annas, "National Bill of Patients' Rights."

149. Terry M. Neal, "Bashing the HMO-Bashers," *Washington Post National Weekly Edition* 15, no. 36 (July 6, 1998): 16.

150. Robert Pear, "H.M.O.'s Fight Plan to Pay for Some Emergency Care," *New York Times*, June 25, 1997.

151. Neal, "Bashing the HMO-Bashers."

152. Alvarez, "After Polling, A Patients' Bill."

153. "Patients' Rights: Senate Republicans Quash Floor Action," American Political Network, Inc., Health Line, 1998. Internet document found through Lexis/Nexis.

154. Ceci Connolly, "Clinton Sets to Work on Health Care," *Washington Post*, August 30, 1998.

155. Robert Pear, "States Take Lead in Health Legislation," *New York Times*, September 14, 1998.

156. Ibid.

157. Ibid.

158. William Schneider, "Fear of Bureaucrats Strikes Again."

Chapter 11: Conclusion: Health Care Policy at the End of the Twentieth Century

1. However, Mayhew argues that, even under conditions of divided government, significant policy initiatives can be enacted. See David R. Mayhew, *Divided We Govern*. Freedman finds that the Reagan and Nixon administrations, periods of divided government, were especially good times for health care legislation. See Grace Roegner Freedman, "Toward a Macro Theory for Health Care Policy Making."

2. For a discussion of how major changes can occur, see Frank R. Baumgartner and Bryan D. Jones, *Agendas and Instability in American Politics*; and John W. Kingdon, *Agendas, Alternatives, and Public Policies*.

3. For a discussion of markets and health care that focuses on the twenty-first century, see the special issue of *Journal of Health Politics, Policy and Law* 22, no. 2 (April 1997).

4. See Daniel Yergin and Joseph Stanislaw, *The Commanding Heights*.

5. Jonathan Rauch, *Demosclerosis*.

6. Jonathan B. Oberlander, "Medicare." The authors recall attending a conference panel of the Committee on Health Politics, during a meeting of the American Political Science Association, when Theda Skocpol expressed a passing thought that the Clinton administration would kill Medicare.

7. Robert Pear, "Congress Alarmed at Failure of Medicare to Bring Change," *New York Times*, September 27, 1998; and Milt Freudenheim, "So Far, 'Medicare Plus Choice' Is Minus Most of the Options," *New York Times*, October 4, 1998.

8. One co-author saw a new ad by the Business Roundtable decrying managed care regulation for this very reason, as well as because it adds layers of new bureaucracy—exactly the arguments made against the Clinton Health Security Act.

9. Jonathan Cohn, "Cosmetic Surgery."

10. See Carrie J. Gavora, "A Progress Report on the Clinton Health Plan"; K. Daniel Glover, "From 'Universal Coverage' to 'Incremental Reform'"; Robert Pear, "New Approach to Overhauling Health Insurance: Step by Step," *New York Times*, November 11, 1996; and Jill Lawrence and Susan Page, "Clinton Health Plan Lives Again, One Bill at a Time," *USA Today*, July 2, 1997.

11. Robert Pear, "H.M.O.'s Are Retreating from Medicare, Citing High Costs," *New York Times*, October 2, 1998; Freudenheim, "So Far, 'Medicare Plus Choice' Is Minus Most Options."

12. Freudenheim, "So Far, 'Medicare Plus Choice' Is Minus Most Options."

13. See Holcomb B. Noble, "Struggling to Bolster Minorities in Medicine," *New York Times*, September 29, 1998. For a vigorous defense of affirmative action, one that argues that it leads to more minorities in medical and other professional schools, see William G. Bowen and Derek Bok, *The Shape of the River*.

14. Sheila Smith et al., "The Next Ten Years of Health Spending." See also Paul B. Ginsburg and Jon R. Gabel, "Tracking Health Care Costs."

15. William Schneider, "Fear of Bureaucrats Strikes Again."

16. See George Anders, *Health against Wealth*.

17. See Milt Freudenheim, "(Loosely) Managed Care Is in Demand," *New York Times*, September 29, 1998.

18. Peter T. Kilborn, "Reality of the H.M.O. System Doesn't Live Up to the Dream," *New York Times*, October 5, 1998.

19. Robert L. Bennefield, "Health Insurance Coverage: 1997." See also Robert Pear, "Americans Lacking Health Insurance Put at 16 Percent," *New York Times*, September 26, 1998.

20. Pear, "Americans Lacking Health Insurance Put at 16 Percent."

21. See Marilyn Moon and Joanne Silberner, "What about Health Care for the Uninsured?"; and Brian J. LeClair, "What about a Bill of Rights for the Uninsured?" LeClair argues that patients'-bill-of-rights legislation will raise health insurance premiums and make it more difficult for many to afford health insurance.

22. See Sandy Lutz, Woodrin Grossman, and John Bigalke, *Med Inc.*; and Mark A. Peterson, "Introduction: Health Care into the Next Century."

23. Kilborn, "Reality of the H.M.O. System."

24. See Atul A. Gawande et al., "Does Dissatisfaction with Health Plans Stem from Having No Choices?"

25. Eric B. Schnurer, "A Health-Care Plan Most of Us Could Buy." This is much higher than for people outside FEHBP. See Kilborn, "Reality of the H.M.O. System."

26. Betty Leyerle, *The Private Regulation of American Health Care*.

27. Robert J. Samuelson, "Having It All." See also Eli Ginzberg, *The Limits of Health Reform*.

Selected Bibliography

"A Survey of Health Care: Surgery Needed." *Economist*, July 6, 1991, 4–5.

Aaron, Henry J. *Serious and Unstable Condition: Financing America's Health Care*. Washington, D.C.: Brookings Institution, 1991.

Aaron, Henry J., and Robert D. Reischauer. "'Rethinking Medicare Reform' Needs Rethinking." *Health Affairs* 17, no. 1 (January/February 1998): 69–71.

Aaron, Henry J., and William B. Schwartz. *The Painful Prescription: Rationing Hospital Care*. Washington, D.C.: Brookings Institution, 1984.

———. "Rationing Health Care: The Choice before Us." *Science* 247, no. 4941 (January 26, 1990): 418–22.

Abraham, Kenneth S., and Paul C. Weiler. "Enterprise Liability and the Evolution of the American Health Care System." *Harvard Law Review* 108, no. 2 (1994): 381–436.

Abramson, Elliot M. "The Medical Malpractice Imbroglio: A Non-Adversarial Suggestion." *Kentucky Law Review* 78 (1989–1990): 293–310.

Aday, Lu Ann. *At Risk in America: The Health and Health Care Needs of Vulnerable Populations in the United States*. San Francisco: Jossey-Bass, 1993.

———. "Equity, Accessibility, and Ethical Issues: Is the U.S. Health Care Reform Debate Asking the Right Questions?" *American Behavioral Scientist* 36, no. 6 (July/August 1993): 724–40.

Alder, Henry C. "Technology Assessment: A Vital Tool for Managers." *Hospitals* 65, no. 8 (April 20, 1991): 56–57.

Alford, Robert A. *Health Care Politics: Ideological and Interest Group Barriers to Reform*. Chicago: University of Chicago Press, 1975.

Allison, Graham. *The Essence of Decision*. Boston: Little, Brown, 1971.

Altenstetter, Christa. *Health Policy-Making and Administration in West Germany and the United States*. Beverly Hills: Sage, 1974.

Altman, Drew E. "Health Care for the Poor." *Annals of the American Academy of Political and Social Sciences* 468 (July 1983): 103–21.

Altman, Drew E., and Douglas H. Morgan. "The Role of the State and Local Government in Health." *Health Affairs* 2, no. 4 (Winter 1983): 7–31.

Altman, Stuart H., and Marc A. Rodwin. "Halfway Competitive Markets and Ineffective Regulation: The American Health Care System." *Journal of Health Politics, Policy and Law* 13, no. 2 (Summer 1988): 323–39.

Altman, Stuart H., and Sanford L. Weiner. "Regulation As a Second Best Choice." In Bureau of Economics, U.S. Federal Trade Commission, *Competition in the Health Care Sector: Past, Present, and Future*, 421–27. Washington, D.C.: Government Printing Office, 1978.

American Tort Reform Association. "Issue-by-Issue Look at the Number of States Enacting Tort Reform Legislation." December 31, 1996. http://www.aaabiz.com/ATRA/atri2.htm.

Anders, George. *Health against Wealth: HMOs and the Breakdown of Medical Trust*. Boston: Houghton Mifflin, 1996.

Anderson, Gerald F., and Earl P. Steinberg. "Role of the Hospital in the Acquisition of Technology." In *Adopting New Medical Technology*, ed. Annetine C. Gelijns and Holly V. Dawkins, 61–70. Washington, D.C.: National Academy Press, 1994.

399

Anderson, James E. *Public Policy Making: An Introduction*. 2d ed. New York: Holt, Rinehart and Winston, 1979.

Anderson, Maren D., and Peter D. Fox. "Lessons Learned from Medicaid Managed Care Approaches." *Health Affairs* 6, no. 1 (Spring 1987): 71–88.

Anderson, Odin W. *Health Services in the United States: A Growth Enterprise Since 1875*. Ann Arbor, Mich.: Health Administration Press, 1985.

Anderson, Odin W. *HMO Development: Patterns and Prospects*. Chicago: Pluribus Press, 1985.

Anderson, Stephanie. "Revenge of the HMO Patients." *Business Week* no. 3518 (March 17, 1997): 30.

Angell, Marcia. "Prisoners of Technology: The Case of Nancy Cruzan." Editorial. *New England Journal of Medicine* 322, no. 17 (April 26, 1990): 1226–1228.

Annas, George J. "A National Bill of Patients' Rights." *New England Journal of Medicine* 338, no. 10 (March 5, 1998). http://www.nejm.org/content/1998/0338/0010/0695.asp.

Ashcraft, Marie L.F., and S.E. Berki. "Health Maintenance Organizations as Medicaid Providers." *Annals of the American Academy of Political and Social Science* 468 (July 1983): 122–31.

Atchinson, Brian K., and Daniel M. Fox. "The Politics of the Health Insurance Portability and Accountability Act."

Atkins, G. Lawrence, and John L. Bauer. "Taming Health Care Costs Now." *Issues in Science and Technology* 9, no. 2 (Winter 1992): 54–60.

Atkinson, Graham, W. David Helms, and Jack Needleman. "State Trends in Hospital Uncompensated Care." *Health Affairs* 16, no. 4 (July/August 1997): 233–41.

Ayanian, John Z., Betsy A. Kohler, Toshi Abe, and Arnold M. Epstein. "The Relation between Health Insurance Coverage and Clinical Outcomes among Women with Breast Cancer." *New England Journal of Medicine* 329, no. 5 (July 29, 1993): 326–31.

Baily, Mary A. "The Administrative Approach to Medical Malpractice Disputes." *Courts, Health Science and the Law* 1, no. 1 (1990): 29–34.

Baird, Karen L. *Gender Justice and the Health Care System*. New York: Garland Publishing, 1998.

Baker, David W., Carl D. Stevens, and Robert H. Brook. "Patients Who Leave a Public Hospital Emergency Department without Being Seen by a Physician." *Journal of the American Medical Association* 266, no. 8 (August 28, 1991): 1085–1090.

———. "Regular Source of Ambulatory Care and Medical Care Utilization by Patients Presenting to a Public Hospital Emergency Department." *Journal of the American Medical Association* 271, no. 24 (June 22, 1994): 1909–1912.

Ball, Robert M. "Background of Regulation in Health Care." In *Controls of Health Care*, ed. Institute of Medicine, 3–22. Washington, D.C.: National Academy of Sciences, 1975.

Balz, Dan, and Ronald J. Brownstein. *Storming the Gates: Protest Politics and the Republican Revival*. New York: Little, Brown, 1996.

Banta, David H., and Stephen B. Thacker. "The Case for Reassessment of Health Care Technology: Once Is Not Enough." *Journal of the American Medical Association* 265, no. 2 (July 11, 1990): 235–40.

Banta, David H., and Hindrik Vondeling. "Strategies for Successful Evaluation and Policy-Making toward Health Care Technology on the Move: The Case of Medical Lasers." *Social Science and Medicine* 38, no. 12 (1994): 1663–1674.

Baruch, Elaine H., Amadeo F. D'Adamo, Jr., and Joni Seager, eds. *Embryos, Ethics, and Women's Rights: Exploring the New Reproductive Technologies*. New York: Haworth Press, 1988.

Battista, Renaldo N. "Health Care Technology Assessment: Linking Science and Policy Making." *Canadian Medical Association Journal* 146, no. 4 (February 15, 1992): 461–62.

Bauman, Patricia. "The Formulation and Evolution of the Health Maintenance Organization Policy, 1970–1973." *Social Science and Medicine* 10 (March–April 1976): 129–42.

Baumgartner, Frank R., and Bryan D. Jones. *Agendas and Instability in American Politics.* Chicago: University of Chicago Press, 1993.

Bayes, Jane H. *Ideologies and Interest-Group Politics.* Novato, Calif.: Chandler and Sharp, 1982.

Beer, S.H. *Modern British Politics.* London: Faber and Faber, 1965.

Bennefield, Robert L. "Who Loses Coverage and for How Long?" *Current Population Reports.* Washington, D.C.: U.S. Department of Commerce, Census Bureau, Economics and Statistics Administration, May 1996.

———. "Health Insurance Coverage: 1996." *Current Population Reports.* Washington, D.C.: U.S. Department of Commerce, Census Bureau, Economics and Statistics Administration, September 1997.

———. "Health Insurance Coverage: 1997." *Current Population Reports.* Washington, D.C.: U.S. Department of Commerce, Census Bureau, Economics and Statistics Administration, September 1998.

Bennett, James T., and Thomas J. DiLorenzo. *Destroying America: How Government Funds Partisan Politics.* Washington, D.C.: Cato Institute, 1985.

Berg, Robert N. "Malpractice Reform Under President Clinton: Through the Looking Glass." *The Journal of the Medical Association of Georgia* 83, no. 6 (1994): 364–66.

Berger, Mitchell S. "Following the Doctor's Orders—Caps on Non-Economic Damages in Medical Malpractice Cases." *Rutgers Law Review* 23, no. 1 (1990): 173–98.

Berk, Marc L., and Claudia L. Schur. "Access to Care: How Much Difference Does Medicaid Make?" *Health Affairs* 17, no. 3 (May/June 1998): 169–80.

Berki, S.E. "Health Care Policy: Lessons from the Past and Issues of the Future." *Annals of the American Academy of Political and Social Science* 468 (July 1983): 231–46.

Berlinger, Howard S. *Strategic Factors in U.S. Healthcare: Human Resources, Capital, and Technology.* Boulder, Colo.: Westview Press, 1987.

Berman, Howard. "Rochester: Community Rating = Insurance Access." *Hospitals* 66, no. 20 (October 20, 1992): 56.

Bernstein, Merton C., and Joan Broadshaug Bernstein. *Social Security: The System That Works.* New York: Basic Books, 1988.

Besharov, Douglas J."Beware the Real Agenda." *New York Times,* August 5, 1997.

Bicknell, William J., and Diana C. Walsh. "Critical Experiences in Organizing and Administering a State Certificate-of-Need Program." *Public Health Reports* 91 (January/February 1976): 29–45.

Bilodeau, A. "Jury Still Out on Plan That Pays for Infants Injured at Birth." *South Florida Business Journal* 11, no. 43 (1991): 3.

Bindman, Andrew, Kevin Grumbach, Dennis Keane, Loren Rauch, and John M. Luce. "Consequences of Queuing for Care at a Public Hospital Emergency Department." *Journal of the American Medical Association* 266, no. 8 (August 28, 1991): 1091–1096.

Biskupic, Joan. "Oregon's Assisted Suicide Law Lives on." *Washington Post,* October 15, 1997, p. A03.

Blackman, N.S., and C.P. Bailey. *Liability in Medical Malpractice: A Reference for Physicians.* New York, Harwood Academic Publishers, 1990.

Blank, Robert H. *Rationing Medicine.* New York: Columbia University Press, 1988.

———. "Introduction." In *Biomedical Technology and Public Policy,* ed. Robert H. Blank and Miriam K. Mills, vii–xv. New York: Greenwood Press, 1989.

Blank, Robert H., and Miriam K. Mills, eds. *Biomedical Technology and Public Policy.* New York: Greenwood Press, 1989.

Blendon, Robert J., Mollyann Brodie, and John Benson. "What Happened to Americans' Support for the Clinton Plan?" *Health Affairs* 14, no. 2 (Summer 1995): 7–23.

Blendon, Robert J., Mollyann Brodie, John W. Benson, Drew E. Altman, Larry Levitt, Tina Hoff, and Larry Hugwick. "Understanding the Managed Care Backlash," *Health Affairs* 17, no. 4 (July/August): 80–94.

Blendon, Robert J., Robert Leitman, Ian Morrison, and Karen Donelan. "Satisfaction with Health Systems in Ten Nations." *Health Affairs* 9, no. 2 (Summer 1990): 185–92.

Blumberg, Linda J., and David W. Liska. *The Uninsured in the United States: A Status Report.* Washington, D.C.: Urban Institute, April 1966. http://www.urban.org/pubs/hinsure/uninsure.htm.

Blumberg, Mark S. "Health Status and Health Care Use by Type of Private Health Coverage." *Milbank Memorial Fund Quarterly/Health and Society* 58, no. 4 (Fall 1980): 633–55.

Blumstein, James F. "A Perspective on Federalism and Medical Malpractice." *Yale Journal on Regulation,* Supplemental Issue (1996): 411–28.

Bodenheimer, Thomas, and Kip Sullivan. "How Large Employers Are Shaping the Health Care Marketplace" (first of two parts). *New England Journal of Medicine* 338, no. 14 (April 2, 1998): 1003–1007.

———. "How Large Employers Are Shaping the Health Care Marketplace" (second of two parts). *New England Journal of Medicine* 338, no. 15 (April 9, 1998): 1084–1087.

Bovbjerg, Randall R. "Reforming a Proposed Tort Reform: Improving on the American Medical Association's Proposed Administrative Tribunal for Medical Malpractice." *Courts, Health Science and the Law* 1, no. 1 (1990): 19–28.

Bovbjerg, Randall R., Esq. and John Holahan. *Medicaid in the Reagan Era: Federal Policy and State Choices.* Washington, D.C.: Urban Institute, 1982.

Bovbjerg, Randall R. et al. "Juries and Justice: Are Malpractice and Other Personal Injuries Created Equal?" *Law and Contemporary Problems* 54, no. 5 (1991).

Bowen, Otis. "Congressional Testimony on Senate Bill S.1804." *Journal of American Medical Association* 257, (1987): 816.

Bowen, William G., and Derek Bok. *The Shape of the River: Long-Term Consequences of Considering Race in College and University Admissions.* Princeton, N.J.: Princeton University Press, 1998.

Bowman, Karlyn H. *The 1993–1994 Debate on Health Care Reform: Did the Polls Mislead the Policy Makers?* Washington, D.C.: AEI Press, 1994.

Brady, David, and Kara M. Buckley. "Health Care Reform in the 103d Congress: A Predictable Failure." *Journal of Health Politics, Policy and Law* 20, no. 2 (Summer 1995): 447–54.

Braverman, Paula A., Susan Egerter, Trude Bennett, and Jonathan Showstack. "Differences in Hospital Resource Allocation among Sick Newborns According to Insurance Coverage." *Journal of the American Medical Association* 266, no. 23 (December 18, 1991): 3300–3308.

Braverman, Paula A., V. Mylo Schaaf, Susan Egerter, Trude Bennett, and William Schecter. "Insurance-Related Differences in the Risk of Ruptured Appendix." *New England Journal of Medicine* 333, no. 7 (August 18, 1994): 444–49.

Breen, N., L.G. Kessler, and M.L. Brown. "Breast Cancer Control among the Underserved: An Overview." *Breast Cancer Research and Treatment* 40, no. 1 (1996):105–15.

Brennan, Troyen A. "Medical Malpractice Reform: The Current Proposals." *Journal of General Internal Medicine* 10, no. 4 (April 1, 1995): 211–18.

Breyer, S. "Analyzing Regulatory Failure: Mismatches, Less Restrictive Alternatives and Reform." *Harvard Law Review* 92, no. 1 (1979): 549–609.

Brienza, Julie. "Changes Ahead for Lawyers Who Handle Medical Malpractice, Insurers Study Says." *Trial* 33, no. 10 (1997): 84.

Brink, Susan. "HMOs Were the Right Rx: America Got Lower Medical Costs—But Also More Worries." *U.S. News and World Report* 124, no. 9 (March 9, 1998): 47–50.

Brink, Susan, and Nancy Shute. "Are HMOs the Right Prescription?" *U.S. News and World Report* 123, no. 14 (October 13, 1997): 60–64.

Britton: Homicide, ed. and trans. by F.M. Nichols. London, Macmillan, 1864.

Brodie, Mollyann, and Robert J. Blendon. "The Public's Contribution to Congressional Gridlock on Health Care Reform." *Journal of Health Politics, Policy and Law* 20, no. 2 (Summer 1995): 403–10.

Brodie, Mollyann, Lee Ann Brady, and Drew E. Altman. "Media Coverage of Managed Care: Is There a Negative Bias?" *Health Affairs* 17, no. 1 (January/February 1998): 9–25.

Bronzino, Joseph D., Vincent H. Smith, and Maurice L. Wade. *Medical Technology and Society: An Interdisciplinary Perspective.* Cambridge, Mass.: Massachusetts Institute of Technology Press, 1990.

Brooks, Durado D., David R. Smith, and Ron J. Anderson. "Medical Apartheid: An American Perspective." *Journal of the American Medical Association* 266, no. 9 (November 20, 1991): 2746, 2747.

Brooks, Robert H., et al. "Does Free Care Improve Adult Health?" *New England Journal of Medicine* 309, no. 23 (1983): 1426–1434.

Brostoff, Steve. "Eliminate Defensive Medicine, Save $36B: Study." *National Underwriter Life and Health-Financial Services Edition* 6 (February 8, 1993): 5.

Brown, J.H.A. *The Politics of Health Care.* Cambridge, Mass: Ballinger, 1978.

Brown, Lawrence D. "The Formulation of Federal Health Care Policy." *Bulletin of the New York Academy of Medicine* 54, no. 1 (January 1978).

———. "Competition and Health Cost Containment: Cautions and Conjectures." *Milbank Memorial Fund Quarterly/Health and Society* 59, no. 2 (Spring 1981): 145–89.

———. "Competition and Health Care Policy: Experience and Expectations." *Annals of the American Academy of Political and Social Science* 468 (July 1983): 48–59.

———. *Health Policy in the Reagan Administration: A Critical Appraisal.* Washington, D.C.: Brookings Institution, 1984.

———. "Introduction to a Decade of Transition." *Journal of Health Politics, Policy and Law* 11, no. 4 (1986): 569–83.

———. "Politics, Money, and Health Care Reform." *Health Affairs* 13, no. 2 (Spring 1994): 175.

Brown, Randall S., Dolores G. Clement, Jerold W. Hill, Sheldon M. Retchin, and Jeanette W. Bergeron. "Do Health Maintenance Organizations Work for Medicare?" *Health Care Financing Review* 15, no. 1 (Fall 1993): 7–23.

Brown, Richard E. "Medicare and Medicaid: Band-Aids for the Old and Poor." In *Reforming Medicine: Lessons of the Last Quarter Century*, ed. Victor W. Sidel and Ruth Sidel, 50–76. New York: Pantheon, 1984.

Bryce, Cindy L., and Kathryn Ellen Cline. "The Supply and Use of Selected Technologies." *Health Affairs* 17, no. 1 (January/February 1998): 213–24.

Buchanan, Allen. "Managed Care: Rationing without Justice, but Not Unjustly." *Journal of Health Politics, Policy and Law* 23, no. 4 (1998); 617–34.

Buck, Jeffrey A., and Mark S. Kamlet. "Problems with Expanding Medicaid for the Uninsured." *Journal of Health Politics, Policy and Law* 18, no. 1 (Spring 1993): 1–25.

Burner, Sally T., Daniel R. Waldo, and David R. McKusick. "National Health Expenditures Projections through 2030." *Health Care Financing Review* 14, no. 1 (Fall 1992): 1–29.

Burns, Chester R. "Malpractice Suits in American Medicine before the Civil War." *Bulletin of the History of Medicine* 43 (1969): 41–56.

Burstin, Helen R., Stuart R. Lipsitz, and Troyen A. Brennan. "Socioeconomic Status and Risk for Substandard Medical Care." *Journal of the American Medical Association* 268, no. 17 (November 4, 1994): 2383–2387.

Butler, Stuart M. "A Tax Reform Strategy to Deal with the Uninsured." *Journal of the American Medical Association* 265, no. 19 (May 15, 1991): 2541-2543.

————. "Rube Goldberg, Call Your Office." *New York Times*, September 28, 1993.

————. "Medicare Price Controls: The Wrong Prescription." *Health Affairs* 17, no. 1 (January/February 1998): 72–74.

Callahan, Daniel. *Setting Limits: Medical Goals in an Aging Society.* New York: Simon and Schuster, 1987.

————. "Why We Must Set Limits," in "A Good Old Age?" In *The Paradox of Setting Limits*, ed. Paul Homer and Martha Holstein, 23–43. New York: Simon and Schuster, 1990.

————. "Bioethics: Private Choice and Common Good." *Hastings Center Report* 24, no. 3 (May 1, 1994): 28–31.

————. *What Kind of Life: The Limits of Medical Progress.* Washington, D.C.: Georgetown University Press, 1995.

Campbell, Ellen S. "Unpaid Hospital Bills: Evidence from Florida." *Inquiry* 29, no. 1 (Spring 1992): 92–98.

Campion, Frank D. *The AMA and U.S. Health Policy Since 1940.* Chicago: University of Chicago Press, 1984.

"Can Malpractice Be Kept Out of the Court?" *Medical Economics* 71, no. 16 (August 22, 1994): 111.

Canaham-Clyne, John P. "Clinton's Folly—The Health Care Debacle." *New Politics* 5, no. 2 (Winter 1995): 27.

Cantor, Norman L. *Advance Directives and the Pursuit of Death with Dignity.* Indianapolis: Indiana University Press, 1993.

Capron, Alexander Morgan. "Biomedical Technology and Health Care: Transforming Our World." *Southern California Law Review* 65, no. 1 (November 1, 1991): 1–10.

Carlisle, David M., Barbara D. Leake, Robert H. Brook, and Martin F. Shapiro. "The Effect of Race and Ethnicity on the Use of Selected Health Care Procedures: A Comparison of South Central Los Angeles and the Remainder of Los Angeles County." *Journal of Health Care for the Poor and Underserved* 7, no. 4 (November 1996): 308–22.

Carmen, Ira H. "Bioethics, Public Policy and Political Science." *Politics and Life Sciences* 13, no. 1 (February 1, 1994): 79–81.

Carter, Douglas, and Philip R. Lee, eds. *Politics of Health.* Huntington, N.Y.: Robert F. Krieger, 1979.

Cassell, Eric J. "The Sorcerer's Broom: Medicine's Rampant Technology." *Hastings Center Report* 23 (November/December 1993): 32–39.

Cassidy, Robert. "Can You Really Speak Your Mind in Peer Review?" *Medical Economics* 61 (January 23, 1984): 246–62.

Cecil, Joe S. et al. "Citizen Comprehension of Difficult Issues: Lessons from Civil Jury Trials." *American University Law Review* 40 (1991): 727, 749.

Center for the Study of Social Policy. *Kids Count Data Book 1994.* Washington, D.C.: Center for the Study of Social Policy, 1994.

"Challenge to Oregon's Assisted-Suicide Law Dies in Appeals Court." Associated Press, February 28, 1997. http://www.wcinet.com/news/02029/national/48387.htm.

Chapman, Audry R. "Introduction." In *Health Care Reform: A Human Rights Approach*, ed. Audrey R. Chapman, 1–32. Washington, D.C.: Georgetown University Press, 1994.

Chernew, Michael, A., Mark Fendrick, and Richard A. Hirth. "Managed Care and Medical Technology: Implications for Cost Growth." *Health Affairs* 16, no. 2 (March/April 1997): 196–206.

Cherouny, Peter, and Colleen Nadolski. "Underreimbursement of Obstetric and Gynecologic Invasive Services by the Resource-Based Relative Value Scale." *Obstetrics and Gynecology* 87, no. 3 (March 1996): 328–31.

Chesebro, Kenneth I. "Galileo's Retort: Peter Huber's Junk Scholarship." *American University Law Review* 42 (1993).

Children's Defense Fund. "Medicaid Coverage of Children in the States, 1996." http://www.childrendefense.org/health_coverage.html.

————. *States Should Consider Building on Medicaid.* December 3, 1997: 1–4. http://www.childrensdefense.org/health_medicaid.html.

————. "State Children's Health Insurance Program: States Should Consider Building on Medicaid." December 3, 1997: 1–4. http://www.childrensdefense.org/health_medicaid.html.

————. *The State of America's Children.* Washington, D.C.: Children's Defense Fund, 1998.

————. *CHIP Checkup: A Health Start for Children.* May 27, 1998. http://www.childrensdefense.org/chipckeck.

Chollet, Deborah J. *Employer-Provided Health Benefits: Coverage, Provisions and Policy Issues.* Washington, D.C.: Employees Benefit Research Institute, 1984.

————. "Employer-Based Health Insurance in a Changing Work Force." *Health Affairs* 13, no. 1 (Spring 1994): 313–26.

Chulis, George S., Franklin P. Eppig, Mary O. Hogan, Daniel R. Waldo, and Ross H. Arnett III. "Health Insurance and the Elderly." *Health Affairs* 12, no. 1 (Spring 1993): 111–18.

Clancy, Carolyn M., and Charlea T. Massion. "American Women's Health Care: A Patchwork Quilt with Gaps." *Journal of the American Medical Association* 268, no. 14 (October 24, 1992): 1918–1920.

Clarke, Leslie L., Christine A. Bono, Michael K. Miller, and Susan C. Malone. "Prenatal Care Use in Nonmetropolitan and Metropolitan America: Racial/Ethnic Differences." *Journal of Health Care for the Poor and Underserved* 6, no. 4 (November 1995): 410–33.

Clayton, Ellen W., Gerald B. Hickson, Penny B. Githens, and Frank A. Sloan. "Doctor-Patient Relationships." In *Suing for Medical Malpractice,* Frank A. Sloan, Penny B. Githens, Ellen Wright Clayton, David F. Partlett, Gerald B. Hickson, and Stephen S. van Wert. Chicago: University of Chicago Press, 1993.

Coelen, Craig, and Daniel Sullivan. "An Analysis of the Effects of Prospective Reimbursement Programs on Hospital Expenditures." *Health Care Financing Review* 1, no. 3 (Winter 1981): 62–73.

Cohen, Alan B., and Donald R. Cohodes. "Certificate of Need and Low Capital-Cost Medical Technology." *Milbank Memorial Fund Quarterly/Health and Society* 60, no. 2 (Spring 1982): 307–28.

Cohen, Cynthia B., and Elizabeth L. McCloskey. "Private Bioethics Forums: Counterpoint to Government Bodies." *Kennedy Institute of Ethics Journal* 4, no. 2 (September 1, 1994): 283–89.

Cohen, Harold. "State Rate Regulation." In *Controls on Health Care,* ed. Institute of Medicine, 123–35. Washington, D.C.: National Academy of Sciences, 1975.

Cohen, Richard E. "Ready, Aim, Reform." *National Journal* 25, no. 44 (October 30, 1993): 2581–2586.

Cohn, Jonathan. "Cosmetic Surgery." *New Republic* nos. 4,361, 4,362 (August 17, 24, 1998): 20–23.

Commonwealth Fund. "Majority of Employers Do Not Consider Reports on HMO Quality When Choosing Employee Health Plans." September 15, 1998. http://www.cmsf.org./media/gabel293-0915.html.

"Congress Says Some Medicaid Planning Is a Federal Crime." *Elder Law Issues* 4, no. 7 (August 19, 1996). http://www.elder-law.com/elder/1996/issue407.html.

Congressional Budget Office, U.S. Congress. *The Impact of PSROs on Health-Care Costs: Update of CBO's 1979 Evaluation.* Washington, D.C.: U.S. Government Printing Office, 1981.

————. Office of Technology Assessment, U.S. Congress. *Defensive Medicine and Medical Malpractice.* Washington, D.C.: U.S. Government Printing Office, 1994. Publication OTA-H-602.

————. *Long-Term Budgetary Pressures and Policy Options.* Washington, D.C: Congressional Budget Office, U.S. Congress, 1997.

————. *Predicting How Changes in Medicare's Payment Rates Would Affect Risk Sector Enrollment and Costs.* Washington, D.C.: Congressional Budget Office, U.S. Congress, 1997.

————. *Trends in Spending by the Private Sector.* Washington, D.C.: Congressional Budget Office, U.S. Congress, 1997.

————. Expanding Health Insurance Coverage for Children under Title XXI of the Social Security Act. Washington, D.C.: Congressional Budget Office, U.S. Congress, 1997. http://www.cbo.html.

————. "Expanding Health Insurance Coverage for Children under Title XXI of the Social Security Act." U.S. Congress, February 1998. http://www/cbo.gov/showdoc.cfm?index=333&sequence=0&from=1.

————. "Expanding Health Insurance Coverage for Children under Title XXI of the Social Security Act." U.S. Congress, August 1, 1998. http://www/cbo.gov/showdoc.cfm?index=353&sequence=0&from=1.

————. *H.R. 3605/S. 1890 Patients' Bill of Rights Act of 1998.* Washington, D.C.: U.S. Congressional Budget Office, 1998. http://www.cbo.gov.

Cook, Karen, Steven M. Shortell, Douglas A. Conrad, and Michael A. Morrisey. "A Theory of Organizational Response to Regulation: The Case of Hospitals." *Academy of Management Review* 8, no. 2 (1983): 193–205.

Cooper, Phillip F., and Barbara Steinberg Schone. "More Offers, Fewer Takers for Employment-Based Health Insurance: 1987–1996." *Health Affairs* 16, no. 6 (November/December 1997): 142–49.

"Cost/Benefits of High-Tech Medicine." *Health Systems Review* 25, no. 1 (January 1, 1992): 16–18.

Corrigan, Janet M., Jill S. Eden, Marsha R. Gold, and Jeremy D. Pickreign. "Trends toward a National Health Care Marketplace." *Inquiry* 34, no. 1 (Spring 1997): 11–28.

Coughlin, Teresa A. *Medicaid Since 1980: Costs, Coverage, and the Shifting Alliance between the Federal Government and the States.* Washington, D.C.: Urban Institute, 1994.

Craig, Stephen C. *The Malevolent Leaders: Popular Discontent in America.* Boulder, Colo.: Westview Press, 1993.

Crittenden, Robert. "Managed Competition and Premium Caps in Washington State," *Health Affairs* 12, no. 2 (Summer 1993): 82–88.

Crozier, David A. "State Rate Setting: A Status Report." *Health Affairs* 1, no. 2 (Summer 1982): 66–83.

Culliton, Barbara J. "Critics Condemn NIH Women's Study." *Nature* 366, no. 6450 (November 4, 1993): 11.

Cunningham, Peter J., and Ha T. Tu. "A Changing Picture of Uncompensated Care." *Health Affairs* 16, no. 4 (July/August 1997): 167–75.

Curtis, Rick. "The Role of the State Government in Assuring Access to Care." *Inquiry* 23, no. 1 (Fall 1986): 277–85.

Cust, Kenneth F.T. *A Just Minimum of Health Care.* New York: University Press of America, 1997.

Dahl, Robert A., and Charles E. Lindblom. *Politics, Economics and Planning.* New York: Harper and Row, 1953.

Dallek, Geraldine. *The Crushing Costs of Medicare Supplemental Policies.* Washington, D.C.: Families USA, 1996. http://epn.org/families/famsup.html.

Daniels, Mark R., ed. *Medicaid Reform and the American States: Case Studies on the Politics of Managed Care.* Westport, Conn.: Auburn House, 1998.

Daniels, Norman. "Rationing Fairly: Programmatic Consideration." *Bioethics* 7, no. 2/3 (April 1, 1993): 224–33.

Daniels, Norman, Donald W. Light, and Ronald L. Caplan. *Benchmarks of Fairness for Health Care Reform*. New York: Oxford University Press, 1996.

Daniels, Norman, and James Sabin. "The Ethics of Accountability in Managed Care Reform." *Health Affairs* 17, no. 5 (September/October 1998): 50–64.

Daniels, Stephen. "Verdicts in Medical Malpractice Cases: Shedding Light on the Issues." *Trial* 25, no. 5 (May 1, 1989): 23–30.

———. "Tracing the Shadow of the Law: Jury Verdicts in Medical Malpractice Cases." *Justice System Journal* 14, no. 1 (1990): 4–39.

Danzon, Patricia M. "The Frequency and Severity of Medical Malpractice Claims." *Journal of Law and Economics* 27 (1984): 115–48.

———. *Medical Malpractice: Theory, Evidence, and Public Policy*. Cambridge, Mass.: Harvard University Press, 1985.

———. "The 'Crisis' in Medical Malpractice: A Comparison of Trends in the United States, Canada, the United Kingdom and Australia." *Law, Medicine and Health Care* 18, no. 1–2 (Spring/Summer 1990).

———. "Liability for Medical Malpractice." *Journal of Economic Perspective*. 5, no. 3 (Summer 1991): 51–69.

———. "Tort Reform: The Case of Medical Malpractice." *Oxford Review of Economic Policy* 10, no. 1 (Spring 1994): 84–98.

Darling, Helen. "The Role of the Federal Government in Assuring Access to Health Care." *Inquiry* 23, no. 1 (Fall 1986): 286–95.

David, Sheri I. *With Dignity: The Search for Medicare and Medicaid*. Westport, Conn.: Greenwood Press, 1985.

Davis, Karen. "Expanding Medicare and Employer Plans to Achieve Universal Health Insurance." *Journal of the American Medical Association* 265, no. 19 (May 15, 1991): 2525–2528.

Davis, Karen, and Roger Reynolds. *The Impact of Medicare and Medicaid on Access to Medical Care*. Washington, D.C.: Brookings Institution, 1977.

Davis, Karen, and Cathy Schoen. *Health and the War on Poverty: A Ten-Year Proposal*. Washington, D.C.: Brookings Institution, 1978.

———. "Universal Coverage: Building on Medicare and Employer Financing." *Health Affairs* 13, no. 2 (Spring 1994): 7–20.

Davis, Karen, Gerard F. Anderson, Diane Rowland, and Earl P. Steinberg. *Health Care Cost Containment*. Baltimore: Johns Hopkins University Press, 1990.

Davis, William R. "Medical Technology Investing in the '90s." *Medical World News* 33, no. 11 (November 1992): 35.

Delfico, Joseph F. *Long-Term Reform: Program Eligibility, States' Service Capacity, and Federal Role in Reform Need More Consideration*. Testimony before the Subcommittee on Aging, Committee on Labor and Human Resources, U.S. Senate. Washington, D.C.: General Accounting Office, April 14, 1994.

Demkovich, Linda E. "Adding Competition to the Health Industry." *National Journal* 11 (October 27, 1979): 1796–1800.

———. "Vermont Takes on LTC Financing." *State Health Notes* 15, no. 175 (March 7, 1994): 1–2, 8.

———. "ERISA: States Push to Raze the Biggest Barrier to Health Reform," *State Health Notes* 15, no. 192 (November 14, 1994): 1–2, 7.

———. "HCFA, States Spar—Again—Over Medicaid Provider Taxes," *State Health Notes* 16, no. 200 (March 20, 1995): 1–3.

Depperschmidt, Thomas O. "The Legality of State Limitations on Medical Malpractice Tort Damage Awards." *Hospital and Health Services Administration* 37, no. 3 (1992): 417–26.

Derbyshire, Robert C. *Medical Licensure and Discipline in the United States.* Westport, Conn: Greenwood Press, 1969.

De Ville, Kenneth A. *Medical Malpractice in Nineteenth Century America: Origins and Legacy.* New York: New York University Press, 1990.

DiCicco, Domenick C., Jr. "Liability of the HMO for the Medical Negligence of Its Providers." *For the Defense* 38, no. 3 (1996):10–15.

Dickenson, L.B. *Update on the Florida Birth-Related Neurological Injury Compensation Association: Internal Report.* Tallahassee, Fla.: Neurological Injury Compensation Association, 1994.

Dickersin, Kay, and Lauren Schauper. "Reinventing Medical Research." In *Man-Made Medicine: Women's Health, Public Policy, and Reform,* ed. Kary L. Moss, 57–76. Durham, N.C.: Duke University Press, 1996.

DiIulio, John J., Jr., and Richard P. Nathan, eds. *Making Health Reform Work: The View from the States.* Washington, D.C.: Brookings Institution, 1994.

Dolnec, D.A., and C.J. Dougherty. "DRGs: The Counterrevolution in Financing Health Care." *Hasting Center Report* 15, no. 3 (June 1985): 19–29.

d'Oronzio, Joseph C. "Bioethics and the Body Politic." *Cambridge Quarterly of Health Care Ethics* 3, no. 2 (1994): 300–1.

Dubin, Elliot J. "Medicaid Reform: Major Trends and Issues." *Intergovernmental Perspective* 18, no. 2 (Spring 1992).

Durda, David. "Number of Medicaid Lawsuits Belies Complexities Involved in Such Filings." *Modern Health Care* 21, no. 8 (February 25, 1991): 31–32.

Durenberger, David F. "The Politics of Health." In *Competition in the Marketplace: Health Care in the 1980s,* ed. James R. Gay and Barbara J. Sax Jacobs, 4. New York: Spectrum Publications, 1982.

Easterbrook, Gregg. "Healing the Great Divide: How Come Patients and Doctors Ended Up on Opposite Sides?" *U.S. News and World Report* 123, no. 14 (October 13, 1997): 64–67.

Eddy, David M. "Connecting Value and Costs: Whom Do We Ask, and What Do We Ask Them?" *Journal of the American Medical Association* 254, no. 13 (October 3, 1990): 1737–1739.

Editorial, "Bush Plans a Good First Step on Tort Reform." *American Medical News* 34, no. 9 (March 4, 1991): 19.

Ehrenreich, Barbara, and John Ehrenreich. *The American Health Empire: Power, Profit and Politics.* New York: Vintage Books, 1970.

"Elections: What Impact on Health Care Reform?" *State Health Notes* 15, no. 194 (December 12, 1994): 4–5.

Ellwood, Paul M., "Health Maintenance Strategy." *Medical Care* 9 (May/June 1971): 291–98.

———. "Alternative to Regulation: Improving the Market." Institute of Medicine, *Controls on Health Care,* ed. Institute of Medicine, 49–72. Washington, D.C.: National Academy of Sciences, 1975.

Emanuel, Linda L. "Professional Standards in Health Care: Calling All Parties to Account." *Health Affairs* 16, no. 1 (January/February 1997): 52–54.

Enthoven, Alain C. "Consumer Choice Health Plans" (first of two parts). *New England Journal of Medicine* 298 (March 23, 1978): 650–58.

———. "Consumer Choice Health Plans" (second of two parts). *New England Journal of Medicine* 298 (March 30, 1978): 709–20.

———. *Health Plan: The Only Practical Solution to the Soaring Cost of Medicare Care.* Reading, Mass.: Addison-Wesley, 1980.

———. "Competition in the Marketplace: Health Care in the 1980s." In *Competition in the Marketplace: Health Care in the 1980s,* ed. James R. Gay and Barbara J. Sax Jacobs, 11–19. New York: Spectrum Publications, 1982.

————. "Managed Competition of Alternate Delivery System." *Journal of Health Politics, Policy and Law* 13, no. 2 (Summer 1988): 305–21.

————. "Universal Health Insurance through Incentives Reform." *Journal of American Medical Association* 265, no. 19 (May 15, 1991): 2532–2536.

————. "The History and Principles of Managed Competition." *Health Affairs* 12 (Supplement 1993): 24–48.

————. "Why Not the Clinton Health Plan?" *Inquiry* 31, no. 2 (Summer 1994): 129–35.

Enthoven, Alain C., and Richard Kronick. "A Consumer-Choice Health Plan for the 1990s: Universal Health Insurance in a System Designed to Promote Quality and Economy" (first of two parts). *New England Journal of Medicine* 320, no. 1 (January 5, 1989): 29–37.

————. "A Consumer-Choice Health Plan for the 1990s: Universal Health Insurance in a System Designed to Promote Quality and Economy" (second of two parts). *New England Journal of Medicine* 320, no. 2 (January 12, 1989): 94–101.

Enthoven, Alain C., and Sara J. Singer. "Markets and Collective Action in Regulating Managed Care." *Health Affairs* 16, no. 6 (November/December 1997): 26–32.

"Eroding Employer-Based Insurance." *CDF Reports* 15, no. 5 (April 1994): 4.

Escarce, Jose J., Judy A. Shea, and Wei Chen. "Segmentation of Hospital Markets: Where Do HMO Enrollees Get Care?" *Health Affairs* 16, no. 6 (November/December 1997): 181–92.

Esposito, Alfonso, et al. "Abstracts of State Legislated Hospital Cost-Containment Programs." *Health Care Financing Review* 4, no. 2 (December 1982): 129–58.

Etheredge, Lynn. "Reagan, Congress and Health Spending." *Health Affairs* 2, no. 1 (Spring 1983): 14–24.

————. "Promarket Regulation: An SEC-FASB Model." *Health Affairs* 16, no. 6 (1997): 22–25.

Evans, Robert G. "Incomplete Vertical Integration in the Health Care Industry: Pseudomarkets and Pseudopolicies." *Annals of the American Academy of Political and Social Science* 468 (July 1983): 60–87.

————. "Finding the Levers, Finding the Courage: Lessons from Cost Containment in North America." *Journal of Health Politics, Policy and Law* ll, no. 4 (1986): 585–615.

————. "Going for the Gold: The Redistributive Agenda behind Market-Based Health Care Reform," *Journal of Health Politics, Policy and Law* 22, no. 2 (1997): 427–66.

Everette, James A., et al. "The Diffusion of Medical Technology: Free Enterprise and Regulatory Models in the USA." *Journal of Medical Ethics* 17, no. 3 (1991): 150–55.

Falkson, Joseph L. *HMOs and the Politics of Health Service Reform*. Chicago: American Hospital Association and Robert J. Brady, 1980.

————. "Market Reform, Health Systems, and HMOs." *Policy Studies Journal* 9, no. 2 (1980–1981): 213–20.

Fallows, James. "A Triumph of Misinformation," *Atlantic Monthly* 275, no. 1 (January 1995): 26–37.

Families USA. *HMO Consumers at Risk: States to the Rescue*. Washington, D.C.: Families USA, July 1996. http://epn.org/families/farisk.html.

————. *Health Legislation Enacted by the 104th Congress*. Washington D.C.: Families USA, December 1996. http://epn.org/families/fah104.html.

————. *Leading Health Plans and National Consumer Groups Announce Unprecedented Agreement for Consumer Protection Standards in Managed Care*. Washington, D.C.: Families USA, 1997. http://www.familiesusa.orghmoagre.htm.

————. *Hit and Miss: State Managed Care Laws*. Washington, D.C.: Families USA, July 1998.

————. *Premium Pay II: Corporate Compensation in America's HMOs*. Washington, D.C.: Families USA, September 1998.

Farber, Henry S., and Michelle J. White. "Medical Malpractice: An Empirical Examination of the Litigation Process." *RAND Journal of Economics* 22, no. 2 (Summer 1991): 199–217.

Feder, Judith M. *Medicare: The Politics of Federal Hospital Insurance*. Lexington, Mass.: D.C. Heath, 1977.

Feder, Judith, and Jeanne Lambrew. "Why Medicare Matters to People Who Need Long-Term Care." *Health Care Financing Review* 18, no. 2 (Winter 1996): 99–112.

Fein, Rashi. *Medical Care, Medical Costs: The Search for a Health Insurance Policy*. Cambridge, Mass.: Harvard University Press, 1986.

Feldman, Roger, John Kralewski, and Bryan Dowd. "Health Maintenance Organizations: The Beginning or the End?" *Health Research Service* 24, no. 2 (June 1989): 191–211.

Feldman, Roger, Bryan Dowd, Don McCann, and Allan Johnson. "The Competitive Impact of Health Maintenance Organizations on Hospital Finances: An Exploratory Study." *Journal of Health Politics, Policy and Law* 10 (Winter 1986): 675–97.

Feldstein, Paul J. "Health Associations and the Legislative Process." In *Health Politics and Policy*, ed. Theodore J. Litman and Leonard S. Robins, 223–42. New York: Wiley, 1984.

Fendrick, Mark A., and J. Sanford Schwartz. "Physicians' Decisions Regarding the Acquisition of Technology." In *Adopting New Medical Technology*, ed. Annetine C. Gelijns and Holly V. Dawkins, 71–84. Washington, D.C.: National Academy Press, 1994.

Ferrari, Herbert A. "Suing for Restitution: The Medical Malpractice Crisis." *USA Today* (January 1, 1990).

Fielding, Stephen L. "Changing Medical Practice and Medical Malpractice Claims." *Social Problems* 42, no. 1 (February 1, 1995): 38–55.

Fineberg, H.V., and H.H. Hiatt. "Evaluation of Medical Practices: The Case for Technology Assessment." *New England Journal of Medicine* 301, no. 20 (1979): 1086–1091.

Flexner, A. *Medical Education in the United States and Canada*, Bulletin No. 4. New York: The Carnegie Foundation for the Advancement of Teaching, 1910.

Flint, Samuel S. "Insuring Children: The Next Steps." *Health Affairs* 16, no. 4 (July/August 1997): 79–81.

Folkemer, Donna. "Shifts to Community Long-Term Care Looms on Horizon." *State Health Notes* 15, no. 184 (July 11, 1994): 1–2, 8.

Fossett, James W. "Cost Containment and Rate Setting." In *Making Health Reform Work: The View from the States*, ed. John J. DiIulio, Jr., and Richard P. Nathan, 60–84. Washington, D.C.: Brookings Institution, 1994.

Foundation for Public Affairs. *Public Interest Profiles 1988–1989*. Washington, D.C.: Congressional Quarterly, 1988.

Fournier, Gary M., and Melayne M. Mcinnes. "Medical Board Regulation of Physician Licensure: Is Excessive Malpractice Sanctioned?" *Journal of Regulatory Economics* 12, no. 2 (1997): 113–26.

Fox, Daniel M. *Health Policies, Health Politics: The British and American Experience: 1911–1965*. Princeton, N.J.: Princeton University Press, 1986.

Fox, Daniel M., and John K. Iglehart (eds.). *Five States That Could Not Wait: Lessons for Health Reform from Florida, Hawaii, Minnesota, Oregon, and Vermont*. Cambridge, Mass.: Blackwell Publishers, 1994.

Fox, Peter D., Thomas Rice, and Lisa Alecxih. "Medigap Regulation: Lessons for Health Care Reform." *Journal of Health Politics, Policy and Law* 20, no. 1 (Spring 1995): 31–48.

Fox-Grage, Wendy. *The Task Force Report: Long-Term Care Reform in the States*. Washington, D.C.: National Conference of State Legislatures, 1997.

Franks, Peter, Carolyn M. Clancy, and Marthe R. Gold. "Health Insurance and Mortality: Evidence from a National Cohort." *Journal of the American Medical Association* 270, no. 6 (August 11, 1993): 737–41.

Franks, Peter, Carolyn M. Clancy, Marthe R. Gold, and Paul A. Nutting. "Health Insurance and Subjective Health Status: Data from the 1987 National Medical Expenditure Survey." *American Journal of Public Health* 83, no. 9 (September 1993): 1295–1299.

Frech, H.E., III, and Paul B. Ginsburg. "Competition Among Health Insurers, Revisited." *Journal of Health Politics, Policy and Law* 13, no. 2 (Summer 1988): 279–91.

Freed, David H. "Toward Redefining Expectations About Medical Technology." *Trends in Health Care, Law and Ethics* 9, no. 2 (Spring 1994): 21–28.

Freedman, Grace Roegner. "Toward a Macro Theory for Health Care Policymaking: Lessons from the Enactment of Health Care Legislation 1945–1992." Paper prepared for delivery at the annual meeting of the American Political Science Association, Chicago, August 31–September 3, 1995.

Freeman, Howard E., and Bradford L. Kirkman-Liff. "Health Care Under AHCCCS: An Examination of Arizona's Alternative to Medicaid." *Health Services Research* 20, no. 3 (August 1985): 245–66.

Freund, Deborah A., Louis F. Rossiter, and Peter D. Fox. "Evaluation of the Medicaid Competition Demonstrations." *Health Care Financing Review* 11 (Winter 1989): 81–97.

Friedman, Milton. *Capitalism and Freedom*. Chicago: University of Chicago Press, 1962.

Frum, David. "What's Wrong with This Plan?" *New York Times* (April 2, 1997).

Fubini, Sylvia. "Medicaid under Welfare Reform." *Health Care Trends* 1, no. 2 (February 1997): 1–2, 15.

Fuchs, Victor R. *The Health Economy*. Cambridge: Harvard University Press, 1986.

———. "The New Technology Assessment." *New England Journal of Medicine* 323, no. 19 (September 6, 1990): 673–77.

———. "The Clinton Plan: A Researcher Examines Reform." *Health Affairs* 13, no. 1 (Spring 1994): 102–14.

———. *Who Shall Live? Health, Economics and Social Choice*. New York: Basic Books, 1995.

Gabel, Jon R. "Ten Ways HMOs Have Changed during the 1990s," *Health Affairs* 16, no. 3 (1997): 134–45.

Gabel, Jon, Kelly Hunt, and Jean Kim. "The Financial Burden of Self-Paid Insurance for the Poor and Near-Poor." New York: Commonwealth Foundation, 1997. http://www.cmwf.org.health_care/gabel251.html.

Gabel, Jon R., and Alan C. Monheit. "Will Competition Plans Change Insurer-Provider Relationships?" *Milbank Memorial Fund Quarterly/Health and Society* 61, no. 4 (Fall 1983): 614–40.

Gadd, Cyril J. *Hammurabi and the End of His Dynasty*, rev. ed. (*Ancient History*, vol. 2, chap. 5). New York: Cambridge University Press, 1965.

Gallup, Cynthia L. "Can No-Fault Compensation of Impaired Infants Alleviate the Malpractice Crisis in Obstetrics?" *Journal of Health Politics, Policy and Law* 14, no. 4 (Winter 1989): 691–718.

Garber, Alan M., and Paul M. Romer. "Evaluating the Federal Role in Financing Health-Related Research." *Proceedings of the National Academy of Sciences* 93, no. 23 (November 12, 1996): 12717–12725.

Garner, M.O., S.P. Cliver, S.F. McNeal, and R.L. Goldenberg. "Ethnicity and Sources of Prenatal Care; Findings from a National Survey." *Birth* 23, no. 2 (1996): 84–87.

Garrett, Thomas M., Harold W. Baillie, and Rosellen M. Garrett. *Health Care Ethics: Principles and Problems*. Englewood Cliffs, N.J.: Prentice Hall, 1989.

Gavora, Carrie J. "A Progress Report on the Clinton Health Plan." Washington, D.C.: The Heritage Foundation, February 25, 1998. http://www.heritage.org/heritage/library/backgrounder/bg1158.html.

Gawande, Atul A., Robert J. Blendon, Mollyann Brodie, John M. Benson, Larry Levitt, and Larry Hugick. "Does Dissatisfaction with Health Plans Stem from Having No Choice?" *Health Affairs* 17, no. 5 (September/October 1998): 184–94.

Gay, E. Greer, Jennie J. Kronenfeld, and Samuel L. Baker. "An Appraisal of Organizational Response to Fiscally Constraining Regulation: The Case of Hospitals and DRGs." *Journal of Health and Social Behavior* 30, no. 1 (March 1989): 41–55.

Geisel, Jerry. "Bush Budget Proposes Malpractice Reform." *Business Insurance* 25, no. 6 (February 11, 1991): 1, 26.

———. "How the National Practitioner Data Bank Affects Medical Malpractice Clients." *Practical Litigator* 5, no. 1 (1994): 35–44.

Gelijns, Annetine, and Nathan Rosenberg. "The Dynamics of Technological Change in Medicine." *Health Affairs* 13, no. 3 (Summer 1994): 28–46.

Gelman, Judith. *Competition and Health Planning. An Issue Paper*. Bureau of Economics, U.S. Federal Trade Commission. Washington, D.C.: Government Printing Office, 1982.

General Accounting Office. *Medical Malpractice Insurance Costs Increased but Varied among Physicians and Hospitals*. Washington, D.C.: Government Accounting Office, 1986.

———. *Long-Term Care for the Elderly: Issues of Need, Access, and Cost*. Washington, D.C.: Government Printing Office, 1988.

———. *Medicare PROs: Extreme Variation in Organizational Structure and Activities*. Washington, D.C.: Government Printing Office, November 1988.

———. *Heart Transplants: Concerns about Cost, Access, and Availability of Donor Organs*. Washington, D.C.: Government Printing Office, May 1989.

———. *Health Insurance: Cost Increases Lead to Coverage Limitations and Cost Shifting*. Washington, D.C.: Government Printing Office, 1990.

———. *Medicaid Expansions*. Washington, D.C.: Government Printing Office, June 1991.

———. *Hospital Costs: Adoption of Technologies Drives Cost Growth*. Washington, D.C.: Government Printing Office, September 1992.

———. *Health Insurance: California Public Employees' Alliance Has Reduced Recent Premium Growth*. Washington, D.C.: General Accounting Office, 1993.

———. *Medicaid: States Turn to Managed Care to Improve Access and Control Costs*. Gaithersburg, Md.: General Accounting Office, March 1993.

———. *Long-Term Care: Diverse, Growing Population Includes Millions of Americans of All Ages*. Washington, D.C.: General Accounting Office, 1994.

———. *Long-term Care: Private Sector Elder Care Could Yield Multiple Benefits*. Washington, D.C.: Government Printing Office, 1994.

———. *Long-Term Care: Support for Elder Care Could Benefit the Government Workplace and the Elderly*. Washington, D.C.: Government Printing Office, 1994.

———. *Health Insurance for Children: Many Remain Uninsured Despite Medicaid Expansion*. Washington, D.C.: U.S. General Accounting Office, 1995.

———. *Medicare: Home Health Utilization Expands While Program Controls Deteriorate*. Washington, D.C.: Government Printing Office, March 1996.

———. *Employment-Based Health Insurance: Costs Increase and Family Coverage Decreases*. Washington, D.C.: General Accounting Office, February 1997.

———. *Private Health Insurance: Continued Erosion of Coverage Linked to Cost Pressures*. Washington, D.C.: General Accounting Office, July 1997.

———. *Retiree Health Insurance: Erosion in Employer-Based Health Benefits for Early Retirees*. Washington, D.C.: U.S. General Accounting Office, July 1997.

———. *Health Insurance: Coverage Leads to Increased Health Care Access for Children*. Washington, D.C.: General Accounting Office, November 1997.

———. *Medicare Home Health Agencies: Certification Process Ineffective in Excluding Problem Agencies*. Washington, D.C.: Government Printing Office, December 1977.

————. *Health Insurance Standards: New Federal Law Creates Challenges for Consumers, Insurers, Regulators.* Washington, D.C.: U.S. General Accounting Office, February, 1998.

Gibson, Robert M., and Daniel R. Waldo. "National Health Expenditures, 1980." *Health Care Financing Review* 3, no. 1 (September 1981): 1–54.

Gibson, Robert M., Katherine R. Levit, Helen Lazenby, and Daniel R. Waldo. "National Health Expenditures, 1983." *Health Care Financing Review* 6, no. 2 (Winter 1984): 1–29.

Gillam, Lynn. "Bioethics and Public Policy in Australia." *Politics and Life Science* 13, no. 1 (February 1, 1994): 87–88, 97.

Ginsburg, Paul B. "Public Insurance Programs: Medicare and Medicaid." In *Health Care in America: The Political Economy of Hospitals and Health Insurance*, ed. H.E. Frech III, 179–215. San Francisco: Pacific Research Institute for Public Policy, 1988.

Ginsburg, Paul B., and Jon R. Gabel. "Tracking Health Care Costs: What's New in 1998? *Health Affairs* 17, no. 5 (September/October 1998): 141–46.

Ginzberg, Eli. *The Limits of Health Reform: The Search for Realism.* New York: Basic Books, 1977.

————. "Procompetition in Health Care: Policy or Fantasy?" *Milbank Memorial Fund Quarterly/Health and Society* 60, no. 3 (Summer 1982): 386–398.

————. "Balancing Dollars and Quality." *Midwest Medical Ethics* 5, no. 4 (Fall 1989): 1–5.

————. "High-Tech Medicine and Rising Health Care Costs." *Journal of the American Medical Association* 263, no. 13 (April 4, 1990): 1820–1822.

————. "Improving Health Care for the Poor." *Journal of the American Medical Association* 271, no. 6 (February 9, 1994): 464–65.

Glover, K. Daniel. "From 'Universal Coverage' to 'Incremental Reform.'" Intellectual Capitol.com, April 23, 1998. http://www.intellectualcapital.com/issues/98.-423/icissues.asp.

Goff, Barbara A., H.G. Muntz, and J.M. Cain. "Is Adam Worth More than Eve? The Financial Impact of Gender Bias in the Federal Reimbursement of Gynecological Procedures." *Gynecological Oncology* 64, no. 3 (March 1997): 372–77.

————. "Comparison of 1997 Medicare Relative Value Units for Gender-Specific Procedures: Is Adam Still Worth More than Eve?" *Gynecological Oncology* 66, no. 2 (August 1997): 313–19.

Gold, Marsha, and Robert Hurley. "The Role of Managed Care 'Products' in Managed Care Plans." *Inquiry* 34, no. 1 (Spring 1997): 29–37.

Gold, Marsha, Karyen Chu, and Suzanne Felt. "Effects of Selected Cost-Containment Efforts: 1971–1993." *Health Care Financing Review* 14, no. 3 (Spring 1993): 183–225.

Gold, Marsha, Lyle Nelson, Randall Brown, Anne Ciemnecki, Anna Aizer, and Elizabeth Docteur. "Disabled Medicare Beneficiaries in HMOs." *Health Affairs* 16, no. 5 (September/October 1997): 149–62.

Gold, Steven D. "Health Care and the Fiscal Crisis of the States." In *Health Policy, Federalism, and the American States*, ed. Robert F. Rich and William D. White, 97–125. Washington, D.C.: Urban Institute, 1996 .

Goldfarb, Bruce. "Uncompensated Care Pushes Trauma Centers Out of Business." *Medical World News* 33, no. 4 (April 1992): 32.

Goldstein, Amy. "Medicare Recipients to Face a Dizzying Array of Choices." *Washington Post,* August 18, 1997.

Goodman, John C. *The Regulation of Medical Care: Is the Price Too High?* San Francisco: Cato Institute, 1980.

Gordon, V.M. "The Origin, Basis and Nature of Medical Malpractice Liability." *Connecticut Medicine* 35 (1970): 73–77.

Gornick, Marian. "Physician Payment Reform under Medicare: Monitoring Utilization and Access." *Health Care Financing Review* 14, no. 3 (Spring 1993): 77–96.

Gosfield, Alice G. "Who Is Holding Whom Accountable for Quality?" *Health Affairs* 16, no. 3 (May/June 1996): 26–40.

Graig, Laurence A. *Health of Nations: An International Perspective on U.S. Health Care Reform*. Washington, D.C.: CQ Press, 1993.

Grannemann, Thomas W., and Mark V. Pauly. *Controlling Medicaid Costs: Federalism, Competition, and Choice*. Washington, D.C.: American Enterprise Institute for Public Policy Research, 1983.

Gray, Bradford, H. "Trust and Trustworthy Care in the Managed Care Era." *Health Affairs* 16, no. 1 (January/February 1997): 34–49.

Greene, Risa B. "Federal Legislative Proposals for Medical Malpractice Reform: Treating the Symptom or Effecting a Cure?" *Cornell Journal of Law and Public Policy* 4, no. 2 (1996): 563–607.

Greifinger, Robert B., and Victor William Sidel. "Three Centuries of Medical Care." In *Medical Care in the United States*, ed. Eric F. Oatman, 12–26. New York: H.W. Wilson Company, 1978.

Griner, Paul F. "New Technology Adoption in the Hospital." In *Technology and Health Care in an Era of Limits*, ed. Annetine C. Gelijns, 123–132. Washington, D.C.: National Academy Press, 1992.

Gross, George. "Reagan's 'Bold' Aid Reform." *Nation's Cities Weekly* 5, no. 5 (February 1, 1982): 1, 8.

Grumbach, Kevin, and Thomas Bodenheimer. "Reins or Fences: A Physician's View of Cost Containment." *Health Affairs* 9, no. 4 (Winter 1990): 120–26.

Guterman, Stuart. "The Balanced Budget Act of 1997: Will Hospitals Take a Hit on Their PPS Margins? *Health Affairs* 17, no. 1 (January/February 1998): 159–66.

Guyer, Jocelyn. "States' Options for Implementing Medicaid Managed Care." Princeton, N.J.: Center for Health Care Strategies, 1998. http://www.chcs/jg_waive.htm.

Hacker, Jacob S. *The Road to Nowhere: The Genesis of President Clinton's Plan for Health Security*. Princeton, N.J.: Princeton University Press, 1997.

Hadley, Jack. *More Medical Care: Better Health?* Washington, D.C.: Urban Institute Press, 1982.

Hadley, Jack, Earl P. Steinberg, and Judith Feder. "Comparison of Uninsured and Privately Insured Hospital Patients: Condition on Admission, Resource Use, and Outcome." *Journal of the American Medical Association* 265, no. 3 (January 19, 1991): 374–79.

Hadley, Jack, and Katherine Swartz. "The Impact of Hospital Costs between 1980 and 1984 on Hospital Rate Regulation, Competition, and Change in Health Insurance Coverage." *Inquiry* 26, no. 1 (Spring 1989): 35–47.

Hafner-Eaton, Chris. "Physician Utilization Disparities between the Uninsured and Insured: Comparisons of the Chronically Ill, Acutely Ill, and Well Nonelderly Populations." *Journal of the American Medical Association* 269, no. 6 (February 10, 1993): 787–82.

———. "Will the Phoenix Rise, and Where Should She Go? The Women's Health Agenda." *American Behavioral Scientist* 36, no. 6 (July/August 1993): 841–56.

Hamilton, Alexander, James Madison, and John Jay. *The Federalist Papers*. New York: New American Library, 1961.

Hanlon, John T., and George E. Picker. *Public Health: Administration and Practice*. St. Louis: C.V. Mosby, 1974.

Hanna, Kathi E., Robert M. Cook-Deegan, and Robyn Y. Nishimi. "Finding a Forum for Bioethics in U.S. Public Policy." *Politics and Life Sciences* 12 (1993): 205–19.

Harris, John. *Wonderwoman and Superman: The Ethics of Human Biotechnology*. New York: Oxford University Press, 1992.

Hart, Bruce G. Jr., "Medical Malpractice Protection under the Federal Tort Claims Act: Protecting Both Physicians and Claimants." *Fordham Law Review* vol. 58, no. 5 (1990): 1107–1120.

Harway, Robert A. "'Hired Guns' Isn't a Synonym for 'Medical Whore,'" *Medical Economics* 69, no. 6 (March 16, 1992): 41–45.

Havard, John. "No-Fault Compensation for Medical Accidents." *Medical Science Law* 32, no. 3 (1992): 187–98.

Havighurst, Clark C. "Health Maintenance Organizations and the Market for Health Services." *Law and Contemporary Problems* 35, no. 1 (Autumn 1970): 716–95.

———. "Regulation of Health Facilities and Services by 'Certificate of Need.'" *Virginia Law Review* 59, no. 7 (October 1973): 1143–1233.

———. "Medical Adversity Insurance: Has Its Time Come?" *Duke Law Journal* 75 (1975).

———. *Deregulating the Health Care Industry.* Cambridge, Mass.: Ballinger, 1982.

———. "The Questionable Cost-Containment Record of Commercial Health Insurers." In *Health Care in America: The Political Economy of Hospital and Health Insurance,* ed. H.E. Frech III, 221–58. San Francisco: Pacific Research Institute for Public Policy, 1988.

———. "'Putting Patients First': Promise or Smoke Screen?" *Health Affairs* 16, no. 6 (November/December 1997): 123–25.

Havighurst, Clark C., and Laurence R. Tancredi "Medical Adversity Insurance: A No-Fault Approach to Medical Malpractice and Quality Insurance." *Insurance Law Journal,* no. 613 (1974): 69–100.

Hayek, Frederick. *The Road to Serfdom.* Chicago: University of Chicago Press, 1944.

Hayes, Michael T. *Incrementalism and Public Policy.* New York: Longman, 1992.

Health Care Financing Administration. "Children's Insurance Program: State Plans." http://www.hcfa.gov/init/chip-map.htm.

———. *Children's Health Insurance Program.* December 13, 1998. HCFA Web page at http://www.hcfa.gov/init/statepln.htm.

———. "Medicaid Managed Care." http://www.hcfa.gov/medicaid/medata97.htm.

Health Care Financing Review. *Medicare and Medicaid: Statistical Supplement,* 1997. Washington, D.C.: U.S. Government Printing office, 1998.

Health Care Liability Alliance. "State Enactment of Selected Health Care Liability Reforms." http://www.wp.com/hcla/statetab.htm.

———. *HCLA Fact Sheet: State Constitutional Impediments.* http://www.wp.com/hcla/ffedjuri.htm.

———. *HCLA Fact Sheet: Non-Economic Damage Cap.* 1997. http://www.wp.com/hcla/fcap.htm.

———. *HCLA Fact Sheet: State Constitutional Limitations.* 1997. http://www.wp.com/hcla/ffedjuri.htm.

Health Insurance Association of America. *Sourcebook of Health Insurance Data.* Washington, D.C.: Health Insurance Association of America, 1998.

———. "Response to Democrats' Medicare Buy-In Bill." March 18, 1998. http://www.hiaa.org.newsroom/press-releases/release4.html.

Helbing, Charles. "Medicare Program Expenditures." *Health Care Financing Review,* 1992 Annual Supplement, 26–41.

Hellinger, F.J. "Selection Bias in Health Maintenance Organizations: Analysis of Recent Evidence." *Health Care Financing Review* 9, no. 2 (winter 1987): 55–63.

Henk, A.M.J. ten Have. "Medical Technology Assessment and Ethics: Ambivalent Relations." *Hastings Center Report* 25, no. 5 (September/October 1995): 13–20.

Henifin, Mary S. "New Reproductive Technologies: Equity and Access to Reproductive Health Care." *Journal of Social Issues* 49, no. 2 (Summer 1993): 61–74.

Hibbard, Judith H., Jacquelyn J. Jewett, Mark W. Legnini, and Martin Tusler. "Choosing a Health Plan: Do Large Employers Use the Data?" *Health Affairs* 16, no. 6 (November/December 1997): 172–80.

"High Tech Medicine for the '90s." *Health Systems Review* 25, no. 1 (January 1, 1992): 18.

Hill, D.W. "25 Years of Medical Technology." *British Journal of Hospital Medicine* 46, no. 4 (October 1991): 242–43.

Hill, Lister. "Health in America: A Personal Perspective." In *Health in America: 1776–1976*, ed. U.S. Department of Health, Education and Welfare, Washington, D.C.: Government Printing Office, 1976.

Hillman, Alan L. "Financial Incentives for Physicians in HMOs: Is There a Conflict of Interest?" *New England Journal of Medicine* 317, no. 27 (December 31, 1987): 1734–1748.

Hillman, Bruce J. "Physicians' Acquisition and Use of New Technology in an Era of Economic Constraints." In *Technology and Health Care in an Era of Limits,* ed. Annetine C. Geligns, 133–149. Washington, D.C.: National Academy Press, 1992.

"Hispanic Health in the United States." *Journal of the American Medical Association* 265, no. 2 (January 9, 1991): 248–52.

Hochstein, Madelyn. "American Attitudes and Values Regarding Medicare." (n.d.) http://www.aarp.org/monthly/medicare3/viewmh.htm.

Holahan, John. "The Impact of Alternative Hospital Payment Systems on Medicaid Costs." *Inquiry* 25, no. 4 (Winter 1988): 519–520.

Holahan, John F., and Joel W. Cohen. *Medicaid: The Trade-Off between Cost-Containment and Access to Care.* Washington, D.C.: Urban Institute Press, 1986.

Holahan, John, and David Liska. "The Slowdown in Medicaid Spending Growth: Will It Continue?" *Health Affairs* 16, no. 2 (March/April 1997): 157–63.

Holahan, John, and John L. Palmer. "Medicare's Fiscal Problems: An Imperative for Reforms." *Journal of Health Politics, Policy and Law* 13, no. 1 (Spring 1988): 66–68.

Holahan, John, and Len Nichols. "State Health Policy in the 1990s." In *Health Policy, Federalism, and the American States,* ed. Robert F. Rich and William D. White, 39–70. Washington, D.C.: Urban Institute, 1996.

Holahan, John, Stephen Zuckerman, Allison Evans, and Suresh Rangarajan. "Medicaid Managed Care in Thirteen States." *Health Affairs* 17, no. 3 (May/June 1998): 43–63.

Hoppszallern, Suzanna, Christine Hughes, and Robert A. Zimmerman. "MRI Aquisition: How Appropriate Is It for Hospitals?" *Hospitals* 65, no. 8 (April 20, 1991): 58.

Hospital Insurance Association of America. *Source Book of Health Insurance Data*. Washington, D.C.: Hospital Insurance Association of America, 1990.

Hsiao, William C., and Daniel L. Dunn. "The Impact of DRG Payment on New Jersey Hospitals." *Inquiry* 24, no. 3 (1987): 212–20.

Huber, Peter W. *The Legal Revolution and Its Consequences.* New York: Basic Books, 1988.

———. *Galileo's Revenge: Junk Science in the Courtroom.* New York: Basic Books, 1991.

Hudson, Terese. "States Scramble for Solutions under New Medicaid Law." *Hospitals* 66, no. 11 (June 5, 1992): 52–56.

Hughes, James W., and Edward A. Snyder. "Evaluating Medical Malpractice Reforms." *Contemporary Policy Issues* 7, no. 2 (1989): 83–98.

Huitt, Ralph. "Political Feasibility." In *Policy Analysis in Political Science*, ed. Ira Sharkansky. Chicago: Markham, 1970.

Huston, Patricia. "Is Health Technology Assessment Medicine's Rising Star?" *Canadian Medical Association Journal* 147, no. 12 (December 15, 1992): 1839–1841.

Hutkins, Allen K. "Resolving the Medical Malpractice Crisis: Alternatives to Litigation." *Journal of Law and Health* 4, no. 1 (1989–90): 21–55.

Hyams, Andrew L., David D. Shapiro, and Troyen A. Brennan. "Medical Practice Guidelines in Malpractice Litigation: An Early Retrospective." *Journal of Health Politics, Policy and Law* 21, no. 2 (1996): 289–313.

Iglehart, John K. "The Federal Government as Venture Capitalist: How Does It Fare?" *Milbank Memorial Fund Quarterly/Health and Society* 59, no. 4 (Fall 1980): 656–66.

————. "Health Care and American Business." *New England Journal of Medicine* 306, no. 2 (1981): 120–24.

————. "Health Care Reform: The States." *New England Journal of Medicine* 330, no. 1 (January 6, 1994): 75–79.

————. "Health Policy Report: Republicans and the New Politics of Health Care." *New England Journal of Medicine* 332, no. 14 (April 6, 1995): 972–75.

Ignagni, Karen. "Covering a Breaking Revolution: The Media and Managed Care." *Health Affairs* 17, no. 1 (January/February, 1998): 26–34.

"Incidence of Adverse Events and Negligence in Hospitalized Patients." (Part I and II), *New England Journal of Medicine* 324, no. 5 (February 7, 1991): 370–84.

Institute of Continuing Legal Education. "Balanced Budget Act Targets Medicaid Planning Advice." <http://www.icle.org/new/alerts/97/10/ep2n.htm>.

Intergovernmental Health Policy Project. *Expanding Access to Health Care: An Overview of 1992 State Legislation.* Washington, D.C.: George Washington University Press, 1993.

International Anti-Euthanasia Task Force. "The Facts about the Oregon 'Death with Dignity Act' Initiative." http://www.iaetf.prg/fctorgn.htm.

Jacobs, Lawrence R., and Robert Y. Shapiro. "Don't Blame the Public for Failed Health Care Reform." *Journal of Health Politics, Policy and Law* 20, no. 2 (Summer 1995): 411–23.

Jajich-Toth, Cindy, and Burns W. Roper. "Americans' Views on Health Care: A Study in Contradictions." *Health Affairs* 9, no. 4 (Winter 1990): 149–57.

James, A. Everette, Seymour Perry, and Susan E. Warner. "The Diffusion of Medical Technology: Free Enterprise and Regulatory Models in the USA." *Journal of Medical Ethics* 17 (1991): 150–55.

Jamieson, Kathleen Hall. "When Harry Met Louise." *Washington Post National Weekly Edition* 11, no. 43 (August 22–28, 1994): 29.

Jaros, G.G., and D.A. Boonzaier. "Cost Escalation in Health-Care Technology—Possible Solutions." *South African Medical Journal* 83, no. 6 (June 1, 1993): 420–22.

Jasper, Margaret C. *The Law of Medical Malpractice.* Dobbs Ferry, N.Y.: Oceana Publications, 1996.

Jecker, Nancy S. "Can an Employer-Based Health Insurance System Be Just?" *Journal of Health Care Politics, Policy and Law* 18, no. 3 (Fall 1993): 657–73.

Jensen, Gail A., Michael A. Morrisey, Shanon Gaffney, and Derek K. Liston. "The New Dominance of Managed Care: Insurance Trends in the 1990s." *Health Affairs* 16, no. 1 (January/February 1997): 125–36.

Johnson, Allan N., and David Aquilina. "The Competitive Impact of Health Maintenance Organizations and Competition on Hospitals in Minnneapolis/St. Paul." *Journal of Health Politics, Policy and Law* 10, no. 4 (Winter 1986): 659–74.

Johnson, Haynes, and David S. Broder. *The System: The American Way of Politics at the Breaking Point.* Boston: Little, Brown, 1996.

Johnson, Kirk B., Carter G. Phillips, David Orentlicher, and Martin J. Hatlie. "The American Medical Association/Specialty Society Tort Reform Proposal: A Fault Based Administrative System." *Courts, Health Science and the Law* 1, no. 1 (1990): 6–18.

Johnson, Richard L. "Should Hospital Planning Continue to Be Regulated?" *Health Affairs* 2, no. 1 (Spring 1983): 83–91.

Johnsson, Julie. "High-Tech Health Care: How Much Can We Afford?" *Hospitals* 65, no. 16 (August 20, 1991): 80.

Jones, Charles O. *An Introduction to the Study of Public Policy.* North Scituate, Mass.: Duxbury Press, 1978.

Jones, David A. "'Putting Patients First': A Philosophy in Practice." *Health Affairs* 16, no. 6 (November/December 1997): 115–20.

Jones, James R. "Cost Pressures and Health Policy Reforms." *Health Affairs* 1, no. 3 (Summer 1982): 39–47.

Jones, Stanley B. "Multiple Choice Health Insurance: The Lessons and Challenges to Private Insurers." *Inquiry* 27, no. 2 (Summer 1990): 161–66.

Jordan, Fred. "Governors OK Alternative Plan on Federalism." *Nation's Cities Weekly* 5, no. 5 (March 1, 1982): 1, 9.

Joskow, Paul L. "Alternative Regulatory Mechanism for Controlling Hospital Costs." In *A New Approach to the Economics of Health Care*, ed. Mancur Olson, 219–57. Washington, D.C.: American Enterprise Institute for Public Policy Research, 1981.

Kadar, Andrew G. "The Sex-Bias Myth in Medicine." *Atlantic Monthly* 274, no. 2 (August 1994): 66–70.

Kaiser Commission on the Future of Medicaid. *Health Reform Legislation: A Comparison of Major Proposals*. Washington, D.C.: Henry J. Kaiser Family Foundation, January 1994.

Kalb, Paul E. "Controlling Health Care Costs by Controlling Technology: A Private Contractual Approach." *Yale Law Journal* 99, no. 4 (March 1990): 1109–1126.

Kambert, Mary-Lan. "High-Tech Health Care: Medical Devices and Treatments for the Future—and Present." *Current Health* 16, no. 8 (April 2, 1990): 4–9.

Kamisar, Yale. "Who Should Live—or Die? Who Should Decide?" An interview with Professor Kamisar at the University of Michigan Law School. *Trial* 27, no. 12 (December 1, 1991): 20–26.

Kane, N., and P. Manoukian. "The Effect of the Medicare Prospective Payment System on the Adoption of New Technology: The Case of Cochlear Implants." *New England Journal of Medicine* 321 (1989): 1378–1383.

Kane, Robert L., Rosalie A. Kane, Wendy Nielson Veazie. "Variation in State Spending for Long-Term Care: Factors Associated with More Balanced Systems," *Journal of Health Politics, Policy and Law* 23, no. 2 (April 1998): 363–90.

Kapp, Marshall B. "Solving the Medical Malpractice Problem: Difficulties in Defining What Works." *Law, Medicine, and Health Care* 17, no. 2 (1989): 156–65.

———. "Medical Malpractice Reform as Part of Health Care Reform: 1994 Version." *The Florida Bar Journal* 68, no. 5 (1994): 28–34.

Kari, Nancy, Harry C. Boyte, and Bruce Jennings. "Health as a Civic Question." Prepared for the American Civic Forum, 1994. Madison, Wisc. http://www.journalism.wisc.edu/cpn/sections/topics/health/civic_perspectives/health_as_quest.html.

"Kassebaum-Kennedy Health Insurance Bill Clears Congress." Washington: Families USA, August 1996. http://www.epn.org/families/Kafeka.html.

Keigher, Sharon M. "Health Care Reform and Long-Term Care: Uneasy Political Partners." *Health and Social Work* 19, no. 3 (August 3, 1994): 223–26.

Kennedy, Edward M. "Remarks on Introducing the Health Security Act." *Congressional Record*, January 25, 1971.

Kennedy, Edward M., and Orrin Hatch. "Health Insurance for Every Child." *Washington Post National Weekly Edition* 14, no. 42 (August 25, 1997): 26.

Kennedy, Louanne, and Bernard M. Baruch. "Health Planning in an Age of Austerity." *Policy Studies Journal* 9, no. 2 (Special #1, 1980-81): 232–41.

Kern, Rosemary G., and Susan R. Windham, with Paula Griswold. *Medicaid and Other Experiments in State Health Policy.* Washington, D.C.: American Enterprise Institute for Public Policy Research, 1986.

Kerner, J.F. "Breast Cancer Prevention and Control Among the Medically Underserved." *Breast Cancer Research and Treatment* 40, no. 1 (1996): 1–9.

Kerr, John K., and Richard Jelinek. "Impact of Technology in Health Care and Health Administration: Hospitals and Alternative Care Delivery Systems." *Journal of Health Administration Education* 8, no. 1 (Winter 1990): 5–10.

Kilborn, Peter T. "Illness Is Turning into Financial Catastrophe for More of the Uninsured." *New York Times,* August 1, 1997.

Kilner, John F. "Age as a Basis for Allocating Lifesaving Medical Resources: An Ethical Analysis." *Journal of Health Politics, Policy and Law* 13, no. 3 (Fall 1988): 405–23.

———. *Who Lives? Who Dies? Ethical Criteria in Patient Selection.* New Haven: Yale University Press, 1991.

———. *Life on the Line: Ethics, Aging, Ending Patients' Lives, and Allocating Vital Resources.* Grand Rapids, Mich.: W.B. Eerdmans, 1992.

Kilpatrick, Anne O., Krishna S. Dhir, and John M. Sanders. "Health Care Technology Assessment: A Policy Planning Tool." *International Journal of Public Administration* 14, no. 1 (1991): 59–82.

King, Josephine Y. "No-Fault Compensation for Medical Injuries." *Journal of Contemporary Health Law and Policy* 8, no. 201 (1992): 227–36.

Kingdon, John W. *Agendas, Alternatives, and Public Policies.* Boston: Little, Brown, 1984.

Kinney, Eleanor D., and Suzanne K. Steinmetz. "Notes from the Insurance Underground: How the Chronically Ill Cope." *Journal of Health Politics, Policy and Law* 19, no. 3 (Fall 1994): 637–41.

Kitzhaber, John. "A Healthier Approach to Health Care." *Issues in Science and Technology* 7, no. 2 (Winter 1991): 59–65.

Klein, Rudolf. "The Political Ideology vs. the Reality of Politics: The Case of Britain's Health Services in the 1980s." *Milbank Memorial Fund Quarterly/Health and Society* 62, no. 1 (Winter 1984).

Kopstein, David M., and Karen R. Ristuben. "Privilege Denied—Hospital Liability for Credentialing." *Trial* 33, no. 5 (1997): 30–34.

Korcok, A. "I Will See You in Court: US Still Looking for Malpractice Cure." *Canadian Medical Association Journal* 138, no. 9 (1988): 846–847.

Kosterlitz, Julie. "Buying into Trouble," *National Journal* 20, no. 57 (December 31, 1988): 3245–3249.

———. "Rationing Health Care." *National Journal* 22, no. 26 (June 30, 1990): 1590–1595.

———. "Softening Resistance." *National Journal* 23, no. 2 (January 12, 1991): 64–68.

———. "Middle-Class Medicaid." *National Journal* 23, no. 45 (November 9, 1991): 2738–2731.

———. "Paying for Miracles." *National Journal* 25, no. 32 (August 7, 1993): 1967–1971.

———. "Health Lobby Cranks Up Its Postage Meter." *National Journal* 25, no. 42 (October 16, 1993).

———. "Winners and Losers." *National Journal* 25, no. 50 (December 11, 1993).

———. "Brinksmanship." *National Journal* 26, no. 28 (July 9, 1994): 1648.

———. "Signs of Life in the Wreckage." *National Journal* 26, no. 43 (October 22, 1994).

———. "Unmanaged Care." *National Journal* 26, no. 50 (December 10, 1994): 2903–2907.

———. "Harry, Louise and Doublespeak." *National Journal* 26, no. 26 (June 25, 1995): 1542.

Kotelchuck, Ronda. "Medicaid Managed Care: A Mixed Review." *Health/PAC Bulletin* 22, no. 3 (Fall 1992): 4–11.

Krause, Elliott A. *Power and Illness: The Political Sociology of Health and Medical Care.* New York: Elsevier, 1977.

Krauss, Clifford. "Under Political Steam, Health-Care Issue Gains Wider Support in Congress." *New York Times,* January 12, 1992.

Krieger, Nancy, and Elizabeth Fee. "Man-Made Medicine and Women's Health." In *Man-Made Medicine: Women's Health, Public Policy, and Reform,* ed. Kary L. Moss, 17–35. Durham, N.C.: Duke University Press, 1996.

Kruse, Lowell C. "Some Thoughts about Resource Allocation in Health Care." *Midwest Medical Ethics* 5, no. 4 (Fall 1989): 15–16.

Kuttner, Robert."Medicare Extension a Step in the Right Direction." 1998. http://
www.epn.org/Kuttner/bk980111.html.
———. "Must Good HMOs Go Bad?" (first of two parts). *New England Journal of Medi-
cine* 338, no. 21 (May 21, 1998): 1558–1563.
———. "Must Good HMOs Go Bad?" (second of two parts). *New England Journal of
Medicine* 338, no. 22 (May 28): 1635–1639.
Ladd, Everett C. "Health Care Hysteria, Part II." *New York Times,* July 23, 1998.
Ladenheim, Kala. *Expanding Access to Health Care: An Overview of 1992 State Legisla-
tion.* Washington, D.C: Intergovernmental Health Policy Project, George Washington
University, 1993.
———. "Health Insurance in Transition: The Health Insurance Portability and Account-
ability Act of 1996." *Publius* 27, no. 2 (Spring 1997): 33–51.
Laham, Nicholas. *A Lost Cause: Bill Clinton's Campaign for National Health Insurance.*
Westport, Conn.: Praeger, 1996.
Lamphere, Jo Ann, Patricia Newman, Kathryn Langwell, and Daniel Sherman. "The Surge
in Medicare Managed Care: An Update." *Health Affairs* 16, no. 3 (May/June 1997):
127–33.
Lantz, Paul M., J.S. House, and J. Chen. "Socioeconomic Factors, Health Behaviors, and Mor-
tality." *Journal of the American Medical Association* 279, no. 21 (June 3, 1998): 1703–1708.
Larkin, Howard. "Firm to Offer Insurance with No-Fault Features." *American Medical News*
33, no. 24 (1990): 9–10.
Latham, Bryan W. *Health Care Costs: There Are Solutions.* New York: American Manage-
ment Association, 1983.
Latz, Ronald S. "No-Fault Liability and Medical Malpractice: A Viability Analysis." *Jour-
nal of Legal Medicine* 10, no. 3 (1989): 479–525.
Laudicina, Susan S., and Brian Burwell. "Profile of Medicaid Home and Community-Based
Care Waivers, 1985: Findings of a National Survey." *Journal of Health Politics, Policy
and Law* 13, no. 3 (Fall 1988): 525–46.
Lauritzen, Paul. *Pursuing Parenthood: Ethical Issues in Assisted Reproduction.* Bloomington:
Indiana University Press, 1993.
Lave, Judith R. "Hospital Reimbursement under Medicare." *Milbank Memorial Fund Quar-
terly/Health and Society* 62, no. 2 (1984): 251–78.
Lazenby, Helen C., and Suzanne W. Letsch. "National Health Expenditures, 1989." *Health
Care Financing Review* 12, no. 2 (Winter 1990): 1–26.
LeClair, Brian J. "What about a Bill of Rights for the Uninsured?" *New York Times,* July 28,
1998.
Lee, Peter V. "The True Test of Whether Health Plans Put Patients First." *Health Affairs*16,
no. 6 (November/December 1997): 129–32.
Lee, Philip R., and Carroll L. Estes. "New Federalism and Health Policy." *Annals of the
American Academy of Political and Social Science* 468 (July 1983): 88–102.
Leeds, Helen. *Health Care Cost Containment in the States: Strategies from the 1990s.* Wash-
ington, D.C.: Intergovernmental Health Policy Project, 1996.
Legal Medicine: Legal Dynamics of Medical Encounters. American College of Legal Medi-
cine. St. Louis: C.V. Mosby, 1988.
Leichter, Howard M. "Rationing of Health Care in Oregon: Making the Implicit Explicit."
In *Health Policy Reform in America: Innovations from the States,* 2d ed., ed. Howard M.
Leichter, 138–62. Armonk, N.Y.: M.E. Sharpe, 1997.
Lemov, Penelope. "States and Medicaid: Ahead of the Feds." *Governing* 6, no. 10 (July
1993): 27–28.
———. "An Acute Case of Health Care Reform." *Governing* 7, no. 8 (May 1994): 44–50.
———. "Nursing Homes and Common Sense." *Governing* 7, no. 10 (July 1994): 44–49.

Letsch, Suzanne W. "Data Watch: National Health Care Spending in 1991." *Health Affairs* 12, no. 1 (Spring 1993): 94–110.

Letsch, Suzanne W., Helen C. Lazenby, Katharine R. Levit, and Cathy A. Cowan. "National Health Expenditures, 1991." *Health Care Financing Review* 14, no. 2 (Winter 1992): 1–30.

Leutz, Walter N., Merwyn R. Greenlick, and John A. Capitman. "Integrating Acute and Long-Term Care." *Health Affairs* 13, no. 4 (Fall 1994): 58–74.

Levit, Katharine R., Helen C. Lazenby, and Madie W. Stewart. "DataView: National Health Expenditures, 1995." *Health Care Financing Review* 18, no. 1 (Fall 1996): 175–214.

Levit, Katharine R. et al. "National Health Expenditures, 1996." *Health Care Financing Review* 19, no. 1 (Fall 1997): 161–200.

Levit, Katharine R., Gary L. Olin, and Suzanne W. Letsch. "Americans' Health Insurance Coverage, 1980-1991." *Health Care Financing Review* 14, no. 1 (Fall 1992): 31–57.

Levit, Katharine R., Arthur L. Sensebig, Cathy A. Cowen, Helen C. Lazenby, Patricia A. McDonnell, Darleen K. Won, Lekha Sivarajan, Jean M. Stiller, Carolyn S. Donham, and Madie S. Stewart. "National Health Expenditures, 1993." *Health Care Financing Review* 16, no. 1 (Fall 1994): 247–94.

Levitats, Meron J. "How to Get Rid of the Hired Guns." *Medical Economics* 68, no. 4 (March 4, 1991): 21–28.

Lewin and Associates, Inc. *Evaluation of the Efficiency and Effectiveness of the Section 1122 Review Process*. Springfield, Va.: National Technical Information Service, 1975.

Leyerle, Betty. *The Private Regulation of American Health Care*. Armonk, N.Y.: M.E. Sharpe, 1994.

Liang, Bryan A. "Medical Malpractice: Do Physicians Have Knowledge of Legal Standards and Assess Cases as Juries Do?" *Roundtable* 3 (1996): 59–111.

Light, Donald W. "The Practice and Ethics of Risk-Related Insurance." *Journal of the American Medical Association* 267, no. 18 (May 13, 1992): 2503–2508.

Lindblom, Charles E. "The Science of Muddling Through." *Public Administration Review* 19 (Spring 1959): 79–88.

———. *Politics and Markets: The World's Political Economic System*. New York: Basic Books, 1977.

Lindblom, Charles E., and Edward J. Woodhouse. *The Policy-Making Process*. Englewood Cliffs, N.J.: Prentice-Hall 1993.

Littell, Candace L., and Robin J. Strongin, "The Truth about Technology and Health Care Cost." *IEEE Technology and Society* 15, no. 3 (Fall 1996): 10–15.

Locke, Adrienne C. "Bush Unveils Malpractice Reform Proposal." *Business Insurance* 25, no. 20 (May 20, 1991): 3–4.

Lohr, Kathleen N. "How Do We Measure Quality?" *Health Affairs* 16, no. 3 (May/June 1997): 22–-25.

Long, Stephen H., and M. Susan Marquis. "Gaps in Employer Coverage: Lack of Supply or Lack of Demand?" *Health Affairs* 12 (Supplement 1993): 282–93.

Long, Stephen H., and Russell F. Settle. "Medicare and the Disadvantaged Elderly: Objectives and Outcomes." *Milbank Memorial Fund Quarterly/Health and Society* 62, no. 4 (Fall 1984): 609–56.

Lotlarz, Virginia. "History of Medical Technology in the United States." *Clinical Laboratory Science* 4, no. 4 (July/August 1991): 233–36.

Lowi, Theodore. "The Public Philosophy: Interest Group Liberalism." *American Political Science Review* 61, no. 1 (March 1967): 5–24.

Ludwig, William C. "The Medical Profession and the 'Health Care Crisis.'" *Ohio Lawyer* 8, no. 5 (September/October 1994): 25–35.

Luft, Harold S. "How Do Health Maintenance Organizations Achieve Their Savings? Rhetoric and Evidence." *New England Journal of Medicine* 298, no. 24 (1978): 1336–1343.

———. "Trends in Medical Costs: Do HMOs Lower the Rate of Growth? *Medical Care* 18, no. 1 (1980): 1–17.

———. *Health Maintenance Organizations: Dimensions of Performance.* New York: Wiley, 1981.

Luft, Harold S., Susan C. Maerki, and Joan B. Trauner. "The Competitive Effects of Health Maintenance Organizations: Another Look at Evidence from Hawaii, Rochester, and Minneapolis/St. Paul." *Journal of Health Politics, Policy and Law* 10, no. 4 (Winter 1986): 625–58.

Luft, Harold S., and R.H. Miller. "Patient Selection in a Competitive Health Care System." *Health Affairs* 7, no. 3 (1988): 97–119.

Lurie, N. "Termination from Medical Care: Does It Affect Health?" *New England Journal of Medicine* 311, no. 7 (1984): 480–84.

Lutz, Sandy, Woodrin Grossman, and John Bigalke. *Med Inc.: How Consolidation Is Shaping Tomorrow's Healthcare System.* San Francisco: Jossey-Bass, 1998.

Mabie, Margot C.J. *Bioethics and the New Medical Technology.* New York: Atheneum, 1993.

McBride, David. "Black America: From Community Health Care to Crisis Medicine." *Journal of Health Politics, Policy, and Law* 18, no. 2 (Summer 1993): 319–37.

McCall, Nelda. "Lessons from Arizona's Medicaid Managed Care Program." *Health Affairs* 16, no. 4 (July/August 1997): 194–99.

Macchiaroli, Jean A. "Medical Malpractice Screening Panels: Proposed Model Legislation to Cure Judicial Ills." *George Washington Law Review* 58, no. 2 (1990): 181–260.

McClellan, Mark. "Are the Returns to Technological Change in Health Care Declining?" *Proceedings of the National Academy of Sciences of the United States* 93, no. 23 (November 12, 1996): 12701–12709.

McClure, Walter. "Structural and Incentive Problems in Economic Regulation of Medical Care." *Milbank Memorial Quarterly/Health and Society* 59, no. 2 (Spring 1981): 107–44.

———. "The Competitive Strategy for Medical Care." *Annals of the American Academy of Political and Social Science* 469 (July 1983): 30–47.

McCombs, Jeffrey S., and Jon B. Christianson. "Applying Competitive Bidding to Health Care." *Journal of Health Politics, Policy and Law* 12, no. 4 (Winter 1987): 703–21.

McConnell, Grant. *Private Power and American Democracy.* New York: Knopf, 1966.

McCormack, Lauren A., Peter D. Fox, and Marcia L. Graham. "Medigap Reform Legislation of 1990: Have the Objectives Been Met?" *Health Care Financing Review* 18, no. 1 (Fall 1996): 157–74.

McCormick, Brian. "Study: Defensive Medicine Costs Nearly $10 Billion." *American Medical News* 36, no. 7 (February 15, 1993): 4–5.

McCormick, Richard A. "Clear and Convincing Evidence: The Case of Nancy Cruzan." *Midwest Medical Ethics* 6, no. 4 (Fall 1990): 10–12.

McDonough, John E. "Tracking the Demise of State Hospital Rate Setting." *Health Affairs* 16, no. 1 (January/February 1997): 142–49.

McGregor, Maurice. "Hospital Costs: Can They Be Cut?" *Milbank Memorial Fund Quarterly/Health and Society* 59, no. 1 (Winter 1981): 89–98.

McLeod, Don. "Home-Care Patients Feel Unfairly Targeted." *AARP Bulletin* 39, no. 4 (April 1998): 1, 8–9.

McMillan, Alma. "Trends in Medicare Health Maintenance Organization Enrollment: 1986–1993." *Health Care Financing Review* 15, no. 1 (Fall 1993): 135–46.

McMillen, Scott R. "The Medical Malpractice Statute of Limitations: Some Answers and Some Questions." *Trial Lawyers Forum* 70, no. 2 (1996): 44–47.

McMullen, Andrew. "Comment: Mediation and Medical Malpractice Disputes: Potential Obstacles in the Traditional Lawyer's Perspective." *Journal of Dispute Resolution* 1990 no. 2 (1990): 371–86.

McNamee, David. "Living with HUGO." *Lancet* 346, no. 8973 (August 19, 1995): 497.

McNay, Don, and Thomas L. Gentry. "Structured Settlements and the Federally Supported Health Centers Assistance Act of 1995." *Trial Diplomacy Journal* 20, no. 3 (1997): 173–75.

McNeil, Richard, Jr., and Robert E. Schlenker. "HMOs, Competition and Government." *Milbank Memorial Fund Quarterly/Health and Society* 53, no. 1 (Spring 1975): 195–224.

McQuade, J.S. "The Medical Malpractice Crisis—Reflections on the Alleged Causes and Proposed Cures: Discussion Paper." *Journal of Royal Society of Medicine* 84 (July 1991): 408–11.

Magleby, James E. "The Constitutionality of Utah's Medical Malpractice Damages Cap under the Utah Constitution." *Journal of Contemporary Law* 21, no. 2 (1995): 217–58.

Mahood, H.R. *Interest Group Politics in America: A New Intensity*. Englewood Cliffs, N.J.: Prentice Hall, 1990.

Malinowski, Michael J. "Capitation, Advances in Medical Technology, and the Advent of a New Era in Medical Ethics." *American Journal of Law and Medicine* 22, no. 2–3 (Summer/Fall 1996): 331–60.

Mann, Cindy, and Jocelyn Guyer. "Overview of the New Child Health Block Grant." Washington, D.C.: Center for Budget and Policy Priorities, August 6, 1997. http://www.cbpp.org/chhlth.htm.

Mann, Joyce M., Glenn A. Melnick, Anil Bamezai, and Jack Zwanziger. "A Profile of Uncompensated Care, 1983–1995." *Health Affairs* 16, no. 4 (July/August 1997): 223–32.

Manning, Bayless, and Bruce Vladeck. "The Role of State and Local Government in Health." *Health Affairs* 2, no. 4 (Winter 1983): 134–40.

Manning, William G., Arleen Leibowitz, George A. Goldber, William H. Roger, and Joseph P. Newhouse. "A Controlled Trial of the Effects of a Prepaid Group Practice on Use of Services." *New England Journal of Medicine* 310, no. 23 (June 1984): 1505–1510.

Marmor, Theodore. *The Politics of Medicare*. Chicago: Aldine, 1973.

———. "Forecasting American Health Care: How We Got Here and Where We Might Be Going." *Journal of Health Care Politics and Policy* 23, no. 3 (June 1998): 551–71.

Marmor, Theodore, and James Morone. "HSAs and the Representation of Consumer Interests: Conceptual Issues and Litigation Problems." *Health Law Project Library Bulletin* 4 (April 1979): 117–28.

Marmor, Theodore, and Jonathan Oberlander. "Rethinking Medicare Reform." *Health Affairs* 17, no. 1 (January/February 1998): 52–68.

Marmor, Theodore R., Donald A. Wittman, and Thomas C. Heagy. "The Politics of Medical Inflation." In *Political Analysis and American Medical Care*, ed. Theodore R. Marmor. Cambridge, England: Cambridge University Press, 1983.

Mawrick, Charles. "Women's Health Action Plan Sees First Anniversary." *Journal of the American Medical Association* 268, no. 14 (October 14, 1992): 1816–1818.

Mayhew, David R. *Divided We Govern: Party Control, Lawmaking, and Investigations*. New Haven, Conn.: Yale University Press, 1991.

Mechanic, David. "Some Dilemmas in Health Care Policy." *Milbank Memorial Fund Quarterly/Health and Society* 59, no. 1 (Winter 1981): 1–14.

———. "Changing Medical Organization and the Erosion of Trust." *Milbank Quarterly* 74, no. 2 (1996): 171–89.

———. "Muddling Through Elegantly: Finding the Proper Balance in Rationing." *Health Affairs* 16, no. 5 (September/October 1997): 83–92.

———. "The Functions and Limitations of Trust in the Provision of Medical Care." *Journal of Health Politics, Policy and Law* 23, No. 4 (August 1998): 661–86.

Meilaender, Gilbert. "The Cruzan Decision: 9.5 Theses for Discussion." *Midwest Medical Ethics* 6, no. 4 (Fall 1990): 3–5.

Meir, Kenneth J. *Regulation: Politics, Bureaucracy and Economics*. New York: St. Martin's Press, 1985.

Mellow, Wesley S. "Determinants of Health Insurance and Pension Coverage." *Monthly Labor Review* 105, no. 5 (May 1982): 30–32.

Melski, John W. "Price of Technology: A Blind Spot." *Journal of the American Medical Association* 267, no. 11 (March 18, 1992): 1516–1518.

Menon, Jody W. "Adversarial Medical and Scientific Testimony and Lay Jurors: A Proposal for Medical Malpractice Reform." *American Journal of Law and Medicine* 21, no. 2, 3 (1995): 281–300.

Menzel, Paul T. *Strong Medicine: The Ethical Rationing of Health Care*. New York: Oxford University Press, 1990.

Merrell, Katie, David C. Colby, and Christopher Hogan. "Medicare Beneficiaries Covered by Medicaid Buy-In Agreements." *Health Affairs* 16, no. 1 (January/February 1997): 175–84.

Merrill, Jeffrey, and Catherine McLaughlin. "Competition versus Regulation: Some Empirical Evidence." *Journal of Health Politics, Policy and Law* 10, no. 4 (Winter 1988): 613–23.

Merrill, Richard A. "Regulation of Drugs and Devices: An Evolution." *Health Affairs* 13, no. 3 (Summer 1994): 47–69.

Meyer, Harris A. "Doctors Fight Fees for No-Fault Patient Compensation Upheld." *American Medical News* 34, no. 46 (1991): 4.

———. "Doctor Fee for No-Fault Patient Compensation Upheld." *American Medical News* 34, no. 46 (1991): 7.

Meyerhoff, Allen S., and David A. Crozier. "Health Care Coalitions: The Evolution of a Movement." *Health Affairs* 3, no. 1 (Spring 1984): 120–27.

Mick, Stephen S., and John D. Thompson. "Public Attitude toward Health Planning under the Health Systems Agencies." *Journal of Health Politics, Policy and Law* 9, no. 4 (Winter 1984): 783–800.

Miller, Judith. "What to Do until the Philosopher Kings Come: Bioethics and Public Policy in Canada." *Politics and the Life Sciences* 13, no. 1 (February 1, 1994): 93–95.

Miller, Mark E., Stephen Zuckerman, and Michael Gates. "How Do Medicare Physician Fees Compare with Private Payers?" *Health Care Financing Review* 14, no. 3 (Spring 1993): 25–39.

Miller, Stephen. *Special Interest Groups in American Politics*. New Brunswick, N.J.: Transaction, 1985.

Miller, Velvet G., and Janis L. Curties. "Health Care Reform and Race-Specific Policies." *Journal of Health Politics, Policy and Law* 18, no. 3 (Fall 1993): 748.

Millman, Michael, ed. *Access to Health Care in America*. Washington, D.C.: National Academy Press, 1993.

Mitchell, Chester N., and Shona McDiarmid. "Medical Malpractice: A Challenge to Alternative Dispute Resolution." *CJLS/RCDS* 3, (1988): 227–45.

Mitchell, Samuel A. "Issues, Evidence, and the Policymaker's Dilemma." *Health Affairs* 1, no. 3 (Summer 1982): 84–98.

Molina, Carlos W., and Marilyn Aguirre-Molina, eds. *Latino Health in the US: A Growing Challenge*. Washington, D.C.: American Public Health Association, 1994.

Monheit, Alan C., and Jessica Primoff Vistnes. "Implicit Pooling of Workers from Large and Small Firms." *Inquiry* 13, no. 1 (Spring 1994): 301–14.

Monreleone, J. Michael. "Trial Lawyers and the Health Care Crisis." *Ohio Lawyer* 8, no. 5 (September/October 1994): 25–33.

Moon, Marilyn. "Ensuring a Future for Medicare." (n.d.) <http://www.aarp.org/monthly/medicare3/viewmm.htm>.

————. *Medicare Now and in the Future*, 2d ed. Washington, D.C.: Urban Affairs Press, 1996.

Moon, Marilyn, Barbara Gage, and Alison Evans. *An Examination of Key Medicare Provisions in the Balanced Budget Act of 1997*. Baltimore, Md. Urban Institute, 1997. http://www.urban.org/entitlements/moonfinal.htm.

Moon, Marilyn, and Janemarie Mulvey. *Entitlements and the Elderly: Protecting Promises, Recognizing Realities*. Washington, D.C.: Urban Institute Press, 1996.

Moon, Marilyn, and Joanne Silberner. "What about Health Care for the Uninsured?" *Washington Post National Weekly Edition* 15, no. 36 (July 6, 1998): 26.

Mooney, Gavin. *Economics, Medicine and Health Care*. Atlantic Highlands, N.J.: Humanities Press, 1986.

Moran, Donald W. "HMOs, Competition, and the Politics of Minimum Benefits." *Milbank Memorial Fund Quarterly/Health and Society* 59, no. 2 (Spring 1981): 190–208.

————. "Federal Regulation of Managed Care: An Impulse in Search of a Theory?" *Health Affairs* 16, no. 6 (November/December1997): 7–21.

Morone, James A., and Andrew B. Dunham. "Slouching toward National Health Insurance: The Unanticipated Politics of DRGs." *Bulletin of the New York Academy of Medicine* 62, no. 6 (July/August 1986): 646–62.

Morris, Jonas. *Searching for a Cure: National Health Policy Considered*. New York: Pica Press, 1984.

Mueller, Keith J. "Organ Transplant Legislation." In *Biomedical Technology and Public Policy*, ed. Robert H. Blank and Miriam K. Mills, 143–65. New York: Greenwood Press, 1989.

Muller, Charlotte. *Health Care and Gender*. New York: Russell Sage Foundation, 1990.

————. "Objective Health Care Technology Evaluation—It Isn't Easy." *Social Work in Health Care* 16, no. 1 (1991): 119–32.

Mullis, Jeffrey. "Medical Malpractice, Social Structure, and Social Control." *Sociological Forum* 10, no. 1 (March 1, 1995): 135–63.

Nadel, Mark V. *Health Care Reform: Supplemental and Long-Term Care Insurance*. Testimony before the Subcommittees on Health and the Environment and on Energy and Commerce, U.S. House of Representatives. Washington, D.C.: General Accounting Office, September 9, 1993.

Nathan, Richard. *The Administrative Presidency*. New York: Wiley, 1983.

Nathan, Richard P., et al. "Initial Effects of the Fiscal Year 1982 Reductions in Federal Domestic Spending." In *Reductions in U.S. Domestic Spending: How They Affect State and Local Governments*, ed. John W. Ellwood, 315–49. New Brunswick, N.J.: Transaction, 1982.

National Center for Health Statistics. *Health US, 1998*. Washington, D.C.: Government Printing Office, 1998.

National Commission on the State and Local Public Service. *Frustrated Federalism: Rx for State and Local Health Care Reform*. Albany, N.Y.: Nelson A. Rockefeller Institute of Government, 1993.

National Conference of State Legislatures. *Health Care Legislation 1996*. Denver, Colo.: National Conference of State Legislatures 1997.

Navarro, Peter. *The Policy Game: How Special Interests and Ideologues Are Stealing America*. New York: Wiley, 1984.

Navarro, Vicente. "Why Congress Did Not Enact Health Care Reform." *Journal of Health Politics, Policy and Law* 20, no. 2 (Summer 1995): 455–62.

Nelson, Harry. *Federalism in Health Reform: Views from the States That Could Not Wait*. New York: Milbank Memorial Fund, 1994.

Nelson, Lyle. "Access to Care in Medicare HMOs, 1996." *Health Affairs* 16, no. 2 (March/April 1997): 148–56.

Nelson, Lyle, Randall Brown, Marsha Gold, Anne Ciemnecki, and Elizabeth Docteur. "Access to Care in Medicare HMOs, 1996." *Health Affairs* 16, no. 2 (March/April 1997): 148–56.

Neubauer, Deane. "Hawaii: A Pioneer in Health System Reform." *Health Affairs* 12, no. 12 (Spring 1993): 3–39.

———. "Hawaii: The Health State Revisited." In *Health Policy Reform in America: Innovations from the States*, 2d ed., ed. Howard M. Leichter, 163–88. Armonk, N.Y.: M.E. Sharpe, 1997.

Neuman, Patricia, Ed Maibach, Katharine Dusenbury, Michelle Kitchman, and Pam Zupp. "Marketing HMOs to Medicare Beneficiaries." *Health Affairs* 17, no. 4 (July/August 1998): 132–39.

Newacheck, P.W., J.J. Stoddard, D.C. Hughes, and M. Pearl. "Health Insurance and Access to Primary Care for Children." *New England Journal of Medicine* 338, no. 8 (February 19, 1998): 513–19.

Newcomer, Lee N. "Measures of Trust in Health Care." *Health Affairs* 16, no. 1 (January/February 1997): 50–51.

Newhouse, Joseph P., Melinda Beeuwkes Buntin, and John D. Chapman. "A Risk Adjustment and Medicare: Taking a Closer Look." *Health Affairs* 16, no. 5 (September/October 1997): 26–43.

Newhouse, Joseph P., et al. "Some Interim Results from a Controlled Trial of Cost Sharing in Health Insurance." *New England Journal of Medicine* 305, no. 25 (December 1981): 1501–1507.

New York Times. *The Downsizing of America*. New York: Times Books, 1996.

Nichols, Len M. *Health Care Quality: At What Cost?* Washington, D.C.: Urban Institute, 1998. http://www.urban.org/PERIODCL/pubsect/pub_13.htm.

Nichols, Len M., and Linda J. Blumberg. "A Different Kind of 'New Federalism'? The Health Insurance Portability and Accountability Act of 1996." *Health Affairs* 17, no. 3 (May/June 1998): 25–42.

Nichols, Mark. "Tinkering with Mother Nature: A Controversial Report on Reproductive Technologies." *Maclean's* 106, no. 48 (November 29, 1993): 38–40.

Nishimi, Robyn Y. "From the Congressional Office of Technology Assessment." *Journal of the American Medical Association* 270, no. 24 (December 22, 1993): 2911.

Nitzkin, Joel L. "Technology and Health Care—Driving Costs Up, Not Down." IEEE *Technology and Society Magazine* 15, no. 3 (Fall 1996): 40–46.

Nixon, Richard M. "Message to Congress." *Weekly Compilation of Presidential Documents*. Washington, D.C.: Office of the Federal Register, February 18, 1971.

Noll, Roger G. "The Consequences of Public Utility Regulation of Hospitals." In *Controls on Health Care*, ed. Institute of Medicine, 23–48. Washington, D.C.: National Academy of Sciences, 1975.

Norris, Jonas. *Searching for a Cure: National Health Policy Considered*. New York: PICA Press, 1984.

Norsigian, Judy. "The Women's Health Movement in the United States." In *Man-Made Medicine: Women's Health, Public Publicy, and Reform*, ed. Kary L. Moss, 79–97. Durham, N.C.: Duke University Press, 1996.

Nye, Joseph S., Jr., Philip D. Zelikow, and David C. King, eds. *Why People Don't Trust Government*. Cambridge, Mass.: Harvard University Press, 1997.

Nyman, John. "Costs, Technology, and Insurance in the Health Care Sector." *Journal of Policy Analysis and Management* 10, no. 1 (Winter 1991): 106–11.

Oberg, Charles, Betty Lia-Hoagberg, Ellen Hodkinson, Catherine Skovholt, and Renee Vanman. "Prenatal Care Comparisons among Privately Insured, Uninsured, and Medicaid-Enrolled Women." *Public Health Reports* 105, no. 5 (September/October 1990): 533–35.

BIBLIOGRAPHY 427

Oberlander, Jonathan B. "Managed Care and Medicare Reform." *Journal of Health Care Politics, Policy and Law* 22, no. 2 (April 1997): 595–631.

———. "Medicare: The End of Consensus." Paper prepared for delivery at the annual meeting of the American Political Science Association, Boston, Mass., September 3–6, 1998.

O'Connell, Jeffrey. "No-Fault Insurance for Injuries Arising from Medical Treatment: A Proposal for Elective Coverage." *Emory Law Journal* 24, no. 1 (1975): 21–42.

O'Connell, Jeffrey, and C. Brian Kelly. *The Blame Game.* New York: Lexington, 1987.

Office of the Federal Register, National Archives and Records Administration. *The United States Government Manual 1990/91.* Washington, D.C.: Government Printing Office, 1990.

Oliver, Thomas R. "Analysis, Advice and Congressional Leadership: The Physician Payment Review Commission and the Politics of Medicare." *Journal of Health Politics, Policy and Law* 18, no. 1 (Spring 1993): 113–74.

Oliver, Thomas R., and Pamela Paul-Shaheen. "Translating Ideas into Actions: Entrepreneurial Leadership in State Health Care Reforms." *Journal of Health Politics, Policy and Law* 22, no. 3 (June 1997): 721–88.

Olsen, Reed N. "The Reform of Medical Malpractice Law: Historical Perspectives." *American Journal of Economics and Sociology* 55, no. 3 (July 1996): 257–275.

Olson, Mancur. *The Logic of Collective Action: Public Goods and the Theory of Groups.* Cambridge: Harvard University Press, 1965.

———. *The Rise and Decline of Nations: Economic Growth, Stagflation, and Social Rigidities.* New Haven: Yale University Press, 1983.

O'Neill, Patrick. "Oregon's Health Care Rationing Plan Causing Fight." *Health Career News* (September 12, 1990): 17–21.

"Oregon Upholds Suicide Law." ABC News. http://www.abcnews.aol.com/sections/us/Daily/News/election97-suicide.htm.

"Oregon's Assisted Suicide Law Stokes the Fires of Controversy." *State Health Notes*, February 20, 1995, 1–3.

"Oregon's Right to Die Movement." Denver, Colo.: The Hemlock Society, USA, 1995. http://www2.privatei.com/hemlock.orertd.htm.

Parsons, T.E. "Suggestions for a Sociological Approach to a Theory of Organizations." *Administrative Science Quarterly* 1 (1956): 63–85.

Patel, Kant. "No-Fault Medical Liabililty in Virginia and Florida: A Preliminary Evaluation." *Evaluation and the Health Professions* 18, no. 2 (1995): 137–51.

———. "Medicaid: Perspectives from the States." *Journal of Health and Social Policy* 7, no. 3 (1996): 1–20.

Patel, Kant, and Mark Rushefsky. "Health Care Elites and Health Care Reform." *Health: An Interdisciplinary Journal of the Social Study of Health, Illness and Medicine* 2, no. 4 (October 1998): 459–84.

Paul-Shaheen, Pamela A. "The States and Health Care Reform: The Road Traveled and Lessons Learned from Seven That Took the Lead." *Journal of Health Politics, Policy and Law* 23, no. 2 (April 1998): 319–90.

Pauly, Mark V. *Medical Care at Public Expense: A Study in Applied Welfare Economics.* New York: Praeger, 1971.

———. "Is Medical Care Different?" In *Competition in the Health Care Sector: Past, Present and Future*, ed. Bureau of Economics, U.S. Federal Trade Commission, 19–48. Washington, D.C.: Government Printing Office, 1978.

———. "Is Medical Care Different? Old Questions, New Answers." *Journal of Health Politics, Policy and Law* 13, no. 2 (Summer 1988): 227–37.

Paxton, Harry T. "Just How Heavy Is the Burden of Malpractice Premiums?" *Medical Economics* 66, no. 2 (January 16, 1989): 168–83.

————. "Which Practice Expenses Are Out of Control?" *Medical Economics* 75, no. 22 (November 6, 1998): 91–117.

Pear, Robert. "Another Set of Dire Warnings on Social Security and Medicare Trust Funds." *New York Times,* April 4, 1995.

————. "Clinton Proposes U.S. Rules for Private Health Insurance." *New York Times,* June 15, 1995.

————. "The Tricky Business of Keeping Doctors Quiet." *New York Times,* September 22, 1996.

————. "Greenspan, Issuing Warning, Urges Changes in Medicare." *New York Times,* April 21, 1998.

Pearlstein, Steven, and Dana Priest. "Some Spoonfuls of Sugar Help the Medicine Go Down with Special Interests." *Washington Post National Weekly Edition* 10, no. 47 (September 27–October 3, 1993): 7.

Pence, Gregory E. *Classic Cases in Medical Ethics,* 2d ed. New York: McGraw Hill, 1995.

Penhallegon, John R. "Emerging Physician and Organization Liability under Managed Health Care." *Defense Counsel Journal* 64, no. 3 (1997): 347–56.

Perin, Joshua. "Long-Term Care Insurance: Partnership Model Offers an Option." *State Health Notes* 15, no. 193 (November 28, 1994): 4–5.

Peters, Philip G., Jr. "The Constitution and the Right to Die." *Midwest Medical Ethics* 6, no. 4 (Fall 1990): 13–16.

Peterson, Mark A. "Introduction: Health Care into the Next Century." *Journal of Health Politics, Policy and Law* 22, no. 2 (April 1997): 291–313.

Petrie, John T. "Overview of the Medicare Program." *Health Care Financing Review,* 1992 Annual Supplement, 1–14.

Petrie, John T., and Herbert A. Silverman. "Medicare Enrollment." *Health Care Financing Review,* 1992 Annual Supplement, 13–22.

Phelps, Charles E., and Stephen T. Parente. "Priority Setting in Medical Technology and Medical Practice Assessment." *Medical Care* 28, no. 8 (August 1990): 703–23.

Phillips, Carter G., and Paul E. Kalb. "Replacing the Tort System for Medical Malpractice." *Stanford Law and Policy Review* 91, no. 3 (Fall 1991): 210–15.

Physician Payment Review Commission. "A New Law Changes Practice Expense." *PPRC Update* no. 24 (August 1997).

Pollard, Michael R. "The Essential Role of Antitrust in a Competitive Market for Health Services." *Milbank Memorial Fund Quarterly/Health and Society* 59, no. 2 (Spring 1981): 256–68.

Priest, Dana, and Michael Weisskopf. "Health Care Reform: The Collapse of a Quest." *Washington Post,* October 11, 1994.

"PROs: Peering Harder in the 1990s." *Hospitals* 63, no. 3 (February 5, 1989): 42–46.

Quade, E.S. *Analysis for Public Decisions,* 3d ed. New York: Elsevier, 1989.

Quinn, Jane Bryant. "Medicare for Boomers." *Newsweek* 130, no. 15 (October 13, 1997): 55.

————. "Reinventing Medicare." *Newsweek* 132, no. 13 (September 28, 1998): 88.

Quintana, J.M., D. Goldmann, and C. Homer. "Social Disparities in the Use of Diagnostic Tests for Children with Gastroenteritis." *International Journal of Quality of Health Care* 9, no. 6 (December 1997): 419–25.

Raffel, Marshall W. *The U.S. Health System: Origins and Functions.* New York: Wiley, 1980.

Rake, Buddy, and Bobby Thrasher. "Medical Malpractice Myths, Truths and Solutions." *Arizona Attorney* 32, no. 7 (1996): 21–27.

Rask, Kimberly J., Mark V. Williams, Ruth M. Parker, and Sally E. McNagny. "Obstacles Predicting Lack of a Regular Provider and Delays in Seeking Care for Patients at an Urban Public Hospital." *Journal of the American Medical Association* 271, no. 24 (June 22, 1994): 1931–1933.

Rauch, Jonathan. *Demosclerosis: The Silent Killer of American Government.* New York: Times Books, 1994.

Raymond, Janice G. *Women as Wombs: Reproductive Technologies and the Battle over Women's Freedom.* San Francisco: Harper, 1993.

Rettig, Richard A. "Medical Innovation Duels Cost Containment." *Health Affairs* 13, no. 3 (Summer 1994): 7–27.

Rhodes, Robert P. *Health Care: Politics, Policy and Distributive Justice: The Ironic Triumph.* New York: State University of New York Press, 1992.

Rice, Berkeley. "Where Doctors Get Sued the Most." *Medical Economics* 72, no. 4 (February 27, 1995): 98–108.

Rice, Thomas. "Can Markets Give Us the Health System We Want?" *Journal of Health Politics, Policy and Law* 22, no. 2 (1997): 383–426.

Rice, Thomas, Katherine Desmond, and Jon Gable. "The Medicare Catastrophic Coverage Act: A Post-Mortem." *Health Affairs* 9, no. 3 (Fall 1990): 75–87.

Rice, Thomas, and Jon Gable. "Protecting the Elderly against High Health Care Costs." *Health Affairs* 5, no. 3 (Fall 1986): 5–21.

Rice, Thomas, and Kathleen Thomas. "Evaluating the New Medigap Standardization Regulations." *Health Affairs* 11, no. 1 (Spring 1992): 194–207.

Rice, Thomas, Kathleen Thomas, and William Weissert. *The Impact of Owning Private Long-Term Care Insurance Policies on Out-of-Pocket Costs.* Washington, D.C.: American Association of Retired Persons, 1989, 7.

Rice, Thomas, and Kenneth E. Thorpe. "Income-Related Cost Sharing in Health Insurance." *Health Affairs* 12, no. 1 (Spring 1993): 22.

Riley, Gerald F., Melvin J. Ingber, and Cynthia G. Tudor. "Disenrollment of Medicare Beneficiaries from HMOs." *Health Affairs* 15, no. 5 (September/October 1997): 117–24.

Riley, Trish. "The Role of States in Accountability for Quality." *Health Affairs* 16, no. 3 (May/June 1996): 41–43.

Rinella, Lore. "The Use of Medical Practice Guidelines in Medical Malpractice Litigation—Should Practice Guidelines Define the Standard of Care?" *University of Missouri Kansas City Law Review* 64, no. 2 (1995j): 337–55.

Rivlin, Alice M., David M. Cutler, and Len M. Nichols. "Financing, Estimation, and Estimation Effects." *Health Affairs* 13, no. 1 (Spring 1994): 30–49.

Robertson, John A. *Children of Choice: Freedom and the New Reproductive Technologies.* Princeton, N.J.: Princeton University Press, 1994.

Robinson, Glen. "Rethinking the Allocation of Medical Malpractice Risks between Patients and Providers." *Law and Contemporary Problems*, 49, no. 2 (1991): 173–99.

Robinson, William T. "New Deep Pocket: Managed Care Entity Liability for Alleged Improper Denial of Access." *Defense Counsel Journal* 64, no. 3 (1997): 357–63.

Rochefort, David A. "Commentary—The Pragmatic Appeal of Employment-Based Health Care Reform." *Journal of Health Care Politics, Policy and Law* 18, no. 3 (Fall 1993): 683–93.

Rockefeller, John D., IV. "The Pepper Commission Report on Comprehensive Health Care." *New England Journal of Medicine* 323, no. 14 (October 4, 1990): 1005–1007.

Roemer, Milton I. "Hospitals Utilization and the Supply of Physicians." *Journal of the American Medical Association* 178, no. 1 (December 1961): 933–89.

———. "The Politics of Public Health in the United States." In *Health Politics and Policy*, ed. Theodore J. Litman and Leonard S. Robins, 261–73. New York: Wiley, 1984.

———. *An Introduction to the U.S. Health Care System*, 2d ed. New York: Springer, 1986.

Romer, Paul M. "Evaluating the Federal Role in Financing Health-Related Research." *Proceedings of the National Academy of Sciences of the United States* 93, no. 23 (November 12, 1996): 12712–12725.

Rosenbaum, Sara H., Kay Johnson, Colleen Sonosky, Anne Markus, and Chris DeGraw. "The Children's Hour: The State Children's Health Insurance Program." *Health Affairs* 17, no. 1 (January/February 1998): 75–89.

Rosenbaum, Walter A. *Environmental Politics and Policy*. Washington, D.C.: CQ Press, 1985.

Rosenberg, Charlotte L. "Why Doctor-Policing Laws Don't Work." *Medical Economics* 61 (March 5, 1984): 84–96.

Rosenbloom, David. "New Ways to Keep Old Promises in Health Care." *Health Affairs* 2, no. 4 (Winter 1983): 41–53.

Rosoff, Arnold J. "Phase Two of the Federal HMO Development Program: New Directions after a Shaky Start." *American Journal of Law and Medicine* 1, no. 2 (Fall 1975): 209–43.

Ross, Jacqueline. "Will States Protect Us, Equally, from Damage Caps in Medical Malpractice Legislation?" *Indiana Law Review* 30, no. 2 (1997): 575–60.

Ross, Jane L. "Long-Term Care: Demography, Dollars, and Dissatisfaction Drive Reform." Testimony before the Special Committee on Aging, U.S. Senate. General Accounting Office, Washington, D.C., April 12, 1994, 1–6.

Rother, John C. "A Medicare in the 21st Century." (n.d.) http://www.aarp.org/monthly/medicare3/viewjr.htm.

Rothstein, Richard, and Karen Hawley Mills. *Where the Money's Gone: Changes in the Level and Composition of Education Spending*. Washington, D.C.: Economic Policy Institute, 1990.

Rovner, Julie. "Climbing Medigap Premiums Draw Attention on Hill." *Congressional Quarterly Weekly Report* 48, no. 7 (February 17, 1990): 527–30.

Rowland, Diana, Barbara Lyons, Alina Salganicoff, and Peter Long. "A Profile of the Uninsured in America." *Health Affairs* 13, no. 2 (Spring 1994): 283–89.

Rowland, Diana, and Alina Salganicoff. "Commentary: Lessons from Medicaid—Improving Access to Office-Cased Physician Care for the Low-Income Population." *American Journal of Public Health* 84, no. 4 (April 1994): 550–52.

Rublee, Dale A. "Medical Technology in Canada, Germany, and the United States: An Update." *Health Affairs* 13, no. 4 (Fall 1994): 113–17.

Rushefsky, Mark E. "A Critique of Market Reform in Health Care: The 'Consumer-Choice Health Plan.'" *Journal of Health Politics, Policy and Law* 5, no. 4 (Winter 1981): 720–41.

Rushefsky, Mark E., and Kant Patel. *Politics, Power and Policy Making: The Case of Health Care Reform in the 1990s*. Armonk, N.Y.: M.E. Sharpe, 1998.

Rustad, Michael, and Thomas Koenig. "Reconceptualizing Punitive Damages in Medical Malpractice: Targeting Amoral Corporations, Not 'Moral Monsters.'" *Rutgers Law Review* 47, no. 3 (Spring 1995): 975–1083.

Rutten, Frans F.H., and Gouke J. Bonsel. "High Cost Technology in Health Care: A Benefit or a Burden?" *Social Science and Medicine* 35, no. 4 (1992): 567–77.

Ruttenberg, Joan E. "Commentary—Revisiting the Employment-Insurance Link." *Journal of Health Care Politics, Policy and Law* 18, no. 3 (Fall 1993): 675–81.

Ryan, William F. *Blaming the Victim*. New York: Pantheon Books, 1971.

Sage, William M., Kathleen E. Hastings, and Robert A. Berenson. "Enterprise Liability for Medical Malpractice and Health Care Quality Improvement." *American Journal of Law and Medicine* 20, no. 1, no. 2 (1994): 1–28.

Salkever, David S., and Thomas W. Bice. "The Impact of Certificate of Need Controls on Hospital Investment." *Milbank Memorial Fund Quarterly/Health and Society* 54, no. 1 (Spring 1976): 185–214.

———. *Hospital Certificate-of-Need Controls: Impact on Investment, Costs and Use*. Washington, D.C.: American Enterprise Institute for Public Policy Research, 1979.

Samuelson, Paul. *Economics*. New York: McGraw-Hill, 1970.

Samuelson, Robert J."Having It All." *Newsweek* 32, no. 13 (Sepember 28, 1998): 71.

Sapolsky, Harvey M., Drew Altman, Richard Greene, and Judith D. Moore. "Corporate Attitude toward Health Care Costs." *Milbank Memorial Fund Quarterly/Health and Society* 59, no. 4 (Fall 1981): 561–85.

Sardell, Alice. *The U.S. Experiment in Social Medicine: The Community Health Center Program, 1965–1986.* Pittsburgh: University of Pittsburgh Press, 1988.

Schear, Stuart. "A Medicaid Miracle?" *National Journal* 27, no. 5 (February 4, 1995): 294–98.

Schmidt, Winsor C., D. Alex Keckert, and Alice A. Mercer. "Factors Associated with Medical Malpractice: Results from a Pilot Study," *Journal of Contemporary Health, Law and Policy* 7, no. 157 (1991): 157–82.

Schneider, Saundra K. "Intergovernmental Influences on Medicaid Program Expenditures." *Public Administration Review* 48, no. 4 (July/August 1988): 756–63.

Schneider, William. "Health Care Reform: What Went Right." *National Journal* 25, no. 40 (October 2, 1993): 2404.

———. "Health Care: So Where's the Crisis?" *National Journal* 26, no. 24 (June 11, 1994): 1378.

———. "Fear of Bureaucrats Strikes Again." *National Journal* 30, no. 29 (July 18, 1998): 1714.

Schnurer, Eric B. "A Health-Care Plan Most of Us Could Buy." *Washington Monthly* 30, no. 4 (April 1998): 20–25.

Schoen, Cathy, Barbara Lyons, Diane Rowland, Karen Davis, and Elaine Pulco. "Insurance Matters for Low-Income Adults: Results from a Five-State Survey." *Health Affairs* 16, no. 3 (September/October 1997): 163–71.

Scholle, Sara H., Kelly J. Kelleher, George Childs, John Mendelhoff, and William P. Gardner. "Changes in Medicaid Managed Care Enrollment among Children." *Health Affairs* 16, no. 2 (March/April 1997): 164–70.

Schur, Claudia L., Marc L. Berk, and Penny Mohr. "Understanding the Cost of a Catastrophic Drug Benefit." *Health Affairs* 9, no. 3 (Fall 1990): 88–100.

Schwartz, Gary T. "Considering the Proper Federal Role in American Tort Law." *Arizona Law Review* 38, no. 3 (1996): 917–51.

Schwartz, M.R. "Liability Crisis: The Physician's Viewpoint." In *Medical Malpractice: Tort Reform*, ed. J.E. Hammer and B.R. Jennings, 15–28. Memphis, Tenn.: University of Tennessee Press, 1987.

Schwartz, William B. "In the Pipeline: A Wave of Valuable Medical Technology." *Health Affairs* 13, no. 3 (Summer 1994): 70–79.

Schwartz, William B., and Henry J. Aaron. *Health Care Costs: The Social Tradeoffs.* Washington, D.C.: Brookings Institution, 1985.

———. "The Achilles Heel of Health Care Rationing." *New York Times*, July 9, 1990, A15.

Selden, Thomas M., Jessica S. Banthin, and Joel W. Cohen. "Medicaid's Problem Children: Eligible but Not Enrolled." *Health Affairs* 17, no. 3 (May/June 1998): 192–200.

Serafini, Marilyn Werber. "Managed Medicare." *National Journal* 27, no. 15 (April 15, 1995): 920–23.

———. "No Strings Attached!" *National Journal* 27, no. 20 (May 20, 1995): 1230–1234.

———. "Quality Time." *National Journal* 29, no. 21 (May 24, 1997): 1035–1037.

———. "Children's Crusade." *National Journal* 29, no. 26 (June 28, 1997): 1323–1326.

———. "Medicare Crooks." *National Journal* 29, no. 29 (July 19, 1997): 1458–1460.

———. "Brave New World." *National Journal* 29, no. 33 (August 16, 1997): 1636–1639.

———. "A Return to Medi-Scare Tactics?" *National Journal* 29, no. 50 (December 13, 1997): 2517.

———. "The Deal Maker." *National Journal* 30, no. 7 (February 14, 1998): 332–37.

Shaffer, Franklin A. "DRGs: History and Overview." *Nursing and Health Care* 4, no. 7 (September 1983), 388–89.

Shavers-Hornaday, V.L., C.F. Lynch, L.F. Burmeister, and J.C. Torner. "Why Are African Americans Under-Represented in Medical Research Studies? Impediments to Participation." *Ethnicity and Health* 2, nos. 1-2 (1997): 31–45.

Shaw, Linda R., et al. "Ethics of Lung Transplantation with Live Donors." *Lancet* 338, no. 8768 (September 14, 1991): 678–81.

Shear, Jeff. "The Big Fix." *National Journal* 27, no. 12 (25 March 1995): 734–38.

Sheils, John F., and Lawrence S. Lewin. "Perspective: Alternative Estimate: No Pain, No Gain." *Health Affairs* 13, no. 1 (Spring 1993): 50–55.

Sheri, David I. *With Dignity: The Search for Medicare and Medicaid.* Westport, Conn.: Greenwood Press, 1985.

Shikles, Janet L. "Long-Term Care Insurance: Risk to Consumers Should Be Reduced." Washington, D.C.: General Accounting Office, 1991, 2.

Shindell, S. "A Survey of the Law of Medical Practice." *Journal of the American Medical Association,* 193 (1965): 601–7.

Short, Pamela Farley, and Jessica Primoff Vistnes. "Multiple Sources of Medicare Supplementary Insurance." *Inquiry* 29 (Spring 1992): 33-43.

Shreve, Maggie, and June Isaacson Kailes. "The Right to Die or the Right to Community Support." *Midwest Medical Ethics* 6, no. 2, 3 (Spring/Summer 1990): 11–15.

Sibley, David. "What the Texas Experiment Shows about H.M.O. Liability." *New York Times,* August 7, 1998.

Siliciano, John A., and James A. Henderson, Jr. "Universal Health Care and the Continued Reliance on Custom in Determining Medical Malpractice." *Cornell Law Review* 79, no. 6 (September 1994): 1382–1405.

Silver, George A. "Health Care Systems." *Grolier Multimedia Encyclopedia,* 1998.

Silverman, Herbert A. "Medicare-Covered Skilled Nursing Facility Services, 1967-88." *Health Care Financing Review* 12, no. 3 (Spring 1991): 103–8.

Simborg, Donald W. "DRG Creep: A New Hospital Acquired Disease." *New England Journal of Medicine* 304, no. 26 (1981): 1602–1604.

Simendinger, Alexis. "Another Problem, Another Commission." *National Journal* 29, no. 50 (December 13, 1997): 2514–2515.

Simmons, Walter O. "An Economic Analysis of Mandatory Mediation and the Disposition of Medical Malpractice Claims." *Journal of Legal Economics* 6, no. 2 (Fall 1996): 41–74.

Simpson, G., B. Bloom, R.A. Cohen, and P.E. Parsons. "Access to Health Care. Part 1: Children." *Vital Health Statistics* 196 (July 10, 1997): 1–46.

Skidmore, Max J. *Medicare and the American Rhetoric of Reconciliation.* University: University of Alabama Press, 1970.

Skocpol, Theda. *Boomerang: Clinton's Health Security Effort and the Turn against Government in U.S. Politics.* New York: Norton, 1996.

Sloan, Frank A. "Government and the Regulation of Hospital Care." *Journal of American Economic Review* 72 (May 1982): 196–201.

———. "Reviews: An Economist." *Health Affairs* 1, no. 3 (Summer 1982): 113–18.

Sloan, Frank A., Randall R. Bovbjerg, and Penny B. Githens. *Insuring Medical Malpractice.* New York: Oxford University Press, 1991.

Sloan, Frank A., Janet Mitchell, and Jerry Cromwell. "Physician Participation in State Medicaid Programs." *Journal of Human Resources* 13 (Supplement 1978): 211–45.

Sloan, Frank A., Michael A. Morrisey, and Joseph Valvona. "Effects of the Medicare Prospective Payment System on Hospital Costs Containment: An Early Appraisal." *Milbank Memorial Fund Quarterly/Health and Society* 66, no. 2 (1988): 191–220.

Sloan, Frank A., P.M. Mergenhagen, and W.B. Burfield. "Medical Malpractice Experience of Physicians: Predictable or Haphazard?" *Journal of American Medical Association* 262, no. 23 (December 15, 1989): 3291–3297.

Sloan, Frank A., Penny B. Githens, Gerald B. Hickson, and Stephen S. van Wert. "Compensation." In *Suing for Medical Malpractice*, ed. Frank A. Sloan, Penny B. Githens, Ellen Wright Clayton, David F. Partlett, Gerald B. Hickson, and Stephen S. van Wert, 187–210. Chicago: University of Chicago Press, 1993.

Sloan, Irving J. *Professional Malpractice*. Dobbs Ferry, N.Y.: Oceana Publications, 1992.

Smith, Adam. *An Inquiry into the Nature and Causes of the Wealth of Nations: A Concordance*. Savage, Md.: Rowman and Littlefield, 1993.

Smith, Hubert W. "Legal Responsibility for Medical Malpractice." *Journal of the American Medical Association*, 116 (14 June 1941): 2672–2673.

Smith, Judith G., ed. *Political Brokers: Money, Organizations, Power and People*. New York: Liveright, 1972.

Smith, Sheila, Mark Freeland, Stephen Heffler, David Mckusick, and the Health Expenditures Project Team. "The Next Ten Years of Health Spending: What Does the Future Hold?" *Health Affairs* 17, no. 5 (September/October 1998): 128–40.

Sorkin, Alan L. *Health Care and the Changing Economic Environment*. Lexington, Mass.: D.C. Heath, 1986.

Southwick, Lawrence, and Gary J. Young. "Lawyers and Medical Torts: Medical Malpractice Litigation as a Residual Option." *Applied Economics* 24, no. 9 (September 1, 1992): 989–98.

Sparer, Michael S. "Devolution of Power: An Interim Report Card." *Health Affairs* 17, no. 3 (May/June 1998): 7–16.

Spencer, Peter L. "Technology Gatekeepers." *Consumers' Research Magazine* 78, no. 7 (July 1995): 43.

Spiegel, Allen D., and Florence Kavaler. "America's First Medical Malpractice Crisis: 1835–1865." *Journal of Community Health* 22, no. 4 (1997): 283–308.

Srinivasan, Srija, Larry Levitt, and Janet Lundy. "Wall Street's Love Affair with Health Care." *Health Affairs* 17, no. 4 (July/August 1998): 126–31.

Stanley, Harold W., and Richard G. Niemi. *Vital Statistics on American Politics*. Washington, D.C.: CQ Press, 1988.

Starr, David S. "Does Malpractice Litigation Deter Substandard Care?" *Medical Trial Technique Quarterly* 37, no. 3 (Spring 1991): 360–84.

Starr, Paul. "Changing the Balance of Power in American Medicine." *Milbank Memorial Fund Quarterly/Health and Society* 58 (Winter 1980): 170.

———. *The Social Transformation of American Medicine*. New York: Basic Books, 1982.

———. *The Logic of Health Care Reform: Why and How the President's Plan Will Work*. New York: Penguin Books, 1994.

———. "Why the Clinton Plan Is Not the Enthoven Plan." *Inquiry* 31, no. 2 (Summer 1994): 136–40.

———. "What Happened to Health Care Reform?" *American Prospect*, no. 20 (Winter 1995): 20–31.

Stauch, Marc S. "Causation Issues in Medical Malpractice: A United Kingdom Perspective." *Annals of Health Law* 5 (1996): 247–58.

Steinmo, Sven, and Jon Watts. "It's the Institutions, Stupid! Why Comprehensive National Health Insurance Always Fails in America." *Journal of Health Politics, Policy, and Law* 20, no. 2 (Summer 1995): 329–72.

Steinwald, Bruce, and Frank A. Sloan. "Regulatory Approaches to Hospital Cost Containment: A Synthesis of the Empirical Evidence." In *A New Approach to the Economics of Health Care*, ed. Mancur Olson, 273–308. Washington, D.C.: American Enterprise Institute for Public Policy, 1981.

Stephenson, Joan. "Ethics Group Drafts Guidelines for Control of Genetic Material and Information." *Journal of the American Medical Association* 279, no. 3 (1998): 184.

Stern, Robert S., Joel E. Weissman, and Arnold M. Epstein. "The Emergency Department as a Pathway for Admission for Poor and High-Cost Patients." *Journal of the American Medical Association* 266, no. 16 (October 23, 1991): 2238–2246.

Stevens, Carol. "Is George Bush the White Knight of Malpractice Reform?" *Medical Economics* 68, no. 17 (September 2, 1991): 87–91.

———. "Will the Clinton Plan End Your Malpractice Woes?" *Medical Economics* 70, no. 11 (June 14, 1993): 24–49.

Stevens, Rosemary. *In Sickness and in Wealth: American Hospitals in the Twentieth Century.* New York: Basic Books, 1989.

Stimson, James A. *Public Opinion in America: Moods, Cycles, and Swings.* Boulder, Colo.: Westview Press, 1991.

Stoddard, Jeffrey J., Robert F. St. Peter, and Paul W. Newacheck. "Health Insurance Status and Ambulatory Care for Children." *New England Journal of Medicine* 330, no. 20 (May 19, 1994): 1421–1425.

Stone, Deborah A. "Why States Can't Solve Health Care Crisis." *American Prospect*, no. 9 (Spring 1992): 51–60.

———. "When Patients Go to Market: The Workings of Managed Competition." *American Prospect* 13 (Spring 1993), 109–15.

———. "The Struggle for the Soul of Health Insurance." *Journal of Health Politics, Policy and Law* 18, no. 2 (Summer 1993): 287–317.

Strathern, Marilyn. *Reproducing the Future: Essays on Anthropology, Kinship and the New Reproductive Technologies.* New York: Routledge, Chapman and Hall, 1992.

Strosberg, Martin A., Joshua M. Wiener, Robert Baker, and I. Alan Fein, eds. *Rationing America's Medical Care: The Oregon Plan and Beyond.* Washington, D.C.: Brookings Institution, 1992.

Strumwasser, Ira, Nitin V. Paranjpe, and David W. Kee. "The Triple Option Choice: Self Selection Bias in Traditional Coverage, HMOs, and PPOs." *Inquiry* 26, no. 4 (Winter 1989): 432–41.

Sugarman, Stephen D. "Doing Away with Tort Law." *California Law Review* 73 (1985): 555–664.

———. "The Need to Reform Personal Injury Law Leaving Scientific Disputes to Scientists." *Science* 248 (1990): 823.

Sullivan, Cynthia B., Marianne Miller, Roger Feldman, and Bryan Dowd. "Employer-Sponsored Health Insurance in 1991." *Health Affairs* 11, no. 4 (Winter 1992): 173.

Sullivan, Sean. *Managing Health Care Costs: Private Sector Innovations.* Washington, D.C.: American Enterprise for Public Policy Research, 1984.

Summer, Laura, Sharon Parrott, and Cindy Mann. *Millions of Uninsured and Underinsured Children Are Eligible for Medicaid.* Washington, D.C.: Center for Budget and Policy Priorities, 1996. http://www.cbpp.org/mcaidprt.htm.

Sun Valley Forum on National Health, Harrison Conference Center. "The Role of State and Local Government in Health." *Health Affairs* 2, no. 4 (Winter 1983): 134–39.

Sussman, Jason H. "Financial Considerations in Technology Assessment." Topics in Health Care Financing 17, no. 3 (Spring 1991): 30–41.

Tabbush, Victor. "Changing Paradigm in Medical Payment." *Archives of Internal Medicine* 156, no. 4 (February 26, 1996): 357–61.

Taragin, M.I. et al. "The Influence of Standard of Care and Severity of Injury on the Resolution of Medical Malpractice Claims." *Annals of Internal Medicine* 117 (1992): 780–84.

Taylor, Kathryn S. "Technology's Next Test: Regional Systems Laying Groundwork for Post-Reform Technology Planning." *Hospitals and Health Networks* 67, no. 11 (June 5, 1993): 42–44.

Tell, Eileen J., Marilyn Falik, and Peter D. Fox. "Private-Sector Health Care Initiatives: A Comparative Perspective from Four Communities." *Milbank Memorial Fund Quarterly/ Health and Society* 62, no. 3 (Summer 1984): 357–79.

Terris, Milton. "A Wasteful System That Doesn't Work." *Progressive* 54, no. 10 (October 1990): 14–16.

Thomas, Lewis. *The Lives of a Cell.* New York: Bantam Books, 1975.

Thomas, Richard K., Louis Pol, and William F. Sehnert, Jr. *Health Care Book of Lists.* Winter Park, Fla.: PMD Publishers Group, 1993.

Thomas, W. John."Clinton Health Care Reform Plan: A Failed Dramatic Presentation." *Stanford Law and Policy Review* 7, no. 1 (1995): 83–104.

Thompson, Frank J. *Health Policy and the Bureaucracy: Politics and Implementation.* Cambridge, Mass.: MIT Press, 1981.

Thompson, Frank J., and John J. DiIulio, Jr., eds. *Medicaid and Devolution: A View from the States.* Washington, D.C.: Brookings Institution, 1998.

———. "New Federalism and Health Care Policy: States and the Old Questions." *Journal of Health Politics, Policy and Law* 11, no. 4 (Tenth Anniversary Issue, 1986): 647–69.

———. "The Faces of Devolution." In *Medicaid and Devolution: A View from the States,* ed. Frank J. Thompson, 15–55. Washington, D.C.: Brookings Institution, 1998.

Thompson, Joseph W., James Bost, Faruque Ahmed, Carrie E. Ingalls, and Caly Sennett. "The NCQA's Quality Compass: Evaluating Managed Care in the United States." *Health Affairs* 17, no. 1 (January/February 1998): 152–58.

Thorpe, Kenneth E. *The Rising Number of Uninsured Workers: An Approaching Crisis in Health Care Financing.* Washington, D.C.: National Coalition on Health Care, October 1997. http://www.americashealth.org/emerge.uninsured.html.

———. *Changes in the Growth in Health Care Spending: Implications for Consumers.* Washington, D.C.: National Coalition on Health Care, April 1997. http://www.americashealth.org/implications/implications.html.

Tiefer, Charles. *The Semi-Sovereign Presidency: The Bush Administration's Strategy for Governing without Congress.* Boulder, Colo.: Westview Press, 1994.

Toner, Robin. "This Time Clinton Tries a Selective Health Care Strategy." *New York Times,* June 14, 1995.

Trebilcock, Michael J., Donald N. Dewees, and David G. Duff. "The Medical Malpractice Explosion: An Empirical Assessment of Trends, Determinants and Impacts." *Melbourne University Law Review* 17, no. 4 (1990): 539–65.

Trevino, Fernando M., M. Eugene Moyer, R. Burciaga Valdez, and Christine A. Stroup-Benham. "Health Insurance Coverage and Utilization of Health Services by Mexican Americans, Mainland Puerto Ricans, and Cuban Americans." *Journal of the American Medical Association* 265, no. 2 (January 9, 1991): 233–37.

Tucker, William. "A Leak in Medicaid." *Forbes* 148, no. 1 (July 8, 1991): 46–48.

Tudor, Cynthia G., Gerald Riley, and Melvin J. Ingber. "Satisfaction with Care: Do Medicare HMOs Make a Difference?" *Health Affairs* 17, no. 2 (March/April 1998): 165–76.

Tussing, Dale A., and Martha A. Wojtowycz. "Malpractice, Defensive Medicine, and Obstetric Behavior." *Medical Care* 35, no. 2 (1997): 172–91.

Urban Institute. *Hospital Prospective Payment: Cost Control and Windfall Profits: Policy and Research Report,* Washington, D.C.: Urban Institute (Winter 1988): 12–13.

U.S. Bureau of the Census. *Statistical Abstract of the United States, 1966.* Washington, D.C.: U. S. Government Printing Office, 1966.

———. *Statistical Abstract of the United States, 1992.* Washington, D.C.: U. S. Government Printing Office, 1992.

———. *Statistical Abstract of the United States, 1994.* Washington, D.C.: U. S. Government Printing Office, 1994.

———. "Health Insurance Coverage: 1995." http://www.census.gov/hhes/hlthins/cover95/c95taba.html.

———. *Statistical Abstract of the United States, 1997*. Washington, D.C.: U.S. Government Printing Office, 1997.

———. *Statistical Abstract of the United States, 1997*. Washington, D.C.: U.S. Government Printing Office, 1998.

———. "Low Income Uninsured Children by States." August 9, 1998. <http://www.cbo.gov/hhes/hlthins/lowinckid.htm>.

U.S. Department of Health, Education, and Welfare. *Toward a Comprehensive Health Policy for the 1970s: A White Paper*. Washington, D.C.: U. S. Government Printing Office, 1971.

———. *Certificate of Need/1122 Project Reviews: An Annotated Bibliography*. Washington, D.C.: U. S. Government Printing Office, 1977.

———. *Health in America: 1776–1976*. Washington, D.C.: U. S. Government Printing Office, 1977.

U.S. Department of Health and Human Services. *Health Status of Minorities and Low-Income Groups*, 3d ed. Washington, D.C.: U. S. Government Printing Office, 1991.

Valdez, R. Burciaga, Hal Morgenstern, E. Richard Brown, Roberta Wyn, Wang Chao, and William Cumberland. "Insuring Latinos against the Costs of Illness." *Journal of the American Medical Association* 269, no. 7 (February 17, 1993): 889–94.

Van DeVeer, Donald. "Introduction." In *Health Care Ethics: An Introduction*, ed. Donald Van DeVeer and Tom Regan, 3–57. Philadelphia: Temple University Press, 1987.

Van Rossum, Wouter. "Decision-Making and Medical Technology Assessment: Three Dutch Cases." *Knowledge in Society* 4, no. 1, 2 (September 1991): 107–24.

Varlova, John. "A $2.2 Million Lesson in the Perils of Peer Review." *Medical Economics* 61 (December 24, 1984): 56–61.

Varner, Theresa, and Jack Christy. "Consumer Information Needs in a Competitive Health Care Environment." *Health Care Financing Review* (Annual Supplement, 1986), 99–104.

"Victory: Family Physicians Make Gains in Medicare Fee Schedule." *AAFD Directors' Newsletter*, November 13, 1997. http://www.aafp.org/dn;/971113dl/2.html.

Vidmar, Neil. "Are Juries Competent to Decide Liability in Tort Cases Involving Scientific/Medical Issues? Some Data from Medical Malpractice." *Emory Law Journal* 43, no. 3 (Summer 1994): 883–911.

———. *Medical Malpractice and the American Jury: Confronting the Myths about Jury Incompetence, Deep Pockets, and Outrageous Damage Awards*. Ann Arbor, Mich.: University of Michigan Press, 1995.

Vikhanski, Luba. "Emergency Departments Face a Growing Crisis in Care." *Medical World News* 33, no. 3 (March 1992): 50–51.

Virts, John R., and George W. Wilson. "Inflation and Health Care Prices." *Health Affairs* 3, no. 1 (Spring 1984): 88–100.

Vladeck, Bruce C. "Interest Group Representation and the HSAs: Health Planning and Political Theory." *American Journal of Public Health* 67, no. 1 (January 1977): 23–29.

———. *Unloving Care: The Nursing Home Tragedy*. New York: Basic Books, 1980.

———. "The Market vs. Regulation: The Case for Regulation." *Milbank Memorial Fund Quarterly/Health and Society* 59, no. 2 (Spring 1981): 209–23.

———. "Comment on Hospital Reimbursement under Medicare." *Milbank Memorial Fund Quarterly/Health and Society* 62, no. 2 (Spring 1984): 269–78.

———. "Variation Data and the Regulatory Rationale." *Health Affairs* 3, no. 2 (Summer 1984): 102–9.

Vladeck, Bruce C., Nancy A. Miller, and Steven B. Clauser. "The Changing Face of Long-Term Care." *Health Care Financing Review* 14, no. 4 (Summer 1993): 5–23.

Vogel, Ronald J. "An Analysis of Structural Incentives in the Arizona Health Care Cost-Containment System." *Health Care Financing Review* 5, no. 4 (Summer 1984): 13–32.

Volpp, Kevin G., and J. Sanford Schwartz. "Myths and Realities Surrounding Health Reform." *Journal of the American Medical Association* 271, no. 17 (May 4, 1994): 1372.
Wagner, Lynn. "Access for All People." *Modern Healthcare* 19, no. 30 (July 28, 1989): 28.
————. "Health PACs Modest Donors—Study." *Modern Healthcare* 20, no. 29 (September 23, 1990).
————. "28 States Face Potential Deficits." *Modern Healthcare* 21, no. 1 (January 7, 1991).
Wagner, Mary. "Weighing the Cost of New Technology." *Modern Healthcare* 18, no. 47 (November 18, 1988): 43–58.
————. "Colorado Considers Establishing Its Own Health Plan for Needy." *Modern Healthcare* 22, no. 16 (April 20, 1992): 5.
Wall, Brett M. "Sympathy for the Devil: How the Ohio Tort Reform Act Creates a Flawed System of Punitive Damages." *Ohio State Law Journal* 58, no. 3 (1997): 1023–1054.
Wallace, Cynthia. "Hospital PACs Ring Up More Clout." *Modern Healthcare* 12, no. 10 (October 1982): 52–53.
Ward, Paul D. "Health Lobbies: Vested Interests and Pressure Politics." In *Politics of Health*, ed. Douglass Carter and Philip R. Lee, 28–47. Huntington, N.Y.: Robert F. Krieger, 1979.
Ware, John E., Jr., William H. Rogers, Allyson R. Davies, George A. Goldberg, Robert H. Brook, Emmett B. Keeler, Cathy D. Sherbourne, Patricia Camp, and Joseph P. Newhouse. "Comparison of Health Outcomes at a Health Maintenance Organization with Those for Fee-for-Service Care." *Lancet* 1, no. 8488 (May 3, 1986): 1017–1022.
Watson, Sidney Dean. "Minority Access and Health Reform: A Civil Right to Health Care." *Journal of Law, Medicine and Ethics* 22, no. 2 (Summer 1994): 127–37.
Weeks, Lewis E., and Howard J. Berman. *Shapers of American Health Care Policy: An Oral History*. Ann Arbor, Mich.: Heath Administration Press, 1985.
Wehr, Elizabeth. "Competition in Health Care: Would It Bring Costs Down?" *Congressional Quarterly* 37, no. 31 (August 4, 1979): 1587–1595.
Weigel, Charles J., II. "Medical Malpractice in America's Middle Years," *Texas Reports on Biology and Medicine* 32 (Spring 1974): 203.
Weil, Alan. "The New Children's Health Insurance Program: Should States Expand Medicaid?" Series A, no. A-13. Washington, D.C.: Urban Institute, October 1997.
Weiler, Paul C. *Medical Malpractice on Trial.;* Clark C. Havighurst and Laurence R. Tancredi. " 'Medical Adversity Insurance'—A No-Fault Approach to Medical Malpractice and Quality Insurance." *Insurance Law Journal*, no. 613 (1974): 69–100.
————. *Medical Malpractice on Trial*. Cambridge, Mass.: Harvard University Press, 1991.
Weiler, Paul C., Howard H. Hiatt, Joseph P. Newhouse, William G. Johnson, Troyen A. Brennan, and Lucian I. Leape. *A Measure of Malpractice: Medical Injury, Malpractice Litigation and Patient Compensation*. Cambridge, Mass.: Harvard University Press, 1993.
Weinder, Jonathan P., and Gregory de Lissovoy. "Razing a Tower of Babel: A Taxonomy for Managed Care and Health Insurance Plans." *Journal of Health Politics, Policy and Law* 18, no. 1 (Spring 1993): 75–103.
Weiner, Joshua M., and David G. Stevenson. "State Policy on Long-Term Care for the Elderly." *Health Affairs* 17, no. 3 (May/June 1998): 81–100.
Weiner, Joshua M., and Laurel Hixon Illston. "How to Share the Burden: Long-Term Care Reform in the 1990s." *Brookings Review* 12, no. 2 (Spring 1994): 16–21.
Weiner, Joshua M., and David G. Stevenson. *Long-Term Care for the Elderly and State Health Policy*. Washington, D.C.: Urban Institute. (n.d.) http://mewfederalism.urban.org/html/abf17.html.
Weiner, Stephen M. "On Public Values and Private Regulation: Some Reflections on Cost Containment Strategies." *Milbank Memorial Fund Quarerly/Health and Society* 59, no. 2 (1982): 269–96.
Weinick, Robin M., Margaret E. Weigers, and Joel W. Cohen. "Children's Health Insurance,

Access to Care, and Health Status: New Findings." *Health Affairs* 17, no. 2 (March/April 1998): 127–36.

Weisbrod, Burton A. "The Nature of Technological Change: Incentives Do Matter!" In *Adopting New Medical Technology: Medical Innovation at the Crossroads*, ed. Annetine C. Gelijns and Holly V. Dawkins, 8–48. Washington, D.C.: National Academy Press, 1994.

Weisman, Joel S., Constantine Gatsonis, and Arnold M. Epstein, "Rates of Avoidable Hospitalization by Insurance Status in Massachusetts and Maryland." *Journal of the American Medical Association* 268, no. 17 (November 4, 1992): 2388–2394.

Welch, W.P. "The New Structure of Individual Practice Associations." *Journal of Health Politics, Policy and Law* 12, no. 4 (Winter 1987): 723–39.

Wencl, Annette, and Margaret Brizzolara. "Survey of States." *Trial* 32, no. 5 (1996): 20–26.

Wetch, C.H. "Legal Medicine: An Historical Review and Future Perspectives." *New York Law School Law Review* 22 (1977): 873–903.

White House Domestic Policy Council. *The President's Health Security Act: The Clinton Blueprint*. New York: Times Books, 1993.

White, Joseph. *Competing Solutions: American Health Care Proposals and International Experience*. Washington, D.C.: Brookings Institution, 1995.

———. "'Saving' Medicare—From What?" Paper prepared for delivery at the annual meeting of the American Political Science Association, Committee on Health Politics, Boston, Mass., September 3–6, 1998.

Whol, Stanley. *The Medical Industrial Complex*. New York: Harmony Books, 1984.

Wholey, Douglas R., Jon B. Christianson, John Enberg, and Cindy Bryce. "HMO Market Structure and Performance: 1985-1995," *Health Affairs* 16, no. 6 (1997): 75–84.

"Why States Can't Solve the Health Care Crisis." *American Prospect* 9 (Spring 1992): 57–60.

Wildavsky, Ben. "Who's Entitled?" *National Journal* 29, no. 30 (July 26, 1997): 1509–1511.

Wildes, Kevin W. "Health Reform and the Seduction of Technology." *America* 170, no. 12 (April 9, 1994): 30.

Wilensky, Gail, and L. Rossiter. "Patient Self-Selection in HMOs." *Health Affairs* 5, no. 2 (1986): 66–80.

Wilensky, Gail R. "Promoting Quality: A Public Policy View." *Health Affairs* 16, no. 3 (May/June 1997): 77–81.

Wilsford, David. *Doctors and the State: The Politics of Health Care in France and the United States*. Durham, N.C.: Duke University Press, 1991.

Wilson, William Julius. *The Declining Significance of Race*. Chicago: University of Chicago Press, 1987.

———. *The Truly Disadvantaged: The Inner City, the Underclass, and Public Policy*. Chicago: University of Chicago Press, 1987.

Wissert, William G., Timothy Lesnick, Melissa Musliner, and Kathleen A. Foley. "Cost Savings from Home and Community-Based Services: Arizona's Capitated Medicaid Long-Term Care." *Journal of Health Politics, Policy and Law* 22, no. 6 (December 1997): 1329–1357.

Wolf, Charles, Jr. "A Theory of Non-Market Failures." *Public Interest* 55 (Spring 1979): 114–23.

Wood, Cece L. "Historical Perspectives on Law, Medical Practice and the Concept of Negligence." *Emergency Medicine Clinic of North America*, 11, no. 4 (1993): 819–832.

Wright, Robert. "The Technology Time Bomb." *New Republic* 208, no. 13 (March 29, 1993): 25–30.

Yergin, Daniel, and Joseph Stanislaw. *The Commanding Heights: The Battle between Government and the Marketplace That Is Remaking the Modern World*. New York: Simon and Schuster, 1998.

Zatkin, Steve. "A Health Plan's View of Government Regulation." *Health Affairs* 16, no. 6 (November/December 1997): 33–35.

Zedlewski, Sheila R., Gregory P. Acs, and Colin W. Winterbottom. "Play-or-Pay Employer Mandates: Potential Effects." *Health Affairs* 11, no. 1 (Spring 1992): 69.

Zellers, Wendy K., Catherine G. McLaughlin, and Kevin D. Frick. "Small-Business Health Insurance: Only Healthy Need Apply." *Health Affairs* 11, no. 1 (Spring 1992): 174–75.

Zelman, Walter A. "The Rationale behind the Clinton Health Reform Plan." *Health Affairs* 13, no. 1 (Spring 1994): 9–29.

Zollinger, Terrel W., Robert M. Saywell, Jr., and David K.W. Chu. "Uncompensated Hospital Care for Pregnancy and Childbirth Cases." *American Journal of Public Health* 81, no. 8 (August 1991): 1017–1022.

Zuckerman, Stephen, Allison Evans, and John Holahan. "Questions for States As They Turn to Medicaid Managed Care." Series A, no. A-11. Washington, D.C.: Urban Institute, 1998. http://newfederalism.urban.org/html/anf_a11.htm.

Index

Kant Patel (Ph.D., University of Houston, 1976) is professor of political science at Southwest Missouri State University. He teaches health policy, policy analysis, and intergovernmental relations. He has published articles in journals such as *Evaluation and Health Profession, Health Policy and Education, Political Methodology, Journal of Political Science, International Journal of Policy Analysis and Information Systems, and Journal of Health and Social Policy*, among others. He is co-author (with Mark E. Rushefsky) of *Politics, Power, and Policy Making: The Case of Health Care Reform in the 1900s* (M.E. Sharpe, 1998)

Mark E. Rushefsky (Ph.D., State Uiversity of New York at Binghamton, 1977) is professor of political science at Southwest Missouri State University. He teaches and writes on public policy and public administration. He is the author of *Making Cancer Policy in the United States: Toward the Twenty-First Century*, 2nd ed. (Harcourt Brace, 1996), as well as articles and chapters on health care and the environment. He is co-author (with Kant Patel) of *Politics, Power, and Policy Making: The Case of Health Care Reform in the 1990s* (M.E. Sharpe, 1998).